ROYAL HORTICULTURAL SOCIETY

GARDEN PLANTS & FLOWERS

THROUGH THE YEAR

ROYAL HORTICULTURAL SOCIETY

GARDEN PLANTS & FLOWERS

THROUGH THE YEAR

IAN SPENCE

LONDON, NEW YORK,
MUNICH, MELBOURNE, DELHI

REVISED EDITION

Editors	Emma ...
Art Editor	Kathryn Gammon
Senior Editor	Helen Fewster
Acting Project Art Editor	Vicky Read
Managing Editor	Esther Ripley
Managing Art Editor	Alison Donovan
Associate Publisher	Liz Wheeler
Production Editor	Joanna Byrne
Production Controller	Hema Gohil
Publisher	Jonathan Metcalf
Art Director	Bryn Walls

RHS Editors   Simon Maughan, Rae Spencer-Jones

FIRST EDITION 2003

Senior Editor	Annelise Evans
Senior Art Editor	Alison Donovan
Project Art Editor	Murdo Culver
Designers	Gillian Andrews, Vanessa Hamilton, Rachael Smith
Additional Editors	Louise Abbott, Pamela Brown, Candida Frith-Macdonald, Letitia Luff
Managing Editor	Anna Kruger
Managing Art Editor	Lee Griffiths
Media Resources	Lucy Claxton, Richard Dabb
Picture Researcher	Samantha Nunn

First published in Great Britain in 2003 by
Dorling Kindersley Limited, London

This revised edition published in 2009,
in association with the Royal Horticultural Society,
by Dorling Kindersley Limited
80 Strand, London WC2R ORL

A Penguin Company

2 4 6 8 10 9 7 5 3 1

A CIP catalogue record for this book is available from
The British Library

ISBN 978 1 4053 4738 9

Printed and bound in Singapore by Star Standard

see our complete catalogue at
www.dk.com

Contents

Key to symbols used in the text

♔ RHS Award of Garden Merit
↕ Height of mature plant
↔ Spread of mature plant
❉❉❉ Fully hardy: plant can withstand temperatures down to -15°C (5°F)
❉❉ Frost-hardy: plant can withstand temperatures down to -5°C (23°F)
❉ Half-hardy: plant can withstand temperatures down to 0°C (32°F)
⌂ Frost-tender: plant may be damaged by temperatures below 5°C (41°F)

Introduction

Gardening has never been more popular than it is today. It has become a huge industry, supplying everything from garden ornaments and gadgets to hard landscaping materials, with a proliferation of expert advice in the media on all aspects of gardening from design to topiary.

In the midst of this, we sometimes forget that the real stars of the show are the plants. There is an astonishing diversity and a huge number of garden plants available to the gardener, from tiny alpines to large trees. Plant breeders also introduce more and more new cultivated varieties, or cultivars, each year. Some of these new plants go out of fashion just as quickly, but others go on to become firm favourites.

It can therefore seem daunting and confusing, especially to those new to gardening, to have to select from this vast array of plants and mass of information. This is where I hope this book will help.

RHS Garden Plants and Flowers includes a selection of plants that have proved to be reliable performers in the garden. Most are robust, hardy, and not difficult to grow. Some may need a little tender loving care to see them through harsh winters, but the results are well worth the effort. There are also a few more unusual plants.

To make your choice as easy as possible, every entry is illustrated so that you can judge the plant's appeal for yourself. The entries are divided into several chapters, dealing with different types of plant. Then, within each chapter, the plants are arranged alphabetically by botanical name because not all plants have a common name, and some common names are shared by more than one plant; where they exist, common names are listed too.

As well as basic information on each featured plant, there is practical advice on caring for plants as well as quick-reference lists of plants for different sites and uses in the garden (*see pp.334–337*). Once you start growing plants, like me, you may be hooked for life.

Happy gardening!

Ian Spence

Trees and shrubs

Trees and shrubs are an essential part of any garden. They act as a backdrop to other plants and provide structure when herbaceous perennials and annuals have died away over winter. Some are beautiful enough to grow as solitary specimens, but most are grown in borders and used for hedging. Choose the right ones, and they will provide interest all year round.

Top: *Rhus typhina*
From left to right: *Betula nigra*; *Clerodendrum trichotomum* var. *fargesii*; *Picea abies*; *Paeonia suffruticosa* 'Cardinal Vaughan'; *Weigela* 'Looymansii Aurea'

Woody plants through the year

Trees and shrubs are long-lived woody plants. Trees usually have a single main stem or trunk with a head of branches growing out from it. Shrubs have several branches that emerge near the base of the plant, without a central trunk. However, some trees have shrubby tendencies and naturally develop more than one stem; others, such as *Amelanchier*, can be pruned and grown as shrubs with several stems.

Size and shape

Before you select trees and shrubs, consider their final shape and size. There is a wide variety, and each one will affect the style and feel of the garden. If you are planning an informal scheme, then trees and shrubs with a more lax or bushy growth habit will fit in well. However, if you are after a formal design, then columnar shapes, like the Italian cypress (*Cupressus*), may be more suitable.

Of course, you can also modify the shape of some trees and shrubs by pruning, or you could try your hand at topiary. Dense evergreens like yew (*Taxus*) and box (*Buxus*) are among the plants that adapt well to this kind of treatment, and you can let your imagination run riot, as long as what you do fits in with the style of the garden.

Do also be aware of the ultimate height and spread of the trees and shrubs you choose. Those with a columnar habit cast smaller shadows than those that spread out; equally, small trees create less shade than large ones. If you only have a small plot, remember that too large a tree might throw most of the garden into shade. So, select your trees and shrubs with care: it is not so easy to move them once they are established.

Planting trees and shrubs

You can plant trees and shrubs at any time of year if they have been raised in containers. Water the plants thoroughly before and after planting and continue to do so during the first growing season. Bare-root trees and shrubs, however, must be planted during the dormant season, from November to March (*see pp.320–321*).

SPRING INTEREST

Camellia japonica 'Adolphe Audusson' *p.28*

Abutilon megapotamicum *p.15*

SUMMER INTEREST

Callistemon pallidus p.27

Hypericum calycinum p.66

AUTUMN INTEREST

Acer palmatum 'Sango-kaku' *p.17*

Cotoneaster x *watereri* 'John Waterer' *p.41*

WINTER INTEREST

Viburnum tinus 'Variegatum' *p.109*

Daphne bholua 'Jacqueline Postill' *p.44*

Salix helvetica *p.99*

Abies nordmanniana 'Golden spreader' *p.13*

Daphne cneorum *p.45*

Cassiope 'Edinburgh' *p.31*

Brachyglottis 'Sunshine Improved' *p.25*

Hydrangea macrophylla 'Ayesha' *p.65*

Elaeagnus x ebbingei 'Gilt Edge' *p.46*

Calluna vulgaris 'Silver Knight' *p.27*

Acer palmatum 'Garnet' *p.16*

Viburnum opulus 'Xanthocarpum' *p.109*

Berberis thunbergii 'Dart's Red Lady' *p.23*

Ilex aquifolium 'Ferox Argentea' *p.66*

Arctostaphylos x media 'Woods Red' *p.21*

Prunus x subhirtella 'Autumnalis Rosea' *p.89*

Skimmia japonica *p.100*

Erica carnea 'December Red' *p.49*

Abelia

SUMMER AND AUTUMN

These deciduous and evergreen shrubs are grown for their profuse clusters of white, pink, or cerise flowers and glossy, rounded foliage. The flowers are borne on slender, arching stems during summer and autumn, and in some species, such as *Abelia chinensis* and *A. schumannii*, they are scented. The size of different cultivars can vary dramatically, from 1.5m (5ft) to 5m (15ft) or more in height, and between 2m (6ft) and 4m (12ft) in width. Abelias are generally trouble-free and ideal for sunny border sites. If you have room, they make attractive planting partners for lespedezas (*see p.72*) and hydrangeas (*see pp.64–65*). In areas prone to frost, plant less hardy species against a warm, south- or west-facing wall.

■ **HARDINESS** Frost-hardy ✳✳ to half-hardy ✳.
■ **CULTIVATION** Grow in any fertile, well-drained soil in full sun and shelter from cold, drying winds. ■ **Prune** deciduous species in late winter or early spring, removing misplaced or crossing shoots to maintain a good shape. For evergreen species, lightly trim back after flowering any flowered shoots that would spoil the symmetry. ■ **Take** softwood cuttings in early summer, or semi-ripe cuttings in late summer (*see pp.329–330*).

Abelia schumannii ♀
‡2m (6ft) ↔3m (10ft), deciduous, lightly scented flowers in late summer to autumn ✳✳

Abelia x grandiflora ♀
‡3m (10ft) ↔4m (12ft), semi-evergreen, fragrant flowers in midsummer to autumn ✳✳

Abelia floribunda ♀
‡3m (10ft) ↔4m (12ft), evergreen, flowers early summer ✳

Abeliophyllum distichum
White forsythia

LATE WINTER TO EARLY SPRING

Clusters of flowers borne on the bare wood of this deciduous shrub open from late winter to delicately perfume the garden. Matt green leaves follow, and turn purple before falling. This open, spreading shrub is related to the forsythia (*see p.54*) and you can grow it as a freestanding shrub in a sunny border, but train it against a sheltered, south- or west-facing wall and it will reward you by bursting into flower earlier and more profusely. It is a fine companion for other early-flowering shrubs such as mahonias (*see p.76*) and viburnums (*see pp.108–109*).

■ **HARDINESS** Fully hardy ✳✳✳, provided that the wood was well ripened by a good summer. Early flowers may potentially be damaged by frosts.
■ **CULTIVATION** Grow in fertile, well-drained soil in full sun. ■ **Prune** after flowering; if freestanding, cut back flowered shoots to strong buds or shoots close to the base. If wall-trained, cut back all flowered shoots to within 2–4 buds of a permanent framework. ■ **Take** semi-ripe cuttings, or layer low-growing shoots, in summer (*see pp.329–330*).

Abeliophyllum distichum
‡↔1.5m (5ft), taller if grown against a wall, white flowers sometimes tinged with pink

Abies
Silver fir

Long, sweeping branches are a typical feature of these stately, evergreen conifers. They make excellent specimen trees, and can also be used to provide shelter from wind or as a screen. The needles usually range in colour from mid-green to bluish-green, with silvery undersides. In late spring and early summer, some plants produce decorative cones; erect, purplish-blue ones on the upper branches will be female, while the pendent cones lower down are male. For small gardens there are several small and even dwarf firs, such as *Abies balsamea* 'Nana' which grows to just 1m (3ft), ideal for a rock garden. For the largest spaces, *A. grandis* attains a majestic stature of up to 45m (150ft).

■ **HARDINESS** Fully hardy ❋❋❋, but frost may damage young foliage.
■ **CULTIVATION** Grow in any fertile, moist but well-drained, neutral to slightly acid soil in sun, sheltered from cold winds. Most tolerate a little shade. Like most conifers, they need no pruning. ■ **Sow** seed (*see pp.328–329*) in containers when ripe or in winter; expose seed to cold for three weeks before sowing. Firs are prone to infestation by adelgids, black aphid-like insects covered in a fluffy white secretion. They may cause foliage to yellow, but can usually be tolerated.

Abies veitchii (Veitch fir)
‡15–20m (50–70ft) ↔ 4–6m (12–20ft), fast-growing, with 5–8cm (2–3in) long female cones

Abies lasiocarpa 'Compacta' ♀
‡3–5m (10–15ft) ↔ 2–3m (6–10ft), small, slow-growing type of corkbark fir, with a neat conical shape

Abies koreana (Korean fir)
‡10m (30ft) ↔ 6m (20ft), produces decorative female cones that are 5–8cm (2–3in) long, from a young age

Abies nordmanniana 'Golden Spreader' ♀
‡1m (3ft) ↔ 1.5m (5ft), slow-growing, shrubby dwarf conifer with spreading branches and greenish-brown cones

Abutilon

Flowering maple, Indian mallow

SPRING TO AUTUMN

A long flowering season is a key attraction of these rather spindly-stemmed shrubs, most of which benefit from some support. They flower in shades of red, orange, soft violet-blue, pink, and white; some even have bicoloured blooms. There are also several that have variegated leaves. Tender and half-hardy types can be planted out with summer bedding, staked with canes if necessary; hardier species can be trained against a sunny, sheltered wall, or in warmer areas are excellent for adding height to a border.

■ **HARDINESS** Frost-hardy ✽✽ to frost-tender ⌖.
■ **CULTIVATION** Grow in any fertile, well-drained soil or loam-based compost in a container. Position in full sun; in frost-prone areas grow abutilons in pots in a sheltered site and bring the plants under frost-free cover during winter. ■ **Prune** in late winter or early spring, cutting back flowered shoots to a permanent framework of main stems (*see p.323*), and taking out any misplaced or crossing shoots. ■ **Sow** seed (*see pp.328–329*) in heat in spring; take softwood cuttings in spring, or semi-ripe cuttings in summer (*see pp.329–330*). If whiteflies or red spider mite infest plants under cover, you might find that biological controls are effective (*see p.332*).

Abutilon 'Boule de Neige'

‡to 4m (12ft) ↔ to 3m (10ft), vigorous evergreen, erect to spreading habit, flowers from spring to autumn ✽

Abutilon vitifolium var. album

‡5m (15ft) ↔ 2.5m (8ft), fast-growing, deciduous shrub, sometimes tree-like, flowering in early summer ✽✽

Abutilon pictum 'Thompsonii'

‡5m (15ft) ↔ 2–5m (6–15ft), evergreen, erect shrub or small tree, flowers from spring to autumn ✽

Abutilon vitifolium 'Veronica Tennant' ♀

‡to 5m (15ft) ↔ 2.5m (8ft), deciduous, upright shrub, flowers in early summer ✽✽

Abutilon megapotamicum ♀
(Trailing abutilon)
↔2m (6ft), semi-evergreen or evergreen, ideal
against a wall; flowers borne from summer to
autumn ✲✲

Acacia
Wattle

Clusters of tiny, often sweetly fragrant,
bright yellow flowers clothe these
fast-growing, deciduous and evergreen
trees and shrubs in winter or spring.
In frost-prone climates, the hardier
species that will survive outdoors need
a warm, sheltered site to flower well.
Grow them with other winter-
flowering evergreens, such as
mahonias (*see p.76*), sarcococcas
(*p.100*), and viburnums (*pp.108–109*),
for an uplifting winter display.

■ **HARDINESS** Half-hardy ✲ to frost-tender ❀
■ **CULTIVATION** Grow in reasonably fertile,
neutral to acid (lime-free) soil. Position in full
sun, out of cold winds. In colder areas, grow in
pots of loam-based compost and take under
frost-free cover in winter. ■ **Prune** (*see
pp.322–323*) deciduous species in spring,
removing any crossing or misshapen branches
to maintain a good framework, and evergreens
after flowering, lightly trimming shoots that
spoil the shape of the tree. ■ **Cut** flowered
shoots on wall-trained shrubs to within two to
four buds of the permanent framework in late
winter or early spring. ■ **Sow** seed (*see
pp.328–329*) at 18°C (64°F) in spring after
soaking in warm water until the seeds are
swollen. Take semi-ripe cuttings (*see pp.329–
330*) in summer.

Acalypha

These tropical shrubs make exotic
bedding plants for summer in a cool
climate, where they are also often
cultivated as pot plants. Some, for
example *Acalypha hispida*, the chenille
plant or red-hot cat's tail, are grown
for their long, catkin-like clusters of
usually pinky-crimson or scarlet
flowers. Others, such as *A. wilkesiana*,
have inconspicuous flowers but
ornamental foliage, that is mottled or
variegated. Given the right conditions,
acalypha can grow very quickly and
make fine accent plants, although you
may find that they will not reach full
height in a single season.

■ **HARDINESS** Frost-tender ❀.
■ **CULTIVATION** Outdoors, grow in fertile,
well-drained soil in full sun or partial shade. If
growing them in pots, use a soilless compost and
position in full light. ■ **Keep** plants in frost-free
conditions throughout the winter; they are
susceptible to damage at temperatures below
10–13°C (50–55°F). ■ **Feed** with a balanced
fertilizer at monthly intervals in spring and
summer, and water regularly during summer.
■ **Lightly trim** shoots that spoil the shape
of the plant. ■ **Take** softwood cuttings in
spring or semi-ripe cuttings in late summer
(*see pp.329–330*).

***Abutilon* 'Souvenir de Bonn'** ♀
‡to 3m (10ft) ↔2–3m (6–10ft), vigorous,
erect evergreen, flowers from spring into early
autumn ✲

Acacia baileyana ♀
(Cootamundra wattle)
‡5–8m (15–25ft) ↔3–6m (10–20ft), small tree
or large shrub, evergreen, flowers winter to spring ✲

Acalypha wilkesiana (Copperleaf)
‡to 2m (6ft) ↔1–2m (3–6ft), spreading shrub,
green- or copper-tinted flowers often hidden by
blue, pink, or coppery leaves

Acer

Maple

Acers are prized for their delicate foliage, which is particularly fine and fern-like in some cultivars of Japanese maple (*Acer palmatum*). There is enough variety in the group to provide interest at any time of the year. Some have brightly coloured leaves in spring, others have variegated grey-green, white, or pink foliage, and many give a brilliant display of intense reds, yellows, and oranges in autumn. Nearly all maples are deciduous. Several also have handsome bark, which helps to enliven the winter months; on *Acer griseum* it peels attractively, while on *A. davidii* and *A. pensylvanicum* it is striped and streaked in green and white. The inconspicuous spring flowers are followed by winged fruits. Maples include trees and shrubs. The largest trees make striking specimens if you have the space, while smaller trees and those of shrubby habit can be grown in gardens of any size. Many cultivars are excellent grown in containers; the restricted root space keeps them compact, and less hardy varieties can also be moved to a sheltered position close to the house during the coldest months.

■ **HARDINESS** Most fully hardy ✻✻✻, some frost-hardy ✻✻.
■ **CULTIVATION** Maples prefer well-cultivated soil in sun or partial shade. ■ **Plant** container-grown trees at any time of the year, but bare-root trees only when dormant, from late autumn to early spring. Water well before and after planting, and water regularly during the first year. ■ **Shelter** those with delicate foliage from cold winds and late frosts that can scorch the young leaves. ■ **Stake** taller maples and those grown in exposed gardens. ■ **Prune** young plants to form the basic framework for the tree or shrub; after this maples need minimal pruning. Remove badly placed and crossing shoots to maintain a well-balanced shape (*see p.332*), and cut out any dead or diseased wood from late autumn to midwinter, or in spring for plants in containers. ■ **Sow** seed outside as soon as it is ripe (*see pp.328–329*) and take softwood cuttings of cultivars in early summer (*see pp.329–330*). In some cultivars, mites may cause small growths called galls, which are harmless.

Looking after maples in containers

Maples grown in containers require more care than those planted in open ground. A thick mulch (*see p.388*) will help retain moisture, but you will still need to water regularly – probably daily during dry spells. Top-dress the container annually in early spring to remove weeds and algal growths in the surface layer and ensure the plant has the nutrients it requires. Every three to five years, repot your maple, either back into the same container with fresh compost, or into a slightly larger one. Remove the plant from its pot, gently tease out the roots and cut back any large, coarse ones. Put the tree in the new container, then fill in with fresh compost so the root ball sits at the same level as before. Water in well and mulch.

A. cappadocicum ‡20m (70ft) ↔15m (50ft)

A. circinatum ‡5m (15ft) ↔6m (20ft)

A. negundo 'Variegatum' ‡15m (50ft) ↔10m (30ft)

A. palmatum atropurpureum ‡8m (25ft) ↔10m (30ft)

A. palmatum Dissectum Atropurpureum Group ‡2m (6ft) ↔3m (10ft)

A. palmatum 'Garnet' ♀ ‡2m (6ft) ↔3m (10ft)

A. platanoides 'Crimson King' ♀ ‡25m (80ft) ↔15m (50ft)

A. pseudoplatanus 'Brilliantissimum' ‡6m (20ft) ↔8m (25ft)

A. davidii 'George Forrest' ♀
‡↔15m (50ft), interesting bark

A. griseum ♀ ‡↔10m (30ft), attractive bark

A. japonicum 'Aconitifolium' ♀ ‡5m (15ft)
↔6m (20ft)

A. negundo 'Flamingo' ‡15m (50ft)
↔10m (30ft)

A. palmatum 'Bloodgood' ♀
‡↔5m (15ft)

A. palmatum 'Butterfly' ‡3m (10ft)
↔1.5m (5ft)

A. palmatum 'Chitose-yama' ♀ ‡2m (6ft)
↔3m (10ft)

A. palmatum 'Corallinum' ‡1.2m
(4ft) ↔1m (3ft)

A. palmatum var. heptalobum
‡5m (15ft) ↔6m (20ft)

A. palmatum 'Linearilobum' ‡5m (15ft)
↔4m (12ft)

A. palmatum 'Red Pygmy' ♀ ‡↔1.5m (5ft)

A. palmatum 'Sango-kaku' ♀
‡6m (20ft) ↔5m (15ft)

A. rubrum 'October Glory' ♀
‡20m (70ft) ↔10m (30ft)

A. rubrum 'Schlesingeri' ‡20m (70ft)
↔10m (30ft)

A. saccharinum ‡20m (70ft) ↔12m (40ft)

A. shirasawanum 'Aureum' ♀
‡↔6m (20ft)

Aeonium

Prized for their exotic forms, aeoniums bear tight rosettes of fleshy leaves in shades of light green to a striking black-purple. From spring to summer, they send up clusters of small starry flowers in pale to bright yellow, white, pink, or copper-red. With some species, the flowering stem dies back once the seed is set. Aeoniums look stunning in containers, especially grouped with other succulents. Grow them in pots on a patio or in a well-drained border in sun or partial shade. They are tender, so will have to be brought into frost-free conditions for the winter.

■ **HARDINESS** Frost-tender ❀; they can withstand short periods of frost in dry conditions.
■ **CULTIVATION** Grow in fertile, very well-drained soil or gritty compost, in sun or partial shade. ■ **Keep** the plants fairly dry during their dormant period in winter.
■ **Sow** seed (*see pp.328–329*) in heat in spring.
■ **Take** cuttings (*see pp.329–330*) in early summer, waiting until the cut surface heals over before inserting them in gritty compost. Place them in good light and keep warm and on the dry side until rooted. Aeoniums are prone to attack by aphids (*see p.332*).

Aeonium 'Zwartkop' ♀
↕↔to 1m (3ft), pyramid-shaped spikes of yellow flowers appear in late summer, superb architectural plant for summer display

Aesculus

Horse chestnut, Buckeye

Horse chestnuts are handsome trees with fingered leaves that turn golden yellow or glowing orange in autumn. In spring and early summer, they are covered in large spikes or "candles" of white or pink flowers. In autumn, their smooth- or prickly-coated, rounded fruits split to reveal shiny, brown seeds or conkers; they can cause stomach upsets if eaten. Because of their size, most horse chestnuts can be grown only in large gardens. Their spreading branches and large leaves cast a deep shade under which little will grow. However, *Aesculus* x *mutabilis* 'Induta' and *A. parviflora* are shrubby and smaller in size and look impressive in medium-sized gardens.

■ **HARDINESS** Most garden species are fully hardy ❅❅❅.
■ **CULTIVATION** Grow in any fertile soil in sun or partial shade. ■ **Prune** young trees to remove misplaced or crossing shoots (*see p.322*) in late winter or early spring. ■ **Sow** seed (*see pp.328–329*) in a seedbed outdoors as soon as it is ripe. *A. parviflora* can be propagated by removing suckers – cut away a stem with its own roots and replant it.

Aesculus parviflora ♀
↕3m (10ft) ↔5m (15ft), suckering shrub that will grow in all but very poorly-drained soils, smooth-skinned fruits

Agave

Native to deserts and mountains, these bold, structural succulents have fleshy, spiked leaves up to 2m (6ft) long, in wide-spreading rosettes. In summer, mature plants may produce funnel-shaped flowers on leafless stems that soar up to 8m (25ft). With most species, the main rosette dies after flowering and fruiting, but leaves a number of offsets – smaller rosettes that develop around it – to mature in later years. These can be split off to make new plants. In frost-prone areas, grow agaves in containers that can be moved into frost-free conditions. If frost is not a problem, grow them as specimen plants in borders protected from excessive winter wet. The spiked leaves are very sharp.

■ **HARDINESS** Half-hardy ❅ to frost-tender ❀.
■ **CULTIVATION** Grow in slightly acid, fertile, very well-drained soil or gritty compost in full sun. ■ **Sow** seed (*see pp.328–329*) in heat in early spring. ■ **Remove** agave offsets in autumn or spring. Insert unrooted offsets in pots containing equal parts peat-free compost and sharp sand. Rooted offsets can be treated like mature plants.

***Agave americana* 'Mediopicta'** ♀
↕2m (6ft) ↔3m (10ft), impressive specimen plant when mature, in warm regions flowers in summer on stems up to 8m (25ft) tall ❀

Alnus
Alder
SPRING TO SUMMER

Fast-growing and tolerant of poor soils, alders are useful trees and shrubs. They are deciduous, and broadly conical in shape, with toothed leaves, and delicate catkins appearing in late winter to spring. The catkins, usually yellow, are followed by green fruits that turn brown in autumn and look like tiny pine cones. Alders, especially those with ornamental foliage such as *Alnus rubra*, *A. glutinosa*, and *A. incana*, make attractively light, slender specimen trees. They do not mind wet feet, so they are a sound choice for a damp site or by a stream or pond. As they are quick-growing, they make ideal screens or windbreaks.

■ **HARDINESS** Fully hardy ✳✳✳.
■ **CULTIVATION** Grow in fertile, moist, but well-drained soil in full sun; *A. cordata* and *A. incana* will tolerate dry soils. Pruning is rarely necessary: remove branches that cross or spoil the shape of the tree between the time of leaf-fall and midwinter to avoid sap bleeding.
■ **Sow** seed (*see pp.328–329*) in a seedbed as soon as it is ripe. ■ **Take** hardwood cuttings in winter (*see pp.329–330*).

Alnus cordata ♀
‡25m (80ft) ↔ 6m (20ft), originates from the Mediterranean and tolerates dry soil, catkins appear in late winter before the leaves

Amelanchier
Juneberry, Snowy mespilus
SPRING AND AUTUMN

A tree for all seasons, the amelanchier is superb value in the garden. Spring to early summer is a high point, when these broad, shrubby trees bear masses of beautiful, star- or saucer-shaped, pink to white flowers, just as the bronze-pink young leaves are opening. Add to this their richly coloured autumnal foliage, juicy fruits, and light, airy growing habit, and you have a plant that has something of interest all year round. The small, maroon to purple-black fruits are very attractive to birds. Make the most of this fine tree by growing it as a specimen. Amelanchiers also make substantial additions to shrub borders.

■ **HARDINESS** Fully hardy ✳✳✳.
■ **CULTIVATION** Grow in acid (lime-free), fertile, well-drained soil in sun or partial shade. *A. asiatica* is lime-tolerant. ■ **Prune out** any branches that cross or spoil the shape in late winter or early spring. ■ **Remove** suckers in winter. ■ **Sow** seed (*see pp.328–329*) outdoors as soon as it is ripe. ■ **Take** greenwood or semi-ripe cuttings (*see pp.329–330*) in summer. Peg low branches into the soil in autumn to root (*see layering, p.330*).

Amelanchier lamarckii ♀
‡10m (30ft) ↔ 12m (40ft), upright-stemmed, leaves emerge as bronze, then turn dark green, white flowers appear mid-spring

Andromeda
Bog rosemary
SPRING TO EARLY SUMMER

Imagine a heather with long, narrow, green leaves, and you have the bog rosemary, a small, wiry-stemmed, evergreen shrub that enjoys the same conditions as ericas (*see pp.48–49*) and callunas (*see p.27*), being native to peat bogs in cool regions. *Andromeda polifolia* is the most commonly grown species; its cultivars vary in size, from 5cm (2in) to 40cm (16in) tall, and in flower colour – either pink or white. Bog rosemaries only thrive in moist, acid (lime-free) soils. If your soil is not suitable, a raised bed or container filled with ericaceous (acid) soil or compost will suffice. They very much enjoy a woodland setting or a shady rock garden.

■ **HARDINESS** Fully hardy ✳✳✳.
■ **CULTIVATION** Grow in moist, acid soil with plenty of well-rotted organic matter added to it, in sun or partial shade. If your soil is dry, spread a layer of leafmould or garden compost around the plants each spring, ideally after heavy rain; this will help retain moisture and keep down weeds. ■ **Take** softwood cuttings in summer (*see pp.329–330*), or pot up rooted layers in autumn or spring (*see p.330*).

***Andromeda polifolia* 'Alba'**
‡15cm (6in) ↔ 20cm (8in), semi-prostrate, free-flowering

Aralia

SPRING TO EARLY AUTUMN

These exotic-looking trees grow mainly in mountainous woodland. Their large, handsome leaves are arranged in pairs; in some, they are covered in large bristles. *Aralia elata* is the largest species. In late summer and early autumn, they produce clusters or spikes of small, white or greenish-white flowers (with no hint of pink), followed by black fruits. Aralias are suitable only for large gardens, in prominent positions where their striking leaves can be admired. They look good in shady borders, woodland plantings, and by streams.

■ **HARDINESS** Fully hardy ✳✳✳ to frost-hardy ✳✳.
■ **CULTIVATION** Grow in fertile soil with plenty of well-rotted organic matter added, in an open or part-shaded site, sheltered from strong winds that may damage the leaves. Trees in very fertile soil can produce soft growth prone to damage by frost. ■ **Remove** badly placed branches or frost-damaged shoots in early spring, and remove suckers. If variegated forms produce shoots with all-green leaves, prune them out. ■ **Sow** seed (*see pp.328–329*) in containers as soon as ripe; place in a cold frame. ■ **Take** root cuttings (see *pp.329–330*) in winter. ■ **Aphids** may attack the soft flower stalks.

***Aralia elata* 'Variegata'** ♀
↕↔10m (30ft) vigorous, deciduous tree, leaves grow to 1.2m (4ft) long with good autumn colour, flowers late summer to early autumn

Araucaria araucana

Monkey puzzle

YEAR-ROUND

One of the most ancient trees, the monkey puzzle is so-called because its branches are clad in sharp, scale-like leaves that make them uncomfortable, if not impossible, to climb. Although hailing from the tropical rainforest, this araucaria is fully hardy, and has long been a garden favourite for its novelty value. Many, unfortunately, are planted in gardens that are far too small, necessitating unsightly lopping that ruins their shape. They need plenty of room for their forms to develop – at first conical, then losing the lower branches to form a graceful, rounded head atop a tall, clear trunk. Male and female cones tend to be borne on different trees; female cones are more rounded than the male ones.

■ **HARDINESS** Fully hardy ✳✳✳.
■ **CULTIVATION** Grow in any fertile, well-drained soil in an open site, but sheltered from cold winds. ■ **Sow** seed (*see pp.328–329*) in a seedbed as soon as it is ripe. Take cuttings (*see pp.329–330*) from vertical shoot tips in midsummer and root them in a cold frame. Cuttings from horizontal branches never make upright trees.

Araucaria araucana
↕15–25m (50–80ft) ↔7–10m (22–30ft), tough, dark grey-brown bark with horizontal ridges

Arbutus

Strawberry tree

YEAR-ROUND

Arbutus are broad, sometimes bushy trees with attractive, peeling, red-brown bark and dark, glossy leaves. Clusters of tiny white or pink flowers are produced from autumn to spring. These are followed by bright orange to red, strawberry-like fruits, which are edible, if tasteless. Although they can reach up to 15m (50ft), they are slow-growing and many remain small shrubs for several years. They are excellent for a large shrub border or as specimens, where their handsome barks can be admired.

■ **HARDINESS** Fully hardy ✳✳✳ when mature (young trees not so) to frost-hardy ✳✳.
■ **CULTIVATION** Grow in fertile soil, enriched with plenty of bulky, well-rotted organic matter, in a sheltered site in full sun with protection from cold winds, even when mature. Both *A.* x *andrachnoides* and *A. unedo* will tolerate alkaline (limy) soils; other species, such as *A. menziesii*, need acid soils. ■ **Prune out** any misplaced shoots to maintain a good shape in winter or late spring when the tree is dormant, but keep pruning to a minimum. ■ **Sow** seed (*see pp.328–329*) in containers as soon as it is ripe and place in a cold frame. ■ **Take** semi-ripe (stem-tip) cuttings in summer (*see pp.329–330*).

Arbutus* x *andrachnoides ♀
↕↔8m (25ft), white, sometimes pink-tinged, flowers in autumn to spring, grown mostly for red bark, fruits are rare ✳✳✳

Arctostaphylos
Bearberry
WINTER, SPRING, AND AUTUMN

These mostly evergreen shrubs originate from western North America. They range in habit from mat-forming to upright and some eventually reach 6m (20ft) tall with a similar spread, while *Arctostaphylos alpina* is just 5cm (2in) tall and 20cm (8in) across. All bear bunches of delicate, white to pink, urn-shaped flowers in winter or spring. Small berries, usually scarlet, follow in autumn. Low-growing bearberries look excellent as ground cover in a shrub border or large rock garden. The larger, upright species look at home in an open, woodland garden.

■ **HARDINESS** Fully hardy ✵✵✵ to half-hardy ✵.
■ **CULTIVATION** Grow in moist, fertile, well-drained, acid (lime-free) soil in full sun or partial shade. Less hardy species need shelter.
■ **Sow** seed (*see pp.328–329*) in containers in a cold frame in autumn, immersing the seeds in boiling water for about 20 seconds before sowing. This softens the hard seed coats.
■ **Take** semi-ripe cuttings (*see pp.329–330*) in summer or layer in autumn (*see p.330*). Shoots growing along the soil surface often produce roots at the leaf joints. Lift, sever, and pot up.

***Arctostaphylos* x *media* 'Wood's Red'**
‡to 10cm (4in) ↔to 50cm (20in), low-growing and densely branched, suitable for a rockery or the front of a shrub border ✵✵✵

Argyranthemum
Marguerite
SUMMER TO AUTUMN

Argyranthemums are hard-working shrubs that produce a succession of cheery, daisy blooms from early summer right through to autumn. There are both single- and double-flowered types, in hues of white, soft yellow to apricot, and pale pink to deep cerise. Formerly classed as chrysanthemums, they have similar foliage: almost fern-like, and either green or greyish-green. They are invaluable in pots, in summer bedding schemes, or in mixed borders. Some make elegant specimens or are trained as standards (in a "lollipop" shape with a single, bare stem and a bushy head).

■ **HARDINESS** Frost-hardy ✵✵ (in mild areas) to half-hardy ✵.
■ **CULTIVATION** Grow in well-drained fertile soil in full sun. Most tolerate salt-laden winds in coastal areas. ■ **Pinch out** the tips of young plants to encourage a bushy habit. ■ **Prune** flowered shoots to within 2.5cm (1in) of their base after flowering or in early spring. Apply a winter mulch if the temperature falls below –5°C (23°F), taking cuttings in late summer as an insurance against losses; or lift and overwinter in frost-free conditions. ■ **Take** softwood cuttings in spring or semi-ripe cuttings in summer (*see pp.329–330*).

***Argyranthemum* 'Jamaica Primrose'** ♀
‡1.1m (3½ft) ↔1m (3ft), open habit with long branching stems, flowers are 6cm (2½in) across, good to train as a standard ✵

Artemisia
Mugwort, Sagebrush, Wormwood
YEAR-ROUND

Artemisias have ferny, aromatic, grey or silver foliage that gives year-round interest and acts as a foil for flowering plants or those with bolder leaves. There are evergreen and deciduous types, all bearing tiny flowers – the leaves are the chief draw. They look good in herb gardens (French tarragon is a form of *Artemisia dracunculus*), rock gardens, and shrub or flower borders (*see p.159*). Artemisias are often featured in drought-tolerant, Mediterranean-style gardens, although a few, notably *A. lactiflora*, do need moist soil.

■ **HARDINESS** Fully hardy ✵✵✵ to frost-hardy ✵✵.
■ **CULTIVATION** Grow in fertile, well-drained soil in a sunny position. *A. arborescens* needs the extra protection of a warm wall in frost-prone areas. In heavy clay soil, dig in plenty of coarse grit to improve drainage; plants can be short-lived in wet conditions. ■ **Prune** plants that have grown over-large and leggy to the ground, in autumn or spring, to encourage a compact habit.
■ **Sow** seed (*see pp.328–329*) in containers in a cold frame in autumn or spring. ■ **Take** heel cuttings in early summer (*see pp.329–330*).
■ **Prone to mildew** (*see p.333*) if damp.

Artemisia arborescens ♀
‡1m (3ft) ↔1.5m (5ft), evergreen with silky leaves ✵✵✵

Aucuba

YEAR-ROUND

Aucubas are useful, evergreen shrubs grown for their bold, glossy foliage and large fruits. They hardly ever suffer from pests and diseases, and tolerate all sorts of difficult growing conditions, including full shade, dry soils, pollution, and salt-laden winds. This makes them a popular choice for town gardens. Aucubas can be used as specimen plants in lawns, in mixed and shrub borders, or for informal hedging (if trimmed, they do not fruit as well). The variegated and spotted cultivars (such as 'Sulphurea Marginata' and 'Crotonifolia') make a bright splash in a dark corner.

■ **HARDINESS** Fully hardy ✳✳✳.
■ **CULTIVATION** Grow in any fertile soil except waterlogged conditions, in full sun or full shade; variegated species prefer partial shade. In areas with hot summers, grow in full shade. Use soil-based potting compost if growing it in a container. ■ **Feed** plants in pots once a month with a liquid fertilizer, and water freely when in full growth, but sparingly in winter. ■ **Trim** aucubas in spring to shape and cut back hard if they are growing too large. ■ **Prune** wayward shoots by cutting them well back into the centre of the bush. Sow seed (*see pp.328–329*) in containers in autumn. ■ **Take** semi-ripe cuttings (*see pp.329–330*) in summer.

Aucuba japonica
↕↔3m (10ft), female plants will produce bright red berries if a male is grown nearby

Azara

MIDWINTER TO MIDSUMMER

Strongly vanilla-scented flowers are the main attraction of this group of evergreen shrubs and small trees. The flowers are produced in tight clusters or spikes carried on the undersides of the branches, with different species flowering at times ranging from midwinter to midsummer. The flowers have no petals, but showy stamens give them a decorative, fluffy appearance. Berries may follow after hot summers. These trouble-free shrubs need a sunny and sheltered position, ideally against a warm wall: they are often wall-trained. The green leaves vary in size and are sometimes in distinctive unequal pairs, with a small leaf opposite a much larger one.

■ **HARDINESS** Fully hardy ✳✳✳ to half-hardy ✳.
■ **CULTIVATION** Grow in moist soil enriched with plenty of well-rotted organic matter. Site in sun or partial shade, sheltered from cold winds, which will scorch the leaves and cause them to drop. In colder areas, grow and train azaras against warm, sunny walls. ■ **Prune out** shoots that spoil the shape of the shrub after flowering; if wall-trained, prune back flowered shoots to two to four buds above the permanent framework of branches.

Azara microphylla ♀
↕10m (30ft) ↔ 4m (12ft), hardiest of the species, will also tolerate full shade ✳✳✳

Ballota

YEAR-ROUND

These evergreen or semi-evergreen plants form mounds or mats of rounded, aromatic, yellow-green to grey-green leaves. Small, funnel-shaped flowers in shades of green, purple, white, or pink are produced from late spring until late summer, but the attractive foliage is the main reason for growing ballotas. They make an excellent foil for more colourful plants, such as brightly flowered border phloxes (*see pp.254–255*) and daylilies (*Hemerocallis, see p.216*). For a more subtle effect, grow them alongside plants such as lavender (*Lavandula, see p.71*) for contrasting foliage textures within the same colour range.

■ **HARDINESS** Fully hardy ✳✳✳ to frost-hardy ✳✳.
■ **CULTIVATION** Grow in poor, dry soil that is free-draining. Position in full sun. ■ **Trim back** all flowered shoots to within 2.5cm (1in) of old growth after flowering or in mid- to late spring; alternatively, trim back in spring. ■ **A thick**, dry winter mulch helps protect borderline hardy plants in cold areas. ■ **Divide** perennials (*see p.330*) in spring or take softwood cuttings of shrubs in late spring or semi-ripe cuttings in early summer (*see p.329–330*).

***Ballota* 'All Hallows Green'** (syn. *Marrubium bourgaei* 'All Hallows Green')
↕60cm (24in) ↔75cm (30in) ✳✳✳

Berberis
Barberry

Barberries are grown for their ornamental foliage and their glowing, yellow to dark orange flowers. The flowers are produced in spring and summer, usually in small clusters, and are often followed by colourful fruits in autumn. There are evergreen and deciduous barberries, many of the latter showing fiery autumn colours. All have spiny stems, making an excellent choice for an impenetrable hedge, but with a wide range of species and cultivars to choose from, you can find a barberry for almost any aspect in the garden.

■ **HARDINESS** Fully hardy ✽✽✽ to frost-hardy ✽✽.
■ **CULTIVATION** Grow in any moist but well-drained soil. Position in full sun or partial shade: autumn colours and fruiting are best in full sun. ■ **Prune** after flowering: lightly trim or prune shoots that spoil the shape of evergreens and cut back flowered shoots of deciduous types to strong shoots or buds.
■ **Trim** hedges after flowering. ■ **Take** semi-ripe cuttings of both types or softwood cuttings of deciduous types in summer (*see pp.329–330*).
■ **Powdery mildew** can be a problem (*see p.333*); cut out badly affected parts and apply a fungicide.

Berberis thunbergii 'Dart's Red Lady'
↕1m (3ft) occasionally more ↔2.5m (8ft), deciduous, deep red-purple leaves turning bright red in autumn ✽✽✽

Berberis x stenophylla 'Corallina Compacta' ♀
↕↔ to 30cm (12in), evergreen, a dwarf cultivar of this usually large species, makes good edging ✽✽✽

Berberis thunbergii 'Rose Glow' ♀
↕1m (3ft) occasionally more ↔2.5m (8ft), rounded and deciduous, with the first leaves of the season unvariegated ✽✽✽

Berberis darwinii ♀
↕↔3m (10ft), upright, evergreen, flowering in spring, sometimes again in autumn, with blue-black fruits in autumn ✽✽✽

Betula
Birch

These graceful, deciduous trees provide a display in every season: the textured bark, often peeling and silvery-white or coppery-brown, looks stunning in winter when there is little else to see; male and female flowers are borne in separate catkins on the same tree during spring, and the small, toothed, mid- to dark green leaves generally turn a soft yellow in autumn. This is a large group, with several species suitable for small gardens. The slender forms of many species of birch look particularly attractive if room can be found in the garden for

a small group of trees. The spreading *Betula medwedewii* and the popular weeping birches are among the most beautiful and elegant of specimen trees for a garden.

■ **HARDINESS** Fully hardy ✳✳✳.
■ **CULTIVATION** Grow in reasonably fertile, well-drained soil. Site in sun or light, dappled shade; most will tolerate exposed positions.
■ **Prune out** any misplaced or crossing branches during winter, when the trees are dormant, to maintain a healthy framework of branches. ■ **Sow** seed (*see pp.328–329*) in a seedbed outdoors in autumn. ■ **Take** softwood cuttings (*see pp.329–330*) in summer.
■ **Mildew** (*see p.333*) may appear, but mature trees should recover without spraying, which would in any case be impractical. Young trees could be treated if badly affected.

Betula nigra (Black birch, River birch)
‡18m (60ft) ↔12m (40ft), conical to spreading in habit, the bark becoming fissured and grey-white or blackish on old trees

Betula papyrifera (Canoe birch, Paper birch)
‡20m (70ft) ↔10m (30ft), newly exposed bark is pale orange-brown, paling with age, and autumn leaves are yellow to orange

Betula utilis var. **jacquemontii** 'Silver Shadow' ♀
‡18m (60ft) ↔10m (30ft), with larger leaves than many other birches and particularly bright white bark

Brachyglottis
Senecio

SUMMER

Evergreen shrubs with clusters of creamy-white to deep yellow flowers in summer, these are ideal for exposed and coastal gardens. 'Sunshine', the most widely grown, belongs to a popular group of small cultivars called the Dunedin Group. Usually about 75cm (30in) tall, these form mounds of oval, wavy-edged leaves, hairy at first, and produce clusters of bright yellow flowerheads from summer until autumn. Other choices include *Brachyglottis repanda*, a spreading shrub to 3m (10ft) tall and wide with dark-green leaves and creamy-white flowers, and the compact *B. rotundifolia*, at 1m (3ft) more suitable for small gardens. Grow them in shrub borders; the foliage makes an effective contrast to narrow-leaved shrubs such as hebes (*see p.61*).

■ **HARDINESS** Fully hardy ✳✳✳ to half-hardy ✳, very cold spells may damage soft stems.
■ **CULTIVATION** Grow in well-drained soil in full sun. ■ **Trim back** or lightly prune shoots that spoil the shape of the shrub after flowering.
■ **Take** semi-ripe cuttings (*see pp.329–330*) in summer.

***Brachyglottis* 'Sunshine'** ♀
‡75cm (30in) ↔1m (3ft), tolerant of all but the shadiest positions, thrives in seaside gardens ✳✳✳

Buddleja
Butterfly bush

EARLY TO LATE SUMMER

The fragrant flowers of buddlejas are wonderful for attracting hordes of butterflies. Most widely grown is the hardy *Buddleja davidii* and its cultivars, most growing to 2.5–3m (8–10ft) tall in a single season, with pink, purple, lilac, or white flowers in conical spikes on tall shoots from late summer to early autumn. *B. globosa*, the orange ball tree, is a larger, rounded shrub, also hardy, that flowers in early summer. Buddlejas may be deciduous, semi-evergreen, or evergreen. They are a good backdrop to other summer-flowering shrubs.

■ **HARDINESS** Fully hardy ✳✳✳ to frost-tender ✿.
■ **CULTIVATION** Grow in fertile, well-drained soil in full sun; poorer soils are tolerated. ■ **Prune** *B. davidii* and its cultivars by cutting old stems back to the base, in early spring (*see p.323*). ■ **Trim** other buddlejas after flowering to keep within bounds. Take semi-ripe cuttings (*see pp.329–330*) in summer or hardwood cuttings of *B. davidii* in autumn. If caterpillars are troublesome, pick them off by hand.

***Buddleja davidii* 'Royal Red'** ♀
‡3m (10ft) ✳✳✳

***Buddleja davidii* 'White Profusion'** ♀
‡3m (10ft) ✳✳

Bupleurum fruticosum
Shrubby hare's ear, Thorow-wax

MIDSUMMER TO AUTUMN

Excellent for coastal areas because it will withstand salt spray from the sea, this evergreen has a spreading habit, making it ideal for covering a wall or bank. The small, starry, yellow flowers surrounded by leafy bracts are borne in rounded clusters from midsummer until autumn. This can grow to be a large and dense shrub, so it needs positioning near the back of a shrub or mixed border. Grow with other shrubs such as hawthorns (*Crataegus, see p.62*), St. John's wort (*Hypericum, see p.66*), and buddlejas (*see left*).

■ **HARDINESS** Fully hardy ✳✳✳ (borderline in cold areas).
■ **CULTIVATION** Will grow in any well-drained soil, preferring full sun in a warm, sheltered site. ■ **Prune** off the fading flowers to prevent seeds forming. ■ **Trim back** shoots that spoil the shape of the shrub in mid- or late spring: it will also tolerate hard pruning if it outgrows its space. ■ **Sow** seed (*see pp.328–329*) in a container in a cold frame in spring. ■ **Take** semi-ripe cuttings (*see pp.329–330*) in summer.

Bupleurum fruticosum
‡2m (6ft) ↔2.5m (8ft)

Buxus
Box, Boxwood

YEAR-ROUND

Evergreen box is one of the garden's most versatile plants. Although many varieties are naturally large and shrubby, all respond well to regular trimming, making them equally at home in formal and informal settings. Tiny, yellow-green flowers appear in spring, but it is the neat, leathery foliage that steals the show. Used in hedges or screens, it furnishes a constant backdrop for seasonal action in the borders. You can clip box into ornamental topiary shapes; simple forms need trimming only once or twice a year. Dwarf boxes were traditionally used to create knot gardens and parterres; they are also excellent for edging paths and borders, and as ground cover.

■ **HARDINESS** Fully hardy ✳✳✳ to frost-hardy ✳✳.
■ **CULTIVATION** Box needs fertile, well-drained soil, ideally in partial shade; dry soil and full sun can cause dull or scorched foliage.
■ **Trim** shrubs and hedges in summer; box tolerates hard pruning in late spring if fed and well watered after. ■ **Take** semi-ripe cuttings in summer (*see pp.329–330*). ■ **Box suckers**, pale green, aphid-like insects that excrete white honey dew, may impede growth on young plants from spring to summer.

Buxus sempervirens 'Elegantissima' ♀
‡↔1.5m (5ft)

Buxus sempervirens 'Handsworthiensis'
‡↔5m (15ft)

Buxus 'Latifolia Maculata' ♀
‡2.5m (8ft) ↔2m (6ft)

Buxus sempervirens 'Suffruticosa' ♀
‡1m (3ft) ↔1.5m (5ft)

Callicarpa
Beauty berry

AUTUMN TO WINTER

Aptly named, the beauty berry is valued for its vibrantly coloured, bead-like, autumn berries. These remain on bare stems of deciduous species after the leaves fall, bringing colour to a winter garden. Berries may be violet, lilac, white, or dusky purple and are most abundant after a long, hot summer. If you have space, plant groups of three or more to maximize fruiting. These shrubs are deciduous or evergreen with green or bronze leaves and varied habits. They bear clusters of small flowers in summer. Other berrying shrubs and trees, such as cotoneasters (*see p.41*) and sorbus (*see p.101*), make good companions.

■ **HARDINESS** Fully hardy ✳✳✳ to frost-tender ❀.
■ **CULTIVATION** Fertile, well-drained soil in full sun or light, dappled shade is suitable.
■ **Cut back** the previous year's growth to the main stems in early spring (*see p.322*). If drastic pruning is required, cut back flowered shoots close to the base. ■ **Sow** seed (*see pp.328–329*) in pots in a cold frame in autumn or spring.
■ **Take** softwood cuttings in spring or semi-ripe cuttings in summer (*see pp.329–330*).

Callicarpa bodinieri var. **giraldii**
‡3m (10ft) ↔2.5m (8ft), deciduous, upright bush, clusters of small pink flowers in midsummer ✳✳✳

Callistemon
Bottlebrush
SPRING TO AUTUMN

The distinctive, bristly flower spikes that give these evergreen shrubs and trees their common name emerge in spring or summer. *Callistemon linearis* and *C. speciosus* bloom into autumn. Bold hues of crimson, purple, pink, white, or gold flowers are set off by simple, leathery leaves. *C. citrinus* 'Firebrand' also boasts silvery-pink shoots. Habits vary, but many have a spreading form. Natives of Australia, bottlebrushes thrive at the base of a warm wall in a shrub border, with ceanothus (*see p.32*) and lavenders (*see p.71*). Grow tender species in containers and overwinter them under cover.

■ **HARDINESS** Fully hardy ✳✳✳ (borderline) to frost-tender ❆.
■ **CULTIVATION** Bottlebrushes like moist but well-drained, neutral to acid (lime-free) soil, in full sun. ■ **Lightly trim** any shoots that spoil the shape of the shrub, after flowering; the plants tolerate hard pruning if frost-damaged or grown out of their space. ■ **Sow** seed (*see pp.328–329*) on the surface of moist compost, in spring at 16–18°C (61–64°F). ■ **Take** semi-ripe cuttings in late summer (*see pp.329–330*).

Callistemon pallidus (Lemon bottlebrush)
↕↔2–4m (6–12ft), erect to spreading shrub, downy shoots, dark to grey-green leaves, 10cm (4in) flowers late spring to midsummer ✳

Calluna vulgaris
Scot's heather, Ling
MIDSUMMER TO LATE AUTUMN

Beloved by bees, this evergreen shrub and its cultivars has stems thickly encrusted with purple, red, pink, or white bell-shaped flowers from midsummer to late autumn. The flower spikes can be up to 10cm (4in) long, but become shorter as the plants age. The foliage usually is dark green, and purple-tinged in winter; the linear leaves lie flat along the stems. There are over 500 prostrate to upright cultivars to choose from; all make excellent ground cover, and some have striking foliage, like the terracotta 'Firefly'. Make space for heathers in wildlife gardens, in bold groups of three or five, or more, together with dwarf rhododendrons (*see pp.92–93*) and conifers. (*See also p.44 and pp.48–49.*)

■ **HARDINESS** Fully hardy ✳✳✳.
■ **CULTIVATION** Callunas need an open site with well-drained, acid (lime-free) soil.
■ **Cut back** flowered shoots to within 2.5cm (1in) of older growth in early spring.
■ **Mulch** with leafmould or composted bark (*see p.326*) in spring or autumn to encourage growth. ■ **Take** semi-ripe cuttings 5cm (2in) long in midsummer (*see pp.329–330*). Layer shoots in spring as for ericas (*see p.48*).

***Calluna vulgaris* 'Gold Haze'** ♥
↕10–60cm (4–24in) ↔ 45cm (18in), pale yellow foliage is retained all year, white flower spikes are 5–10cm (2–4in) long

***Calluna vulgaris* 'Anthony Davis'** ♥
↕45cm (18in) ↔ to 75cm (30in), grey-green leaves, white flowers over 10cm (4in) long, good for cutting

***Calluna vulgaris* 'Silver Knight'**
↕40cm (16in) ↔ to 75cm (30in), downy grey foliage darkens to purple-grey in winter, flower spikes are 5–10cm (2–4in) long

***Calluna vulgaris* 'Robert Chapman'** ♥
↕25cm (10in) ↔ 65cm (26in), gold foliage turns red and orange in winter and spring, purple flower spikes are 5–10cm (2–4in) long

Camellia

These elegant, evergreen shrubs suit a range of uses from borders to woodland settings. They are also excellent container plants, and this is an ideal way of growing them if your soil is alkaline (high lime content), since camellias prefer a neutral to acid soil. There are over 250 species, and the largest are very tall, but there are many smaller cultivars that are more suited to most gardens. The exquisite flowers in shades of pink, scarlet, and white appear in spring and last for several weeks. Borne singly or in clusters, they last well as cut flowers and some are slightly fragrant. Flowers may be single or double, and vary considerably in size, the largest measuring 13cm (5in) or more across, but the average bloom is about half that size. Most commonly grown camellias are hardy, although *Camellia reticulata* and its cultivars are half-hardy and need a sheltered site. Dark green, glossy foliage ensures that camellias stay handsome all year.

■ **HARDINESS** Fully hardy ❋❋❋ to frost-tender ❀.
■ **CULTIVATION** Grow in moist but well-drained, humus-rich, acid soil (pH 5.5–5.6). Shelter from cold winds and position in partial shade, since early sun may damage the buds and flowers on frosty mornings.
■ **Plant** with the top of the root ball just below the surface of the soil.
■ **Mulch** in spring with 5–8cm (2–3in) leafmould or shredded bark.
■ **Feed** with a balanced fertilizer in mid-spring and again in early summer, and keep well watered during dry spells to prevent bud drop.
■ **Protect** roots with a thatch of bracken or straw during prolonged cold spells. ■ **Prune** lightly to shape in late spring or early summer after flowering, and deadhead. ■ **Take** semi-ripe cuttings from late summer until early winter (*see pp.329–330*). Virus disease may blemish flowers, and camellias may be attacked by vine weevils (*see p.332*).

C. **'Inspiration'** ♀ ‡4m (12ft) ↔2m (6ft)

C. *japonica* **'Adolphe Audusson'** ♀ ‡9m (28ft) ↔8m (25ft)

C. *japonica* **'Betty Sheffield Supreme'** ‡2–4m (6–12ft) ↔1.5–3m (5–10ft)

C. *japonica* **'Elegans'** ♀ ‡9m (28ft) ↔8m (25ft)

C. *japonica* **'Mrs D.W. Davis'** ‡9m (28ft) ↔8m (25ft)

C. *japonica* **'R.L. Wheeler'** ♀ ‡9m (28ft) ↔8m (25ft)

C. *tsaii* ‡10m (30ft) ↔5m (15ft)

C. x *williamsii* **'Anticipation'** ♀ ‡4m (12ft) ↔2m (6ft)

Pruning young camellias

Young camellias develop a variety of habits. Careful pruning of young plants can help produce a well-balanced shape and encourage new, bushy growth. Reduce any thin, weak growth by cutting back to two or three buds or pruning it out entirely and shorten any vigorous main shoots to give the plant a balanced shape. To encourage branching at the base, pinch out the tips. If you are planning to train your camellia against a wall, then look for a plant with a tall central stem. Established plants require very little pruning. If plants have outgrown their space, they can be cut back hard in early spring.

C. japonica 'Alexander Hunter' ♀
↕9m (28ft) ↔8m (25ft)

C. japonica 'Apollo' ↕9m (28ft) ↔8m (25ft)

C. japonica 'Ave Maria' ♀ ↕9m (28ft)
↔8m (25ft)

C. japonica 'Bella Romana'
↕↔2m (6ft)

C. japonica 'Gloire de Nantes' ♀
↕9m (28ft) ↔8m (25ft)

C. japonica 'Guilio Nuccio' ♀ ↕9m (28ft)
↔8m (25ft)

C. japonica 'Hagoromo' ♀ ↕9m (28ft)
↔8m (25ft)

C. japonica 'Jupiter' ♀ ↕9m (28ft)
↔8m (25ft)

C. japonica 'Rubescens Major' ♀
↕9m (28ft) ↔8m (25ft)

C. reticulata ↕10m (30ft) ↔5m (15ft)

C. reticulata 'Arch of Triumph' ↕3m (10ft)
↔5m (15ft)

C. reticulata x *williamsii* 'Leonard
Messel' ↕↔2m (6ft)

C. x *williamsii* 'Bow Bells' ♀
↕4m (12ft) ↔1–3m (3–10ft)

C. x *williamsii* 'Donation' ♀ ↕5m (15ft)
↔2.5m (8ft)

C. x *williamsii* 'J.C. Williams' ♀
↕2–5m (6–15ft) ↔1–3m (3–10ft)

C. x *williamsii* 'Saint Ewe' ♀ ↕2–5m
(6–15ft) ↔1–3m (3–10ft)

Caragana

These deciduous shrubs or small trees thrive in exposed sites with dry soils. They are found from Eastern Europe to China and their tolerance of difficult conditions makes them very garden-worthy. They have attractive leaves, and delicate, pea-like flowers in yellow, white, or pink, followed in autumn by long, slender, brown pods. Caraganas are useful as a windbreak or can be grown in a shrub or mixed border with other trees and shrubs. *Caragana arborescens* 'Pendula' is often sold grafted on top of a straight, clear stem to form a small weeping standard. The dwarf *C. arborescens* 'Nana' is slow-growing, to 75cm (30in) tall and wide, with twisted branches; it makes an unusual rock-garden plant.

■ **HARDINESS** Fully hardy ✳✳✳.
■ **CULTIVATION** Grow in well-drained, reasonably fertile soil in full sun. Will also tolerate poor, dry soils in exposed places.
■ **Prune** minimally, only to remove any misplaced shoots, in late winter or early spring.
■ **Sow** seed in containers in a cold frame as soon as it is ripe (*see pp.328–329*); or sow in spring, pre-soaking the seeds before sowing to soften the seed coat. Take softwood cuttings in spring (*see pp.329–330*).

Caragana arborescens (Pea tree)
‡6m (20ft) ↔ 4m (12ft), thorny shrub, light green leaves made up of 12 leaflets, pale lemon flowers in late spring

Carpinus
Hornbeam

There are 35–40 species of these deciduous, woodland trees, several of which make good garden trees and can also be grown as handsome hedges. Grown as trees, they have an elegant habit, ranging from columnar and pyramid-shaped – the flame-like *Carpinus betulus* 'Fastigiata' being particularly popular – to rounded and spreading. Their beech-like foliage is mid- to dark green and often glossy; smooth, fluted grey bark is another pleasing feature. In spring, they produce yellow-green catkins, followed by drooping, hop-like, green fruits, maturing to brown or yellow. Autumn foliage colour is striking, too, the leaves turning to gold and amber.

■ **HARDINESS** Fully hardy ✳✳✳.
■ **CULTIVATION** Grow in reasonably fertile, well-drained soil in sun or partial shade.
■ **Prune** young trees to remove any misplaced or crossing branches in late winter or early spring; trim hedges in mid- to late summer. Hornbeams can withstand severe pruning if they outgrow their space. ■ **Sow** seed in a seedbed outdoors in autumn (*see pp.328–329*).
■ **Take** greenwood cuttings in early summer (*see pp.329–330*).

Carpinus betulus ♀
‡25m (80ft) ↔ 20m (70ft), as a tree pyramid-shaped, rounded when mature; as hedge (*see above*) retains brown leaves over winter

Caryopteris

Small, dainty shrubs with a mound-forming habit, caryopteris bear masses of small, fluffy flowers in shades of blue. The group includes both these deciduous shrubs and some perennials, found in a variety of habitats from dry, hot slopes to woodland. They flower from late summer until autumn; most have grey- or silvery-green foliage, giving a cool look, although 'Worcester Gold' has warm yellow foliage. Caryopteris are elegant front-of-border shrubs, especially planted in groups; they make a striking contrast with yellow-flowered potentillas (*see p.87*) or St. John's wort (*Hypericum, p.66*).

■ **HARDINESS** Fully hardy ✳✳✳ to frost-hardy ✳✳.
■ **CULTIVATION** Grow in light but moderately fertile soil, in full sun. Plant against a warm wall in very cold areas, especially if summers are also cool. ■ **Prune** previous year's flowered shoots in early spring, cutting back to three or four good buds, so that a permanent stubby framework of shoots develops. If necessary, cut down almost to soil level. ■ **Sow** seed in autumn in a cold frame (*see pp.328–329*). ■ **Take** softwood cuttings in late spring, or semi-ripe cuttings in early summer (*see pp.329–330*).

Caryopteris x clandonensis 'Kew Blue'
‡1m (3ft) ↔ 1.5m (5ft), excellent on chalky soils, leaves silver-grey underneath, attractive seedheads ✳✳✳

Cassiope

Originating from windswept arctic and alpine regions, this is a small group of dwarf, evergreen shrubs with a ground-hugging habit. They have tiny, overlapping, almost scale-like leaves that clasp the short, slender stems. In late spring and early summer, they produce tiny, nodding, bell-shaped flowers that hang singly or in pairs. The flowers are white, sometimes tinged red. Cassiope do best in acid (lime-free) soil and need plenty of moisture. They are so small that they are really only suitable for the rock garden or alpine trough, or perhaps planted in drifts in open woodland. 'Edinburgh' is the easiest to grow, and looks good with dwarf rhododendrons and conifers in an open position.

■ **HARDINESS** Fully hardy ✳✳✳. Late frosts may damage the flowers.
■ **CULTIVATION** Best grown in a sheltered site in moist, acid (lime-free) soil in partial shade or an open sunny site. *C. tetragona* tolerates some lime. ■ **Sow** seed in a container in a cold frame in autumn (*see pp.328–329*). ■ **Take** semi-ripe cuttings in summer (*see pp.329–330*), and layer shoots in autumn or early spring (*see p.330*).

***Cassiope* 'Edinburgh'** ♀
↕↔ to 25cm (10in), low-growing but with upright shoots, flowers produced at stem tips in late spring

Catalpa

Catalpas are deciduous trees with year-round appeal, with their showy, often beautifully coloured foliage, large flowers, and distinctive seed pods. The bell-shaped flowers are borne in upright clusters in mid- and late summer. They are followed in autumn by bean-like seed pods, usually more than 30cm (1ft) long. Catalpas have a wide, spreading habit and are best admired when grown as specimen trees in a lawn. Several varieties can be pollarded (cutting the trunk to a metre, then cutting stems back to this stubby head each year) to produce lollipop-shaped, foliage shrubs with very large, ornamental leaves. They will thrive in sheltered town gardens.

■ **HARDINESS** Fully hardy ✳✳✳, although soft, young shoots can be prone to frost damage.
■ **CULTIVATION** Grow in fertile, moist but well-drained soil in full sun, with shelter from strong winds. In cold gardens, protect young plants from severe frosts with fleece. ■ **Prune** in late winter or early spring, either to pollard (*see above*), or in trees, only to maintain a healthy branch framework. ■ **Sow** seed in pots in autumn (*see pp.328–329*). Take softwood cuttings in late spring or summer (*pp.329–330*).

Catalpa speciosa
↕↔15m (50ft), spreading habit, flowers larger and showier than most other catalpas, seed pods to 50cm (20in) long

***Catalpa bignonioides* 'Aurea'** ♀
↕↔10m (30ft), slow-growing, leaves bronze when young and unfold in early summer, good pollarded to form a shrub

Catalpa bignonioides ♀
(Indian bean tree)
↕↔15m (50ft), broad heart-shaped leaves, fragrant flowers, pencil-thin seed pods to 40cm (16in) long

Ceanothus
California lilac

Vigorous, spreading shrubs, California lilacs are grown for their masses of usually blue, but sometimes white or pink flowers. They flower abundantly, in small fluffy clusters at the tips of stems or on small sideshoots. Most of the evergreen ceanothus are best suited to growing against a wall or fence or in a sheltered spot. Prostrate or low-growing species make superb ground-cover plants and are ideal for sloping banks. The deciduous types, generally hardier than the evergreens, make more compact plants, especially if pruned annually back to a stubby framework of stems, and are ideal in a border. California lilacs are not very long-lived, and dislike being transplanted.

■ **HARDINESS** Fully hardy ✻✻✻ to frost-hardy ✻✻.
■ **CULTIVATION** Grow in any reasonably fertile soil in full sun, sheltered from strong, cold winds. Tolerant of limy soils, but may develop yellow leaves (chlorosis) on shallow, chalky soils.
■ **Prune** in early spring, lightly trimming evergreens to maintain a good shape, and cutting deciduous types back to a permanent framework; treat all wall-trained plants as for deciduous species. ■ **Take** greenwood cuttings of deciduous types in summer or semi-ripe cuttings of all types in late summer (*see pp.329–330*).

Ceanothus x *pallidus* **'Perle Rose'**
↕↔1.5m (5ft), bushy, deciduous type, flowering from midsummer to autumn ✻✻✻

Ceanothus **'Cascade'** ♀
↕↔4m (12ft), vigorous, arching evergreen, flowering from spring to early summer ✻✻

Ceanothus **'Blue Cushion'**
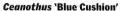 ↕45–75cm (18–30in) ↔1–2m (3–6ft), spreading but dense and tidy evergreen, ideal as a ground-cover plant, flowering profusely in summer ✻✻

Ceanothus **'Blue Mound'** ♀
↕1.5m (5ft) ↔2m (6ft), prostrate, mound-forming evergreen, flowering in late spring ✻✻

Cedrus
Cedar
YEAR-ROUND

These large, evergreen conifers make impressive specimen trees, needing plenty of space if their stature is to be fully appreciated (although there are some dwarf cultivars). Conical when young, they later develop spreading, horizontal branches. Cedars are best grown on their own, or with other large trees where space allows; they are very long-lived. Their needles are arranged in clusters on short shoots; there are cedars with either bright golden or glaucous blue foliage, as well as plain green. Male cones are cylindrical and light brown; female cones are oblong or barrel-shaped, and green when they first appear, ripening and turning brown over two years.

■ **HARDINESS** Fully hardy ✳✳✳.
■ **CULTIVATION** Grow in any reasonably fertile soil in an open, sunny position. ■ **Prune** only if the trees happen to produce two leading shoots, cutting out the weaker shoot in autumn. ■ **Sow** seed (see pp.328–329) in spring after keeping them moist and in a refrigerator at 0–5°C (32–41°F) for three weeks.

Cedrus deodara 'Aurea' ♀
↕5m (15ft), a slow-growing cultivar with golden-yellow spring foliage that becomes greener in summer

Ceratostigma
Chinese plumbago
LATE SUMMER TO AUTUMN

True blue, late-summer flowers distinguish these small shrubs, all growing to about 1m (3ft) tall. The group includes the woody perennial *Ceratostigma plumbaginoides*, which is half the height and perfect for the front of a border. There are deciduous, evergreen, or semi-evergreen species, the leaves of all turning red in autumn to provide a foil for late flowers. Their colouring is particularly dramatic in a mixed or shrub border next to yellow daylilies (*Hemerocallis, see p.216*) or St. John's wort (*Hypericum, see p.66*). Growth often dies back in very cold winters, but usually regrows in spring.

■ **HARDINESS** Fully hardy ✳✳✳.
■ **CULTIVATION** Grow in light, reasonably fertile soil, in full sun. ■ **Prune back** to within 2.5cm (1in) of a permanent framework after flowering or in early spring. ■ **Remove** any growth that has been damaged during winter in spring. ■ **Take** softwood cuttings in spring or semi-ripe cuttings in summer (see pp.329–330). Shoots can be layered (see p.330) in autumn. ■ **Susceptible** to powdery mildew (see also Mildew, p.333); treat badly affected plants with fungicide.

Ceratostigma willmottianum ♀
↕1m (3ft) ↔1.5m (5ft), bushy deciduous shrub with purple-edged leaves, turning red in autumn

Cercidiphyllum
Katsura tree
AUTUMN

Fiery autumn displays of yellow, orange, and red leaves that smell of burnt sugar when crushed are the chief attraction of this tree. The mid-green leaves are also bronze when young. The best colour is produced on acid (lime-free) soils. All katsuras belong to one species, *Cercidiphyllum japonicum*. There is a weeping form, and also a variety that is a smaller tree, despite being called *magnificum*. Planted as a specimen tree, the katsura can show off its form, pyramidal when young and becoming more rounded with age.

■ **HARDINESS** Fully hardy ✳✳✳, although the young leaves may be damaged by late frosts. New foliage should grow again.
■ **CULTIVATION** Grow in good, fertile soil enriched with plenty of well-rotted organic matter in sun or partial shade, sheltered from cold, drying winds. ■ **Prune out** any crossing branches or those that spoil the shape of the tree in late winter or early spring. Plants often develop several main stems, but these can be reduced to one if desired, provided that the tree is still young. ■ **Take** semi-ripe cuttings in midsummer (see pp.329–330).

Cercidiphyllum japonicum ♀
(Katsura tree)
↕20m (70ft) ↔15m (50ft), the tree tends to remain smaller in cooler areas

Cercis
Redbud

SPRING AND AUTUMN

Deciduous trees from woodland edges, these make excellent specimen plants in a lawn or in a large shrub border. They are grown for their foliage and their clusters of pink or purple flowers, borne in profusion in spring before the leaves. The flowers of the Judas tree, *Cercis siliquastrum*, appear directly on the branches and even the trunk. This is the largest species; choose *C. chinensis* or *C. canadensis* for a smaller garden; the latter can also be kept small by pollarding (cut the trunk to a metre, then cut the shoots that emerge back to this head each year). The leaves of all species are heart-shaped, and turn yellow in autumn.

■ **HARDINESS** Fully hardy ✲✲✲; frosts may damage young growth.
■ **CULTIVATION** Grow in fertile, moist but well-drained soil in full sun or partial shade. Plant while the trees are young; older plants resent root disturbance. ■ **Prune out** branches that are crossing in late winter or early spring. *C. canadensis* 'Forest Pansy' can be pollarded in early spring for larger, showier foliage.
■ **Sow** seed (*see pp.328–329*) in containers in a cold frame in autumn. ■ **Take** semi-ripe cuttings (*see pp.329–330*) in summer.

***Cercis canadensis* 'Forest Pansy'** ♀
(Eastern redbud)
↕↔5m (15ft), may not flower in all locations, but the purple foliage gives a reliable display

Chaenomeles
Flowering quince, Japanese quince, Japonica

WINTER, SPRING, AND AUTUMN

These versatile shrubs, among the first to flower, are usually grown in shrub borders or trained against a wall or fence, but also make useful ground cover or an informal hedge, even in shade. Deciduous and spiny-branched, they flower in shades of red and pink. The flowers, single or double, are borne all along the stems, appearing before and with the leaves. They are followed in autumn by apple-like, yellow to green fruits, which are edible after being cooked, although the true edible quince is a different tree, *Cydonia*.

■ **HARDINESS** Fully hardy ✲✲✲.
■ **CULTIVATION** Grow in reasonably fertile soil: flowering quinces are best not planted in very limy (alkaline) soil, where the leaves may yellow (chlorotic). Position in full sun or partial shade. ■ **Cut back** flowered shoots after flowering: cut to strong buds lower down, or if wall-trained cut back to the permanent framework. ■ **Sow** seed (*see pp.328–329*) in containers in a cold frame or outdoors in a seedbed. ■ **Take** semi-ripe cuttings (*see pp.329–330*) in summer or layer shoots (*see p.330*) in autumn.

***Chaenomeles* x *superba* 'Crimson and Gold'** ♀
↕1m (3ft) ↔2m (6ft), flowers into late spring, green fruit ripening to yellow in autumn

Chamaecyparis
False cypress

YEAR-ROUND

Ideal for hedging, these evergreen, coniferous trees are not overly vigorous and tolerate some clipping; their attractive growth habit also makes many of them handsome specimen plants. Grow them with other conifers such as *Cupressus* (*see p.43*), or with large rhododendrons (*see pp.92–93*). There are also many dwarf or slow-growing cultivars, and these can be used in smaller borders or even in large rock gardens. The leaves are scale-like and flattened;

***Chamaecyparis obtusa* 'Nana Aurea'** ♀
↕2m (6ft)

***Chamaecyparis lawsoniana* 'Pembury Blue'** ♀
↕15m (50ft)

contact with the foliage may aggravate some skin allergies. False cypresses bear round or oval male cones in spring, which are followed in summer by round or angular female cones that ripen in autumn.

■ **HARDINESS** Fully hardy ✻✻✻.
CULTIVATION Grow in moist but well-drained, preferably neutral to acid (lime-free) soil, although they will tolerate deep, chalky soils. Position in full sun. ■ **Trim** trees used for hedging from late spring to autumn, but do not cut into older wood. ■ **Sow** seed (*see pp.328–329*) in a seedbed outdoors in spring or take semi-ripe cuttings (*see pp.329–330*) in late summer. If heavy infestations of conifer aphids cause browning of foliage on false cypress, use insecticide in spring.

Chamaecyparis pisifera 'Filifera Aurea' ♀
‡12m (40ft)

Chamaecyparis nootkatensis 'Pendula' ♀
‡30m (100ft)

Chimonanthus praecox
Wintersweet

Powerfully fragrant, waxy flowers hang from the bare shoots of *Chimonanthus praecox* throughout winter. This deciduous shrub has flowers that are pale sulphur-yellow. Young plants take a few years to reach flowering age. The shrub is not unattractive in leaf, but winter is its real season of interest, so plant it near a doorway or where you will come across it and its extraordinary scent on winter walks. It can also be trained against a sunny wall, and this may be advisable in cooler areas, because good, sunny summers are needed to ripen the wood in an open position.

■ **HARDINESS** Fully hardy ✻✻✻; frosts may damage unripened wood.
CULTIVATION Grow in any fertile, well-drained soil in full sun. Prune only mature shrubs that flower regularly in late winter, when dormant, or in early spring. ■ **Cut out** any crossing or misshapen branches; cut back the shoots of wall-trained plants to 2–4 buds above the permanent framework of branches. ■ **Sow** seed (*see pp.328–329*) in a cold frame as soon as it is ripe. Take softwood cuttings (*see pp.329–330*) in summer.

Chimonanthus praecox 'Grandiflorus' ♀
‡4m (12ft) ↔3m (10ft), flowers that are both larger and a deeper yellow than the species

Chionanthus
Fringe tree

Large, attractive shrubs, fringe trees are grown for their long, narrow leaves and fragrant, white flowers, borne in clusters during summer. Two spreading, deciduous shrubs from this large and varied genus are grown in gardens: *Chionanthus retusus* has upright flower clusters and peeling bark, while *C. virginicus* has hanging flower clusters and larger leaves that have bright, golden-yellow autumn colour. In autumn, the flowers of both are followed by blue-black fruits. Fringe trees make excellent specimen plants; they also work well grown in a shrub border along with plants such as abelias (*see p.12*), choisyas (*see p.36*), or camellias (*see pp.28–29*).

■ **HARDINESS** Fully hardy ✻✻✻.
CULTIVATION Grow in reasonably fertile soil in full sun: *C. retusus* tolerates limy (alkaline) soil, but *C. virginicus* needs an acid soil. Flowering and fruiting are best in climates with hot summers. ■ **Prune out** crossing or badly placed branches in winter or early spring, to prevent growth becoming unhealthily crowded. ■ **Sow** seed (*see pp.328–329*) in containers in a cold frame in autumn; germination may take as long as 18 months.

Chionanthus virginicus
‡3m (10ft) ↔3m (10ft) or more, the lower branches can be pruned back to the trunk to encourage a more tree-like form

Choisya

Mexican orange blossom

YEAR-ROUND

The glossy, aromatic foliage of these evergreen shrubs ensures they have year-round appeal in any garden, quite apart from the fact that most give a superb, late summer and autumn show of abundant, starry, sweetly fragrant flowers. Of the commonly available Mexican orange blossoms, 'Aztec Pearl' and *Choisya ternata* are particularly good value, since they also produce an early flush of blooms in late spring before the main flowering towards the end of summer. Although *C. ternata* SUNDANCE rarely flowers, this is more than made up for by its spring foliage, which can light up the dullest border with a ray of sunshine.

■ **HARDINESS** Fully hardy ✳✳✳ to frost-hardy ✳✳.
■ **CULTIVATION** Choisyas prefer a fertile, well-drained soil in full sun, but tolerate partial shade. The frost-hardy varieties benefit from the extra warmth of a south-facing wall, and a winter mulch. ■ **Trim** any shoots that spoil the shape of the shrub after flowering.
■ **Take** semi-ripe cuttings in summer (*see pp.329–330*). ■ **Snails** and slugs like these shrubs; while the plant is small and vulnerable, it is well worth discouraging them (*see p.218*).

***Choisya ternata* SUNDANCE** ('Lich') ♀
↕↔2.5m (8ft), the buttery young foliage of this cultivar is best in bright sun, achieving only a greenish-yellow in shade ✳✳

Cistus

Rock rose, Sun rose

EARLY TO LATE SUMMER

Rock roses are evergreens, grown for their profuse, saucer-shaped flowers in white to purplish-pink. They appear from early to late summer. Rock roses thrive in sunny spots in a shrub border, at the base of a wall, around a patio, or spilling over the side of a raised bed. Usefully, they appreciate dry conditions and poor soil, and so grow very well as low-maintenance container plants and alongside demanding plants such as shrub roses that take a lot out of the soil. They can be short-lived; it is worth taking cuttings to make replacement plants.

■ **HARDINESS** Frost-hardy ✳✳.
■ **CULTIVATION** Grow in full sun, in poor to reasonably fertile, well-drained soil, including chalky soil. ■ **Pinch out** the growing tips of young plants to encourage a bushy habit; lightly trim shoots that spoil the shape of the shrub in spring, or after flowering. Old, woody plants are best replaced. ■ **Sow** seed (*see pp.328–329*) in a cold frame when it is ripe, or in spring. ■ **Take** softwood cuttings in summer (*see pp.329–330*).

***Choisya* x *argenteus* 'Peggy Sammons'** ♀
↕↔to 1m (3ft)

***Choisya* x *dansereaui* 'Decumbens'** ♀
↕↔1m (3ft)

Clerodendrum

LATE SUMMER TO AUTUMN

This is a large group of tropical and subtropical plants, although some of the elegant, shrubby species are robust enough to be grown outdoors in cooler, temperate climates. The hardy, deciduous shrubs include *Clerodendrum trichotomum*, a large shrub for a large garden, and the glory flower (*C. bungei*), smaller but still up to 2m (6ft) tall. This species is only frost-hardy and will be happiest in a warm, sheltered border. Both are valued for their large clusters of often fragrant flowers, usually produced from late summer to autumn.

■ **HARDINESS** Fully hardy ✳✳✳ to frost-tender 🌡.
■ **CULTIVATION** Grow in soil enriched with well-rotted organic matter to make sure it is fertile and moist but well-drained, in full sun.
■ **Pruning** is rarely needed by *C. trichotomum*; remove wayward branches, or trim shoots, in late winter or early spring. Cut back *C. bungei* to a low, permanent framework in early spring.
■ **Sow** seed (*see pp.328–329*) at 13–18°C (55–64°F) in spring. ■ **Take** semi-ripe cuttings in summer (*see pp.329–330*), rooting them in a heated propagator. *C. bungei* tends to produce suckers that can make new plants: scrape back the soil to find one that has developed roots in autumn or spring; cut it away; and pot it up.

Clerodendrum trichotomum* var. *fargesii ♀
↕↔5–6m (15–20ft), fruits follow the pinky-white flowers in midsummer to late autumn ✳✳✳

Clethra
Summer-sweet, Sweet pepper bush, White alder
MID- TO LATE SUMMER

These evergreen and deciduous shrubs and trees are grown for their spikes of white flowers and foliage. The blooms are fragrant and are borne from mid- to late summer; beneath the canopy of a woodland garden, they perfume the still air. Summer-sweets can also be grown in a shady corner of a shrubbery, or close to a seating area where their scent can be enjoyed. The lily-of-the-valley tree (*Clethra arborea*) is tender, and in temperate climates is best grown in a large tub so it can be moved under cover to a conservatory or greenhouse for the winter.

■ **HARDINESS** Fully hardy ❋❋❋ to half-hardy ❋.
■ **CULTIVATION** Grow in dappled shade in acid (lime-free), fertile, moist, well-drained soil. In containers, use an ericaceous compost.
■ **Prune out** wayward branches in late winter, and for *C. alnifolia*, once mature, cut back a few of the old stems to the base for strong new growth. Only deadhead *C. arborea*, although it can be pruned to fit its space. ■ **Sow** seed (*see pp.328–329*) at 6–12°C (43–54°F) in spring or autumn. Take semi-ripe cuttings of deciduous species in mid- or late summer (*see pp.329–330*).

Clethra arborea
(Lily-of-the-valley tree)
↕8m (25ft) ↔ 6m (20ft), young shoots are red, the spikes of flowers may be up to 15cm (6in) long ❋

Colutea
Bladder senna
SUMMER

Decorative, greenish-brown, inflated seed pods give these deciduous shrubs their common name. They are good all-round plants with soft, pale or blue-green foliage and, in summer, large, yellow or brown, pea-like flowers that are followed by the fat pods. Bladder sennas are very resilient plants, and can be used in problematic sites such as exposed and coastal areas, sloping, free-draining banks, gardens affected by urban pollution, and sites with poor, dry soils.

■ **HARDINESS** Fully hardy ❋❋❋ to frost-hardy ❋❋.
■ **CULTIVATION** Bladder sennas will tolerate most conditions although they prefer reasonably fertile, well-drained soil in full sun. ■ **Prune** them according to the available space; either removing only wayward, dead or damaged branches, or keeping the shrub small by cutting it down to a low, permanent framework in late winter or early spring. *C. arborescens* can also be trained as a standard. ■ **Sow** seed (*see pp.328–329*) in autumn or early spring and germinate with the protection of a cold frame.

Colutea arborescens (Bladder senna)
↔3m (10ft), flowers over a very long period in summer, often still in bloom as the first pods are developing ❋❋❋

Cordyline
Cabbage palm, Cabbage tree
YEAR-ROUND

The palm-like cordylines are architectural shrubs that can bring a touch of the exotic to a temperate garden. In frost-free areas, use them as focal points; given the time and space most species will become tree-like in stature. In colder areas, grow them in pots and move under frost-free cover in winter; they make handsome plants in a conservatory or greenhouse. These plants are mainly valued for their spiky, leathery leaves, often variegated or brightly coloured. An occasional bonus in summer are tall, heavy stems of white, perfumed flowers, followed by bead-like berries in white, red, purple, or blue.

■ **HARDINESS** Half-hardy ❋❋ to frost-tender ❋; some cultivars can withstand freezing, but the top-growth may be damaged.
■ **CULTIVATION** Grow in fertile, well-drained soil in full sun or semi-shade; the cultivars with coloured foliage prefer some shade. In containers, use any good potting compost with some added grit and top-dress annually in spring (*see p.325*). ■ **Sow** seed (*see pp.328–329*) in spring at 16°C (61°F), or for an instant result cut well-rooted suckers away from the parent plant in spring and pot them up individually.

***Cordyline australis* 'Torbay Red'** ♥
↕3–10m (10–30ft) ↔1–4m (3–12ft), the eventual size of *C. australis* is largely dependent on the prevailing climate ❋❋

Cornus
Dogwood

YEAR-ROUND

Beautiful flowerheads, decorative bark, and vibrant autumn leaves make these outstanding garden plants. Dogwoods include deciduous shrubs, small trees, and woody-based perennials. Some, such as *Cornus alternifolia*, have an airy, tiered shape, and make graceful specimen trees. Many of the shrubby types, such as *C. alba*, *C. sanguinea*, and *C. sericea* and their cultivars, are grown principally for their bright red, yellow, or green bark. These dogwoods are especially welcome in winter, when the thickets of stems seem to glow with colour, at its most intense if the plants are regularly coppiced. Creeping *C. canadensis* can be used in woodland or as ground cover in a shrub border. The small, starry flowers are borne in clusters at the tips of the shoots, and in dogwoods grown for their flowering displays, for example *C. capitata*, *C. florida*, *C. kousa*, *C. nuttallii*, and many hybrids, they are surrounded by prominent bracts (modified leaves) that look like petals, which may be cream, white, or pink. In some plants, the berries or strawberry-like fruits that follow the flowers in autumn could cause mild stomach upset if eaten.

■ **HARDINESS** Fully hardy ✳✳✳ to frost-hardy ✳✳.
■ **CULTIVATION** Dogwoods can be grown in sun or partial shade.
■ **Plant** flowering dogwoods (those with large bracts) in fertile, neutral to acid soil with plenty of well-rotted organic matter added to it. All other types tolerate a wide range of conditions. Those that are grown for their winter stem colour are best positioned in full sun. ■ **Prune** those grown for stem colour hard (coppice) every spring to produce young shoots, which have the brightest colour (*see below*). Other dogwoods require little pruning except to keep them within bounds or to maintain the shape of the shrub; cutting out one in four of the older shoots in late winter or early spring every year will restrict the spread of the shrub. ■ **Renovate** neglected plants by cutting out old wood at the centre of the shrub. ■ **Sow** seed in a seedbed in autumn, or expose it to a period of cold weather and sow in spring (*see pp.328–329*). ■ **Take** hardwood cuttings (*see pp.329–330*) of dogwoods grown for stem colour in autumn.

How to coppice dogwoods

In the first year after planting, cut back all the stems to 5–8cm (2–3in) from the base. Afterwards apply a general organic fertilizer around the shrub to encourage strong new growth and mulch with a thick layer of well-rotted organic matter. In subsequent years the stems can be cut back each spring to just above two buds of the previous year's growth; this allows the plant to develop into a larger shrub. Where shrubby dogwoods are planted in a group, coppicing to varying levels creates a sloping effect rather than a dense mass of stems of uniform height. This is particularly useful for breaking up a border and making it look more interesting.

C. alba '**Aurea**' ↕↔3m (10ft)

C. alba '**Elegantissima**' ♀
↕↔3m (10ft), stems, leaves

C. capitata ↕↔12m (40ft), flowers, fruits

C. controversa '**Variegata**' ♀
↕↔8m (25ft), flowers, leaves

C. kousa var. *chinensis* ♀ ↕7m (22ft)
↔5m (15ft), bark, flowers, autumn leaves

C. kousa '**China Girl**' ↕7m (22ft)
↔5m (15ft), bark, flowers, autumn leaves

C. nuttallii ↕12m (40ft) ↔8m (25ft),
flowers, fruits

C. nuttallii '**Colrigo Giant**' ↕12m
(40ft) ↔8m (25ft), flowers, fruits

***C. alba* 'Kesselringii'** ↕↔3m (10ft), stems, leaves

***C. alba* 'Sibirica'** ♀ ↕↔3m (10ft), stems

***C. alba* 'Spaethii'** ♀ ↕↔3m (10ft), stems, leaves

***C. alternifolia* 'Argentea'** ♀ ↕3m (10ft) ↔2.5m (8ft), leaves

***C.* 'Eddie's White Wonder'** ↕6m (20ft) ↔5m (15ft), flowers, leaves

***C. florida* 'Cherokee Chief'** ♀ ↕6m (20ft) ↔8m (25ft), flowers, autumn leaves

***C. florida* 'Spring Song'** ↕6m (20ft) ↔8m (25ft), flowers, autumn leaves

***C. florida* 'Welchii'** ↕6m (20ft) ↔8m (25ft), flowers, autumn leaves

***C. kousa* 'Miss Satomi'** ♀ ↕7m (22ft) ↔5m (15ft), bark, flowers, autumn leaves

***C. macrophylla* ↕12m (40ft) ↔8m (25ft), flowers

***C. mas* ↕↔5m (15ft), flowers, fruits, autumn leaves

***C.* 'Norman Hadden'** ♀ ↕↔8m (25ft), flowers, fruits

***C.* 'Porlock'** ♀ ↕10m (30ft) ↔5m (15ft), flowers

***C. sanguinea* 'Winter Beauty'** ↕3m (10ft) ↔2.5m (8ft), stems

***C. sericea* 'Flaviramea'** ♀ ↕2m (6ft) ↔4m (12ft), stems

***C. sericea* 'Kelseyi'** ↕75cm (30in) ↔1.5m (5ft), stems

Corylopsis

SPRING

The slender, bare shoots of these small trees and shrubs bear fragile, pendent clusters of bell-shaped flowers in spring before the leaves emerge. The flower clusters are fragrant and are up to 15cm (6in) long. The leaves are broadly oval, and pale to dark green. These are graceful shrubs with open, spreading habits, and look handsome in partly shaded sites, such as in a woodland setting. Combine these trouble-free plants with other early flowering trees and shrubs, such as *Corylus avellana* 'Contorta' (*see right*), small willows (*Salix, see pp.98–99*), and magnolias (*see p.76*).

■ **HARDINESS** Fully hardy ✼✼✼, although late frosts may damage the flowers.
■ **CULTIVATION** Corylopsis prefer reasonably fertile, acid (lime-free) soil that is reliably moist but well-drained and in partial shade. ■ **Prune out** misplaced or crossing shoots if necessary, to maintain a good shape and healthy framework of shoots, immediately after flowering. ■ **Take** greenwood cuttings – from slightly more mature shoots than softwood – in summer (*see pp.329–330*). Layer shoots in autumn (*see p.330*).

Corylopsis glabrescens
↕↔5m (15ft), upright shrub, dark green leaves with blue-green undersides, flowers in mid-spring

Corylus

Hazel

LATE WINTER, SPRING, AND AUTUMN

Long catkins and attractive foliage and habits make hazels worthy garden plants. These small to medium-sized, deciduous shrubs and trees begin the season in late winter or spring by producing yellow, occasionally purple, male catkins. Broadly heart-shaped, toothed leaves follow that may be coloured. Some foliage displays autumnal tints. *Corylus avellana* 'Contorta', also called Harry Lauder's walking stick, has strikingly twisted stems that enhance the winter garden and are favourites with flower arrangers. Edible hazelnuts and filberts are produced by *C. avellana* and *C. maxima* in autumn. Larger hazels look good as specimens; use smaller species in a border with shrubs such as hamamelis (*see p.61*) or mahonias (*see p.76*).

■ **HARDINESS** Fully hardy ✼✼✼.
■ **CULTIVATION** Hazels grow well in fertile, well-drained, preferably chalky (limy) soil, in sun or partial shade. ■ **Remove** suckers as soon as you see them. Layer shoots (*see p.330*) in autumn. ■ **Prune** only to keep them in shape, in winter or early spring (*see p.322*).

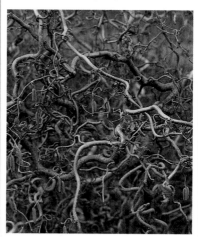

***Corylus avellana* 'Contorta'**
(Corkscrew hazel)
↕↔5m (15ft), upright shrub with mid-green leaves, 6cm (2½in) catkins in late winter and early spring

Cotinus

Smoke bush

SUMMER AND AUTUMN

This small group of deciduous shrubs and small, bushy trees is prized for its ornamental, colourful foliage and unusual flowers. These are tiny, but mass in great plumes above the foliage in summer. They resemble puffs of smoke from a distance – hence the common name. The flowers are followed by tiny fruits lasting into autumn, when the foliage usually changes colour. That of *Cotinus coggygria* 'Royal Purple' turns from dark red-purple to red; that of *C.* 'Grace' from purple to a bright, translucent scarlet. They look particularly good in autumn as specimens or planted in groups.

■ **HARDINESS** Fully hardy ✼✼✼.
■ **CULTIVATION** Cotinus prefer reasonably fertile, well-drained soil, in sun or partial shade. Purple-leaved types have the best-coloured foliage in full sun. ■ **Cut out** misplaced or crossing shoots to maintain a well-shaped shrub, in late winter or early spring (*see p.322*). For the best foliage display, keep 3–5 main stems to 60–90cm (24–36in) long and in early spring cut all shoots to 2–3 buds above the main stems. ■ **Take** softwood cuttings (*see p.329–330*) in summer or layer shoots (*see p.330*) in spring.

***Cotinus coggygria* 'Royal Purple'** ♀
↕↔5m (15ft), flowers green, turning grey in autumn

Cotoneaster

Dense but dainty foliage, a variety of ornamental forms and autumn berries ensure this plant a place in many gardens. There are many deciduous, semi-evergreen, and evergreen shrubs to choose from. Tiny, pink or white flowers in summer are followed by masses of berries in vivid reds and yellows – all much appreciated by birds. The wide range of growth habits makes cotoneasters suitable for many sites. They can be grown as freestanding shrubs, weeping trees, hedging, trained against walls, or as ground cover. You can also use dwarf species in a rock garden.

■ **HARDINESS** Fully hardy ✳✳✳.
■ **CULTIVATION** Reasonably fertile, well-drained soil in sun or partial shade is best, but most cotoneasters tolerate dry conditions. Larger shrubs need protection from cold, drying winds. Dwarf evergreens fruit better if they are sheltered. Most cotoneasters require very little pruning, but they will tolerate hard renovation pruning (*see p.323*) if it is required.
■ **Trim** formal hedges in mid- or late summer.
■ **Take** greenwood cuttings of deciduous species of cotoneaster in early summer and semi-ripe cuttings of evergreen species in late summer (*see pp.329–330*).

***Cotoneaster atropurpureus
'Variegatus'*** ♀
‡45cm (18in) ↔ 90cm (35in), deciduous shrub, leaf edges pink and red in autumn, orange-red berries

***Cotoneaster* x *watereri* 'John Waterer'** ♀
‡↔5m (15ft), vigorous, evergreen or semi-evergreen shrub or tree, white flowers in summer

Cotoneaster divaricatus
‡2.5m (8ft) ↔ 3m (10ft), erect, deciduous shrub, dense leaves turn red in autumn, pink-tinged white flowers in summer

Cotoneaster horizontalis ♀
(Fishbone cotoneaster)
‡1m (3ft) ↔ 5m (15ft), deciduous shrub, spreads in herringbone pattern, red autumn leaves, pinky-white flowers in late spring

Crataegus
Hawthorn
LATE SPRING AND AUTUMN

These extremely hardy trees and shrubs are particularly valuable in exposed or coastal gardens. They are usually spiny, deciduous, and medium-sized, with a rounded or spreading habit. Their mid- to dark green foliage often has attractive tints in autumn. Hawthorns produce flat clusters of white or pink blossoms at the ends of the branches. Birds enjoy the berries that follow in autumn, which are mostly scarlet, but sometimes they are coloured black, orange, yellow, or blue-green. *Crataegus laevigata* and *C. monogyna* make good hedging plants. The berries may cause stomach upsets if eaten.

■ **HARDINESS** Fully hardy ✳✳✳.
■ **CULTIVATION** Hawthorns will grow in any soil, except waterlogged ground, in full sun or partial shade. ■ **Prune out** any crossing or misshapen branches in winter or early spring, to maintain a good shape and healthy framework of branches. ■ **Trim** hedges after flowering or in autumn. ■ **Remove** seed from the berries as soon as they are ripe and sow in a seedbed or in containers (*see pp.328–329*). Germination may take up to 18 months.

***Craetaegus laevigata* 'Paul's Scarlet'** ♀
↕↔ to 8m (25ft), thorny, deciduous tree, lobed leaves, abundant flower clusters in late spring are occasionally followed by red berries

Cryptomeria japonica
Japanese cedar
YEAR-ROUND

This coniferous tree from the forests of China and Japan is grown for its neat, conical or columnar habit and evergreen foliage produced in cloud-like clumps of soft, glossy, dark green needles. Large, round, female cones are borne singly and the smaller, male cones cluster at the shoot tips. The red-brown bark is rugged and fibrous. This is a large tree, reaching up to 25m (80ft), but there are also several smaller cultivars that have pleasingly tinted foliage. Japanese cedars make handsome specimen trees, and the smaller types blend well in a border with rhododendrons and azaleas (*see pp.92–93*). Try dwarf forms in a large rock garden.

■ **HARDINESS** Fully hardy ✳✳✳.
■ **CULTIVATION** The Japanese cedar tolerates most well-drained soils, including chalky (limy) soils, in full sun or partial shade. It grows best in deep, fertile, moist but well-drained soil that has been enriched with organic matter. ■ **Provide** shelter from cold, drying winds. ■ **Cut back** stems to within 60–90cm (24–36in) of ground level in spring, to reshape specimens.

***Cryptomeria japonica* 'Elegans Compacta'** ♀
↕2–4m (6–12ft) ↔6m (20ft), conical shrub, leaves are dark green when new, turning bronze in autumn, as shown here

x Cupressocyparis leylandii
Leyland cypress
YEAR-ROUND

This widely grown coniferous tree is most often used as a hedging or screening plant. It has a tapering habit and smooth bark that becomes stringy as it ages. The dense sprays of scale-like foliage are dark green with grey tints. Its dark brown female cones are larger than its male cones, which are yellow. Cultivars with tinted foliage are available, in tones of gold, grey-green, blue-grey, bronze, and lime-green. It is a very fast-growing tree – if well maintained, it forms a fine hedge or specimen tree, but if neglected, it can become a monster. If it grows too big, take it out and start again: you cannot cut it back into old wood because it will not regrow.

■ **HARDINESS** Fully hardy ✳✳✳.
■ **CULTIVATION** Any deep, fertile, well-drained soil in full sun or partial shade will suit this vigorous tree. When grown as a specimen, it needs no formal pruning.
■ **Trim** hedging plants two to three times a year (without cutting into the old wood), finishing in early autumn (*see p.323*). Take semi-ripe cuttings (*see pp.329–330*) in late summer.

x Cupressocyparis leylandii ♀
↕35m (120ft) ↔5m (15ft), often grown as a hedge, which must be trimmed several times a year to keep it under control

Cupressus
Cypress

YEAR-ROUND

From the slender silhouette of the Italian cypress (*Cupressus sempervirens*) to the more stately Monterey cypress (*C. macrocarpa*), these evergreen, coniferous trees have attractive columnar habits. There are also a few weeping cypresses. They have scale-like, sometimes glaucous foliage in dark, grey- or blue-green. The bark sometimes peels; the smooth cypress (*C. arizonica* var. *glabra*) has reddish-purple bark. Female cones are small and round and remain for several years; male cones are green and found on the shoot tips. Large cypresses are fine specimen trees; group smaller ones with other conifers or shrubs.

■ **HARDINESS** Fully hardy ✳✳✳ to half-hardy ✳.
■ **CULTIVATION** Tolerate dry soils and grow in any well-drained soil in full sun. Provide shelter from cold, drying winds. ■ **Trim** hedges in late spring (*see p.323*), but do not cut into old wood because it will not regrow. ■ **Take** semi-ripe cuttings (*see pp.329–330*) in late summer.
■ **Canker** may cause bark to recede, killing twigs and then the tree; cut affected branches back to healthy wood to stop it spreading.

Cupressus macrocarpa 'Goldcrest' ♀
↕to 5m (15ft) ↔2.5m (8ft), narrowly conical, shallowly ridged bark, dense foliage ✳✳✳

Cytisus
Broom

SPRING AND SUMMER

Abundant, pea-like flowers are produced by these deciduous to evergreen shrubs in spring and summer. The flowers are often fragrant and are borne singly or in clusters, in a variety of shades from white and crimson to bright orange-yellow. Long, flat, often downy seed pods follow. The usually small, palm-like leaves of broom are mostly mid-green, but the shrubs often become leafless as they mature. Brooms vary in habit from prostrate or spreading to upright, arching, or bushy. Smaller species and cultivars suit a rock garden and larger species a shrub or mixed border. The splendid, tree-like *Cytisus battandieri* (or Pineapple broom, *see below*) can be trained to grow against a south-facing wall or fence, where it benefits from the shelter and its silvery leaves reflect the sun.

■ **HARDINESS** Fully hardy ✳✳✳ to frost-tender ❀.
■ **CULTIVATION** Grow brooms in reasonably fertile soil in full sun. Less hardy species need protection from cold, drying winds. Brooms thrive in poor, acid soils, but some may become chlorotic (show yellowing leaves) on shallow, chalky soils. ■ **Plant** young container-grown shrubs because older plants resent root disturbance. ■ **Prune** flowered shoots to 2–3 buds above the main stems, after flowering. Do not cut into old wood because they do not regrow readily.

Cytisus scoparius (Common broom)
↕↔1.5m (5ft), deciduous, upright shrub with arching stems, abundant flowers in late spring ✳✳✳

Cytisus battandieri ♀ (Pineapple broom)
↕↔5m (15ft), deciduous, upright shrub, silvery leaves, pineapple scented flowers from mid- to late summer, needs shelter ✳✳

Cytisus x praecox 'Warminster' ♀
(Warminster broom)
↕1.2m (4ft) ↔1.5m (5ft), deciduous, compact shrub with arching stems, flowers in mid- to late summer ✳✳✳

Daboecia cantabrica

Cantabrican heath, St. Dabeoc's heath

This evergreen, heather-like shrub has given rise to a large number of garden plants. They are grown for their spikes of urn-shaped flowers, appearing from early summer to mid-autumn, in white and purple-crimson, and are typically larger than those of other heaths and heathers. The leaves are small, thin, and dark green. The species grows up to 40cm (16in) and spreads to 65cm (26in), but the cultivars vary in size. They make useful ground-cover plants, around taller heathers or other acid-loving shrubs. If your soil is alkaline, grow them in large pots or a raised bed, in ericaceous compost.

■ **HARDINESS** Fully hardy ✳✳✳ to half-hardy ✳.
■ **CULTIVATION** These shrubs need well-drained, acid (lime-free) soil in full sun; they will tolerate neutral soil in partial shade. Daboecias are susceptible to root rot, particularly on heavy, wet soils, so on clay soil dig in some coarse grit to improve drainage.
■ **Prune** flowered growth in early or mid-spring to keep the plant shapely. ■ **Take** semi-ripe cuttings (*see pp.329–330*) in midsummer.

Daboecia cantabrica 'William Buchanan' ♀
‡35cm (14in) ↔ 55cm (22in) ✳✳

Daphne

Deliciously fragrant flowers are borne very early, or sometimes very late, in the year on these shrubs, so plant them where the wonderful scent can be fully appreciated. The flowers, in shades of red-purple, pink, white, and yellow, may be followed by round, white, pink, red, orange, or purple fruits. Mostly slow-growing, daphnes are generally compact enough for even small gardens. They may be upright, bushy, or prostrate in habit, and there are deciduous, semi-evergreen, and evergreen species, all with neat, usually dark but sometimes variegated leaves. All parts of these plants are toxic, and the sap may irritate skin.

Daphne mezereum f. *alba* 'Bowles' Variety'
‡to 2m (6ft) ↔ 1m (3ft), deciduous shrub, flowers in late winter or early spring, yellow fruits ✳✳✳

■ **HARDINESS** Fully hardy ✳✳✳ to frost-hardy ✳✳.
■ **CULTIVATION** Grow in reasonably fertile soil that is well-drained but does not dry out, and is preferably neutral (neither acid nor alkaline). Position in sun or partial shade; all resent root disturbance, so choose the site carefully.
■ **Mulch** annually with organic matter around the base (*see p.326*) to keep the roots cool and moist. ■ **Prune** only if absolutely necessary, in late winter or early spring. ■ **Sow** seed in a cold frame as soon as it is ripe (*see pp.328–329*).
■ **Take** softwood cuttings in early and midsummer, and semi-ripe cuttings in late summer (*see pp.329–330*).

Daphne bholua 'Jacqueline Postill' ♀
‡2–4m (6–12ft) ↔ 1.5m (5ft), upright evergreen, fragrant flowers in winter or early spring, black-purple fruits ✳✳✳ (borderline)

Daphne laureola subsp. *philippi*
‡45cm (18in) ↔ 60cm (24in), low, spreading evergreen, lightly scented flowers in late winter and early spring, black fruits ✳✳✳

Daphne cneorum (Garland flower)
‡15cm (6in) or more ↔to 2m (6ft), trailing
evergreen with pink or occasionally white,
very fragrant flowers in late spring ✳✳✳

Daphne mezereum (Mezereon)
‡1.2m (4ft) ↔1m (3ft), upright, deciduous
cottage-garden classic, flowers in late winter
or early spring, fleshy red fruits ✳✳✳

Davidia involucrata
Dove tree, Ghost tree,
Handkerchief tree

SPRING

This extraordinarily beautiful tree is
festooned with white bracts (modified
leaves) along the branches in spring.
The leaves are up to 15cm (6in) long,
oval in shape with heart-shaped bases
and sharply pointed tips. Mid-green
with strong veins, they have reddish
stalks and soft hairs underneath. The
bracts surround small flowerheads,
which are followed by greenish-brown
fruits in autumn. Davidia is a large
tree; it is related to the dogwoods
(*Cornus, see pp.38–39*), which include
more compact, but less dramatic,
species suited to smaller gardens.

■ **HARDINESS** Fully hardy ✳✳✳.
■ **CULTIVATION** Grow in fertile, well-drained
but moisture-retentive soil, in sun or partial
shade. Position where there is shelter from
strong, cold winds. ■ **Trim out** any crossing
or misplaced branches on young trees in late
winter or early spring. ■ **Sow** whole fruits in
a container as soon as ripe (*see pp.328–329*):
germination will take at least two winters
outdoors. Seed-raised trees may take up to ten
years to reach flowering size. ■ **Take** hardwood
cuttings in winter (*see p.330*).

Davidia involucrata ♀
‡15m (50ft) ↔10m (30ft), this tree needs plenty
of space to develop its shape and also to be seen
at its best

Deutzia

SPRING TO SUMMER

Clusters of starry, white or pink
flowers, fragrant on *Deutzia gracilis*
and *D. scabra*, almost smother these
deciduous shrubs from mid-spring
to midsummer. Most have oval leaves
and all are are easy to grow. The
larger ones make good specimen
plants, often developing attractively
peeling bark as they mature, although
in colder regions it is best to grow the
less hardy types among other trees
and shrubs, or in the shelter of a warm
wall. Try them alongside mock orange
(*Philadelphus, see p.82*) and weigelas
(*see p.110*) for an early-summer show.

■ **HARDINESS** Fully hardy ✳✳✳ to
frost-hardy ✳✳.
■ **CULTIVATION** Grow in fertile soil that is
not too dry, in full sun; some tolerate partial
shade. ■ **Cut back** flowered stems to strong
buds or young shoots. Encourage new growth
on mature plants by cutting one in four of the old
branches to the base. ■ **Sow** seed in containers
in a cold frame in autumn (*see pp.328–329*).
■ **Take** softwood cuttings in summer or
hardwood cuttings in autumn (*see pp.329–330*).

Deutzia x hybrida 'Mont Rose' ♀
‡↔1–2m (3–6ft) ✳✳✳

Deutzia ningpoensis ♀
‡↔2m (6ft) ✳✳✳

Dipelta

These upright or arching, deciduous shrubs bloom in late spring to early summer, bearing clusters of tubular flowers at the tips of the branches and where the leaf stems join the shoots. The white or pink flowers are fragrant and backed by two papery bracts (modified leaves) that stay on the plant as the fruits develop. Narrow, pointed, pale to mid-green leaves and pale brown, peeling bark add to the attraction. Suitable for a shrub border or as specimen plants, these Chinese natives complement lilacs (*Syringa, see p.104*) and flowering currants (*Ribes, p.95*). Dipeltas can be tricky to propagate and may take a little finding, but once off they are easy to grow, so the search is worthwhile.

■ **HARDINESS** Fully hardy ✷✷✷.
■ **CULTIVATION** Grow in fertile, well-drained, and preferably alkaline (limy) soil, in sun or partial shade. ■ **Prune back** flowered shoots to strong buds lower down after flowering. Once mature, encourage new growth by cutting about one in three or four of the old stems back to the base of the shrub. ■ **Sow** seed (*see pp.328–329*) in a seedbed in autumn or spring. ■ **Take** softwood cuttings (*see pp.329–330*) in summer.

Dipelta floribunda ♀
↕↔4m (12ft), upright shrub, flowers in late spring and early summer, tolerates quite poor soils

Disanthus cercidifolius

Brilliant autumn hues of yellow, orange, red, and purple, often all on display at the same time, are the main attraction of this rounded shrub. The round leaves are similar to those of cercis (*see p.38*), as the name suggests, but the two have very different flowers. In mid-autumn, disanthus produces small, slightly fragrant, spidery, bright rose-red flowers. This shrub is native to mountain and forest habitats, and is ideal as a specimen in a woodland setting. For a superb show of leaf colour in contrasting shapes in autumn, combine it with acers (*see pp.16–17*).

■ **HARDINESS** Fully hardy ✷✷✷, but late frosts may damage the young growth.
■ **CULTIVATION** Grow in preferably well-drained, lime-free soil that has been enriched with well-rotted organic matter. Position in sun or partial shade where it will be sheltered from strong, cold winds. ■ **Prune** minimally after flowering, cutting out only any crossing stems and those that spoil the shape of the shrub (*see p.322*). ■ **Sow** seed in a seedbed in autumn or spring (*see pp.328–329*). ■ **Layer** low-growing shoots (*see pp.329–330*) in autumn.

Disanthus cercidifolius ♀
↕↔3m (10ft), the leaves are a cloudy blue-green before they take on these vibrant autumn colours

Elaeagnus

Tough, fast-growing, and resistant to coastal winds, these are immensely useful shrubs. Evergreen or deciduous, they have ornamental, lance-shaped to oval leaves. These may be plain green or silvery, and there are also many with silver or gold variegation. Evergreen elaeagnus make good hedging plants, and the variegated types are great for brightening up a dull border when used as specimen plants. As a bonus, small clusters of bell-shaped, sometimes very fragrant flowers are borne in summer or autumn, and these are occasionally followed by small berries.

***Elaeagnus x ebbingei* 'Gilt Edge'** ♀
↕↔4m (12ft), dense, rounded to spreading evergreen, leaves silver-scaly beneath, creamy white flowers in autumn

■ **HARDINESS** Fully hardy ✳✳✳.
■ **CULTIVATION** Grow in fertile, well-drained soil; dry soils are tolerated, but leaves may turn yellow on shallow, chalky soils. Position in full sun; evergreens tolerate partial shade. ■ **Prune** deciduous plants in early spring, evergreens in mid- or late spring, removing crossing branches and any that spoil the shape (see p.322). Trim hedges in late summer. ■ **Cut out** any shoots that revert to green leaves on variegated types. ■ **Take** greenwood cuttings in late spring or early summer, or semi-ripe cuttings of deciduous species in late summer (see pp.329–330).

Elaeagnus 'Quicksilver' ♀
↕↔4m (12ft), fast-growing, deciduous, clump-forming shrub, flowers in summer and bears yellow fruits in autumn

Elaeagnus pungens 'Maculata'
↕4m (12ft) ↔5m (15ft), dense, slightly spiny evergreen, pendent silvery-white flowers in autumn, brown berries ripening to red

Embothrium coccineum
Chilean fire bush, Flame flower
LATE SPRING AND EARLY SUMMER

Spectacular when in flower, this evergreen tree or shrub have an upright, but freely branching or suckering habit, and are capable of very rapid growth in mild conditions. The glowing scarlet flowers are carried in dense clusters in late spring and early summer. The lance-shaped leaves are up to 13cm (5in) long. In cool climates, the plant is happiest in a sheltered spot; in areas where there are few frosts, it tolerates a more open aspect and makes a good specimen tree, especially the slightly hardier cultivar 'Norquinco'.

■ **HARDINESS** Fully hardy ✳✳✳ (borderline) to frost-hardy ✳✳.
■ **CULTIVATION** Grow in fertile, neutral to acid (lime-free) soil enriched with well-rotted organic matter, in full sun or partial shade. ■ **Trim off** crossing shoots and any that spoil the shape in early spring. ■ **Sow** seed at 13–16°C (55–61°F) in spring (see pp.328–329). ■ **Take** greenwood cuttings in early summer, or semi-ripe cuttings in mid- or late summer (see pp.329–330). Take root cuttings, or dig up suckers growing by the main plant, in winter.

Embothrium coccineum
↕10m (30ft) ↔5m (15ft) or more, ✳✳

Enkianthus
SPRING TO AUTUMN

Pendent flower clusters and rich autumnal foliage tints give these plants two seasons of interest. A small group, they are for the most part deciduous shrubs, sometimes trees. The small, delicate flowers are borne at the branch tips from mid-spring to early summer. They are urn- to bell-shaped, in shades from cream or pure white to pink and deep purple-red, with contrasting veins. The autumn display is if anything more distinctive and varies according to the species from yellow through to a brilliant scarlet. They make ideal specimens in a woodland garden.

■ **HARDINESS** Fully hardy ✳✳✳.
■ **CULTIVATION** Grow in acid (lime-free), moist but well-drained soil enriched with well-rotted organic matter. Position in an open site in full sun or partial shade. ■ **Prune** in early spring, only to remove misplaced or crossing branches. ■ **Sow** seed at 18–21°C (64–70°F) in late winter or early spring (see pp.328–329). ■ **Take** semi-ripe cuttings in summer (see pp.329–330) or layer in autumn (see p.330).

Enkianthus deflexus
↕2.5–4m (8–12ft) ↔3m (10ft)

Enkianthus cernuus f. rubens ♀
↕↔2.5m (8ft)

Erica
Heath

YEAR-ROUND

Heaths are evergreens with masses of tiny, usually bell-shaped flowers ranging from shades of red and pink to white, with some bicolours. In some cultivars, the small, tightly curled leaves are tinted with red or gold, or colour in cold weather, so the right choice of cultivars can ensure interest all through the year. Hardy prostrate species make colourful ground cover, while the taller, upright types, such as *Erica arborea*, can make excellent specimen plants in borders. Heaths, which are related to heathers (*Calluna*, see p.27), are mainly found in wet moorland, but will grow in a variety of conditions. Ericas are easy plants to grow providing you have acid soil and, apart from possibly getting honey fungus, they are generally trouble-free. Taller types of heath can be used as low hedging. To get the best cultivars visit a specialist nursery.

■ **HARDINESS** Fully hardy ✲✲✲ to frost-hardy ✲✲.
■ **CULTIVATION** Grow in well-drained, acid soil in an open site in full sun. A few winter- and spring-flowering types such as *E. carnea* and *E. x darleyensis*, will tolerate a slightly alkaline (limy) soil, as will summer-flowering *E. manipuliflora, E. terminalis,* and *E. vagans.*
■ **Cut back** flowered shoots to within 2.5cm (1in) of the old growth after flowering. For taller, tree-like cultivars cut back the stems to within two or three buds of the base, or to a permanent framework of shoots in early spring. ■ **Layer** (see below) or take semi-ripe cuttings in mid- or late summer (see p.329–330). Heaths may be susceptible to fungal root rot in warm and wet conditions: improve drainage to avoid this.

Using heaths in the garden
Heaths are valuable plants because they can provide colour and interest throughout the year. They require very little attention beyond clipping over once a year after flowering, making them ideal for a low-maintenance garden. Different colours can be grouped en masse in their own bed, but they are also effective growing with dwarf conifers such as junipers (see p.68) and with rhododendrons (see pp.92–93). If you have alkaline soil, lime-hating heaths can be grown in a raised bed filled with ericaceous (lime-free) compost or in large pots on the patio.

Layering to increase your plants
Heaths and heathers root readily from the stems, so propagating them by layering is much easier than taking cuttings. From early to mid-autumn or in spring, make a shallow trench around the plant and refill with soil mixed with a little sharp sand and peat substitute, for example leafmould, to provide a good rooting medium. Bend down healthy shoots and cover with some of the prepared soil. Peg down the shoots with wire staples or weigh down with a stone. The stems need not be cut. The next year, cut off the rooted stems; replant where they can grow into new plants.

E. arborea var. *alpina* ♀ ‡2m (6ft) ↔85cm (34in)

E. carnea 'Ann Sparkes' ♀ ‡15cm (6in) ↔25cm (10in)

E. carnea 'Vivellii' ♀ ‡15cm (6in) ↔35cm (14in)

E. ciliaris 'David McClintock' ‡40cm (16in) ↔45cm (18in)

E. cinerea 'Hookstone White' ♀ ‡35cm (14in) ↔65cm (26in)

E. cinerea 'Purple Beauty' ‡30cm (1ft) ↔55cm (22in)

E. tetralix 'Alba Mollis' ♀ ‡20cm (8in) ↔30cm (1ft)

E. vagans 'Birch Glow' ♀ ‡30cm (1ft) ↔50cm (20in)

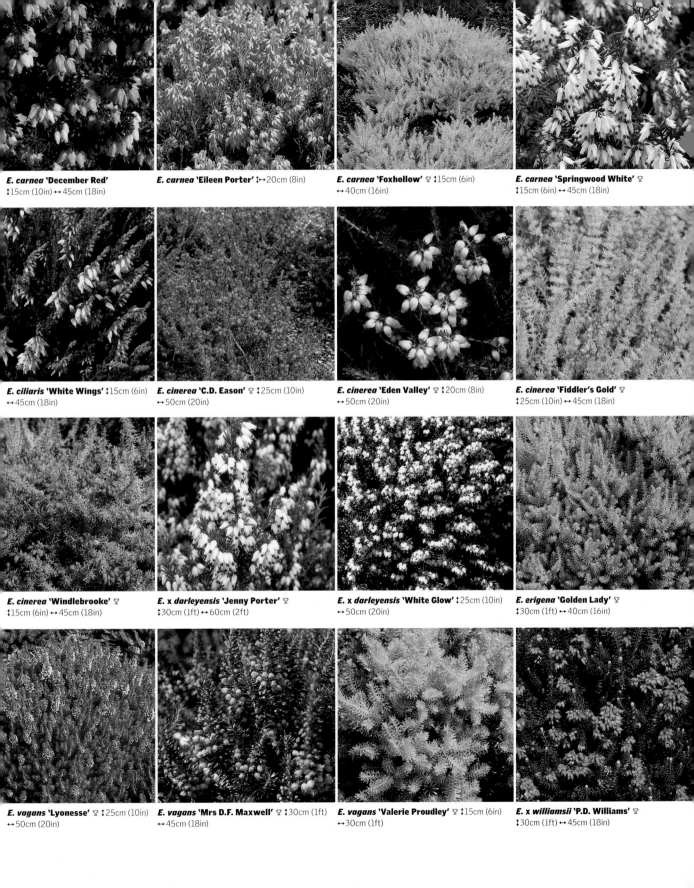

E. carnea 'December Red'
‡15cm (10in) ↔ 45cm (18in)

E. carnea 'Eileen Porter' ‡↔20cm (8in)

E. carnea 'Foxhollow' ♀ ‡15cm (6in) ↔ 40cm (16in)

E. carnea 'Springwood White' ♀
‡15cm (6in) ↔ 45cm (18in)

E. ciliaris 'White Wings' ‡15cm (6in) ↔ 45cm (18in)

E. cinerea 'C.D. Eason' ♀ ‡25cm (10in) ↔ 50cm (20in)

E. cinerea 'Eden Valley' ♀ ‡20cm (8in) ↔ 50cm (20in)

E. cinerea 'Fiddler's Gold' ♀
‡25cm (10in) ↔ 45cm (18in)

E. cinerea 'Windlebrooke' ♀
‡15cm (6in) ↔ 45cm (18in)

E. x darleyensis 'Jenny Porter' ♀
‡30cm (1ft) ↔ 60cm (2ft)

E. x darleyensis 'White Glow' ‡25cm (10in) ↔ 50cm (20in)

E. erigena 'Golden Lady' ♀
‡30cm (1ft) ↔ 40cm (16in)

E. vagans 'Lyonesse' ♀ ‡25cm (10in) ↔ 50cm (20in)

E. vagans 'Mrs D.F. Maxwell' ♀ ‡30cm (1ft) ↔ 45cm (18in)

E. vagans 'Valerie Proudley' ♀ ‡15cm (6in) ↔ 30cm (1ft)

E. x williamsii 'P.D. Williams' ♀
‡30cm (1ft) ↔ 45cm (18in)

Escallonia

The attractions of these excellent shrubs are the glossy, evergreen foliage and a profusion of flowers. Borne over a long period, mainly in summer, the flowers are tubular or saucer-shaped, in shades of white, pink, or red. Escallonias are undemanding plants, being fairly fast-growing and drought-tolerant. Widely grown as tough, wind-resistant hedging, they also make fine freestanding shrubs in a shrub or mixed border. They are particularly good in coastal areas, where the tough leaves stand up to salt-laden winds. Try them with other robust shrubs, such as cotinus (see p.40), lilacs (Syringa, see p.104), St John's wort (Hypericum, see p.66), and potentillas (see p.87).

■ **HARDINESS** Fully hardy ✳✳✳ to half-hardy ✳.
■ **CULTIVATION** Grow in fertile, well-drained soil. Position in full sun, with shelter from cold, drying winds. Half-hardy types grow best with the protection of a sheltered wall. ■ **Trim** back shoots that spoil the shape of the shrub lightly in mid- or late spring. ■ **Clip** hedges after flowering. ■ **Take** softwood cuttings in early summer or semi-ripe cuttings in late summer; or try hardwood cuttings from late autumn to winter (see p.330).

Escallonia 'Pride of Donard' ♀
↕1.5m (5ft) ↔2.5m (8ft), compact, erect shrub, flowers are larger than most and borne in early to midsummer, suitable for hedging ✳✳

Escallonia 'Apple Blossom' ♀
↕↔2.5m (8ft), compact bush, slow-growing, flowers in early and midsummer, suitable for hedging ✳✳

Escallonia 'Langleyensis' ♀
↕2m (6ft) ↔3m (10ft), arching, evergreen to semi-evergreen shrub, flowers in early and midsummer ✳✳✳

Escallonia rubra 'Woodside'
↕75cm (30in) ↔1.5m (5ft), dwarf form, flowers from summer to early autumn, cut out any overly vigorous shoots promptly ✳✳✳

Eucalyptus
Gum, Ironbark
YEAR-ROUND

These distinctive trees and shrubs are grown for their handsome, often aromatic, evergreen foliage, and their ornamental bark. The foliage of eucalyptus is usually mid- or grey-green and leathery. The young, or juvenile, leaves are most attractive, and look rather like silvery-blue pennies on *Eucalyptus gunnii*. They grow longer and droop as the plants mature. Small clusters of petalless flowers open in summer, and may be white, creamy yellow, or red. The bark is smooth and white in some species, flaking or striped in shades of green or tawny brown in others. As specimen trees they grow quickly and need space. However, with hard pruning (coppicing) each year, they may be grown as shrubs, which retain the appealing juvenile foliage.

Eucalyptus dalrympleana ♀
(Mountain gum)
↕20m (70ft) ↔ 8m (25ft), vigorous tree, blue-green new leaves, flowers late summer to autumn, tolerates chalk soil ✳✳✳ (borderline)

■ **HARDINESS** Fully hardy ✳✳✳ to frost-tender ❄.
■ **CULTIVATION** Grow in fertile, neutral to slightly acid soil that does not easily dry out, in full sun, preferably with shelter from cold winds.
■ **Prune** crossing or misplaced branches in late winter or early spring; to form a shrub, cut back stems to within two or three buds of the base.
■ **Sow** seed at 13–18°C (55–64°F) in spring or summer (*see pp.328–329*).

Eucryphia
SUMMER TO AUTUMN

Valued for their late flowering, this a small group comprises mostly evergreen, columnar trees and shrubs. Their beautiful, often fragrant flowers are white, occasionally pink or with pink edges to the petals, and have a fluffy mass of stamens at the centre. They are borne from summer to early autumn, once the plants are a few years old. The leaves are leathery, usually oval but sometimes made up of narrow leaflets along a central stalk. They make glorious specimen plants or flowering hedges in a sheltered spot.

■ **HARDINESS** Fully hardy ✳✳✳ to frost-hardy ✳✳
■ **CULTIVATION** Grow in fertile, moist but well-drained soil that is neutral to acid (lime-free). *E.* x *nymansensis* tolerates alkaline soil. Position with roots in shade and the crown in full sun. Needs shelter from cold winds in all but mild areas. ■ **Remove** fading flowers if the plant is small enough to make this practical.
■ **Prune out** any crossing branches in early spring, or trim shoots that spoil the shape in late spring (for *E. lucida*, after flowering). Do not overprune, or you will lose flowers. ■ **Take** semi-ripe cuttings (*see pp.328–329*) in summer, and overwinter plants in frost-free conditions.

Eucryphia glutinosa ♀
↕10m (30ft) ↔ 6m (20ft), deciduous or semi-evergreen tree or shrub, flowers in mid- to late summer, tolerates exposed sites ✳✳✳

Eucalyptus pauciflora **subsp.**
niphophila ♀ (Snow gum)
↕6m (20ft) ↔ 6–15m (20–50ft), flowers late spring to summer, bark shed late summer ✳✳✳

Eucalyptus gunnii ♀ (Cider gum)
↕10–25m (30–80ft) ↔ 6–15m (20–50ft), flowers in summer or autumn, bark shed in late summer ✳✳✳ (borderline)

Euonymus
Spindle tree

`YEAR-ROUND`

Colourful foliage is the main feature of this large group of shrubs and trees. Deciduous types have fiery autumn foliage and decorative, lobed fruits, while most of the evergreens have bright variegation that brings colour to the garden all year. The leaves are variable, but usually broadly oval, and small clusters of purple-red or red-brown flowers appear in late spring or summer. The evergreen spindle trees can be used as specimen shrubs in borders, or as hedging or ground cover. Some *Euonymus fortunei* types will climb if planted by a wall. Young plants are useful in winter windowboxes and containers. All parts may cause mild stomach upset if eaten.

■ **HARDINESS** Fully hardy ✳✳✳ to frost-hardy ✳✳.
■ **CULTIVATION** Grow in any well-drained soil; deciduous species are more drought-tolerant. Site in full sun (especially variegated types) or partial shade; in full sun they need moist soil. Shelter evergreens from cold winds.
■ **Prune** deciduous types in late winter or early spring if needed and evergreens if necessary after flowering (*see pp.322–323*). ■ **Sow** seed (*see pp.328–329*) in a container in a cold frame as soon as it is ripe. ■ **Take** softwood cuttings of deciduous species, and semi-ripe cuttings of evergreens in summer (*see pp.329–330*).

Euonymus alatus ♥ (Winged spindle)
‡2m (6ft) ↔3m (10ft), dense, deciduous shrub, red-purple fruits with orange seeds, dark green leaves until autumn ✳✳✳

***Euonymus fortunei* 'Emerald 'n' Gold'** ♥
‡60cm (24in) ↔90cm (36in), dense, bushy, evergreen shrub, gold leaf edges turn pink in winter, white fruits and orange seeds ✳✳✳

***Euonymus fortunei* 'Silver Queen'**
‡2.5m (8ft) ↔1.5m (5ft), upright, evergreen bush, occasional, pale green flowers and pink fruits, climbs if given support ✳✳✳

***Euonymus japonicus* 'Ovatus Aureus'** ♥
‡4m (12ft) ↔2m (6ft), slow-growing, evergreen bush or tree, good for hedging, rarely fruits, tends to revert to all-green shoots ✳✳

Euonymus oxyphyllus
‡2.5m (8ft) or more ↔2.5m (8ft), upright, slow-growing deciduous species, dull-green leaves before autumn ✳✳✳

Euphorbia
Milkweed, Spurge
SPRING AND SUMMER

In this large and widely varied group of plants, there are a few evergreen shrubs. They are grown for their impressive foliage and distinctive flowerheads. The leaves are mostly narrow and lance-shaped – in *Euphorbia characias* they are blue-green and very architectural. *E.* x *martini* has leaves that are flushed purple when young, on red-tinged stems; its flowerheads are long-lasting and borne in spring and summer. The flowers are brown and honey-scented in *E. mellifera*, the honey spurge, and yellow-green with dark-red nectar glands in *E.* x *martini*. Spurges are suitable for coastal gardens. All parts can cause severe discomfort if eaten, and contact with the milky sap may irritate skin. (*See also p.201.*)

■ **HARDINESS** Fully hardy ✲✲✲ to frost-hardy ✲✲.
■ **CULTIVATION** Grow in well-drained soil in full sun. Dig in plenty of coarse grit on heavy clay soils to improve drainage. ■ **Take** softwood cuttings (*see pp.329–330*) in spring or early summer, wearing gloves, and dipping the ends in lukewarm water to stem the bleeding of sap.

Euphorbia characias subsp. *wulfenii* **'John Tomlinson'** ♀
↕↔1.2m (4ft), upright shrub, huge flowerheads from early spring to early summer ✲✲

Exochorda
Pearl bush
SPRING TO SUMMER

Showy, pure white blooms wreath the branches of these shrubs in spring to summer; not for nothing is the most popular variety named 'The Bride'. All cultivars are deciduous, with an attractive, arching habit, and are equally impressive grown with other shrubs in a border or as isolated specimen plants. They flower at around the same time or a little later than the spring-flowering magnolias (*see p.76*), but the pearl bush flowers are more resistant to frost, which makes them an excellent alternative for a blossom display in frost-prone areas where magnolia flowers might be spoiled.

■ **HARDINESS** Fully hardy ✲✲✲.
■ **CULTIVATION** Grow in fertile, moist, but well-drained soil; these shrubs will tolerate all but the shallowest, chalky soils, where the leaves may become yellow (chlorotic). Position in full sun or partial shade. ■ **Cut back** flowered shoots to strong buds or young lower growths after flowering. Encourage fresh growth on mature plants by cutting one in three or four older branches back to the base every few years. ■ **Take** softwood cuttings (*see pp.329–330*) of pearl bush in summer.

Exochorda x *macrantha* **'The Bride'** ♀
↕2m (6ft) ↔3m (10ft), forms a compact, arching mound with fragrant flowers in late spring and early summer

Fagus
Beech
SUMMER TO AUTUMN

These stately, deciduous trees are grown for their fine forms and handsome foliage. They are large, with wavy edged or toothed, oval leaves. In most, these are pale green when they first open in spring, maturing to dark green and then taking on soft yellow or russet-brown tones in autumn, but there are several with dark, purple or coppery foliage. All make fine specimen trees; the common beech, *Fagus sylvatica*, is also popular as a hedge; when clipped, it retains its brown leaves all winter. For smaller gardens, look for compact forms, such as 'Purpurea Pendula', with branches that often trail to the ground.

■ **HARDINESS** Fully hardy ✲✲✲; the North American beech *F. grandiflora* needs long, warm summers to thrive.
■ **CULTIVATION** Grow in any well-drained soil; even chalk is tolerated. Position in sun or partial shade; purple-leaved types have the best foliage colour in full sun. ■ **Prune out** crossing branches and any that spoil the shape of the tree in late winter or early spring. ■ **Trim** hedges of *F. sylvatica* in mid- to late summer. ■ **Sow** seed in a seedbed in autumn or spring (*see pp.328–329*).

Fagus sylvatica **'Dawyck Purple'** ♀
↕20m (70ft) ↔5m (15ft), particularly good purple-leaved type, also one of the narrowest columnar forms

Fatsia japonica

Japanese aralia, Japanese fatsia

YEAR-ROUND

The large, glossy green leaves of these evergreen, spreading shrubs are ideal for creating a jungly garden, and make a dramatic contrast to feathery foliage plants such as ferns (*see pp.300–309*). An architectural plant for a shady border, it tolerates pollution and thrives in city gardens, but is also a good choice for coastal areas, where the tough leaves will withstand salt-laden winds. Clusters of rounded, creamy white flowerheads are produced in autumn, followed by small, round, inedible black berries. There are also variegated cultivars, but they tend to be less hardy.

■ **HARDINESS** Fully hardy ✳✳✳ (species) to frost-hardy ✳✳ (cultivars).
■ **CULTIVATION** Will thrive in any fertile, moist but well-drained soil in full sun or partial shade, but needs shelter from cold, drying winds. ■ **Trim** or prune shoots that spoil the shape in mid- or late spring. ■ **Remove** fading flowers unless seed is wanted. ■ **Sow** seed (*see pp.328–329*) at 15–21°C (59–70°F) in autumn or spring. ■ **Take** greenwood cuttings (*see pp.329–330*) in early or midsummer. Cold winds may cause blackening and die-back of shoots and leaves.

Fatsia japonica ♀
↕↔1.5–4m (5–12ft), leaves are 15–40cm (6–16in) across ✳✳✳

Ficus carica

Common fig

SUMMER

Unlike most figs, *Ficus carica* is hardy. It can be grown as a free-standing tree, but will quickly spread to cover a large area if trained against a wall. The handsome, deciduous foliage is its main attraction; it does produce edible figs, but these do not always mature in cooler climates. The fruits are green when young, but they mature after a second, long, hot summer into dark green, purple, or dark brown figs. The leaves can cause skin rashes in sunlight (photodermatitis).

■ **HARDINESS** Fully hardy ✳✳✳.
■ **CULTIVATION** Figs prefer moist but well-drained soil, enriched with plenty of organic matter, in full sun or partial shade, with shelter from cold, drying winds. ■ **Restrict** the roots in a large pot or by a barrier in the soil for better fruiting. ■ **Tie in** regularly new shoots of wall-trained plants. ■ **Prune out** misplaced or crossing shoots that spoil the shape in late winter or early spring; prune wall-trained plants to fit available space. ■ **For best fruits**, pick off larger, green fruitlets on the main stems in autumn to leave smaller ones to ripen next year; protect them with fleece from cold winds and frosts. Wasps attack ripe fruits.

Ficus carica
↕3m (10ft) ↔ 4m (12ft), leathery leaves can reach 24cm (10in) across and are tolerant of salty air

Forsythia

LATE WINTER TO SPRING

These superbly reliable, deciduous shrubs will be covered in flowers every spring and sometimes in late winter, no matter what the weather throws at them. The bright yellow blooms appear in profusion all along the length of the stems, singly or in small clusters, before the leaves open. Most forsythias are medium-sized, bushy or upright shrubs; a few are semi-evergreen. These versatile shrubs can be grown either freestanding or trained against a wall or a fence, and *Forsythia* x *intermedia* also makes a good hedging plant. A classic spring

planting combination involves forsythias along with red-flowering currants (*Ribes, see p.95*).

■ **HARDINESS** Fully hardy ✳✳✳.
■ **CULTIVATION** Reasonably fertile, moist but well-drained soil is needed. Position in full sun or partial shade. ■ **Prune** flowered shoots to strong shoots lower down after flowering. ■ **Cut** about one-third of old stems on mature plants to the base every 4–5 years: cut back hard leggy plants over two years (*see p.323*). ■ **Trim** hedges in summer. ■ **Take** greenwood cuttings in early summer or semi-ripe cuttings in late summer (*see pp.329–330*).

Forsythia x *intermedia* **'Lynwood Variety'** ♀
‡↔3m (10ft), bushy habit, sharply toothed leaves, flowers are 2.5–3.5cm (1¼–1½in) across and borne in early and mid-spring

Fothergilla

SPRING AND AUTUMN

There are just two species of these deciduous, low-growing shrubs from woodlands and swamps. They are grown for their bottlebrush-like clusters of scented flowers, which are produced before the leaves unfold. Fothergillas also have attractive, dark green foliage, which has toothed edges and turns brilliant shades of red, orange, and golden yellow in autumn. The witch alder (*Fothergilla gardenii*) is the smaller of the two, forming a dense bush with a height and spread of 1m (3ft); it flowers in spring. The slow-growing *F. major* is an upright shrub with glossy leaves; its flowers are occasionally tinged with pink.

■ **HARDINESS** Fully hardy ✳✳✳.
■ **CULTIVATION** Grow fothergillas in moist but well-drained, acid (lime-free) soil that has been enriched with well-rotted organic matter. ■ **Position** in full sun or partial shade; full sun encourages flowers and better autumn colour. ■ **Prune off** crossing shoots or those that spoil the shape in late winter or early spring, only if necessary (*see p.322*). ■ **Sow** seed (*see pp.328–329*) in a container in autumn or winter; it will take two years to germinate. ■ **Take** softwood cuttings (*see pp.329–330*).

Fothergilla major ♀
‡2.5m (8ft) ↔2m (6ft), flowers in late spring and early summer, found naturally in dry woods and rocky riverbanks

Fraxinus
Ash

SPRING TO AUTUMN

These deciduous trees tolerate pollution, wind, and coastal conditions, and have fine foliage and sometimes coloured winter bark. The leaves are made up of small leaflets along central stalks up to 50cm (20in) long. Fast-growing, they have attractive habits, ranging from narrow or columnar to round or spreading. Ash trees have tiny flowers, but those of *Fraxinus ornus* and *F. sieboldiana* are decorative. Most are suitable only for large gardens: *F. excelsior* 'Pendula' is smaller than many. Ashes seed themselves about quite prolifically, so root out any seedlings. They look good with trees such as birches (*Betula, see p.24*) and beeches (*Fagus, see p.53*).

■ **HARDINESS** Fully hardy ✳✳✳ to frost-hardy ✳✳.
■ **CULTIVATION** Need fertile, moist soil that is well-drained and neutral to acid (lime-free); *F. angustifolius* and *F. ornus* tolerate fairly dry soils from acid to alkaline (limy). ■ **Position** in full sun. ■ **Sow** seed (*see pp.328–329*) in autumn or spring in an open cold frame; the seed requires 2–3 months of cold before it germinates.

Fraxinus excelsior **'Jaspidea'** ♀
‡30m (100ft) ↔20m (70ft), yellow shoots and leaves in winter and spring, leaves dark green in summer, distinct black buds in winter

Fuchsia

SUMMER TO LATE AUTUMN

The brightly coloured, pendulous flowers of fuchsias are unmistakeable. They vary from elegant, single and semi-double forms to frilly, fully double blooms, appearing from summer until late autumn. Deciduous or evergreen shrubs, fuchsias are very versatile. They can be planted in mixed borders and as hedging, some can be trained against walls or grown as standards or pillars (*see below*), and cultivars with a trailing habit are ideal in raised containers, where the flowers spill over the edges to great effect. Fuchsias can be divided into two groups, hardy to frost-hardy and half-hardy to tender. The former may lose all their leaves in harsh winters, but will reshoot in the spring if they have been well planted and mulched. Grow half-hardy to tender fuchsias, with their wide range of extravagant flowers, outdoors in the summer. They make showy plants either in borders or in containers, but need some protection during severe winters: keep half-hardy types in a frost-free greenhouse, shed, or garage, and tender plants in a slightly warmer place.

■ **HARDINESS** Hardy ✻✻✻ to frost-tender ❀.
■ **CULTIVATION** Grow in fertile, moist but well-drained soil in full sun or partial shade, with shelter from cold, drying winds. ■ **Plant** hardy fuchsias with the base of the stem 5cm (2in) below the soil surface, and protect with a deep winter mulch of bark chippings or similar. ■ **Plant out** tender cultivars in early summer, when the threat of frost has passed. Water well in summer and feed with a balanced liquid fertilizer every two weeks. ■ **Cut** the old stems of hardy fuchsias to the ground in spring. ■ **Lift** tender cultivars in autumn and keep in a frost-free place, watering sufficiently to keep them just moist. ■ **Take** softwood cuttings in spring (*see pp.329–330*). ■ **Vine weevils** can cause damage, especially in pots where larvae may eat large areas of root (*see p.332*).

Pruning and training

Bush When each shoot has made about three pairs of leaves, pinch out the tip. This encourages the plant to produce sideshoots. Do this three or four times and then allow the plant to flower.

Standard This shape is achieved by training a shoot up a cane, removing sideshoots. When the main stem reaches the required height, pinch out the tip and treat the top as for a bush. Training takes 2–3 years.

Pyramid Allow the main stem to grow to 23cm (9in). Pinch out the tip, keeping one shoot to continue as a new leader. Pinch out all sideshoots at three pairs of leaves. Repeat until the right height and shape is reached.

Column Allow two shoots to develop as central stems, and stop them at the desired height. Pinch the sideshoots regularly to create dense, bushy growth. As with a standard, this takes 2–3 years.

F. **'Alice Hoffman'** ♥ ↕↔45–60cm (18–24in) ✻✻

F. **'Annabel'** ♥ ↕↔30–60cm (12–24in) ✻

F. **'Genii'** ♥ ↕↔75–90cm (30–36in) ✻✻

F. **'Jack Shahan'** ♥ ↕30–45cm (12–18in) ↔45–60cm (18–24in) ✻

F. **'Marinka'** ♥ ↕15–30cm (6–12in) ↔45–60cm (18–24in) ✻

F. **'Mieke Meursing'** ♥ ↕↔30–60cm (12–24in) ✻

F. **'Riccartonii'** ♥ ↕2–3m (6–10ft) ↔1–2m (3–6ft) ✻✻✻

F. **'Royal Velvet'** ♥ ↕45–75cm (18–30in) ↔30–60cm (12–24in) ✻

F. 'Autumnale' ♀ ↕15–30cm (6–12in) ↔30–60cm (1–2ft) ✳

F. 'Ballet Girl' ♀ ↕30–45cm (12–18in) ↔45–75cm (18–30in) ✳

F. 'Celia Smedley' ♀ ↕↔45–75cm (18–30in) ✳

F. 'Dark Eyes' ♀ ↕45–60cm (18–24in) ↔60–75cm (24–30in) ✳

F. 'La Campanella' ♀ ↕15–30cm (6–12in) ↔30–45cm (12–18in) ✳

F. 'Lena' ♀ ↕30–60cm (12–24in) ↔60–75cm (24–30in) ✳✳

F. 'Machu Picchu' ↕↔30–60cm (12–24in) ✳

F. magellanica ↕↔2–3m (6–10ft) ✳✳

F. 'Mrs Popple' ♀ ↕↔1–1.1m (3–3½ft) ✳✳✳

F. 'Other Fellow' ↕↔30–45cm (12–18in) ✳

F. 'Peppermint Stick' ↕↔45–75cm (18–30in) ✳

F. 'Red Spider' ↕15–30cm (6–12in) ↔30–60cm (12–24in) ✳

F. 'Swingtime' ♀ ↕30–60cm (12–24in) ↔45–75cm (18–30in) ✳

F. 'Thalia' ♀ ↕↔45–90cm (18–36in) ❦

F. 'Tom Thumb' ♀ ↕↔15–30cm (6–12in) ✳✳

F. 'Winston Churchill' ♀ ↕↔45–75cm (18–30in) ✳

Garrya

Long catkins adorn these tough, large, evergreen shrubs from mid- to late winter. Male and female flowers are borne on separate plants, the male catkins being more dramatic. Most widely grown is the silk-tassel bush, *Garrya elliptica*. *G.* x *issaquahensis* 'Pat Ballard' has red-purple shoots, glossy leaves, and purple-tinged catkins. Garryas are versatile: they can be grown in a border, trained against a wall, or even used as hedging. They tolerate urban pollution, and the leathery leaves stand up to salt-laden winds and sea spray in coastal areas. For best effect, grow garryas with other winter-flowering shrubs like *Jasminum nudiflorum* (*see p.67*) trained against a wall, mahonias (*see p.77*), and Christmas box (*Sarcococca, see p.100*).

■ **HARDINESS** Fully hardy ✳✳✳ (borderline) to half-hardy ✳.
■ **CULTIVATION** Grow garryas in reasonably fertile, well-drained soil, in full sun or partial shade; shelter from cold winds in areas with severe frosts. ■ **Prune** lightly after flowering, cutting out shoots that spoil the shape. Garryas tolerate hard renovation pruning (*see p.323*). ■ **Take** semi-ripe cuttings (*see pp.329–330*) in summer.

Garrya elliptica 'James Roof' ♀
↕↔4m (12ft), vigorous shrub, male plants noted for particularly long catkins up to 20cm (8in) ✳✳✳

Gaultheria
Pernettya

Colourful autumn fruits are the main attraction of these trouble-free, evergreen shrubs. They bear small flowers just 7mm (¼in) long, usually in small clusters, in spring or summer. These are followed in autumn by berries in dusky shades of red, purple, and pink to white. These are edible; all other parts cause stomach upsets if eaten. Small to medium-sized, these shrubs have neat, dark green, leathery leaves and varied habits. Gaultherias can be grown in shrub borders, rock gardens, or woodland settings, and they make excellent companions for rhododendrons (*see pp.92–93*). Some have been subject to name changes, and they are often sold simply as pernettyas.

■ **HARDINESS** Fully hardy ✳✳✳ to half-hardy ✳.
■ **CULTIVATION** Need acid (lime-free), moist soil, ideally in partial shade, although they will tolerate full sun where the soil is permanently moist. ■ **Prune** lightly after flowering, cutting back shoots that spoil the shape. Restrict the spread of plants by removing suckering growths. ■ **Sow** seed (*see pp.328–329*) in containers outdoors in a cold frame in autumn. ■ **Take** semi-ripe cuttings (*see pp.329–330*) in summer or remove rooted suckers in spring and replant.

Gaultheria mucronata 'Mulberry Wine' ♀
↕↔1.2m (4ft), female, suckering shrub, berries if a male, for example *G. mucronata*, is nearby ✳✳✳

Genista
Broom

These elegant shrubs are grown for their pretty, pea-like yellow flowers, borne in small clusters from spring to summer. They are related to the other brooms, cytisus (*see p.43*) and spartiums (*see p.101*). The leaves are small. Although some species are almost leafless and almost all of them are deciduous, the green stems give some colour to a garden even in winter. Habits vary from upright to arching, tree-like forms. Brooms contrast well with broader-leaved plants such as ceanothus (*see p.32*) and fatsias (*see p.54*). The Mount Etna broom makes a graceful specimen in a border, while dwarfer species, like the dense, spiny *Genista hispanica*, suit rock gardens. Some have sharp spines.

■ **HARDINESS** Fully hardy ✳✳✳ to half-hardy ✳.
■ **CULTIVATION** Genistas like light, poor to reasonably fertile, well-drained soil, in full sun. Little pruning is required apart from removing misplaced or crossing shoots that spoil the shape, in late winter or early spring. ■ **Avoid** cutting into old wood, because it will not produce new shoots. ■ **Sow** seed (*see pp.328–329*) in a cold frame in autumn or take semi-ripe cuttings (*see pp.329–330*) in summer.

Genista lydia ♀
↕to 60cm (24in) ↔to 1m (3ft), domed shrub with spine-tipped, blue-green shoots, flowers in early summer ✳✳✳

Ginkgo biloba
Maidenhair tree
SUMMER AND AUTUMN

Perhaps the most ancient of all living trees, the ginkgo is upright or columnar when young and spreads as it ages. The deciduous foliage, similar to that of maidenhair ferns (*Adiantum, see p.304*) and gives the tree its common name, turns a soft, golden yellow in autumn. Catkin-like, yellow male flowers and tiny female flowers are produced on separate trees. Given warm summers, female flowers produce yellow-green fruits in autumn that smell unpleasant but contain large, edible nuts that are traditionally roasted. Easy to grow, ginkgos will tolerate atmospheric pollution and are excellent as landscape trees and as specimens in borders.

■ **HARDINESS** Fully hardy ✳✳✳.
■ **CULTIVATION** Any fertile, well-drained soil, in full sun will suit ginkgos. ■ **Cut** out any crossing or misshapen branches that spoil the shape of the tree, in late winter or early spring, to maintain a healthy framework (*see p.322*).
■ **Sow** seed (*see pp.328–329*) in a cold frame as soon as it is ripe. ■ **Take** semi-ripe cuttings (*see pp.329–330*) in summer.

Gingko biloba ♀
↕ to 30m (100ft) ↔ to 8m (25ft), extinct in the wild, the ginkgo has long been grown in temples and as a street tree in China and Japan

Gleditsia
SPRING TO AUTUMN

Decorative foliage and seed pods, and an elegant, spreading habit, make these deciduous trees beautiful specimen plants. The glossy, ferny leaves are divided into as many as 24 smaller, pale to dark green leaflets. In autumn, long, curved and twisted, pendent seed pods and foliage in yellow tints give further interest. The widely grown honey locust, *Gleditsia triacanthos*, usually has spiny trunks and shoots. 'Elegantissima' is a much smaller and thornless form of this tree, while 'Rubylace' has dark bronze-red young leaves that turn to dark bronze-green by midsummer. To highlight the autumn foliage of these trees, grow them alongside dark-leaved shrubs like cotinus (*see p.40*).

■ **HARDINESS** Fully hardy ✳✳✳, but they are susceptible to frost damage when young.
■ **CULTIVATION** Grow gleditsias in any fertile, well-drained soil, in sun. ■ **Pruning** is rarely necessary ■ **Sow** seed (*see pp.328–329*) in an open frame in autumn. ■ **Prepare** the seed by chipping each seed coat with knife or rubbing it with sandpaper to allow moisture in. ■ **Gall midges** may cause swellings on the leaves.

Gleditsia triacanthos 'Sunburst' ♀
↕12m (40ft) ↔10m (30ft), fast-growing and thornless, light canopy can be underplanted so particularly suited to gardens

Griselinia littoralis
Broadleaf
YEAR-ROUND

This vigorous, dense, evergreen, upright shrub or small tree can make a superb windbreak hedge in an exposed garden. It is grown for its tough and handsome foliage. Tiny flowers are borne in late spring, with male and female blossoms on separate plants. They are followed by purple fruits in autumn if plants of both sexes are grown together. Although most often used as hedging, griselinias also make handsome specimen plants in a border. *Griselinia littoralis* is particularly good in coastal areas, where the leathery leaves can withstand salt-laden winds and sea spray.

■ **HARDINESS** Fully hardy ✳✳✳ (borderline).
■ **CULTIVATION** Griselnias like light, fertile, well-drained soil in full sun, with shelter from cold, drying winds, also required. ■ **Prune** the shrub lightly in mid- or late spring, cutting back any shoots that spoil that shape of the shrub. ■ **Trim** hedges once or twice a year.
■ **Sow** seed (*see pp.328–329*) in spring at 13–18°C (55–64°F) or take semi-ripe cuttings (*see pp.329–330*) in summer.

Griselinia littoralis ♀
↕ to 8m (25ft) ↔ to 5m (15ft); there are variegated forms, but the plain green is best for hedging

Halesia
Silver bell, Snowdrop tree
SPRING AND AUTUMN

Beautiful in spring, this small group of deciduous, trouble-free shrubs and trees is grown for its pendent, bell-shaped, pure white flowers. These are generally borne in late spring, sometimes in early summer, and are followed in autumn by winged green fruits and golden foliage. The forms can vary from conical, as in *Halesia monticola*, to spreading, as in *H. carolina* or *H. diptera*. The more spreading types can be grown as trees or shrubs in gardens of any size. Found naturally in woodland and woodland margins and near riverbanks, halesias make pleasing specimens as shrubs for the back of a border or as trees in a woodland setting.

■ **HARDINESS** Fully hardy ✽✽✽.
■ **CULTIVATION** Prefer fertile, moist but well-drained, neutral to acid (lime-free) soil enriched with well-rotted organic matter. Position in sun or partial shade sheltered from cold winds. ■ **Remove** crossing shoots, in winter or late spring. ■ **Sow** seed (*see pp.328–329*) at 14–25°C (57–77°F) in autumn. ■ **Take** softwood cuttings (*see pp.329–330*) in summer, or layer low shoots (*see p.330*) in spring.

x Halimiocistus
LATE SPRING TO LATE SUMMER

Charming, fragile flowers are the main attraction of these small, evergreen shrubs. They are crosses between cistus (*see p.36*) and halimiums (*see right*). The flowers resemble rock roses (*Helianthemum, see p.62*) and are usually pure white or blotched with deep red at the bases of the petals. Several of these trouble-free, often spreading hybrids are grown in gardens, with flowering periods from late spring to late summer. Found where their parent species grow together in hot, dry, Mediterranean areas, these shrubs are happy in a rock garden or dry, sunny border alongside roses (*see pp.96–97*) and other shrubs such as lavenders (*Lavandula, see p.71*) and cistus.

■ **HARDINESS** Fully hardy ✽✽✽ to frost-hardy ✽✽; less hardy if grown in shade or in very fertile soil.
■ **CULTIVATION** Plant these shrubs in very well-drained soil in full sun and provide shelter from cold, drying winds. ■ **Pruning** is rarely needed, but if necessary in mid- or late spring, lightly trim shoots that spoil the shape of the shrub. ■ **Take** semi-ripe cuttings (*see pp.329–330*) in late summer.

Halimium
LATE SPRING TO EARLY SUMMER

Upright to spreading, but almost all compact, these small, evergreen shrubs bear sprays of flowers from late spring to early summer. These are golden yellow, occasionally white, and their petals are sometimes blotched at the bases with maroon-purple. They will flower best in long, hot summers. Their leaves are generally small, light to grey-green, and sometimes silver-scaly or hairy. These trouble-free shrubs usually have an upright or spreading habit. Halimiums are naturally found in dry, rocky places and thrive in rock gardens or at the front of a sunny border. You can also display them in pots in the sunniest corner for the best show of flowers.

■ **HARDINESS** Frost-hardy ✽✽.
■ **CULTIVATION** Halimiums like moderately fertile, well-drained, sandy soil, in full sun, with shelter from cold, drying winds. Choose the planting site carefully, since plants resent disturbance or transplanting once they are established. ■ **Trim** lightly or prune back shoots that spoil the shape after flowering; deadheading plants will help to prolong flowering. ■ **Sow** seed (*see pp.328–329*) at 19–24°C (66–75°F) in spring. ■ **Take** semi-ripe cuttings (*see pp.329–330*) of halimium in late summer.

Halesia monticola
‡12m (40ft) ↔ 8m (25ft), usually conical, vigorous tree, flowers in late spring before or just as leaves unfold, fruits heavily (*as shown*)

x *Halimiocistus sahucii* ♀
‡45cm (18in) ↔ 90cm (36in), compact, mounding or spreading, narrow-leaved, flowers in summer, one of most reliably hardy ✽✽✽

***Halimium* 'Susan'** ♀
‡45cm (18in) ↔ 60cm (24in), spreading shrub, flowers appear in summer and are often semi-double

Hamamelis
Witch hazel

AUTUMN AND WINTER

Fragrant, spidery blooms and autumn colour make these medium-sized to large, deciduous shrubs essential in the winter garden. The striking flowers cluster thickly on bare stems from autumn to early spring. Frost does not damage them. The broad, oval leaves turn yellow in autumn. Try witch hazels as specimen plants in borders, or grow them in groups. Evergreen Christmas box (*Sarcococca confusa, see p.100*), which is also scented and winter-flowering, will show off the upright, open forms of witch hazels and fill the garden with delicious scent on the coldest of days.

■ **HARDINESS** Fully hardy ✳✳✳.
■ **CULTIVATION** Witch hazels prefer reasonably fertile, moist but well-drained, ideally neutral to acid (lime-free) soil. They will stand chalk if in deep, humus-rich soil. ■ **Position** them in sun or partial shade, in an open but not exposed spot. ■ **Prune** any crossing shoots, in late winter or early spring, to maintain a good shape. Named witch hazels are grafted and are best bought from a nursery or garden centre.

***Hamamelis* x *intermedia* 'Pallida'** ♥
↕↔4m (12ft), vase-shaped habit, bright green leaves turn gold in autumn, large flowers in mid- to late winter

Hebe

YEAR-ROUND

Varied and attractive, evergreen foliage and pretty flowers, in a huge range of shrubs from low, sprawling plants to large domed bushes, means that there is a hebe for almost any situation. Hebes have neat, matt or glossy foliage in tones of grey-, blue- or true green, sometimes with coloured edges. Spikes up to 30cm (12in) long or clusters of small flowers are usually borne from early to midsummer. They vary in hue from white to pinks, blues, purples, or red. Hebes provide year-round interest in mixed or shrub borders, rock gardens, gravel gardens, or even in pots on the patio. In mild areas, particularly coastal ones, they can be used as hedging or as ground cover.

***Hebe* 'Great Orme'** ♥
↕↔1.2m (4ft), open, rounded bush, flowers from midsummer right through to mid-autumn, fading to white as they age ✳✳

Hebe albicans ♥
↕60cm (24in) ↔90cm (36in), dense, mound-forming or spreading shrub, flowers from early to midsummer ✳✳✳

■ **HARDINESS** Fully hardy ✳✳✳ to half-hardy ✳.
■ **CULTIVATION** Hebes grow in poor to reasonably fertile, moist but well-drained, preferably neutral to slightly alkaline (limy) soil. Sun or partial shade, with shelter from cold, drying winds, is best. ■ **Remove** any growths that spoil the shape, in late winter or early spring, but otherwise little pruning is needed. ■ **Take** semi-ripe cuttings (*see pp.329–330*) in summer or autumn. ■ **Downy mildew** may infect leaves in damp conditions: avoid watering from above and pick off spoiled leaves.

***Hebe pinguifolia* 'Pagei'** ♥
↕30cm (12in) ↔90cm (36in), erect, then semi-prostrate habit, purple stems, flowers from late spring to early summer ✳✳✳

Hedera
Ivy

YEAR-ROUND

Although it is known as a climbing plant (*see p.121*), there are a few named cultivars of the common ivy, *Hedera helix*, that have an unusual, shrubby habit. Like the climbing ivies, they are evergreen and famously tough plants. *Hedera helix* 'Congesta' forms a neat, dense bush with erect, spire-like shoots. It is compact and would make a striking addition to a rock garden. *Hedera helix* 'Erecta' is more vigorous, with stiffly upright stems, and slow-growing. It is better suited to a shrub or mixed border, perhaps where its small leaves contrast with, for example, ferns (*see pp.300–309*) or broad-leaved plants such as bergenias (*see p.198*). The stems are quite brittle, so are best grown in a sheltered spot, or with the support of other shrubs or a wall.

■ **HARDINESS** Fully hardy ✳✳✳.
■ **CULTIVATION** Grow in a variety of soils, but do best in fertile, moist but well-drained, preferably alkaline (limy) soil, in sun or partial shade, sheltered from wind. ■ **Trim** to shape the shrubs at any time of the year. ■ **Take** semi-ripe cuttings (*see pp.329–330*) in summer.

Hedera helix 'Congesta' ♀
↕↔45cm (18in)

Helianthemum
Rock rose, Sun rose

LATE SPRING TO MIDSUMMER

The pretty, papery, saucer-shaped flowers of these little evergreen shrubs have ensured that they remain a firm favourite of gardeners. Most grow to only 15–30cm (6–12in) tall. A profusion of blooms, in a wide range of vivid and pale colours, are borne over a long period from late spring to midsummer against a background of silver to grey- or mid-green foliage. They love to bask in sunshine and, with their compact habit, thrive in dry conditions, such as a rock garden, or a raised bed, or at the front of a mixed or herbaceous border, or as ground cover on a sunny bank. A gravel mulch suits rock roses very well, as it both looks good and gives them a dry, warm, free-draining surface over which to spread.

■ **HARDINESS** Fully hardy ✳✳✳ to frost-hardy ✳✳.
■ **CULTIVATION** Rock roses enjoy well-drained, neutral to alkaline (limy) soil, in full sun. ■ **Pruning** is easy; after flowering use shears to trim the flowered shoots back to the old growth. ■ **Take** softwood cuttings (*see pp.329–330*) in late spring or early summer.

Helianthemum 'Rhodanthe Carneum' ♀
↕30cm (12in) ↔45cm (18in), sometimes sold as 'Wisley Pink', with an especially long flowering season ✳✳✳

Heliotropium
Heliotrope, Cherry pie

SUMMER

Heliotrope is a treasured cottage-garden plant, loved for its dense, sweetly-scented flowerheads. Most heliotropes on sale are related to *Heliotropium arborescens*, the only commonly grown species, which although it is a woody shrub is quite tender – hence heliotropes are most often used in frost-prone climates as bedding or container plants, for summer display. They can be overwintered under cover, but new plants grown over winter from cuttings taken from the parent often make more successful, bushier plants to set out the following year. The wrinkled leaves are sometimes tinged purple, complementing the tiny blue or purple flowers borne in large clusters throughout summer.

■ **HARDINESS** Half-hardy ✳.
■ **CULTIVATION** Grow in any fertile, moist but well-drained soil, in full sun. In containers such as pots, tubs, and windowboxes, use any good-quality potting compost. ■ **Sow** seed (*see pp.328–329*) at 16–18°C (61–64°F) in spring. ■ **Take** softwood or semi-ripe cuttings (*see pp.329–330*) in summer.

Heliotropium arborescens 'Marine'
↕45cm (18in) ↔30–45cm (12–18in), flowerheads to 15cm (6in) across

Hibiscus

SPRING TO AUTUMN

Famous for their spectacular flowers from spring until autumn, hibiscus are available in a rainbow of bright hues. The blooms are carried against glossy-green, occasionally variegated foliage. The group includes annuals and perennials, as well as shrubs, but the woody, fully hardy, deciduous *Hibiscus syriacus* and its cultivars are the most commonly grown in cool climates. They thrive in large pots: useful if growing tender species, since the container can be moved under cover over winter.

■ **HARDINESS** Fully hardy ✳✳✳ to frost-tender ❀.
■ **CULTIVATION** Grow in moist, well-drained, preferably slightly alkaline (limy) soil, in full sun. The longer and hotter the summer, the more flowers are produced, so give hibiscus a warm, sheltered position in cooler areas, and apply a winter mulch (*see p.326*). ■ **Prune** only to remove wayward branches and any damaged wood. ■ **Sow** seed (*see pp.328–329*) at 13–18°C (55–64°F) in spring. ■ **Take** semi-ripe cuttings in summer (*see pp.329–330*), or layer shoots (*see p.330*) in late spring.

Hibiscus syriacus **'Woodbridge'** ♀
‡3m (10ft) ↔ 2m (6ft), with flatter, more mallow-like, but intensely coloured blooms ✳✳✳

Hibiscus syriacus **'Diana'** ♀
‡3m (10ft) ↔ 2m (6ft), bears some of the largest flowers for this species, to 13cm (5in) across ✳✳✳

Hibiscus syriacus **'Oiseau Bleu'** ♀
‡3m (10ft) ↔ 2m (6ft), very popular for its novel colour, and frequently sold under the name 'Blue Bird' ✳✳✳

Hippophae
Sea buckthorn

AUTUMN

These tough, deciduous shrubs or small trees are popular plants with a handsome, upright habit and narrow, silvery leaves. In autumn, abundant orange berries are borne if a male and a female are grown together; those of the willow-leaved sea buckthorn (*Hippophae salicifolia*) are said to be the most nutritious fruits that can be grown in temperate climates. They have a sharp taste like lemon and can be used in juice and preserves. The common sea buckthorn (*H. rhamnoides*) has spiny stems and is invaluable in areas buffeted by salt-laden winds and sea spray, where it can be used for hedges.

■ **HARDINESS** Fully hardy ✳✳✳.
■ **CULTIVATION** Ideally in full sun in moist but well-drained, slightly alkaline (limy) soil; in practice, these resilient plants will survive most well-drained and sandy soils and periods of drought, strong winds, and heavy rain. ■ **Prune** only those stems that are crossing or spoiling the shape of the shrub. ■ **Sow** seed (*see pp.328–329*) in a cold frame as soon as it is ripe or in spring. ■ **Take** semi-ripe cuttings in summer or hardwood cuttings in autumn (*see pp.329–330*), or layer shoots (*see p.330*) in autumn.

Hippophae rhamnoides ♀
‡↔ 6m (20ft), bushy shrub or small tree, the berries persist on female plants through to winter

Hydrangea

These shrubs have long been garden favourites for their large, stately flowerheads. These may be flat or domed and are made up of clusters of tiny, fertile flowers and larger, sterile flowers with petal-like sepals. The many cultivars of the most common species, *Hydrangea macrophylla*, include two types: hortensias have round "mopheads" of sterile flowers, whereas lacecaps have flat flowerheads of fertile flowers edged with sterile ones. Flower colour is affected by the acidity or alkalinity of the soil. Hydrangea blooms are blue on acid soils and pink on alkaline (limy) soils; on neutral soils, the hues can be mixed, often being bluish-pink. The white-flowered cultivars are not affected. Most garden hydrangeas are deciduous. Some hydrangeas also have flaky, peeling bark and handsome foliage, which has good autumn colour. These excellent plants can be used in many sites, especially as specimen plants or in borders. The flowers dry to parchment shades and are useful in arrangements. (*See also p.122.*)

■ **HARDINESS** Fully hardy ✳✳✳ to frost-hardy ✳✳
■ **CULTIVATION** Hydrangeas thrive in moist, well-drained, fertile soil in sun or partial shade, if sheltered from cold, drying winds. Pruning, for most cultivars except those mentioned below, consists of cutting out misplaced or crossing shoots in late winter or early spring. ■ **Sow** seed (*see pp.328–329*) in containers in spring. ■ **Root** soft stem-tip cuttings in early summer or take hardwood cuttings in winter (*see pp.329–330*). Blooms may be spoiled by grey mould (botrytis) in very wet summers.

How to prune hydrangeas

Hard pruning of *H. paniculata* in early spring – before it produces its flowering shoots – results in a much better show of flower. If not pruned, the plants become very tall and the flowers appear only at the tips, where they are difficult to see. Cut off all the previous year's flowering wood to leave a base of woody stems, as low as 25cm (10in) in exposed gardens or 60cm (24in) at the back of a border. Cut each stem back to a pair of healthy buds at the required height. Neglected plants also respond well to this type of hard pruning.

Light pruning is advisable for hortensias, all other *H. macrophylla* cultivars, *H. serrata* and its cultivars, and 'Preziosa'. These hydrangeas all flower on stems formed in the previous year. On the whole, they manage this without much attention, but a little annual pruning enhances flowering and keeps the shrubs healthy. Leave old flowerheads over winter to protect the new buds. Then, in late winter or early spring, prune the previous year's flowered shoots by up to 30cm (12in) to just above two strong buds. Cut out weak and thin shoots and prune one or two of the oldest stems to the base.

H. arborescens 'Annabelle' ♀ ↕↔2.5m (8ft) ✳✳✳

H. arborescens 'Grandiflora' ♀ ↕↔2.5m (8ft) ✳✳✳

H. macrophylla 'Blue Bonnet' (hortensia) ↕2m (6ft) ↔2.5m (8ft) ✳✳✳

H. macrophylla 'Bouquet Rose' (hortensia) ↕2m (6ft) ↔2.5m (8ft) ✳✳✳

H. paniculata 'Brussels Lace' ↕3–7m (10–22ft) ↔2.5m (8ft) ✳✳✳

H. paniculata 'Floribunda' ↕3–7m (10–22ft) ↔2.5m (8ft) ✳✳✳

H. 'Preziosa' ♀ ↕↔1.5m (5ft) ✳✳

H. quercifolia ♀ ↕2m (6ft) ↔2.5m (8ft) ✳✳✳

H. aspera Villosa Group ♀ ‡↔1–4m (4–12ft) ✱✱✱

H. involucrata 'Hortensis' ♀ ‡1m (3ft) ↔2m (6ft) ✱✱

H. macrophylla 'Ami Pasquier' ‡60cm (2ft) ↔1m (3ft) ✱✱✱

H. macrophylla 'Ayesha' (hortensia) ‡1.5m (5ft) ↔2m (6ft) ✱✱✱

H. macrophylla 'Hamburg' (hortensia) ‡2m (6ft) ↔2.5m (8ft) ✱✱✱

H. macrophylla 'Lanarth White' ♀ (lacecap) ‡↔1.5m (5ft) ✱✱✱

H. macrophylla 'Mariesii Perfecta' ♀ (lacecap) ‡2m (6ft) ↔2.5m (8ft) ✱✱✱

H. macrophylla 'Veitchii' ♀ (lacecap) ‡2m (6ft) ↔2.5m (8ft) ✱✱✱

H. paniculata 'Grandiflora' ♀ ‡3–7m (10–22ft) ↔2.5m (8ft) ✱✱✱

H. paniculata PINK DIAMOND ('Interhydia') ♀ ‡3–7m (10–22ft) ↔2.5m (8ft) ✱✱✱

H. paniculata 'Praecox' ‡3–7m (10–22ft) ↔2.5m (8ft) ✱✱✱

H. paniculata 'Unique' ♀ ‡3–7m (10–22ft) ↔2.5m (8ft) ✱✱✱

H. quercifolia SNOW QUEEN ('Flemygea') ‡2m (6ft) ↔2.5m (8ft) ✱✱✱

H. serrata ‡↔1.2m (4ft) ✱✱

H. serrata 'Bluebird' ♀ (lacecap) ↔1.2m (4ft) ✱✱

H. serrata 'Rosalba' ♀ (lacecap) ‡↔1.2m (4ft) ✱✱

Hypericum
St. John's wort

SUMMER TO AUTUMN

This diverse group ranges from large shrubs to small annuals and perennials, but in summer all bear similar, distinctive, bright yellow flowers with a central boss of golden stamens. Some are decorated with berries through autumn. The shrubs are most commonly cultivated: both evergreen and deciduous species provide lovely autumn colour. There is a hypericum for most situations: the larger species are good for a border, smaller ones for a rock garden. The spreading Rose of Sharon (*Hypericum calycinum*) makes ideal ground cover, although it can become invasive so is not recommended for borders.

■ **HARDINESS** Fully hardy ✻✻✻ to half-hardy ✻✻.
■ **CULTIVATION** Larger shrubs prefer moist but well-drained soil in sun or partial shade, the small rock-garden types sun and good drainage. *H. androsaemum* and *H. calycinum* tolerate deep shade. ■ **Trim** in spring to keep them neat; cut back hard larger deciduous species to a permanent framework in early spring. ■ **Take** semi-ripe cuttings in summer (*see pp.329–330*).

Hypericum calycinum (Aaron's beard, Rose of Sharon)
↕60cm (24in) ↔ indefinite, evergreen or semi-evergreen, flowers summer to autumn ✻✻✻

Ilex
Holly

YEAR-ROUND

Hollies are best known for winter berries and stiff, prickly, evergreen foliage, but not all are spiny. Their glossy leaves may be plain dark or mid-green, or edged, splashed, or striped with silver or gold. The flowers are tiny, the berries usually red or black; they can cause a stomach upset if eaten. Female plants berry only if a male is nearby; hollies are often sold by sex so you can be sure of fruiting. Grow hollies in woodland, with winter-flowering shrubs like sarcococcas (*see p.100*) or mahonias (*see p.77*), or as specimens, so their shapely forms and pale grey bark can be appreciated. *Ilex* x *altaclerensis* and *I. aquifolium* cultivars can be used as formal hedging, but frequent trimming can mean fewer berries.

■ **HARDINESS** Fully hardy ✻✻✻ to half-hardy ✻✻.
■ **CULTIVATION** Best planted in late winter or early spring. Full sun encourages bright colour in variegated hollies, but can site in sun or shade in moist, well-drained soil. ■ **Prune** free-standing specimens only if needed to maintain a well-balanced shape; trim hedges in late summer. ■ **Take** semi-ripe cuttings in late summer or autumn (*see pp.329–330*).

***Ilex aquifolium* 'Amber'** ♀
↕6m (20ft) ↔2.5m (8ft), compact, pyramid-shaped, female tree, reliably bears abundant fruit when a male holly is close by ✻✻

***Ilex* x *altaclerensis* 'Golden King'** ♀
↕6m (20ft) ↔ 4m (12ft), compact, female shrub, good conical form but berries can be sparse in some years ✻✻

***Ilex aquifolium* 'J.C. van Tol'** ♀
↕6m (20ft) ↔ 4m (12ft), broadly shaped female tree, self-fertile so berries are guaranteed every year without a male nearby ✻✻

***Ilex aquifolium* 'Ferox Argentea'** ♀
(Hedgehog holly)
↕8m (25ft) ↔ 4m (12ft), slow-growing, upright, prickly male with spines over and on the leaves ✻✻

Indigofera

EARLY SUMMER TO AUTUMN

The evergreen and deciduous shrubby indigoferas are the most commonly cultivated in this large group. They need space to grow and show off their elegant habits, for example in a shrub border, perhaps with euonymus (*see p.52*) and escallonias (*see p.50*), or trained against a sunny wall. They bear masses of pea-like flowers from early summer until early autumn, against a background of soft-green leaves. *Indigofera amblyantha* and *I. heterantha* are the hardiest species, and thus the best choice in temperate climates, unless you can provide a sheltered, south-facing wall. They respond well to annual pruning.

■ **HARDINESS** Fully hardy ✳✳✳ to frost-hardy ✳✳.
■ **CULTIVATION** Grow in moist but well-drained soil, in full sun. ■ **Prune** hard in frost-prone climates only; in early spring, cut all stems down to within a few buds of their bases, leaving a low stubby framework (*see pp.322–323*). For wall-trained shrubs, in late winter or early spring, remove or tie in branches, and trim sideshoots to within four buds of the main branches. ■ **Take** semi-ripe cuttings in early or midsummer (*see pp.329–330*).

Indigofera amblyantha ♀
↕2m (6ft) ↔2.5m (8ft), deciduous shrub, particularly free-flowering ✳✳✳

Itea

SUMMER TO AUTUMN

Itea ilicifolia and *I. virginica* are widely cultivated – for their tiny white flowers, borne in catkin-like clusters in summer, and their foliage, similar to that of holly. The leaves of the evergreen *I. ilicifolia* are valuable for providing year-round greenery; those of the deciduous *I. virginica* give a spectacular autumn display of reds and purples before they fall.

■ **HARDINESS** Fully hardy ✳✳✳ to frost-hardy ✳✳.
■ **CULTIVATION** The less hardy evergreen iteas like fertile, moist, well-drained soil in a sunny, sheltered position; they thrive against a sunny, south-facing wall and with a thick winter mulch (*see p.326*), especially while young. Deciduous species prefer the shady, damp, slightly acid conditions of a woodland garden or dense shrub border. ■ **Trim** evergreens only as necessary to keep them neat, or to keep shapely, cut the flowered shoots back to strong, non-flowering sideshoots; once plants are mature, cut back one stem in four to the base each year to prevent congestion (*see pp.322–323*). If wall-trained, cut back flowered shoots to a few buds from the framework branches.
■ **Sow** seed when ripe (*see pp.328–329*).
■ **Take** soft stem-tip cuttings in spring, or semi-ripe cuttings in summer (*see pp.329–330*).

Itea virginica (Sweetspire, Tassel-white)
↕1.5–3m (5–10ft), flowers in summer ✳✳✳

Jasminum nudiflorum

Winter jasmine

WINTER

Most commonly grown jasmines are climbers (*see p.123*), but this one is a shrub, albeit a rather lanky one. The winter jasmine (*Jasminum nudiflorum*) may not be quite as intensely perfumed as its summer-flowering cousins, but is highly valued for its golden flowers through the barest months of the year. This slender-stemmed, arching, often quite untidy, plant is best wall-trained, perhaps with other winter favourites such as garryas (*see p.58*). Cut sprigs and bring indoors while the buds are still closed; the warmth of a room should force them into flower for a touch of winter cheer and delicate scent.

■ **HARDINESS** Fully hardy ✳✳✳.
■ **CULTIVATION** Grow in fertile, well-drained soil in full sun or partial shade.
■ **Prune** flowered shoots back to strong buds, and once plants are older, after flowering, remove up to one in four of the main stems at the base to encourage fresh growth (*see pp.322–323*). ■ **Take** semi-ripe cuttings in summer or autumn (*see pp.329–330*); or shoots can be layered (*see p.330*) in autumn.

Jasminum nudiflorum ♀ (Winter jasmine)
↕↔3m (10ft), deciduous shrub with fragrant flowers in winter, leaves are dark green and appear after flowering

Juniperus
Juniper
YEAR-ROUND

These evergreen, coniferous trees and shrubs are grown for their sculptural habits and colourful foliage. They come in all shapes and sizes; large trees, dwarf cultivars, and spreading shrubs, and their leaves, or needles, can be dark green, golden yellow or even blue. A fantastic tapestry of shapes, colours and of textures can be built up by growing a collection of junipers together, or with other conifers. The females bear round, fleshy cones, rather like berries; these are used in cooking and also as one of the flavourings of gin. Junipers will tolerate a wide range of conditions: larger trees can be used as specimens, small shrubs in a rock garden with alpines, and prostrate cultivars as ground cover.

■ **HARDINESS** Fully hardy ✳✳✳ to frost-hardy ✳✳.
■ **CULTIVATION** Junipers are unfussy and will grow in any well-drained soil, in sun or partial shade. Pruning is generally unnecessary, although if prostrate species spread too far you can remove selected stems carefully to keep them within bounds. ■ **Propagation** is tricky, and seed may take up to five years to germinate, so new plants are probably best bought from a nursery.

Juniperus squamata 'Blue Star' ♥
↕40cm (16in) ↔ to 1m (3ft), a compact, spreading bush forming wave-like, cascading shapes ✳✳✳

Juniperus scopulorum 'Skyrocket'
↕6m (20ft) ↔ 50–60cm (20–24in), pencil-thin, columnar tree that provides a spectacular focal point ✳✳✳

Juniperus communis 'Compressa' ♥
↕80cm (32in) ↔ 45m (18in), dwarf and very slow-growing, suitable for combining with alpine plants in a trough or rock garden ✳✳✳

Kalmia
MID-SPRING TO EARLY SUMMER

Kalmias are acid-loving, evergreen shrubs with clusters of pretty, pink, bowl-shaped flowers in mid-spring and early summer. Throughout the year, the branches are clothed with the glossy, leathery leaves. The larger kalmias, such as *Kalmia latifolia* and its cultivars, are spectacular in borders or among groves of trees. Small species, for example *K. microphylla*, can be used in a rock or woodland garden with heathers and dwarf rhododendrons, which require similar soil conditions.

■ **HARDINESS** Fully hardy ✳✳✳.
■ **CULTIVATION** Grow in moist, acid (lime-free) soil, preferably in partial shade unless the ground remains continually damp; a layer of leafmould, pine needles, or compost around the plants in spring will help retain moisture. If you live in an area with limy soil, grow kalmias in pots filled with ericaceous (lime-free) compost. ■ **Prune** after flowering only if necessary to trim shoots that spoil the shape of the shrub. If you have a leggy specimen, then renovate it over several seasons (*see p.323*) – except *K. angustifolia*, which can be cut back hard in a single year, and will regrow well.
■ **Take** semi-ripe cuttings in midsummer (*see pp.329–330*), or layer low-growing shoots in late summer (*see p.330*).

Kalmia angustifolia ♥ (Sheep laurel)
↕60cm (24in) ↔ 1.5m (5ft), mound-forming shrub, flowers are occasionally white

Kerria japonica
Jew's mantle

Kerria and its cultivars are vigorous, suckering shrubs that are good value all year-round. In mid and late spring, they bear single or double, golden yellow flowers. The deciduous foliage is bright green, grey-green, or variegated with creamy white. When the leaves fall, winter interest is then provided by the dense clumps of arching, light green stems. Grow kerrias in a border where they have room to spread out among other shrubs, or as part of a display of winter stems together with dogwoods (*Cornus, see pp.38–39*).

■ **HARDINESS** Fully hardy ✳✳✳.
■ **CULTIVATION** Grow kerrias in fertile, well-drained soil in full sun or partial shade.
■ **Prune** the stems when they have flowered to sideshoots or strong buds lower down on the shrub (*see pp.322–323*). ■ **Divide** the bush in autumn (*see p.330*), or propagate from suckers (stems growing up from the roots) in spring. To do this, find a sucker and dig down to check that it has developed some roots of its own. Cut it away from its parent, cut back its stem by a half, and replant it.

***Kerria japonica* 'Picta'**
‡1.5m (5ft) ↔2m (6ft)

***Kerria japonica* 'Golden Guinea'** ♀
‡2m (6ft) ↔2.5m (8ft), very large single flowers up to 6cm (2½in) across

Koelreuteria

These make fine specimen trees throughout the year. They have a spreading shape, elegant, deciduous leaves, large clusters of yellow flowers in summer, and unusual, bladder-like fruits in the autumn. The golden rain tree (*Koelreuteria paniculata*) is the most widely available, and also perhaps the most impressive, of the three species. Its leaves emerge reddish-pink in spring, mature to mid-green, and give a lovely show of butter-yellow tints in autumn. In mid- and late summer, it bears sprays of small, golden flowers, up to 30cm (12in) long, followed by pink- or red-flushed fruit capsules. The flowers are more abundant in areas with long, hot summers.

■ **HARDINESS** Fully hardy ✳✳✳ to frost-hardy ✳✳.
■ **CULTIVATION** Grow in fertile, well-drained soil in full sun. ■ **Prune out** any damaged or dead wood (*see p.322*) when dormant in winter, but no further pruning is necessary. ■ **Sow** seed (*see pp.328–329*) in autumn, in a container, and place in a cold frame.

***Koelreuteria paniculata* ♀**
(Golden rain tree, Pride of India)
‡↔10m (30ft), leaves to 45cm (18in) long ✳✳✳

Kolkwitzia amabilis
Beauty bush

In full flower, the beauty bush is an amazing sight. From late spring to early summer, the pale- to deep-pink blooms are borne in such numbers that they almost completely obscure the tapered, dark green leaves. This is a deciduous, suckering shrub with an elegant, arching habit. It makes an excellent border plant and is also wonderful grown as a specimen, so that its charms can be enjoyed to the full. Cultivars with brighter pink flowers or orange-yellow young foliage are available.

■ **HARDINESS** Fully hardy ✷✷✷; foliage may be damaged by late frost.
■ **CULTIVATION** This shrub prefers well-drained soil, preferably in full sun, although it will tolerate some shade. ■ **Prune** shoots after they have flowered, to strong buds or shoots lower down on the plant. On mature plants, cut out about one-third to a quarter of old branches to the ground to encourage new growth (see pp.322–323). ■ **Propagate** the shrub from suckers (stems growing up from the roots) in spring. To do this, find a sucker and dig down to check that it has developed some roots of its own. Cut it away from its parent, cut back its stems by half, and then replant it. Water the beauty bush well.

Laburnum
Golden rain

As the common name suggests, these spreading trees are grown for their bright-yellow, pea-like flowers, which are produced in long pendent clusters in late spring and early summer. Any one of this small group of compact trees is an excellent choice for a specimen tree in a small garden. Create a lovely arch, tunnel, or pergola of golden rain – simply tie in the branches to a frame while they are young and supple. In this way, the pendent flowers can be enjoyed at their best. Plant purple flowers, such as alliums (see p.147), beneath them for a pleasing contrast. Weeping cultivars are available.

■ **HARDINESS** Fully hardy ✷✷✷.
■ **CULTIVATION** Site laburnums in well-drained soil in full sun. ■ **Train** them by tying in shoots as they grow. In late summer, trim the sideshoots to two or three buds from the main stems to encourage branching, and more flowers. Remove any wayward shoots when they are still young, in late winter (see p.322). ■ **Sow** seed of species (see pp.328–329) in a cold frame in autumn; when it's time to plant out the seedlings, do so quickly because they resent root disturbance.

Laurus nobilis
Sweet bay, Bay laurel

The sweet bay forms a large shrub or small, conical tree with evergreen, aromatic foliage that is used as a culinary flavouring. Cultivars with golden leaves are also available. Both male and female flowers are greenish-yellow, but are borne on separate plants in spring; if grown together, then black berries may follow on the female. Bay is often clipped and looks elegant with other formal topiary, such as box (Buxus, see p.26), or in a pot as a patio plant. Neat bushes or standards in containers have the bonus of being easily moved under cover in winter, if needed. Bay can also be grown in its natural form as a specimen, in borders, or against a wall.

■ **HARDINESS** Frost-hardy ✷✷; foliage may be damaged by cold winds.
■ **CULTIVATION** Grow in moist, well-drained soil, in sun or partial shade, with some shelter. Remove wayward or crossing shoots of naturally shaped bay (see p.322). ■ **Clip** topiary once or twice in summer to keep it neat. ■ **Sow** seed (see pp.328–329) in pots in a cold frame in autumn; take semi-ripe cuttings (see pp.329–330) in summer. ■ **Scale insects** may be a problem on plants growing under cover.

Kolkwitzia amabilis 'Pink Cloud' ♥
↕3m (10ft) ↔ 4m (12ft), widely available

Laburnum x *watereri* 'Vossii' ♥
↕↔8m (25ft), flower clusters up to 60cm (2ft) long

Laurus nobilis ♥
↕12m (40ft) ↔10m (30ft), widely available, contact with foliage may inflame skin allergies

Lavandula
Lavender

Lavenders are deservedly popular plants, grown for their evergreen, aromatic foliage, and scented flowers in mid- to late summer. There are many types, some more strongly perfumed than others, most with silvery foliage and nectar-rich blooms irresistible to pollinating bees. To dry the flowers, cut them before they are fully open and hang upside down in bunches in a dry place. Lavenders can be used in borders and are classic partners for roses; they are wonderful grown as low edging for a bed, sending up great wafts of scent as you brush past. Some species are not fully hardy but can be grown in pots and taken into a conservatory over winter.

■ **HARDINESS** Fully hardy ❋❋❋ to half-hardy ❋.
■ **CULTIVATION** Lavenders are undemanding, provided that they have well-drained soil in full sun. ■ **Trim** in early or mid spring: use shears to create a neat, rounded mound, taking off shoot tips but never cutting into old, bare wood. Trim lightly again to remove faded flower stalks (see right). ■ **Sow** seed in a container in a cold frame in spring (*see pp.328–329*). ■ **Take** semi-ripe cuttings in summer (*see pp.329–330*) for quicker results.

***Lavandula angustifolia* 'Munstead'**
↕45cm (18in) ↔ 60cm (24in), more compact than the species so better for border edging ❋❋❋

Lavandula pedunculata* subsp. *pedunculata ♀
↕↔ 60cm (24in), attractive relative of the vigorous French lavender, *L. stoechas* ❋❋❋ (borderline)

***Lavandula* 'Marshwood'**
↕↔ 60cm (24in), bushy plant with similar flowers to the French lavenders ❋❋❋ (borderline)

***Lavandula angustifolia* 'Hidcote'** ♀
↕60cm (24in) ↔ 75cm (30in), compact lavender whose vivid flowers contrast spectacularly with the grey leaves ❋❋❋

Lavatera
Mallow

There are lots of mallows; the shrubby ones need space to grow as they get quite large, but they respond well to hard pruning. They are valued for their profusion of ice-cream-coloured flowers in summer and autumn. The foliage of both deciduous and evergreen types is soft green, with downy hairs, rather coarse in appearance, so these shrubs are best used to provide a substantial backdrop for smaller ornamental plants; put them near the back of the border, preferably against a wall in areas with very cold winters. Mallows are ideal for coastal gardens, enjoying the sandy soil and often mild, frost-free conditions. (See also p.226.)

■ **HARDINESS** Fully hardy ✳✳✳ to frost-hardy ✳✳.
■ **CULTIVATION** Mallows prefer light, sandy soil in full sun, but tolerate heavier ground. In cold regions, the frost-hardy species may need shelter from cold, drying winds, for example a south-facing wall. ■ **Prune** in early spring to keep the shrub compact, cutting stems back almost to the base. ■ **Take** softwood cuttings (see pp.329–330) in early summer; lavateras can be short-lived so grow replacements.

***Lavatera* x *clementii* 'Burgundy Wine'** ♀
↕↔2m (6ft) vigorous, semi-evergreen ✳✳✳

Lespedeza
Bush clover

The bush clovers are named for their blue-green leaves, borne in groups of three and looking like those of the common clover. There are annual and perennial species, but the most commonly available are the deciduous shrubs, which are mainly grown for their pea-like flowers. They hang in long, dense clusters from the arching branches towards the end of summer and into autumn. This late flowering time makes lespedezas invaluable plants to team with rudbeckias (see p.265) and Michaelmas daisies (*Aster,* see pp.162–163) for a fabulous display of warm, glowing colours late in the season. Very cold winters may cut these plants down, but bush clover will regrow.

■ **HARDINESS** Fully hardy ✳✳✳.
■ **CULTIVATION** Grow in light, well-drained soil in full sun. ■ **Prune** in early spring by cutting back all the stems to a low framework; if severe winters cause the top-growth to die back, then cut stems right down to the base of the plant. ■ **Sow** seed in containers outdoors in spring (see pp.328–329). *L. thunbergii* can be divided (see p.330), also in spring.

Lespedeza thunbergii ♀
↕2m (6ft) ↔3m (10ft), flowers in early autumn, may only achieve full height in warmer areas where the top-growth survives winter

Leucothoe

These deciduous, evergreen and semi-evergreen shrubs resemble pieris (see pp.96–97) in many ways, with an upright habit, arching branches, and attractive, bell-like, white flowers that appear in spring. The leaves of all are handsome, but novel foliage colour is an added attraction in cultivars of *Leucothoe fontanesiana* such as 'Rainbow' and 'Scarletta', which has dark red-purple young foliage that turns dark green in summer and then bronze in winter. Leucothoes grow best in a shady position, accompanying shrubs such as rhododendrons (see pp.92–93), ericas (see pp.48–49) and pieris, which all like similar soil conditions. Most are good choices for a woodland garden.

■ **HARDINESS** Fully hardy ✳✳✳ to frost-hardy ✳✳.
■ **CULTIVATION** Grow in partial or deep shade, in soil that is acid (lime-free) and reliably moist; add plenty of well-rotted organic matter. ■ **Prune** in late winter or early spring, only to take out any crossing or badly placed branches. ■ **Sow** seed in containers in a cold frame in spring (see pp.328–329). ■ **Take** semi-ripe cuttings (see pp.329–330) in summer.

***Leucothoe fontanesiana* 'Rainbow'**
↕1.5m (5ft) ↔2m (6ft), clump-forming variety that makes good underplanting for a woodland garden, flowers in late spring ✳✳✳

Leycesteria formosa
Himalayan honeysuckle

SUMMER TO AUTUMN

A fast-growing shrub with hollow, bamboo-like stems, this has unusual flowers appearing in summer, followed by small, round berries. The white flowers are covered by distinctive bracts, forming drooping, pagoda-like clusters. These bracts persist to enclose purple-red berries. It is less widely grown today, which is a pity as it provides a long season of interest, from blue-green shoots in spring to good autumn colour. The stems remain attractive during winter and look effective among other shrubs with colourful winter stems, such as the dogwoods (*Cornus, see pp.38–39*).

■ **HARDINESS** Fully hardy ✳✳✳ (borderline).
■ **CULTIVATION** Grow in reasonably fertile, well-drained soil, in full sun or partial shade.
■ **Protect** from cold, drying winds and protect with a thick layer (mulch) of organic matter around the base of the plant in winter if severe frosts are forecast (*see p.326*). ■ **Prune** after flowering by cutting back flowered shoots to young sideshoots or strong buds lower down – or, in spring, cut all the stems back hard (*see p.323*). ■ **Sow** seed in containers in a cold frame in autumn (*see pp.328–329*). ■ **Take** softwood cuttings in summer (*see pp.329–330*).

Leycesteria formosa ♀
↕↔2m (6ft), upright, thicket-forming habit, suited to a woodland garden or shrub border, flowers from late summer to early autumn

Ligustrum
Privet

YEAR-ROUND

Most commonly used as hedging, privets are evergreen or semi-evergreen shrubs found in many an urban garden, since they withstand shade and pollution. Easy to grow, they thrive in most soils. Musty scented white flowers appear in spring or summer, followed by black fruits, but the dense, neat foliage is the main feature. The habit can be upright or conical, rounded or spreading. Some species, like *Ligustrum japonicum*, are used as specimen shrubs or in a border; others, such as the golden privet (*L. ovalifolium* 'Aureum'), make the best hedges.

■ **HARDINESS** Fully hardy ✳✳✳ to frost-hardy ✳✳.
■ **CULTIVATION** Grow in any well-drained soil in full sun or partial shade; variegated cultivars do best in full sun. ■ **Prune** shrubs in late winter, cutting out any crossing branches. Clip hedges at least twice a year. ■ **Sow** seed in containers in a cold frame in autumn or spring (*see pp.328–329*). ■ **Take** semi-ripe cuttings in summer, or hardwood cuttings in winter (*see pp.329–330*). ■ **Leaf miners** may attack, making characteristic ribbon-like markings, but they do no lasting damage.

Ligustrum lucidum 'Excelsum Superbum' ♀
↕↔10m (30ft), conical-shaped tree or shrub, evergreen leaves, flowers in late summer ✳✳✳

Linum arboreum
Flax

LATE SPRING TO SUMMER

This tough little shrub has flowers of deep yellow. Individual blooms are short-lived (and usually close in the afternoon), but there are always plenty to take their place, following on from late spring through summer. A dwarf evergreen, this flax originates in scrubby regions of Greece and western Turkey, and is very suitable for sloping, free-draining banks, rock gardens, or the front of a sunny border. Create a Mediterranean feel by growing it with other sun-loving, green and gold plants such as golden marjoram (*Origanum, see p.80*), helianthemum (*see p.62*), or gold-variegated elaeagnus (*see pp.46–47*). (*See also p.232.*)

■ **HARDINESS** Frost-hardy ✳✳.
■ **CULTIVATION** Grow in light, reasonably fertile soil with added organic matter; dig in coarse grit on heavy clay soils to improve drainage (*see p.319*). The plant must have a warm, sunny spot. ■ **Protect** it from winter wet, if possible, by placing a cloche over it. ■ **Sow** seed in spring or autumn in containers in a cold frame (*see pp.328–329*). ■ **Take** semi-ripe cuttings (*see pp.329–330*) in summer.

Linum arboreum ♀
↕↔30cm (12in), thick, glaucous leaves often produced in rosettes

Liquidambar

AUTUMN

These deciduous trees bear maple-like leaves that turn to stunning shades of purple, crimson, orange, and gold in autumn. In late spring, tiny, yellow-green flowers are produced, followed by spiky, round fruit clusters. Liquidambars have an upright, open habit and look attractive either in a woodland setting or as specimens, isolated from other trees. The sweet gum (*Liquidambar styraciflua*), in particular, is really excellent value as a garden tree, pyramid-shaped with glossy, dark-green leaves and grey, deeply grooved bark. In autumn, its leaves are a blaze of fiery colour for up to six weeks.

■ **HARDINESS** Fully hardy ✳✳✳ to frost-hardy ✳✳.
■ **CULTIVATION** Grow in reasonably fertile, preferably acid (lime-free), moist but well-drained soil. The best autumn colour is produced in full sun, but they will tolerate partial shade.
■ **Prune** young trees to remove any crossing or misplaced branches, in late winter or early spring (*see p.322*). ■ **Sow** seed in containers in a cold frame in autumn (*see pp.328–329*).
■ **Take** soft stem-tip cuttings (*see pp.329–330*) of liquidambar in summer.

***Liquidambar styraciflua* 'Golden Treasure'**
‡10m (30ft) ↔6m (20ft)

Liriodendron

Tulip tree

SUMMER AND AUTUMN

Excellent as a specimen, the tulip tree has distinctive leaves that turn from dark green to butter-yellow in autumn. The trees are deciduous, with a stately, broadly columnar habit. In summer, mature trees produce curiously tulip-shaped, pale green flowers, although these are not really visible from a distance. It is only in warm summers, when the wood has been well ripened, that the tree is likely to flower well. It is well worth growing for the foliage alone, but only if you have plenty of space. For a smaller garden, choose the more compact *Liriodendron tulipifera* 'Aureomarginatum'.

■ **HARDINESS** Fully hardy ✳✳✳.
■ **CULTIVATION** Grow in reasonably fertile soil that is moist but well-drained, and preferably slightly acid (lime-free). Will grow in full sun or partial shade. ■ **Prune out** any crossing or misshapen branches while trees are young, in late winter or early spring, to create a healthy, well-shaped framework of branches (*see p.322*). ■ **Sow** seed in containers in a cold frame in autumn (*see pp.328–329*).

Liriodendron tulipifera ♀
‡30m (100ft) ↔15m (50ft), vigorous, broadly columnar to conical tree, leaves to 15cm (6in) long, flowers 6cm (2½in) long

Lithodora

SUMMER

Lithodoras are small, spreading, evergreen shrubs grown for their profusion of funnel-shaped, blue or white flowers mainly in the summer. Previously known as lithospermums, they can be upright or prostrate, and have spear-shaped leaves that vary from dark green to grey-green. The leaves are hairy, which helps the plants conserve moisture. They originate from southern Europe and enjoy free-draining hot, dry conditions. They make good ground-cover plants in a rock garden, at the front of a border, or in an alpine trough where they can cascade over the edge.

■ **HARDINESS** Fully hardy ✳✳✳ to frost-hardy ✳✳.
■ **CULTIVATION** Grow most lithodoras in well-drained, ideally alkaline (limy) soil, in full sun; however, *L. diffusa* 'Heavenly Blue' needs acid soil with well-rotted organic matter added to it. If growing it in an alpine trough, use a compost mix of equal parts loam, leafmould, and grit. ■ **Trim** shoots that spoil the shape after flowering, or to rejuvenate plants, shear over flowered shoots to within 2.5cm (1in) of the old growth in early spring. ■ **Take** semi-ripe cuttings in summer (*see pp.329–330*). ■ **Aphids** are occasionally troublesome (*see p.332*).

***Lithodora diffusa* 'Heavenly Blue'** ♀
‡15cm (6in) ↔60cm (24in), fast-growing, mat-forming shrub with many branches, popular rockery plant, leaves hairy on both sides, flowers from late spring through summer ✳✳✳

Lonicera
Honeysuckle
WINTER AND YEAR-ROUND

These honeysuckles are shrubs, not the climbers that are most commonly grown (*see pp.124–125*). There are two distinct types: deciduous species grown for their perfumed flowers (such as *Lonicera fragrantissima*, bearing these in winter), and small-leaved evergreens, such as *L. nitida* and *L. pileata*, which have tiny flowers and a dense, neat habit, so are valuable for hedging and ground cover respectively. All tolerate a wide range of conditions and need little maintenance. Their berries can cause mild stomach upset if eaten.

■ **HARDINESS** Fully hardy ✳✳✳.
■ **CULTIVATION** Grow in any well-drained soil in full sun or partial shade. ■ **Trim** deciduous shrubs after flowering if needed to restrict size, cutting back flowered shoots to strong sideshoots lower down. When plants grow old and growth is crowded, take out a main branch at the base. Evergreens can be trimmed as necessary. If *L. nitida* is grown as a hedge, it will need trimming at least twice, in summer. ■ **Sow** seed (*see pp.328–329*) in a container when ripe, placing it in a cold frame. ■ **Take** semi-ripe cuttings of evergreens in summer, and hardwood cuttings of deciduous types in autumn (*see pp.329–330*). ■ **Aphids** (*see p.332*) can be troublesome.

***Lonicera x purpusii* 'Winter Beauty'** ⚘
↕2m (6ft) ↔2.5m (8ft), twiggy habit, deciduous or semi-evergreen, heavily scented winter flowers, berries rarely produced

Luma
YEAR-ROUND

These South American evergreen shrubs and small trees have aromatic, leathery leaves and cup-shaped, white flowers, blooming in summer and autumn. *Luma apiculata* is also prized for its striking peeling bark. The oval leaves are usually dark green, though *L. apiculata* 'Glanleam Gold' has foliage that features creamy yellow margins. The flowers are followed by purple or black berries. Grow lumas in small groups, or as a specimen in a lawn. In areas with cold winters, these plants perform at their best against a warm wall. *L. apiculata* can also be used as a hedging plant.

■ **HARDINESS** Frost-hardy ✳✳
■ **CULTIVATION** Grow in fertile soil, enriched with well-rotted organic matter, in full sun or partial shade. ■ **Prune out** any crossing or misshapen branches (*see p.322*) in late winter or early spring to maintain a good shape and a healthy framework of branches and clip the shrub or tree regularly to keep it neat. ■ **Trim** hedges of luma in spring. ■ **Sow** seed in containers in a cold frame in spring (*see pp.328–329*); lumas may also self-seed in the garden. ■ **Take** semi-ripe cuttings in late summer (*see pp.329–330*).

***Luma apiculata* ⚘**
↕↔10–15m (30–50ft), upright, vigorous, cinnamon-brown and cream bark, flowers from midsummer to mid-autumn, purple berries

Maackia
MID- TO LATE SUMMER

If you are looking for an unusual specimen tree for the garden, consider a maackia. Deciduous, it has fine leaves made up of several oval leaflets. In summer, it produces erect clusters of tiny, white, pea-like flowers, followed by long, flat seed pods. Native to woodland in East Asia, maackias are slow-growing trees. Although it may ultimately reach 15m (50ft), *Maackia amurensis* would be suitable for smaller gardens for many years. *M. chinensis* is slightly smaller, at 10m (30ft) tall, with attractive, silvery grey-blue leaves. As well as specimen trees, maackias look good alongside other slender, delicate trees such as birches (*Betula, see p.24*) and rowan (*Sorbus, see p.101*).

■ **HARDINESS** Fully hardy ✳✳✳.
■ **CULTIVATION** Maackias like reasonably fertile, well-drained soil that is neutral to acid (lime-free), in full sun. ■ **Little pruning** is needed; remove any shoots that spoil the shape of young trees (*see p.322*). ■ **Sow** seed, after soaking, in containers or in a seedbed in autumn (*see pp.328–329*). ■ **Take** stem-tip cuttings in early or midsummer (*see pp.329–330*).

Maackia amurensis
↕15m (50ft) ↔10m (30ft), open, spreading habit, flowers in mid- and late summer

Magnolia

EARLY SPRING TO EARLY SUMMER

Splendid, solitary, often fragrant, cup- or saucer-shaped flowers distinguish these stately, slow-growing, deciduous and evergreen trees and shrubs. A magnolia in full flower is a sight never to be forgotten. The range of flower colours includes pure white, pink, rich purple, and shades of creamy and greenish-yellow. Most magnolias flower between early spring and early summer, many before the tough, but handsome leaves unfurl. Some produce cone-like pods studded with red-coated seeds in autumn. Magnolias make fine specimens; some can be wall-trained.

■ **HARDINESS** Fully hardy ✳✳✳ to frost-tender ❄.
■ **CULTIVATION** Grow in moist but well-drained, fertile soil in sun or partial shade. They prefer neutral to acid (lime-free) soil, but some tolerate alkaline soil. ■ **Prune** only if necessary, in late winter or early spring. ■ **Take** softwood cuttings of deciduous species in early summer; take semi-ripe cuttings of evergreens in late summer or early autumn (see pp.329–330). ■ **Coral spot**, orange pustules on dying stems can occur; remove affected wood and burn it.

Magnolia stellata ♥ (Star magnolia)
↕3m (10ft) ↔4m (12ft), deciduous shrub, flowers in early to mid-spring before the leaves unfurl ✳✳✳

Magnolia wilsonii ♥
↕↔6m (20ft), deciduous shrub or tree, red-purple shoots, leaves felted red-brown underneath, flowers in late spring ✳✳✳

Magnolia x soulangeana
↕↔6m (20ft), deciduous shrub or tree, may be wall-trained, flowers open in mid- and late spring, on bare branches ✳✳✳

Mahonia

WINTER AND SPRING

These evergreen shrubs are valued for their honey-scented, winter (occasionally spring) flowers and attractive foliage. The large, leathery leaves are divided into spiny leaflets. Most have either rounded clusters or star-burst spikes of usually yellow flowers that last for many weeks over winter, followed by purple to black berries. Most are upright, but some have a low-growing, spreading habit and make good ground cover. Taller ones are ideal at the back of a border or as specimen plants. Use with other winter-interest plants such as holly (*Ilex, see p.66*) and *Viburnum* x *bodnantense (see pp.108–109)*.

■ **HARDINESS** Fully hardy ✳✳✳ to frost-hardy ✳✳.
■ **CULTIVATION** Mahonias prefer reasonably fertile soil enriched with well-rotted organic matter. Most prefer full or partial shade, but tolerate full sun where the soil is moist at all times. ■ **Prune** after flowering, lightly cutting back shoots that spoil the shape. Mahonias regrow well from hard pruning if necessary (see p.323). ■ **Take** semi-ripe cuttings (see pp.329–330) from late summer until autumn.

Mahonia x media 'Charity'
↕to 5m (15ft) ↔to 4m (12ft), vigorous hybrid with prominent flower clusters from late autumn to late winter ✳✳✳

Malus
Crab apple
SPRING AND AUTUMN

Among the most popular of flowering trees, especially since so many are ideally sized for the smaller garden, crab apples are renowned for their pink or white spring blossom. Golden or scarlet fruits follow in the autumn; inedible raw, they can be made into wine and jellies. The fruits attract birds, and the autumn foliage colour of these trees is often brilliant. All crab apples are deciduous; some form a rounded crown, while others (such as *Malus floribunda*) have long, graceful, arching branches. They look equally good as specimens or with other small trees, such as hawthorns (*Crataegus, see p.42*), birches (*Betula, see p.24*), and rowans (*Sorbus, see p.101*).

■ **HARDINESS** Fully hardy ✴✴✴.
■ **CULTIVATION** Grow in reasonably fertile soil that is moist but well-drained, in full sun; most tolerate partial shade. ■ **Prune** young trees to remove any shoots that spoil a good branch framework in late winter or early spring (*see p.322*). ■ **Sow** cleaned seed of *M. baccata* and *M. hupehensis* in autumn, in a seed bed (*see pp.328–329*).

Malus floribunda ♀
(Japanese crab apple)
↕↔10m (30ft), dense, spreading habit, flowers in mid- and late spring, small, yellow fruits in autumn

Mespilus germanica
Medlar
SPRING, SUMMER, AND AUTUMN

The medlar is a deciduous tree or large shrub that originates in mountainous regions of southern Europe and Asia. It makes an interesting specimen tree, with a pleasing, spreading habit, bowl-shaped, white (occasionally pink-tinged) flowers that appear from late spring to early summer, and round, fleshy fruits that follow in autumn. The fruits can be made into jelly. Raw fruits are an acquired taste; they are edible, but only when well ripened or partly rotted ("bletted"). The medlar is lovely in autumn with other fruiting trees, such as hawthorns (*Crataegus, see p.42*) or crab apples (*Malus, see left*).

■ **HARDINESS** Fully hardy ✴✴✴.
■ **CULTIVATION** Grow in reasonably fertile, moist but well-drained soil in full sun or partial shade. ■ **Pruning** is unnecessary except to remove any shoots that are crossing, dead or misshapen in late winter or early spring (*see p.322*). ■ **Sow** seed in a seedbed in autumn (*see pp.328–329*).

Mespilus germanica
↕6m (20ft) ↔8m (25ft), foliage turns yellow-brown in autumn

Metasequoia glyptostroboides
Dawn redwood
SPRING TO AUTUMN

This prehistoric tree was once known only from fossils, and following its rediscovery was introduced to British gardens in 1948. It makes an outstanding specimen tree standing alone in grass or on the edge of woodland. Native to the valley forests of central China, it is one of the few conifers that are deciduous, and has a narrow, conical shape and fibrous bark. The soft, feathery leaves are a bright, fresh green; in autumn, they turn gold and then russet-brown. The female cones are light brown, on stalks; male cones are pendent. Only grow in a very large garden.

■ **HARDINESS** Fully hardy ✴✴✴.
■ **CULTIVATION** Grow in moist but well-drained soil enriched with well-rotted organic matter, in full sun. In early years, growth is fast but will slow down once the tree starts to reach around 10m (30ft) tall. ■ **Sow** seed in a seedbed (*see pp.328–329*) in autumn. ■ **Take** hardwood cuttings in autumn or root semi-ripe cuttings in midsummer with bottom heat in a propagator (*see pp.329–330*).

Metasequoia glyptostroboides ♀
↕20–40m (70–130ft) ↔5m (15ft) or more, tolerates waterlogged sites, growth is slower on dry sites

Morus
Mulberry

`SUMMER TO AUTUMN`

The black, white, and red mulberries, native to China, South-western Asia, and the Americas respectively, were first cultivated to provide leaves for the silkworm industry. All have raspberry-shaped, edible fruits, ripening to dark purple, yellow, or red, among attractive leaves that turn yellow in autumn. Orange, scaly bark provides winter interest. Mulberries become beautifully shaped trees with age, so grow them as specimens – the small, weeping, white mulberry (*Morus alba* 'Pendula') is an excellent choice for small gardens. Do not site mulberries overhanging paving, or the fruits will stain it badly.

■ **HARDINESS** Fully hardy ✻✻✻.
■ **CULTIVATION** Grow in reasonably fertile soil enriched with well-rotted organic matter, in full sun, with shelter from cold, drying winds.
■ **Prune** only in late autumn or early winter, if necessary. If pruned at any other time, the cuts will "bleed" sap badly. ■ **Sow** seed in containers in a cold frame in autumn (*see pp.328–329*).
■ **Take** semi-ripe cuttings in summer, or hardwood cuttings in autumn (*see pp.329–330*).
■ **Susceptible** to powdery mildew (*see p.333*).

Morus nigra ♀ (Black mulberry)
‡12m (40ft) ↔15m (50ft), fruits pleasant if a little dull eaten raw, but good for jam and wine

Myrtus communis
Common myrtle

`SPRING TO AUTUMN`

Grown for its rich, delicate scent, myrtle is a bushy, upright, evergreen shrub or tree with glossy, dark-green, aromatic leaves. It produces white, sweet-smelling, bowl-shaped flowers in abundance from spring to autumn. Both the flowers and the purple-black berries that follow in autumn are dependent on long, hot summers. Myrtles only thrive in a warm, sheltered position. They look well in shrub and mixed borders, or as an informal hedge. They can also be trained against a wall, or grown in containers for a patio where their scent can be best appreciated.

■ **HARDINESS** Frost-hardy ✻✻.
■ **CULTIVATION** Grow in reasonably fertile, moist but well-drained soil or loam-based compost, in full sun with shelter.
■ **Lightly trim** or prune shoots that spoil the shape in mid- or late spring. If wall-trained, after flowering or in late winter or early spring, cut back flowered shoots to within 2–4 buds of the main stems. ■ **Trim** hedges in spring (*see p.323*). ■ **Sow** common myrtle seed in containers in a cold frame in autumn (*see pp.328–329*). ■ **Take** semi-ripe cuttings in late summer (*see pp.329–330*).

Myrtus communis ♀
‡↔3m (10ft), branches arching with age, thrives in town and seaside gardens

Nandina domestica
Heavenly bamboo

`SPRING, SUMMER, AND AUTUMN`

Growing wild in the mountain valleys of India, China, and Japan, heavenly bamboo is an elegant shrub, grown for its flowers, fruits, and handsome foliage. The leaves are red to reddish-purple when young, mature to green, and then turn vivid crimson again in late autumn. In midsummer, small clusters of star-shaped, white flowers with yellow centres are produced, followed, in warmer climates or after hot summers, by bright red fruits. Nandinas are evergreen or semi-evergreen, but may not survive very cold winters. Grow it with other shrubs that have good autumn leaf colour. The low-growing *Nandina domestica* 'Firepower' makes an excellent ground cover.

■ **HARDINESS** Frost-hardy ✻✻.
■ **CULTIVATION** Grow in moist but well-drained soil in full sun. ■ **Prune** back hard after planting, then prune in mid-spring to keep the plant tidy and maintain a good shape (*see pp.322–323*). ■ **Sow** seed in containers in a cold frame as soon as it is ripe (*see pp.328–329*).
■ **Take** semi-ripe cuttings of heavenly bamboo in summer (*see pp.329–330*).

Nandina domestica ♀
‡2m (6ft) ↔1.5m (5ft), can be invasive and "weedy" in hot climates, but behaves well in temperate gardens

Neillia

LATE SPRING TO EARLY SUMMER

Unusual shrubs with handsome foliage and flowers, neillias provide plenty of year-round interest. They are deciduous, originating from the Himalayas and East Asia, and are characterized by graceful, arching stems and dark, glossy leaves and, in late spring to early summer, masses of handsome, bell-shaped, pinkish-white or rose-pink flowers. Neillias have a thicket-forming habit, ideal for the back of a shrub or mixed border, or as a screen. If you have room for a single-season show, they look fantastic with other shrubs that flower at the same time, such as weigelas (see p.110) or mock oranges (Philadelphus, see p.82).

■ **HARDINESS** Fully hardy ✻✻✻.
■ **CULTIVATION** Grow in fertile, well-drained soil in full sun or partial shade.
■ **Prune** back flowered shoots after flowering to strong buds or shoots lower down on the stem. On mature plants, cut out an entire old branch every three or four years to encourage new growth from the base of the shrub (see pp.322–323). ■ **Take** greenwood cuttings in early summer (see pp.329–330), or dig up well-rooted, naturally layered stems from the edges of the plant (see p.330).

Neillia thibetica
↕↔2m (6ft), suckering shrub with an upright then arching habit, tolerates most soils, blooms best in sun

Nyssa
Tupelo

AUTUMN

The tupelo is a deciduous tree prized for its foliage, which is bronze when young, matures to dark green, then turns to brilliant hues of amber, ruby, and gold in autumn. It does produce tiny green flowers, followed by small, blue fruits, which are enjoyed many by birds. However, the autumn foliage tints are the main attraction. Tupelo makes an ideal specimen tree, and looks effective planted near water (it thrives in wet, swampy areas). Try *Nyssa sinensis* with birches (*Betula*, see p.24) as the golden autumn foliage of the birch will contrast brilliantly with the tupelo's scarlet leaves.

■ **HARDINESS** Fully hardy ✻✻✻, but best in areas with hot summers.
■ **CULTIVATION** Grow in fertile, moist but well-drained, neutral to acid soil, in sun or partial shade with shelter from cold, drying winds. Choose young, container-grown specimens, since they increasingly resent root disturbance as they get older. ■ **Trim** crossing shoots in late winter or early spring for a good shape and healthy framework (see p.322). ■ **Sow** seed in a seedbed in autumn (see pp.328–329). ■ **Take** greenwood cuttings in early summer, or semi-ripe cuttings in midsummer (see pp.329–330).

Nyssa sinensis ♀
↕↔10m (30ft), broadly conical, often multi-stemmed habit, usually with sweeping lower branches, green leaves turn fiery in autumn

Olearia
Daisy bush

SPRING TO AUTUMN

This group of evergreen shrubs is grown for its leathery leaves and and daisy-like flowers borne singly or in clusters from spring to autumn. Flower colours are predominantly white. *Olearia* x *haastii* is a dense, bushy shrub with fragrant flowers. It is tolerant of salt-laden winds and can be grown as an informal hedge. *O. nummulariifolia* is a rounded, slow-growing shrub that does best planted against a warm, sunny wall where it is protected from drying winds. *O. solandri* is dense and heather like with strongly scented flowers.

■ **HARDINESS** Fully hardy ✻✻✻ to frost-tender ✿.
■ **CULTIVATION** Grow in fertile, well-drained soil in full sun, with shelter from cold, drying winds. ■ **Prune** daisy bush lightly in early spring, removing shoots that spoil the shape of the shrub. ■ **Trim** hedges after flowering. They all tolerate hard pruning. ■ **Take** semi-ripe cuttings in summer (see pp.329–330).

Olearia x haastii
↕2m (6ft) ↔3m (10ft) ✻✻✻

Olearia solandri
↕↔2m (6ft), scented ✻✻

Origanum
Marjoram, Oregano
SUMMER

Aromatic plants from the Mediterranean, marjorams may be shrubs, subshrubs (woody only at the base), or herbaceous perennials (*see p.246*). All are very similar: small, with an upright to spreading habit and tiny, pink to mauve flowers borne through summer amid more conspicuous, often brightly coloured bracts. Larger species are suited to a herb bed, raised bed, or in containers near the house, where the fragrant leaves can be rubbed to release their scent. They also look good as edging plants for borders or paths, where they sprawl contentedly. Grow the tiniest species, such as *Origanum amanum*, in a rock garden or alpine trough, so they are not swamped by larger plants.

■ **HARDINESS** Fully hardy ✷✷✷ to frost-hardy ✷✷.
■ **CULTIVATION** Grow in full sun in poor to reasonably fertile soil. Marjorams prefer a free-draining, alkaline (limy) soil. ■ **Cut back** old flowered stems in early spring (*see p.322*). ■ **Take** cuttings of new shoots growing from the base in late spring and treat as softwood cuttings (*see pp.329–330*).

Origanum 'Kent Beauty'
↕10cm (4in) ↔20cm (8in), prostrate, with trailing stems, semi-evergreen, named for its hop-like flowers ✷✷✷

Osmanthus
EARLY TO MID-SPRING

Useful for a shrub border or woodland garden, this group of evergreen shrubs is grown for its glossy, dark green foliage, and white, occasionally yellow or orange flowers, scented like jasmine. These are produced in early and mid-spring and are followed by round, blue-black fruits. *Osmanthus heterophyllus* and *O.* x *fortunei* have spiky, holly-like foliage. Osmanthus has a dense, neat habit, and is an effective foil to showier shrubs in the border. *O. delavayi* and *O. burkwoodii* are good for hedging, while *O. heterophyllus* 'Aureomarginatus' will liven up a dull corner with its yellow-margined leaves.

■ **HARDINESS** Fully hardy ✷✷✷ to frost-tender ✿.
■ **CULTIVATION** Grow in fertile, well-drained soil in sun or partial shade and shelter from cold, drying winds. ■ **Trim** lightly or prune back shoots after flowering, taking out any that spoil the shape of the shrub (*see p.322*). Trim hedges in summer. All species tolerate hard pruning if necessary (*see p.323*). ■ **Sow** osmanthus seed in a container in a cold frame once ripe (*see pp.328–329*). ■ **Take** semi-ripe cuttings in summer and put in a propagator with bottom heat, or layer low-growing shoots in autumn or spring (*see pp.329–330*).

Osmanthus x burkwoodii ♀
↕↔3m (10ft), rounded habit, osmanthus is good for topiary ✷✷✷

Oxydendrum arboreum
Sorrel tree, Sourwood
SUMMER AND AUTUMN

The sorrel tree is a deciduous tree or large shrub with a conical or columnar habit. It is a dual-season tree for interest, with white flowers in the summer and boldly coloured foliage in the autumn. Its flowers, produced during in late summer and early autumn, are tiny, about 6mm (¼in) long, but gain impact by being borne in large, airy plumes, up to 25cm (10in) long, at the ends of the shoots. The leaves are glossy, toothed, and dark green, turning brilliant shades of red, yellow, and purple in autumn. Grow it as a specimen tree or in a woodland setting.

■ **HARDINESS** Fully hardy ✷✷✷.
■ **CULTIVATION** Grow a sorrel tree in fertile, moist but well-drained soil, preferably acid (lime-free), avoiding exposed sites.
■ **Prune** young trees in late winter or early spring to remove any crossing or misplaced branches. ■ **Sow** seed in a container in a cold frame in autumn (*see pp.328–329*).
■ **Take** semi-ripe cuttings of sorrel tree in summer (*see pp.329–330*).

Oxydendrum arboreum
↕10–15m (30–50ft) ↔8m (25ft), dark green leaves turning red, yellow, and purple in autumn, white flowers in late summer to autumn ✷✷✷

Paeonia
Tree peony
LATE SPRING TO EARLY SUMMER

Shrubby peonies, as opposed to the herbaceous kinds that die down each year (*see p.248*), are commonly known as tree peonies. These peonies also have the characteristically voluptuous flowers in a wide range of colour, occasionally scented, borne from late spring to early summer, with the bonus of permanent stature in a mixed planting. Flowers can be single or double, cup- or saucer-shaped, and up to 30cm (12in) across. The stamens in the centre are often in a contrasting colour. Leaves are usually mid- to dark green, often feathery. Grow these peonies in a shrub, mixed, or herbaceous border.

■ **HARDINESS** Fully hardy ❋❋❋ to frost-hardy ❋❋. Late frosts may damage young growths and flower buds.
■ **CULTIVATION** Grow in deep, fertile soil enriched with well-rotted organic matter, in full sun or partial shade. Peonies prefer shelter from cold, drying winds. ■ **Prune out** flowered shoots and, from time to time, old wood to encourage bushy growth (*see p.322*). ■ **Take** semi-ripe cuttings in summer (*see pp.329–330*).

***Paeonia suffruticosa* 'Cardinal Vaughan'** (Moutan)
↕↔to 2.2m (7ft), flowers 15–30cm (6–12in) across in late spring and early summer, dark green leaves blue-green beneath ❋❋❋

Paeonia delavayi ♀
↕2m (6ft) ↔1.2m (4ft), flowers up to 10cm (4in) across in early summer, leaves dark green and blue-green underneath ❋❋❋

Paulownia
LATE SPRING AND SUMMER

These vigorous, deciduous trees make striking additions to the garden. They grow and flower best in areas with long, hot summers. The fast-growing foxglove tree (*Paulownia tomentosa*) (*see below*) is tolerant of air pollution and *P. fortunei* is smaller, to 8m (25ft) tall. Both bear their fragrant flowers in late spring, often on near-bare branches. Although they can make fine specimen trees in a lawn, they are best coppiced (*see Cornus, pp.38–39*) for bold, "tropical" foliage, a good way to get the best from them in areas where they do not flower reliably, or in small gardens.

■ **HARDINESS** Fully hardy ❋❋❋. Young trees may be damaged by frosts unless protected in their early years.
■ **CULTIVATION** Grow these trees in fertile, well-drained soil in full sun. In frost-prone areas, shelter paulownias from cold, drying winds.
■ **Prune** paulownias grown as trees only if necessary. To obtain big leaves, cut back stems to within 2–3 buds of the main framework of shoots in early spring. ■ **Sow** seed in containers in a cold frame in spring or autumn (*see pp.328–329*). ■ **Take** root cuttings in winter (*see pp.329–330*). Young plants benefit from growing on in pots and under glass in winter.

Paulownia tomentosa ♀
(Foxglove tree, Empress tree)
↕12m (40ft) ↔10m (30ft), flowers well the year after a hot summer; coppice for big velvety leaves

Perovskia

LATE SUMMER TO EARLY AUTUMN

A graceful shrub, perovskia has tall, wand-like stems of tiny, violet-blue flowers in late summer or early autumn. Both stems and leaves are usually grey-white or grey-green, and the foliage is aromatic, with a pleasantly sharp, lemony scent. The stems can reach a height of up to 1.2m (4ft) in a single season, bearing small flowers along about half their length. Perovskias add height and a cloud of hazy blue in a massed herbaceous planting, and like perennials, are best cut back hard each spring, or they will become leggy and bare. They also look striking against a grey or white-painted wall.

■ **HARDINESS** Fully hardy ✳✳✳.
■ **CULTIVATION** Grow in well-drained soil that is poor or reasonably fertile in full sun. Perovskias will grow in dry, chalky soils and in coastal areas. ■ **Prune** hard in spring, cutting back the previous season's growth to within 5–10cm (2–4in); gradually, a permanent, stubby, woody framework will develop. ■ **Take** softwood cuttings in late spring, or semi-ripe cuttings in summer (*see pp.329–330*).

Perovskia **'Blue Spire'** ♀
‡1.2m (4ft) ↔1m (3ft), leaves slender and silver-grey, hugging the stems

Philadelphus
Mock orange

EARLY TO MIDSUMMER

Deliciously fragrant flowers are a feature of this group of mainly deciduous shrubs. The flowers are cup or bowl-shaped, single, semi-double, and double, and usually white, often with yellowish stamens; and they are produced either singly or in clusters. The leaves are mid-green; *P. coronarius* has white-variegated and golden-leaved forms. There is no missing a mock orange in flower, since the scent drifts in the air for a long way. Grow them in a shrub border, with other early and midsummer-flowering shrubs like weigelas (*see p.110*), or as specimen plants.

■ **HARDINESS** Fully hardy ✳✳✳ to half-hardy ✳.
■ **CULTIVATION** Grow in any reasonably fertile, well-drained soil, in full sun or partial shade. *P. microphyllus* needs full sun, while the golden-leaved *P. coronarius* 'Aureus' must have some shade. ■ **Prune** after flowering, cutting back flowered stems to strong buds or new shoots. On mature plants, cut one or two old branches to the base each year to encourage new growth. ■ **Take** softwood cuttings in summer, or hardwood cuttings in autumn or winter (*see pp.329–330*). ■ **Aphids** may be troublesome, as may powdery mildew (*see pp.332–333*), pick off mildew-affected leaves.

Philadelphus **'Belle Etoile'** ♀
‡1.2m (4ft) ↔2.5m (8ft)

Philadelphus **'Virginal'**
‡3m (10ft) or more ↔2.5m (8ft)

Philadelphus microphyllus
‡↔1m (3ft)

Philadelphus coronarius **'Aureus'** ♀
‡2.5m (8ft) ↔1.5m (5ft)

Phlomis

EARLY TO MIDSUMMER

These attractive and undemanding, evergreen shrubs are grown for their sage-like foliage and their unusual, often hooded, flowers. The leaves are variable in shape: narrow and lance-shaped to more oval. In colour, they range from light green to grey-green, and are often hairy. The flowers are produced in early and midsummer in shades of golden yellow, lilac-pink, purple to pink, and occasionally white, and are borne on tall, erect stems. Ornamental seedheads extend the interest into winter. Phlomis have an upright or rounded habit and look particularly at home among herbs such as sage and lavender (*see p.71*), but they can also be grown in mixed borders. There are some herbaceous phlomis (*see p.254*).

■ **HARDINESS** Fully hardy ✽✽✽ to frost-hardy ✽✽.
■ **CULTIVATION** Grow these shrubs in fertile, well-drained soil in full sun. ■ **Deadhead** for a longer flowering display and lightly trim shoots that spoil the shape when flowering has finished. ■ **Sow** seed (*see pp.328–329*) in spring, or take softwood cuttings (*see pp.329–330*) in summer.

Phlomis fruticosa ♀ (Jerusalem sage)
↕1m (3ft) ↔1.5m (5ft), mound-forming
✽✽✽ (borderline)

Phormium
New Zealand flax

YEAR-ROUND

With striking, sword-like foliage and exotic-looking flowers, these architectural plants develop into large, handsome clumps that can act as focal points in a border or gravel, by a building, or even as specimen plants in a lawn or pot on a patio or terrace. Their versatility is enhanced by the range of leaf colours available, from bronze-green with rose-pink margins to dark green with red, orange, or pink stripes. In summer, in milder areas, they produce tall, leafless spikes bearing abundant tubular flowers in erect clusters.

■ **HARDINESS** Frost-hardy ✽✽ to half-hardy ✽.
■ **CULTIVATION** Grow phormiums in fertile, moist but free-draining soil where they receive full sun. Although these plants are not completely hardy, in frost-prone areas they may survive winter temperatures as low as -12°C (10°F) if they are given a deep mulch (*see p.326*) around their roots. ■ **Sow** seed (*see pp.328–329*) in spring. ■ **Divide** the woody crowns of large, established clumps, also in spring, to increase stocks (*see p.330*); you may need a large knife to cut through the crown.

Phormium tenax ♀
↕4m (12ft) ↔2m (6ft), dull red flower spikes are up to 4m (12ft) tall ✽✽

Phormium 'Dazzler'
↕1m (3ft) ↔1.2m (4ft), flowers are 5cm (2in) long ✽✽

Phormium 'Sundowner' ♀
↕↔2m (6ft), yellow-green flower spikes to 2m (6ft) tall ✽✽

Photinia

These evergreen or deciduous shrubs and trees are grown for their attractive foliage and varied habits. Some are spreading trees, but many are upright or rounded shrubs, ranging in height from 3m (10ft) to 12m (40ft). They produce small clusters of tiny, white flowers in summer, although the deciduous species are mainly prized for their autumn leaf colours and fruits. Evergreen types often have striking, reddish new leaves in spring before they turn glossy dark or mid-green. Photinias look good in a shrub border or as specimen plants. They can also be used as hedging or standard plants in large pots.

■ **HARDINESS** Fully hardy ✽✽✽ to frost-hardy ✽✽; young growth may be damaged by late spring frosts.
■ **CULTIVATION** Grow in fertile, moist but well-drained soil, in full sun or partial shade with protection from cold winds. ■ **Trim** any crossing shoots in winter or early spring, to maintain a good shape and framework of shoots. Trim hedges in summer when young growth colour has faded. ■ **Propagate** all types by semi-ripe cuttings in summer; sow seed of deciduous types in autumn (*see pp.328–329*). ■ **Powdery mildew** may spoil the leaves (*see p.333*).

Photinia x fraseri **'Red Robin'** ♀
↕↔5m (15ft), upright evergreen shrub or small tree, bronze to scarlet young foliage, flowers in mid- to late spring ✽✽

Phygelius

Hanging clusters of flowers produced over a long period in summer, and often into autumn, are the main reason for growing these evergreen or semi-evergreen shrubs. They have oval- to lance-shaped leaves, and flowers in shades of yellow, orange-red, creamy yellow, and orange. Phygelius thrives in a shrub border or at the base of a warm wall and spreads by suckers. If temperatures often fall below freezing, treat them as herbaceous perennials – the top-growth may be killed off, but they should grow again in spring.

■ **HARDINESS** Frost-hardy ✽✽.
■ **CULTIVATION** Phygelius like fertile, moist, well-drained soil in full sun. Deadhead to encourage more flowers. ■ **Protect** roots in frost-prone areas with a winter mulch of straw or bracken. Overwinter young plants in frost-free conditions. ■ **Cut back** the stems in spring of plants treated as herbaceous perennials; or trim shoots that spoil the shape. ■ **Take** softwood cuttings (*see pp.329–330*) in late spring or remove rooted suckers for replanting in spring.

Phygelius x rectus **'Salmon Leap'** ♀
↕1.2m (4ft) ↔1-1.5m (3–5ft)

Phygelius aequalis **'Yellow Trumpet'** ♀
↕1m (3ft) ↔1-1.5m (3–5ft)

Picea

Spruce

Spruces are evergreen, coniferous trees grown mainly for their dense foliage and attractive shapes. The most familiar is the Norwegian spruce, *Picea abies*. The needles vary from dark green to the silvery blue of *P. pungens* 'Koster', and make a good textural contrast to plants with bolder leaves. In summer and autumn, older trees produce cones. The larger spruces are useful on their own, to show off their handsome forms, or in groups, especially to create shelter. Like all evergreen conifers, they provide a year-round backdrop and add structure to the garden. The dwarf or slow-growing spruces are suitable for small spaces and rock gardens.

■ **HARDINESS** Fully hardy ✽✽✽ to frost-hardy ✽✽.
■ **CULTIVATION** Grow in any deep, moist, but well-drained soil, ideally neutral to acid (lime-free), in full sun. No pruning required. ■ **Sow** seed in containers in a cold frame in spring (*see pp.328–329*). ■ **Take** stem-tip cuttings (*see pp.329–330*) of dwarf forms in late summer. ■ **Aphids** (*see p.332*) may appear; treat only young or dwarf plants.

Picea abies
↕to 40m (130ft) ↔6m (20ft)

Picrasma quassioides
Quassia

AUTUMN

This elegant, upright tree is grown mainly for its attractive foliage, which fades to lovely shades of yellow, orange, and scarlet before the leaves drop in autumn. Oriental in origin, *Picrasma quassioides* bears a passing resemblance to the tree of heaven, *Ailanthus altissima*, to which it is related. Each glossy, mid-green leaf is divided into several leaflets. In early summer, minute, bowl-shaped green flowers are borne in clusters, but they have little ornamental value. Site this fine tree in an open position in a shrub border, or on the edge of a woodland setting with other trees and shrubs that also have good autumn colour, such as *Disanthus cercidifolius* (*see p.46*) and *Nyssa sinensis* (*see p.79*).

■ **HARDINESS** Fully hardy ✳✳✳.
■ **CULTIVATION** Grow in fertile, well-drained soil in full sun or partial shade. In frost-prone areas, choose a site that is not exposed to cold, drying winds. ■ **Prune out** any crossing branches and those that spoil the shape of the tree in late winter or early spring. ■ **Sow** seed in containers in a cold frame in autumn (*see pp.328–329*).

Picrasma quassioides
↕↔8m (25ft), autumn foliage shown here

Pieris

LATE WINTER AND SPRING

These colourful evergreen shrubs are valued for their glossy, leathery foliage and delightful flowers. They are best placed in a shrub border or woodland garden, or in a container. Not all are large; 'Little Heath' and 'Purity' are popular for small gardens or pots. The young leaves of pieris are often brilliantly coloured, and, in spring, clusters of small, white, or pink flowers almost cover the shrub. Rhododendrons and azaleas (*see pp.92–93*) and ericas (*see pp.48–49*) make good companions, as all require similar soil.

■ **HARDINESS** Fully hardy ✳✳✳ to frost-hardy ✳✳; the young growth may be damaged by late frosts in spring.
■ **CULTIVATION** Grow in reasonably fertile, moist but well-drained, acid (lime-free) soil, or ericaceous compost, in full sun or partial shade. In frost-prone areas, shelter from cold, drying winds and early morning sun (which can damage frosty leaves). ■ **Trim back** shoots that spoil the shape after flowering, and remove faded flowers if the shrubs are not too large. ■ **Sow** seed in containers in a cold frame in spring or autumn (*see pp.328–329*). ■ **Take** softwood cuttings in early summer, or semi-ripe cuttings from mid- to late summer (*see pp.329–330*).

Pieris japonica 'Blush' ♥
↕4m (12ft) ↔3m (10ft), compact and rounded shrub, pink-flushed, later all-white flowers in late winter and spring ✳✳✳

Pinus
Pine

YEAR-ROUND

The pines comprise a large and varied group of evergreens, both trees and shrubs, with distinctive, needles, ornamental cones, and attractive, scaly bark. The larger species are very tall trees with striking, sparsely branched silhouettes. Habits vary, from slender giants, such as the Scots pine (*Pinus sylvestris*), to the umbrella-shaped stone pine (*P. pinea*). In a spacious garden they make grand specimen trees and also excellent windbreaks; *P. radiata* and *P. nigra* tolerate coastal exposure. There are medium-sized and dwarf pines, often very slow-growing, for the smaller garden and for rock gardens; look especially among the cultivars of *P. sylvestris*, *P. densiflora*, and *P. mugo*.

■ **HARDINESS** Fully hardy ✳✳✳ to frost-hardy ✳✳.
■ **CULTIVATION** Grow in any well-drained soil in full sun. Some species may be short-lived in shallow, chalky soils; *P. nigra* and *P. mugo* both tolerate chalk. No pruning required. ■ **Sow** seed in a cold frame in spring (*see pp.328–329*).
■ **Aphids** (*see p.332*) can appear, but rarely need treatment.

Pinus nigra ♥ (Austrian pine, European black pine)
↕to 30m (100ft) ↔6–8m (20–25ft), domed tree, bark becomes deeply fissured with age ✳✳✳

Pittosporum

YEAR-ROUND

Glossy, leathery leaves, often with wavy edges and sometimes variegated, are the main attraction of these evergreen shrubs. They have a naturally dense, neat habit but also respond well to pruning. The lower branches may be removed to produce a more tree-like shape, allowing for some underplanting. In mild areas, they make handsome specimen plants or windbreak hedges for coastal gardens. Dark-leaved forms form an excellent contrast to bright-leaved or variegated shrubs such as elaeagnus (*see pp.46–47*) and euonymus (*see p.52*). In spring, they bear small, five-petalled flowers.

■ **HARDINESS** Frost-hardy ✳✳ to frost-tender ❀
■ **CULTIVATION** Grow in fertile, moist but well-drained soil, in full sun or partial shade; site those with variegated or purple foliage in sun for the best colour. Must be sheltered from cold winds in frost-prone areas. ■ **Prune** out any crossing or misplaced shoots in late winter or early spring; trim hedges in spring and late summer. ■ **Sow** seed (*see pp.328–329*) as soon as it is ripe, or in spring in containers in a cold frame. ■ **Take** semi-ripe cuttings (*see pp.329–330*) in summer.

Pittosporum tenuifolium ♀
‡to 10m (30ft) ↔to 6m (20ft) ✳✳

Pittosporum tobira ♀
‡2–10m (6–30ft) ↔to 6m (20ft) ✳✳

Poncirus trifoliata
Japanese bitter orange

SPRING, SUMMER, AND AUTUMN

This rounded, bushy, deciduous shrub deserves to be more widely grown for its beautiful and fragrant flowers and orange-like fruits; although Poncirus is related to citrus trees, these are inedible. White flowers, again similar to orange blossom, appear in late spring and early summer, to be followed by the fruits; as these ripen, they may be accompanied by a second, smaller flush of blossom. The dark green leaves gradually turn yellow in autumn. Grow in a shrub border, or against a sunny wall in colder areas. Sharp spines on the stems also make it a good choice for a thick hedge.

■ **HARDINESS** Fully hardy ✳✳✳.
■ **CULTIVATION** Grow in fertile, well-drained soil in full sun and provide shelter from cold, drying winds. ■ **Prune off** any crossing or misshapen shoots that spoil the shape in late winter or early spring. ■ **Trim** hedges once or twice in summer. ■ **Sow** seed (*see pp.328–329*) in a container in a cold frame in autumn. ■ **Take** semi-ripe cuttings (*see pp.329–330*) in summer and root in a propagator with bottom heat.

Poncirus trifoliata
‡↔5m (15ft), the fruits are green at first and then ripen to yellow-orange; they resemble miniature oranges but are inedible

Populus
Aspen, Cottonwood, Poplar

SUMMER AND AUTUMN

The leaves of these vigorous, deciduous trees are their prettiest feature, usually showing silvery undersides when ruffled by the wind. Some are also balsam-scented. In a large garden, these make fine specimen trees or windbreaks, and look good with birches (*Betula, see p.24*) or beeches (*Fagus, see p.53*), but plant them well away from buildings and drains; they have invasive roots. Shapes vary, from the spreading common aspen (*Populus tremula*) to the columnar Lombardy poplar (*P. nigra* var. *italica*) and conical Canadian poplar (*P.* x *canadensis*). Catkins grow in early spring, usually with male and female flowers on separate trees.

■ **HARDINESS** Fully hardy ✳✳✳.
■ **CULTIVATION** Poplars tolerate all but waterlogged soils, but grow best in fertile, moist but well-drained soil. Position in full sun.
■ **Prune** crossing or dead branches that spoil the shape of young trees in late winter or early spring. Remove suckers growing up around the tree in autumn or winter. ■ **Take** hardwood cuttings (*see pp.329–330*) in winter.

Populus x ***jackii* ‘Aurora’**
‡15m (50ft) ↔6m (20ft), has leaves marked with both cream and pink splashes

Potentilla
Cinquefoil
SUMMER TO AUTUMN

Bearing bright flowers for many weeks over summer and autumn, these reliable shrubs are excellent value for a border. There are also many non-woody potentillas, with very similar flowers – most shrubby types are cultivars of *Potentilla fruticosa*. Their flowers are cup- to saucer-shaped, borne singly or in small clusters, and produced in colours from purest white to shades of pink, red, orange, and yellow. Because they flower over such a long period, they make good foils for other plants with a briefer flowering display. Wider than they are tall, they also make good low hedging. (*See also p.259.*)

■ **HARDINESS** Fully hardy ✳✳✳.
■ **CULTIVATION** Grow in poor to reasonably fertile soil that is well drained. Position most in full sun, red-flowered types in light shade. ■ **Cut** back flowered shoots to within 2.5cm (1in) of old growth after flowering or in early spring; the easiest way to do this is with shears. ■ **Sow** seed (*see pp.328–329*) in containers in a cold frame in autumn or spring. ■ **Take** softwood cuttings (*see pp.329–330*) in early summer.

Potentilla fruticosa **'Primrose Beauty'** ♥
‡1m (3ft) ↔1.5m (5ft), a tidy, densely growing cultivar with larger flowers than many, to 3.5cm (1½in) across

Potentilla fruticosa **'Daydawn'**
‡1m (3ft) ↔1.2m (4ft), a compact plant with flowers flushed with both yellow and pink shades

Potentilla fruticosa **'Red Ace'**
‡1m (3ft) ↔1.5m (5ft), the flowers have yellow backs and their colour tends to fade if the plant is sited in full sun

Prostanthera
Mint bush
LATE SPRING TO SUMMER

These evergreen shrubs are grown for their aromatic leaves and clusters of bell-shaped flowers. Bushy or spreading, they have mid- to dark green or grey-green leaves that smell of mint, and flower from late spring until summer. In frost-prone areas, the purple- to pink-flowered *Prostanthera ovalifolia* and *P. rotundifolia* need protection in winter. In milder areas, they thrive in the shelter of a warm wall; the hardier, white-flowered *P. cuneata* may be grown in sheltered borders. Position it towards the back or centre of a grouping with lower plants in front, because it often becomes bare at the base, and hard pruning to correct this is not possible.

■ **HARDINESS** Frost-hardy ✳✳ to half-hardy ✳
■ **CULTIVATION** Grow in fertile, well-drained soil, and site in full sun. In pots, use a loam-based compost and grow in full light. ■ **Trim** or lightly prune back shoots that spoil the shape of the shrub after flowering. Avoid hard pruning, which can be detrimental. ■ **Sow** seed (*see pp.328–329*) indoors in spring. ■ **Take** semi-ripe cuttings (*see pp.329–330*) in summer.

Prostanthera cuneata ♥
(Alpine mint bush)
‡↔30–90cm (1–3ft), has small, aromatic, glossy leaves and flowers profusely in late spring ✳✳

Prunus
Ornamental cherry

SPRING, AUTUMN, AND WINTER

This group contains two very different types of plant: ornamental or flowering cherries that are deciduous, and evergreen laurels. In spring, ornamental cherries billow with blossom in shades of pink, white, and sometimes red. *Prunus* x *subhirtella* produces its delicate flurries of flowers in mild spells from autumn to spring. Some, such as *P. maackii* and *P. serrula*, are also grown for their rich cinnamon-coloured bark, and others, like *P. sargentii*, have leaves that colour well in autumn. Laurels, on the other hand, are dense, bushy evergreens, such as *P. laurocerasus* and *P. lusitanica*, with much less showy flowers but handsome, glossy leaves. Prunus also includes many trees grown for fruit, including plum, peach, and cherry, but the fruits of laurels and most ornamental cherries can cause severe discomfort if eaten. Ornamental cherries are upright, rounded or spreading trees or shrubs; many of them are suitable for smaller gardens, and make excellent specimen plants. Laurels are reliable hedging plants.

■ **HARDINESS** Fully hardy ✳✳✳ to frost-hardy ✳✳.
■ **CULTIVATION** Grow in any moist, well-drained soil in full sun or partial shade. Water young trees well until they are established.
■ **Prune** each of the types slightly differently. For most deciduous shrubs and trees, simply remove any misplaced shoots to maintain a good shape. This is best done in summer to avoid the fungal disease silver leaf, to which cherries are susceptible. For *P. glandulosa* and *P. triloba*, prune hard after flowering. ■ **Trim** deciduous hedges after flowering and use secateurs to cut back evergreens in early to mid-spring. ■ **Sow** seed of species in containers outside in autumn (*see pp.328–329*), or propagate deciduous cultivars by greenwood cuttings, which are taken slightly later than softwood cuttings when the stem is a little firmer and darker (*see pp.329–330*).

Using ornamental cherries in the garden

Wall of blossom Ornamental cherries can be trained against a wall to provide a generous display in even the smallest garden. Once the shrub has formed a framework, all that is needed is some routine pruning (*see pp.322–323*) and tying in. Cut out older shoots that produce little growth and tie in younger shoots as replacements.

Ornamental hedging Several ornamental cherries are suitable for growing as hedging. Evergreen shrubs such as *P. laurocerasus* and *P. lusitanica* make dense screens, and deciduous species, such as *P. spinosa*, *P. cerasifera*, and its cultivars like 'Nigra', will be more open.

P. **'Accolade'** ♀ ‡↔8m (25ft), early spring

P. avium **'Plena'** ♀ ‡↔12m (40ft), mid-spring

P. **'Kiku-shidare-zakura'** ♀ ‡↔3m (10ft), mid- and late spring

P. laurocerasus **'Otto Luyken'** ♀ ‡1m ↔1.5m (5ft), evergreen, spring and autumn

P. **'Pandora'** ♀ ‡10m (30ft) ↔8m (25ft), early spring

P. **'Pink Perfection'** ♀ ‡↔8m (25ft), late spring

P. spinosa ‡5m (15ft) ↔4m (12ft), early to mid-spring, followed by blue-black fruit (sloes)

P. **'Spire'** ♀ ‡10m (30ft) ↔6m (20ft), mid-spring

P. cerasifera **'Nigra'** ♀ ↕↔10m (30ft),
early spring, followed by plum-like fruit

P. **x** *cistena* ♀ ↕↔1.5m (5ft), late spring

P. glandulosa **'Alba Plena'** ↕↔1.5m (5ft),
late spring

P. **'Kanzan'** ♀ ↕↔10m (30ft), mid- and
late spring

P. lusitanica **subsp.** *azorica* ↕↔20m
(70ft), evergreen, early summer

P. maackii ↕10m (30ft) ↔ 8m (25ft),
mid-spring

P. **'Okame'** ♀ ↕10m (30ft) ↔ 8m (25ft),
early spring

P. padus **'Watereri'** ♀ ↕15m (50ft)
↔10m (30ft), late spring

P. sargentii ♀ ↕20m (70ft)
↔15m (50ft), mid-spring

P. serrula ♀ ↕↔10m (30ft), late spring

P. **'Shirofugen'** ♀ ↕8m (25ft) ↔10m (30ft),
late spring

P. **'Shogetsu'** ♀ ↕5m (15ft) ↔8m
(25ft), late spring

P. **x** *subhirtella* **'Autumnalis Rosea'** ♀
↕↔8m (25ft), autumn to spring

P. **'Taihaku'** ♀ ↕8m (25ft) ↔10m (30ft),
mid-spring

P. triloba ↕↔3m (10ft), early and mid-spring

P. **'Ukon'** ♀ ↕8m (25ft) ↔10m (30ft),
mid-spring

Pyracantha
Firethorn
SPRING AND AUTUMN

Evergreen foliage, dainty white flowers, and bright autumn berries make these spiny shrubs both popular and useful. From late spring to midsummer, flat clusters of small, 5-petalled, open flowers, like those of the hawthorn, appear. Berries in vivid shades of orange, scarlet, and golden yellow follow and often persist through the winter – unless the birds eat them. Firethorns are spreading or upright in habit, and can be grown as freestanding shrubs, as hedging, or, more commonly, trained against a wall or fence in a fan or espalier (several horizontal tiers) shape.

■ **HARDINESS** Fully hardy ✻✻✻ to frost-hardy ✻✻.
■ **CULTIVATION** Firethorns like fertile, well-drained soil in full sun or partial shade and tolerate north-facing walls. In frost-prone areas, give shelter from cold winds. ■ **Prune** freestanding shrubs in late winter or early spring by removing shoots that spoil the shape. In midsummer, prune each sideshoot of wall-trained shrubs to two or three buds from the base; tie in shoots regularly. Trim hedges in midsummer. ■ **Sow** seed in containers in a cold frame in autumn (*see pp.328–329*) or root semi-ripe cuttings with bottom heat in summer (*see pp.329–330*). ■ **Scab**, a fungus which causes dark, scabby patches in damp weather, may affect berries and leaves; if this occurs, spray with fungicide.

Pyracantha '**Orange Glow**' ♀
‡↔3m (10ft), upright, then spreading habit, flowers in late spring followed by dark orange to orange-red berries-✻✻✻

Pyracantha '**Soleil d'Or**'
‡3m (10ft) ↔2.5m (8ft), upright habit, flowers in early summer ✻✻✻

Pyracantha '**Mohave**'
‡4m (12ft) ↔5m (15ft), vigorous, bushy habit, flowers in early summer followed by long-lasting berries ✻✻

Pyracantha '**Golden Charmer**' ♀
‡↔3m (10ft), vigorous, bushy habit with arching branches, flowers in early summer ✻✻✻

Pyrus
Pear

Pears are valued not only for their sometimes edible fruits, but also for their flowers, and in some cases, their attractive habits exemplified by the silvery weeping pear (*see below*). The trees are usually deciduous, and some have good autumn colour. The flowers, which appear in spring, are white or pink. Fruit shapes vary from the typical pear shape to round; many varieties have been developed over the centuries for their fine-flavoured fruits. Ornamental varieties include *Pyrus calleryana*, which is thorny and develops red foliage and round, brown fruits in autumn, and the snow pear (*P. nivalis*), which has silvery grey leaves – both have conical habits and flower in spring. The more compact ornamental pears are ideal for a small garden as specimens in a lawn.

■ **HARDINESS** Fully hardy ✳✳✳.
■ **CULTIVATION** Grow pears in fertile, well-drained soil in full sun. ■ **Prune out** any shoots that spoil the shape of the tree in late winter or early spring. ■ **Fruiting pears** in particular may suffer from canker, areas of sunken, split bark, which can kill branches as it spreads: cut back stems to healthy wood. Aphids and caterpillars may also attack foliage.

Pyrus salicifolia 'Pendula' ♀
↕5m (15ft) ↔4m (12ft), ideal for smaller gardens, willowy, silvery felted leaves, pear-shaped green fruits 3cm (1¼in) long

Quercus
Oak

Oaks are large, stately trees, known for their longevity, with attractive foliage and fissured bark. They form a large group of deciduous and evergreen trees with a great range of leaf shapes and colours and growth habits. Male flowers appear as catkins in late spring and early summer alonside tiny female flowers. Acorns 1–3cm (½–1¼in) long are borne in autumn. Many deciduous oaks are excellent for autumn colour, with foliage in a variety of brilliant shades. The classic common or English oak (*Quercus robur*) with the typical oak leaf is a huge, spreading tree so is suited only to parks or woods, but if you have a large garden, there are smaller – although still large – oaks that are well worth growing as specimen trees. Plant the sapling in its permanent position because it may not survive later transplanting.

Quercus ilex ♀ (Holm oak)
↕25m (80ft) ↔20m (70ft), evergreen with smooth, dark grey bark, variable leaves silvery grey when young, thrives in coastal sites ✳✳

■ **HARDINESS** Fully hardy ✳✳✳ to frost-hardy ✳✳.
■ **CULTIVATION** Oaks need deep, fertile, well-drained soil in partial shade. Evergreens prefer full sun and frost-hardy species shelter from cold, drying winds. ■ **Prune out** any shoots that spoil the shape of the tree on planting; mature oaks need little pruning except the removal of dead wood (*see p.322*). ■ **Sow** acorns in a seedbed or cold frame as soon as they fall (*see pp.328–329*).

Quercus coccinea (Scarlet oak)
↕20m (70ft) ↔15m (50ft), rounded canopy, pale grey-brown bark, dark green leaves turn red in autumn, needs lime-free soil ✳✳✳

Quercus laurifolia
↕↔20m (70ft), rounded habit with grey-black bark, leaves bronze when young and lasting well into winter, needs lime-free soil ✳✳✳

Rhododendron

Rhododendron, Azalea

Dramatic, sometimes strongly scented flowers are borne on these shrubs from late autumn through until summer. The flowers vary in size and shape, but they are mainly bell-shaped, often with attractive, contrasting markings on the petals, and are carried singly or in large clusters known as trusses. This is a large and highly variable group being both deciduous and evergreen, and with flowers of every colour. Their natural habitats include dense forest and high alpine slopes, and they range in habit from huge trees up to 25m (80ft) tall to dwarf shrubs no more than 15cm (6in) high. All require acid (lime-free) soil. The young growth of some leaves can be attractive, with colours of red to bronze-brown or metallic blue-green, and many deciduous rhododendrons have strong autumn leaf colours. Dwarf alpine species are at home in a rock garden, and larger woodland types are excellent for brightening shady spots. More compact varieties are good for growing in containers on the patio, and this is useful if you do not have acid (lime-free) soil.

■ **HARDINESS** Fully hardy ✳✳✳ to frost-tender ❀.
■ **CULTIVATION** Grow in moist but well-drained, acid (lime-free) soil, ideally pH 4.5–5.5. Site in dappled shade if possible, but most dwarf alpine species will tolerate full sun. Shallow planting is essential; the top of the root ball should be level with the surface of the soil.
■ **Mulch** rhododendrons annually with leafmould or lime-free compost (see p.326). ■ **Snap off** the old flowerheads when the flowers have faded. Be careful not to damage the developing new buds just below, which contain the flowers for the following year. ■ **Propagate** by layering (see p.330). If leaves are affected by powdery mildew or rusts, treat with fungicide. Ensure good drainage to avoid root rot.

Rhododendrons versus azaleas

Tree rhododendrons Tree rhododendrons are very large plants, most often seen in public parks and too large to be suitable for many gardens. Hardy evergreens, they are spectacular when in flower.

Shrub rhododendrons The most common and well-known type of rhododendron, these are rounded and range in size from less than 1m (3ft) to 4m (12ft). The flower clusters vary from quite small to large trusses in a wide range of bold colours. Most of them are evergreen.

Azaleas Azaleas have generally small to medium-sized leaves and small flowers. Most are deciduous, and often colour wonderfully in autumn. In spring and early summer, they are an almost solid mass of flowers in colours ranging from salmon-pink to red and various shades of yellow, typically with a delicious scent. They are easily controlled with occasional, but not hard, pruning.

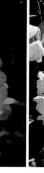

R. arboreum ↕12m (40ft) ↔4m (12ft), tree ✳✳

R. argyrophyllum ↕6m (20ft) ↔2.5m (8ft), evergreen shrub ✳✳✳

R. cinnabarinum ↕6m (20ft) ↔2m (6ft), evergreen shrub ✳✳✳

R. 'Cynthia' ♀ ↕↔6m (20ft), evergreen shrub ✳✳✳

R. 'John Cairns' ♀ ↕↔1.5m (5ft), evergreen azalea ✳✳✳

R. 'Lavender Girl' ♀ ↕↔2.5m (8ft), evergreen shrub ✳✳✳

R. rex subsp. *fictolacteum* ♀ ↕↔12m (40ft), tree ✳✳✳

R. 'Strawberry Ice' ♀ ↕↔2m (6ft), deciduous azalea ✳✳✳

R. augustinii ‡↔2.2m (7ft), tree ✽✽✽

R. 'Beauty of Littleworth' ‡↔4m (12ft), evergreen shrub ✽✽✽

R. 'Beethoven' ♀ ‡↔1.3m (4⅜ft), evergreen azalea ✽✽✽

R. 'Blue Peter' ♀ ‡↔3m (10ft), evergreen shrub ✽✽✽

R. davidsonianum ♀ ‡4m (12ft) ↔3m (10ft), evergreen shrub ✽✽✽

R. 'Golden Torch' ♀ ‡↔1.5m (5ft), evergreen shrub ✽✽✽

R. 'Hinomayo' ♀ ‡↔60cm (24in), dwarf evergreen azalea ✽✽✽

R. 'Hydon Dawn' ♀ ‡↔1.5m (5ft), evergreen shrub ✽✽✽

R. 'Linda' ♀ ‡↔1m (3ft), evergreen shrub ✽✽✽

R. occidentale ♀ ‡↔3m (10ft), deciduous shrub ✽✽✽

R. 'Pink Pearl' ‡↔4m (12ft), evergreen shrub ✽✽✽

R. 'Purple Splendour' ♀ ‡↔3m (10ft), evergreen shrub ✽✽✽

R. 'Susan' ♀ ‡↔3m (10ft), evergreen shrub ✽✽✽

R. 'Vuyk's Rosyred' ♀ ‡75cm (30in) ↔1.2m (4ft), evergreen azalea ✽✽✽

R. yakushimanum ‡↔2m (6ft), evergreen shrub ✽✽✽

R. yunnanense ‡6m (20ft) ↔4m (12ft), tree ✽✽✽

Rhamnus

AUTUMN

Cultivated for their foliage, which in deciduous species usually colours well in autumn, rhamnus are mostly thorny shrubs, native to a range of habitats, from woodland, heath and scrub, to fen and bog. They bear small, cup-shaped flowers, often fragrant and attractive to bees, followed by decorative red fruits that usually ripen to purple or black. These make a very striking contrast with the leaves of white-variegated *R. alaternus* 'Argenteovariegata', a popular evergreen, but one that needs some shelter in cold areas. Grow rhamnus in a shrub border, or a wild or woodland garden. They also make good informal hedges.

■ **HARDINESS** Fully hardy ✳✳✳ to frost-hardy ✳✳.
■ **CULTIVATION** Grow in reasonably fertile, reliably moist soil, in full sun or partial shade.
■ **Prune out** any crossing or misplaced shoots that spoil the shape in late winter or early spring. Trim hedges in early spring. ■ **Sow** seed in containers in a cold frame as soon as it is ripe (*see pp.328–329*). ■ **Take** softwood cuttings in early summer (*see pp.329–330*).

Rhamnus cathartica
↕6m (20ft) ↔5m (15ft), dense, spiny shrub producing yellowish green flowers in spring, leaves turn yellow in autumn, decorative fruit ✳✳✳

Rhaphiolepis

EARLY SUMMER AND AUTUMN

These are evergreen shrubs with glossy, dark-green foliage and fragrant flowers that look similar to apple-blossom. The white or pink flowers appear in small clusters in spring or summer. They are good companions to small flowering trees such as crab apples (*Malus, see p.77*) and hawthorns (*Crataegus, p.42*). Rhaphiolepis generally grow into dense, compact shapes, around 2m (6ft) tall and wide, although there are one or two much smaller varieties. However, they are not fully hardy, so need the protection of a warm, sunny wall. Alternatively, grow the smaller types in containers, and take them under frost-free cover for the winter.

■ **HARDINESS** Frost-hardy ✳✳ to half-hardy ✳.
■ **CULTIVATION** Grow outdoors in moist but well-drained soil in full sun, with shelter from cold, drying winds. If growing in pots, use a loam-based compost and water moderately in summer, giving monthly feeds of a balanced fertilizer. ■ **Trim** lightly after flowering, removing stems that spoil the shape. ■ **Take** semi-ripe cuttings in late summer (*see pp.329–330*), or layer shoots in autumn (*see p.330*).

Rhaphiolepis umbellata ♀
↕↔1.5m (5ft), slow-growing, bushy, rounded habit, flowers in early summer, berries only after long, hot summers ✳✳

Rhus

Sumach

SUMMER AND AUTUMN

The shrubs and trees in this group are grown for their bold, dissected leaves, which turn to vivid hues of ruby, gold, and amber as the temperature falls in autumn. The tiny flowers are borne in candle-like clusters in spring or summer; more impressive are the spikes of usually crimson fruits, although these appear only when male and female plants are grown together. Sumachs look best at the back of a shrub border or in a woodland garden. Some, such as *Rhus typhina* with its craggy form, also make architectural specimens. Sumachs can be invasive; cut out suckers whenever they appear.

■ **HARDINESS** Fully hardy ✳✳✳ to frost-tender ❄.
■ **CULTIVATION** Grow in reasonably fertile, moist, but well-drained soil, in full sun for best autumn colour. ■ **Prune out** shoots that are crossing or spoil the shape in late winter or early spring. Or in early spring cut back stems to within 2–3 buds from the base. ■ **Sow** seed in a seedbed in autumn (*see pp.328–329*). ■ **Take** semi-ripe cuttings in summer, or root cuttings in winter (*see pp.329–330*). ■ **Prone** to coral spot; cut affected growth right out and burn it.

Rhus typhina ♀ (Stag's horn sumach, Velvet sumach)
↕5m (15ft) ↔6m (20ft), deciduous, arching, suckering shrub or tree, dense velvety coating on stems, brilliant autumn colour ✳✳✳

Ribes
Flowering currant

Closely related to edible currant bushes, most ornamental ribes have a blackcurrant- or even cat-like scent, both in flower and when the leaves are crushed. These are old-fashioned, cottage-garden-style, mainly deciduous shrubs, grown for their cheering spring flowers; pink-flowered *Ribes sanguineum* is a traditional partner for yellow forsythias (*see p.54–55*). It is also often seen as a flowering hedge. There are ribes that flower in cerise, pale pink, white, or greenish-yellow. They do bear fruits, although these are usually inedible. Most make quite large shrubs, but they can be wall-trained, and there are compact varieties, including one or two with golden foliage.

■ **HARDINESS** Fully hardy ✳✳✳ to frost-hardy ✳✳.
■ **CULTIVATION** Grow ribes in reasonably fertile, well-drained soil, in full sun. *R. laurifolium* tolerates partial shade. ■ **Prune** after flowering, cutting back flowered shoots to strong buds or shoots lower down the stem. Prune out one or two old main branches on mature plants

***Ribes sanguineum*
'Pulborough Scarlet'** ♀
↕3m (10ft) ↔2.5m (8ft), upright, vigorous habit, flowers with white centres in spring, blue-black fruits ✳✳✳

every three or four years. If wall-trained, after flowering or in late winter, cut back flowered shoots to within two to four buds of the permanent framework. ■ **Trim** hedges after flowering. ■ **Take** hardwood cuttings of deciduous flowering currant in winter and semi-ripe cuttings of evergreens in summer (*see pp.329–330*).

Ribes odoratum (Buffalo currant)
↕↔2m (6ft), upright, deciduous shrub, aromatic flowers in mid- to late spring, black fruits, leaves turn red and purple in autumn ✳✳✳

Ribes laurifolium
↕1m (3ft) ↔1.5m (5ft), spreading, evergreen, leathery leaves, flowers in late winter and early spring, tolerates semi-shade ✳✳✳

Robinia

Robinias are trees and shrubs found in woodland and thickets in North America. They are usually thorny and have bright, graceful, long leaves, and, in late spring and early summer, sprays of white or pink, pea-like flowers. These are followed by large, dark brown seedpods. Grow the trees as specimens in a lawn, and the shrubby species in a large shrub border. *Robinia pseudoacacia* 'Frisia', which may be coppiced (*see p.38*) and grown as a foliage shrub, and *Acer palmatum* 'Rubrum', with dark red-purple leaves (*see pp.16–17*), make striking companions.

■ **HARDINESS** Fully hardy ✳✳✳.
■ **CULTIVATION** Robinias like full sun in reasonably fertile soil, ideally moist but well-drained, but will tolerate dry, poor soils.
■ **Shelter** from strong winds; the branches are rather brittle and break easily. ■ **Prune out** any misplaced or crossing branches that spoil the shape of young trees in late summer or early autumn (*see p.322*). Remove any suckers (shoots growing up from the ground around the tree).
■ **Sow** seed in a container in a cold frame in autumn (*see pp.328–329*). ■ **Take** root cuttings (*see pp.329–330*) in autumn.

***Robinia pseudoacacia* 'Frisia'** ♀
(False acacia, Black locust)
↕15m (50ft) ↔8m (25ft), fast-growing, suckering tree, fragrant flowers, foliage turns orange-yellow in autumn

Rosa
Rose

Superb, often highly scented flowers in summer and autumn make roses enduring garden favourites. They are mostly deciduous shrubs and there are hundreds of colourful varieties to choose from. Shrub roses look best mixed with other plants in borders; the miniature varieties can be grown in rock gardens and in large pots. The flowers, borne in clusters at the tips of stems, are excellent for cutting. They vary enormously in form and size, from small single or double blooms to immense, rounded doubles. The red autumn fruits (hips) of some roses also make a striking display. (See also pp.128–129.)

■ **HARDINESS** Fully hardy ✱✱✱.
■ **CULTIVATION** Grow in an open, sunny position, in fertile soil with plenty of well-rotted organic matter. ■ **Plant** bare-root roses when dormant, from late autumn to early spring, container-grown plants at any time. ■ **Feed** with a balanced fertilizer in spring and mulch with organic matter (see pp.325 and 326). ■ **Prune** in late winter or early spring; deadhead to encourage more flowers. ■ **Take** hardwood cuttings (see p.330) in autumn. ■ **Blackspot**, powdery mildew, or rust affect roses. Spray with fungicide and try to choose resistant cultivars.

Rose groups

Modern bush roses These upright shrubs are useful in borders and beds, being compact and repeat-flowering with single or double flowers. They bear large flowers singly or in small clusters (hybrid tea) or small flowers in large clusters (floribunda). Prune hard.

Standard roses Ideal for pots, formal schemes, or to add height in borders, these are modern bush roses top-grafted onto clear stems of rootstocks. They need permanent staking. Prune the head according to the rose type used.

Dwarf patio roses Compact shrubs with a bushy habit, these are ideal for growing at the front of borders and in containers. They produce abundant clusters of single to double, sometimes scented flowers in many colours in the summer. Only light pruning is needed.

Modern shrub roses A diverse group of roses, varying in size, habit, and flower type. Most are upright with flowers similar to modern bush roses, and make impressive specimen plants. Heavy pruning can spoil their character.

Ground-cover roses Spreading in habit, numerous stems bear clusters of small flowers, usually double or semi-double and lightly scented. They are ideal for ground cover and also for edging paths or growing in large pots. Prune to keep plants to the desired size.

Old garden roses A varied group, upright or arching, most flowering once but some repeat-flowering, most with semi-double or double flowers, often fragrant. Position arching types so they do not crowd plants, and give only a light annual pruning.

R. AMBER QUEEN ('Harroony') ♀
↕↔60cm (24in), floribunda

R. ANNA FORD ('Harpiccolo') ♀
↕↔45cm (18in), patio

R. 'Chinatown' ♀ ↕1.2m (4ft) ↔1m (3ft), modern shrub

R. 'Crimson Glory' ↕↔60cm (24in), hybrid tea

R. 'Ispahan' ♀ ↕1.5m (5ft) ↔1.2m (4ft), old rose

R. 'Just Joey' ♀ ↕↔75cm (30in), hybrid

R. 'Perle d'Or' ♀ ↕1.2m (4ft) ↔1m (3ft), old rose

R. rugosa ↕↔1–2.5m (3–8ft), species

R. 'Ballerina' ♀ ‡1.5m (5ft) ↔1.2m (4ft), modern shrub

R. 'Boule de Neige' ‡1.5m (5ft) ↔1.2m (4ft), old rose

R. 'Bourbon Queen' ‡2.5m (8ft) ↔1.5m (5ft), old rose

R. 'Charles de Mills' ♀ ‡↔1.2m (4ft), old rose

R. 'Fru Dagmar Hastrup' ♀ ‡1m (3ft) ↔1.2m (4ft), old rose

R. gallica var. officinalis 'Versicolor' ♀ ‡80cm (32in) ↔1m (3ft), old rose

R. 'Geranium' ♀ ‡2.5m (8ft) ↔1.5m (5ft), old rose

R. GRAHAM THOMAS ('Ausmas') ♀ ‡↔1.2–1.5m (4–5ft), modern shrub

R. 'Madame Isaac Pereire' ♀ ‡2.2m (7ft) ↔2m (6ft), old rose

R. 'Maiden's Blush' ♀ ‡1.2m (4ft) ↔90cm (36in), old rose

R. 'National Trust' ‡↔60cm (24in), hybrid tea

R. 'Nevada' ♀ ‡↔2.2m (7ft), modern shrub

R. 'Silver Jubilee' ♀ ‡1.1m (3½ft) ↔60cm (24in), hybrid tea

R. 'Souvenir de la Malmaison' ‡↔1.5m (5ft), old rose

R. 'The Fairy' ♀ ‡↔60–90cm (24–36in), floribunda

R. 'The Queen Elizabeth' ‡2.2m (7ft) ↔1m (3ft), modern bush

Rosmarinus
Rosemary

YEAR-ROUND

Aromatic and evergreen, these shrubs add height and structure to a herb garden, and also grow well in pots. Native to Mediterranean regions, they can, although hardy, suffer badly in cold wet winters. The upright types benefit from the shelter of a sunny wall, while the less hardy, prostrate forms prefer spreading over a gravel mulch or even a stony bank, rather than sitting on chilly wet soil. The leaves are dark green and from mid-spring to early summer, and now and again in late summer, they bear clusters of blue, mauve, or white, tubular flowers towards the tips.

■ **HARDINESS** Frost-hardy ✳✳; *Rosmarinus officinalis* and cultivars withstand -10°C (14°F) if well-drained.
■ **CULTIVATION** Grow in well-drained to dry, relatively poor soil, in full sun. ■ **Trim** lightly but regularly to keep plants bushy and to encourage soft shoots. ■ **Sow** seed (*see pp.328–329*) in a container in a cold frame in spring. ■ **Take** semi-ripe cuttings (*see pp.329–330*) in summer.

Rosmarinus officinalis
‡↔1.5m (5ft)

***Rosmarinus officinalis* 'McConnell's Blue'** ♀
‡↔1.5m (5ft)

Rubus

EARLY SUMMER, AUTUMN, AND WINTER

These arching shrubs, related to brambles, bear simple, rose-like flowers in early summer, in white, red, purple, or pink. In some, such as the thornless 'Benenden' and the spectacularly bright *Rubus spectabilis* 'Olympic Double', the flowering period is the main season of interest; these suit a wild or woodland garden. *R. biflorus*, *R. cockburnianus*, and *R. thibetanus* are also grown for winter interest, with a white bloom on their prickly stems that makes them stand out. They look good with willows (*Salix, see right*) and dogwoods (*Cornus, see pp.38–39*) grown for colourful winter stems, and, like them, are best pruned hard annually. (*See also p.130.*)

■ **HARDINESS** Fully hardy ✳✳✳.
■ **CULTIVATION** Grow in well-drained, reasonably fertile soil. Position in full sun for the brightest winter stems. ■ **Prune** rubus grown for their flowers lightly, cutting back flowered shoots to strong buds or shoots lower down. Prune those grown for winter stems hard, in early spring, cutting stems to within three buds of the base, then feed and mulch. ■ **Take** hardwood cuttings in early winter (*see p.330*).

Rubus cockburnianus
‡↔2.5m (8ft), thicket-forming, small, purple flowers in summer, black fruits, attractive although unpalatable

Salix
Willow

SPRING, SUMMER, AND WINTER

This is a large and varied group of deciduous trees and shrubs. Spring catkins are one of the striking features, but they also have attractive habits, and in some cases decorative stems. Willows seen growing in the wild are often massive trees, but there are many small and medium-sized ones – the weeping *Salix caprea* 'Kilmarnock' is a favourite centrepiece for a small lawn or border. Some of the larger species, generally too vigorous for most gardens, can be grown as shrubs, cut back annually to make them compact and encourage brightly coloured stems. *S. alba* 'Britzensis', for example, makes a fine winter display with mahonias (*see p.77*) together with Christmas box (*Sarcococca, see p.100*), and dogwoods (*Cornus, see pp.38–39*).

***Salix alba* var. *vitellina* 'Britzensis'** ♀
‡25m (80ft) ↔10m (30ft), naturally a large tree, annual coppicing will keep it in bounds, dull-green leaves, catkins in spring

■ **HARDINESS** Fully hardy ✻✻✻.
■ **CULTIVATION** Grow in any deep, moist but well-drained soil, except chalky soils, in full sun.
■ **Pruning** is rarely necessary except for those grown for winter stems; in early spring, cut back to within three or four buds of the base or to a permanent stubby framework (*see pp.322–323*).
■ **Take** greenwood cuttings in early summer, or hardwood cuttings in winter (*see pp.329–330*).

Salix gracilistyla 'Melanostachys'
‡3m (10ft) ↔ 4m (12ft), upright shrub, silky-hairy grey-green leaves turn glossy green, dramatic black catkins in early to mid-spring

Salix helvetica ♀ (Swiss willow)
‡60cm (2ft) ↔ 40cm (16in), an upright, bushy shrub, leaves grey-green above and silvery white beneath, catkins in early spring

Sambucus
Elder

MID-SPRING TO AUTUMN

These deciduous shrubs and trees are grown for their flowers and ornamental foliage. From spring to early summer, they produce dense, flat clusters of white or creamy yellow flowers followed by black or glossy red fruits. The leaves may be blackish-purple, dark green, or golden yellow, and are made up of small leaflets, deeply fringed in some cultivars. Elders are suitable for shrub and mixed borders or as specimens. *Photinia* x *fraseri* 'Red Robin' (*see p.84*) with its red young foliage is a good companion.

■ **HARDINESS** Fully hardy ✻✻✻.
■ **CULTIVATION** Grow in reasonably fertile soil that is moist but well-drained. Position in full sun or partial shade: leaves colour most strongly in full sun, but retain colour better in dappled shade. ■ **Prune** only to remove misplaced shoots, in winter or early spring; or, for the best leaf colour, cut back stems to within two or three buds of the base in early spring. ■ **Sow** seed (*see pp.328–329*) in a container in a cold frame in autumn. ■ **Take** hardwood cuttings in winter, or softwood cuttings in early summer (*see pp.329–330*). ■ **Blackfly** (*see Aphids, p.332*) may infest young growth, but can be treated.

Sambucus racemosa 'Plumosa Aurea'
(Red-berried elder)
‡↔3m (10ft), bushy shrub, new leaves are bronze and can scorch in full sun, flowers in mid-spring

Santolina
Cotton lavender

SUMMER

Compact, rounded, evergreen – or rather, "evergrey" – shrubs, these can be used as low hedges or to edge borders, and are ideal for rock gardens, being naturally found in dry sites. They are grown principally for their fine, aromatic foliage. The long-stemmed flowerheads are button-like, yellow or creamy-yellow, surrounded by broad rings of similarly coloured bracts (modified leaves) that make them more conspicuous. The plants spread to cover the ground, and effectively suppress weeds. For a heady mix of scents, grow with other aromatic herbs, such as lavender (*Lavandula, see p.71*) and rosemary (*Rosmarinus, see p.98*).

■ **HARDINESS** Frost-hardy ✻✻.
■ **CULTIVATION** Grow in poor to reasonably fertile soil that is well-drained and in full sun.
■ **Cut back** flowered shoots to within 2.5cm (1in) of old growth in spring. ■ **Sow** seed (*see pp.328–329*) in containers in a cold frame in autumn or spring. ■ **Take** semi-ripe cuttings (*see pp.329–330*) in late summer and root in a propagator with bottom heat.

Santolina pinnata 'Sulphurea' ♀
‡75cm (30in) ↔ 1m (3ft), feathery, finely divided, grey-green leaves, flowers in midsummer

Sarcococca
Christmas box, Sweet box
WINTER AND YEAR-ROUND

A small group of tough evergreen shrubs, sarcococcas are invaluable in the garden in winter. Their dense forms with dark green leaves, add visual interest by blooming in winter, bearing clusters of white flowers followed by glossy berries. Their greatest attraction, however, is scent: the flowers are not showy, but this is more than made up for by the sweet and powerful fragrance. Grow them with other winter-flowering plants, such as *Viburnum* x *bodnantense* 'Dawn' (*see pp.108–109*) and *Helleborus niger* (*see p.215*), or as an informal hedge.

■ **HARDINESS** Fully hardy ✳✳✳.
■ **CULTIVATION** Grow in reasonably fertile, moist but well-drained soil, enriched with well-rotted organic matter. Position in deep or partial shade: they tolerate full sun if the soil is reliably moist. ■ **Trim** any stems that spoil the shape of the shrub after flowering, but not too much or the result may be fewer flowers.
■ **Sow** seed (*see pp.328–329*) in containers outdoors in autumn or spring. ■ **Take** semi-ripe cuttings (*see pp.329–330*) in late summer, or remove suckers for transplanting in late winter.

Sarcococca confusa ♀
‡2m (6ft) ↔1m (3ft), dense and rounded, slow-growing shrub that is very useful for fairly dry, shady areas

Senecio cineraria
Cineraria
SPRING, SUMMER, AND AUTUMN

These mounding evergreen shrubs are grown chiefly for their leaves, soft like felt, in a range of delicate shapes and shades of silvery green and grey. Yellow flowerheads are produced in the second year after sowing, but the plants are often discarded after one season. The flowers are not particularly attractive, and the foliage is at its pristine best only when plants are young. They can be grown in shrub borders, but are mainly used as dot plants or edging in bedding schemes, where their foliage can act as a foil for flowering plants. A classic combination is cinerarias with red salvias (*see p.266*); for a more subdued effect, pair it with purple heliotropes (*see p.62*). (*See also p.325.*)

■ **HARDINESS** Frost-hardy ✳✳.
■ **CULTIVATION** Grow cinerarias in reasonably fertile soil in full sun. ■ **Trim** plants if necessary to improve the shape. ■ **Sow** seed (*see pp.328–329*) in spring at 19–24°C (66–75°F). ■ **Take** semi-ripe cuttings (*see pp.329–330*) in mid- or late summer. ■ **Prone to rust**; affected plants are best removed to prevent it from spreading.

***Senecio cineraria* 'White Diamond'**
‡30–40cm (12–16in) ↔30cm (12in), usually grown as perennial

Skimmia
LATE WINTER TO SUMMER

Skimmias are handsome evergreens, all with similar looks but varying widely in size, with many compact varieties for the smaller garden. Clusters of starry flowers, sometimes scented, open in spring, but are prominent in bud through the winter in several forms. The flowers are followed by fleshy, round, black, red, or white berries; some skimmias have male and female plants, so both are needed for fruit. The pointed leaves are dark, glossy, and aromatic. Skimmias are reliable players in winter-interest schemes, adding structure and colour next to deciduous shrubs like hamamelis (*see p.61*), and height to groupings of winter- and spring-flowering heathers (*Calluna*, *see p.27*).

■ **HARDINESS** Fully hardy ✳✳✳.
■ **CULTIVATION** Grow in reasonably fertile, moist but well-drained soil, with well-rotted organic matter added. Position in light or dappled shade; *S.* x *confusa* 'Kew Green' will tolerate full sun. ■ **Prune** only if necessary.
■ **Sow** seed (*see pp.328–329*) in containers in a cold frame in autumn. ■ **Take** semi-ripe cuttings (*see pp.329–330*) in late summer.

Skimmia japonica
‡↔to 6m (20ft), variable in shape, fragrant white flowers in mid- and late spring, male and female forms

Sophora

SPRING TO LATE SUMMER

Grown for their fine foliage and their clusters of bright flowers, these trees and shrubs need long, hot spells to flower well, but are worth growing for the leaves alone. These are composed of small leaflets arranged along a central leaf stalk, and have a very elegant appearance. There are both deciduous and evergreen sophoras. The pea-like flowers are carried in clusters at the end of the branches, in colours that include purple-blue to white and golden-yellow. Sophoras look good in a shrub border, or near a sheltered wall in cooler regions to encourage flowering. In cold areas, grow the less hardy types in pots, and take under frost-free cover for the winter.

■ **HARDINESS** Fully hardy ✳✳✳ to frost-hardy ✳✳.
■ **CULTIVATION** Grow in reasonably fertile, well-drained soil, in full sun. Use a loam-based compost in pots, water freely in summer and feed at monthly intervals with a balanced fertilizer. ■ **Prune out** any misplaced shoots that spoil the shape in late winter or early spring, and to create a framework. ■ **Sow** ripe seed (*see pp.328–329*) in a container in a cold frame.

Sophora davidii
‡2.5m (8ft) ↔3m (10ft), bushy or spreading, deciduous shrub or tree, flowering in late summer or early autumn when mature

Sorbus

Mountain ash, Rowan, Whitebeam

SPRING TO AUTUMN

Upright, columnar, or spreading trees and shrubs, sorbus have an attractive branch structure and flowers in spring or summer. Ornamental foliage has leaves in a range of shapes, often colouring well in autumn, and the bark is textured when mature, but the main highlight is the autumn show of berries. These are mostly in shades of red, orange, and yellow, but some have white berries, often tinted pink, as in the tree *Sorbus cashmiriana* (syn. *S. rosea*). The thicket-forming shrub *S. reducta* has crimson berries that become white. Use sorbus as specimens or grow in a border together with hawthorns (*Crataegus, see p.42*) or amelanchiers (*see p.19*) for a richly coloured autumn display.

■ **HARDINESS** Fully hardy ✳✳✳.
■ **CULTIVATION** Grow in any fertile, moist but well-drained soil, in full sun or dappled shade. ■ **Prune out** crossing or misplaced shoots in late winter or early spring, but only if necessary. ■ **Sow** seed (*see pp.328–329*) in a container in a cold frame in autumn.

Sorbus aucuparia
‡15m (50ft) ↔7m (22ft)

Sorbus 'Joseph Rock'
‡10m (30ft) ↔7m (22ft)

Spartium junceum

Broom, Spanish broom

EARLY SUMMER TO EARLY AUTUMN

This plant is closely related to cytisus (*see p.43*) and genistas (*see p.58*), both also commonly called broom. Spanish broom is a wonderful plant for coastal gardens, suitable for a shrub border or for training against a warm, sunny wall. It is an upright shrub, with slender, dark green shoots and few leaves. From early summer until early autumn, it produces masses of fragrant, pea-like flowers, followed by flattened, dark brown seed pods. The intense yellow of the flowers of *Spartium junceum* would make a lively contrast to the similarly shaped, rich blue flowers of *Sophora davidii* (*see p.101*).

■ **HARDINESS** Frost-hardy ✳✳.
■ **CULTIVATION** This plant likes reasonably fertile, well-drained soil; thrives in coastal areas and on chalky soils. Needs full sun. ■ **Trim** or prune shoots that spoil the shape of the shrub, lightly in mid- or late spring. Older specimens may be renovated by cutting back fairly hard in spring. ■ **Sow** seed (*see pp.328–329*) in containers in a cold frame in spring or autumn. It is a plant that will often self-seed.

Spartium junceum ♀
‡↔to 3m (10ft), plants in sheltered positions may become tall and leggy; in an exposed seaside garden, winds will keep the growth dense

Spiraea

SPRING TO SUMMER

There is a spiraea for almost any position in the garden. This varied group of semi-evergreen and deciduous shrubs contains many elegant and easily cultivated plants, in various sizes. They are grown mainly for their dense clusters of small, saucer-shaped or bowl-shaped flowers, carried at the branch tips in spring and summer. These range from white, pink, and yellow, to purple. Some spiraeas have coloured leaves, like *Spiraea japonica* 'Goldflame', which has bronze-red young leaves that turn to bright yellow, then to mid-green; its flowers are dark pink.

■ **HARDINESS** Fully hardy ✲✲✲, although new growth may be damaged by frosts.
■ **CULTIVATION** Grow in fertile, moist but well-drained soil in full sun. ■ **Prune** most spiraeas, which flower on older wood, after flowering, cutting back the flowered shoots to strong buds or shoots lower down the shrub. Encourage new growth from the base of mature plants by cutting out about one in every three or four old stems each year. Prune *S. japonica* and its cultivars, which flower on the current year's growth, differently, cutting them back to a permanent low framework of shoots in early spring. ■ **Take** greenwood cuttings in summer (*see pp.329–330*).

Spiraea x vanhouttei
↕2m (6ft) ↔1.5m (5ft), a graceful, arching, deciduous shrub, profuse flowers almost obscure the leaves in early summer

***Spiraea nipponica* 'Snowmound'** ♥
↕↔1.2–2.5m (4–8ft), fast-growing, deciduous, smothered with white flowers in early summer

***Spiraea japonica* 'Anthony Waterer'**
↕to 1.5m (5ft) ↔1.5m (5ft), deciduous, leaves are bronze when young and often edged pink or white, flowers in mid- and late summer

Stachyurus

LATE WINTER TO EARLY SPRING

A small group of spreading, deciduous and semi-evergreen shrubs, these are grown for their late winter and early spring flowers, which are small, bell-shaped, and pale yellow. The yellow buds are produced in clusters along the bare stems in autumn, opening in spring before the leaves appear. Only *Stachyurus chinensis* and *S. praecox* are reliably and widely grown; *S. chinensis* is the smaller of the two. Both shrubs have pointed, dark green leaves on arching, slender, glossy shoots, which are red-brown in *S. praecox* and purplish in *S. chinensis*. 'Magpie' is a popular variegated cultivar. Grow them in a shrub or mixed border, or against a wall.

■ **HARDINESS** Fully hardy ✲✲✲.
■ **CULTIVATION** Grow in light, moist, but well-drained, acid (lime-free) soil in full sun or partial shade. Position in a spot sheltered from cold, drying winds. ■ **Prune out** any crossing or misplaced shoots after flowering. Mature plants may be rejuvenated, when necessary, by cutting them to the base after flowering. ■ **Sow** seed (*see pp.328–329*) in a cold frame in autumn. ■ **Take** semi-ripe cuttings (*see pp.329–330*) consisting of a sideshoot with a sliver of older stem (a "heel") attached in summer.

Stachyurus praecox ♥
↕1–4m (3–12ft) ↔to 3m (10ft), deciduous shrub and one of the first to flower in late winter and early spring

Stewartia

A succession of flowers in the summer, fine autumn colour, and beautifully textured bark on older specimens all make these large, evergreen or deciduous trees and shrubs worth growing. The rose-like, white flowers have creamy yellow stamens in the centre and are produced singly or in pairs. Stewartias are related to camellias (*see pp.28–29*) and prefer broadly similar conditions, making excellent specimen trees in a woodland setting or shady border. Try them with eucryphias (*see p.51*), which bear similar open, white flowers at different times of the year depending on the species.

■ **HARDINESS** Fully hardy ✱✱✱ to frost-hardy ✱✱.
■ **CULTIVATION** Grow in moist but well-drained, reasonably fertile, neutral to acid (lime-free) soil. Position in full sun or partial shade, with shelter from strong, cold winds. Buy container-grown plants and choose the right spot first time; they resent root disturbance.
■ **Sow** stewartia seed (*see pp.328–329*) in a cold frame in autumn. ■ **Take** greenwood cuttings in early summer or semi-ripe cuttings from mid- to late summer (*see pp.329–330*), or layer low-growing shoots in autumn (*see p.330*).

Stewartia pseudocamellia ♀
‡20m (70ft) ↔8m (25ft), peeling bark, leaves turn yellow and then orange and red, flowers in midsummer ✱✱✱

Styrax
Snowbell

Bell-shaped, pure white or pink-tinged flowers give these graceful plants their common name. A large group of deciduous or evergreen shrubs and small trees, most are compact enough to be included in almost any garden. The dainty, fragrant flowers are produced in summer on short branches formed in the previous year. The leaves are variable in shape. Shrubby snowbells are ideal for a border with mock oranges (*Philadelphus, see p.82*), weigelas (*see p.110*), and potentillas (*see p.87*); plant trees where the flowers can be seen from below.

■ **HARDINESS** Fully hardy ✱✱✱.
■ **CULTIVATION** Grow in moist but well-drained soil that has been enriched with well-rotted organic matter, and is preferably neutral to acid (lime-free). Position in full sun or partial shade, with protection from cold, drying winds. ■ **Prune out** any misplaced or crossing shoots that spoil the shape of shrubs or young trees in late winter or early spring. ■ **Sow** seed (*see pp.328–329*) as soon as ripe: this needs some care, maintaining 15°C (59°F) for three months and then keeping the seedlings frost-free until they are established. ■ **Take** greenwood cuttings (*see pp.329–330*) in summer.

Styrax obassia ♀ (Fragrant snowbell)
‡12m (40ft) ↔7m (22ft), broadly columnar tree, downy leaves that turn yellow and red in autumn, flowers in early and midsummer

Symphoricarpos
Snowberry

These deciduous shrubs are grown for their autumn and winter show of berries, which are usually white or rose-tinted. In summer, they bear clusters of small, bell-shaped flowers which, although too small to have impact, are rich in nectar and attract bees into the garden. The berries last well into winter as they are not eaten by wildlife; they may irritate the skin. Often forming thickets, these are very hardy plants and tolerant of a wide range of conditions including poor soil and pollution. They are best grown in a wild garden along a boundery with other shrubs, such as hawthorn (*Crataegus, see p.42*), to form a screen or mixed informal hedge.

■ **HARDINESS** Fully hardy ✱✱✱.
■ **CULTIVATION** Grow in any reasonably fertile, well-drained soil, and position in full sun or partial shade. ■ **Prune out** misplaced shoots that spoil the shape of the shrub in late winter or early spring (*see p.322*); reduce by cutting back flowered stems to strong shoots, after flowering. ■ **Divide** clumping plants in autumn (*see p.330*). ■ **Take** greenwood cuttings in summer, or hardwood cuttings in autumn (*see pp.329–330*).

Symphoricarpos x doorenbosii '**White Hedge**'
‡1.5m (5ft) ↔indefinite, an upright shrub, flowers in mid- and late summer, densely clustered fruits

Syringa
Lilac

Renowned for their beautiful and exquisitely scented flowers in early summer, these deciduous shrubs, traditionally mauve-flowered, are also available in white, cream, pale yellow, pink, magenta, and wine red. Most lilacs in gardens are the familiar cultivars of *Syringa vulgaris*, with a relatively short season in bloom, their flowers borne in distinctive conical clusters. These can grow quite large, and suit the back of a border or a wild garden area well, or can be pruned to a more shapely form. However, there are others, such as *S. meyeri* 'Palibin', that can be trained as standards.

■ **HARDINESS** Fully hardy ❊❊❊; late frosts may damage new growth.
■ **CULTIVATION** Grow in fertile soil enriched with well-rotted organic matter, preferably neutral to alkaline. Site in full sun. ■ **Deadhead** young lilacs to prevent the plant's energy going into setting seed. ■ **Prune out** any misshapen branches in late winter or early spring (*see p.322*). *S. vulgaris* and its cultivars can be renovated by pruning hard. ■ **Sow** ripe seed (*see pp.328–329*) in a cold frame. ■ **Layer** low-growing shoots (*see p.330*) in early summer.

***Syringa meyeri* 'Palibin'** ♀
↕1.5–2m (5–6ft) ↔1.2m (4ft), slow-growing, rounded shrub, smaller but profuse flower clusters in late spring and early summer

Syringa vulgaris* var. *alba
↕↔7m (22ft), white-flowered form of this highly fragrant, spreading shrub or small tree, which usually has lilac-blue flowers

***Syringa vulgaris* 'Primrose'**
↕↔7m (22ft), spreading shrub or small tree, small clusters of flowers in unusual colour for lilacs, flowers in late spring to early summer

***Syringa x josiflexa* 'Bellicent'** ♀
↕4m (12ft) ↔5m (15ft), upright shrub, flower clusters are larger than many, up to 20cm (8in) long, in late spring and early summer

Tamarix
Tamarisk

Invaluable in seaside gardens, these are graceful deciduous shrubs or small trees with red-brown, arching stems. Their flowers are pink and carried in dense, plume-like sprays. Naturally found in coastal sites, tamarisks happily withstand salt-laden winds and sea spray. They have tiny, tough, feathery leaves from which little water evaporates; this makes them ideal for a windbreak hedge or screen where winds are not cold. In a sheltered site, they do grow leggy if not checked by regular pruning. The most widely seen types are *Tamarix tetrandra*, flowering in mid- to late spring, and *T. ramosissima*, which flowers from late summer.

■ **HARDINESS** Fully hardy ❊❊❊.
■ **CULTIVATION** In coastal areas, grow in full sun, in well-drained soil or, inland, in moist soil with shelter from winds. ■ **Prune** young plants almost to ground level after planting and trim regularly to stop plants becoming top-heavy (*see p.323*). Cut flowered stems of spring-flowering types back to strong new shoots; prune autumn-flowering types slightly harder, in early spring; all tolerate renovation pruning, almost to the base. ■ **Sow** seed (*see pp.328–329*) as soon as it is ripe in containers in a cold frame. ■ **Take** hardwood cuttings in winter or semi-ripe cuttings in summer (*see pp.329–330*).

***Tamarix ramosissima* 'Pink Cascade'**
↕↔5m (15ft), flowers in clusters in late summer and early autumn, on the new year's shoots

Taxus
Yew
YEAR-ROUND

Versatile and adaptable conifers, yews are grown for their handsome evergreen foliage and sculptural forms. They have reddish-brown, often peeling bark and narrow, very dark green leaves (there are also golden forms). Female plants bear red berries in autumn. Grow yews as freestanding trees or clip into topiary shapes, and they make the best formal hedges; while prostrate ones make good ground cover. Yews grow faster than many people think, and will make a dense hedge in under ten years. They can be pruned hard into old wood, so are easy to renovate if overgrown or damaged. All parts except the red fruits' flesh are poisonous.

■ **HARDINESS** Fully hardy ✳✳✳.
■ **CULTIVATION** Grow in any except wet soil, and in any site, from full sun to full shade. ■ **Trim** hedges and clipped shapes in summer and early autumn. Renovate in autumn to early winter. ■ **Sow** seed (*see pp.328–329*) as soon as they are ripe in a cold frame or seedbed; they may take two years or more to germinate. ■ **Take** semi-ripe cuttings (*see pp.329–330*) in late summer, choosing upright shoots (except for prostrate forms), otherwise they may not form a central upright stem.

Taxus baccata 'Fastigiata Aureomarginata' ♈
↕3–5m (10–15ft) ↔1–2.5m (3–8ft), broadly conical tree, female, gold-variegated cultivar

Teucrium
Germander
SUMMER

Grown for their aromatic foliage and attractive summer flowers, these small evergreen and deciduous shrubs are part of a large group that also includes non-woody plants. The leaves are often grey-green, and the flowers are tubular or bell-shaped, in shades of pink, yellow, or blue, and are borne in clusters in summer. A sheltered border is necessary in colder areas, but wall germanders (*Teucrium chamaedrys*) make good hedging and edging plants in milder regions. For an aromatic mix, grow germander with other shrubs that enjoy the same conditions, such as lavenders (*Lavandula, see p.71*), artemisias (*see p.21*), and rosemary (*Rosmarinus, see p.98*).

■ **HARDINESS** Fully hardy ✳✳✳ to frost-hardy ✳✳.
■ **CULTIVATION** Grow in well-drained soil that is slightly alkaline (limy); the smaller species require very sharply drained soil. Position in full sun. ■ **Trim back** growth to maintain a good shape in spring or late summer, after flowering. ■ **Take** softwood cuttings in early summer, or semi-ripe cuttings in late summer, rooting both in a heated propagator (*see pp.329–330*). Overwinter young plants in frost-free conditions.

Teucrium polium
↕↔30cm (12in), mound-forming and deciduous, this flowers abundantly in summer ✳✳✳

Thuja
Arborvitae
YEAR-ROUND

These conifers, both large and small, make handsome specimen trees, and also hedges because they stand up well to clipping. They have flattened sprays of scaly foliage, usually aromatic. The white cedar, *Thuja occidentalis*, is a rounded tree that can reach 20m (70ft), with billowing branches, peeling, orange-brown bark, and apple-scented leaves. It has many forms, and widely varying colours and sizes. 'Caespitosa', for example, is cushion-like and slow-growing, reaching only 30cm (12in) high, suitable for a rock garden. *T. plicata* is a popular hedge, but otherwise only suitable for large gardens. It also has a range of smaller forms.

■ **HARDINESS** Fully hardy ✳✳✳.
■ **CULTIVATION** Grow thuja in deep, moist but well-drained soil. Position in full sun, with shelter from cold, drying winds. ■ **Trim** hedging in spring and late summer. ■ **Sow** seed (*see pp.328–329*) in late winter in containers in a cold frame or take semi-ripe cuttings in late summer (*see pp.329–330*). ■ **Prone to aphids** (*see p.332*) and small, limpet-like pests known as scale insects: if these become a problem, control with insecticide.

Thuja occidentalis 'Rheingold' ♈
↕1–2m (3–6ft) ↔to 1–1.2m (3–4ft), yellow leaves are tinted pink when young

Thymus
Thyme
`SUMMER`

Low-growing evergreen shrubs with small, aromatic leaves and pretty flowers, thymes attract bees and other beneficial insects. In summer, they produce clusters of tiny flowers, usually in pink, purple, or white. Provided that they do not sit in the wet, thymes can be grown in a range of situations, with border plants or with other decorative herbs, such as lavenders (*Lavandula, see p.71*) and chives. They are ideal for the front of a bed, and mat-forming types can be planted in crevices between paving. In containers, perhaps with other herbs, they trail attractively.

■ **HARDINESS** Fully hardy ✳✳✳ to frost-hardy ✳✳.
■ **CULTIVATION** Grow in neutral to alkaline (limy) soil that is well-drained. Position in full sun. ■ **Trim back** after flowering to keep the plants compact. ■ **Sow** seed (*see pp.328–329*) in a container in a cold frame in spring or divide plants (*see p.330*) in spring. ■ **Take** softwood cuttings (*see pp.329–330*) in mid- to late summer.

***Thymus doerfleri* 'Bressingham'**
‡10cm (4in) ↔ to 60cm (2ft) ✳✳✳

***Thymus pulegioides* 'Bertram Anderson'** ♀
‡to 30cm (12in) ↔ to 60cm (2ft) ✳✳✳

Tilia
Lime, Linden
`SPRING, SUMMER, AND AUTUMN`

Large, stately, deciduous trees, limes are grown for their habit, foliage, and scented flowers. All have broadly oval to rounded, bright or dark green leaves that turn yellow in autumn. From midsummer, they produce hanging clusters of creamy-white or pale yellow flowers, which attract pollinating insects into the garden. They are followed by inedible dry fruits. As the trees age, the silver-grey bark becomes fissured. In large gardens, limes can be used as specimen trees.

■ **HARDINESS** Fully hardy ✳✳✳.
■ **CULTIVATION** Grow in moist, but well-drained soil; limes prefer alkaline (limy) or neutral soil, but will tolerate acid soils. Avoid wet sites or very dry conditions, and sites exposed to strong, cold winds. Position in full sun or partial shade. ■ **Prune** limes in late winter or early spring, cutting out any misplaced shoots that spoil the shape of young trees. ■ **Keep** seed cold for 3–5 months before sowing in containers in a cold frame in spring (*see pp.328–329*).
■ **Aphids** attack limes without harming them; but the sticky honeydew they excrete can be a nuisance as it rains from the tree in summer: do not plant where they overhang paths or cars.

Tilia henryana
‡↔ to 25m (80ft), a spreading tree, leaves red-tinged when young, flowering in late summer to early autumn

Trachycarpus
Fan palm
`YEAR-ROUND`

These evergreen palms have dark green leaves made up of many pointed segments joined in a fan shape. They usually form a strong single main stem, as in the Chusan palm *Trachycarpus fortunei*, which is the most widely seen in gardens. Small yellow flowers are borne in summer in large, hanging clusters. Male and female flowers are borne on separate plants in early summer: if they are grown together, female plants produce round, blue-black fruits. Superb feature plants, Chusan palms can be grown in large pots in cold areas and brought into frost-free conditions for the winter. Grow among bamboos and ornamental grasses (*see pp.284–299*) or with ferns (*see pp.300–309*) for a jungle look in a sheltered courtyard.

■ **HARDINESS** Frost-hardy ✳✳.
■ **CULTIVATION** Grow in well-drained, fertile soil. Position in full sun or partial shade with shelter from cold, drying winds. ■ **Pruning** is unnecessary, but trim off dead leaves (do not cut close to the trunk). ■ **Sow** seed (*see pp.328–329*) in spring or autumn at 24°C (75°F).

***Trachycarpus fortunei* ♀** (Chusan palm)
‡to 20m (70ft) ↔ 2.5m (8ft), seldom reaches anything like this height in temperate gardens, generally remaining a small tree

Tsuga
Hemlock

YEAR-ROUND

A graceful form, usually broadly conical and made up of tiers of sweeping branches, is the main attraction of these evergreen conifers. They come in almost every size you can imagine, from 30cm (12in) to 30m (150ft) tall, with needle-like leaves that vary in colour from bright green to blue-grey to silvery-grey, so there should be one to suit almost every garden. *Tsuga heterophylla*, the western hemlock, makes a fine hedge. All hemlocks grow very well in shade. Male and female flowers appear in separate clusters on the same tree, and the small, hanging cones ripen in the same year as they are produced.

■ **HARDINESS** Fully hardy ✻✻✻.
■ **CULTIVATION** Grow in moist but well-drained, preferably neutral to slightly acid soil, enriched with organic matter. Position in sun or partial shade with shelter from cold, drying winds. ■ **Pruning** is unnecessary, as for most conifers, unless removing damaged growth.
■ **Trim** hedges from early to late summer.
■ **Sow** seed (*see pp.328–329*) in containers in a cold frame in spring or take semi-ripe cuttings (*see pp.329–330*) in late summer.

Tsuga canadensis
‡to 25m (80ft) ↔to 10m (30ft), the best choice if your soil tends to be alkaline (limy), this tree has many smaller cultivars

Ulex
Furze, Gorse

SPRING

Evergreen and prickly, gorse is ideal for a tough barrier hedge. *Ulex europaeus* is an upright, rounded to bushy shrub with spine-tipped green shoots, and even the leaves are reduced to rigid spines, making it almost impossible to penetrate. The main flowering period is in spring, but flowers are borne singly or in clusters almost all year round in mild climates. The pea-like, bright yellow blooms have a coconut-like scent, bringing a surprisingly exotic element to the spring garden. The equally spiny dwarf gorse, *U. gallii*, is more spreading in shape, reaching only 2m (6ft), and flowers from late summer. Both suit a hot border or a sunny, sloping site, where little else will grow apart from other robust, drought-tolerant shrubs.

■ **HARDINESS** Fully hardy ✻✻✻.
■ **CULTIVATION** Grow in poor, sandy, acid to neutral, well-drained soil; plants may become very leggy on rich, fertile soils. Position in full sun.
■ **Cut** back flowered shoots to within 2.5cm (1in) of old growth after flowering or in mid-spring every two or three years. ■ **Take** semi-ripe cuttings in summer (*see pp.329–330*).

Ulex europaeus 'Flore Pleno' ♑
‡to 2.5m (8ft) ↔2m (6ft), has double flowers and does not produce seed

Ulmus
Elm

SUMMER AND AUTUMN

In spite of popular belief, there are several elms that can be grown in countries that have suffered the ravages of Dutch elm disease. These deciduous trees have appealing foliage, which turns golden-yellow in autumn. They also produce clusters of tiny, red-tinted, bell-shaped flowers, usually in spring but sometimes in autumn, followed by winged green fruits. Larger elms such as *Ulmus pumila* are suitable as specimen trees in larger gardens. *U.* x *hollandica* 'Jacqueline Hillier' is a shrubby elm reaching only 2.5m (8ft), and is also suitable for use as hedging.

■ **HARDINESS** Fully hardy ✻✻✻.
■ **CULTIVATION** Grow in any well-drained soil in full sun or partial shade. ■ **Prune out** any crossing or misplaced branches that spoil the shape of the tree in late winter or early spring.
■ **Sow** seed (*see pp.328–329*) in containers outdoors in spring or autumn, or take softwood cuttings (*see pp.329–330*) in summer. ■ **Dutch elm disease** is a fatal and incurable problem, however the elms suggested here are partially resistant, as are Asian elms such as the Chinese elm *U. parvifolia* and its cultivars.

Ulmus pumila
‡20–30m (70–100ft) ↔12m (40ft), bears tiny, red flowers in early spring and has lance-shaped leaves

Viburnum

YEAR-ROUND

Flowers, fruits, and foliage are all valued in this large, widely varying group of evergreen, semi-evergreen, and deciduous shrubs. The flowers are pink, or pink-flushed white or cream, and in some plants intensely fragrant. They are borne in winter, spring, or summer, often in rounded clusters at the ends of the branches. The red or black berries that follow may also be ornamental; if space allows, grow several plants of the same species together to ensure good pollination and a more generous show of berries. On a species such as *Viburnum opulus* these help to attract wildlife into the garden. The foliage also provides interest. On some viburnums, the leaves are rough-textured, on others smooth and glossy, while many have striking, prominent veins. Most deciduous types colour brilliantly in autumn. Viburnums are usually grown in shrub borders or mixed borders or in woodland settings, but *V. macrocephalum* is less hardy and best grown against a sunny wall.

■ **HARDINESS** Fully hardy ✳✳✳ to frost-hardy ✳✳.
■ **CULTIVATION** Grow in any good soil that is moist but well-drained. Position in full sun or partial shade, and in areas prone to heavy frosts shelter evergreen species from cold, drying winds. ■ **Prune** deciduous species after flowering, lightly trimming shoots that spoil the shape of the shrub. Most deciduous types and *V. tinus* will tolerate hard pruning.
■ **Remove** misplaced branches or crossing shoots from evergreens in late winter or early spring to maintain a good framework. ■ **Sow** seed in containers in a cold frame in autumn (*see pp.328–329*), or propagate deciduous species by greenwood cuttings, which are taken slightly later than softwood cuttings when the stem is a little firmer and darker (*see pp.329–330*). ■ **Sooty moulds** may form on the foliage of *V. tinus* if colonized by whiteflies: control with a suitable insecticide if necessary. Remove the affected leaves of plants suffering from leaf spot.

Using viburnums in the garden

In the border Viburnums are ideal shrubs for hedging or for a mixed border, since many, such as *V. opulus*, have an attractive, naturally rounded habit that requires little or no pruning; 'Compactum' is especially neat. Others are more architectural, for instance the tiered *V. plicatum* 'Mariesii'. *V. davidii* is a useful evergreen for shade.

As a standard The evergreen *V. tinus* is suitable for training as a standard and underplanting will add interest beyond the viburnum's own flowering period. Training takes three or four years. Train the main stem to the desired height and pinch out the tip to encourage lots of new sideshoots to form the head. Keep pinching out sideshoots to keep it dense and rounded. Remove any shoots appearing on the stem to ensure all growth remains in the head.

V. acerifolium ↕1–2m (3–6ft) ↔1.2m (4ft), deciduous

V. x *bodnantense* 'Charles Lamont' ↕3m (10ft) ↔2m (6ft), deciduous

V. carlesii 'Aurora' ♀ ↕↔2m (6ft), deciduous

V. 'Chesapeake' ↕2m (6ft) ↔3m (10ft), semi-evergreen

V. x *juddii* ♀ ↕1.2m (4ft) ↔1.5m (5ft), deciduous

V. macrocephalum ↕↔5m (15ft), evergreen

V. 'Pragense' ♀ ↕↔3m (10ft), evergreen

V. rhytidophyllum ↕5m (15ft) ↔4m (12ft), semi-evergreen

V. **x** *bodnantense* **'Dawn'** ♀ ‡3m (10ft) ↔2m (6ft), deciduous

V. **x** *burkwoodii* ‡↔2.5m (8ft), evergreen

V. **x** *burkwoodii* **'Anne Russell'** ♀ ‡2m (6ft) ↔1.5m (5ft), evergreen

V. **x** *carlcephalum* ♀ ‡↔3m (10ft), deciduous

V. davidii ♀ ‡↔1–1.5m (3–5ft), evergreen

V. dentatum ‡↔3m (10ft), deciduous

V. farreri ♀ ‡3m (10ft) ↔2.5m (8ft), deciduous

V. **x** *globosum* **'Jermyns Globe'** ‡2.5m (8ft) ↔3m (10ft), evergreen

V. opulus **'Compactum'** ♀ ‡↔1.5m (5ft), deciduous

V. opulus **'Xanthocarpum'** ♀ ‡5m (15ft) ↔4m (12ft), deciduous

V. plicatum **'Mariesii'** ♀ ‡3m (10ft) ↔4m (12ft), deciduous

V. plicatum **'Pink Beauty'** ♀ ‡3m (10ft) ↔4m (12ft), deciduous

V. sargentii ‡↔3m (10ft), deciduous

V. sieboldii ‡4m (12ft) ↔6m (20ft), deciduous

V. tinus **'Eve Price'** ♀ ‡↔3m (10ft), evergreen

V. tinus **'Variegatum'** ‡↔3m (10ft), evergreen

Weigela

LATE SPRING TO EARLY SUMMER

For a showy display of flowers in spring or summer, few shrubs are more reliable than weigelas. The flowers, bell- or funnel-shaped, come in shades of ice-cream pink to ruby red and occasionally pure white or yellow. Weigelas are deciduous, and most grow to around 1.5m (5ft), making them suitable for even small backyards. They do well in almost any reasonable garden soil and can withstand neglect. If space allows, plant them with other shrubs that flower around the same time, such as potentillas (*see p.87*) or mock oranges (*Philadelphus, see p.82*). Just make sure they have room to show off their arching stems.

■ **HARDINESS** Fully hardy ✳✳✳.
■ **CULTIVATION** Grow in any fertile, well-drained soil in full sun or partial shade. Variegated types produce the best coloured foliage in full sun, golden-leaved forms in partial shade. ■ **Cut back** stems after flowering to strong buds or shoots lower down the shrub. Once plants are mature and growth is crowded, cut out an entire old branch or two, to encourage new growth from the base. ■ **Take** greenwood cuttings in early summer or semi-ripe cuttings in midsummer, or try hardwood cuttings from autumn until winter (*see pp.329–330*).

Weigela florida 'Foliis Purpureis' ♀
↕1m (3ft) ↔1.5m (5ft), low, spreading habit, tolerant of pollution, likes a warm, sunny site, flowers in late spring and early summer

Weigela 'Florida Variegata' ♀
↕↔2–2.5m (6–8ft), large but dense and bushy, tolerant of urban pollution, flowers profusely in late spring and early summer

Weigela 'Looymansii Aurea'
↕↔1.5m (5ft), slow-growing, spreading, arching habit, leaf colour is best in partial shade, flowers in late spring and early summer

Weigela 'Eva Rathke'
↕↔1.5m (5ft), compact, upright then cascading shrub, flowers open from ruby buds to pink in late spring and early summer

Yucca

YEAR-ROUND

Perhaps best known as a house plant, the yucca makes a spectacular architectural plant for the garden. Yuccas include around 40 evergreen shrubs and trees, all of which come from hot, dry deserts and plains. They usually have a stout, upright stem, and with maturity, some spread and become branched. Their sword-like leaves are produced in shades of mid- to dark green or blue-green. A few have cream or yellow edges. Towering spikes of bell-shaped, usually white flowers rise above the leaves in summer and autumn, making a dramatic focal point in a border or pot. They grow and flower particularly well in mild coastal areas. In cold, frost-prone areas, yuccas must be taken under frost-free cover for winter.

■ **HARDINESS** Fully hardy ❅❅❅ (in mild areas) to frost-tender ❦.
■ **CULTIVATION** Grow yuccas in any well-drained soil in full sun. If growing them in pots, use a loam-based compost; water freely during summer and feed with a balanced fertilizer at monthly intervals. ■ **Sow** seed in spring at 13–18°C (55–64°F) (*see pp.328–329*).
■ **Take** root cuttings in winter (*see pp.329–330*), or remove suckers in spring and replant.

Yucca gloriosa ♀ (Spanish dagger)
↕↔2m (6ft), long, blue-green leaves mature to dark green, mature plants flower in late summer ❅❅

Zauschneria

Californian fuchsia

LATE SUMMER TO AUTUMN

This exotic-looking shrub offers spectacular colour late in the season when most other plants are past their peak. Evergreen in its native California, it may die back in temperate regions, but should recover. It bears show-stopping, narrow trumpets on the tips of shoots, which appear over a long period in late summer and autumn. Californian fuchsias thrive in hot, sunny sites with sharp drainage. Rock gardens or dry stone walls are perfect. They can also be planted in a mixed or herbaceous border alongside other late-flowering shrubs and perennials, such as hardy fuchsias (*see pp.56–57*), rudbeckias (*see p.265*), asters (*see pp.162–163*), and sedums (*see p.270*).

■ **HARDINESS** Fully hardy ❅❅❅ to frost-hardy ❅❅.
■ **CULTIVATION** Grow in reasonably fertile, well-drained soil in full sun, with shelter from cold, drying winds. ■ **Protect** in winter in cold areas by spreading a layer of organic matter around the crown of the plant to shield from severe frosts. ■ **Sow** seed in a container in a cold frame in spring (*see pp.328–329*).
■ **Take** cuttings of strong young shoots from the base in spring, treat as softwood cuttings (*see pp.329–330*), and root in a propagator.

Zauschneria californica
↕to 30cm (12in) ↔50cm (20in), evergreen or semi-evergreen, clump-forming ❅❅❅ (borderline)

Zelkova

AUTUMN

These stately trees combine a distinctive, upright, then spreading habit with dark green leaves that turn to fiery shades of yellow, orange, and red in autumn. There are about six species in the group; all are deciduous and are often confused with their close relatives, the elms (*Ulmus, see p.107*). They have tiny, green flowers in spring followed by small, green fruits. Zelkovas make handsome specimens for large gardens or open spaces, or to flank wide avenues. Good companions to grow with zelkova include limes (*Tilia, see p.106*) and birches (*Betula, see p.24*). For smaller gardens, choose a dwarf cultivar of *Z. serrata*, such as 'Goblin', which makes a 1m (3ft) tall, bushy shrub.

■ **HARDINESS** Fully hardy ❅❅❅.
■ **CULTIVATION** Grow in deep, fertile soil that is moist but well-drained, in full sun or partial shade. Protect from cold, drying winds in frost-prone areas. ■ **Prune** young trees in late winter or early spring, removing any branches that are crossing or misplaced and that spoil the shape of the tree (*see p.322*).
■ **Sow** seed in containers outdoors in autumn (*see pp.328–329*). ■ **Take** softwood cuttings in summer (*see pp.329–330*).

Zelkova serrata ♀
↕to 30m (100ft) ↔18m (60ft), spreading habit, smooth grey bark peels to show orange patches beneath, rich autumn colour (*above*)

Climbing plants

Thanks to their upward mobility, climbers are extremely versatile. Use them to create scented archways or pergolas, build living screens over trellis, or train them up an obelisk to add height. They are also superb in small spaces where the only way to go is up, and you can achieve stunning effects and prolong the season of interest by simply planting two together.

Top: *Lonicera* x *americana*
From left to right: *Rosa* 'Felicité Perpétue'; *Parthenocissus henryana*;
Clematis 'Bees' Jubilee'; *Cobaea scandens*; *Parthenocissus tricuspidata*

Climbers through the year

Most climbers are perennial, but a few are annual, grown from seed each year, such as the morning glory *Ipomoea purpurea*, some species of plumbago, and black-eyed Susan (*Thunbergia alata*). In the wild, climbing plants work their way up their hosts naturally by different means. Some, like ivy (*Hedera*), have aerial roots that attach themselves to their support. Sweet peas (*Lathyrus*) and passion flowers (*Passiflora*) send out tendrils, which quickly coil around anything they touch, while others, such as clematis, have twining leaf stalks that spiral tightly around their host.

Planting climbers

Before planting climbers, take into consideration the soil and site. Bear in mind that soil at the base of a wall can be very dry so dig your planting hole at least 45cm (18in) away from the wall, incorporate plenty of organic matter to help your climber establish, and angle the plant back towards the wall. You may need to supply some initial encouragement to get tendril and twining types to travel up their supports. Usually inserting a cane next to the plant and attaching it to the support is sufficient in the early stages, tying the plant to the cane regularly until it reaches the permanent support.

Climbers in containers

Most climbing plants can be grown in containers (*see p.321*), which is particularly useful if you have only a small garden: train them against walls or fences from the pot, just as you would if they were growing in the open ground. Insert the support system right at the start, so that plants can be trained to it. You could also try growing them up obelisks or wigwams to enjoy features that can be enjoyed from every angle. Containers are also ideal for less hardy climbers like some jasmines; move the pot to a sheltered spot or greenhouse for the winter months. And keep the pots well watered throughout the year, especially during dry spells; a decorative grit or pebble mulch may help conserve moisture.

SPRING INTEREST

Thunbergia mysorensis p.131

Clematis montana var. *grandiflora* p.119

SUMMER INTEREST

Lathyrus odoratus 'Mars' p.123

Hydrangea anomala subsp *petiolaris* p.122

AUTUMN INTEREST

Vitis coignetiae p.133

Solanum rantonnetii 'Roya Robe' p.131

WINTER INTEREST

Akebia quinata p.116

Hedera helix 'Buttercup' p.121

Actinidia kolomikta
p.116

Wisteria floribunda 'Multijuga'
p.133

Gelsemium sempervirens *p.121*

Lonicera x tellmanniana
p.124

Thunbergia alata *p.131*

Rosa 'Zéphirine Drouhin' *p.129*

Trachelospermum jasminoides
p.132

Lonicera x brownii
'Dropmore Scarlet' *p.124*

Ipomoea lobata *p.122*

Passiflora 'Star of Bristol' *p.126*

Parthenocissus tricuspidata *p.126*

Plumbago auriculata *p.127*

Hedera hibernica *p.121*

Clematis tibetana *p.119*

Hedera colchica 'Dentata
Variegata' *p.121*

Hedera helix 'Little Diamond'
p.121

Actinidia

The attractions of these large, clambering plants are their deciduous foliage, and, in warm climates, their flowers and fruits. They will twine through mesh, or taut wires, on a sunny wall. The leaves of variegated actinidias look like they have been splashed with white, and sometimes pink, paint. The effect is that of huge petals, and is as pretty but much longer-lasting than a floral display. White, often scented flowers appear in early summer. These are followed by edible fruits provided that you have a self-fertile cultivar or have planted a male and a female close to each other. The crop needs plenty of sun to set and ripen. *Actinidia deliciosa*, the kiwi fruit or Chinese gooseberry, is the only species grown commercially.

■ **HARDINESS** Fully hardy ✳✳✳ to frost-hardy ✳✳.
■ **CULTIVATION** Choose a spot with fertile, well-drained soil in a sheltered position; full sun will encourage fruiting. ■ **Prune** in late winter to keep within the available space (*see p.322*).
■ **Sow** seed (*see pp.328–329*) in containers in a cold frame in spring or autumn, or take semi-ripe cuttings (*see pp.329–330*) in late summer.

Actinidia kolomikta ♀
↕5m (15ft) or more, leaves emerge purple and become striped with broad bands of pink and white as they mature ✳✳✳

Akebia

Chocolate vine

The cocoa-coloured flowers of this small group of twining, woody climbers give them their common name. They hang from the branches in long clusters through early spring and, if the summer is long and hot, are followed by impressive fruits that ripen from green to purple. In milder areas, the dark green leaves of the semi-evergreen *Akebia quinata* do not fall in winter and become tinged purple in the cool weather. Spring interest is provided by the new bronze leaves of the deciduous *A. trifoliata*. Chocolate vines are splendid plants for a pergola or archway, where the spicy fragrance of the flowers can be enjoyed fully. They can grow quite large, so provide a sturdy support.

■ **HARDINESS** Fully hardy ✳✳✳, but late frosts may damage flowers.
■ **CULTIVATION** Can be grown in any moist but well-drained soil, in sun or partial shade.
■ **Pruning** is minimal – trim back after flowering to keep it under control (*see p.323*).
■ **Sow** seed (*see pp.328–329*) in containers in a cold frame as soon as it is ripe, or take semi-ripe cuttings (*see pp.329–330*) in summer.

Akebia quinata
↕10m (30ft), the undersides of the leaves are blue-green and are evergreen in milder climates ✳✳✳

Ampelopsis

Using twisting tendrils, these handsome, deciduous climbers can cling to walls or fences or can be trained over pergolas or old trees. Ampelopsis are grown for their large leaves, which give a fiery display of colour in autumn. Variegated cultivars, such as *Ampelopsis brevipedunculata* 'Elegans' are less vigorous than the species, so suit smaller spaces, and the white and pink mottling on the leaves provides a welcome splash of colour on a dull wall. In warm areas, following the tiny, late-summer flowers, you may get masses of ornamental pink, blue, black, or orange berries.

■ **HARDINESS** Fully hardy ✳✳✳, although *A. brevipedunculata* 'Elegans' benefits from the shelter of a warm wall.
■ **CULTIVATION** Grow in any moist but well-drained soil in sun or partial shade. Fruits are more abundant in sun or if the roots are restricted in a container. ■ **Trim** vigorous plants in spring (*see p.323*), making sure that tendrils are kept clear of roof tiles and gutters.
■ **Sow** seed (*see pp.328–329*) in a cold frame in autumn, or take softwood cuttings (*see pp.329–330*) in summer.

Ampelopsis brevipedunculata
↕5m (15ft), the pink or purple berries change colour to a clear sky-blue as they ripen ✳✳✳

Berberidopsis corallina
Coral plant

This is a twining, woody perennial with long, heart-shaped leaves, but it is mainly grown for its fuchsia-like flowers that hang from the shoots like baubles through summer to early autumn. It is excellent scrambling through a tree, which will provide it with the ideal conditions of some shelter and partial shade. The snowy mespilus (*Amelanchier, see p.19*) or rowan (*Sorbus, see p.101*) make good supports since the red flowers of the coral plant bridge the gap between the spring flowers and autumn colour of the tree. Alternatively, train it against a shaded wall.

■ **HARDINESS** Frost-hardy ✳✳.
■ **CULTIVATION** Plant in neutral or acid (lime-free) soil and dig in plenty of well-rotted organic matter. Choose a shady area with shelter from cold winds and protect roots in winter with a thick mulch (*see p.326*). ■ **Tie in** young shoots to their support (*see p.321*). ■ **Trim** in late winter or early spring (*see p.323*). ■ **Sow** seed (*see pp.328–329*) in a cold frame in spring; root semi-ripe cuttings (*see pp.329–330*) in late summer; or layer shoots (*see p.330*) in autumn.

Campsis
Trumpet creeper, Trumpet vine

The only two campsis, *Campsis radicans* and *C. grandiflora*, have been crossed to produce the popular hybrid *C.* x *tagliabuana*. From late summer until autumn, they produce exotic flowers, usually in shades of yellow, orange, or red, in small clusters amongst dark green leaves. These woody-stemmed climbers cling with aerial roots, although they will need some extra support. They are impressive growing up a wall, fence, or pergola, or through a large tree.

■ **HARDINESS** Fully hardy ✳✳✳ to frost-hardy ✳✳.
■ **CULTIVATION** Grow in moist but well-drained soil. In areas with sharp frosts, they are best grown against a warm, sunny wall.
■ **Fan out** the young stems to provide good coverage of the support and cut away misplaced shoots; it may take 2–3 years to establish a main framework of branches. You will need to tie in young shoots until the aerial roots take firm hold. Once the framework is in place, prune sideshoots back to two or three buds every year, after flowering. Keep clear of roofs and gutters.
■ **Sow** seed (*see pp.328–329*) in containers in autumn or root semi-ripe cuttings in summer (*see pp.329–330*).

Celastrus
Bittersweet, Staff vine

Bittersweet comes into its own in autumn. When many other plants are starting to die down, it is beaded with yellow berries that split open when they are ripe to reveal pink or red seeds within. They follow discreet clusters of green flowers, but the males and females are on separate vines so you need more than one plant for fruit unless you choose a self-fertile cultivar. The most commonly cultivated are the woody, deciduous climbers: American bittersweet (*Celastrus scandens*) and Oriental bittersweet (*C. orbiculatus*) and its cultivars. Train them against a wall, fence, or pergola, or encourage one to scramble up through a large tree.

■ **HARDINESS** Fully hardy ✳✳✳ to frost-tender ✳✳.
■ **CULTIVATION** Prefers full sun in any well-drained soil. It needs a strong support, so if you want to grow it through a tree choose one at least 10m (30ft) tall. ■ **Prune** in late winter or early spring to keep it within its space (*see p.323*). ■ **Sow** seed (*see pp.328–329*) as soon as it is ripe or in spring, or take semi-ripe cuttings in summer (*see pp.329–330*).

Berberidopsis corallina
‡5m (15ft), widely available climber

Campsis x tagliabuana 'Madame Galen' ♀
‡10m (30ft), by far the most widely available and popular of this group of climbers ✳✳

Celastrus scandens
‡10m (30ft), bears yellow-orange fruits with red seeds ✳✳✳

Clematis

Old man's beard, Traveller's joy, Virgin's bower

LATE WINTER TO LATE SUMMER

Often known as the queen of climbers, the climbing clematis have been favourites of gardeners for many years because of their beautiful blooms. There are hundreds to choose from with varied habits, from clump-forming herbaceous plants to evergreen scramblers up to 15m (30ft) or more that will clothe large trees. Many more are less vigorous and suited to growing on fences or through shrubs. The flowers vary widely in size, shape, and hue – from large, flat blooms to small nodding bells in soft and bold shades of white, gold, orange, and blue to pinks and scarlets, often with contrasting anthers. Some, such as *Clematis tangutica*, have attractive, silky seedheads. (*See also p.180.*)

■ **HARDINESS** Hardy ✽✽✽ to half-hardy ✽✽.
■ **CULTIVATION** Clematis are divided into groups for pruning (*see below*), but other cultivation needs are similar for all types. ■ **Grow** in well cultivated soil with plenty of organic matter, in sun or partial shade. Plant deeply, with the top of the rootball 8cm (3in) below the soil surface to help overcome clematis wilt, a disease that causes the plant to die back suddenly to soil level. If this happens, the stems may shoot again from buds below the surface. ■ **Tie in** a new clematis to a cane and angle to the permanent support. ■ **Sow** seed of species when they are ripe in autumn (*see pp.328–329*) and place in a cold frame. ■ **Take** softwood cuttings in spring or semi-ripe cuttings in summer (*see pp.329–330*).

Pruning groups

Pruning group 1 This group produces flowers in spring from the previous year's growth. The flowers are usually bell-shaped or single and 2–5cm (¾–2in) long or saucer-shaped and 4–5cm (1½–2in) across. Prune after flowering to remove damaged shoots; shorten others to the allotted space. Once established, vigorous montana types need regular pruning to stop them outgrowing their space. Cut back overgrown plants hard, then leave for at least three years.

Pruning group 2 These large-flowered hybrids flower in late spring and early summer on sideshoots produced in the previous year. They are deciduous. The flowers are held upright and may be single, semi-double, or fully double, 10–20cm (4–8in) across, and are mostly saucer-shaped. In late winter or early spring, prune out any weak or damaged shoots back to their point of growth or cut out entire shoots if they are damaged.

Pruning group 3 All the clematis in this group bear flowers on the current year's wood. The large-flowered hybrids are deciduous with single, saucer-shaped flowers, 8–15cm (3–6in) across, in summer and early autumn. Species and small-flowered hybrids flower from summer to late autumn. Their blooms may be single or double, star- or bell-shaped, or tubular and 1–10cm (½–4in) across. Prune this group in late winter or early spring by cutting all the stems back to about 30cm (12in) above the ground, just above a pair of healthy buds. Make sure that any dead growth is completely cut out.

C. **'Abundance'** ♀ ‡3m (10ft) ↔1m (3ft), group 3

C. alpina ♀ ‡2–3m (6–10ft) ↔1.5m (5f group 1, fluffy seedheads

C. **'Comtesse de Bouchaud'** ♀ ‡2–3m (6–10ft) ↔1m (3ft), group 3

C. **'Doctor Ruppel'** ‡2.5m (8ft) ↔1m (3ft), group 2

C. **'Jackmanii'** ♀ ‡3m (10ft), group 3

C. **'Lasurstern'** ♀ ‡2.5m (8ft), group 2

C. **'Nelly Moser'** ♀ ‡3m (10ft), group 2, fades in full sun

C. **'Niobe'** ♀ ‡2–3m (6–10ft), group 2, fades in full sun

C. armandii ‡3–5m (10–15ft) ↔2–3m (6–10ft), group 1, evergreen ✵✵

C. 'Beauty of Worcester' ‡2.5m (8ft) ↔1m (3ft), group 2 ✵✵

C. 'Bees' Jubilee' ‡2.5m (8ft) ↔1m (3ft), group 2, partial shade

C. 'Bill MacKenzie' ♀ ‡7m (22ft) ↔2–3m (6–10ft), group 3

C. 'Etoile Violette' ♀ ‡3–5m (10–15ft) ↔1.5m (5ft), group 3

C. 'Gravetye Beauty' ‡2.5m (8ft) ↔1m (3ft), group 3

C. 'Hagley Hybrid' ‡2m (6ft) ↔1m (3ft), group 3, fades in sun

C. 'Huldine' ♀ ‡5m (15ft) ↔2m (6ft), group 3

C. 'Madame Julia Correvon' ♀ ‡3m (10ft), group 3

C. 'Minuet' ♀ ‡3m (10ft), group 3

C. montana var. *grandiflora* ♀ ‡10m (30ft), group 1

C. 'Mrs George Jackman' ♀ ‡2.5m (8ft), group 2

C. 'Paul Farges' ♀ ‡9m (28ft), group 3

C. 'Rouge Cardinal' ‡3m (10ft), group 3, prefers full sun

C. 'The President' ♀ ‡3m (10ft), group 2

C. tibetana ‡2–3m (6–10ft), group 3

Cobaea

Only the cup and saucer vine (*Cobaea scandens*) is commonly cultivated. Although a perennial climber, it is tender and so in frost-prone climates it is best used as an annual. It has rich green leaves and creamy-white, fragrant blooms that become purple as they age. Cultivars that remain white are also available. Grow this lovely plant over an arbour or an archway, where the perfume of the flowers can easily be enjoyed, or train it on a sunny wall. In colder areas, a good option is to grow a cobaea through a tree or shrub so that there is no ugly, bare support left at the end of the season. Alternatively, plant a cobaea in containers and hanging baskets and let the shoots trail attractively over the rim.

■ **HARDINESS** Frost-tender ❀, although *C. scandens* can survive cold snaps close to 0°C (32°F).
■ **CULTIVATION** Grow cobaea in well-drained soil, in a sheltered spot with full sun. ■ **Sow** seed (*see pp.328–329*) at 18°C (64°F) in spring, and plant out when the threat of frost has passed, or root softwood cuttings (*see pp.329–330*) in summer.

Cobaea scandens ♀ (Cathedral bells, Cup and saucer vine)
‡10–20m (30–70ft), less if grown as an annual

Dicentra

These climbing perennials have unusual flowers that appear on the scrambling, slender stems throughout summer. In common with the non-climbing, spreading or clump-forming dicentras, the flowers look as if they have been gently inflated. There are two commonly available climbing species: *Dicentra scandens*, which has deeply lobed, mid-green leaves, and *D. macrocapnos*, which has ferny foliage and yellow flowers into late autumn. Dicentras are excellent plants for growing up walls or fences at the back of a border, or for training through a shrub or a hedge. (*See also p.190.*)

■ **HARDINESS** Fully hardy ✳✳✳, but frost may damage early growth.
■ **CULTIVATION** Dicentras prefer moist, slightly alkaline (limy), humus-rich soil and partial shade. They are perfect for a woodland garden or other shady spot, but will tolerate more sun in reliably damp soil. ■ **Sow** seed (*see pp.328–329*) in containers in a cold frame as soon as it is ripe, or wait until spring. ■ **Slugs** (*see p.332*) may leave large holes in the leaves of dicentras, so it is worth protecting young plants against them.

Dicentra scandens
‡1m (3ft), flowers may also be white or tipped with pink ✳✳✳

Fallopia

These enthusiastic vines can grow very fast, so if you have a vast expanse of bare wall, or an ugly structure such as a shed, that needs cover quickly, they are a good choice. Before you buy, however, check that you have room to grow this rampant climber; in too small an area it will need constant pruning just to keep it under control. If you do have the space, these deciduous, woody plants have attractive leaves and, from late summer until autumn, bear large clusters of tiny, white flowers followed by pinkish-white fruits. All fallopias are vigorous but *Fallopia japonica*, also known as Japanese knotweed, is a pernicious weed. Its underground roots spread quickly, taking over your own, and your neighbour's, garden.

■ **HARDINESS** Fully hardy ✳✳✳.
■ **CULTIVATION** Grow in almost any soil, in full sun or partial shade, with a strong, long-lasting support. ■ **Trim** in early spring if it gets too big (*see p.323*). ■ **Sow** seed (*see pp.328–329*) in containers in a cold frame in spring, or as soon as it is ripe. ■ **Root** semi-ripe cuttings in summer or hardwood cuttings in autumn (*see pp.329–330*).

Fallopia baldschuanica (Mile-a-minute plant, Russian vine)
‡12m (40ft), often confused with the equally popular *F. aubertii*

Gelsemium sempervirens

Carolina jasmine, Evening trumpet, False yellow jasmine

Of these twining perennials, *Gelsemium sempervirens* is the only common ornamental. It has handsome, glossy leaves and from spring to late summer clear-yellow, perfumed flowers. In places prone to frost, it needs the protection of a warm wall, or it can be grown in a container and brought under cover in winter. In warmer areas, it is lovely climbing over a pergola or arch, beneath which you can linger to enjoy the sweet fragrance of the flowers. All parts of the plant are toxic and have been used historically as a poison.

■ **HARDINESS** Frost-tender ❀; will survive a short spell at 0°C (32°F).
■ **CULTIVATION** Grow in well-drained soil, in full sun or semi-shade, with shelter from cold, drying winds. ■ **Plant** in containers in frost-prone areas so it is easy to move under cover in winter. Use a loam-based potting compost and repot or top-dress annually.
■ **Thin out** the flowered stems when they have faded. ■ **Sow** seed (*see pp.328–329*) at 13–18°C (55–64°F) in spring, or take semi-ripe cuttings (*see pp.329–330*) in summer.

Hedera

Ivy

Ivy leaves come in many shapes and shades of green, some with bright gold or silver variegation. Young ivies creep flat against surfaces using aerial roots, but at maturity they become tree-like, with large, bushy growths high in the air. In summer, mature ivies bear tiny flowers, followed by attractive, globe-shaped heads of black, orange, or yellow berries. These woody, evergreen climbers vary hugely in size, hardiness, and shade tolerance, so there is bound to be one suited to your garden. Grow them up a wall or tree, or let them scramble as ground cover. Contrary to popular belief, ivies do not damage walls unless there are already cracks in the mortar. (*See also p.62.*)

■ **HARDINESS** Fully hardy ✳✳✳ to half-hardy ✳✳.
■ **CULTIVATION** Tolerate most soils, especially alkaline (limy), and most positions, but all grow best in fertile soil enriched with well-rotted organic matter. Green-leaved types thrive in shade; variegated cultivars prefer more light and some shelter from cold winds. ■ **Prune** to fit the available space at any time of year (*see p.322*); keep clear of roofs and gutters. ■ **Root** semi-ripe cuttings in summer (*see pp.329–330*).

Hedera hibernica ♀ (Irish ivy)
‡10m (30ft), this vigorous climber can provide fast ground cover or clothe a wall, leaves are 5–8cm (2–3in) across ✳✳✳

***Hedera helix* 'Little Diamond'**
‡30cm (12in), a tiny, slow-growing ivy, perfect for a rock garden, leaves are 4–6cm (1½–2½in) across ✳✳

Gelsemium sempervirens ♀
‡3–6m (10–20ft) ✳ (borderline)

***Hedera colchica* 'Dentata Variegata'** ♀
‡5m (15ft), use as ground cover or train up a wall, leaves are 15cm (6in) across ✳✳✳

***Hedera helix* 'Buttercup'**
‡2m (6ft), compact ivy, butter-yellow in sun – a good contrast for coppery bark, leaves 6cm (2½in) or more across ✳✳✳

Humulus
Hop
SPRING TO AUTUMN

Hops are twining, perennial climbers, with soft, hairy shoots that die down in winter. They are admired for their large, ornamental leaves, which are often patterned with white or yellow. In summer, male and female flowers are borne on separate plants; males in clusters and females in unusual spikes that resemble papery, green pine-cones. The female hop flowers are used in brewing beer, and also in fresh or dried flower arrangements. Hops are vigorous but not rampant, perfect for any area if provided with trellis, wires, or mesh to wind around, or for growing through a large shrub or small tree.

■ **HARDINESS** Fully hardy ✻✻✻.
■ **CULTIVATION** Grow in moist, well-drained soil in sun or partial shade. ■ **Root** softwood cuttings in spring (*see pp.329–330*). ■ **Cut** back dead stems in winter, or in spring in cold areas.
■ **If your hop** looks floppy, and after watering and feeding it fails to perk up, remove a little of the outer bark at the base of one of the stems. If you see brown stripes in the tissue beneath, remove the entire plant, and the soil around its roots, because it is likely to have verticillium wilt: this action will prevent the disease from spreading. If the stem seems healthy, cut it off cleanly below the wound and stay on the look-out for a possible cause.

***Humulus lupulus* 'Aureus'** ♀
(Golden hop)
↕6m (20ft), the golden leaves are brightest in full sun, fragrant flowers

Hydrangea
Climbing hydrangea
EARLY TO MIDSUMMER

The climbing hydrangeas are popular for their abundance of huge, frothy white flowers in summer. Evergreen species such as *Hydrangea seemannii* and *H. serratifolia* are only frost-hardy, but are great year-round plants, with large, leathery leaves. The deciduous *H. anomala* subsp. *petiolaris* is commonly grown in cooler areas and has the bonus of leaves that turn golden-yellow in autumn. These sturdy plants will cling, using aerial roots, to large areas of wall, fence, or even old tree stumps. Once established, climbing hydrangeas grow quickly to provide invaluable cover, particularly on a shady, north- or east-facing wall where little else can thrive. (*See also pp.64–65.*)

■ **HARDINESS** Fully hardy ✻✻✻ to frost-hardy ✻✻.
■ **CULTIVATION** Grow in any moist, well-drained soil in sun or shade. ■ **Prune** to fit space after flowering (*see p.322*). ■ **Root** softwood cuttings in early summer or hardwood cuttings in autumn (*see pp.329–330*) or layer in spring (*see p.330*). ■ **Mildew** (*see p.333*) and grey mould (botrytis) can be troublesome: cut back affected parts and dispose of the trimmings, but not onto the compost heap.

Hydrangea anomala* subsp. *petiolaris ♀
↕15m (50ft), flowerheads may reach an impressive 25cm (10in) across ✻✻✻

Ipomoea
Morning glory
SUMMER TO AUTUMN

These annuals and perennials can flower through the year in warm climates. In cooler areas, they are successful as annuals during summer, or the perennials can be grown in containers and brought under cover in winter. They are mostly fast-growing, twining climbers or trailing plants, with abundant trumpet- or tube-shaped flowers in reds and purples, and pretty whites and pinks. The mid- to deep-green leaves vary in shape. Train it through trellis in a sunny site with other climbers such as sweet peas (*Lathyrus, see facing page*) for a fine floral show.

■ **HARDINESS** Frost-tender ✿.
■ **CULTIVATION** Grow in well-drained soil in full sun with shelter from winds. ■ **Tie** young stems into their supports. ■ **Trim** perennials in spring if getting too big (*see p.323*). ■ **Sow** seed (*see pp.328–329*) singly in pots at 18°C (64°F) in spring. Chip each seed coat or soak in water for 24 hours before sowing.

Ipomoea lobata
↕2–5m (6–15ft), perennial

Ipomoea purpurea
↕3m (10ft), annual

Jasminum
Jasmine, Jessamine
SUMMER

Many of the twining, climbing jasmines are tender, but are worth growing because of their honeyed, fragrant, usually yellow or white flowers. They are lovely in any situation, although in frost-prone areas even the hardier species need the shelter of a sunny wall. In cool climates it is worth taking cuttings in case of a harsh winter; in very cold areas, grow in pots and move under cover in winter. The common jasmine (*Jasminum officinale*), *J. beesianum* and *J. x stephanense*, are quite hardy and bear heavily perfumed flowers in summer. Common jasmine is vigorous and may smother a small arch or trellis. (*See also p.67.*)

■ **HARDINESS** Frost-hardy ✳✳ to frost-tender ✿.
■ **CULTIVATION** Grow jasmines in fertile, well-drained soil in full sun, or in containers using a loam-based potting compost. ■ **Prune** *J. mesnyi* after flowering: cut back flowered shoots to two or three buds from the old wood. ■ **Thin out** the old and flowered shoots from *J. officinale*; thin other jasmines after flowering (*see p.323*).
■ **Root** semi-ripe cuttings in summer (*see p.329*).

Jasminum mesnyi ♀ (Primrose jasmine) ↕3m (10ft) ↔1–2m (3–6ft), habit is naturally that of an open shrub, but it is usually trained as a climber ✳

Lapageria rosea
Chilean bellflower
SUMMER TO LATE AUTUMN

The Chilean bellflower is a woody, twining climber, with leathery, dark green leaves. It is prized for its exotic, fleshy, raspberry-red flowers, borne in summer and late autumn. There are also luscious white and pink cultivars available. It is native to dense forest and in cultivation prefers a similarly still, shady environment. A sheltered site, close to the house for extra warmth, but away from full sun, is perfect for this climber. In cold areas, the Chilean bellflower is best grown in a container and then moved under cover in winter.

■ **HARDINESS** Frost-hardy ✳✳ (borderline).
■ **CULTIVATION** Grow in well-drained, slightly acid soil improved with plenty of well-rotted organic matter. In containers, use an ericaceous potting compost. ■ **Mulch** thickly over the rooting area through the winter (*see p.326*), especially in cool climates. ■ **Trim** over-long stems to fit the available space (*see p.323*) if needed, but leave unpruned if at all possible.
■ **Sow** seed (*see pp.328–329*) at 13–18°C (55–64°F) in spring, or root semi-ripe cuttings (*see pp.329–330*) in summer.

Lapageria rosea ♀ ↕5m (15ft)

Lathyrus odoratus
Sweet pea
SUMMER TO LATE AUTUMN

Sweet peas are prized for their showy, usually fragrant flowers in opulent shades of red, pink, mauve, blue, and white. If they are deadheaded regularly, and have the nutrients from rich soil or regular feeding, they will bloom from summer until late autumn. The climbers of this group are very versatile: they cling with tendrils that corkscrew tightly around almost any support. Train them on trellis, netting, wires, obelisks, through shrubs, or over an arch. There are other perennial peas, also with richly-coloured, sweet-smelling flowers, such as *Lathyrus latifolius*. (*See also p.226.*)

■ **HARDINESS** Fully hardy ✳✳✳ to frost-hardy ✳✳.
■ **CULTIVATION** Grow in fertile soil in sun or dappled shade. Dig well-rotted organic matter into the ground. Feed plants fortnightly (*see p.325*). ■ **Sow** seed (*see pp.328–329*) in deep, preferably bottomless, pots or sweet peas tubes in a cold frame, or in situ under cloches, in early spring. ■ **Deadhead** regularly (*see p.327*).
■ **Slugs**, snails, and aphids (*see p.332*) are common pests on sweet peas.

Lathyrus odoratus ↕2m (6ft) or more, sweetly scented ✳✳

Lonicera
Honeysuckle

A classic cottage-garden favourite, honeysuckles are valued for their delicate flowers that are often fragrant enough to perfume the entire garden. The twining climbers are especially popular. They are very adaptable and can be trained on walls, through large shrubs or trees, or used as spreading ground cover. They are particularly lovely around a seating area where the scent can be enjoyed while you relax. There are many available that produce flowers in many shades. Snowy white and double-cream are traditional, but there are exotic, rich scarlet, coral, and gold honeysuckles available. The red or black berries can cause a slight stomach upset if they are eaten. There are also shrubby species (see p.75).

■ **HARDINESS** Fully hardy ✳✳✳ to half-hardy ✳.
■ **CULTIVATION** Grow honeysuckle in any moist but well-drained soil, in full sun or preferably partial shade, ideally with the roots in shade. ■ **Prune** to fit the available space in early spring or after flowering (see p.323). The easiest way to tidy up larger specimens is to cut them with a hedgetrimmer. ■ **Sow** seed (see pp.328–329) in a cold frame as soon as it is ripe.
■ **Aphids** (see p.332) are fond of honeysuckles.

Lonicera x *brownii* 'Dropmore Scarlet'
↕4m (12ft), compact, deciduous or semi-evergreen, slightly fragrant flowers for a long period in summer, has red berries in autumn, best grown in partial shade ✳✳✳

Lonicera japonica 'Halliana' ♀
↕10m (30ft), vigorous evergreen or semi-evergreen, very fragrant flowers from late spring to late summer, red berries in autumn ✳✳✳

Lonicera x *tellmanniana*
↕5m (15ft), deciduous, flowers from late spring to midsummer, leaves are blue-white beneath ✳✳✳

Lonicera periclymenum **'Serotina'** ♀
‡7m (22ft), deciduous, very fragrant flowers in
mid- and late summer, red berries ✳✳✳

Lonicera **x** *americana*
‡7m (22ft), deciduous, very fragrant flowers
during summer and early autumn, red berries
in autumn ✳✳✳

Lophospermum
SUMMER TO AUTUMN

This small group of perennial climbers
includes evergreen and deciduous
plants. Their trumpet-shaped flowers
are produced for a long period
through the summer and autumn.
The rose-pink, or occasionally white
or purple, blooms are shown off
beautifully by the velvety, fresh-green
leaves. They cling to their support
using twining leaf-stalks, and in warm
areas are wonderful for training
through shrubs and trees, or up an
obelisk or trellis. Lophospermum will
also scramble without support as
ground cover. In temperate climates,
the tender species are best grown as
annuals, or planted in containers
and then moved under cover during
the winter months.

■ **HARDINESS** Half-hardy ✳ to
frost-tender ❄.
■ **CULTIVATION** Plant in a spot in full sun.
The soil should be moist but quite well drained:
dig some grit into the planting area to improve
drainage on heavy soils (*see p.319*). In a
container, it is a good idea to use standard
loam-based compost with added sharp sand or
grit. ■ **Propagate** with seed (*see pp.328–329*)
sown at 19–24°C (66–75°F) in spring, or root
semi-ripe cuttings (*see pp.329–330*) in summer.

Lophospermum erubescens ♀
(Creeping gloxinia, Climbing foxglove)
‡1.2–3m (4–10ft), evergreen, widely available ❄

Maurandella antirrhiniflora
Violet twining snapdragon
SUMMER TO AUTUMN

Delicate and slender-stemmed, this
twining climber is a herbaceous
perennial with lush, bright green
leaves that provide a splendid
backdrop for the main attraction: the
flowers. They are borne in abundance
throughout the summer and autumn
and are usually violet, but sometimes
purple or white. Plant twining
snapdragon so it can wind its way
through trellis, taut wires, or netting
attached to any vertical surface. It is
grown as an annual in cool climates,
but the shorter season means it does
not grow to full size; instead, combine
it with other climbers to cover a larger
area and prolong the display.

■ **HARDINESS** Half-hardy ✳.
■ **CULTIVATION** Grow in moist but
well-drained soil in light shade, or in sun with
some shade at midday. Protect from cold, drying
winds. ■ **Deadhead** twining snapdragons
regularly (*see p.327*), and if growing it as a
perennial, remove the dead top-growth at the
end of the season. ■ **Sow** seed (*see pp.328–
329*) at 13–18°C (55–64°F) in spring. Take
softwood cuttings (*see pp.329–330*) in spring
and root in a propagator.

Maurandella antirrhiniflora
‡1–2m (3–6ft), flowers have violet, purple, or
sometimes pink lobes

Parthenocissus
Virginia creeper
AUTUMN

Virginia creepers can cling strongly to almost any surface using tiny suckers at the end of their tendrils. These deciduous, woody climbers are grown for their leaves, which give a bonfire-like show of colour in autumn. The dense foliage has the added bonus of providing a home for a variety of beneficial wildlife. Tiny, summer flowers may be followed by toxic black berries. These are vigorous vines that can be trained to cover walls, fences, and any ugly garden structures, or can be used to scramble up a large tree.

■ **HARDINESS** Fully hardy ✻✻✻; *Parthenocissus henryana* is frost-hardy ✻✻ unless grown against a wall.
■ **CULTIVATION** Grow in fertile, well-drained soil in sun or shade; grow *P. henryana* in partial shade. ■ **Support** until they attach themselves (*see p.327*). ■ **Trim** in winter and summer to keep within bounds (*see p.323*). ■ **Sow** seed (*see pp.328–329*) in pots in a cold frame in autumn, or take softwood cuttings in summer or hardwood cuttings in winter (*see pp.329–330*).

Parthenocissus henryana ♀
‡10m (30ft)

Parthenocissus tricuspidata ♀
(Boston ivy)
‡20m (70ft)

Passiflora
Passion flower, Granadilla
SUMMER TO AUTUMN

Despite their tropical appearance, some of these mostly evergreen climbers, notably the blue passion flower (*Passiflora caerulea*), can be grown outdoors in cool climates. They climb using tendrils, so need the support of stretched wires, netting, trellis, or a large shrub. They are good all-round plants, with pleasing foliage, and unusual and exotic flowers through summer and autumn that are followed by edible, but not always tasty, fruits. In warm climates, they can be used in almost any situation, but in cold areas the tender species are best grown in containers and moved under cover in autumn, well before the first frosts.

■ **HARDINESS** Frost-hardy ✻✻ to frost-tender ❋; *P.* 'Amethyst', *P. manicata*, and *P.* 'Star of Bristol' may survive a frost if well-ripened.
■ **CULTIVATION** Grow in soil that is moist but well-drained, in full sun or partial shade, or in tubs of loam-based potting compost. ■ **Give shelter** from cold winds and apply a winter mulch (*see p.326*) if grown outside in cold areas. ■ **Root** semi-ripe cuttings (*see pp.329–330*) in summer or layer (*see p.330*) in spring or autumn.

***Passiflora* 'Star of Bristol'** ♀
‡to 4m (12ft), flowers from summer to autumn, bright-orange fruits ❋

***Passiflora caerulea* 'Constance Elliott'**
‡to 10m (30ft), fragrant flowers from summer to autumn, orange-yellow fruits ✻✻

Passiflora caerulea ♀ (Blue passion flower)
‡to 10m (30ft), flowers from summer to autumn, orange-yellow fruits ✻✻

Passiflora x exoniensis ♀
‡to 6m (20ft), downy, rich-green leaves, flowers in summer followed by yellow, banana-shaped fruits ❀

Passiflora 'Amethyst' ♀
‡to 4m (12ft), flowers from late summer to autumn, orange fruits ❀

Pileostegia viburnoides

LATE SUMMER TO AUTUMN

This woody climber is valued for its sprays of starry, creamy-white flowers that are borne from late summer to autumn, and its leathery, evergreen leaves that are up to 15cm (6in) long. This vigorous plant can cling to almost any surface with aerial roots, and will make short work of covering a large tree trunk, fence, or wall. *Pileostegia viburnoides* can also be grown over a sturdy pergola or arch. Use its rich-green foliage as a background for showy spring- and summer-flowering annuals such as morning glories (*Ipomoea, see p.122*) and sweet peas (*Lathyrus, see p.123*). It is also a good plant to combine with deciduous climbers such as clematis (*see pp.118–119*), as well as being invaluable for shady north- and east-facing walls.

■ **HARDINESS** Frost-hardy ✳✳✳.
■ **CULTIVATION** Grow in any soil in sun or shade. ■ **Trim** in early spring to keep it under control (*see p.323*). ■ **Root** semi-ripe cuttings (*see pp.329–330*) in summer or layer shoots (*see p.330*) in spring.

Pileostegia viburnoides ♀
‡6m (20ft), flower clusters are up to 15cm (6in) across

Plumbago
Leadwort

SUMMER TO LATE AUTUMN

Plumbago is grown for its large clusters of simple, flat flowers. There are annuals, perennials, and shrubs in the group, but the evergeen climbers are most commonly cultivated. Their bright, matt-green leaves provide the perfect foil for the sky-blue, pure white, or deep rose-pink flowers.
In mild climates, grow plumbago over a pergola or arch, or against a wall. In cool areas, where temperatures fall below 7°C (45°F), it is best grown in a container placed in a sheltered, sunny spot, and moved under cover during the cold winter months.

■ **HARDINESS** Half-hardy ✳ to frost-tender ❀.
■ **CULTIVATION** Grow in fertile, well-drained soil in full sun, or in containers of loam-based potting compost, and top-dress or repot in spring. ■ **Tie** shoots of young plants into the support as they grow to create a permanant framework. ■ **Prune** in early spring once fully established; cut back sideshoots to within two or three buds of the main branches. ■ **Sow** seed (*see pp.328–329*) at 13–18°C (55–64°F) in spring or take semi-ripe cuttings (*see pp.329–330*) in midsummer. ■ **Whitefly** may attack if the plant is grown under glass or moved under cover through winter.

Plumbago auriculata ♀ (Cape leadwort)
‡3–6m (10–20ft) ↔1–3m (3–10ft), flower clusters from summer to late autumn are up to 15cm (6in) across ✳

Rosa (climbing and rambling)

Rose

The glorious displays produced by climbing and rambling roses are one of the delights of the summer garden, but the thorny, arching stems need some form of support and, in most cases, regular tying in. Climbers tend to have stiff stems, with the flowers, often scented, carried singly or in clusters. Some have one main show of blooms on wood produced the previous year, while others flower in succession on the current season's growth. Ramblers are generally more rampant and have more flexible stems. The sometimes scented flowers are usually borne in clusters in one main flush on the previous year's growth. (See also pp.96–97.)

■ **HARDINESS** Fully hardy ✿✿✿ to frost-hardy ✿✿.
■ **CULTIVATION** Roses tolerate a wide range of conditions, but prefer fertile soil in a sunny site. Plant bare-root roses while dormant, from late autumn to early spring. Container-grown roses can be planted at any time. ■ **Water** well after planting and keep watered until established. ■ **Prune** sideshoots back to two or three buds in autumn or spring once the basic framework is established; cut one or two old stems to the base every three or four years to encourage new growth. Ramblers produce shoots from the base, so cut out one in three main stems after flowering each year. ■ **Take** hardwood cuttings (see p.330) in autumn. Plants may be affected by mildew, blackspot, or rust. If possible, choose a disease-resistant variety, improve air circulation around the plant, or spray with a suitable fungicide.

Training climbing and rambling roses

Covering an arch with a rose The arch must be strong enough to bear the weight of the numerous shoots and flowers. Check, too, that it is securely anchored into the ground. Tie in the stems as they grow, spreading them evenly over the frame. This is much easier done while the shoots are still young and flexible, especially on climbers. Deadhead faded blooms.

Training a rambler into a tree Ramblers with far-reaching stems will scramble into trees to provide a spectacular display. Check that the tree can support the mass of growth, especially if choosing a vigorous rose. Plant the rose at least 1–1.2m (3–4ft) away from the trunk, and add plenty of organic matter to the planting hole. Site the rose on the windward side so shoots are blown towards the tree, and train it into the tree up a length of rope leading from a stake at the rose's roots to a low branch. Protect the bark with a piece of rubber hose. No further training should be needed.

Growing a climber up a pillar or tripod Choose one of the less vigorous climbers to reduce the need for pruning. Keeping stems close to the horizontal encourages the development of flowering sideshoots so, where possible, train stems in a spiral around the pillar or tripod. Tie in stems as they grow, while they are still young and flexible. Prune out any unwanted or over-long stems as necessary.

R. **'Albertine'** ♀ ‡5m (15ft) ↔ 4m (12ft), rambler

R. **'Aloha'** ♀ ‡3m (10ft) ↔2.5m (8ft), climber

R. **'Climbing Iceberg'** ♀ ‡↔3m (10ft), climber

R. **'Compassion'** ♀ ‡3m (10ft) ↔2.5m (8ft), climber

R. filipes **'Kiftsgate'** ♀ ‡10m (30ft) ↔6m (20ft), rambler

R. **'Gloire de Dijon'** ‡5m (15ft) ↔4m (12ft), climber

R. **'New Dawn'** ♀ ‡3m (10ft) ↔2.5m (8ft), climber

R. **'Paul's Lemon Pillar'** ‡4m (12ft) ↔3m (10ft), climber

R. **'American Pillar'** ‡5m (15ft)
↔4m (12ft), rambler

R. *banksiae* **'Lutea'** ♀ ‡↔6m (20ft),
rambler ✻✻

R. BREATH OF LIFE ('Harquanne')
‡2.5m (8ft) ↔2.2m (7ft), climber

R. **'Chaplin's Pink Climber'**
‡5m (15ft) ↔2.5m (8ft), climber

R. **'Danse du Feu'** ‡↔2.5m (8ft),
climber

R. **'Dortmund'** ♀ ‡3m (10ft) ↔2m (6ft),
climber

R. DUBLIN BAY ('Macdub') ♀ ‡↔2.2m (7ft),
climber

R. **'Félicité Perpétue'** ♀ ‡5m (15ft)
↔4m (12ft), rambler

R. **'Golden Showers'** ♀ ‡3m (10ft)
↔2m (6ft), climber

R. HANDEL ('Macha') ♀ ‡3m (10ft) ↔2.2m
(7ft), climber

R. *laevigata* ‡2–6m (6–20ft), vigorous
rambler

R. **'Madame Grégoire Staechelin'** ♀
‡6m (20ft) ↔ 4m (12ft), climber

R. **'Pink Perpétué'** ‡3m (10ft)
↔2.5m (8ft), climber

R. **'Rosy Mantle'** ‡2.5m (8ft)
↔2m (6ft), climber

R. **'Sander's White Rambler'** ♀
‡↔4m (12ft), rambler

R. **'Zéphirine Drouhin'** ‡3m (10ft)
↔2m (6ft), thornless climber

Rubus

Rubus is a large group of climbers and shrubs that includes blackberries and raspberries. The ornamental climbers are mainly slender, prickly, or bristly evergreens and the handsome, dark green foliage is felted white on the undersides. The clusters of flat, usually pink, summer flowers are similar to those of wild roses, and are followed by glossy fruits. Some species are very vigorous, and are best reserved for wild and woodland gardens. Others are well-behaved and splendid grown with other climbers such as jasmine (*Jasminum, see p.123*). (*See also p.98.*)

■ **HARDINESS** Fully hardy ❋❋❋ to frost-hardy ❋.
■ **CULTIVATION** Grow in well-drained soil in sun or partial shade. The young stems need tying into their support regularly to keep them neat. ■ **Trim** large species only if necessary keep them in check, after flowering (*see p.323*).
■ **Root** semi-ripe cuttings of evergreens in summer or hardwood cuttings of deciduous species in early winter (*see pp.329–330*).
■ **Grey mould** can result in fuzzy, fungal growth on any part of the plant; remove affected areas promptly to prevent it spreading.

Rubus henryi* var. *bambusarum
↕6m (10ft), evergreen, white hairy shoots have sharp spines, bears black fruits in autumn ❋❋❋

Schisandra

If you have a large area to cover, then schisandras are good all-rounders with attractive flowers, foliage, and fruits. These twining, woody, usually deciduous climbers have glossy, mid-green leaves and pretty, white, or red flowers. They are borne in spring and summer, and are followed by bright bunches of pink or red berries if a male and female plant are grown together. Train them through trees, or over trellis attached to walls or fences. They can be grown with plants such as golden hops (*Humulus lupulus* 'Aureus', *see p.122*) for a spectacular colour contrast.

■ **HARDINESS** Fully hardy ❋❋❋.
■ **CULTIVATION** Grow schisandra in fertile, moist, well-drained soil in sun or partial shade.
■ **Tie in** the shoots of young plants until they begin to twine, encouraging them to form a regularly spaced framework. Once this is accomplished, maintain schisandra by cutting back sideshoots to within three or four buds of the main stems in early spring. ■ **Sow** seed (*see pp.328–329*) in pots in a cold frame when they are ripe, or root semi-ripe cuttings (*see pp.329–330*) in the summer.

Schisandra rubriflora
↕10m (30ft), vigorous species, young shoots are red, flowers in late spring and summer, fleshy fruits in autumn

Schizophragma

These woody, deciduous climbers are in the same family as hydrangeas (*see p.122*). The resemblance can be clearly seen in their huge, flat clusters of creamy-white, subtly fragrant flowers. They are borne in abundance in midsummer, against a background of dark green leaves. The foliage of some cultivars is mottled silver or edged with pink. These variegated plants provide unusual ground cover when grown without support in the dappled shade beneath deciduous trees and shrubs. Train schizophragmas up walls or large tree trunks, to which they cling strongly using aerial roots. They are very heavy when mature, so choose a suitably robust support that will not collapse under the weight.

■ **HARDINESS** Fully hardy ❋❋❋ to frost-hardy ❋❋.
■ **CULTIVATION** Grow in moist, well-drained, humus-rich soil in sun or partial shade. ■ **Tie in** the shoots of young plants to their support until the aerial roots take hold.
■ **Trim** them in spring if they outgrow their space (*see p.323*). ■ **Root** semi-ripe cuttings (*see pp.329–330*) in late summer.

Schizophragma integrifolium ♀
↕12m (40ft) ❋❋

Solanum

SPRING TO AUTUMN

This huge group of plants contains varieties that are annuals, perennials, shrubs, and trees, but the climbing solanums are especially popular. They are grown for their bell- or trumpet-shaped flowers in regal blues and purples, or pure white, from spring through to autumn. In some years, shiny berries follow. Most of the ornamental species are toxic if eaten, so take care as the fruits can be very appealing to children. Solanums need a warm, sunny wall to thrive in temperate climates. Grow them with other sun-worshippers such as jasmines (*see p.123*) and roses (*see pp.128–129*).

■ **HARDINESS** Frost-hardy ✳✳ to frost-tender ❀.
■ **CULTIVATION** Grow in well-drained soil in full sun. ■ **Mulch** (*see p.326*) over winter, particularly young plants. In cold areas, use containers of loam-based compost and move under cover in winter. ■ **Tie in** shoots regularly. ■ **Prune** sideshoots to within two or three buds of main branches in late winter (*see pp.322–323*). ■ **Sow** seed (*see pp.328–329*) at 18–20°C (64–68°F) in spring or root semi-ripe cuttings (*see pp.329–330*) in summer in a propagator.

***Solanum rantonnetii* 'Royal Robe'**
‡1–2m (3–6ft), flowers from summer to autumn ✳✳

Thunbergia

SUMMER TO AUTUMN

Valued for their abundance of exotic, brightly coloured flowers, the tropical, perennial climbers are usually grown as annuals in cool areas, or in pots and taken under cover in winter. The blooms come in shades of gold, orange, or blue, and are borne against a background of soft green leaves. Their slender, twining stems can wind round a freestanding arch or obelisk, or through a shrub. Otherwise attach trellis, wires, or netting to a fence or wall to provide a support to scramble up. Create a jewel-like display through summer by growing thunbergias with other annual climbers, such as sweet peas (*Lathyrus, see p.123*), on a single support.

■ **HARDINESS** Half-hardy ✳ to frost-tender ❀.
■ **CULTIVATION** Grow thunbergias in a reasonably sheltered site in moist, well-drained soil and full sun. In containers, use a loam-based potting compost. ■ **Train** the young plants towards their support. ■ **Trim** thunbergias grown as perennials in early spring if they are taking up too much room (*see p.323*). ■ **Sow** seed (*see pp.328–329*) at 16–18°C (61–64°F) or take semi-ripe cuttings (*see pp.329–330*) in summer.

***Thunbergia grandiflora* ♀**
(Bengal clock vine, Blue trumpet vine)
‡5–10m (15–30ft), flowers are occasionally white ❀

***Thunbergia mysorensis* ♀**
‡6m (20ft), flowers in spring ❀

Thunbergia alata (Black-eyed Susan)
‡1.5–2m (5–6ft) as an annual, 2.5m (8ft) as a perennial, flowers from summer to autumn, often raised from seed ❀

Trachelospermum

MID- TO LATE SUMMER

These woody, evergreen climbers are widely available. They are grown for their glossy, dark green leaves and immaculate white, perfumed flowers in mid- and late summer, which, on *Trachelospermum asiaticum*, age to yellow. Train them against a warm wall in frost-prone areas: trellis or taut, horizontal wires, fixed 5cm (2in) away from the wall, provide perfect support for twining stems. In very cold areas, grow trachelospermum in a container and always move under cover in winter. The mature plants can be used successfully to support spring- and summer-flowering annuals, such as tropaeolums (*see right*), to create a stunning mass of colour.

■ **HARDINESS** Frost-hardy ✵✵.
■ **CULTIVATION** Choose a spot with fertile, well-drained soil, in sun or partial shade, with shelter from cold, drying winds. ■ **Mulch** (*see p.326*) over winter, particularly young plants. For containers, use a loam-based potting compost.
■ **Trim back** long shoots of trachelospermum in spring if you find the plant is outgrowing its support (*see p.323*). ■ **Root** semi-ripe cuttings of these climbers in summer (*see pp.329–330*).

Tropaeolum

SUMMER TO AUTUMN

Climbing tropaeolums use long, twining leaf-stalks to scale fences, trellises, or pergolas. They can also scramble through shrubs, or without support grow as ground cover. In summer, they are decorated with masses of flamboyant flowers, often in glowing shades of red and yellow. Some cultivars have the bonus of variegated foliage. Many species are tender, but even the perennials can be grown successfully as annuals in cold climates. The climbing nasturtiums (*Tropaeolum majus* and some cultivars) flower best on poor soil. The leaves and flowers of annual species are edible and can be used as a tasty addition to salads. (*See also p.277.*)

■ **HARDINESS** Frost-hardy ✵✵ to frost-tender ❋.
■ **CULTIVATION** Grow these plants in moist but well-drained soil in full sun. ■ **Tie in** young stems to their support to encourage them in the right direction. ■ **Sow** seed of perennials in containers in a cold frame when ripe. Annual seed needs temperatures of 13–16°C (55–61°F) in early spring, or can be sown in situ in mid-spring (*see pp.328–329*). ■ **Blackfly** can smother shoots; pick or wash them off, or use a suitable insecticide.

***Tropaeolum tuberosum* 'Ken Aslet'** ♀
‡2–4m (6–12ft), perennial, lift tubers and store in frost-free conditions over winter (as for dahlias, *see pp.186–187*) ❋

Tropaeolum peregrinum
(Canary creeper)
‡2.5–4m (8–12ft), annual, the flowers are said to resemble flying canaries ❋

***Trachelospermum jasminoides* ♀**
(Confederate jasmine, Star jasmine)
‡9m (28ft), aging flowers remain pure white, bronze winter foliage

***Tropaeolum speciosum* ♀**
(Flame nasturtium)
‡3m (10ft), perennial, prefers acid (lime-free) soil, flowers are followed by blue berries in red, papery jackets, mulch in winter ✵✵

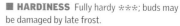

Vitis
Vine

SUMMER TO AUTUMN

The ornamental vines in this group, unlike those that are grown for grapes or to make wine, are valued for their large leaves, which turn brilliant shades of bright red or plum-purple in autumn. They do bear small, blue-black fruits, but these are usually unpalatable. Strong tendrils fasten these vigorous, woody, deciduous climbers to the nearest support. Train a vine against a wall or fence, or through a large shrub or tree. A vine also makes a handsome and practical cover for an arbour or pergola, especially over an eating area, because the leafy growth provides cool shade.

■ **HARDINESS** Fully hardy ❊❊❊.
■ **CULTIVATION** Grow vines in well-drained, neutral or slightly alkaline (limy) soil, in full sun or semi-shade. ■ **Prune** in winter and again in summer if growth needs to be restrained (*see p.323*). If your vine is more formally trained against a wall, prune sideshoots to two or three buds from the main framework in winter. ■ **Sow** seed (*see pp.328–329*) in a cold frame in autumn or spring or take hardwood cuttings (*see pp.329–330*) in winter. ■ **Mildew** (*see p.333*) can be troublesome for a vine.

Vitis coignetiae ♀
↕15m (50ft), widely available, dark green leaves are up to 30cm (12in) long (shown here with autumn colour)

Wisteria
Wistaria

SPRING TO EARLY SUMMER

The oriental elegance of wisterias ensures that they remain very popular. Before you buy, always check the stem for a healthy graft union: seedling plants (those growing on their own roots) take years to bloom and then only bear few, or no, flowers. They are very fragrant and borne in long clusters in spring or early summer and are followed by green, bean-like pods. These woody, deciduous, twining climbers can be trained over a sturdy arch or pergola so you can enjoy the perfume as you walk beneath, or against a wall. Wisterias are long-lived and can grow very large if they are on too rich a soil. Prune plants twice a year to keep them within bounds and maximize flowering. A low-maintenance option is to scramble wisteria through a large tree where it will need no pruning.

***Wisteria brachybotrys* 'Shiro-kapitan'**
↕9m (28ft) or more, foliage is softly hairy, flowers clusters to 15cm (6in) long, occasionally produces double flowers

■ **HARDINESS** Fully hardy ❊❊❊; buds may be damaged by late frost.
■ **CULTIVATION** Grow in moist but well-drained soil, in sun or semi-shade. ■ **Tie in** shoots to form a permanent framework. Keep the main stems horizontal. ■ **Trim** sideshoots in late summer to 4–6 leaves, or about 15cm (6in), from the main branches. Shorten again in winter, to 2–3 buds. ■ **Leaf spot** (*see p.333*) can be a problem.

***Wisteria floribunda* 'Alba'** ♀
↕9m (28ft) or more, flower clusters up to 60cm (24in) long open from base to tip, followed by velvety, green pods

***Wisteria floribunda* 'Multijuga'** ♀
↕9m (28ft) or more, flower clusters up to 30cm (12in) long open from base to tip, followed by velvety, green pods

Flowering plants

If shrubs and trees provide the structural backdrop to your garden, and climbing plants give height and drama, it is the flowering plants that add the detail. Whatever you favour – subtle tones, jewel bright clashes, striking architectural blooms, or small and dainty flowers – you can find the perfect fit among the wide range of plants included in this chapter.

Top: *Dahlia* 'Conway'
From left to right: *Euphorbia dulcis* 'Chameleon'; *Kniphofia* 'Bees' Sunset';
Helleborus x *hybridus*; *Hosta sieboldiana* var. *elegans*; *Aster novi-belgii* 'Marie Ballard'

Flowering plants through the year

Flowering plants are the mainstay of the garden display, providing the "understorey" of planting to complement your trees and shrubs. Most flowering plants are at their peak in summer, but plenty of them flower happily at other times of year as well.

Designing planting schemes

Before you visit the garden centre or nursery, take the time to decide which plants you want and the theme or atmosphere you aim to create. The plants you choose may be used to evoke different moods. Colour is important – more of that below – but so, too, are the texture and shape of plant leaves and stems. For instance, lots of brightly coloured small-leaved plants will help you achieve a cottage-garden effect, whereas a few plants with large leaves in cooler colours will give the garden a more contemporary feel.

To determine how many plants you'll need, it helps to find out their ultimate height and spread. You can work out how much space to leave between two plants by adding together their spreads, then dividing by two. Logically, tall plants go at the back of the border and small ones at the front, but don't be afraid to bring some tall plants forward, towards the centre; the undulating effect will break up what might otherwise have been too flat a scheme. It also introduces an element of mystery, by partly obscuring other plants.

It's fun to experiment with colour combinations, and if you change your mind, after the first season or two most plants can be moved. Create harmonious effects using different shades of similar colours or liven things up by opting for a more contrasting scheme.

Reds, yellows, and oranges are hot colours and pack a punch, while cool shades of white, blue, and purple provide a reflective atmosphere. The size of the border can also apparently change just through the use of colour. Hot reds and oranges draw the eye and make it seem shorter, while cool colours recede into the distance, creating the impression of a larger space.

SPRING INTEREST

Scilla siberica 'Spring Beauty' *p.269*

Aquilegia vulgaris 'Nora Barlow' *p.156*

SUMMER INTEREST

Inula hookeri p.221

Scabiosa 'Butterfly Blue' *p.268*

AUTUMN INTEREST

Schizostylis coccinea 'Major' *p.269*

Chrysanthemum 'Pavilion' *p.178*

WINTER INTEREST

Eranthis hyemalis p.196

Iris 'Katherine Hodgkin' *p.222*

Narcissus 'Grand Soleil d'Or' *p.241*   **Tulipa 'Queen of Night'** *p.279*   **Hesperis matronalis var. albiflora** *p.217*   **Bellis perennis** *p.166*

Paeonia lactiflora 'Festiva Maxima' *p.249*   **Nymphaea 'Fire Crest'** *p.244*   **Erigeron aureus 'Canary Bird'** *p.197*   **Gladiolus 'Elvira'** *p.210*

Tricyrtis ohsumiensis *p.276*   **Aster x frikartii 'Mönch'** *p.163*   **Colchicum speciosum 'Album'** *p.181*   **Sedum spectabile 'Brilliant'** *p.270*

Primula allionii *p.260*   **Galanthus 'Atkinsii'** *p.205*   **Hacquetia epipactis** *p.212*   **Iris unguicularis 'Mary Barnard'** *p.223*

Choosing flowering plants

There is an enormous range of non-woody or herbaceous plants. They include annuals, biennials, perennials, and bulbs, and they tolerate a wide range of soil types and differing conditions in sun or shade although some, like *Meconopsis*, require an acid (lime-free) soil.

Perennial plants

Herbaceous perennials are non-woody plants that grow and flower over several years. Some are evergreen, but with most the top-growth dies down in winter while the roots remain alive; in spring, new growth sprouts up from the base or crown of the plant. Perennial plants have astonishing variety in foliage shapes, colour, flower forms, textures, and growth habits. They range from hardy geraniums no more than 15cm (6in) tall, to stately plants like *Cephalaria gigantea*, which grows up to 2m (6ft).

Annuals and biennials

Annual plants complete their life cycle – germination, flowering, seed production, and death – within one year. Biennials take two growing seasons: they produce leafy growth in the first year and flower in the next. Biennials and many annuals withstand frost. Annuals killed by cold temperatures are described as "half hardy": wait until all danger of frost has passed before planting them out. Growing so quickly, this group can make a cheerful splash while you wait for trees and shrubs to mature.

Bulbous plants

Bulbous plants are perennials equipped with a food storage organ (a swollen part of the stem or root). This enables them to stay dormant until conditions are favourable for growth. Bulbs are generally not too fussy about soil conditions and most are very hardy. They tolerate almost any aspect except deep shade, with many preferring hot, sunny sites. Bulbs are not only for spring displays; if you choose correctly, you can have bulbs in flower for most months of the year – snowdrops in winter, tulips in spring, alliums in summer, and colchicums in autumn.

PERENNIALS

Actaea rubra p.142

Osteospermum 'Whirlygig' p.247

PERENNIALS

Eryngium x oliverianum p.198

Physalis alkekengi p.256

ANNUALS/BIENNIALS

Argemone mexicana p.158

Nicotiana 'Lime Green' p.24

BULBS

Lilium 'Enchantment' p.231

Allium unifolium p.147

Hosta 'Shade Fanfare' p.219

Helleborus x hybridus p.215

Chrysanthemum 'Pennine Oriel' p.179

Cynara cardunculus p.185

Rudbeckia laciniata 'Herbstsonne' p.265

Dodecatheon dentatum p.192

Dianthus 'Brympton Red' p.189

Phlox 'Kelly's Eye' p.255

Felicia amelloides 'Santa Anita' p.202

Anethum graveolens p.153

Silybum marianum p.272

Echium vulgare 'Blue Bedder' p.195

Dahlia 'Candy Cane' p.186

Gladiolus tristis p.211

Iris 'Eyebright' p.222

Anenome blanda 'White Splendour' p.152

Acaena
New Zealand burr

SUMMER

These low, creeping herbaceous perennials form dense mats of evergreen foliage by virtue of their rooting stems. This makes for good ground cover in a rock garden or at the front of a flower border, but plants can be invasive. In summer, the plant is covered with round flowerheads, which develop into the characteristic, spiny, red burrs for which these plants are known. New Zealand burr are valued for their colourful leaves: *Acaena caesiiglauca* has glaucous blue foliage, and *A. microphylla* 'Kupferteppich' has bronze leaves and bright red burrs. Other mat-forming plants that combine well with it are *Sedum rupestre* and *S. obtusatum*.

■ **HARDINESS** Fully hardy ✳✳✳.
■ **CULTIVATION** Grow New Zealand burr in reasonably fertile soil in full sun or part shade. If necessary, curb a spreading plant by pulling out unwanted rooted stems. ■ **Sow** seed (*see pp.328–329*) in containers in a cold frame in autumn. ■ **Make new plants** by digging up rooted stems and transplanting them to a new position, in autumn or early spring.

***Acaena saccaticupula* 'Blue Haze'**
↕10–15cm (4–6in) ↔1m (3ft), the steely grey-blue foliage lasts throughout the year and sets off the dark red burrs in summer

Acanthus
Bear's breeches

LATE SPRING TO MIDSUMMER

With their tall spikes of unusual flowers above the striking spiny, dark green foliage, acanthus make valuable architectural plants for a border. The tubular flowers, each up to 5cm (2in) long, come in combinations of white, green, yellow, pink, or purple, and are borne on spikes up to 1.2m (4ft) tall. These are produced from late spring to midsummer. Leave a few spikes on the plant over winter, since they look good when covered in frost. Acanthus are vigorous perennials and associate well with other perennials such as *phloxes* (*see p.254*) and hardy geraniums (*see pp.208–209*).

HARDINESS Fully hardy ✳✳✳ to frost-tender ✳✳.
CULTIVATION Grow in any reasonably fertile soil in sun or partial shade, although they do best in deep, fertile, well-drained loam. ■ **Remove** dead foliage and old flower spikes in late winter or early spring. ■ **Sow** seed in pots in a cold frame (*see pp.328–329*) in spring, or divide clumps in spring or autumn (*see p.330*). ■ **Take** root cuttings in winter (*see pp.329–330*). ■ **Powdery mildew** may mar leaves, but only in very dry conditions.

***Acanthus spinosus* ♀**
↕1.5m (5ft) ↔60–90cm (24–36in) ✳✳✳

Achillea
Yarrow

SUMMER TO AUTUMN

The ferny, grey-green foliage and flat-topped flowerheads of yarrows are mainstays of the cottage garden or herbaceous border. Low-growing types are ideal for rock gardens. Herbaceous perennials, yarrows quickly form spreading, drought-resistant clumps that are suited to most soil types, including chalky and gravelly soils. Their summer flowerheads, in a wide range of colours, attract beneficial insects, making them a good choice for wildflower borders.

***Achillea* 'Fanal'**
↕75cm (30in) ↔60cm (24in), the bold crimson flowerheads are ideal cutting material; a good contrast to grey or silvery plants

***Achillea filipendulina* 'Gold Plate' ♀**
↕1.2m (4ft) ↔45cm (18in), this classic variety, with golden yellow flowerheads throughout summer, is also one of the tallest

The flowerheads can be dried for indoor decoration. Grow with other herbaceous perennials such as lythrums (*see p.235*), phloxes (*see p.254*), and sidalceas (*see p.271*). Contact with the foliage may aggravate some skin allergies.

■ **HARDINESS** Fully hardy ✳✳✳.
■ **CULTIVATION** Grow in moist, but well-drained soil in an open site in full sun, although most yarrows tolerate a wide range of soils and conditions. ■ **Remove** faded flowers to encourage more to follow. ■ **Sow** seed outdoors (*see pp.328–329*) in situ, or divide clumps every 2–3 years in spring (*see p.330*) to increase stock and maintain vigour. In dry, overcrowded conditions, powdery mildew may spoil foliage.

Achillea 'Moonshine' ♀
↕↔60cm (24in), once the bright yellow flowers start to open in summer, 'Moonshine' puts on a fine display well into autumn

Achillea 'Forncett Candy'
↕85cm (34in) ↔45cm (18in), the pale pink flowerheads fade to almost white as they age

Aconitum
Aconite, Monkshood

EARLY SUMMER TO AUTUMN

Monkshoods are named for their hooded flowers, which come in shades of lilac, blue, and pale yellow. These are arranged on tall spires held well above the clumps of divided green foliage. The flowers, which appear from early summer to autumn depending on variety, attract bees and butterflies into the garden. Monkshoods are spreading herbaceous perennials, at their best in reasonably moist beds and borders where they associate well with other perennials such as achilleas (*see p.140*), hemerocallis (*see p.216*), phloxes (*see p.254*), and delphiniums (*see p.188*). The flowers are good for cutting, but take care when handling this plant because all parts are toxic if eaten and contact with the foliage may aggravate some skin allergies.

■ **HARDINESS** Fully hardy ✳✳✳.
■ **CULTIVATION** Monkshoods prefer cool, moist, fertile soil in partial shade, but most soils are tolerated, as is sun if the site is damp enough. ■ **Stake** taller monkshoods to prevent them

Aconitum 'Bressingham Spire' ♀
↕90–100cm (36–39in) ↔30cm (12in), a long-flowering plant, from midsummer to autumn, and a little shorter than many monkshoods

keeling over. ■ **Cut** down the previous year's growth in late winter or early spring. ■ **Sow** seed (*see pp.328–329*) in pots in a cold frame in spring. Divide clumps every three years in autumn or late winter to maintain vigour (*see p.330*).

Aconitum x cammarum 'Bicolor' ♀
↕to 1.2m (4ft) ↔30cm (12in), an unusual monkshood, flowers in mid- and late summer

Aconitum carmichaelii 'Arendsii' ♀
↕to 1.2m (4ft) ↔30cm (12in), flowers in early and mid-autumn

Actaea
Baneberry, Bugbane
MID-SPRING TO AUTUMN

This group of plants, which now includes those formerly known as cimicifugas, comprises a range of clump-forming perennials for woodland gardens, shady borders, or streamsides. All have attractive foliage and flowers, and in some cases fruits. Plumes or spires of small, white or pink-tinged flowers appear above the foliage from mid-spring to late summer and autumn. Varieties such as *Actaea rubra* and *A. spicata* also develop clusters of shiny white, red, or black berries, which are highly poisonous. The divided leaves are usually green, although some of the bugbanes, for instance *Actaea simplex* 'Brunette', are prized for their bronze or purple foliage. Bugbanes combine well with other perennials such as sidalceas (*see p.271*), goldenrods (*see Solidago, p.272*), and rudbeckias (*see p.265*).

■ **HARDINESS** Fully hardy ✱✱✱.
■ **CULTIVATION** Grow in moist, fertile soil, enriched with well-rotted organic matter, in partial shade. Keep well watered in dry spells.
■ **Sow** baneberry seed in containers in a cold frame in autumn (*see pp.328–329*); divide plants in spring (*see p.330*).

***Actaea simplex* Atropurpurea Group 'Brunette'** ♀
↕1–1.2m (3–4ft) ↔ 60cm (24in), fine foliage plant, has flower plumes like those of *A. simplex* (*see below left*) but tinged with pink

Actaea simplex
↕1–1.2m (3–4ft) ↔ 60cm (24in), feathery spires of flowers appear in late summer and autumn

Actaea rubra ♀
↕45cm (18in) ↔ 30cm (12in), the white flowers, as well as the red berries that follow, will enliven areas of light shade in woodland

Adonis
Pheasant's eye
LATE WINTER TO SPRING

The solitary flowers of these relatively obscure, clump-forming perennials and annuals have a delicate anemone-like appeal. Some, such as *Adonis amurensis*, appear from late winter to spring, before the fine ferny foliage has had time to develop. *A. brevistyla* and *A. vernalis* also bloom in spring and, like many flowers at this time of year, come in shades of white and yellow. These three are all perennial. Good early-flowering companions include snowdrops (*see p.205*), doronicums (*see p.193*), and cyclamens (*see p.185*). *A. aestivalis* is a charming annual that opens its red flowers in midsummer. Adonis vary in their cultivation requirements, suiting either cool, shady, woodland conditions or sunny, open sites. Check before you buy.

■ **HARDINESS** Fully hardy ✱✱✱.
■ **CULTIVATION** Grow *A. amurensis* and *A. brevistyla* in cool, humus-rich soil that is acidic (lime-free) in shade; *A. aestivalis* needs well-drained, alkaline (limy) soil in sun. ■ **Sow** seed (*see pp.328–329*) in a cold frame as soon as ripe; germination is slow. Perennial adonis do not respond well to being divided.

Adonis brevistyla
↕20–40cm (8–16in) ↔ 20cm (8in), a faint flush of blue on the outside of the petals adds to the charm of this adonis

Aegopodium podagraria
Ground elder

SUMMER

Of the five or so species of ground elder, most are invasive weeds that spread by underground stems, but the variegated cultivars of *Aegopodium podagraria* are worthy of the garden. *A. podagraria* 'Variegatum' makes a decorative ground cover, spreading over those moist, shady areas of the garden where little else will grow. The leaves are up to 10cm (4in) across. In early summer, it produces clusters of white flowers, but its main value lies in its foliage. Confining this perennial to poor soil, where other plants will not thrive, prevents it from becoming troublesome. Alternatively, grow it in an island bed on its own. Other plants that enjoy similar conditions include bergenias (*see p.167*) and hardy geraniums (*see pp.208–209*).

■ **HARDINESS** Fully hardy ✱✱✱.
■ **CULTIVATION** Can be grown in any soil, even very poor ground, in full or partial shade. Removing fading flowers before they set seed and slicing off unwanted growth with a spade help to confine its spread. ■ **Divide** rhizomes in autumn or spring (*see p.330*).

Aegopodium podagraria '**Variegatum**'
‡30–60cm (12–24in) ↔indefinite

Aethionema
Stone cress

SPRING TO EARLY SUMMER

Clusters of dainty flowers, in cheerful shades of red, pink, creamy-white, and pure white, are the main reason for growing these annuals and evergreen or semi-evergreen, woody-based perennials. The flowers are produced on short stems from spring to early summer. The leaves are small, usually stalkless, and rather fleshy. They tend to be short-lived plants and are best increased from cuttings every two or three years to make sure they perform well. As petite plants, they are obvious candidates for the front of a mixed or herbaceous border or as part of a rock garden. Try growing stone cress with dicentras (*see p.190*), *Euphorbia polychroma* (*see p.201*), and doronicums (*see p.193*).

Aethionema grandiflorum ♥
‡↔20–30cm (8–12in), perennial, flowers in late spring and early summer

■ **HARDINESS** Fully hardy ✱✱✱ (given good drainage).
■ **CULTIVATION** These plants grow best in fertile, well-drained, alkaline (limy) soil in full sun, but they also tolerate poor, acid (lime-free) soils.
■ **Sow** seed (*see pp.328–329*) in containers in a cold frame in spring; sow seed of annuals in autumn directly where they are to grow.
■ **Take** softwood cuttings (*see pp.329–330*) in late spring or early summer.

Aethionema armenum
‡↔15–20cm (6–8in), perennial, flowers in late spring

Agapanthus
African blue lily
MIDSUMMER TO EARLY AUTUMN

Vigorous and clump-forming, these large perennials bear round or pendent heads of bell-shaped flowers in deep shades of blue and violet-blue, or in white, from midsummer to early autumn. African blue lily generally have handsome, long, strappy leaves. The majority of hybrids are deciduous, while some species are evergreen. Agapanthus blooms make excellent cut-flower displays, although if they are left on the plant attractive seedheads will follow. These late-flowering perennials also look particularly good in containers.

■ **HARDINESS** Fully hardy ✳✳✳ to half-hardy ✳.
■ **CULTIVATION** Agapanthus prefer fertile, moist but well-drained soil, in full sun. Mulch them in late autumn, in cold areas, with a layer of well-rotted organic matter. ■ **Container-grown** plants are best in loam-based compost. Water them freely during summer; sparingly in winter. During summer, feed the plants with a balanced liquid fertilizer until flowering commences. *A. campanulatus* 'Albovittatus' does better under cover if winters are very cold.

■ **Sow** seed (*see pp.328–329*) when ripe or in spring. Keep the seedlings in a frost-free cold frame for their first winter. Most seedlings do not come true to type. ■ **Divide** large clumps (*see p.330*) in spring.

***Agapanthus* 'Bressingham White'**
‡90cm (36in) ↔ 60cm (24in), flowers in mid- and late summer ✳✳✳

Agapanthus campanulatus
‡60–120cm (24–48in) ↔ 45cm (18in), deciduous, grey-green leaves, flowers – sometimes white – in mid- and late summer ✳✳✳

***Agapanthus* 'Blue Giant'**
‡1.2m (4ft) ↔ 60cm (24in), flowers in mid- to late summer ✳✳✳

Agastache
MIDSUMMER TO AUTUMN

These perennials are grown for their long-lasting, loose spikes of small, tubular flowers, which are up to 30cm (12in) long and borne from midsummer until autumn. These are erect, bushy plants, with lance-shaped to oval, aromatic leaves. *Agastache* 'Tutti-frutti' has strongly aromatic foliage and pinkish-red flowers and can be grown as an annual where winters are harsh, as can the rosy-flowered *A. mexicana*. Suitable for herbaceous and mixed borders, agastaches associate well with perennials such as yarrows (*see p.140*) and phloxes (*see p.254*).

■ **HARDINESS** Fully hardy ✳✳✳ to half-hardy ✳.
■ **CULTIVATION** Grow agastache in fertile, well-drained soil in full sun. In warm areas, less hardy species survive winter conditions outside if planted in a sheltered site. In cold areas, overwinter young plants in frost-free conditions.
■ **Sow** seed (*see pp.328–329*) in early spring.
■ **Take** semi-ripe cuttings (*see pp.329–330*) in late summer. ■ **Powdery mildew** may be a problem on the leaves in dry summers; keep the soil watered, but avoid splashing the foliage.

Agastache foeniculum (Anise hyssop)
‡90–150cm (3–5ft) ↔ 30cm (12in), flowers from midsummer to early autumn ✳✳

Agrostemma
Corn cockle

At one time, the corn cockle was a weed in cornfields, but these days this delightful annual is used to bring summer colour to the garden. The purple to plum-pink or white flowers are borne on slender, downy stems, and are set off by the thin, grey-green leaves. The corn cockle's delicate, lax appearance works best in a cottage garden, wildflower meadow, or annual border – or try it in containers. Growing it with other types of hardy annual allows you to create a bright tapestry of colour. The flowers are suitable for cutting and attract bees.

■ **HARDINESS** Fully hardy ✳✳✳.
■ **CULTIVATION** Grow in poor, well-drained soil in full sun. Too fertile a soil results in leaf growth at the expense of flowers. ■ **Sow** seed in the soil in early spring or autumn where it is to grow (see pp.328–329), and thin seedlings to 23–30cm (9–12in) apart. The rather lax growth often needs staking with twiggy sticks (see p.327). ■ **Remove** fading flowers to prolong flowering of corn cockle, or leave on to allow plants to self-seed.

Agrostemma githago
‡60–90cm (24–36in) ↔30m (12in), one of several varieties grown from seed, the flowers measure up to 5cm (2in) across

Ajuga
Bugle

Bugles make excellent ground cover in the shade or partial shade, particularly in moist ground. They have a dense, spreading habit and can carpet large areas quickly, yet are easy to pull up if they start to grow into other plants. A few are annuals but, for the most part, those grown in gardens are evergreen or semi-evergreen perennials. The leaves of some bugles have a metallic sheen, but for added colour, choose those that are tinted bronze or purple-red, or splashed with cream and pink. From late spring until early summer, the mats of foliage are studded with short spikes of usually blue or mauve flowers. Undemanding and easy to grow, bugles are a good choice for the edge of a shady border or for growing under shrubs.

■ **HARDINESS** Fully hardy ✳✳✳.
■ **CULTIVATION** Grow bugle in any moist but well-drained soil in partial shade or, for good leaf colour, sun. *Ajuga reptans* and its cultivars tolerate poor soils and full shade.

■ **Separate** rooted stems to make new plants, or take softwood cuttings in early summer (see pp.329–330). ■ **Powdery mildew** may spoil the leaves in overcrowded, dry condition. After flowering, remove old flower stems and excess growth to avoid it.

Ajuga reptans 'Multicolor'
‡15cm (6in) ↔60–90cm (24–36in), evergreen, will tolerate full shade but needs sun to bring out the lovely colours in its leaves

Ajuga reptans 'Atropurpurea'
‡15cm (6in) ↔60–90cm (24–36in), the lustrous evergreen leaves look particularly effective with shade-loving primroses (*Primula*)

Ajuga reptans 'Catlin's Giant' ♀
‡15cm (6in) ↔60–90cm (24–36in), the dark blue flowerheads are up to 20cm (8in) tall on this large-leaved, evergreen

Alcea
Hollyhock
`SUMMER`

An old-fashioned, cottage garden favourite, hollyhocks are short-lived perennials or biennials. The tall, showy spires of flowers, up to 2.5m (8ft) tall, come in a variety of shades including shell pink, apricot, lemon, cerise, white, and purplish-black. The flowers, especially if single, are attractive to butterflies and bees. At their most impressive when grown at the back of a border or along a wall or fence, hollyhocks associate well with cottage garden favourites with soft colours and billowing outlines, such as rambling roses (*see pp.128–129*) and lilacs (*see Syringa, p.104*). Mix the brightest types with delphiniums (*see p.188*).

■ **HARDINESS** Fully hardy ✳✳✳.
■ **CULTIVATION** Grow in reasonably fertile, well-drained soil in full sun. In exposed places, stems may require staking. Treat as annuals or biennials (sow one year to flower the next year) to limit the spread of hollyhock rust, the most common disease, which causes orange-brown pustules on the leaves. Rust-resistant varieties are available and fungicides may be used.
■ **Sow** seed (*see pp.328–329*) of annuals at 13°C (55°F) in late winter or where it is to grow in spring. For biennials, sow in midsummer where plants are to flower and thin out or transplant seedlings, as necessary, in autumn.

Alcea rosea Chater's Double Group
↕2–2.5m (6–8ft) ↔ to 60cm (24in), vigorous, flowers in many bright or pale shades

Alcea rosea 'Nigra'
↕to 2m (6ft) ↔ to 60cm (24in)

Alchemilla
Lady's mantle
`EARLY SUMMER TO EARLY AUTUMN`

The most widely grown plant in this group of perennials, all with greyish-green leaves and frothy, luminous yellow flowers, is *Alchemilla mollis*. Drought tolerant and clump-forming, it makes excellent ground cover. The flowers appear for long periods from early summer and are good for cutting, and for drying. Most other alchemillas, such as *A. erythropoda*, are smaller. Lady's mantle self-seeds prolifically unless fading flowers are removed before they set seed. Grow it in beds and borders or along paths to soften hard lines. Alchemilla associates especially well with shrub roses (*see pp.96–97*) and penstemons (*see p.252*), and contrasts beautifully with blue flowers.

■ **HARDINESS** Fully hardy ✳✳✳ to frost-hardy ✳✳.
■ **CULTIVATION** Grow in any reasonably fertile soil in sun or partial shade. ■ **Deadhead** *A. mollis* and cut back foliage after flowering for fresh leaves. ■ **Sow** seed (*see pp.328–329*) in pots in a cold frame in spring, or divide (*see p.330*) in early spring or autumn.

Alchemilla mollis ♀
↕60cm (24in) ↔75cm (30in), velvety grey-green leaves and yellow-green flowers from early summer to early autumn ✳✳✳

Allium
Ornamental onion

These distinctive, bulbous perennials bear dramatic, round, or pendent clusters of bell- or star-shaped flowers in spring and summer. Some of these are up to 30cm (12in) across; some dry well for use in winter flower arrangements. Alliums range in size from small, rock-garden species to 2m (6ft) giants, but most plants are 30–90cm (1–3ft) tall. Show off their bold flowerheads in borders, among other flowering perennials, or through a drift of grasses. Chives (*Allium schoenoprasum*) and *A. cernuum* are good edging plants. Alliums include the edible onions, and so the strappy or cylindrical foliage has a pungent onion aroma when crushed; it often withers before the flowerheads open.

■ **HARDINESS** Fully hardy ✳✳✳ to frost-hardy ✳✳.
■ **CULTIVATION** Grow in fertile, well-drained soil in full sun. ■ **Plant** bulbs to two or three times their own depth in autumn. ■ **Remove** offsets of bulbs in autumn and divide clumps (*see p.330*) in spring. ■ **Downy mildew**, an off-white fungus, may cause leaves to wither and rot into the bulbs in damp conditions; space plants farther apart and use fungicide. Dig up and destroy any bulbs that are attacked by onion fly maggots.

Allium cristophii ♀
‡30–60cm (12–24in) ↔15–19cm (6–7in), flowerheads to 20cm (8in) across in early summer, grey-green basal leaves ✳✳

Allium karataviense ♀
‡10–25cm (4–10in) ↔10cm (4in), broad, flat leaves, purple- or grey-green with red edges, medium flowerheads in summer ✳✳✳

Allium 'Globemaster' ♀
‡80cm (32in) ↔20cm (8in), grey-green basal leaves, dramatic flowerheads to 15–20cm (6–8in) across in summer ✳✳✳

Allium unifolium ♀
‡30cm (12in) ↔5cm (2in), short, grey-green basal leaves that die before small flowerheads appear in spring ✳✳

Allium cernuum (Nodding onion, Wild onion)
‡30–60cm (12–24in) ↔5cm (2in), vigorous, narrow dark green leaves and stiff stems, mid- to deep pink flowers in summer ✳✳✳

Allium moly (Golden garlic)
‡15–25cm (6–10in) ↔5cm (2in), grey-green flat leaves, medium-sized flowerheads in summer, naturalizes rapidly into drifts ✳✳✳

Alstroemeria
Peruvian lily

SUMMER

Widely grown for cut flowers, these vigorous, tuberous perennials are stalwarts of many a mixed and herbaceous border. The flowers appear in summer, usually in small clusters at the ends of the stems; they are available in such a wide range of shades that there is bound to be one to suit virtually any colour scheme. The long, strappy leaves are mid- to grey-green. Try growing alstroemerias combined with sunflowers (*see Helianthus, p.214*), shrub roses (*see pp.96–97*), and border phloxes (*see pp.254–255*).

■ **HARDINESS** Hardy to -10°C (14°F) ✳✳: *Alstroemeria aurea* and *A. ligtu* hybrids withstand brief periods as low as -15°C (5°F).
■ **CULTIVATION** Alstroemerias like moist but well-drained soil, in sun or partial shade.
■ **Plant** the long tubers 20cm (8in) deep in late summer or early autumn, and handle them carefully, because they break easily. The plants resent being disturbed, so leave them to form large clumps. ■ **Protect** them with a dry mulch of organic matter in winter (*see p.326*).
■ **Sow** seed (*see pp.328–329*) in a container in a cold frame when it is ripe; transplant seedlings to small pots; and plant out from the pots to avoid root disturbance. ■ **Divide** large, established clumps (*see p.330*) in autumn or early spring, if needed. ■ **Slugs** can attack (*see p.332*); remove and destroy plants infected by viruses (*see p.333*).

Alstroemeria aurea
↕1m (3ft) ↔ 45cm (18in)

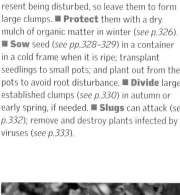

Alstroemeria ligtu hybrids
↕50cm (20in) ↔ 75cm (20in)

Alstroemeria pelegrina
↕↔ to 60cm (24in)

Alstroemeria psittacina
↕1m (3ft) ↔ 45cm (18in)

Althaea

MIDSUMMER TO EARLY AUTUMN

These woody-based perennials and annuals are similar to hollyhocks (*see Alcea, p.146*), but they have smaller flowers which, unlike hollyhocks, are on stalks. The blooms appear from midsummer until early autumn in shades of lilac, deep pink, or rose-pink, sometimes with darker eyes. Althaeas have dark green leaves with lobed or toothed edges and pale undersides. The stems are strong and wiry and rarely need supporting. These are pretty plants for a mixed or herbaceous border as well as a wildflower garden. Grow them with other summer-flowering perennials, like daylilies (*see Hemerocallis, p.216*) and loosestrife (*see Lysimachia, p.235*).

■ **HARDINESS** Fully hardy ✳✳✳.
■ **CULTIVATION** These plants tolerate a range of conditions, but do best in fertile, moist but well-drained soil. ■ **Sow** seed of perennials in rows outdoors (*see pp.328–329*) in midsummer and transplant seedlings in early autumn; for annual althaeas, sow seed in pots in late winter, or directly in the ground in mid-spring.
■ **Rust**, orange-brown pustules, may afflict the leaves; pick them off and destroy them.

Althaea cannabina
↕2m (6ft) ↔ 60cm (24in), perennial

Alyssum

Low masses of brightly colourful flowers make this large group of tufted or mat-forming, evergreen perennials, and sometimes erect annuals, prized in the garden. The flowers open in early summer, in shades of pale and golden-yellow, pale to deep rose-pink, or white, and are occasionally honey-scented. The small leaves form rosettes and are coloured grey to silvery-grey, sometimes with white hairs. Alyssums are spreading, although never invasive, so can be put to many uses. Try them at the front of a border or in a rock garden. They look very effective when planted with other carpeting plants, for example *Arabis* x *arendsii* 'Rosabella', which has rose-pink flowers.

■ **HARDINESS** Fully hardy ✳✳✳.
■ **CULTIVATION** Grow the plants in well-drained, reasonably fertile soil with added grit, in full sun. A light trim after flowering maintains a compact shape. ■ **Sow** seed (*see pp.328–329*) in a container in autumn or spring. ■ **Root** greenwood cuttings – new shoots that are beginning to firm up – as for soft stem-tip cuttings, in early summer (*see pp.329–330*).

Alyssum wulfenianum
‡10–15cm (4–6in) ↔ to 50cm (20in), erect or prostrate evergreen

x Amarygia parkeri

The parents of this hybrid are *Amaryllis belladonna* (*see right*) and *Brunsvigia*. Opening on bare, stout stems before the leaves appear, its large, pink or white flowers make an eye-catching addition to the summer garden. The leaves, which are up to an impressive 45cm (18in) long and grow from the base of the plant, are semi-erect and strappy. In colder areas, the plant benefits from the shelter at the foot of a warm wall, or in an herbaceous or mixed border. Grow it with other bulbous perennials, such as crinums (*see p.184*), and perennials such as achilleas (*see p.140*).

■ **HARDINESS** Frost-hardy ✳✳
■ **CULTIVATION** Plant bulbs from early to late summer with the necks just above soil level, in full sun in sandy soil that has been enriched with well-rotted organic matter. ■ **Water** freely during summer and feed monthly with a well-balanced fertilizer. ■ **Remove** offsets to replant (*see p.330*) from congested plants just before they come into growth in summer. The leaves of x *Amarygia parkeri* are prone to scorch. If flowers fail, eelworms and bulb flies may have eaten the bulb; dig up and discard affected plants.

x Amarygia parkeri 'Alba'
‡1m (3ft) ↔30cm (12in)

Amaryllis belladonna

Stately, scented, and showy, the clusters of flowers of this bulbous perennial open on stout stems in the autumn. It has strappy, fleshy leaves, up to 40cm (16in) long, produced after the flowers open. In warmer areas where frosts are rare, grow it at the base of a sunny, sheltered wall. Where winter temperatures regularly fall below –5°C (23°F), this plant is best grown in a cool greenhouse or in a conservatory. *Amaryllis belladonna* looks attractive partnered with other autumn-flowering bulbs and plants, such as crocuses (*see Colchicum, p.181*) and coneflowers (*see Rudbeckia, p.265*).

■ **HARDINESS** Frost-hardy ✳✳.
■ **CULTIVATION** Plant the bulbs just below soil or compost level when they are dormant, in late summer or in spring. ■ **Outdoors**, grow in reasonably fertile, well-drained soil in full sun and protect foliage from frost. ■ **Indoors**, they need a loam-based compost with additional sharp sand or grit, and full light. In the growing season, water well and feed at monthly intervals with a balanced fertilizer. ■ **Remove** offsets (*see p.330*) in spring and grow indoors for 1–2 seasons before planting. Amaryllis are prone to slug damage (*see p.332*).

Amaryllis belladonna ♀
‡60cm (24in) ↔10cm (4in), each flower is up to 10cm across

Anacyclus

SUMMER

Appealing, daisy flowers and feathery foliage are the attractions of these creeping, low-growing annuals and herbaceous perennials. The flowers, which are usually white with yellow centres, are borne on short stems in summer, held just above a low mound of foliage; the leaves are finely cut and attractive in their own right. Anacyclus hate cold, wet conditions, and are most suited to growing in a rock garden, raised bed, or alpine trough; a top-dressing of grit over the soil will help keep their stems dry, and also enhances their sun-loving, Mediterranean look.

■ **HARDINESS** Frost-hardy ✳✳, but can withstand to -5°C (23°F) if protected from winter wet.
■ **CULTIVATION** Grow in gritty, sharply drained soil in full sun, with shelter from the worst winter rains if possible. If growing in containers, use a mix of equal parts loam-based compost, leafmould, and sharp sand or grit.
■ **Sow** seed in an open frame in autumn (*see pp.328–329*). ■ **Take** softwood cuttings in spring or early summer (*see pp.329–330*).

Anacyclus pyrethrum* var. *depressus
‡2.5–5cm (1–2in) or more ↔10cm (4in), perennial, leaves grey-green, solitary flowers on short, slender stems, petals red on reverse

Anagallis
Pimpernel

LATE SPRING TO SUMMER

The deep blue or deep pink flowers of these annuals and evergreen perennials are produced in late spring and summer, and are borne in such profusion that they almost completely hide the leaves. The flowers are open and saucer-shaped. Pimpernels are low-growing or mat-forming, with branching stems and mid-green leaves. The largest grow to only around 25cm (10in) tall, and look good in a rock garden or at the front of a border. Tiny varieties like *Anagallis tenella* 'Studland' are ideal plants for shallow pots and bowls.

■ **HARDINESS** Fully hardy ✳✳✳ to frost-hardy ✳✳.
■ **CULTIVATION** Grow pimpernels in fertile, moist, but well-drained soil or gritty compost, in full sun. Pimpernels are short-lived so it is best to propagate them every three or four years. ■ **Divide** in spring (*see p.330*). ■ **Sow** pimpernel seed in a container in a cold frame in spring (*see pp.328–329*). ■ **Take** stem-tip cuttings of named varieties in spring or early summer (*see pp.329–330*). Overwinter young plants in a frost-free greenhouse or conservatory and plant out only when any danger of frost has passed.

Anagallis monellii ♀ (Blue pimpernel)
‡10–20cm (4–8in) ↔to 40cm (16in), perennial, red- and pink-flowered forms are available ✳✳

Anaphalis
Pearl everlasting

MIDSUMMER TO AUTUMN

These medium-height, spreading or upright perennials have woolly, grey foliage, and clusters of papery, "everlasting" white flowers, produced from midsummer until autumn and very popular for cutting and drying. The smaller varieties suit a rock garden; grow the more upright varieties in a border. They are ideal for a white-themed scheme, since the flowers and silvery foliage provide several months of colour. Pearl everlasting is also useful in locations that are too moist for growing other grey- or silver-leaved foliage plants that prefer better-drained soils. To dry the flowers, cut them soon after they are open and hang upside down in bunches in a light, airy place.

■ **HARDINESS** Fully hardy ✳✳✳.
■ **CULTIVATION** Grow in reasonably fertile soil that is fairly well-drained, but does not dry out during hot spells in summer. They prefer full sun, but will tolerate partial shade.
■ **Divide** plants in early spring (*see p.330*).
■ **Sow** seed in a container in a cold frame in spring (*see pp.328–329*). ■ **Take** stem-tip cuttings in early summer (*see pp.329–330*).

Anaphalis margaritacea
‡↔60cm (24in), flowers midsummer to early autumn

Anchusa
Alkanet

SPRING TO EARLY SUMMER

The small but numerous flowers are produced in spring and early summer on stems that are upright in taller cultivars or prostrate in the dwarf, mound-forming types, in shades of indigo, clear gentian blue, or ultramarine, some with a white centre. Bees love them. The leaves are long and thin, coarse, and often bristly. Alkanets may be annual, biennial, or perennial. The taller ones give a vivid accent to a herbaceous or mixed border. Dwarfer types, such as *Anchusa cespitosa*, bring jewel-like brilliance to a rock garden or alpine trough.

■ **HARDINESS** Fully hardy ✲✲✲ to frost-hardy ✲✲.
■ **CULTIVATION** Grow in moist, moderately fertile, well-drained soil in full sun. Most resent excessive winter wet and dwarf types must have free-draining soil, or gritty compost. ■ **Stake** taller anchusas (*see p.330*). ■ **Deadhead** after the first flush of flowers to encourage more later on. ■ **Cut back** top-growth after flowering to encourage new growth that will overwinter.
■ **Sow** seed in a container in a cold frame in spring (*pp.328–329*). ■ **Take** basal cuttings in spring (*see pp.329–330*). ■ **Mildew** (*see pp.333*) can be a problem.

***Anchusa azurea* 'Loddon Royalist'** ♀
‡90cm (36in) ↔ 60cm (24in), perennial, forms compact, densely flowering clumps, rarely needs staking, flowers in early summer ✲✲✲

Androsace
Rock jasmine

LATE SPRING TO LATE SUMMER

These pretty perennials make dense cushions or mats of evergreen foliage that is smothered in small pink or white flowers. The flowers are tubular and appear singly or in clusters from late spring to late summer. The cushion-forming species from high mountainous regions are ideal for an alpine house (an unheated, well-ventilated greenhouse) where they are easily protected from winter wet. The rest, however, are suitable for rock gardens, dry-stone walls, and alpine troughs, and look good with other cushion-forming plants such as saxifrages (*see p.267*).

■ **HARDINESS** Fully hardy ✲✲✲.
■ **CULTIVATION** Grow in vertical crevices in walls in moist, well-drained soil in full sun. In containers, use a loam-based compost with extra grit, and add grit at the base of planting holes to improve drainage. ■ **Top-dress** the soil surface with grit (*see p.325*) to protect plants from wet, which causes fungal disease.
■ **Sow** seed in a cold frame when ripe or in autumn (*see pp.328–329*). Take single rosettes as cuttings in early to midsummer; water from below to avoid wetting the rosettes.

Androsace carnea* subsp. *laggeri ♀
‡5cm (2in) ↔ 30cm (12in)

Androsace lanuginosa ♀
‡to 10cm (4in) ↔ 30cm (12in)

Androsace pyrenaica
‡4–5cm (1½–2in) ↔ 30cm (12in)

Androsace villosa* var. *jacquemontii
‡to 4cm (1½in) ↔ 30cm (12in)

Anemone
Windflower

This large and versatile group of perennials has delightful flowers from spring to autumn, and displays a wide range of habits, sizes, and tolerance for different situations. The flowers vary from pink, blue, and violet to red and yellow. They are usually saucer- to cup-shaped with a central boss of stamens and are either solitary or in clusters. Leaves are mid- to dark green with toothed edges. Anemones are divided into three main groups: spring-flowering types, growing in woodland and pastures, some with tubers or rhizomes; tuberous Mediterranean species, flowering in spring or early summer; and larger, tall herbaceous perennials, flowering in late summer and autumn.

■ **HARDINESS** Fully hardy ✳✳✳ to half-hardy ✳.
■ **CULTIVATION** Grow in moist, well-drained soil in sun or partial shade. ■ **Plant** windflowers in autumn or spring and mulch with well-rotted organic matter (*see p.325*) for winter protection. ■ **Sow** seed (*see pp.328–329*) in containers in a cold frame when ripe; germination may be slow and erratic. ■ **Divide** (*see p.330*) autumn-flowering anemones in autumn or spring. Separate tubers of tuberous species in summer when dormant. ■ **Powdery mildew** (*see p.333*) can disfigure foliage.

Anemone blanda 'White Splendour' ♀
↕↔15cm (6in), like 'Radar' (*see below*) in every respect, apart from its white flowers, which can be breathtaking if planted en masse ✳✳✳

Anemone x hybrida 'Max Vogel'
(Japanese anemone)
↕1.2–1.5m (4–5ft) ↔indefinite, prefers moist, humus-rich soil, in sun or light shade, and will flower from late summer to mid-autumn

Anemone pavonina
↕25cm (10in) ↔15cm (10in), tuberous anemone with red, pink, or purple flowers in spring; it needs sun and good drainage ✳✳✳

Anemone blanda var. rosea 'Radar' ♀
↕↔15cm (6in), grows from knobbly tubers and prefers sun or partial shade and well-drained soil; it flowers in spring ✳✳✳

Anethum graveolens
Dill

The aromatic green and blue-green foliage of dill is its distinctive feature, complemented in midsummer by its flattened clusters of greenish-yellow flowers. Dill is annual or biennial and has hollow, ridged stems and aniseed-scented leaves that are finely divided into thread-like leaflets. The seeds and leaves have many culinary uses. Dill looks at its best grown with other herbs, but the fine, ferny foliage also acts as a wonderful contrast to perennials with bolder leaves such as hostas (*see pp.218–219*). The dwarf *Anethum graveolens* 'Fern Leaved' grows to only 45cm (18in) and is suitable for pots on a windowsill.

■ **HARDINESS** Fully hardy ✽✽✽.
■ **CULTIVATION** Grow in fertile, well-drained soil in full sun with shelter from strong, cold winds.
■ **Water** freely during dry spells in summer to prevent it running to seed. ■ **Sow** seed (*see pp.328–329*) from spring to midsummer for a succession of fresh foliage. Young plants do not transplant well so thin seedlings to 10cm (4in) apart. If you have little space, sow a pinch of seed in a large pot and grow on the patio.

Angelica

Angelicas bring both height and drama to a garden. Clump-forming perennials and biennials, their majestic stems are topped with umbrella-shaped flower clusters, followed by attractive seedheads. The flowers are lime yellow on *Angelica archangelica* and open in early summer; those of *A. gigas* appear in late summer and, like the stems, are a striking red-purple. Grow these architectural plants in borders, or as specimens in a woodland setting. They also thrive in damp soil along streams or pond edges.

■ **HARDINESS** Fully hardy ✽✽✽.
■ **CULTIVATION** Grow in deep, moist, fertile soil in full sun or partial shade. *Angelica archangelica* dies after flowering, but if the fading flowers are cut off before the seedheads form, it may survive and flower for a second year. It may also self-seed freely. ■ **Sow** seed (*see pp.328–329*) in a container in a cold frame as soon as it is ripe; do not cover with compost or grit, as it needs light to germinate.
■ **Transplant** the seedlings while they are small since larger plants resent root disturbance. Angelica will take around two years to flower from seed. ■ **Slugs** and snails may be troublesome (*see p.332*).

Anomatheca

Closely related to freesias, this small group of perennials bears delicate flowers in shades of red, green, and pure white. These appear in late spring and early summer and are followed by brown seedheads containing scarlet seeds. Anomathecas grow from corms and, like freesias, in climates subject to winter frosts, are best grown in a container in an unheated or cool greenhouse or conservatory. In frost-free regions, plant them at the front of a sheltered border; they make splendid companions for late-flowering tulips.

■ **HARDINESS** Half-hardy ✽, but will withstand occasional temperatures down to -5°C (23°F).
■ **CULTIVATION** Plant corms in spring 5cm (2in) deep in free-draining, sandy, reasonably fertile soil, in full sun. If growing in containers, use a loam-based compost.
■ **Water** well and feed with a balanced fertilizer at monthly intervals during the growing season. Keep the corms completely dry while dormant.
■ **Divide** clumps in spring, as necessary (*see p.330*). ■ **Sow** seed (*see pp.328–329*) at 13–16°C (55–61°F) in spring, but allow up to two years for the seedlings to flower.

Anethum graveolens
‡60cm (24in) or more ↔30cm (12in)

Angelica archangelica
‡2m (6ft) ↔1.2m (4ft), the leaf stalks of this aromatic herb can be candied for use in sweets and cake decoration

Anomatheca laxa ♀
‡15–30cm (6–12in) ↔5m (2in), each corm produces up to six flowers in early summer

Anthemis

LATE SPRING TO LATE SUMMER

Aromatic foliage and daisy flowers are the chief attributes of these clump-forming and mat-forming perennials. The golden-eyed, yellow or white flowers are produced in succession from late spring until late summer and are excellent for cutting. Anthemis enjoy sunny, well-drained conditions, the smaller types such as *A. punctata* making good plants for a rock garden. In borders, their finely cut foliage can look effective next to other filigree-leaved plants such as artemisias (*see p.21 and p.159*) and argyranthemums (*see p.21*). Alternatively, contrast anthemis with bold, sword-leaved plants such as irises (*see pp.222–223*) and yuccas (*see p.111*).

■ **HARDINESS** Fully hardy ✽✽✽ to frost-hardy ✽✽.
■ **CULTIVATION** Grow in reasonably fertile, well-drained soil in full sun. *Anthemis sancti-johannis* and *A. tinctoria* are short-lived plants. ■ **Cut back** hard, to the new shoots at the base, after flowering to encourage new growth and increase longevity. ■ **Sow** seed (*see pp.328–329*) in pots in a cold frame in spring. ■ **Divide** in spring (*see p.330*) to make new plants or take basal cuttings in spring or late summer (*see pp.329–330*).

Anthemis sancti-johannis
‡60–90cm (24–36in) ↔ 60m (24in), a short-lived but free-flowering plant, best supported with twiggy sticks in exposed sites ✽✽✽

***Anthemis tinctoria* 'E.C. Buxton'**
‡45–70cm (18–28in) ↔ 60–90m (24–36in), flowers are produced in abundance all summer, if deadheaded regularly ✽✽✽

Anthericum

LATE SPRING TO EARLY SUMMER

With graceful, narrow leaves to 40cm (16in) long, these rhizomatous perennials are ideal for naturalizing in grass. In late spring and early summer, the clumps of mid- or grey-green leaves produce delicate, lily-like, white flowers in small clusters on slender stems. The flowers are at their largest, up to 3cm (1¼in) across, in *Anthericum liliago* 'Major'. In autumn, these are followed by decorative brown seedheads. Anthericums are excellent naturalized with other wild flowers, or in a herbaceous or mixed border. They look good alongside early summer-flowering oriental poppies (*see Papaver, p.249*). The flowers are also good for cutting.

■ **HARDINESS** Fully hardy ✽✽✽ to frost-hardy ✽✽.
■ **CULTIVATION** Grow in any fertile, well-drained soil in full sun. ■ **Sow** seed (*see pp.328–329*) in a container in a cold frame in autumn or spring. Seedlings may take up to three years to flower. Alternatively, increase stock by dividing (*see p.330*) in spring as growth begins, although the new plants may not flower until the following year.

Anthericum liliago (St Bernard's lily)
‡60–90m (24–36in) ↔ 30m (12in), this is a versatile plant for naturalistic and sophisticated schemes ✽✽✽

Anthriscus

MID-SPRING TO EARLY SUMMER

The dainty flowerheads and lacy foliage of *Anthriscus sylvestris*, better known as cow parsley, introduce an airy, natural charm into the garden from mid-spring until early summer. This is the most commonly grown ornamental of the various annual, biennial, and perennial types of anthriscus, although *A. cerefolium*, chervil, is an invaluable aniseed-flavoured herb. Cow parsley's tiny, white or creamy-white flowers are followed by flat seedheads. The dark-leaved *A. sylvestris* 'Ravenswing' has flowerheads with a tinge of pink. Cow parsley, usually biennial, but sometimes a short-lived perennial, is at home in meadow-style plantings. In the herbaceous border, team it with spiky-flowered stachys (*see p.273*), veronicas (*p.281*), or salvias (*p.266*).

■ **HARDINESS** Fully hardy ✳✳✳.
■ **CULTIVATION** Grow in any moist but well-drained soil, in full sun or partial shade. It self-seeds prolifically. ■ **Sow** seed (*see pp.328–329*) in a container in a cold frame in spring or autumn. If grown well away from other cow parsleys, 'Ravenswing' produces dark-leaved seedlings.

***Anthriscus sylvestris* 'Ravenswing'**
↕1m (3ft) ↔30cm (12in), like all cow parsleys, this will produce self-seedlings but select only those with dark, purple-brown foliage

Antirrhinum
Snapdragons

EARLY SUMMER TO AUTUMN

Appealingly shaped flowers, usually in a riot of bright colours, make snapdragons hugely cheering. They belong to a group of annuals and perennials that flower from early summer until autumn. The most popular are those grown as annuals in bedding or cottage-garden schemes. Although technically short-lived perennials, the best flowers are usually obtained in their first year, so new plants should be bought, or raised from seed, each spring. The dark green leaves will be almost entirely hidden by the flowers when plants are grown closely together, in blocks or with other summer-bedding plants. There are trailing types especially bred for hanging baskets too. If you have a rock garden, try growing some of the lesser-known, more delicate, shrubby snapdragons.

■ **HARDINESS** Fully hardy ✳✳✳ to half-hardy ✳.
■ **CULTIVATION** Grow in fertile, well-drained soil in full sun. Shrubby species require very well-drained soil and shelter from strong, cold winds. ■ **Remove** fading flowers to prolong flowering. ■ **Sow** seed of *A. majus* cultivars at 16–18°C (61–64°F) in early spring, and of shrubby species in a container in autumn or spring (*see pp.328–329*).

Antirrhinum braun-blanquetii
↕↔45cm (18in), a bedding type, very densely packed flowers, ideal for containers ✳✳✳

Antirrhinum pulverulentum
↕15–20cm (6–8in) ↔20–30cm (8–12in), very small and creeping, needs shelter and hates cold, wet conditions ✳✳✳ (borderline)

Antirrhinum hispanicum
↕20cm (8in) ↔45cm (18in), subshrubby, compact plant, good for small rock gardens or an alpine trough, dislikes winter wet ✳✳✳

Aquilegia
Columbine

`LATE SPRING`

The nodding, bonnet-like flowers of columbines are invaluable in informal planting schemes, from a sunny cottage garden to a lightly shaded woodland area. From late spring, and in some cases until late summer, mostly bell-shaped flowers with spurred petals are borne singly or in small clusters on long stalks. Columbines are upright, vigorous perennials and the larger species, including *Aquilegia vulgaris*, are at home in dappled shade or massed in a border with upright flowering plants such as lupins (*see p.234*), delphiniums (*see p.188*) and other perennials. The alpine columbine is best grown in a rock garden in sharply drained soil.

■ **HARDINESS** Fully hardy ✳✳✳.
■ **CULTIVATION** Grow the larger types in fertile, moist but well-drained soil in full sun or partial shade. Grow alpine species in well-drained soil in full sun and mulch (*see p.326*) with grit. ■ **Sow** seed in a container in a cold frame as soon as it is ripe (*see pp.328–329*). Seed of alpine species may take two years to germinate. Columbines do self-seed freely if seed is allowed to ripen on the plants, so do not be hasty in cutting back stems in autumn.

Aquilegia fragrans
‡15–40cm (6–16in) ↔15–20cm (6–8in), fragrant flowers, needs rich soil, tolerates light shade

Aquilegia vulgaris 'Nora Barlow' ♀
‡90cm (36in) ↔ 45cm (18in), vigorous, with spurless, double pompon flowers, good in a cottage garden

Aquilegia McKana Group
‡75cm (30in) ↔ 60cm (24in), flowers from late spring to midsummer, vigorous but short-lived

Aquilegia vulgaris 'Nivea' ♀
‡90cm (36in) ↔ 45cm (18in), grey-green foliage, flowers in late spring and early summer

Aquilegia alpina (Alpine aquilegia)
‡45cm (18in) sometimes more ↔to 30cm (12in), flowers in late spring, prefers rich soil in sun or partial shade

Arabis
Rock cress

These small, mat-forming, evergreen or semi-evergreen perennials can bring colour to poor or dry sites where many other plants would not survive. Loose clusters of cross-shaped flowers are borne on slender stems during late spring and early summer. The leaves are often hairy, and on some cultivars are variegated white or yellow. Rock cress is very easy to grow and *Arabis alpina* subsp. *caucasica* is a good ground-cover option for dry soils. It is often used as a spreading plant in a rock garden, at the edge of a border, or in crevices in a wall.

■ **HARDINESS** Fully hardy ✳✳✳.
■ **CULTIVATION** Grow rock cress in any well-drained soil in full sun. It will tolerate poor, infertile soils, even in very hot or dry conditions. ■ **Protect** *A. blepharophylla* 'Frühlingszauber' from winter wet (*see p.314*). ■ **Site** vigorous species, such as *A. alpina* subsp. *caucasica*, with care as they may swamp small neighbours. ■ **Trim** with shears, after flowering, to keep plants dense. ■ **Sow** seed (*see pp.328–329*) in a container in autumn and give seedlings the protection of a cold frame. Alternatively, take softwood cuttings (*see pp.329–330*) in summer.

Arabis alpina **subsp.** *caucasica* **'Variegata'**
↕15cm (6in) ↔50cm (20in) or more, when the fragrant flowers have finished, the cream-margined evergreen leaves attract attention

Arctotis
African daisy

Silvery leaves and a South African origin mark out these annuals and perennials as heat-loving plants. Long, sturdy stems support the daisies from midsummer until autumn. They are brightly coloured orange, white, or creamy yellow; the petals are often marked near the base with a contrasting shade. The flowers a tend to close on dull days or mid-afternoon, although modern varieties have been bred to stay open longer. African daisies are often used in summer bedding displays, and are wonderful in gravel gardens or in containers. In cool climates, the perennials are often grown as annuals, or dug up and kept in frost-free conditions over winter.

■ **HARDINESS** Frost-tender ❄.
■ **CULTIVATION** Grow in sharply drained, but preferably moist soil in full sun. ■ **Sow** seed (*see pp.328–329*) at 16–18°C (61–64°F) in early spring or autumn. After gemination, prick out into individual 10cm (4in) pots to minimize root disturbance before planting out. ■ **Root** stem cuttings (*see pp.329–330*) at any time – it is the best method for propagating plants with fine flowers, because seed may not come true.

Arabis blepharophylla
'Frühlingszauber' ♀
↕10cm (4in) ↔20cm (8in), mat- or cushion-forming evergreen that may be short-lived if winter is wet

Arabis procurrens **'Variegata'** ♀
↕5–8cm (2–3in) ↔30–40cm (12–16in), evergreen or semi-evergreen, remove any stems with non-variegated leaves

Arctotis x hybrida **'Flame'**
↕45–50cm (18–20in) ↔30cm (12in)

Arenaria
Sandwort

LATE SPRING TO EARLY SUMMER

Most of the sandworts are low-growing or spreading perennials; some of them are evergreen, although there are a few annual species. All have narrow, greyish-green leaves, borne on wiry stems that can form loose mats or dense cushions. From late spring until early summer, they bear a profusion of small, cup-shaped, usually white flowers. Sandworts thrive in a rock garden or the crevices of dry stone walls. They are excellent, too, for planting between paving slabs to soften the hard edges and will transform a bare patio if grown in this way with other mat-forming plants such as aubrietas (*see p.165*) and arabis (*see p.157*).

■ **HARDINESS** Fully hardy ✳✳✳.
■ **CULTIVATION** Grow sandwort in moist, but well-drained, sandy or poor soil, in full sun. *Arenaria balearica* grows well in partial shade; *A. tetraquetra* needs very well-drained soil.
■ **Divide** (*see p.330*) in early spring. ■ **Sow** seed (*see pp.328–329*) in a cold frame in autumn, or take new shoots from the base and treat as softwood cuttings (*see p.329*) in early summer.

Arenaria montana ♀
‡2–5cm (1–2in) ↔30cm (12in), flowers only in early summer

Argemone
Prickly poppy

SUMMER TO AUTUMN

As you might expect from its common name, an argemone rather resembles a cross between a thistle and a poppy. This group of annuals and short-lived perennials form clumps of grey-green, often very spiky leaves. The main attraction, though, is their paper-thin, white, yellow, or mauve flowers that are borne from summer right through until autumn, and are followed by very spiny seedpods. Complement their colouring by planting them with other silver-leaved plants such as artemisias (*see p.21*) or mulleins (*see Verbascum, p.280*) in a hot, sunny border or gravel garden. Perennial argemones are often grown as annuals. All species self-seed freely.

■ **HARDINESS** Half-hardy ✳.
■ **CULTIVATION** Argemones like very poor, gritty or stony soil in full sun. ■ **Deadhead** regularly (*see p.330*) to prolong the flowering period. ■ **Sow** seed (*see pp.328–329*) at 18°C (6°F) in early spring, and prick out seedlings into 10cm (5in) pots. ■ **Plant out** as soon as possible after the last frost because older plants resent disturbance.

Argemone mexicana (Devil's fig, Prickly poppy)
‡1m (3ft) ↔30–40cm (12–16in), the flowers appear in late summer and early autumn

Armeria
Sea pink, Thrift

LATE SPRING TO SUMMER

Thrifts are a delightful group of clump-forming perennials, familiar to some as seaside plants. They are loved for their small and fluffy, rounded flowerheads in late spring to summer, borne at the tips of slender stems above the rather grassy foliage. Flower colours range from white to pale and dark pink. Whether you garden inland or by the coast, these are ideal plants for growing in a rock garden or at the front of a mixed border. They also make a decorative edging plant alongside a path, and thrive between cracks in paving. Try growing them in a trough with other small rock-garden plants like haberleas (*see p.212*) and rhodiolas (*see p.264*).

■ **HARDINESS** Fully hardy ✳✳✳.
■ **CULTIVATION** Grow in well-drained, poor to reasonably fertile soil in an open spot in full sun. ■ **Sow** seed in a pot or tray (*see pp.328–329*) in a cold frame in spring or autumn. ■ **Divide** plants in early spring (*see p.330*).

Armeria pseudarmeria
‡to 50cm (20in) ↔30cm (12in)

Artemisia

Mugwort, Sagebrush, Wormwood

YEAR-ROUND

Gardeners are attracted by artemisias' silvery and aromatic, ferny foliage, which is shown to advantage when set beside plants with bold or plain leaves. Most artemisias have a bushy habit, but there are some creeping or spreading forms, such as *Artemisia stelleriana* 'Boughton Silver', which make good ground-cover plants. The majority are perennial, and a few are classed as shrubs (*see p.25*). If the small and insignificant flowers spoil the overall appearance, snip these off as they appear in summer. Artemisias make splendid partners for many plants, including silver-leaved shrubs such as lavenders (*see p.71*), and plants with purple, pink, or red flowers. They also look good at the base of roses (*see pp.96–97 and 128–129*).

■ **HARDINESS** Fully hardy ✳✳✳ to frost-hardy ✳✳.
■ **CULTIVATION** Grow in well-drained, fertile soil in full sun. Improve heavy soils before planting by digging in plenty of coarse grit.
■ **Cut** back in spring to maintain a compact habit. ■ **Divide** plants in spring or autumn (*see p.330*). ■ **Sow** seed in containers in a cold frame in spring (*see pp.328–329*). ■ **Take** greenwood or heel cuttings in summer, slightly later than softwood cuttings when the stem is a little firmer (*see pp.329–330*).

***Artemisia schmidtiana* 'Nana'** ♀
‡8cm (3in) ↔30cm (12in), low, compact plant with silky, silvery foliage that is ideal for rock gardens and troughs ✳✳✳

***Artemisia stelleriana* 'Boughton Silver'**
‡to 15cm (6in) ↔30–45cm (12–36in), good for ground cover in well-drained sites, and an attractive plant for large pots ✳✳✳

Artemisia pontica
‡40–80cm (16–32in) ↔90cm (36in), forms dense, all-year ground cover, but it can be too vigorous for small areas ✳✳✳

Arthropodium

MIDSUMMER

The grassy, blue- or grey-green leaves and small, starry flowers in midsummer are the main points of interest of this little-known group of evergreen and deciduous perennials. Relatives of the lily, arthropodiums grow from short rhizomes, producing leaves that are up to 25cm (10in) long. The pendulous, white, pale violet, or blue flowers have a wiry delicacy. *Arthropodium candidum* and *A. milleflorum* are the two most commonly grown plants in this group, suiting sunny rock gardens or sheltered borders, where they mix well with foliage plants such as tradescantias (*see p.275*).

■ **HARDINESS** Frost-hardy ✳✳; will withstand temperatures down to –10°C (14°F) if given good drainage.
■ **CULTIVATION** Grow in fertile, well-drained, gritty soil in full sun. In frosty areas, grow at the base of a warm, sheltered wall, or in a cold or cool greenhouse or conservatory. ■ **Sow** seed in containers in a cold frame in autumn or early spring (*see pp.328–329*). ■ **Divide** arthropodium in early spring (*see p.330*). Young plants are best overwintered in frost-free conditions. ■ **Slugs** (*see p.332*) can be attracted to new growth.

Arthropodium milleflorum
‡to 50cm (20in) ↔to 20cm (8in), the bluish- or greyish-green foliage is spangled with flowers in midsummer

Arum
Lords and ladies

With their arrow-shaped leaves emerging in late autumn and winter, these tuberous perennials make good foliage plants at a time of year when fresh growth is particularly welcomed. Reaching 35cm (14in) long, the leaves can be glossy green and have pale green or cream marbling. Between late spring and summer, leaf-like flowers are produced in pale green, white, or yellow. Enclosed within is a prominent spike, which bears persistent, bright orange-red berries later in the year. The best and largest leaves are produced in light shade, but a sunny, open site is needed for the plant to flower successfully. All parts of the plant are toxic.

■ **HARDINESS** Fully hardy ✽✽✽ to half-hardy ✽.
■ **CULTIVATION** Grow in a sheltered site in well-drained soil enriched with organic matter.
■ **Plant** tubers up to 15cm (6in) deep in autumn or spring. ■ **Divide** after flowering to make new plants (*see p.330*).

***Arum italicum* 'Marmoratum'** ♀
‡30cm (12in) ↔15cm (6in), marbled leaves are striking from winter to late spring, flowers in early summer, berries last to autumn ✽✽✽

Aruncus
Goatsbeard

Feathery plumes of flowers are borne above mounds of heavily veined leaves from early to midsummer. Goatsbeards belong to a small genus, related to filipendulas (*see p.202*) and spiraeas (*see p.102*), containing just a few species, all perennial. The tiny cream or white flowers that form the plumes may be either male or female, with the females subsequently producing small, green seedpods that will scatter seed freely if they are not deadheaded. Both seedheads and flowerheads of aruncus are popular for indoor arrangements. In the garden, this clump-forming plant thrives in moist soil and suits being grown at the edge of a pond or in damp woodland.

■ **HARDINESS** Fully hardy ✽✽✽.
■ **CULTIVATION** Grow goatsbear in moist, fertile soil, in partial shade. ■ **Plant out** in autumn or early spring. ■ **Sow** seed in containers (*see pp.328–329*) placed in a cold frame. ■ **Lift and divide** in spring or autumn every two or three years to make new plants and maintain vigour (*see p.330*).

***Aruncus dioicus* ♀**
‡2m (6ft) ↔1.2m (4ft), will tolerate drier conditions than other types, but much prefers a fairly damp site

Asarina procumbens
Creeping snapdragon

The delicate, pale yellow flowers of this trailing, evergreen perennial closely resemble those of the snapdragon (*see Antirrhinum, p.155*), giving rise to its common name. Appearing from early summer until early autumn, the flowers have deep yellow throats with light purple veining and reach 3.5cm (1¹⁄₂in) long. They are borne above grey-green leaves that are soft, hairy, and slightly sticky. Asarina's trailing habit makes it a favourite for growing as a ground cover over the edge of a shady wall, a raised bed, or the stony slopes of a rock garden. The plant tends to be short-lived, but does seed itself freely about the garden.

■ **HARDINESS** Hardy to –10°C (14°F) ✽✽✽.
■ **CULTIVATION** Grow in well-drained soil enriched with well-rotted organic matter.
■ **Plant** in partial shade for best results.
■ **Sow** seed in early spring (*see pp.328–329*) at a temperature of 16°C (61°F).

Asarina procumbens
‡5cm (2in) ↔to 60cm (24in)

Asclepias
Silkweed, Milkweed

MIDSUMMER TO AUTUMN

Colourful clusters of flowers are produced by this large group of perennials (and a few shrubs) in such abundance that they attract great numbers of butterflies and bees. The flowers range from purple-pink, deep pink, and orange-red to yellow and appear from midsummer until autumn. They are followed by fruits, which split when ripe to reveal rows of seeds with long, silky hairs, hence the common name of silkweed. The leaves and tips of the stems contain a milky sap, which can irritate skin. Silkweeds like a variety of sites from sunny borders to pondsides.

■ **HARDINESS** Fully hardy ✳✳✳ to frost-tender ❀.
■ **CULTIVATION** Most grow well in fertile, well-drained soil in full sun, although *A. incarnata* prefers fairly moist conditions. In frost-prone areas, grow frost-tender types in a cool greenhouse or conservatory. ■ **Sow** seed in spring in containers in a cold frame (*see pp.328–329*). ■ **Divide** in spring to make new plants (*see p.330*) and, if necessary, to keep clumps under control. Some spread quickly by underground suckers and can be invasive.

Asclepias incarnata (Swamp milkweed)
↕1.2m (4ft) ↔ 60cm (24in), likes a moist site and grows well near streams and pools ✳✳✳

Asphodeline
Jacob's rod

SPRING AND SUMMER

Striking spires of yellow or white starry flowers emerge in spring and summer, rising above the clumps of blue-green, grassy leaves. These herbaceous biennial and perennial plants, natives of the Mediterranean, grow from swollen, fleshy roots (rhizomes), which allow them to withstand dry conditions. They thrive in dry, sunny sites such as banks and well-drained beds and borders. Good companions include many annuals, such as the corn marigold (*Xanthophthalum segetum*), eryngiums (*see p.198*), and other Mediterranean plants like rosemary (*p.98*) and phlomis (*p.254*).

■ **HARDINESS** Fully hardy ✳✳✳.
■ **CULTIVATION** Grow in reasonably fertile, well-drained soil in full sun. Mulch for winter protection in very cold areas by spreading a thick layer of straw, bark chippings, or other organic matter over clumps in late autumn. ■ **Sow** seed in a container (*see pp.328–329*) in a cold frame in spring. ■ **Divide** plants (*see p.330*) in late summer or early autumn, taking care not to damage the roots.

Asphodeline lutea (Yellow asphodel, King's spear)
↕1.5m (5ft) ↔30cm 12in), fragrant flowers in late spring, the spires of seedpods are also attractive

Asphodelus
Asphodel

LATE SPRING AND EARLY SUMMER

Grown for their slender spikes of delicate flowers in shades of white or pink, asphodels, like their close cousins asphodelines (*see left*), are excellent plants for a dry, sunny border. Those grown in gardens are mostly perennial, but there are also some annuals. The flowers open in late spring and early summer and often have attractive, contrasting markings on the petals. The tall flower stems rise up from dense tufts of grassy foliage. Natives of warm, well-drained, sometimes quite barren places, asphodels need a sheltered site and free-draining soil in cool climates where winters tend to be wet. A beautifully bold plant for naturalistic plantings.

■ **HARDINESS** Fully hardy ✳✳✳.
■ **CULTIVATION** Grow in well-drained soil in full sun. ■ **Sow** seed in a container (*see pp.328–329*) in a cold frame in spring. *Asphodelus fistulosis* is generally grown as an annual and needs to be raised from seed each year. ■ **Divide** plants (*see p.330*) in late summer or early autumn, taking great care not to damage the roots.

Asphodelus albus
↕90cm (36in) ↔30cm (12in), clumping perennial, flowers in mid- or late spring

Aster

LATE SUMMER TO AUTUMN

Asters bring cheer to the late-summer and autumn garden with masses of daisy flowers, which give *Aster novi-belgii* types the name Michaelmas daisy. Varying in hue from sky blue to white, scarlet, pink, and lavender, all with bright golden centres, flowers are carried at the tips of the stems, either singly or in clusters. Asters are mostly perennial, but also include a few annuals, biennials, and shrubby types; they range from tiny alpines no more than 15cm (6in) tall to upright clumps of 1.2m (4ft) or more. Flowering times vary slightly. Some such as *A. x frikartii* and *A. thomsonii* put on a particularly long display.

■ **HARDINESS** Perennials are mostly hardy ✻✻✻, shrubby types are frost-tender ❅.
■ **CULTIVATION** Grow in a variety of sites from open sun to partial shade. Plant according to which of the three cultivation groups they fall into. **Group 1** needs moist, fertile, well-cultivated soil in sun or partial shade. **Group 2** needs open, well-drained, moderately fertile soil, and a position in full sun. **Group 3** needs moist, moderately fertile soil in partial shade. ■ **Support** taller asters (*see below*), which is best done in early spring. ■ **Cut down** old stems in autumn, making it easier to give plants a winter mulch or, if preferred, leave and cut down in winter or early spring. ■ **Divide** clumps (*see p.330*) every three to four years, both to give more plants and to maintain vigorous growth, especially for *A. novae-angliae* and *A. novi-belgii* cultivars. ■ **Sow** seed (*see pp.328–329*) in spring or autumn in a cold frame. Grey mould (botrytis) and powdery mildew can affect plants, particularly in cultivars of *A. novi-belgii*; remove infected parts and spray with fungicide. *Aster amellus* and *A. x frikartii* types are generally trouble-free.

How to stake asters

Canes and twine This is the most inexpensive method of staking. Space the canes evenly around the plants and among clumps and weave the twine around them, keeping it taut, to provide support. This may look unsightly at first, but both canes and twine will soon be completely hidden by the foliage and flowers. Put a cap on all canes to prevent accidental damage to your eyes. L-shaped linking stakes are an alternative and are adaptable to any size of clump.

Peasticks These branching, twiggy sticks are the most versatile method of staking. The garden may look a little like a forest after they are put in, but they are soon hidden once the plants grow. The tops of peasticks can be bent over, providing additional support for the plants to grow through. The sticks should last for several seasons. Alternatively, try stems from tall shrubs like buddleja (*see p.25*) that are pruned in early spring, just when staking is needed.

Grow-through supports These consist of a mesh or grid of rigid plastic across a hoop supported by four legs. The supports are pushed into place and the plant grows through the mesh. They can gradually be raised as plants become taller. Get them in place early in the season, when the plant has made about 30cm (12in) of growth. They are easily removed when the stems are cut back in autumn.

A. alpinus ♀ ‡25cm (10in) ↔45cm (18in), group 2

A. amellus '**King George**' ♀ ‡↔45cm (18in), group 2

A. novae-angliae '**Harrington's Pink**' ♀ ‡1.2m (4ft) ↔60cm (2ft), group 1

A. novi-belgii '**Carnival**' ‡60cm (2ft) ↔90cm (3ft), group 1

A. novi-belgii '**Little Pink Lady**' ‡40cm (15in) ↔50cm (20in), group 1

A. novi-belgii '**Marie Ballard**' ‡90cm (3ft) ↔60cm (2ft), group 1

A. pilosus '**Monte Cassino**' ♀ ‡1m (3ft) ↔30cm (1ft), groups 1 or 3

A. '**Pink Star**' ‡90cm (3ft) ↔30cm (12in), group 2

A. *cordifolius* 'Silver Spray'
‡1.2m (4ft) ↔ 45cm (18in), group 3

A. x *frikartii* 'Mönch' ♀ ‡70cm (28in)
↔ 35–40cm (14–16in), group 2

A. x *frikartii* 'Wunder von Stäfa' ♀
‡70cm (28in) ↔ 35–40cm (14–16in), group 2

A. *lateriflorus* var. *horizontalis* ♀
‡60cm (2ft) ↔ 30cm (1ft), group 3

A. *novi-belgii* 'Chequers'
‡60cm (2ft) ↔ 90cm (3ft), group 1

A. *novi-belgii* 'Jenny' ‡30cm (1ft)
↔ 45cm (18in), group 1

A. *novi-belgii* 'Kristina' ‡30cm (1ft)
↔ 45cm (18in), group 1

A. *novi-belgii* 'Lady in Blue'
‡30cm (1ft) ↔ 50cm (20in), group 1

A. *novi-belgii* 'Patricia Ballard'
‡90cm (3ft) ↔ 60cm (2ft), group 1

A. *novi-belgii* 'Schöne von Dietlikon'
‡to 1m (3ft) ↔ 45cm (18in), group 1

A. *novi-belgii* 'Snowsprite' ‡25–30cm
(10–12in) ↔ 45cm (18in), group 3

A. *pilosus* var. *demotus* ♀ ‡1.2m (4ft)
↔ 45cm (18in), group 3

A. *pyrenaeus* 'Lutetia' ‡60cm (2ft)
↔ to 1m (3ft), group 2

A. *sedifolius* ‡1.2m (4ft) ↔ 60cm (2ft),
group 2

A. *thomsonii* 'Nanus' ‡45cm (18in)
↔ 25cm (10in), group 3

A. *turbinellus* ‡1.2m (4ft)
↔ 60cm (2ft), group 2

Astilbe

EARLY TO LATE SUMMER

With their plumes of tiny, starry flowers, astilbes bring both elegance and texture to the garden. The flowerheads, in shades of white, cream, pink, and red, are produced in summer and, if left on the plant to fade, turn a rich russet brown, extending the period of interest from autumn into winter. The cut flowers also last well in water in arrangements. Handsome, mid- to dark green, divided leaves add to the attractions of these clump-forming perennials. They particularly suit damp sites close to ponds and streams, or in bog gardens, and combine well with daylilies (*see Hemerocallis, p.216*), ferns (*see pp.300–309*), and grasses (*see pp.254–299*).

■ **HARDINESS** Fully hardy ✳✳✳.
■ **CULTIVATION** Grow in moist soil enriched with plenty of well-rotted organic matter in sun or partial shade. Astilbes will not thrive in soils that dry out in summer. ■ **Divide** plants in late winter or early spring every three or four years to maintain vigour (*see p.330*). The flowers and young leaves can, occasionally, be damaged by late frosts. ■ **Powdery mildew** (*see p.333*) can marr foliage with a greyish-white coating, especially if plants are in too dry a site.

Astilbe 'Irrlicht'
↕↔50cm (18in), flowers in late spring and early summer, somewhat smaller than many astilbes

Astrantia

Hattie's pincushion, Masterwort

EARLY AND MIDSUMMER

The delicate and distinctive flowerheads that grace these clump-forming perennials are in fact composed of an outer circle of papery bracts (modified leaves) and a central cluster of pinhead-like true flowers. In early and midsummer, strong stems hold the blooms of white, pink, or red well above the foliage. *Astrantia major* 'Sunningdale Variegated' has leaves with creamy yellow margins, which are at their most striking early in the season. The flowers look attractive in dried flower arrangements. Astrantias make excellent companions for many other herbaceous perennials, including asters (*see pp.162–163*), astilbes (*see left*), and rudbeckias (*see p.265*).

Astilbe 'Fanal' ♀
↕60cm (24in) ↔ 45cm (18in), the crimson flower plumes appear in early summer

Astilbe 'Straussenfeder' ♀
↕90cm (36in) ↔ 60cm (24in), flowers in late summer and early autumn, young foliage has a bronze tint, needs ample moisture

Astrantia 'Hadspen Blood'
↕60cm (24in) ↔ 45cm (18in), one of the darkest of all astrantias and useful for adding depth of colour to planting schemes

■ **HARDINESS** Fully hardy ✷✷✷.
■ **CULTIVATION** Grow Hattie's pincushion in moist, fertile soil, enriched with well-rotted organic matter, in sun or partial shade. 'Sunningdale Variegated' needs full sun for the best foliage colour. ■ **Remove** faded flowers to prevent self-seeding. ■ **Divide** plants in spring (*see p.330*) to maintain vigour. ■ **Sow** seed in a container in a cold frame as soon as it is ripe (*see pp.328–329*). ■ **Powdery mildew** (*see p.333*) may spoil the leaves if dry or overcrowded.

Astrantia major 'Alba'
↕60cm (24in) ↔ 45cm (18in), the delicate white flowers will enliven a shady corner

Astrantia major 'Rubra'
↕60cm (24in) ↔ 45cm (18in), will tolerate slightly drier conditions

Aubrieta
Aubretia

`SPRING`

Mats or low hummocks of pink, magenta, mauve, and purple flowers make aubretia a mainstay of the spring rock garden and border edge. When in bloom, the small, cross-shaped flowers, which may be single or double, obscure the evergreen foliage, although in silver- or gold-variegated aubretias such as 'Argenteovariegata' this also makes a good show after the flowers have faded. This spreading perennial is most popularly combined with rock-garden plants of a similar habit, such as soapworts (*see Saponaria, p.267*) or saxifrages (*see p.267*).

■ **HARDINESS** Fully hardy ✷✷✷.
■ **CULTIVATION** Grow in reasonably fertile, well-drained soil, preferably neutral to alkaline (limy), in full sun. ■ **Cut back** hard after flowering to maintain a compact habit and prevent the centre from becoming straggly and bare. ■ **Sow** seed (*see pp.328–329*) in a cold frame in spring or autumn; named cultivars rarely come true to type. ■ **Take** softwood cuttings in early summer (*see pp.329–330*).

Aubrieta 'Joy'
↕5cm (2in) ↔ 60cm (24in), mat-forming variety with double flowers in spring

Baptisia
False indigo, Wild indigo

`EARLY SUMMER`

False indigo is a vigorous, clump-forming perennial that sends up tall, lupin-like spires of royal blue, purple, or white, pea-like flowers in early summer, followed by large, puffy seedpods that last into the autumn. Informal in form, it can be used to add height to a wildflower garden, but also thrives when grown among other clump-forming plants of medium height, benefiting from their support. Grow it towards the centre of a traditional border with other robust perennials such as lupins (*see p.234*), eryngiums (*p.198*) and Oriental poppies (*see Papaver, p.249*).

■ **HARDINESS** Fully hardy ✷✷✷.
■ **CULTIVATION** Grow in full sun in a well-drained soil. Take care to choose the right site, because the plants resent root disturbance once established. Plants grown in open or windy sites usually benefit from staking. ■ **Sow** seed (*see pp.328–329*) in pots in a cold frame as soon as it is ripe. ■ **Divide** (*see p.330*) in early spring, keeping the sections of rootball as intact and large as possible.

Baptisia australis ♀ (False indigo)
↕1.5m (5ft) ↔ 60cm (24in), erect to spreading, flowers in early summer followed by pods, at both stages good for cutting

Begonia

SUMMER AND YEAR-ROUND

Most begonias used in the garden produce spectacular flowers – great either in individual size or their sheer number – in whites, yellows, apricots, and pinks, through to bright orange, cerise, and rich reds. There are also types grown chiefly for their heavily patterned foliage. The most familiar are the small, fibrous-rooted *Begonia semperflorens* plants, so widely used for bedding and containers. Larger types make useful dot plants for summer accents in borders and in patio containers; use trailing begonias for hanging baskets. Overwinter in frost-free conditions.

■ **HARDINESS** Half-hardy ✳ to frost-tender ✿.
■ **CULTIVATION** Grow in fertile, well-drained soil in full sun or partial shade. In pots, use a multipurpose compost; keep well watered, and feed weekly with tomato feed. ■ **Deadhead** to prolong the flowering period. ■ **Cut back** semperflorens kinds in autumn; lift and pot if necessary; and bring them into a conservatory or cool room; place in good light and water moderately until spring. ■ **Lift tubers** before first frosts, and store them, clean and dry, over winter; in spring, pot them up, and start into growth by watering. ■ **Sow** seed (*see pp.328–329*) in late winter or early spring at 21°C (70°F). ■ **Take** stem-tip cuttings (*see p.330*) in spring or summer.

Begonia 'Can-can'
‡90cm (36in) ↔ 45cm (18in), tuberous, upright habit, flowers to 18cm (7in) across in summer, ✿ (min. 10°C/50°F)

Begonia sutherlandii ♀
‡45cm (18in), tuberous-rooted, trailing, small but many-flowered, tubers must be lifted and stored each winter ✳

Begonia 'Crystal Brook'
‡15cm (6in) ↔ 1m (3ft), fibrous-rooted perennial, small and spreading, overwinter under cover in pots ✿

Begonia 'Président Carnot'
‡1.5–2m (5–6ft) ↔ 60cm (2ft), pink flowers in summer, good light vital for good leaf colour, cut back in spring, overwinter in pots ✿

Bellis
Daisy, Double daisy

LATE WINTER TO LATE SUMMER

Although bellis are in fact perennials, they are very often grown as biennials; with wallflowers (*see Erysimum, p.199*) and forget-me-nots (*see Myosotis, p.239*), they form a classic triumvirate of spring bedding. Their small, perky flowerheads, to 8cm (3in) across, in white tinged with maroon, pink, or red, are borne from late winter until late summer. These highly bred varieties of the lawn-type daisy make great cottage-garden plants, and are also good for containers. Those with tight, pompon flowerheads can also have a formal, old-fashioned charm; use them in blocks to fill beds in a potager, herb, or knot garden, before summer salads, herbs, or bedding plants go in.

■ **HARDINESS** Fully hardy ✳✳✳.
■ **CULTIVATION** Grow in well-drained soil, in full sun or partial shade. Deadhead to prolong the flowering display of bedding plants, or to prevent plants grown as perennials from self-seeding. ■ **Sow** seed (*see pp.328–329*) in containers in early spring, or outdoors in early summer where the plants are to grow – or, if raising bedding for the next year, in a nursery bed. ■ **Divide** plants grown as perennials just after flowering (*see p.330*).

Bellis perennis
‡↔ 5–20cm (2–8in), flowers to 6cm (2½in) across, raise plants in early summer or buy in late summer to flower early the next spring

Bergenia

Elephant-eared saxifrage,
Elephant's ears

SPRING AND EARLY SUMMER

Bergenias have large, glossy or leathery, tough leaves, and the plant makes excellent ground cover. They are evergreen perennials that produce clusters of creamy-pink to purple-pink flowers on sturdy stems in spring and early summer. The rounded leaves are usually mid- to dark green but in some, such as 'Ballawley', they turn bronze-red in winter. Bergenias can be grown at the front of a border, but may need cutting back if they spread too far. They are particularly useful for covering dry and shady areas in the shadows of walls or shrubs and trees.

■ **HARDINESS** Fully hardy ✳✳✳ to frost-hardy ✳✳.
■ **CULTIVATION** Grow in well-drained soil enriched with well-rotted organic matter, in full sun or partial shade. Poorer soils enhance the winter leaf colour. ■ **Slice down** with a spade to remove growth exceeding the allotted space. ■ **Divide** old, leggy-looking clumps every three to five years after flowering or in autumn (*see p.330*), replanting healthy sections of rhizome with roots and one or more leaves. Pick off any foliage that develops dark leaf spots (*see p.333*).

Bergenia 'Sunningdale'
‡30–45cm (12–18in) ↔ 45–60cm (18–24in) ✳✳✳

Bidens ferulifolia

MIDSUMMER TO AUTUMN

The most popular garden bidens is *Bidens ferulifolia*, which has fresh, finely divided leaves and a succession of flowers from midsummer to autumn. Although perennial, it is usually treated as an annual since it grows quickly. Yellow-flowered, it has orange or orange-red forms too. Its sprawling habit makes it a good choice for growing in hanging baskets or wall pots where the stems will tumble over the edge of the container. Bidens look cheerful with other bedding plants that enjoy similarly warm, well-drained conditions, such as felicias (*see p.202*) and marigolds (*see Tagetes, p.274*), or sit well in a gravel garden with rock roses (*see Cistus, p.36*).

■ **HARDINESS** Frost-hardy ✳✳.
■ **CULTIVATION** Grow in reasonably fertile, moist but well-drained soil, in full sun. If growing in hanging baskets or other containers, water regularly during summer and feed weekly with a balanced fertilizer. ■ **Sow** seed at 13–18°C (55–64°F) in spring (*see pp.328–329*). ■ **Take** stem-tip cuttings after flowering in autumn (*see p.330*). ■ **Cut back** plants in autumn and overwinter in a frost-free greenhouse, keeping the plants on the dry side until spring.

Bidens ferulifolia ♀
‡to 30m (12in) ↔ to 90cm (30in), slender, spreading stems

Bletilla

SPRING TO EARLY SUMMER

These orchids are native to temperate regions of China and Japan. They have delicate, bell-shaped, magenta flowers that are arranged in upright clusters, with up to 12 flowers on each cluster. The narrow, mid-green leaves that spring up from the bulbous, fleshy rootstock die back in winter. Bletillas look charming in a sheltered woodland setting with other small, spring-flowering plants, such as *Anemone blanda* (*see p.152*). They can also be grown in a raised bed, bringing their exquisite flowers nearer the eye. In frost-prone areas they need winter protection, either in situ with a thick mulch or cold frame, or potted up under cover.

■ **HARDINESS** Half-hardy ✳ to frost-tender ❄.
■ **CULTIVATION** Grow in partial shade, in moist but well-drained soil enriched with well-rotted organic matter, or in soil-based compost with added leafmould. ■ **Mulch** in autumn with a layer of organic matter at least 5cm (2in) thick to protect from frost. Alternatively, lift and overwinter in a frost-free place. ■ **Divide** in early spring (*see p.330*).

Bletilla striata
‡↔30–60cm (12–24in), fleshy underground storage organs known as pseudobulbs, flowers from spring to early summer ✳

Boltonia

There are around eight species of these perennials, all of which thrive in moist, sunny sites. They have masses of daisy flowers in shades of white, lilac, or pinkish-purple with canary-yellow centres. The flowers are set off by blue-green or mid-green, sometimes finely toothed foliage. Their loose, relaxed appearance is ideal for a wild garden, or they can add a light, airy feel to a border. The flowers are also good for cutting. Boltonias are tolerant of most garden soils and will put up with partly shaded conditions. Plant alongside other tall perennial daisies, such as Michaelmas daisies (*see Aster, pp.162–163*) and rudbeckias (*p.265*). Stonecrops (*see Sedum, p.270*) are also good companions.

■ **HARDINESS** Fully hardy ✽✽✽.
■ **CULTIVATION** Grow in any reasonably fertile, moist, well-drained soil, in full sun or partial shade. ■ **Divide** plants in spring every two or three years to maintain their vigour (*see p.330*). ■ **Sow** seed in containers in a cold frame in autumn (*see pp.328–329*). ■ **Powdery mildew** (*see pp.333*) can be a problem in dry conditions.

Boltonia asteroides
‡2m (6ft) ↔1m (3ft), glaucous, blue-green leaves become greener with age, flowers in late summer to mid-autumn

Borago
Borage

Borage grows wild in rocky places in western and southern Europe. They are robust plants with hairy stems and leaves, and flower for long periods over summer, producing nodding heads of intensely blue, or occasionally white, starry flowers. *Borago pygmaea* is a shade-loving perennial that is suitable for a rock or gravel garden, growing to about 60cm (24in) tall and wide. The annual, common borage, *B. officinalis*, needs sun and tolerates dry places. It has cucumber-flavoured leaves that are often added to drinks and salads, and the flowers make a pretty garnish. It looks attractive growing with mint, sage, and feverfew, but may be too thuggish for a small, neat herb garden; if so, it looks fine in a border. All species self-seed freely.

■ **HARDINESS** Fully hardy ✽✽✽ to frost-hardy ✽✽.
■ **CULTIVATION** Grow in any well-drained soil, in full sun or partial shade. ■ **Sow** seed of *B. officinalis* where you want it to grow in spring (*see pp.328–329*). ■ **Take** cuttings of young sideshoots of *B. pygmaea* in summer (*see p.329*) and overwinter the young plants in a cold frame.

Borago officinalis (Borage)
‡60cm (24in) ↔ 45cm (18in), freely branching annual, will flower until the first frosts, attractive to bees ✽✽✽

Boykinia

Originating in moist woodland and mountain regions, boykinias are clump-forming perennials with dark green foliage that is occasionally tinted bronze when young. The mounds of round to kidney-shaped leaves that develop around the base of the plants make good ground cover. In spring or summer, lax clusters of crimson or white, bell-shaped flowers rise above the leaves on long stalks. Boykinias thrive in cool, moist soil in partial shade. In the garden, they are best suited to a shady border or rock garden, or woodland edge. Pair them with violas (*see p.282*), or grow in clumps among other low, informal perennials that are not too vigorous and enjoy similar conditions, such as heucheras (*see p.217*) and dicentras (*p.190*). Small species also grow well in troughs and sinks.

■ **HARDINESS** Fully hardy ✽✽✽.
■ **CULTIVATION** Grow boykinia in lime-free (acid) soil, or ericaceous compost with added grit, in partial shade. ■ **Divide** in spring (*see p.330*). ■ **Sow** seed in containers in a cold frame as soon as it is ripe (*see pp.328–329*).

Boykinia jamesii
‡↔15cm (6in), flowering in mid- and late spring, the frilled flowers have green centres

Brodiaea

EARLY SUMMER

These plants are perennials, growing from corms, that in early summer produce funnel-shaped flowers in shades of violet, lilac, deep purple, or pink. The flowers are carried in large, open clusters, with each flower on its own short stalk, at the top of tall stems, and are excellent for cutting. Strappy, blue-green or mid-green leaves grow from the base of the plant, often dying back before the flowers emerge. Altogether they look similar to agapanthus (*see p.144*), but smaller. Grow brodiaeas at the front of a border, or in a rock garden or raised bed, in mild areas, or in shallow pots and bowls where they need to be stored under cover over winter.

■ **HARDINESS** Frost-hardy ✿✿.
■ **CULTIVATION** Grow in light, well-drained soil in full sun or partial shade. ■ **Plant** corms 8cm (3in) deep in autumn. ■ **Water** freely when plants are in full growth, but keep warm and dry after they die down in summer. ■ **Protect** with a winter mulch of well-rotted organic matter (*see p.326*) in frost-prone areas, or bring container-grown brodiaea under cover.
■ **Sow** seed (*see pp.328–329*) at 13–16°C (55–61°F) as soon as ripe. Remove offsets (*see p.330*) when the corms are dormant.

Brodiaea californica
‡50cm (20in) ↔ 8cm (3in), the flowers may be violet, lilac, pink, or white in this species

Brunnera macrophylla

MID- TO LATE SPRING

This clump-forming perennial and its cultivars have both delicate flowers and attractive foliage. In mid- and late spring, they produce clusters of small, usually bright blue flowers similar to those of forget-me-nots (*see Myosotis, p.239*). The softly hairy leaves on the stems are broadly lance-shaped, those at the base larger and more heart-shaped. Excellent for woodland areas beneath deciduous trees and shrubs, brunneras also make good ground cover in borders – especially those with patterned foliage that remain attractive once flowering is over. Grow with other spring-flowering perennials such as leopard's bane (*see Doronicum, p.193*).

■ **HARDINESS** Fully hardy ✿✿✿.
■ **CULTIVATION** Grow in reasonably fertile soil that is moist but well-drained, preferably in a cool site in part shade. Dig in well-rotted organic matter when planting. ■ **Divide** established plants (*see p.330*) in spring. ■ **Sow** seeds (*see pp.328–329*) in a container in a cold frame in early spring and take root cuttings in winter (*see p330*).

Brunnera macrophylla 'Dawson's White'
‡45cm (18in) ↔ 60cm (24in), needs light shade and rich soil to thrive; the 'White' in the plant name refers to the leaf margins rather than the flowers

Buglossoides

EARLY SUMMER

These are fine, fast-growing ground-cover plants – they are fairly vigorous, and the tips of the spreading shoots root easily when they come into contact with the soil, extending the plant ever farther. In spring or early summer, erect stems bear clusters of flat-faced flowers, which are purple when they first open, later maturing to clear blue. There are about 15 species, including annuals, perennials, and subshrubs. The leaves are mid- to dark green, variably shaped, and generally rough or hairy. These plants are at home in a woodland or wild garden, or in a border with other spreading, spring-flowering plants such as aubrietas (*see p.165*) or with bulbs.

■ **HARDINESS** Fully hardy ✿✿✿.
■ **CULTIVATION** Grow in a fertile, well-drained soil that is neutral to alkaline (limy). Position in full sun, but preferably with some shade around midday. ■ **Sow** seed (*see pp.328–329*) in containers in a cold frame in autumn or spring. ■ **Divide** perennials (*see p.330*) in early spring. Take stem-tip cuttings (*see p.330*) of subshrubs in summer.

Buglossides purpurocaerulea
‡to 60cm (24in) ↔ variable, perennial species, with underground stems, or rhizomes, flowers in late spring and early summer

Bulbocodium vernum
Spring meadow saffron
SPRING

This plant resembles the autumn crocus (*see Colchicum, p.181*) but with flowers that appear in spring or even in late winter in mild areas. These are pinkish-purple and turn from funnel- to star-shaped as the petals open. The leaves follow soon after, but do not reach their full height, 15cm (6in), until after the flowers are finished. Although the spring meadow saffron is fully hardy, it has the reputation of being rather fussy, resenting excessive winter wet, but it should thrive in sunny rock gardens, raised beds, and well-drained borders. It also grows well in pots. Pair it with other spring-flowering bulbs such as crocuses (*see p.185*) and small daffodils (*see Narcissus, pp.240–241*).

■ **HARDINESS** Fully hardy ✳✳✳, but protect from excessive winter wet.
■ **CULTIVATION** Plant corms 8cm (3in) deep in autumn, in full sun or partial shade, in soil enriched with well-rotted organic matter.
■ **Sow** seed in a pot in a cold frame in autumn or spring (*see pp.328–329*). Offsets from corms can be removed in summer (*see p.330*).

Bulbocodium vernum
‡4–8cm (1½–3in) ↔ 5cm (2in)

Buphthalmum salicifolium
Yellow oxeye
EARLY SUMMER TO AUTUMN

With flowers like chrysanthemums, *Buphthalmum salicifolium* is an easy-to-grow perennial suitable for most garden soils, including those on chalk. It produces masses of bright yellow daisies from early summer and into autumn, when they almost completely hide the dark green, willowy leaves. The flowers last well when cut, making them useful for indoor arrangements. The plant forms spreading clumps. Well suited to a wildflower planting, this is also a good plant for the front of an informal herbaceous border with other perennials like achilleas (*see p.140*), phloxes (*see p.254*), and monardas (*see p.239*), or try growing it among hostas (*see pp.218–219*) to brighten dappled shade.

■ **HARDINESS** Fully hardy ✳✳✳.
■ **CULTIVATION** Grow in poor soil in full sun or partial shade; tall plants may need to be supported. ■ **Divide** mature plants in early spring (*see p.330*). ■ **Sow** seed in a container in a cold frame in spring (*see pp.328–329*).

Buphthalmum salicifolium
‡60cm (24in) ↔ 45cm (18in)

Calandrinia
SUMMER

These fleshy-leaved perennials form mats of evergreen foliage topped with long-lasting displays of vivid, purple-red, pale pink, or purple flowers in summer. *Calandrinia umbellata* is most often grown; it tends to be short-lived and is usually treated as an annual or as a biennial – where the seeds are sown one year to flower the following year, just like wallflowers (*see Erysimum, p.199*). Each flower lasts for just two days, but there are always plenty to continue the display into late summer. Rock purslanes are drought-tolerant plants for the rock garden, associating well with small pinks (*see Dianthus, p.189*) and other plants with grey or silvery foliage.

■ **HARDINESS** Frost-hardy ✳✳; dislikes cold wet conditions.
■ **CULTIVATION** Grow in slightly acid (lime-free) soil that is sharply drained and in full sun. ■ **Sow** seed at 16–18°C (61–64°F) in early spring (*see pp.328–329*), or in autumn, planting out the following spring. Take stem-tip cuttings in spring (*see p.330*). If growing the plant as a perennial, take cuttings regularly, as it can be short-lived. Young plants may need protection from slugs and snails (*see p.332*).

Calandrinia umbellata (Rock purslane)
‡↔15–20cm (6–8in), blue or grey-green leaves, flowers to 2cm (¾in) across in summer

Calceolaria
Pouch flower, Slipper flower, Slipperwort

SPRING AND SUMMER

The curious flowers of calceolarias always arouse interest, with their vivid colours and strange balloon or pouch shapes. They are a group of annuals and perennials that generally flower throughout spring and summer, depending on when the seeds are sown. On flowering, they form massed or loose clusters of red, orange to yellow, even rich brown blooms, which are often spotted. The bedding forms like 'Bright Bikinis' are short-lived and can be prone to frost damage, but they make striking spring and summer container plants. The hardier perennial and alpine species are ideal for a rock garden or trough.

■ **HARDINESS** Fully hardy ✳✳✳ to frost-tender ❄.
■ **CULTIVATION** Grow in light, reasonably fertile soil in sun or partial shade. They require cool, moist conditions to flower freely. Grow alpine species like *C. arachnoidea* in moist, gritty soil and protect from winter wet. ■ **Sow** seed of hardy and alpine species, which must be exposed to cold, in containers outdoors in a cold frame in autumn (*see pp.328–329*). Cover alpine seeds with grit rather than compost. Sow seed of 'Bright Bikinis' and other bedding types at 18°C (64°F) in late summer or spring. Do not cover these tiny seeds with compost; cover the pots instead to prevent them drying out.

Calceolaria tenella
‡5cm (2in) ↔ to 30cm (12in), perennial, forms creeping mats of pale, evergreen foliage, flowers in summer, rock-garden plant ✳✳✳

Calceolaria 'Walter Shrimpton'
‡10cm (4in) ↔ 23cm (9in), evergreen perennial, glossy, dark green, leafy rosettes, flowers in summer ✳✳✳

Calceolaria arachnoidea
‡20–25cm (8–10in) ↔ to 15cm (6in), evergreen alpine perennial, white-hairy leaves, flowers from summer to autumn ✳✳

Calendula officinalis
English marigold, Marigold, Pot marigold

SUMMER

This annual calendula is the one most widely grown in gardens: they are exceptionally easy, fast-growing plants that bear a succession of vibrant orange, yellow, soft cream, or apricot, daisy-like flowers from summer to autumn. The wide range of cultivars includes many with double or "pompon" flowers, varying from compact, dwarf plants to taller forms. All make good cut flowers. They continue flowering into winter if unchecked by frost and, although annual, can survive into the following year. They make robust plants for hardy annual borders, and are equally useful in bedding schemes or in containers. Plants self-seed prolifically so they can be enjoyed year after year.

■ **HARDINESS** Fully hardy ✳✳✳.
■ **CULTIVATION** Sow seed outdoors in spring or autumn where plants are to grow (*see pp.328–329*), in sun or partial shade. Thin out seedlings to 15cm (6in) apart. Autumn-sown seedlings benefit from cloche protection.
■ **Deadhead** flowers regularly to prolong flowering (*see p.327*).

Calendula officinalis
‡30–75cm (12–18in) ↔ 30–45cm (12–30in), softly hairy, aromatic leaves, flowers 10cm (4in) across

Calla palustris
Bog arum
MIDSUMMER

This easy-to-grow perennial is an excellent marginal aquatic plant and looks particularly attractive growing along slow-moving stream edges. Bog arum spreads through shallow water – no more than 25cm (10in) deep – by means of creeping underground stems (rhizomes) below the soil. In midsummer, large white "hoods" appear that surround the cone-like flower clusters, which in autumn develop into spikes of scarlet berries. The leaves remain on the plant during mild winters. Contact with the foliage may cause skin allergies, so wear gloves when handling the plant.

■ **HARDINESS** Fully hardy ✳✳✳.
■ **CULTIVATION** Grow bog arums in very moist soil at the edge of a stream or pond.
■ **Plant** in aquatic planting baskets using garden soil or aquatic compost, or directly into mud in shallow water, which should be still or slow-moving. Position the plants in full sun to encourage more flowers. ■ **Divide** (*see p.330*) in spring, severing the underground stems carefully. ■ **Sow** seed (*see pp.328–329*) in late summer in containers submerged in shallow water.

Calla palustris
‡25cm (10in) ↔ 60cm (24in)

Caltha palustris
Kingcup, Marsh marigold
SPRING TO EARLY SUMMER

This moisture-loving perennial and its cultivars display striking yellow or white flowers in spring and early summer, which are followed by architectural, heart-shaped leaves up to 15cm (6in) in diameter. The plants spread by means of underground stems (rhizomes), and prefer a moist soil at the edge of water, although they will thrive in non-aquatic garden sites provided that the soil remains reliably moist. *Caltha palustris* will tolerate being grown in water up to 23cm (9in) deep, but prefers more shallow water or a boggy soil. Grow them with other moisture-loving plants such as mimulus (*see p.238*), or with bright pink waterside primulas (*see pp.260–261*).

■ **HARDINESS** Fully hardy ✳✳✳.
■ **CULTIVATION** Marsh marigolds prefer an open site with constantly moist soil in full sun. When planting in water, use an aquatic planting basket and top with gravel. ■ **Divide** plants (*see p.330*) in late summer or early spring. Marsh marigolds are prone to powdery mildew (*see pp.333*) when conditions are hot and dry, especially when they are growing in soil rather than water.

Caltha palustris ♀
‡10–40cm (4–16in) ↔ 45cm (18in)

Camassia
Quamash
LATE SPRING TO EARLY SUMMER

These bulbous perennials are grown for their tall spikes of large flowers, in sky-blue or creamy white. These are borne in late spring and early summer amid clumps of strappy, prominently veined, grey-green leaves. There are many types to choose from, but all are very similar. Grow them near the front or in the middle of a border, in a wildflower or meadow planting, or in containers. The frilly flower spikes would contrast well with the drumstick flowers of alliums such as 'Globemaster' (*see p.147*), perhaps underplanted with soft yellow cowslips (*see Primula veris, p.261*). The flowers are ideal for cutting, lasting well in indoor arrangements.

■ **HARDINESS** Fully hardy ✳✳✳ to frost-hardy ✳✳.
■ **CULTIVATION** Plant bulbs 10cm (4in) deep in autumn, in moist but well-drained soil enriched with well-rotted organic matter, in full sun or partial shade. In heavy clay soils, fork in grit before planting to improve drainage. ■ **Protect** with a winter mulch in cold areas (*see p.326*).
■ **Sow** seed (*see pp.328–329*) in a container in a cold frame when ripe, or remove bulb offsets (*see p.330*) in summer when the bulbs are dormant.

Camassia leichtlinii ♀
‡60–130cm (2–4½ft) ↔ 10cm (4in) ✳✳

Campanula
Bellflower

Campanulas are old favourites in cottage gardens for their tubular, bell- or star-shaped flowers, which are borne in clusters, or occasionally singly, in a range of shades from white to lavender, sky-blue, and soft lilac-pink. Campanulas form a large group of perennial, biennial, or annual plants and vary greatly in habit from spreading mats no more than 5cm (2in) tall, and clump-forming or trailing plants, to upright giants 1.5m (5ft) tall. Smaller species are best for rock gardens. Tall campanulas can punctuate mixed borders or be naturalized in wildflower beds.

■ **HARDINESS** Fully hardy ✳✳✳ to frost-tender ❆.
■ **CULTIVATION** To make cultivation easy, campanulas are divided into groups. ■ **Group 1** need fertile, well-drained, slightly alkaline soil, in sun or partial shade. Taller species require staking. Cut back after flowering to encourage more flowers later. ■ **Group 2** are rock-garden species that need well-drained soil in sun or partial shade. ■ **Groups 3 and 4** are specialist alpine or tender plants that are not often grown in temperate gardens. ■ **Rust**, a fungal disease that causes orange or brown patches to develop on leaves or stems, may afflict some campanulas. Remove affected foliage and thin out congested growth of affected plants. Use an appropriate fungicide if necessary.

Campanula lactiflora **'Loddon Anna'** ♀
‡1.2–1.5m (4–5ft) ↔ 60cm (24in), upright perennial, flowers from early summer to early autumn, cultivation group 1 ✳✳✳

Campanula glomerata **'Superba'** ♀ (Clustered bellflower)
‡60cm (24in) ↔ indefinite, perennial, spreading clumps of upright stems, flowers throughout summer, cultivation group 1 ✳✳✳

Campanula persicifolia **'Telham Beauty'**
‡↔ 90cm (36in), rosette-forming perennial with upright stems, flowers in early and midsummer, cultivation group 1 ✳✳✳

Campanula alliariifolia (Ivory bells)
‡30–60cm (12–24in) ↔ 45cm (18in), clump-forming perennial, flowers from midsummer to early autumn, cultivation group 1 ✳✳✳

Canna
Indian shot plant
MIDSUMMER TO AUTUMN

These striking perennials bring a touch of the exotic to any garden and height to otherwise low borders. They have dramatic foliage, with large leaves in shades of purple-brown to mid-green, sometimes with attractive veining, as well as showy, gladioli-like flowers. The flowers appear in pairs from midsummer to early autumn, in bright shades of scarlet to golden yellow. Cannas have underground stems (rhizomes), which can suffer frost damage in colder areas; lift and store overwinter or grow them as annuals.

■ **HARDINESS** Half-hardy ✳ to frost-tender ✿.
■ **CULTIVATION** Grow cannas in sheltered borders in fertile soil and full sun. In temperate areas, plant outside after all threat of frost is past, in early summer. ■ **Water** these perennials well during summer and feed monthly with a high-potash fertilizer to encourage flowers.
■ **Deadhead** regularly to prolong flowering.
■ **Lift** the plants in autumn, cut them down, and store the rhizomes in peat-free compost in frost-free conditions. ■ **Sow** seed (*see pp.328–329*) in spring or autumn at 21°C (70°F).
■ **Divide** the rhizomes (*see p.330*) in early spring, making sure that each piece has a healthy bud before replanting it.

***Canna* 'Rosemond Coles'**
↕1.5m (5ft) ↔50cm (20in), flowers from midsummer to early autumn ✳

***Canna* 'Durban'**
↕1.2m (4ft) ↔50cm (20in), bears burnt orange flowers in late summer ✳

***Canna* 'Assaut'**
↕2m (6ft) ↔50cm (20in), purple-brown leaves, flowers from midsummer to autumn ✳

Cardamine
Bittercress
LATE SPRING TO EARLY SUMMER

A large group, the bittercresses include both dainty garden plants, which are mostly perennial, and invasive weeds, which are mostly annual. Ornamental types are grown for the four-petalled flowers that they bear in late spring and early summer. The flowers are in shades of pale purple, lilac, white, and occasionally pink. The leaves are variable, sometimes made up of smaller leaflets, and may be lance-shaped and toothed in some species, rounded or kidney-shaped in others. The compact types are ideal for growing in a rock garden or at the front of a border with other plants that flower in late spring, such as camassias (*see p.172*). Other, larger species suit woodland gardens.

■ **HARDINESS** Fully hardy ✳✳✳.
■ **CULTIVATION** Grow in moist soil that has been enriched with plenty of well-rotted organic matter. Position in full sun or partial shade.
■ **Divide** plants (*see p.330*) in spring or after flowering. ■ **Sow** seed in containers in a cold frame in autumn or spring (*see pp.328–329*).

***Cardamine pratensis* 'Flore Pleno'**
↕20cm (8in) ↔30cm (12in), flowers in late spring and has glossy dark green leaves; produces many plantlets at the base

Cardiocrinum
Giant lily
SUMMER

These covetable, stately plants grow to around 4m (12ft) in ideal conditions, so need careful siting. Grow a small group as a specimen planting in woodland or in a shady border. They are bulbous perennials and trumpet-shaped, scented white flowers, occasionally tinged with maroon-purple or green at the base, are borne in clusters in summer. The stems are strong and stout, and the leaves glossy green and heart-shaped. The bulbs die after flowering, but leave many offsets that will flower in four or five years: the spectacular show is well worth the wait.

■ **HARDINESS** Fully hardy ✳✳✳; new growth may be damaged by frost.
■ **CULTIVATION** Plant bulbs just below the soil surface in autumn, in a moist but well-drained, deep, fertile soil. Site in a sheltered spot in partial shade; they will not do well in hot, dry places.
■ **Feed** with a balanced fertilizer two or three times during the growing season to encourage the development of offsets. Top-dress annually with well-rotted organic matter. ■ **Divide** and grow on the bulb offsets (*see p.330*) or sow seed in a deep tray (*see pp.328–329*) in a cool shady place as soon as ripe; they may take seven years to flower.

Cardiocrinum giganteum
↕1.5–4m (5–12ft) ↔ 45cm (18in), has up to 20 strongly scented flowers in each cluster, on tall stout stems

Catananche
Blue cupidone, Cupid's dart
MIDSUMMER TO AUTUMN

Grown for their bright summer flowers, this is a small group of annuals and perennials. Their flowerheads, up to 5cm (2in) across, are similar to those of cornflowers (*see Centaurea, p.176*) and are good for cutting and drying. Produced from midsummer until autumn, they may be lilac-blue, yellow, or white with purple centres. Grass-like, hairy leaves grow from the base. Grow *Catananche caerulea* as an annual with other summer bedding plants like asters (*see pp.162–163*), annual rudbeckias (*see p.265*), and impatiens (*p.221*); *C. caespitosa* is a plant of high, dry meadows, and is best grown in pots and over-wintered under glass.

■ **HARDINESS** Fully hardy ✳✳✳.
■ **CULTIVATION** Grow in any well-drained soil. Position in full sun. ■ **Sow** seed (*see pp.328–329*) in a container in a cold frame in early spring or in drills outside in mid-spring.
■ **Divide** plants that are grown as perennials in spring (*see p.330*). Take root cuttings in winter (*see p.330*) of plants grown as perennials.
■ **Powdery mildew** may be a problem (*see p.333*) and fungicides may be used.

Catananche caerulea 'Bicolor'
↕50–90cm (20–36in) ↔30cm (12in), this perennial is treated as an annual or biennial because it flowers best when young

Celmisia
New Zealand daisy
SPRING AND SUMMER

Ideal for a rock garden, New Zealand daisies are a large group of perennials grown for their attractive evergreen foliage and cheerful daisies. They flower freely in spring and summer, but also have long, thin, leathery leaves, which are silvery green and make them worthwhile for the rest of the year. The flowerheads are around 5cm (2in) across and and are borne on dense, whitish, woolly stems in early summer. They are white, sometimes tinged pink or purple, with yellow centres. Grow them among small shrubs such as lavenders (*see Lavandula, p.71*) and cotton lavenders (*see Santolina, p.99*).

■ **HARDINESS** Fully hardy ✳✳✳.
■ **CULTIVATION** Grow in moist but well-drained, slightly acid (lime-free) soil, in sun or partial shade. Grow smaller types in pots of gritty compost and shelter under glass in winter.
■ **Divide** plants (*see p.330*) in spring or take individual rosettes of leaves with roots and treat as cuttings in spring (*see pp.329–330*).
■ **Sow** seed (*see pp.328–329*) in a container in a cold frame as soon as it is ripe: New Zealand daisies hybridize freely in the garden, but produce few viable seeds.

Celmisia spectabilis
↕↔to 30cm (12in), tufted, clump-forming New Zealand daisy that flowers in early summer

Centaurea

Hardheads, Knapweed

SUMMER

Striking, thistle-like flowerheads that last for many weeks over summer are the main attraction of this group, which includes annuals, biennials, and perennials. The rounded flowerheads may be purple, pink, blue, or yellow, and are often deeply and sometimes darkly fringed. The leaves, which are not particularly attractive, are sometimes toothed, and occasionally grey-green beneath. Try centaureas in a wild planting, or among other bright perennials such as daylilies (*see Hemerocallis, p.216*), achilleas (*see pp.140–141*), phloxes (*see p.254*), or loosestrifes (*see Lythrum, p.235*).

■ **HARDINESS** Fully hardy ✱✱✱ to frost-hardy ✱✱.
■ **CULTIVATION** Most will tolerate some drought and can be grown in well-drained soil in full sun. Taller varieties may need support in the border. ■ **Grow** selections of *C. macrocephala* and *C. montana* in moist but well-drained soil; they tolerate some shade.
■ **Divide** perennials (*see p.330*) in spring or autumn. ■ **Sow** seed in containers in a cold frame (*see pp.328–329*) in spring. ■ **Powdery mildew** may be a problem (*see p.333*) in dry summers; avoid wetting the leaves.

Centaurea 'John Coutts'
‡60cm (24in) ↔ 45cm (18in), clump-forming perennial, flowers are long-lasting and fragrant in summer ✱✱✱

Cerastium

LATE SPRING TO SUMMER

Mainly carpet-forming, this is a large group of annuals and vigorous perennials; a few are grown in gardens, while many others are regarded as invasive weeds. They produce masses of small, starry flowers, singly or in clusters, and have usually simple and hairy leaves. The species grown in gardens, of which the best-known is *Cerastium tomentosum*, make excellent ground-cover plants. They will spread to cover a large area and can become invasive, but are fairly easily to control by simply chopping down with a spade around the edges and uprooting the surplus. These should not be grown among other small plants, however, which they tend to grow into and smother; they are best used to cover an area such as a dry bank where little else will grow.

■ **HARDINESS** Fully hardy ✱✱✱.
■ **CULTIVATION** Grow these plants in any well-drained soil, in full sun; *C. tomentosum* tolerates even poor soils. ■ **Divide** plants (*see p.330*) in early spring. ■ **Sow** seed in a container in a cold frame in autumn (*see pp.328–329*).
■ **Take** stem-tip cuttings (*see p.330*) of established plants in early summer.

Cerastium tomentosum (Snow-in-summer)
‡5–8cm (2–3in) ↔ indefinite, rampant perennial, usually smothered with flowers during late spring and summer

Cerinthe

Honeywort, Wax flower

LATE SPRING TO SUMMER

Exotic-looking but easy-to-grow, these flower from late spring until summer and attract bees. At the tips of the stems, petal-like bracts (modified leaves) that are often sea-blue are packed around small clusters of tubular, nodding flowers, which may be rich purple-blue, dark red, yellow, or white, often combining two colours. The leaves are fleshy and blue-green, and there is often white mottling on the foliage and stems. This small group includes annuals, biennials, and short-lived perennials, but all are usually grown as annuals. Use them in borders or with other summer bedding plants such as China asters (*see pp.162–163*), begonias (*see p.166*), impatiens (*see p.221*), and marigolds (*Tagetes, see p.274*).

■ **HARDINESS** Frost-tender ❀.
■ **CULTIVATION** Grow in any well-drained soil, in full sun. Provide a winter mulch or some other winter protection if grown as perennials; they can also be taken indoors as pot plants.
■ **Sow** seed (*see pp.328–329*) in spring at 20–30°C (65–86°F), and plant out young plants in early summer when threat of frost has passed.

Cerinthe major 'Purpurascens'
‡to 60cm (24in) ↔ 45cm (18in), bracts change from blue-green to purple and then deep blue, from spring to early summer

Chamaemelum
Chamomile

SUMMER

These aromatic, mat-forming, hairy perennials and annuals have feathery or thread-like, fresh green leaves and bear daisy-like white flowerheads with yellow centres in summer. The lawn or Roman chamomile, *Chamaemelum nobile*, is the best known and is attractive in a herb border, as edging or for growing in crevices in paving. The scent from the foliage, which is reminiscent of apples, is released when it is crushed. The non-flowering form 'Treneague' is often used for making a scented lawn; although it does not need mowing, it is not hard-wearing, and so is not suitable for areas that are frequently walked over.

■ **HARDINESS** Fully hardy ✳✳✳.
■ **CULTIVATION** Grow chamomile in well-drained soil, in full sun, in an open site. ■ **Cut back** plants regularly to maintain a compact habit. ■ **Sow** seed where it is to grow (*see p.329*), or divide plants in spring (*see p.330*). 'Treneague' is always grown from divisions. ■ **Plant** divided sections 13–15cm (5–6in) apart to make a lawn, and weed and water regularly until established. Roll lawns occasionally to help keep them level.

Chamaemelum nobile 'Flore Pleno'
‡15cm (6in) ↔ 45cm (18in), double flowers, shorter than the single-flowered form, ideal for edging

Chelone
Turtlehead

LATE SUMMER TO AUTUMN

The curiously shaped, white, purple, or pink flowers of these perennials give them the common name of turtlehead. These showy flowers are carried in short clusters at the tops of the stems from late summer until mid-autumn, and are valuable when many other plants are past their best. Although they are upright in habit, they spread by underground runners so need a bit of space to grow; a clump of them makes good ground cover and suppresses weeds. The flowers stand up well to autumn weather, and make a vivid colour contrast to other late-flowering perennials such as coreopsis (*see p.182*), crocosmias (*see p.184*), and rudbeckias (*see p.265*).

■ **HARDINESS** Fully hardy ✳✳✳.
■ **CULTIVATION** Grow in deep, fertile, moist soil; turtleheads will grow in a bog garden and tolerate heavy clay soils. Position in an open site or in partial shade. ■ **Mulch** with well-rotted organic matter (*see p.326*) in mid-spring. ■ **Sow** seed (*see pp.328–329*) in containers in a cold frame in early spring. ■ **Take** soft-tip cuttings (*see pp.329–330*) in late spring or early summer.

Chelone obliqua
‡40–60cm (16–24in) ↔ 30cm (12in), has spikes of dark pink or purple flowers up to 2cm (½in) long

Chionodoxa
Glory of the snow

EARLY SPRING

In early spring, these easy, bulbous perennials produce starry, clear blue or pink flowers with white eyes. The glossy green leaves usually curve outwards, showing off the flowers. This is a small group of plants, related to the later-flowering scillas (*see p.269*). Grow them in a rock garden or raised bed, or naturalized in grass, where they will self-seed freely. Like cyclamens (*see p.185*), they make a pool of colour if planted around the base of deciduous shrubs, so can be useful in drawing the eye to an interesting winter silhouette such as that of *Corylus avellana* 'Contorta' (*see p.40*).

■ **HARDINESS** Fully hardy ✳✳✳.
■ **CULTIVATION** Grow in any well-drained soil in full sun; only *C. nana* needs protection from winter wet, all others are undemanding plants. Plant bulbs 8cm (3in) deep in autumn. ■ **Sow** seed (*see pp.328–329*) in containers in a cold frame as soon as it is ripe, or remove offsets from bulbs (*see p.330*) in summer; either of these methods should produce bulbs of flowering size after about three years.

Chionodoxa forbesii ♀
‡10–20cm (4–8in) ↔ 3cm (1¼in), species names are sometimes confused on labels, so it may be best to buy it in flower

Chrysanthemum

LATE SUMMER TO AUTUMN

Popular for their bright, showy flowers, these upright, bushy annuals and herbaceous perennials are the stars of late summer and autumn. They are grown primarily for border displays, for cutting, and for exhibition, and come in a range of glowing colours from ivory to pink, crimson, and gold, with blooms that vary vastly in shape, size, and form. There are ten chrysanthemum flowerhead categories. Some, especially the huge exhibition varieties, can be demanding since rain may damage the flowers and many are not hardy. Those classed as Rubellum Group chrysanthemums, such as 'Clara Curtis', are among the easiest to grow and are ideal for beds and borders, as are the many hardy pompon and spray types, which include the 'Pennine' cultivars. Annual *Chrysanthemum* (syn. *Xanthophthalum*) *segetum* (corn marigold) and *X. carinatum* put on a long, colourful display.

■ **HARDINESS** Fully hardy ✽✽✽ to frost tender ✿.
■ **CULTIVATION** Check the plant label or catalogue for growing requirements and hardiness. ■ **Plant** from late spring in a sheltered site in full sun, in fertile, moist, but well-drained soil. ■ **Support** tall varieties with canes and tie in. Pinch out (*see below*) to improve shape and flowering. ■ **Water** freely during dry spells and feed with a balanced fertilizer every 7–10 days from midsummer until the buds begin to show some colour. ■ **Lift** non-hardy types after the first frost and store in a frost-free place for winter. Hardy types can remain in the ground.

Pinch pruning chrysanthemums

Pinch pruning a plant – taking out the growing tip or tips – encourages it to produce plenty of sideshoots from the buds in the leaf axils (where leaf stalk joins stem) lower down the stem. This results in a bushier, more attractive shape, and also in extra flowers on plants such as chrysanthemums and fuchsias. The more frequently a plant is pinch pruned, the greater the number of sideshoots and flowers it will produce. This technique is especially worth doing for plants in containers for a more compact style of growth. For the greatest success, plants need to be growing strongly so, if necessary, feed them with a balanced fertilizer.

Step 1 When the plant is 15–20cm (6–8in) high, pinch out the tip of the shoot just above a leaf joint, using your finger and thumb. Remove only the small tip to encourage the maximum number of flower-bearing sideshoots (known as breaks).

Step 2 Side buds grow and develop into shoots. When these shoots have developed four leaves, repeat the pinching (called the second stop). Pinch pruning stimulates shoots from the tip and lower down the stem, creating a much bushier plant.

Step 3 Keep pinching out the tips of the shoots until the plant is furnished with plenty of bushy growth. Stop pinching in early autumn to let flowering shoots develop.

C. **'Alison Kirk'** ↕1.2m (4ft) ↔40cm (16in) ✽

C. **'Autumn Days'** ↕1.2m (4ft) ↔75cm (30in) ✽

C. **carinatum** ↕60cm (2ft) ↔30cm (1ft), annual ✽

C. **'Clara Curtis'** ↕75cm (30in) ↔60cm (2ft), Rubellum Group ✽✽✽

C. **'Pavilion'** ↕1.3m (4½ft) ↔60–75cm (24–30in) ✽

C. **'Pennine Alfie'** ♀ ↕1.2m (4ft) ↔75cm (30in) ✽✽✽

C. **'Rose Madeleine'** ♀ ↕1.2m (4ft) ↔75cm (30in) ✽✽✽

C. **'Roy Coopland'** ♀ ↕1.4m (4½ft) ↔60cm (24in) ✿

C. 'Brietner's Supreme' ‡1.2m (4ft)
↔75cm (30in) ✽✽   **C. 'Bronze Fairie'** ♀ ‡↔60cm (30in) ✽✽✽   **C. 'Bronze Hedgerow'** ‡1.5m (5ft)
↔75–100cm (30–39in) ❀   **C. 'Bronze Yvonne Arnaud'** ‡1.2m
(4ft) ↔60–75cm (24–30in) ✽✽

C. 'George Griffiths' ♀ ‡1.5m (5ft)
↔1m (3ft) ✽✽   **C. 'Maria'** ‡45cm (18in) ↔30–60cm
(12–24in) ✽✽✽   **C. 'Marion'** ‡1.2m (4ft) ↔75cm (30in) ✽✽✽   **C. 'Marlene Jones'** ‡1m (3ft) ↔60cm
(24in) ✽✽✽

C. 'Pennine Flute' ♀ ‡1.2m (4ft)
→75cm (30in) ✽✽✽   **C. 'Pennine Oriel'** ♀ ‡1.2m (4ft)
↔60–75cm (24–30in) ✽✽✽   **C. 'Primrose Margaret'** ‡1.2m (4ft)
↔60–75cm (24–30in) ✽✽✽   **C. 'Purple Pennine Wine'** ♀ ‡1.2m
(4ft) ↔75cm (30in) ✽✽✽

C. 'Salmon Fairie' ♀ ‡30–60cm
(12–24in) ↔60cm (24in) ✽✽✽   **C. 'Satin Pink Gin'** ♀ ‡1.2m (4ft)
↔75–100cm (30–39in) ❀   **C. 'Wendy'** ♀ ‡1.2m (4ft) ↔60–75cm
(24–30in) ✽✽✽   **C. 'Yvonne Arnaud'** ♀ ‡1.2m (4ft)
↔60–75cm (24–30in) ✽✽

Cirsium
Plumed thistle, Creeping thistle
SUMMER TO AUTUMN

The opulent, jewel-like shades sported by the flowers of the cirsium deserve a place in every garden. The hues range from deep crimson-purple to rich reds, yellows, and sometimes white. The flowers, up to 3cm (1¼in) across, are carried singly or in small clusters over dark green, prickly leaves in summer and autumn. Cirsiums belong to a large group of perennials and biennials; some form clumps, others spread by means of underground stems (rhizomes) and can be invasive. Cirsiums look dramatic grown among fine grasses (*see pp.284–299*) or with other summer-flowering perennials such as coreopsis (*see p.182*), phloxes (*see p.254*), and cranesbills (*see Geranium, pp.208–209*). They also blend in well in naturalistic borders.

■ **HARDINESS** Fully hardy ✿✿✿.
■ **CULTIVATION** Cirsiums need moist but well-drained soil, in full sun. ■ **Deadhead** to avoid self-seeding if growing cirsiums in a formal garden. ■ **Sow** seed (*see pp.328–329*) in a cold frame in spring or divide plants (*see p.330*) in autumn or spring.

Cirsium rivulare 'Atropurpureum'
‡1.2m (4ft) ↔ 60cm (24in), clump-forming perennial, flowers in early and midsummer

Clematis
Old man's beard, Virgin's bower
SUMMER TO LATE AUTUMN

There are a few clematis that are herbaceous perennials, forming open, sometimes woody-based plants smothered in delicate, often scented flowers. These appear in summer to late autumn. All the herbaceous clematis have very attractive, dark, mid- or grey-green leaves that vary in shape. Their soft stems require some support to stop them flopping over with the weight of the flowers. Plant these clematis in large containers or towards the centres of herbaceous or mixed borders among other summer-flowering perennials such as cranesbills (*see Geranium, pp.208–209*), and achilleas (*see p.140*). (*See also pp.118–119.*)

■ **HARDINESS** Fully hardy ✿✿✿ to frost-hardy ✿✿.
■ **CULTIVATION** These clematis require full sun in fertile soil that has been enriched with

well-rotted organic matter. ■ **Prune** (*see pp.322–323*) the previous year's growth back to two or three buds, about 15–20cm (6–8in) from the base of the plant, before new growth starts in early spring. ■ **Support** the stems with twiggy peasticks. ■ **Mulch** with a layer of garden compost or well-rotted manure in late winter. ■ **Divide** in spring (*see p.330*) or take semi-ripe cuttings (*see pp.329–330*) in summer.

Clematis recta
‡1–2m (3–6ft) ↔ 75cm (30in), clump-forming, heavily scented flowers from midsummer to autumn, decorative seedheads ✿✿✿

Clematis integrifolia
‡↔ 60cm (24in), flowers in summer, followed by silvery brown, silky seedheads ✿✿✿

Clematis tubulosa 'Wyevale' ♀
‡75cm (30in) ↔ 1m (3ft), open bush, scented, light to mid-blue flowers that are 4cm (1½in) long in summer ✿✿✿

Colchicum
Autumn crocus, Naked lady

AUTUMN

Autumn crocuses are a late-season treasure, their flowers emerging seemingly from nowhere in autumn before the leaves appear. A few appear in spring. The flowers are sometimes fragrant and come in delicate shades of lilac-pink or white. The strappy leaves of these bulbous perennials last from winter to spring. Sizes vary from large cultivars such as 'The Giant' which has a height of 20cm (8in) and spread of 10cm (4in) to the tiny *Colchicum kesselringii* which, with a height and spread of 2.5cm (1in), is best grown as an alpine. Large-leaved colchicums such as 'Autumn Queen' sprawl untidily after the wind or rain and should be grown in the shelter of deciduous shrubs. Naturalize others such as *C. speciosum* and *C. autumnale* in grass. All are highly toxic.

■ **HARDINESS** Fully hardy ✳✳✳ to half-hardy ✳✳.
■ **CULTIVATION** Plant the corms 10cm (4in) deep, in deep, fertile, well-drained, moisture-retentive soil, in summer or early autumn. Choose an open, sunny site. Small alpine species need gritty, sharply draining soil. ■ **Feed** with a low-nitrogen fertilizer before growth starts. ■ **Divide** large clumps (*see p.330*) in summer.

Colchicum byzantinum ♀
‡13cm (5in) ↔10cm (4in) ✳✳✳

Colchicum autumnale **'Album'**
‡10–15cm (4–6in) ↔8cm (3in) ✳✳✳

Colchicum speciosum **'Album'** ♀
‡18cm (7in) ↔10cm (4in) ✳✳✳

Colchicum **'Waterlily'** ♀
‡13cm (5in) ↔10cm (4in) ✳✳✳

Convallaria majalis
Lily-of-the-valley

LATE SPRING TO EARLY SUMMER

Famed for their strong fragrance, the dainty white flowers of this small, creeping perennial are borne on arching stems in late spring to early summer. Lily-of-the-valley has mid- to dark green leaves, and makes an excellent ground cover in a woodland garden or moist, shady border. It spreads by means of underground stems (rhizomes) and rapidly forms new colonies in favourable conditions. To show off these plants at their best, grow them under deciduous shrubs so that their bell-shaped flowers stand out against a background of newly opening spring leaves. Forms of lily-of-the-valley with pink flowers or variegated leaves are available.

■ **HARDINESS** Fully hardy ✳✳✳.
■ **CULTIVATION** A shady position in moist, fertile soil that has been enriched with well-rotted organic matter is best for lily-of-the-valley. ■ **Lift** some of the rhizomes and pot them up in autumn for a display of fragrant flowers indoors. Replant them outdoors after flowering in the spring. ■ **Sow** seed (*see pp.328–329*) in containers in a cold frame as soon as it is ripe.

Convallaria majalis ♀
‡23cm (9in) ↔30cm (12in), waxy flowers are held in graceful sprays, good for cutting

Convolvulus

Bindweed

SUMMER TO AUTUMN

Do not confuse these annuals and perennials with the pernicious, choking weed that shares their common name. These plants produce flowers in several shades, from white, blue, and creamy white, often with a contrasting coloured centre, and are suitable for mixed borders, rock gardens, and sunny banks. The more compact forms grow to only around 30cm (12in) tall. *Convolvulus sabatius* is good in containers. The perennials are short-lived and are often treated as annuals. Grow bindweed with annuals such as marigolds (*see Calendula officinalis, p.171*).

■ **HARDINESS** Fully hardy ❄❄❄ to frost-hardy ❄❄.
■ **CULTIVATION** These trouble-free plants require poor to moderately fertile, well-drained soil and a sunny, sheltered site. ■ **Deadhead** flowers to prolong the flowering period into autumn. ■ **Container-grown plants** require loam-based compost, frequent watering in dry weather, and a weekly feed with a balanced fertilizer. ■ **Sow** seed (*see pp.328–329*) of annuals directly in the garden in mid-spring, or in autumn with cloche protection over winter. ■ **Divide** (*see p.330*) perennials in spring.

Convolvulus sabatius 🏆
↕15cm (6in) ↔50cm (20in), trailing, slender-stemmed perennial, pale to deep lavender flowers from summer to early autumn ❄❄

Coreopsis

Tickseed

LATE SPRING TO LATE SUMMER

Both the perennials and annuals are grown for their bright, daisy-like, summer-long flowers. Coreopsis has masses of single or double flowers, all in shades of gold, which are produced on stems rising above fine foliage. The flowers not only attract bees into the garden, they also make successful cut flowers. Many of the perennials are short-lived, however, and are grown as annuals – usually flowering freely in their first year from seed sown in spring. Grow them in a sunny border with perennials such as achilleas (*see p.140*) and phloxes (*see p.254*).

■ **HARDINESS** Fully hardy ❄❄❄ to frost-tender ❀.
■ **CULTIVATION** Fertile, well-drained soil and a position in full sun or partial shade are required for this plant. ■ **Remove** fading flowers to prolong flowering. ■ **Stake** taller-growing plants to support the flower stems (*see p.327*). ■ **Sow** seed (*see pp.328–329*) in a seedbed outdoors in spring or indoors at 13–16°C (55–61°F) in late winter or early spring; sow in small batches from early spring to early summer for a longer succession of flowers. ■ **Divide** (*see p.330*) perennials in early spring.

***Coreopsis* 'Schnittgold'**
↕80cm (32in) ↔60cm (24in), flowers in early to midsummer ❄❄❄

Corydalis

SPRING TO AUTUMN

Low-growing and clump-forming, the numerous perennials, annuals, and biennials are favoured by gardeners for their distinctive flowers. These occur in shades of blue, white, and red, and are borne in clusters above the foliage in the spring, summer, or autumn. The ferny leaves are usually mid- to light green and in a few species, such as *Corydalis lutea* and *C. ochroleuca*, are evergreen. The perennials have tuberous ('George Baker') or rhizomatous roots. Some species will self-seed freely. They are

Corydalis lutea
↕40cm (16in) ↔30cm (12in) ❄❄❄

Corydalis flexuosa 🏆
↕30cm (12in) ↔20cm (8in) ❄❄❄

best grown in a border or rock garden, but often survive in soil-filled cracks in walls and paving. Some corydalis require a dry, dormant summer period and protection from winter wet, and are best grown in shallow pots in an unheated greenhouse or cold frame.

■ **HARDINESS** Fully hardy ✽✽✽ to frost-hardy ✽✽.
■ **CULTIVATION** All need free-draining, moderately fertile soil enriched with well-rotted organic matter. Some corydalis prefer sun, others like partial shade. ■ **Sow** seed (*see pp.328–329*) in pots in an open frame as soon as it is ripe; germination can be erratic.
■ **Divide** spring-flowering species in autumn, and summer-flowering ones in spring (*see p.330*).

Corydalis solida **'George Baker'** ♀
‡25cm (10in) ↔20cm (8in) ✽✽✽

Corydalis ochroleuca
‡↔30cm (12in) ✽✽✽

Cosmos

MIDSUMMER TO AUTUMN

Cosmos are invaluable for informal gardens. They include easy-to-grow tuberous perennials and annuals favoured for their crimson-red, pink, or white, bowl- or saucer-shaped flowers, produced on long stems in summer. The perennial chocolate cosmos (*Cosmos atrosanguineus*), with reddish-brown stems and dark green leaves, has velvety, chocolate-scented flowers from midsummer until autumn. Slightly tender, it needs winter protection once the foliage dies back. Grow them with other border plants such as phloxes (*see p.254*) and grey-leaved plants like santolinas (*see p.99*) to contrast with the dark flowers. Sow the annual *C. bipinnatus* in a drift, or plant to fill mid- and late-summer gaps in a border.

■ **HARDINESS** Frost-hardy ✽✽ to frost-tender ❅.
■ **CULTIVATION** Grow in reasonably fertile soil that is moist but well-drained, in full sun. Deadhead to prolong flowering. ■ **Lift** and store tubers in autumn in frost-free conditions.
■ **Sow** annuals where they are to grow in spring or autumn in milder gardens, or in pots (*see pp.328–329*). Thin seedlings to 15cm (6in).

Cosmos atrosanguineus
‡75cm (30in) ↔45cm (18in) ✽✽

Crambe

LATE SPRING TO MIDSUMMER

Tall, but with an airy presence, these woody-based annuals or perennials are grown for their handsome, wavy-edged leaves and sprays of tiny, often white, sometimes fragrant flowers. The flowers appear from late spring to midsummer on strong stems above undulating, dark green or blue-grey foliage. The large leaves are decorative when young, but tend to die down in mid- to late summer. While crambes are magnificent in a mixed border, taller species, such as *Crambe cordifolia*, need lots of space. They are a good choice for coastal sites because the foliage withstands sea spray and salt-laden winds. Grow them with old garden roses (*see pp.96–97*) and philadelphus (*see p.82*).

■ **HARDINESS** Fully hardy ✽✽✽.
■ **CULTIVATION** Grow in deep, fertile, well-drained soil in full sun, although they also tolerate poor soil and partial shade. Shelter from strong winds. ■ **Sow** seed (*see pp.328–329*) in a pot in a cold frame in spring or autumn.
■ **Divide** pants (*see p.330*) in early spring.
■ **Clubroot**, a persistent, soil-borne disease that can affect crambes and other members of the cabbage family, causes deformed roots and stunted plants. Dig out and burn affected plants.

Crambe cordifolia ♀
‡to 2.5m (8ft) ↔1.5m (5ft), perennial, bristly leaves to 35cm (14in) across, flowers from late spring to midsummer ✽✽✽

Crinum

SPRING TO AUTUMN

Reminiscent of lilies, crinums belong to a large group of stately, deciduous and evergreen bulbous perennials. They are grown for their showy, white and pink flowers, which are often deliciously scented. The flowers are borne on long, leafless stalks from spring to autumn, depending on the species. The long, strappy leaves are a glossy, light to mid-green. Crinums are best grown outside in a warm, sheltered border together with other perennials like *Anemone hupehensis* and forms of *A.* x *hybrida* (*see p.152*), border phloxes (*see p.254*) and daylilies (*see Hemerocallis, p.216*).

■ **HARDINESS** Fully hardy ✳✳✳ (borderline) to frost-tender ❦.
■ **CULTIVATION** Plant crambe in spring with the neck of each bulb just above soil level, in deep, fertile soil that is moist but very well-drained, and enriched with well-rotted organic matter. Choose a position in full sun, preferably by a wall. ■ **Water** generously when crinums are in growth and then keep moist after flowering. ■ **Divide** large clumps of the huge bulbs in spring (*see p.330*) to increase your stock.

***Crinum* x *powellii* 'Album'** ♀
↕1.5m (5ft) ↔30cm (12in), deciduous, up to ten fragrant flowers per stem from late summer to autumn ✳✳✳ (borderline)

Crocosmia

Montbretia

MID- TO LATE SUMMER

Perfect for hot-coloured borders, these eye-catching perennials produce arching sprays of flowers in vivid shades of scarlet, orange, and yellow, as well as bicolors in red and orange. From mid- to late summer, long-lasting flowers are held on wiry stems that may be branched or unbranched – they are good for cutting. Crocosmias are robust, forming clumps of flat, sword-like leaves that stand erect but fan out slightly, making a strong accent in a bed or border. Established clumps spread to around 60cm (2ft). Plant crocosmia corms in a shrub border or with other late-summer perennials, such as Michaelmas daisies (*see Aster, pp.162–163*), rudbeckias (*see p.265*), and sedums (*see p.270*).

■ **HARDINESS** Fully hardy ✳✳✳ to frost-hardy ✳✳.
■ **CULTIVATION** Plant corms in spring, 8–10cm (3–4in) deep, in soil enriched with well-rotted organic matter, in sun or partial shade. In frost-prone gardens, plant close to a sheltered wall. ■ **Divide** congested clumps in spring or autumn every three or four years to maintain the vigour of the plants (*see p.330*).

***Crocosmia* 'Lucifer'** ♀
↕1–1.2m (3–4ft) ↔8cm (3in), flowers 5cm (2in) long in midsummer on sparsely branched spikes ✳✳✳ (borderline)

Crocus

SPRING AND AUTUMN

Not just a welcome sign of spring, some crocuses also extend the season well into autumn. This is a large group of dwarf perennials that grow from corms, producing flowers at the same time as, or just before, the narrow, grassy foliage. The flowers come in vivid or pastel shades from yellow to lilac, purple, and white and are sometimes striped or shaded. The leaves are mid-green with a central, silver-green stripe. They are easy to grow and look best planted in drifts in a border or naturalized in short grass for carpets of colour. Grow them with spring-flowering bulbs like dwarf narcissi (*see pp.240–241*) or autumn-flowering hardy cyclamens (*see p.181*).

■ **HARDINESS** Fully hardy ✳✳✳ to frost-hardy ✳✳.
■ **CULTIVATION** Most prefer gritty, not too rich, well-drained soil in full sun or partial shade. ■ **Plant** in situ; spring-flowering types 8–10cm (3–4in) deep in autumn, autumn-flowering ones in late summer. Plant autumn crocuses in containers and bring indoors to flower. ■ **Divide** cormlets (*see p.330*) when dormant and replant or leave to self-seed freely. ■ **Rodents** may feed on the corms; deter them by covering corms at planting with chicken wire before replacing the soil.

Crocus speciosus ♀
↕10–15cm (4–6in) ↔5cm (2in), autumn-flowering crocus that increases rapidly; flowers produced before the leaves ✳✳✳

***Crocus* 'Gipsy Girl'**
‡8cm (3in) ↔ 5cm (2in), flowers in early spring ✽✽✽

***Crocus sieberi* 'Albus'** ♀
‡5–8cm (2–3in) ↔ 2.5cm (1in), flowers 3–4.5cm
(¹/₂–1¹/₂in) long with deep yellow throats, in early
spring ✽✽✽

***Crocus sieberi* 'Hubert Edelsten'** ♀
‡5–8cm (2–3in) ↔ 2.5cm (1in), flowers in late
winter to early spring ✽✽✽

***Crocus* 'Snow Bunting'** ♀
‡8cm (3in) ↔ 5cm (2in), scented flowers in early
spring, up to four per plant ✽✽✽

Cyclamen
Sowbread

AUTUMN TO LATE WINTER

Hardy cyclamen bring winter cheer
to gardens and windowboxes. The
elegant flowers of these tuberous
perennials are held aloft on leafless
flower stalks. They are produced,
depending on the species, from
autumn until late winter and vary in
hue from white to pink to carmine-red.
The leaves are attractively marked
with silver zones or patterns; they last
through winter to spring. Grow hardy
cyclamens under trees, or at the front
of a shrub border with early bulbs
such as snowdrops (*see Galanthus,
p.205*) and spring-flowering crocuses
(*see facing page*); they also do well in
a rock garden or container. Do not
confuse them with cyclamens sold
as houseplants, which are not hardy.

■ **HARDINESS** Fully hardy ✽✽✽ to
frost-hardy ✽✽.
■ **CULTIVATION** Plant the corms 2.5–5cm
(1–2in) deep in well-drained, humus-rich, fertile
soil. They prefer dryish conditions in summer.
■ **Mulch** (*see p.326*) with leafmould every year
after the leaves die down. ■ **Rodents** can be
deterred by covering corms at planting with
chicken wire before replacing the soil.

Cyclamen cilicium ♀
‡5cm (2in) ↔ 8cm (3in), pink or white flowers
in autumn, stained carmine-red at the mouth,
strongly patterned leaves ✽✽

Cynara

SUMMER TO AUTUMN

These imposing, architectural plants
have great presence in a border. The
clump-forming perennials produce tall,
thistle-like flowerheads in shades of
blue and violet from summer until
autumn. The unopened buds of the
globe artichoke (*Cynara scolymus*) are
edible, and the flowers can be dried
and used in indoor arrangements.
The boldly cut, silver or greyish-green
leaves arch elegantly in the manner of
a fountain, making this an impressive
foliage plant for the back of a mixed
or herbaceous border with other
perennials such as veronicas (*see
p.281*), salvias (*see p.266*), or daylilies
(*see Hemerocallis, p.216*). Cynaras also
attract bees and other pollinating
insects into the garden.

■ **HARDINESS** Fully hardy ✽✽✽ to
frost-hardy ✽✽.
■ **CULTIVATION** Grow cynara in any
reasonably fertile soil that is well-drained and
in full sun. Where winters are very cold, protect
with a mulch of organic matter (*see p.326*).
■ **Sow** seed (*see pp.328–329*) in a container in a
cold frame or divide plants (*see p.330*) in spring.
New shoots are vulnerable to slugs and snails.

Cynara cardunculus ♀ (Cardoon)
‡1.5m (5ft) ↔ 1.2m (4ft), spiny leaves, woolly grey
stems, flowers early to late summer, blanched
leaf-stalks and midribs edible ✽✽✽

Dahlia

Dahlias are deservedly popular garden plants, putting on a bravura performance from midsummer until the first frosts of autumn, in shades from white to vivid yellow, orange, scarlet, pink, and purple. In addition to bringing welcome colour as summer plants fade, the blooms are good for cutting, and a few cultivars have rich, chocolate-coloured foliage. Dahlias, which grow from tubers, are generally tender perennials. In permanent plantings, reserve spaces for them because tubers cannot be set out until late spring or early summer, except in mild, frost-free areas. The smaller bedding types are often treated as annuals and grown from seed; they are superb for edging borders or growing in containers. There are several categories of dahlia, including singles and fully doubles, with collarettes and waterlilies somewhere in between. Cactus types have spiky, quill-shaped petals, while pompons and balls have a pleasing geometry. The giant decoratives may have flowers the size of a tea plate.

■ **HARDINESS** Frost-hardy ✱✱.
■ **CULTIVATION** Grow in full sun in deep, fertile soil enriched with plenty of well-rotted farmyard manure or garden compost. Bedding dahlias tolerate less rich conditions. In milder areas, tubers can be left in the ground, covered with a dry mulch over winter. ■ **Plant out** young plants in leaf when the threat of frost has passed in early summer – dormant tubers a little earlier – and lift in mid-autumn (*see below*). ■ **Support** with stout stakes or three canes inserted at planting and tie in new growth. Bedding dahlias do not need staking. ■ **Water** well in dry periods, and feed regularly during the growing season with nitrogenous fertilizer; from midsummer switch to a high-potash fertilizer to encourage flowering. ■ **Cut** flowers regularly to ensure a succession of blooms; for large flowers restrict the plants to two or three shoots. ■ **Propagate** by starting tubers into growth in spring in a greenhouse or cold frame. Divide into sections, each with a growing shoot, and pot up each as a new plant. ■ **Slugs** (*see p.332*) and earwigs (*see p.333*) may eat the leaves and flowers.

Storing dahlias over winter

Step 1 In mid-autumn, ideally after the foliage has been blackened by the first frost, cut the old stems back, taking care to leave 15cm (6in) of stem attached to each tuber. Loosen the soil and lift out the tubers. Clean off excess soil from and attach a label to each.

Step 2 Store the tubers upside-down for about three weeks in a frost-free place, to allow moisture to drain from the stems. When dried out, put in a cool, frost-free place and cover with bark chippings. Keep them dry until spring, but inspect occasionally for disease.

Step 3 In spring, about six weeks before the last frosts are expected, plant out dormant tubers. Before planting tall types, insert a stout 1m (3ft) stake in the planting hole. Add soil around the tuber so that the crown, where the stem and tubers are joined, is 2.5–5cm (1–2in) below soil level. Shoots will show in about six weeks.

D. 'Bishop of Llandaff' ♥ ‡1.1m (3½ft) ↔45cm (18in), peony-flowered miscellaneous group

D. 'Candy Cane' ‡1–1.2m (3–4ft) ↔60cm (2ft), miniature waterlily

D. 'David Howard' ♥ ‡↔90cm (3ft), miniature decorative

D. 'Fascination' ♥ ‡60cm (2ft) ↔45cm (18in), annual bedding

D. 'Noreen' ‡1m (3ft) ↔45cm (18in), pompon

D. 'Pink Giraffe' ♥ ‡↔60–90cm (2–3 orchid-flowered miscellaneous group

D. 'Small World' ♥ ‡1.1m (3½ft) ↔60cm (2ft), pompon

D. 'So Dainty' ♥ ‡1.1m (3½ft) ↔60cm (2ft), miniature semi-cactus

D. **'Clair de Lune'** ♀ ‡1.1m (3½ft) ↔60cm (2ft), collerette

D. **'Conway'** ‡1.1m (3½ft) ↔60cm (2ft), small semi-cactus

D. **'Corton Olympic'** ‡1.2m (4ft) ↔60cm (2ft), giant decorative

D. **'Davenport Sunlight'** ‡1.2m (4ft) ↔60cm (2ft), medium semi-cactus

D. **'Hamari Accord'** ♀ ‡1.2m (4ft) ↔60cm (2ft), large semi-cactus

D. **'Hamari Gold'** ♀ ‡1.2m (4ft) ↔60cm (2ft), giant decorative

D. **'Hillcrest Royal'** ♀ ‡1.1m (3½ft) ↔60cm (24in), medium cactus

D. **'Nina Chester'** ‡1.1m (3½ft) ↔60cm (2ft), small decorative

D. **'Pontiac'** ‡1.2m (4ft) ↔60cm (2ft), semi-cactus

D. **'Preston Park'** ♀ ‡↔45cm (18in), annual bedding

D. **'Rhonda'** ‡1.1m (3½ft) ↔60cm (2ft), pompon

D. **'Rokesly Mini'** ‡1m (3ft) ↔45cm (18in), semi-cactus

D. **'White Alva's'** ♀ ‡1.2m (4ft) ↔60cm (2ft), giant decorative

D. **'Wootton Cupid'** ♀ ‡1.1m (3½ft) ↔60cm (2ft), miniature ball

D. **'Wootton Impact'** ♀ ‡1.2m (4ft) ↔60cm (2ft), semi-cactus

D. **'Zorro'** ♀ ‡1.2m (4ft) ↔60cm (2ft), giant decorative

Darmera peltata

LATE SPRING

Handsome and unusual, this spreading perennial enjoys moisture. In late spring, pink or white flowers are borne in clusters at the tips of sturdy, hairy stems that can grow to 2m (6ft) in height. It is only when the flowers begin to fade that the rounded, long-stemmed leaves, which are up to 60cm (24in) across, begin to unfurl. This impressive foliage turns scarlet in autumn, before dying down over winter. *Darmera peltata* is a large plant that needs plenty of space, and although it will grow in a shady border, darmeras prefer sites in bog gardens or by water. Try it with other moisture-loving plants like astilbes (*see p.164*) or primulas (*see pp.260–261*), or plant a group of them together to emphasize their striking forms.

■ **HARDINESS** Fully hardy ✳✳✳, although flowers may be damaged by late frosts.
■ **CULTIVATION** This plant prefers moist or boggy soil in sun or shade, but it will tolerate drier soil in shade. ■ **Sow** seed (*see pp.328–329*) in containers in a cold frame in spring or autumn, or divide plants (*see p.330*) in spring.

Darmera peltata ♀
‡2m (6ft) ↔1m (3ft) or more

Delphinium

EARLY TO MIDSUMMER

With their towering spikes of flowers, delphiniums are perfect for adding height and form to a border. The blooms are borne in early and midsummer, in a wide range of colours from creamy whites through to lilac-pinks, sky-blues, and deepest, darkest indigo. The mid-green leaves form clumps around the bases of the flower stems. The garden delphiniums are usually herbaceous perennials. Their flower spikes make the stems top-heavy and prone to snapping in winds, so they need support and a sheltered position. This can often be provided by placing them at the back of a border by a wall or fence. Small species and dwarf varieties are suited to more exposed areas. Belladonna types are easier to grow.

***Delphinium* 'Sungleam'** ♀
‡1.5m (5ft) ↔ 60–90cm (24–36in), clump-forming perennial

■ **HARDINESS** Fully hardy ✳✳✳.
■ **CULTIVATION** Delphiniums like fertile, moist but well-drained soil in full sun. Provide support with sturdy bamboo canes.
■ **Deadhead** regularly (*see p.327*) and you may be rewarded with another flush of flowers later in the summer, but do not expect them to be as spectacular as the first. ■ **Sow** seed (*see pp.328–329*) at 13°C (55°F) in early spring.
■ **Slugs** and snails (*see p.332*), and powdery mildew (exacerbated by damp dry soil) can be troublesome.

Delphinium nudicaule
‡60–90cm (24–36in) ↔20cm (8in), short perennial grown as an annual, flowers in midsummer only

***Delphinium* 'Fanfare'**
‡2.2m (7ft) ↔ 60–90cm (24–36in), clump-forming perennial

Delphinium **'Mighty Atom'**
↕1.5m (5ft) ↔ 60–90cm (24–36in), clump-forming perennial, flowers and stems may be deformed if too many flowers are pollinated

Dianthus
Carnation, Pink

`SUMMER`

The main garden plants in this group of evergreen perennials and annuals are pinks and border carnations. In summer, both bear a profusion of bright flowers, which last well when cut, above narrow, silvery leaves. The flowers are single or double in many shades of pink, white, carmine, salmon, and mauve, often with darker, contrasting markings on the petals. Some are fragrant, particularly the rich, spicy "clove-scented" cultivars. Pinks are smaller than carnations and have fewer petals, but other than this their flowers and growth habits are similar. Smaller pinks, including the alpine types like *Dianthus* 'Little Jock', are excellent in rock gardens and troughs. The perpetual carnations, grown under glass for cut flowers, are by far the tallest in the group. Sweet William (*D. barbatus*) is a short-lived perennial usually grown as a biennial from seed sown in summer; plants flower in the following year.

■ **HARDINESS** Fully hardy ✲✲✲; perpetual carnations half-hardy ✲.
■ **CULTIVATION** All dianthus require a well-drained, neutral to alkaline soil enriched with well-rotted manure or garden compost. Position plants in full sun. Alpine cultivars, especially, benefit from sharp drainage in alpine troughs and raised beds. ■ **Plant out** young plants in spring and early summer and feed with a balanced fertilizer in spring. ■ **Support** tall cultivars in spring using thin canes and string.
■ **Deadhead** (remove fading flowers) to encourage plants to produce more flowers and maintain a compact growth habit (*see p.327*). Annuals and biennials are discarded after flowering.

Dianthus **'Brympton Red'**
↕45cm (18in) ↔ 30cm (1ft), pink

Delphinium **'Blue Nile'** ♀
↕1.7m (5½ft) ↔ 60–90cm (24–36in), clump-forming perennial

Dianthus **'Dad's Favourite'**
↕45cm (18in) ↔ 30cm (1ft), pink

Dianthus **'Valda Wyatt'** ♀
↕45cm (18in) ↔ 40cm (16in), scented pink

Diascia

For their length of flowering alone, these annuals and semi-evergreen perennials are worthy of any garden. Loose, densely packed flowerheads bloom from early summer to autumn above heart-shaped, mid-green leaves. The main flush of flowers is in early summer, but if you trim back plants after this, they produce another flush later in the summer. The colour range includes shades of apricot, deep pink, rose-pink, purplish-pink, or salmon-pink. Try growing diascias at the front of a herbaceous border, under roses, or in a rock garden. Most diascias are creeping or mat-forming, but some of them have a trailing habit which makes them excellent in containers. Diascias are not reliably hardy, so take cuttings to ensure that you keep them for next year.

■ **HARDINESS** Most are hardy to -8°C (18°F) ❄❄.
■ **CULTIVATION** Diascias prefer moist but well-drained, fertile soil, in full sun. Water in dry periods. ■ **Sow** seed (see pp.328–329) at 16°C (61°F) once ripe, or in spring. Take semi-ripe cuttings in late summer (see pp.329–330). Overwinter young plants in frost-free conditions.

Diascia rigescens ♀
‡30cm (12in) ↔ 50cm (20in)

Diascia barberae 'Fisher's Flora' ♀
‡25cm (10in) ↔ 50cm (20in)

Diascia barberae 'Blackthorn Apricot' ♀
‡25cm (10in) ↔ 50cm (20in)

Diascia fetcaniensis
‡25cm (10in) ↔ 50cm (20in)

Dicentra

This cottage-garden favourite is grown both for its finely cut foliage and heart-shaped flowers. Most are perennials and form compact clumps with ferny, often greyish leaves and arching stems from which the flowers are suspended. Flowers are produced from spring to early summer in a range of shades from red, purple, and deep pink to white or yellow. Dicentras are also at home in a mixed border, cottage-garden planting, or in woodland garden. They may die down early in dry summers. Their delicate flowers and foliage contrasts nicely with the broad young foliage of hostas (see pp.218–219).

Dicentra cucullaria (Dutchman's breeches)
‡to 20cm (8in) ↔ 25cm (10in), tuberous perennial, compact clumps, white or pink flowers in early spring, needs gritty soil

Dicentra spectabilis ♀ (Bleeding heart, Lyre flower)
‡to 1.2m (4ft) ↔ 45cm (18in), clumping perennial, flowers in late spring and early summer

■ **HARDINESS** Fully hardy ✳✳✳, but frost can damage early growth.
■ **CULTIVATION** Most decentras thrive in partial shade and moist, fertile, slightly alkaline (limy) soil enriched with well-rotted organic matter. *D. chrysantha* needs a dry, sunny site; *D. spectabilis* tolerates sun if in moist soil.
■ **Sow** seed (*see pages 328–329*) in a container in a cold frame as soon as it is ripe, or in spring.
■ **Divide** the fleshy-rooted plants (*see p.330*) carefully in spring or after the leaves die down.

Dicentra formosa (Wild bleeding heart)
↕45cm (18in) ↔ 60–90cm (24–36in), spreading perennial, leaves glaucous below, late spring and early summer flowers fade to white

***Dicentra spectabilis* 'Alba'** ♀
↕to 1.2m (4ft) ↔ 45cm (18in), robust, clump-forming perennial, light green leaves, flowers from late spring until midsummer

Dictamnus albus
Burning bush, Dittany

EARLY SUMMER

This tall, woody-based perennial is grown for its dense spikes of fragrant flowers, produced above lemon-scented foliage in summer. The leathery leaves of burning bush are composed of light green leaflets. Volatile, aromatic oils produced by the flowers and ripening seedpods can be ignited in hot weather, giving rise to the common name of burning bush. This clumping plant mixes well in a herbaceous or mixed border with other tall perennials such as achilleas (*see p.140*), daylilies (*see Hemerocallis, p.216*), phloxes (*see p.254*), and loosestrifes (*see Lythrum, p.235*). Contact with the foliage may cause skin irritation aggravated by sunlight (photodermatitis).

■ **HARDINESS** Fully hardy ✳✳✳.
■ **CULTIVATION** Grow this plant in any well-drained, reasonably fertile soil, in full sun or partial shade. ■ **Sow** seed (*see pp.328–329*) in containers in a cold frame as soon as it is ripe.
■ **Divide** plants (*see p.330*) in autumn or spring; bear in mind that the woody rootstocks may take some time to get established again.

Dictamnus albus
↕40–90cm (16–36in) ↔ 60cm (24in), white or pinkish-white flowers

Dierama
Angel's fishing rod, Wandflower

SUMMER

One of the most delicate-looking and mobile plants in the garden, dieramas carry their flowers on long, gently arching stems, so slender they move in every breeze. The funnel- or bell-shaped flowers in shades of coral-pink to red, bright pink, or purple-pink, are borne in succession on individual flower spikes. The fine, grassy, green to grey-green leaves of these evergreen perennials grow from tufts at the base and can be up to 90cm (30in) long. Grow dieramas with other summer-flowering perennials such as acanthus (*see p.140*), penstemons (*see p.252*), phloxes (*see p.254*), and salvias (*see p.266*).

■ **HARDINESS** Frost-hardy ✳✳ to half-hardy ✳; established clumps tolerate temperatures down to -10°C (14°F).
■ **CULTIVATION** Plant corms 5–8cm (2–3in) deep in spring in well-drained soil enriched with rotted organic matter, in a sheltered site in full sun. Do not let plants dry out in summer. In frost-prone areas, cover with a dry mulch over winter. Young plants take time to settle, but then grow freely. ■ **Sow** seed (*see pp.328–329*) in a seedbed or in containers in a cold frame as soon as it is ripe. ■ **Divide** (*see p.330*) in spring.

Dierama pulcherrimum
↕1–1.5m (3–5ft) ↔ 60cm (24in), flowers pale to deep magenta-pink, occasionally white or purple-red, in summer ✳✳

Digitalis

Foxglove

Classic cottage-garden plants, foxgloves form a large group of biennials and short-lived perennials. Their imposing flower spikes come in a variety of shades, from the classic purple of *Digitalis purpurea* to pink, white, and yellow, and appear from spring through to midsummer in the second year. They are striking plants, with one or more leafy rosettes at the base, and flower stems often reaching 1.5m (5ft) or more. Use them to give height to a mixed or an herbaceous border with other early-flowering perennials such as dicentras (*see p.190*) and doronicums (*see facing page*) or in a woodland planting. They self-seed prolifically, adding a natural charm to the garden. All foxgloves are toxic.

■ **HARDINESS** Fully hardy ✿✿✿ to frost-hardy ✿✿.
■ **CULTIVATION** Grow in almost any soil and situation, except extremely wet or dry conditions. Most prefer soil enriched with well-rotted organic matter in partial shade.
■ **Deadhead** after flowering if you do not want the seedlings springing up everywhere.
■ **Collect** seed and sow in containers in a cold frame in late spring (*see pp.328–329*). The leaves might be disfigured (*see p.333*) by leaf spot and powdery mildew: avoid splashing the foliage when watering and pick off affected leaves.

Digitalis grandiflora ♀
↕to 90cm (3ft) ↔45cm (18in), clumping biennial or perennial, veined leaves up to 25cm (10in), flowers in early and midsummer ✿✿✿

Digitalis* x *mertonensis ♀
↕to 90cm (3ft) ↔30cm (12in), clump-forming perennial, flowers in late spring and early summer, comes true from seed ✿✿✿

Digitalis davisiana
↕to 70cm (28in) ↔45cm (18in), perennial with underground stems (rhizomes), flowers in early summer ✿✿

Dodecatheon

American cowslip, Shooting stars

These perennials make an impressive display in spring and summer. They thrive alongside ponds and at the edge of bog gardens, as well as in rock gardens and borders. Their cyclamen-like flowers, in shades of purple, pink, lavender, or white, are borne in clusters on long, arching stems. They have basal rosettes of lance or spoon-shaped leaves. After flowering in summer, the plants become dormant. Grow with other spring and early summer-flowering perennials like doronicums (*see right*) and lupins (*see p.234*).

■ **HARDINESS** Fully hardy ✿✿✿.
■ **CULTIVATION** Grow in well-drained, moist soil enriched with well- rotted organic matter in sun or partial shade. Keep well watered during the growing season. ■ **Sow** seed (*see pp.328–329*) as soon as ripe in a container and place in an open cold frame, but it needs exposure to cold before germination can take place. ■ **Divide** in spring (*see p.330*). ■ **Protect** young leaves from slugs and snails (*see p.218*).

Dodecathon dentatum ♀
↕↔to 20cm (8in), 2–5 white flowers on each stem in late spring

***Dodecathon pulchellum* 'Red Wings'**
↕35cm (14in) ↔20cm (8in), 20 flowers per stem in late spring and early summer

Doronicum
Leopard's bane

SPRING

Leopard's bane are grown for their delightful yellow flowers, which can be single or double. They are held on slender stems high above the leaves. These perennials flower for several weeks over spring, but may come into bloom in mid- or late winter if the weather is mild. Some species are bulbous and have tubers or rhizomes. Leopard's bane look quite at home in a woodland garden; alternatively, plant in a border with daffodils (*see Narcissus, pp.240–241*), pulmonarias (*see p.262*) and primulas (*see pp.260–261*). They are also good for cutting.

■ **HARDINESS** Fully hardy ✳✳✳.
■ **CULTIVATION** Grow in moist soil enriched with well-rotted organic matter, in part or dappled shade. *D. orientale* and its cultivars are vulnerable to root rot, especially on heavy clay soils: dig in plenty of coarse grit to improve drainage. Raising the soil level by 5–8cm (2–3in) can also help. ■ **Water** well in the growing season and deadhead to prolong flowering.
■ **Sow** seed in containers in a cold frame in spring (*see pp.328–329*). ■ **Divide** plants in early autumn (*see p.330*). ■ **Powdery mildew** may affect the leaves if the soil is dry but the air is damp; avoid splashing leaves when watering.

Doronicum orientale
‡60cm (24in) ↔ 90cm (36in), produces solitary, golden yellow flowers in mid and late spring

Draba
Whitlow grass

SPRING TO EARLY SUMMER

These delicate alpines are usually found in mountainous areas. They are mat- or cushion-forming perennials that produce a mass of yellow or white flowers in spring or early summer. The tiny, grey-green leaves form tight, evergreen or semi-evergreen rosettes. They are best grown in a rock garden or raised bed, although some need protection from winter wet in temperate climates. In the autumn, place a sheet of glass or clear plastic over each plant, supported by short pieces of cane, then put a stone on top to hold it in place. Alternatively, grow the plant in a shallow pot, or pan, and move it over winter into a well-ventilated cold frame or unheated greenhouse.

■ **HARDINESS** Fully hardy ✳✳✳, but protect from winter wet.
■ **CULTIVATION** Grow in gritty, sharply drained soil in full sun, with a gravel mulch. If growing in pots, use loam-based compost with grit. Avoid wetting the foliage. ■ **Sow** seed in an open frame in autumn; they need a cold winter to germinate (*see pp.328–329*). ■ **Take** rosettes of larger species as cuttings in late spring (*see p.330*).

Draba mollissima
‡8cm (3in) ↔ 20cm (8in), hummock-forming evergreen, grey-green, hairy leaves, flowers in late spring

Dracocephalum
Dragon's head

EARLY TO MIDSUMMER

The annuals and perennials in this group are grown for their sage-like, tubular flowers in shades of white and blue. The flowers are produced from early to midsummer in spikes up to 30cm (12in) or more long. Their leaves are often aromatic. They are a bright addition to free-draining, mixed or herbaceous borders, and rock gardens. They associate well with such plants as poppies (*see Papaver, p.249*) or cranesbills (*see Geranium, pp.208–209*). Annuals combine with grasses and are useful gap-fillers in borders. Some will naturalize in partial shade.

■ **HARDINESS** Fully hardy ✳✳✳.
■ **CULTIVATION** Well-drained, fertile soil and full sun are the requirements for these plants, but some shade from the midday sun is also needed. *Dracocephalum forrestii* requires sharply drained soil and protection from too much winter wet. *D. ruyschiana* tolerates dry soil. ■ **Sow** seed (*see pp.328–329*) of annuals in mid-spring directly in the soil. Thin seedlings to around 15cm (6in) apart. ■ **Divide** mature clumps (*see p.330*) or sow seed of perennials in autumn or spring in containers in a cold frame.
■ **Take** new shoots from the base and treat as softwood cuttings (*see pp.329–330*) in spring.

Dracocephalum argunense
‡45cm (18in) ↔ 30cm (12in), clump-forming perennial, hairy leaves 5–8cm (2–3in) long, flowers in midsummer

Echinacea
Coneflower

MIDSUMMER TO AUTUMN

With their large daisies in shades of purple, rose-pink, or white, these tall perennials from dry prairies, open woodland, and gravelly hillsides make an eye-catching display in a late-summer border. The large central cone standing proud of its petals gives rise to the plant's common name and may be brownish-yellow to ochre. Each daisy is up to 15cm (6in) across and is held on stout, upright stems. The flowers persist for about two months. The leaves reach up to 20cm (8in) in length. Grow these undemanding plants in a border with other late-flowering perennials, such as sedums (see p.270) and rudbeckias (see p.265). The seedheads continue looking good into winter.

■ **HARDINESS** Fully hardy ✳✳✳.
■ **CULTIVATION** Coneflowers need deep, fertile, well-drained soil enriched with well-rotted organic matter and full sun, but they tolerate some shade. ■ **Cut** back the stems as the flowers fade for more blooms.
■ **Sow** seed (see pp.328–329) in spring.
■ **Divide** in spring or autumn (see p.330).
■ **Take** root cuttings (see p.330) in late autumn.

***Echinacea purpurea* 'Green Edge'**
‡1.5m (5ft) ↔ 45cm (18in), flowerheads 13cm (5in) across from midsummer to early autumn

Echinacea purpurea
‡1.5m (5ft) ↔ 45cm (18in), stems sometimes red-tinted, flowers are 13cm (5in) across and borne from midsummer to early autumn

***Echinacea purpurea* 'Magnus'** ♀
‡1.5m (5ft) ↔ 45cm (18in), extra-large flowers are 18cm (7in) across and borne from midsummer to early autumn

***Echinacea purpurea* 'White Lustre'**
‡80cm (32in) ↔ 45cm (18in), flowers from midsummer to early autumn

Echinops
Globe thistle

MIDSUMMER TO AUTUMN

Grown for their thistle-like flowers that appear from midsummer until autumn, these perennials, biennials, and annuals are very undemanding plants. The flowers can be up to 4cm (1½in) across, often have bristly bracts (modified leaves), and are usually blue or white and carried on stout stems. Globe thistles usually form clumps and often have dissected foliage that is spiny and greyish-white. The flowers are also good for cutting and drying. Plant them in a wild garden, or grow them with other perennials such as echinaceas (see p.194), monardas (see p.239), and phloxes (see p.254).

■ **HARDINESS** Fully hardy ✳✳✳ to frost-hardy ✳✳.
■ **CULTIVATION** Globe thistles are best grown in poor, well-drained soil in full sun, but they will tolerate almost any situation.
■ **Remove** fading flowers to prevent self-seeding. ■ **Sow** globe thistle seed in a seedbed in mid-spring (see pp.328–329).
■ **Divide** established plants from autumn to spring or take root cuttings in winter (see p.330).

***Echinops ritro* 'Veitch's Blue'**
‡to 90cm (3ft) ↔ 45cm (18in), compact perennial, leaves have white, downy undersides, flowers in late summer ✳✳✳

Echum

SUMMER

This is a large group of annuals, biennials, and evergreen perennials, with charming flowers that appear from early to late summer in shades of deep blue, pink, purple, or white. They are carried either on large, impressive spikes, or in dense clusters close to the stems. The bristly, hairy leaves are usually borne in basal rosettes and on the stems. Grow echiums in borders with echinaceas (*see facing page*), chrysanthemums (*see pp.178–179*), and phloxes (*see p.254*). Wear gloves when handling echiums because contact with the bristly foliage may irritate your skin.

■ **HARDINESS** Fully hardy ✳✳✳ to frost-tender ❀.
■ **CULTIVATION** Grow these plants in reasonably fertile, well-drained soil, in full sun.
■ **Protect** the perennials in winter in frost-prone areas by covering them with horticultural fleece. As a precaution, it is also wise to take cuttings of perennials in summer (*see pp.329–330*). ■ **Sow** seed at 13–16°C (55–61°F) in summer and overwinter the seedlings in a frost-free greenhouse or cold frame; annuals can be sown in spring where they are to grow (*see pp.328–329*).

Epimedium

Barrenwort, Bishop's mitre

SPRING TO EARLY SUMMER

The foliage is prized as much as the flowers with these perennials. The mid- to light-green leaves are lost in autumn in some species or after new leaves have formed in others. They often develop attractive tones in autumn and occasionally bronze tips on the new leaves in spring. From spring until early summer, loose clusters of saucer- to cup-shaped flowers, often with spurs, are produced in a range of colours including gold, beige, white, pink, crimson, and purple. They make excellent ground-cover plants, especially under trees.

■ **HARDINESS** Fully hardy ✳✳✳, although sharp frosts may damage young plants.
■ **CULTIVATION** Grow in fertile soil, enriched with well-rotted organic matter, in partial shade. Provide shelter from strong, cold winds. ■ **Sow** seed in a container in a cold frame as soon as it is ripe (*see pp.328–329*).
■ **Divide** established plants in autumn or just after flowering (*see p.330*). ■ **Vine weevils** can eat the leaves and mosaic virus can cause stunted, mottled growth. Practise good hygiene in the garden (*see pp.331*) and destroy any plants afflicted with virus.

Epimedium x youngianum **'Niveum'** ♀
‡20–30cm (8–12in) ↔30cm (12in), deciduous, red-tinted leaf stalks, flowers mid- to late spring

Epimedium pinnatum subsp. *colchicum*
‡30–40cm (12–16in) ↔25cm (10in), slow-growing, clump-forming evergreen, new leaves have white or red hairs, flowers in spring

Echium vulgare **'Blue Bedder'**
‡45cm (18in) ↔30cm (12in), evergreen biennial with upright, bushy habit, light blue flowers in early summer age to bluish-pink ✳✳✳

Epimedium acuminatum
‡30cm (12in) ↔ 45cm (18in), clumping evergreen, leaf undersides have waxy or powdery bloom, flowers in mid-spring to early summer

Epimedium var. *versicolor* **'Versicolor'**
‡↔30cm (12in), clump-forming evergreen, young leaves copper-red and brown turning mid-green, flowers in mid- and late spring

Epipactis
Helleborine
LATE SPRING TO SUMMER

These hardy orchids come mainly from temperate regions of the northern hemisphere, where they favour marshes, meadows, woodland and even dunes. They are therefore one of the few orchids that can be grown in temperate gardens – in a damp, shady border or a woodland setting. They have fleshy underground stems, or rhizomes, which produce twisted stalks bearing loose or dense clusters of flowers from spring to early summer. Some of the blooms are greenish-white while others are brown-tinted and streaked with violet, white, or pink. Epipactis usually have ribbed, mid-green leaves that are to 20cm (8in) in length.

■ **HARDINESS** Fully hardy ✻✻✻.
■ **CULTIVATION** Epipactis require soil enriched with well-rotted organic matter; it must be moist but well-drained, and in partial or deep shade. Given favourable conditions, they will spread freely by sending out creeping rhizomes. ■ **Divide** clumps (*see p.330*) in early spring, ensuring that each piece of rhizome has at least one healthy growing point before replanting. ■ **Slugs** and snails (*see p.332*) may be attracted to the fleshy flowers and shoots.

Epipactis gigantea (Giant helleborine)
‡30–40cm (12–16in) ↔ to 1.5m (5ft), loose terminal spikes of up to 15 flowers from late spring to early summer

Eranthis hyemalis
Winter aconite
LATE WINTER

Winter aconites provide a splash of gold to signal the end of winter. Their buttercup-like flowers bloom from late winter to early spring; each appears to sit on an elegant ruff of finely dissected leaves. These clump-forming perennials grow from knobbly tubers just below soil level in damp, shady places. They look best under deciduous shrubs or trees where, once established, they rapidly spread to form a carpet of colour, especially on alkaline (limy) soils. Winter aconites also naturalize well in grass and combine well with other winter- and early-spring bulbs, such as snowdrops (*see Galanthus, p.205*). Contact with the sap may aggravate skin allergies.

■ **HARDINESS** Fully hardy ✻✻✻ to frost-hardy ✻✻.
■ **CULTIVATION** Fertile soil that does not dry out in summer and a position in full sun or light, dappled shade are required here.
■ **Plant** the tubers 5cm (2in) deep in autumn. Dried-out tubers will not thrive. *E. pinnatifida* needs acid soil in a raised bed. ■ **Sow** seed (*see pp.328–329*) in containers in a cold frame in late spring. Lift and divide large clumps of winter aconite (*see p.330*) in spring after flowering.

Eranthis hyemalis ♀ (Winter aconite)
‡5–8cm (2–3in) ↔ 5cm (2in), rapid colonizer especially in alkaline (limy) soils, flowers 2–3cm (¹/₂–1¹/₂in) across ✻✻✻

Eremurus
Desert candle, Foxtail lily
SPRING TO EARLY SUMMER

Majestic flower spikes densely covered in pink, white, or golden, starry flowers soar skywards in spring and early summer. Usually, these clump-forming perennials produce only one flowering stem from each crown. Their long, fleshy, strappy leaves deteriorate quickly, however, so foxtail lilies are best positioned toward the middle or back of a border among shrubs or herbaceous perennials. The flowers are long-lasting when cut. Since grasslands and semi-desserts are the natural home of foxtail lilies, their large, starfish-shaped, fleshy rootstocks are prone to rot in damp conditions.

■ **HARDINESS** Fully hardy ✻✻✻; although young growth is often damaged by frosts.
■ **CULTIVATION** Plant in well-drained, fertile soil, in full sun with shelter from winds. To improve drainage on heavy clay soils, dig in plenty of coarse grit around the planting area; fork extra into the bottom of the planting hole.
■ **Support** in exposed sites. ■ **Sow** seed (*see pp.328–329*) in containers in a cold frame in autumn or late winter. ■ **Divide** plants after flowering (*see p.330*); handle the brittle rootstocks gently.

Eremurus robustus ♀
‡3m (10ft) ↔ 1.2m (4ft), blue-green leaves, flowers in early and midsummer

Erigeron
Fleabane

Long-lasting, single or double daisies are borne over many weeks in summer by the annuals, biennials, and perennials in this group. The flowers are available in a wide range of shades, from white, pink, purple, or blue to yellow or orange. All have a bright yellow eye and are borne singly or in small clusters. The leaves are found mostly at the bases of the plants, are sometimes spoon-shaped, and mid- or light green. Erigerons range from low-growing alpines to medium-sized clumps, so need a position at the front of a border. They also stand up well to salt-laden winds, making them invaluable in coastal gardens. The flowers last well if they are cut when fully open.

■ **HARDINESS** Fully hardy ✳✳✳.
■ **CULTIVATION** Erigerons prefer fertile, well-drained soil that does not dry out in summer in sun, preferably with some shade around midday. ■ **Alpine** species need sharply drained soil and protection from winter wet. ■ **Stake** taller species. ■ **Remove** fading flowers for more flowers; cut down old growth in autumn. ■ **Divide** plants every 2–3 years in late spring (*see p.330*). ■ **Take** root cuttings (*see p.330*) in spring or detach new shoots near the base and treat as softwood cuttings.

Erigeron **'Dunkelste Aller'** ♀
↕60cm (24in) ↔45cm (18in), also called 'Darkest of All', clump-forming border perennial, flowers in early and midsummer

Erigeron **'Quakeress'**
↕60cm (24in) ↔45cm (18in), vigorous, clump-forming border perennial, clusters of single flowers in early and midsummer

Erigeron aureus **'Canary Bird'** ♀
↕to 10cm (4in) ↔to 15cm (6in), hairy-leaved perennial, flowers in summer, needs protection from winter wet

Erinus
Fairy foxglove

Dainty, open flowers in shades of pink, purple, or white are borne in clusters by these trouble-free plants. There are only two species, which are semi-evergreen, short-lived perennials. The leaves are lance- to wedge-shaped, softly textured, and produced in rosettes. Fairy foxgloves are ideal for alpine or rock gardens, or for growing in crevices in old walls or between gaps in paving. If you let them, they will self-seed themselves all around the garden.

■ **HARDINESS** Fully hardy ✳✳✳.
■ **CULTIVATION** Grow these plants in light, reasonably fertile soil that is well-drained, in full sun or partial shade. ■ **Sow** seed in the ground where they are to grow or in containers in a cold frame in autumn (*see pp.328–329*). ■ **Take** rosettes as cuttings in spring (*see pp.329–330*).

Erinus alpinus ♀
↕8cm (3in) ↔10cm (4in), sticky leaves, pink, purple, or white flowers from late spring to summer

Erodium
Heron's bill, Stork's bill
SUMMER TO AUTUMN

The foliage and long flowering period of the annual and perennial erodiums make them valuable plants for the garden. The flowers resemble those of cranesbills (*see Geranium, pp.208–209*) and are produced singly from the joints of leaves and stems or in clusters at the ends of the stems. Flower hues range from pink to purple, and occasionally yellow or white. The curious, pointed seed pods give this plant its common name. Grow smaller species in a rock garden and taller ones in a border with other summer-flowering perennials such as achilleas (*see p.140*), cranesbills (*see pp.208–209*), phloxes (*see p.254*), or among shrub roses (*see pp.96–97*).

■ **HARDINESS** Fully hardy ✽✽✽ to frost-hardy ✽✽.
■ **CULTIVATION** Grow the plants in well-drained soil that is neutral to alkaline (limy), in full sun. ■ **Protect** the smaller species from excessive winter wet to avoid them rotting off by covering them with an open-sided cloche.
■ **Sow** seed as soon as it is ripe in containers in a cold frame (*see pp.328–329*). ■ **Divide** plants in spring or take stem cuttings in late spring or early summer (*see pp.329–330*).

Erodium manescavii
↕20–45cm (8–18in) ↔20cm (8in), clumping perennial, flowers summer to autumn ✽✽✽

Eryngium
Eryngo, Sea holly
MIDSUMMER TO AUTUMN

Sea hollies are striking, architectural plants that lift any border, while some can be naturalized in a wildflower meadow. Most form basal rosettes of leaves that are often spiny, with attractive silvery white veins. From midsummer to autumn, they bear thistle-like flowers on branched stems. These consist of round to cone-shaped heads of tiny flowers, that are surrounded by conspicuous ruffs, also usually silvery white. Grow smaller sea hollies in a rock garden and taller ones in a herbaceous border, where their skeletal forms can be enjoyed through winter. The flowers can be dried very successfully, but, for the best effect, they must be cut before they are fully open. Eryngiums are a large group of annuals, biennials, and deciduous and evergreen perennials.

■ **HARDINESS** Fully hardy ✽✽✽ to frost-hardy ✽✽.
■ **CULTIVATION** All sea hollies prefer well-drained soil in full sun, but some like poor to moderately fertile soil and protection from excessive winter wet whereas others need moist, rich soil. ■ **Sow** seed as soon as they are ripe in containers in a cold frame (*see pp.328–329*).
■ **Divide** plants in spring – they can be slow to re-establish; take root cuttings of perennials in winter (*see pp.329–330*). Despite their spines, sea hollies are prey to slugs and snails.

Eryngium alpinum ♀
↕70cm (28in) ↔45cm (18in), rosette-forming perennial, mid-green, spiny leaves are toothed, flowers are steel-blue or white in midsummer to early autumn, keep soil moist, protect from winter rains ✽✽✽

Eryngium x oliverianum ♀
↕90cm (3ft) ↔45cm (18in), clumping perennial, dark green spiny leaf rosettes, blue stems, flowers midsummer to early autumn ✽✽✽

Eryngium variifolium
↕30–40cm (12–16in) ↔25cm (10in), clump-forming evergreen, flowers in mid- and late summer, protect from winter wet ✽✽✽

Erysimum
Wallflower
SPRING TO EARLY SUMMER

The most commonly grown wallflowers are those used as spring bedding plants. They are usually grown as biennials from seed sown in summer or plants bought bare-rooted in autumn. The fragrant flowers are produced in pastel and brilliant hues of scarlet, orange, and gold, with some purples. Wallflowers spread only 20–60cm (8–24in), so are ideal for containers, a rock garden, or the front of a mixed border.

■ **HARDINESS** Fully hardy ✳✳✳ to frost-hardy ✳✳.
■ **CULTIVATION** Grow in poor to reasonably fertile, well-drained, slightly alkaline (limy) soil, or loam-based compost with added grit, in full sun. ■ **Trim** perennials lightly after flowering to keep compact. ■ **Soak** bare-root plants in a bucket of water for an hour before planting. ■ **Sow** seed of perennials in containers in a cold frame in spring; and of biennials in early summer. Transplant to flowering positions in autumn (*see pp.328–329*). ■ **Take** softwood cuttings from woody-based perennials in summer (*see pp.329–330*). Susceptible to club root disease so plant in a different spot each year.

Erysimum **'Bowles' Mauve'** ♀
↕75cm (30in) ↔60cm (24in) ✳✳✳

Erysimum **'John Codrington'**
↕25cm (10in) ↔30cm (12in) ✳✳✳

Erythronium
Dog's-tooth violet, Trout lily
SPRING TO EARLY SUMMER

The elegant, drooping flowers of these perennials are produced from spring until early summer, singly or in clusters on slender, upright stems. They have distinctive, swept-back petals, in shades of purple, violet, pink, yellow, or white, and conspicuously long stamens. The broad leaves grow from the base and may be glossy or glaucous; some have a strong bronze marbling, as in *Erythronium dens-canis*, or are veined with white. The common name derives from the long-pointed, tooth-like bulbs from which these clump-forming perennials grow. Natives of meadows and woodlands, they thrive in a rock garden or beneath deciduous trees, and also if naturalized with other bulbs such as dwarf narcissi (*see pp.240–241*) and crocuses (*see p.184*).

Erythronium revolutum ♀
(American trout lily)
↕20–30cm (8–12in) ↔10cm (4in), sometimes slow to establish, but self-seeds freely freely once it is settled, leaves heavily marbled bronze

■ **HARDINESS** Fully hardy ✳✳✳.
■ **CULTIVATION** These plants like deep, fertile soil that does not dry out, in partial or light, dappled shade. Plant the bulbs at least 10cm (4in) deep in autumn; keep them slightly damp if stored before planting.
■ **Divide** established clumps (*see p.330*) after flowering.

Erythronium californicum **'White Beauty'** ♀
↕15–35cm (6–14in) ↔10cm (4in), vigorous, soon forms a large clump, bears clusters of up to three flowers in spring

Erythronium **'Pagoda'** ♀
↕15–35cm (6–14in) ↔10cm (4in), very vigorous, leaves are glossy green and marbled bronze, clusters of up to ten flowers in spring

Eschscholzia
California poppy
SUMMER

In fiery shades of orange, gold, and scarlet, and sometimes cream, white, pink, or purple, the tissue-thin, satiny flowers of California poppies are carried singly on slender stems. They may be simple and cup-shaped, double, or even ruffled. Although they open fully only in sun, the flowers are still colourful when closed. The ferny foliage is light to blue-green. The most commonly grown Californian poppies are the summer-flowering hardy annuals – often in a border with other annuals such as annual phloxes (*see p.254*) or in a gravel garden. *Eschscholzia californica* types also do well in containers and hanging baskets. These poppies' fragile appearance belies their robust nature; they self-seed freely, even into cracks in paving or concrete.

■ **HARDINESS** Fully hardy ✳✳✳.
■ **CULTIVATION** These thrive in a poor, well-drained soil, in full sun. ■ **Sow** seed (*see pp.328–329*) of annuals where they are to grow in spring or early autumn. Repeat sowings at two or three week intervals to provide a succession of flowers. Thin to around 15cm (6in) apart.

Eschscholzia californica ♀
(California poppy)
↕to 30cm (12in) ↔to 15cm (6in), very variable habit, often sprawling

Eucomis
Pineapple flower, Pineapple lily
LATE SUMMER TO AUTUMN

These striking plants are grown for their unusual clusters of flowers in late summer and early autumn. The starry flowers are usually pale greenish-white or white, but what sets them apart is the tuft of green bracts leaves, similar to that on a pineapple, that tops each tight cluster. The flowers are followed by long-lasting seed pods. In mild or sheltered places, grow these bulbous perennials at the base of a warm wall or in a sunny border, where the upright stems and strappy leaves contrast well with bold foliage plants such as hostas (*see pp.218–219*). Elsewhere grow pineapple flowers in containers so they can be overwintered under cover.

■ **HARDINESS** Fully hardy ✳✳✳ (borderline) to frost-tender ❀.
■ **CULTIVATION** Plant the bulbs 15cm (6in) deep in fertile, well-drained soil in full sun. ■ **Mulch** in winter (*see p.326*). In pots, use a loam-based compost with added coarse grit for drainage, and water freely in summer and sparingly in winter. ■ **Sow** seed (*see pp.328–329*) at 16°C (61°F) in autumn or spring or remove bulb offsets (*see p.330*) in spring.

Eucomis bicolor ♀
↕30–60cm (12–24in) ↔20cm (8in), has maroon-spotted, light green stems and leaves ✳✳✳ (borderline)

Eupatorium
Hemp agrimony
SUMMER TO AUTUMN

Adored by bees and butterflies, the clusters of tiny flowers on upright, leafy stems are the attraction of the hardy eupatoriums. The flowers come in shades of white, pink, violet, or purple and are mostly borne from summer until early autumn. There are many, varied annuals and perennial eupatoriums that are worthy of the garden, with leaves that differ in shape and shade. The large, hardy, herbaceous perennials such as *Eupatorium cannabinum* look lush in large borders, with grasses (*see pp.284–299*) or in a wild or woodland garden. *E. purpureum* is even taller and has similarly strong stems that need no support.

■ **HARDINESS** Fully hardy ✳✳✳ to frost-tender ❀.
■ **CULTIVATION** Eupatoriums thrive in any soil, providing it remains moist, in full sun or partial shade. ■ **Deadhead** fading flowers. ■ **Divide** hardy species (*see p.330*) and take softwood cuttings of tender species (*see pp.329–330*) in spring. Sow seed in spring (*see pp.328–329*).

Eupatorium purpureum (Joe Pye weed)
↕2.2m (7ft) ↔1m (3ft), clump-forming perennial, flowers from midsummer to early autumn, prefers alkaline soil ✳✳✳

Euphorbia
Milkweed, Spurge

SPRING TO AUTUMN

The flamboyant, acid-yellow bracts characteristic of many garden spurges contrast dramatically with other plants, and ensure that they always catch the eye. The bracts, which are really modified leaves, surround tiny flowers, borne in clusters at the stem tips. As well as acid-yellow, plants with bracts in warm shades of red, orange, purple, or brown are available. The leaves are usually green to blue-green. This huge and incredibly varied group includes annuals, biennials, evergreen and semi-evergreen perennials, succulents, and shrubs and trees (*see p.53*), and you can find a euphorbia to suit almost any garden situation. Spurges can be short-lived, particularly in wet soils; luckily, many such as *Euphorbia polychroma* self-seed freely about.

■ **HARDINESS** Fully hardy ✳✳✳ to frost-tender ❋.
■ **CULTIVATION** Most herbaceous euphorbias like either well-drained, light soils in full sun or moist, humus-rich soils in light, dappled shade. ■ **Sow** seed (*see pp.328–329*) in containers in a cold frame. ■ **Divide** plants in early spring (*see p.330*). Tender and succulent species should be overwintered in a cool greenhouse or conservatory.

Euphorbia palustris ♀
‡↔90cm (36in), vigorous perennial, prefers moist situations, leaves turn yellow and orange in autumn, flowers in late spring ✳✳✳

Euphorbia griffithii **'Fireglow'**
‡75cm (30in) ↔1m (3ft), perennial, for moist, light shade, autumn leaves red and gold, flowers in early summer, can be invasive ✳✳✳

Euphorbia polychroma ♀
‡40cm (16in) ↔60cm (24in), perennial, likes sun, flowers mid-spring to midsummer, good ground cover, can be invasive ✳✳✳

Euphorbia dulcis **'Chameleon'**
‡↔30cm, spreading perennial, tolerates dry shade, dark green or bronze leaves colour well in autumn, flowers in summer ✳✳✳

Exacum affine
Persian violet

SUMMER

Fragrant, summer flowers in shades of lavender-blue or, less frequently, rose-pink or white are borne by this annual, or short-lived perennial. The blooms are set off against glossy leaves in a small, bushy, evergreen plant which achieves a maximum height and spread of 30cm (12in). Persian violets, often grown as house or conservatory plants, are best grown outdoors in containers for a summer display and overwintered in a greenhouse or conservatory. In milder areas, they can also be grown as summer bedding, or to fill in mixed beds and borders. Try them with plants such as asters (*see pp.162–163*), begonias (*see p.166*), and petunias (*see p.254*).

■ **HARDINESS** Frost-tender ✸.
■ **CULTIVATION** Position Persian violets in full sun, in moderately fertile, well-drained soil. For plants in containers, mix sharp sand with a preferably loam-based compost to improve the drainage. ■ **Water** well and feed with a balanced fertilizer at weekly intervals in summer. ■ **Sow** seed (*see pp.328–329*) at 18°C (64°F) in early spring.

Felicia
Blue daisy

SUMMER

Masses of daisies of pure blue, or occasionally white, mauve, or lilac, smother felicias throughout summer, making the plant a popular choice for bedding and containers, including hanging baskets. Felicias are not entirely hardy, so are generally treated as annuals or tender perennials. In mild, dry winters, they should survive to form substantial, bushy plants with a maximum height and spread of 30–50cm (12–20in). The plentiful, tiny leaves are grey- or mid-green in colour; those of *Felicia amoena* 'Variegata' have bright creamy-white edges.

■ **HARDINESS** Frost-hardy ✸✸ to half-hardy ✸.
■ **CULTIVATION** Grow felicias in poor to moderately fertile, well-drained soil, in full sun. They do not thrive in damp conditions. For plants in containers, use a loam-based compost; then water them well in summer; and feed at weekly intervals with a balanced fertilizer. ■ **Pinch back** young shoots regularly to encourage a bushy habit. ■ **Sow** seed (*see p.328–329*) at 10–18°C (50–64°F) in spring. Take softwood cuttings (*see pp.329–330*) in late summer and overwinter the young plants in frost-free conditions under glass.

Filipendula

SPRING TO SUMMER

From a distance, the flowers of filipendulas look like a cloud of foam floating above a sea of bright green leaves. At closer quarters, their unusual, musky fragrance can be detected. These perennials bear large heads of fluffy white, cream, pink, or red flowers on branching stems in late spring and summer. They thrive in damp soil, so are most at home in woodland plantings. Try them with other moisture-loving perennials such as eupatoriums (*see p.200*) or hostas (*see pp.218–219*). *Filipendula vulgaris* tolerates drier conditions, and prefers alkaline (limy) soils in full sun; it has dark green, ferny leaves, which look good with lupins (*see p.234*) and poppies (*see Papaver, p.249*).

■ **HARDINESS** Fully hardy ✸✸✸.
■ **CULTIVATION** Grow filipendulas in moderately fertile, moist but well-drained soil, in sun or partial shade. Planting gold-leaved cultivars in shade results in a stronger colour. ■ **Sow** seed (*see pp.328–329*) in autumn in pots and place them in a cold frame, or sow in spring at 10–13°C (50–55°F). ■ **Divide** (*see p.330*) in autumn or spring. Take root cuttings (*see pp.329–330*) from late winter until early spring.

Exacum affine ♀ (Persian violet)
‡↔23–30cm (9–12in), flowers 2cm (¹/₂in) across

***Felicia amelloides* 'Santa Anita'** ♀
‡↔30–60cm (12–24in), subshrub, often grown as annual, deep green leaves, 5cm (2in) flowers from summer to autumn ✸✸

***Filipendula rubra* 'Venusta'** ♀
‡2–2.5m (6–8ft) ↔1.2m (4ft), spreading to large clumps, flowers in early and midsummer, becoming paler as they age

Foeniculum vulgare
Fennel

SUMMER

The large, billowing clumps of green or purple filigree foliage make fennel a star in beds and borders, where the finely cut leaves contrast well with broad-leaved plants or blowsy flowers. Try purple fennel with the huge, dusky pink blooms of the oriental poppy, 'Patty's Plum'. Fennel is perhaps best known as an aromatic herb with a strong anise flavour used for flavouring foods, and all parts have the strong aroma of anise. This perennial reaches a height of 2m (6ft) and spread of 45cm (18in) from large, deep roots. During mid- and late summer, flat clusters of tiny, yellow flowers appear, followed by large, aromatic seeds. Herb fennel and ornamental fennels both work well in borders or in a herb garden.

■ **HARDINESS** Fully hardy ✲✲✲, although new shoots may be damaged by frosts.
■ **CULTIVATION** Fennels prefer fertile, moist but well-drained soil, in full sun.
■ **Deadhead** before the seeds form to prevent prolific self-seeding. ■ **Sow** seed (see pp.328–329) in spring at 13–18°C (55–64°F) or outdoors where the plants are to grow.

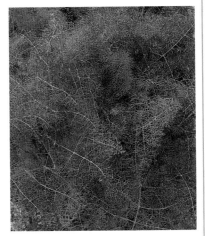

Foeniculum vulgare **'Purpureum'**
↕2m (6ft) ↔ 45cm (18in), bronze-purple foliage when young, turning glaucous green with age

Fragaria
Strawberry

SPRING TO AUTUMN

In the rush for the delicious, early-summer fruits, the ornamental cultivars of the perennial strawberry plants should not be overlooked. These bear clusters of up to ten pink or white flowers from late spring through until mid-autumn. *Fragaria vesca* 'Variegata' has attractively variegated, cream and grey-green leaves. Strawberries increase by means of stems that creep along the ground, producing young plantlets at their tips. They spread rapidly, but without becoming invasive, so useful as a weed-suppressing ground cover. Strawberries are quite vigorous plants and evergreen, except through harsh winters. Use them to edge beds and borders, in cracks and crevices of paving, containers, or hanging baskets.

■ **HARDINESS** Fully hardy ✲✲✲.
■ **CULTIVATION** Fertile, moist but well-drained soil, in full sun or partial shade is required. Strawberries prefer neutral to alkaline soils, but will tolerate acid soil. ■ **Sow** seed (see pp.328–329) in spring at 13–18°C (55–64°F).
■ **Remove** and transplant rooted runners in late summer.

Fragaria **PINK PANDA** ('Frel')
↕10–15cm (4–6in) ↔ indefinite, flowers to 2.5cm (1in) across, borne from late spring to mid-autumn, rarely bears fruit

Francoa
Bridal wreath

SUMMER AND AUTUMN

Widely grown as a flower for cutting, bridal wreath has graceful, dainty flower spikes of pink or white that give an airy feel to a border. The main flowering period of these few evergreen perennials is summer, but often the plants produce a second flush of flowers in autumn. They are 60–90cm (24–36in) tall, and have attractive rosettes of softly hairy leaves with wavy edges that spread to about 45cm (18in). They happily seed themselves about without becoming invasive. Place in mixed borders with plants such as persicarias (see p.253), phloxes (see p.254), and daylilies (see *Hemerocallis, p.216*), or use them in containers or as edging plants.

■ **HARDINESS** Frost-hardy ✲✲, although may survive to -10°C (14°F).
■ **CULTIVATION** Undemanding, these plants like moist but well-drained soil, that has been enriched with well-rotted organic matter, in full sun or partial shade. ■ **Water** freely in summer and apply a balanced feed every four weeks.
■ **Divide** bridal wreath plants (see p.330) in spring. ■ **Sow** seed (see pp.328–329) at 15–24°C (59–75°F) in spring.

Francoa sonchifolia
↕60–90cm (24–36in) ↔ 45cm (18in)

Fritillaria
Fritillary

SPRING TO EARLY SUMMER

Elegant, nodding bells are the common feature of this diverse group of perennial bulbs. The flowers come in muted shades such as soft green, tawny reds, and purples, often with strikingly patterned petals, and are borne in spring and early summer, singly or in clusters. Fritillaries vary from diminutive, delicate types only 8cm (3in) tall to more robust species with stout stems up to 1.5m (5ft). Crown imperials thrive in mixed borders. The more demure snake's head fritillary (*F. meleagris*) can be naturalized in moist meadows or in the dappled shade under trees and shrubs. Alpine species can be tricky to grow and need sharp drainage and usually alpine-house conditions.

■ **HARDINESS** Fully hardy ✻✻✻ to frost-hardy ✻✻.
■ **CULTIVATION** Plant the bulbs at four times their depth. Fritillarias differ in their needs, but most garden plants need fertile, well-drained, moisture-retentive soil in full sun, or moist, humus-rich soil in light shade. ■ **Divide** large clumps (*see p.330*) in late summer. Smaller species such as *F. acmopetala*, produce numerous but tiny bulblets (called "rice"); treat them like seeds and grow on in a seed tray (*see pp.328–329*).

Fritillaria meleagris (Snake's head fritillary)
‡30cm (12in) ↔ 5–8cm (2–3in), purple or white flowers in spring, needs moist, enriched soil in full sun or light shade ✻✻✻

Fritillaria acmopetala ♀
‡40cm (16in) ↔ 5–8cm (2–3in), robust, flowers in late spring, needs fertile, well-drained soil in full sun ✻✻✻

Fritillaria imperialis (Crown imperial)
‡1.5m (5ft) ↔ 25–30cm (10–12in), orange, red, or yellow flowers in early summer, needs fertile, well-drained soil in full sun ✻✻✻

Gaillardia
Blanket flower

SUMMER TO AUTUMN

These plants have cheerful, large daisies that appear for a long period throughout summer and into autumn. The flowers, which are up to 14cm (5½in) across, are yellow, crimson, or orange with contrasting bosses in purple, brown, red, or yellow. These are held on long stems up to 90cm (36in) tall above bushy plants with soft, hairy, long leaves. Cultivars of the short-lived perennial *Gaillardia* x *grandiflora* are most commonly grown of the group, which also includes annuals and biennials. They brighten up containers or borders. Gaillardias are also good for cutting.

■ **HARDINESS** Fully hardy ✻✻✻ to frost-hardy ✻✻.
■ **CULTIVATION** Prefer fertile, well-drained soil in full sun; they will also tolerate poor soils.
■ **Deadhead** to encourage more flowers.
■ **Cut back** perennials to around 15cm (6in) in late summer to encourage fresh growth at the base. ■ **Sow** seed (*see pp.328–329*) at 13–18°C (55–64°F) in early spring. Seed of annuals can also be sown in situ in late spring or early summer. ■ **Divide** perennials (*see p.330*) in spring or take root cuttings (*see p.330*) in winter.

***Gaillardia grandiflora* 'Dazzler'** ♀
‡60–85cm (24–34in) ↔ 45cm (18in), short-lived perennial, mid- to grey-green leaves, flowers from early summer to early autumn ✻✻✻

Galanthus
Snowdrop
WINTER TO EARLY SPRING

Snowdrops need little introduction: this hugely popular flower is a welcome sight in late winter and early spring, appearing when little else is in flower. There are hundreds of different kinds with subtly different petal shapes and green markings; snowdrop fanciers, called galanthophiles, will travel miles to see new forms. Each snowdrop bulb usually produces a single, white, pendent flower on an arching flower stalk. Some have scented flowers. Most snowdrops are vigorous and easily grown, often forming large clumps, and spread by self-seeding. They look particularly good if they are naturalized in grass. *Galanthus reginae-olgae* flowers in autumn. Contact with the bulbs may cause a rash.

■ **HARDINESS** Fully hardy ✻✻✻ to frost-hardy ✻✻.
■ **CULTIVATION** Soil enriched with well-rotted organic matter, that does not dry out in summer, in sun or partial shade, suits snowdrops. ■ **Divide** clumps of bulbs every 3–4 years to stop the plants becoming congested and losing vigour; do this in spring after flowering while the bulbs are "in the green". Snowdrops cross-pollinate freely so may not come true to type from seed.

Galanthus **'Atkinsii'** ♀
↕20cm (8in) ↔8cm (3in), flowers 3cm (1¼in) long appear in late winter ✻✻✻

Galanthus nivalis **'Flore Pleno'** ♀
↕↔10cm (4in), robust, double-flowered, spreads rapidly from offsets, honey-scented, irregular flowers in winter ✻✻✻

Galanthus **'S. Arnott'** ♀
↕20cm (8in) ↔8cm (3in), strongly honey-scented flowers, 2.5–3.5cm (1–1½in) long, in late winter and early spring ✻✻✻

Galax urceolata
Wandflower
LATE SPRING AND SUMMER

This evergreen perennial is grown for its elegant wands of small, white flowers produced in late spring and summer, followed by rich, red-bronze foliage in autumn. The flower spikes are up to 25cm (10in) tall and the leaves up to 8cm (3in) across. It spreads by creeping roots and makes a useful ground cover under shrubs in a shady bed or border or in a woodland garden. It is also happy in a large rock garden. Try growing wandflower with other shade-loving, early summer-flowering perennials, such as cranesbills (*see Geranium, pp.208–209*), lupins (*see p.234*), and poppies (*see Papaver, p.249*).

■ **HARDINESS** Fully hardy ✻✻✻.
■ **CULTIVATION** Thrives in moist, acid (lime-free) soil in partial shade; make sure the roots will not dry out. ■ **Mulch** annually in spring with pine needles or leafmould. ■ **Sow** seed (*see pp.328–329*) in containers of lime-free (ericaceous) compost in an open frame outdoors in autumn. ■ **Separate** rooted runners in early spring: carefully dig up the rooted stem; trim back the stub; and transplant the divided pieces where required.

Galax urceolata
↕30cm (12in) ↔1m (3ft)

Galega
Goat's rue, French lilac
SUMMER TO AUTUMN

The tall, floppy stems of these bushy, spreading perennials are very graceful, but tend to fall over other plants unless staked. The many clusters of pea-like flowers come in shades or bicolours of white, blue, and mauve. Viewed from a distance, the mass of small flowers creates a vivid wash of colour over the bright green foliage. Flowering usually in summer, but also in spring or autumn, galegas are best in borders with summer-flowering plants like lychnis (*see p.234*), lythrums (*see p.235*), monardas (*see p.239*), and sunflowers (*see p.214*). They also naturalize well and are good for cutting. *Galega officinalis* is most often seen in gardens.

■ **HARDINESS** Fully hardy ✷✷✷.
■ **CULTIVATION** Galegas thrive in any moist soil in full sun or partial shade. ■ **Deadhead** to prevent self-seeding; cut back to ground level after flowering. ■ **Sow** seed, soaked overnight, of species (*see pp.328–329*) in containers in a cold frame in spring. ■ **Divide** cultivars (*see p.330*) between late autumn and spring.

Galega 'His Majesty'
‡to 1.5m (5ft) ↔90cm (36in), flowers from early summer to early autumn; 'Lady Wilson' ♀ has similar flowers, 'Alba' ♀ is a white form

Galtonia
LATE SUMMER

Like a late-summer hyacinth, *Galtonia candicans* has tall, elegant spikes of pure white, slightly fragrant flowers. The only commonly grown species, it is particularly useful in the garden, and deserves wider recognition, because few bulbs of this beauty flower at this time of year. The grey-green, strappy leaves are quite fleshy. This trouble-free, bulbous perennial mixes well with grasses and other perennials like dicentras (*see p.190*), lythrums (*see p.235*), monardas (*see p.239*), poppies (*see Papaver, p.249*), sedums (*see p.270*), and rudbeckias (*see p.265*). *G. viridiflora* has pale green, nodding flowers, but is less hardy to frost.

■ **HARDINESS** Fully hardy ✷✷✷ to frost-hardy ✷✷.
■ **CULTIVATION** Fertile, well-drained soil that is reliably moist in summer, in full sun, suits galtonias. ■ **Lift** the bulbs in late autumn in areas with severe winters, and overwinter in pots in a frost-free greenhouse or conservatory. Alternatively, leave the bulbs in the soil and cover with a deep winter mulch (*see p.326*). ■ **Sow** seed in a container (*see pp.328–329*) in a cold frame as soon as it is ripe. ■ **Divide** large clumps (*see p.330*) and replant in early spring.

Galtonia candicans ♀
‡1–1.2m (3–4ft) ↔10cm (4in), tubular flowers open from the base of the flower spike in late midsummer ✷✷✷

Gaura lindheimeri
SUMMER TO AUTUMN

The summer and autumn flowers of this gracious perennial would soften any border with their light, airy growth. Each bloom nestles inside the leaves and is short-lived, but is soon replaced by another, keeping up a continuous display for several weeks. This trouble-free plant forms a bushy clump. *Gaura lindheimeri* has several pretty cultivars – 'Corrie's Gold' has gold-edged leaves and 'Siskiyou Pink' has pinkish flowers. 'Whirling Butterflies' is named after the shape of its reddish flowers; it forms a smaller clump, and is very free-flowering. Gauras contrast well with late-flowering perennials that have large, fleshy blooms, like chrysanthemums (*see pp.178–179*), rudbeckias (*see p.265*), and sedums (*see p.270*).

■ **HARDINESS** Fully hardy ✷✷✷.
■ **CULTIVATION** Any fertile, moist but well-drained soil, in full sun will do; drought and partial shade are tolerated. ■ **Sow** seed (*see pp.328–329*) in containers in a cold frame from spring until early summer. ■ **Divide** clumps (*see p.330*) in spring to increase stock. Take softwood cuttings in spring or heel cuttings in summer (*see pp.329–330*).

Gaura lindheimeri ♀
‡to 1.5m (5ft) ↔90cm (36in), pinkish buds open at dawn to white flowers that fade to pink, from late spring to early autumn

Gazania

SUMMER

The bright and cheery, sunflower-like blooms of these small annuals or evergreen perennials are most often seen in summer bedding displays, windowboxes, and patio containers in climates with frosty winters. Hybrids are usually treated as annuals with other bedding plants like pelargoniums (*see pp.250–251*) and marigolds (*see p.171 and p.274*). The summer flowers come in a wide range of bold colours, often with darker centres and markings on the petals. They need a sunny site because they close up on dull days. The dark green, hairy foliage is a good foil to the flowers.

■ **HARDINESS** Half-hardy ✲ to frost-tender ✿, but most can survive short periods at 0°C (32°F).
■ **CULTIVATION** Grow in light, sandy, well-drained soil, in full sun. ■ **Remove** dead blooms to prolong flowering. ■ **Sow** seed at 18–20°C (64–68°F) in late winter or early spring (*see pp.328–329*). ■ **Take** new shoots from the base and treat as softwood cuttings (*see pp.329–330*) in late summer or early autumn. Overwinter new plants in frost-free conditions; these may suffer from grey mould (botrytis) if poorly ventilated, and aphids may be a problem – remove any plants that are infested.

***Gazania* Talent Series**
↕↔to 25cm (10in), vigorous evergreen perennial, grey felty leaves, flowers in summer; grow well in coastal areas ✲

Gentiana
Gentian

LATE SPRING TO AUTUMN

It is the intense blue, trumpet- or bell-shaped flowers that draw gardeners to gentians, but there are also white-, yellow- and, rarely, red-flowered forms. Flowering times vary, from late spring (*G. acaulis*) to summer (*G. saxosa*), late summer (*G. septemfida*), and autumn (*G. sino-ornata*). Gentians are a large and varied group, but perennials are usually grown; they may be deciduous, evergreen, or semi-evergreen, and range from low mats and trailing types to clumping or upright forms.

***Gentiana acaulis* ♀**
↕8cm (3in) ↔30cm (12in)

***Gentiana septemfida* ♀**
↕15–20cm (6–8in) ↔30cm (12in)

Many are alpines, needing rock-garden conditions; a few suit herbaceous borders, such as the relatively tall, shade-loving *G. asclepiadea* with late-summer flowers. Some gentians have very specific soil needs, so you may have to grow them in containers. Autumn-flowering gentians have rosettes of leaves.

■ **HARDINESS** Fully hardy ✲✲✲.
■ **CULTIVATION** Most need light but rich, well-drained but moist soil, in full sun only where summers are cool. Provide partial shade in warmer areas. Autumn-flowering gentians need neutral to acid soil. ■ **Sow** seed (*see pp.328–329*) of species as soon as it is ripe in a cold frame. ■ **Divide** rooted offshoots (*see p.330*) carefully in spring.

Gentiana saxosa
↕8cm (3in) ↔10cm (4in)

***Gentiana sino-ornata* ♀**
↕to 8cm (3in) ↔15–30cm (6–12in)

Geranium

Cranesbill

EARLY SUMMER TO AUTUMN

Easy-to-grow, versatile, and long-flowering, few plants are as useful in the garden as hardy geraniums. The genus contains about 300 annuals, biennials, and herbaceous perennials, some of them semi-evergreen or evergreen. The flowers are delicate and abundant, with colours ranging from white, shades of pink and purple, to blue, often with contrasting veins. Leaves are usually rounded or palm-like (palmate) and are frequently aromatic. Some types have colourful autumn foliage. They are often confused with the non-hardy bedding and container plant, *Pelargonium* (*see pp.250–251*), which is popularly called geranium. Cranesbills are found in many habitats, except in very wet areas, and can be grown almost anywhere in the garden, and in pots. There are compact varieties to 15cm (6in) tall, suitable for a rock garden, and plants of 1.4m (4ft) or more for mixed and herbaceous borders. Mat-forming species like *Geranium macrorrhizum* are useful as ground cover, including on slopes, where the dense root system helps to prevent soil erosion.

■ **HARDINESS** Fully hardy ✳✳✳ to half-hardy ✳.
■ **CULTIVATION** Grow larger species and hybrids in fertile soil in full sun or partial shade. Small species need a well-drained site in full sun. Avoid soils that are excessively wet in winter. ■ **Water** well during dry spells and feed with a liquid fertilizer monthly. ■ **Trim off** faded blooms and foliage after the first flush of flowers to encourage fresh leaves and more flowers. ■ **Sow** seed (*see pp.328–329*) of hardy species outdoors in containers as soon as it is ripe or in spring. Seed of half-hardy species is sown at 13–18°C (55–64°F) in spring. ■ **Divide** overgrown clumps in spring (*see p.330*). ■ **Take** basal cuttings (the base of the stem and a small piece of the crown) in spring and treat as stem-tip cuttings (*see p.330*).

Using geraniums in the garden

Woodland planting Loose, spreading shapes and plentiful flowers, even in dappled shade, make geraniums an appropriate choice for the

woodland garden. Here, *G. endressii* are an effective contrast to the solid forms of the tree trunks. This species, together with *G. himalayense* and *G. macrorrhizum* and their cultivars, and *G. nodosum*, all make good cover in any shady site.

Ground cover *Geranium* x *magnificum* is used here as ground cover under climbing roses. Roses and geraniums are a classic garden combination. A geranium's vigorous, spreading habit camouflages bare soil and hides dull rose stems – and its small, saucer-shaped flowers are good foils to the showier rose blooms. Geranium and rose hues also harmonize well.

G. 'Ann Folkard' ♀ ‡60cm (24in) ↔1m (3ft)

G. asphodeloides ‡30–45cm (12–18in) ↔30cm (12in), evergreen

G. clarkei 'Kashmir White' ♀ ‡45cm (18in) ↔indefinite

G. dalmaticum ♀ ‡15cm (6in) ↔50cm (20in), evergreen

G. ibericum ‡50cm (20in) ↔60cm (24in)

G. macrorrhizum ‡50cm (20in) ↔60cm (24in), aromatic

G. nodosum ‡30–50cm (12–20in), ↔50cm (20in)

G. orientalitibeticum ‡30cm (12in) ↔1m (3ft)

x cantabrigiense ‡30cm (12in)
↔60cm (24in), evergreen, aromatic

G. x cantabrigiense 'Biokovo' ‡30cm (12in)
↔75–90cm (30–36in), evergreen

G. cinereum 'Ballerina' ♀ ‡15cm (6in)
↔30cm (12in), evergreen

G. cinereum var. subcaulescens ♀
‡15cm (6in) ↔30cm (12in), evergreen

endressii ♀ ‡45cm (18in) ↔60cm
‑4in), evergreen

G. erianthum ‡45–60cm (18–24in) ↔30cm
(12in), good autumn leaf colour

G. himalayense ‡30–45cm (12–18in)
↔60cm (24in)

G. himalayense 'Gravetye' ♀ ‡30cm
(12in) ↔60cm (24in)

macrorrhizum 'Ingwersen's
ariety' ♀ ‡50cm (20in) ↔60cm (24in)

G. maculatum ‡60–75cm (24–30in) ↔45cm
(18in), evergreen

G. maderense ♀ ‡↔1.2–1.5m (4–5ft) ❋

G. x magnificum ♀ ‡↔60cm (24in)

x oxonianum ‡80cm (32in)
‑60cm (24in), evergreen

G. x oxonianum 'Southcombe Star' ‡80cm
(32in) ↔60cm (24in), evergreen

G. x oxonianum 'Winscombe' ‡↔45cm (18in),
evergreen

G. phaeum 'Album' ‡80cm (32in),
↔45cm (18in)

Geum
Avens

Looking rather like buttercups or small roses, the bod flowers of geums come in attractive shades of red, orange, and yellow. They appear from late spring into summer and are held above clumps of deep green, wrinkled and divided leaves. The smaller geums are suitable for growing in a rock garden, while the larger ones are almost tailor-made for the front of a sunny border. Combine them with other herbaceous perennials such as the closely related potentillas (*see p.259*), which have a similar style of flower, and cranesbills (*see Geranium, pp.208–209*).

■ **HARDINESS** Fully hardy ✳✳✳.
■ **CULTIVATION** Grow most geums in fertile, well-drained soil in full sun. *Geum rivale* and its cultivars, need more moisture and plenty of organic matter, but avoid soil that becomes waterlogged in winter. ■ **Sow** seed in containers in a cold frame in spring or autumn (*see pp.328–329*). 'Lady Stratheden'

and 'Mrs J. Bradshaw' generally come true from seed, but the majority of the larger geums cross-pollinate freely and produce unpredictable offspring. ■ **Divide** other named varieties (*see p.330*) to be sure that new plants are true to type.

Geum montanum ♀
↕15cm (6in) ↔ to 30cm (12in), one of the smaller geums that is ideally suited to a rock garden; it flowers in spring and early summer

Gladiolus

With their tall, strongly upright spikes of summer flowers, gladioli can look especially striking in cut-flower displays as well as in the garden. The funnel-shaped flowers open from the bottom of the stem upwards and come in shades of white, red, pink, yellow, orange, and some bicolours, sometimes with dainty splotches on the lower petals. Gladioli grow from corms, with long, sword-like leaves arranged in fans. Many are not hardy and need a warm, sheltered border. Partner them with other herbaceous perennials such as daylilies (*see Hemerocallis, p.216*) and grasses. They are sometimes grown in rows in the vegetable garden specifically for cutting.

■ **HARDINESS** Fully hardy ✳✳✳ to frost-tender ❄.
■ **CULTIVATION** Grow in fertile, well-drained soil in full sun. ■ **Plant** corms 10–15cm (4–6in) deep in spring. In heavy soil, fork coarse grit into the planting area. Large-flowered kinds need staking. ■ **Lift** corms in frost-prone areas once

***Geum* 'Red Wings'**
↕to 60cm (24in) ↔to 40cm (16in), the semi-double, bright red or scarlet flowers appear very freely throughout summer

***Geum* 'Lady Stratheden'** ♀
↕40–60cm (16–24in) ↔ 60cm (24in), a popular geum for a sunny border, where its large flowers will be produced all summer

***Gladiolus* 'Elvira'**
↕80cm (32in) ↔8–10cm (3–4in), each corm produces two or three slender flower spikes in early summer that are ideal for cutting ✳

leaves begin to yellow, dry them for a fortnight or so, then remove all leafy remains.
■ **Separate** the corms, discarding the old, dried-up, dark brown ones, and store over winter in a cool, frost-free place. Check occasionally and remove any that show signs of mould.

Gladiolus tristis
‡45–150cm (1½–5ft) ↔ 5cm (2in), pale yellow or creamy white flowers in spring, strong evening scent ✳

Gladiolus communis subsp. byzantinus ♀
‡to 1m (3ft) ↔ 8cm (3in), flowers in early summer, mulch over winter in cold areas ✳✳✳ (borderline)

Glechoma
Ground ivy
SPRING TO SUMMER

The creeping nature of these perennials makes them useful ground-cover plants, especially in partially shaded areas. The small, toothed leaves appear on long, slender stems, which readily root into the soil. Some forms can be quite invasive and their spread needs to be checked from time to time. The small, violet-blue flowers are borne from spring through summer. Good companions include bugles (*see Ajuga, p.145*), corydalis (*see p.182*), lamiums (*see p.224*), and violets (*see p.282*). The white-marbled leaves of *Glechoma hederacea* 'Variegata', the most commonly grown type, make a good foil for summer bedding plants such as pelargoniums (*see pp.250–251*) and fuchsias (*see pp.56–57*) in container displays, and mixes well with silver-leaved helichrysums.

■ **HARDINESS** Fully hardy ✳✳✳.
■ **CULTIVATION** Grow in reasonably fertile, well-drained soil in full sun or partial shade.
■ **Divide** plants in spring or autumn (*see p.330*), or take softwood cuttings in late spring (*see pp.329–330*).

Glechoma hederacea 'Variegata'
‡to 15cm (6in) ↔ to 2m (6ft) or more, the trailing foliage makes an all-year display in hanging baskets and windowboxes

Gunnera
SPRING TO AUTUMN

The foliage of gunneras is one of gardening's sensations. Although there are diminutive mat-forming gunneras like *Gunnera magellanica*, which is no more than 15cm (6in) tall, it is the giant rhubarb, *G. manicata*, for which this group of perennials is famed. This plant reaches a majestic 2.5m (8ft) or more within a season. The undersides of the rhubarb-like leaves and their thick stalks are coarsely spined. The flower spikes are also attractive in some species. Large-leaved specimens make excellent architectural plants for stream- or pondsides, but in large gardens only. They combine well with other moisture-loving plants, such as astilbes (*see p.164*). The small gunneras are best in a rock garden.

■ **HARDINESS** Fully hardy ✳✳✳ to frost-hardy ✳✳.
■ **CULTIVATION** Grow in deep, permanently moist soil in sun or partial shade in a sheltered position. In frosty areas, protect their crowns in winter with a covering of the old leaves.
■ **Increase** large species by taking cuttings of leafy, basal buds, with a section of root attached, in spring. ■ **Divide** small species in spring (*see p.330*). ■ **Sow** seed (*see pp.328–329*) in containers in a cold frame as soon as it is ripe.

Gunnera tinctoria
‡1.5m (5ft) ↔ 2m (6ft), the enormous leaves and rusty flowerheads are slightly smaller than those of the hardier *G. manicata* ✳✳

Gypsophila

SUMMER

The diffuse, starry sprays of small, white or pink summer flowers of gypsophilas will be familiar to anyone who buys cut flowers. They make a pretty and airy filler for indoor arrangements and the same principle applies to gypsophilas in the garden. Small types are ideal for rock gardens; the annual and larger perennial gypsophilas such as *G. paniculata* suit borders. The clouds of flowers look good with many herbaceous perennials, for example coreopsis (*see p.182*), cranesbills (*see Geranium, pp.208–209*), and geums (*see p.210*). Popular cultivars include 'Bristol Fairy' and 'Perfekta', with double white flowers, and 'Flamingo', with lilac-pink double flowers.

■ **HARDINESS** Fully hardy ✽✽✽ to frost-hardy ✽✽.
■ **CULTIVATION** Grow in deep, light, preferably alkaline (limy) soil that is sharply drained and in full sun. ■ **Sow** seed of annuals where they are to flower in spring (*see p.329*), and thin out seedlings to around 15cm (6in) apart. Seed of perennials should be sown at 13–18°C (55–64°F) in spring (*see pp.328–329*). ■ **Take** root cuttings of perennials in winter (*see p.330*) as an alternative way of making new plants.

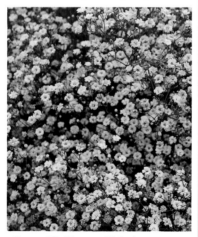

Gypsophila 'Rosenschleier' ♀
↕40–50cm (16–20in) ↔1m (3ft), also known as 'Rosy Veil' for its billowing clusters of pale pink, semi-double flowers ✽✽✽

Haberlea

SPRING TO EARLY SUMMER

Suited to a shady rock garden, these stemless, evergreen perennials can gradually colonize an area with their rosettes of dark green leaves, which are brightened in spring and early summer by loose clusters of nodding, trumpet-shaped flowers. These appear in shades of lavender-blue or pale violet-blue, although *Haberlea rhodopensis* 'Virginalis' (*see below*) has white flowers. They are ideal for growing in the pockets of a dry-stone wall, in rock crevices, or in an alpine house (a well ventilated, cold greenhouse). They combine well with a wide range of other rock plants.

■ **HARDINESS** Fully hardy ✽✽✽.
■ **CULTIVATION** Grow in moist, but well-drained, preferably alkaline (limy) soil in full or partial shade. In an alpine house, grow them in free-draining, loam-based compost. Once planted, they resent root disturbance.
■ **Protect** from excessive winter wet; haberleas prefer to be planted on their sides to prevent water from accumulating in the crowns of the plants. ■ **Sow** seed at 13–18°C (55–64°F) in spring (*see pp.328–329*). ■ **Divide** clumps of rosettes in early summer (*see p.330*). Slugs and snails may attack the foliage (*see p.332*) of plants outside.

Haberlea rhodopensis 'Virginalis'
↕15cm (6in) ↔to 25cm (10in), rosette-forming perennial with white flowers from spring to early summer, leaves are softly hairy

Hacquetia epipactis

EARLY SPRING

The bright, early flowers of this species are composed of a central boss of tiny, yellow true flowers surrounded by bright green bracts (modified leaves). They are borne in dense clusters from late winter to mid-spring. The plant has glossy, green leaves that only fully develop once the flowers are finished. This is a small clump-forming perennial for a moist, shady site. An ideal position would be a damp rock garden in shade or a woodland border with plants such as snowdrops (*see Galanthus, p.205*), anemones (*see p.152*), winter aconites (*Eranthis hyemalis, see p.196*), and corydalis (*see p.182*). Other natural companions include hellebores (*see p.215*) and epimediums (*see p.195*).

■ **HARDINESS** Fully hardy ✽✽✽.
■ **CULTIVATION** This plant will thrive in any reliably moist but not waterlogged, neutral to acid (lime-free) soil, that has been enriched with well-rotted organic matter. ■ **Sow** seed in a container in a cold frame as soon as it is ripe or in autumn (*see pp.328–329*). ■ **Divide** plants in spring (*see p.330*) to increase stock and to maintain vigour, or take root cuttings in winter (*see p.330*).

Hacquetia epipactis ♀
↕5cm (2in) ↔to 15cm (6in), a fascinating colour combination that will help to light up damp areas in shade

Helenium
Helen's flower

A top choice for the autumn border, heleniums make a superb late-flowering contribution to the garden. Their daisy flowers, in wonderfully hot colours, appear over a long period from summer to autumn. These relatively tall, clump-forming perennials slowly spread over the years to create bold expanses of colour in shades of yellow, bronze, orange, and red. The flowers are good for cutting and also attract bees and other beneficial insects into the garden. Grow in a herbaceous border with other late-flowering perennials such as sedums (*see p.270*), rudbeckias (*see p.265*), and asters (*see pp.162–163*). Contact with foliage may aggravate skin allergies.

■ **HARDINESS** Fully hardy ✳✳✳ to frost-hardy ✳✳.
■ **CULTIVATION** Grow in any fertile, moist but well-drained soil in full sun. ■ **Provide** support for tall varieties. ■ **Divide** clumps every few years in autumn or spring (*see p.330*) to increase stock or maintain vigour. ■ **Sow** seed (*see pp.328–329*) of species in containers in a cold frame in spring. ■ **Propagate** cultivars by taking new shoots from the base of the plant in spring and treating them as softwood cuttings (*see pp.329–330*).

Helenium **'Crimson Beauty'**
‡90cm (36in) ↔ 60cm (24in), the shaggy, red flowers take on a brownish tinge with age ✳✳✳

Helenium **'Moerheim Beauty'** ♀
‡90cm (36in) ↔ 60cm (24in), flowers from early to late summer ✳✳✳

Helenium autumnale (Sneezeweed)
‡to 1.5m (5ft) ↔ 45cm (18in), flowers from late summer to mid-autumn; use twiggy sticks to support stems ✳✳✳

Helianthus
Sunflower
SUMMER

A favourite for children's gardens, these annuals and perennials are grown for their dramatic height and often huge, bright, daisy flowerheads. These appear in summer and autumn in shades of yellow, red, bronze, and mahogany, and are borne singly or in loose clusters. The flowers of some annuals may measure up to 30cm (12in) across. Despite their coarse foliage, they make showy plants for the border; some of the dwarfer annuals also do well in containers. Sunflowers are good for cutting; they attract pollinating insects into the garden, and the seedheads may provide food for birds. Tall types make a good, fast-growing summer screen.

■ **HARDINESS** Fully hardy ✳✳✳ to frost-hardy ✳✳.
■ **CULTIVATION** Grow in reasonably fertile soil that is well-drained, neutral to alkaline (limy) and in full sun. Tall types, especially those with large, heavy heads, will need support.
■ **Sow** seed (*see pp.328–329*) of perennials in containers in a cold frame in spring. Sow annuals at 16°C (61°F) in spring. ■ **Divide** (*see p.330*) and replant perennials every two to four years in spring or autumn to maintain vigour.

Helianthus x multiflorus
‡2m (6ft) ↔90cm (36in)

Helianthus 'Monarch' ♀
‡to-2m (6ft) ↔1.2m (4ft) ✳✳

Helianthus 'Soleil d'Or'
‡to 2m (6ft) ↔1.2m (4ft) ✳✳✳

Helianthus 'Lemon Queen' ♀
‡1.7m (5½ft) ↔1.2m (4ft) ✳✳✳

Heliopsis
Ox eye
MIDSUMMER TO AUTUMN

Originating in the dry prairies of North America, these clump-forming perennials are valuable for their long flowering period and for being relatively trouble-free. Their cheerful, golden yellow daisies, up to 8cm (3in) in diameter, are produced from midsummer through to early autumn. Ox eyes have stiff, branching stems to 1m (3ft) tall, clothed with mid- or dark green foliage. The flowers may be single or double. These are useful plants in a mixed or herbaceous border; grow them with other colourful perennials such as achilleas (*see p.140*), rudbeckias (*see p.265*), cranesbills (*see Geranium, pp.208–209*), and campanulas (*see p.173*).

■ **HARDINESS** Fully hardy ✳✳✳.
■ **CULTIVATION** Grow in reasonably fertile, well-drained soil enriched with well-rotted organic matter, in full sun. The taller types may need supporting with twiggy sticks or canes.
■ **Divide** plants (*see p.330*) every two to three years to maintain vigour. ■ **Sow** seed (*see pp.328–329*) in a container in a cold frame in spring. ■ **Take** cuttings of new shoots at the base of the plant in spring and treat as softwood cuttings (*see pp.329–330*). ■ **Slugs** (*see p.332*) can damage young shoots.

Heliopsis helianthoides 'Sommersonne'
‡90cm (36in) ↔60cm (24in), deep gold flowers sometimes flushed orange-yellow, good source of cut flowers for the house

Helleborus
Hellebore
WINTER TO SPRING

Hellebores are stars of the winter garden. All species in this group of mainly evergreen perennials are grown for their handsome, glossy foliage, which sets off the exquisite flowers in subtle shades of purple, pink, green, white, and cream, many with contrasting spots. The flowers of hellebores are extremely long-lasting; some face outwards, others look gracefully to the ground, and a few are scented. Hellebores are most effective when they are grown in groups in a mixed or shrub border or in a natural woodland setting. Grow with other winter-flowering shrubs such as witch hazels (*see Hamamelis, p.61*), Christmas box (*see Sarcococca, p.100*), and viburnums (*see pp.108–109*).

■ **HARDINESS** Fully hardy ✱✱✱ to frost-hardy ✱✱.
■ **CULTIVATION** Hellebores tolerate a fairly wide range of soil types and conditions. Most prefer neutral to alkaline (slightly limy) soil in sun or shade. Avoid dry or waterlogged soils.
■ **Dig in** plenty of well-rotted organic matter before planting and mulch with a layer of organic matter in autumn. ■ **Sow** seed (*see p.328–329*) in containers in a cold frame as soon as it is ripe; named forms will not come true. Hellebores self-seed freely. ■ **Divide** (*see p.330*) in early spring or late summer.

Helleborus* x *hybridus (Lenten rose)
↕↔ to 45cm (18in), flowers, in white, purple, yellow, green, or pink, from midwinter to mid-spring, remove old, tattered leaves before the flowerbuds open ✱✱✱

Helleborus foetidus ♀ (Stinking hellebore)
↕ to 80cm (32in) ↔ 45cm (18in), deeply cut foliage, which smells only when crushed, flowers from midwinter to mid-spring ✱✱✱

***Helleborus* x *hybridus* Ashwood Garden hybrids**
↕↔ 45cm (18in), flowers midwinter to spring ✱✱✱

Helleborus* x *hybridus slaty blue-flowered
↕↔ 45cm (18in), usually grown from seed, flowers from midwinter to mid-spring ✱✱✱

***Helleborus niger* 'Potter's Wheel'** (Christmas rose)
↕ to 30cm (12in) ↔ 45cm (18in), particularly large flowers from early winter to early spring ✱✱✱

Helleborus argutifolius ♀ (Corsican hellebore)
↕ to 1.2m (4ft) ↔ 90cm (3ft), shallow pale green flowers in late winter and early spring ✱✱✱

Hemerocallis
Daylily

`SUMMER`

The exotic blooms of daylilies last for only one day – hence the name – but more buds open to take their place. Thousands of cultivars are available, with blooms in dazzling hues from near-white, gold, and apricot to orange, red, and blue, that vary in shape from spidery or flat to very full doubles. Deciduous, evergreen, or semi-evergreen, these easy-to-grow, clump-forming perennials flower from spring to late summer, adding height and long-lasting colour to a border. Many flower repeatedly through the season (remontant). They are especially successful in drifts in a wild garden. Dwarf daylilies are good in containers.

■ **HARDINESS** Fully hardy ✷✷✷; some evergreens are frost-hardy ✷✷.
■ **CULTIVATION** Daylilies like fertile, moist but well-drained soil; most need full sun for best colour but also grow in partial shade. ■ **Divide** plants (*see p.330*) every 2–3 years to maintain vigour; divide or plant evergreens only in spring. Maggots of hemerocallis gall midges may infest and kill early buds; destroy abnormally swollen buds at once.

Hemerocallis 'Gentle Shepherd'
‡65cm (26in) ↔30cm–1.2m (12in–4ft) ✷✷✷

Hemerocallis 'Golden Chimes' ♀
‡90cm (36in) ↔30cm–1.2m (12in–4ft) ✷✷✷

Hemerocallis 'Lemon Bells' ♀
‡1.2m (4ft) ↔30cm–1.2m (12in–4ft) ✷✷✷

Hemerocallis 'Marion Vaughn' ♀
‡85cm (34in) ↔30cm–1.2m (12in–4ft) ✷✷✷

Hepatica

`LATE WINTER TO EARLY SPRING`

This small group of early-flowering perennials is related to anemones (*see p.152*). Their solitary, bowl- or star-shaped flowers are unusual in that they open from late winter until early spring, before the leaves have fully developed. The flowers come in shades of white, pale pink to crimson, pale blue to mauve, and purple, and are often mottled or marbled. The leaves are often purple underneath and sometimes marbled in silver or white. They form basal rosettes to 13cm (5in) across and last all summer after the flowers fade. Hepaticas do well in moist soil in partial shade, such as in a woodland planting or shady corner of a rock garden. They combine well with small spring bulbs.

■ **HARDINESS** Fully hardy ✷✷✷.
■ **CULTIVATION** Hepaticas grow well in partial shade, in heavy, neutral to alkaline (slightly limy) soils, but will also thrive in well-drained soils that have been enriched with well-rotted organic matter. ■ **Top-dress** with a layer of leafmould or garden compost around the plants in spring or autumn. Hepaticas do not transplant well since they resent root disturbance. ■ **Sow** seed (*see pp.328–329*) in a cold frame as soon as it is ripe. ■ **Divide** plants in spring (*see p.330*); divisions are slow to re-establish.

Hepatica nobilis ♀
‡10cm (4in) ↔15cm (6in), slow-growing, domed, semi-evergreen, white, pink, blue, or purple flowers in early spring

Hesperis matronalis
Sweet rocket, Dame's violet

The sweet-scented flowers of hesperis are borne on tall, swaying stems above rosettes of hairy, dark green leaves. Only the biennial or the short-lived perennial, *Hesperis matronalis*, and its cultivars are usually grown. The blooms are usually lilac or purple, appear in late spring to early summer, and have an intensely spicy fragrance at evening. Some cultivars have double flowers and they are all good for cutting. Hesperis is usually grown as a biennial and freely self-seeds. It works well in a cottage garden, herbaceous border, or wild garden, with other early flowerers, such as poppies (*see Papaver, p.249*).

■ **HARDINESS** Fully hardy ✳✳✳.
■ **CULTIVATION** Grow this plant in fertile, moist but well-drained soil that is neutral to alkaline (limy), in sun or partial shade.
■ **Sow** seed (*see pp.328–329*) in spring or early summer, in spare ground, or where the plants are to grow, and plant out in autumn.

Hesperis matronalis var. albiflora
↕90cm (36in) ↔ 45cm (18in), flowers 3–4cm (1¼–1½in) across, attractive to insects, seedlings are white if no other hesperis are grown nearby

Heuchera
Coral flower

Richly coloured foliage is the chief feature of heucheras. Evergreen and semi-evergreen, the lobed, rounded, or scalloped leaves are often tinted bronze or purple, are mottled or marbled, and have bold veins. They form neat mounds, above which rise airy spikes of dainty flowers in shades of pink to almost pure white from early to midsummer. They are good for cutting and drying, and attract bees into the garden. Commonly used as ground cover in borders and as edging for pathways, heucheras also look good in borders, and woodland and rock gardens. Contrast the foliage with that of plants like *Stachys byzantina* (*see p.273*) or *Choisya ternata* SUNDANCE (*see p.36*).

■ **HARDINESS** Fully hardy ✳✳✳ to frost-hardy ✳✳.
■ **CULTIVATION** Prefer a neutral, fertile soil that is moist but well-drained, in sun or partial shade. They tolerate deep shade if the soil is moist. ■ **Sow** seed in containers (*see pp.328–329*) in a cold frame in spring. ■ **Divide** each autumn (*see p.330*) to stop the woody rootstock pushing up from the soil. ■ **Vine weevil** larvae may eat the roots, causing the plant to wilt; destroy affected plants immediately.

Heuchera cylindrica 'Greenfinch'
↕to 90cm (36in) ↔ 60cm (24in), mound-forming, often hairy leaves, flowers from mid-spring to midsummer ✳✳✳

Heuchera villosa 'Palace Purple'
↕↔ 45–60m (18–24in), mound- or clump-forming, leaves to 15cm (6in) long, free-flowering in early summer, pink seed heads ✳✳✳

Heuchera 'Red Spangles'
↕50cm (20in) ↔ 25cm (10in), clumping, round- to kidney-shaped, dark green leaves are marbled pale green, flowers all summer ✳✳✳

Hosta
Plantain lily

SPRING TO SUMMER

Hostas are among the most impressive of foliage plants, their ribbed, sometimes huge, leaves appearing in shades of green, yellow, blue-green, and blue-grey. In many cultivars, they are edged or banded with white or cream. In summer, spires of trumpet-shaped flowers are held well above the foliage. These herbaceous perennials grow naturally along rocky streamsides, and in woodland and alpine meadows. Most form clumps, but a few spread by underground stems. All make excellent ground-cover plants because the dense, overlapping leaves block out light from the soil surface, preventing weed seeds from germinating. They are ideal, too, for shady sites, but if planted under trees, will need plenty of well-rotted organic matter adding to the soil to retain moisture. Hostas also look effective in pots, where they are easier to protect against slug damage. Their lush, rounded foliage looks pleasing by ponds, or when contrasted with tall, spiky plants, such as grasses. The small-leaved cultivars are good for growing in rock gardens.

■ **HARDINESS** Fully hardy ✲✲✲
■ **CULTIVATION** Grow in fertile, moist but well-drained soil, sheltered from cold, drying winds. Never let the soil dry out and water during dry spells. Most hostas prefer full or partial shade, although yellow-leaved and variegated cultivars have better colour in sun. ■ **Mulch** (see p.326) between plants in spring to help conserve moisture. ■ **Propagate** by division in spring (see p.330). ■ **Prone to damage** from slugs and snails so take protective measures (see below). The roots of container-grown plants may be eaten by vine weevil larvae (see p.332).

Preventing slug and snail damage
The leaves of hostas are stunning, but they also often prove irresistible to slugs and snails. It is not uncommon to find some leaves completely shredded after slugs have been feasting at night. There are several ways to control them without resorting to slug pellets. Buy slug traps or spread coarse grit, gravel, crushed eggshells, or cocoa shells around the plants as they dislike crossing rough surfaces (put the material in place before the leaves emerge and renew when necessary). Collect slugs and snails at nightfall with the aid of a torch, especially in damp weather.

Band of copper Containers can offer hostas a degree of protection. As a further barrier, stick adhesive copper tape, available at garden centres, around the rim. The copper has a natural electric charge to which molluscs are sensitive and they will not cross.

Slug pub An organic way to catch slugs and snails. Sink a container in the ground with the rim about 2.5cm (1in) above soil level (this prevents beneficial creatures tumbling in) and fill it with beer. Attracted by the smell, they fall into the container and drown.

H. **'Aureomarginata'** ‡50cm (20in) ↔1m (3ft), tolerates sun or partial shade

H. **'Blue Blush'** ‡20cm (8in) ↔35–40 (14–16in), lavender blue flowers

H. **'Frances Williams'** ♀ ‡60cm (24in) ↔1m (3ft), greyish-white flowers

H. **'Golden Prayers'** ‡35cm (14in) ↔60cm (24in)

H. plantaginea ‡60cm (24in) ↔1m (3ft), white flowers late summer and autumn

H. **'Regal Splendor'** ‡75cm (30in) ↔1m (3ft)

H. **'Sum and Substance'** ♀ ‡75cm (30in) ↔1.2m (4ft), pale lilac flowers

H. undulata ‡1m (3ft) ↔45cm (18in), mauve flowers

H. 'Emerald Tiara' ‡35cm (14in)
↔65cm (26in), violet flowers

H. fortunei var. **albopicta** ♀ ‡55cm (22in)
↔1m (3ft)

H. fortunei var. **aureomarginata** ♀
‡55cm (22in) ↔1m (3ft)

H. 'Francee' ‡55cm (22in)
↔1m (3ft)

H. 'Halcyon' ‡35–40cm (14–16in)
↔70cm (28in), lavender-grey flowers

H. 'Honeybells' ♀ ‡75cm (30in) ↔1.2m (4ft),
fragrant, white or lavender striped flowers

H. lancifolia ♀ ‡45cm (18in) ↔75cm (30in),
purple flowers, red-dotted stems

H. 'Love Pat' ♀ ‡45cm (18in)
↔1m (3ft), off-white flowers

H. 'Royal Standard' ♀ ‡60cm (24in)
↔1.2m (4ft), fragrant

H. 'September Sun' ‡65cm (26in) ↔1m (3ft)

H. 'Shade Fanfare' ♀ ‡45cm (18in)
↔60cm (24in)

H. sieboldiana var. **elegans** ♀
‡1m (3ft) ↔1.2m (4ft)

H. undulata var. **univittata** ♀
‡45cm (18in) ↔70cm (28in)

H. ventricosa ♀ ‡50cm (20in) ↔1m (3ft)

H. venusta ♀ ‡5cm (2in) ↔25cm (10in)

H. 'Wide Brim' ♀ ‡45cm (18in)
↔1m (3ft)

Hyacinthoides
Bluebell

LATE SPRING

Bluebells are familiar as a shimmering blue carpet of blooms in woodland in late spring. They can become invasive, but are easy to control by digging up unwanted bulbs. The small flowers, usually violet-blue but also white or pink, are held on sturdy stems above strappy foliage. Plant the English bluebell (*Hyacinthoides non-scripta*) in dappled shade beneath deciduous trees; the flower colour will seem all the more intense. When buying, check bulbs have not been collected from the wild, an illegal practice. The larger, more robust Spanish bluebell (*H. hispanica*) tolerates sun and drier conditions. Bluebells may be naturalized in grass or in a wild garden, but in a border *H. hispanica* is likely to become a nuisance.

■ **HARDINESS** Fully hardy ✳✳✳.
■ **CULTIVATION** Plant bulbs 8cm (3in) deep in autumn, in reasonably fertile soil that is well-drained, in partial shade. Remove flowers as they fade to prevent self-seeding, except where planted in woodland. ■ **Sow** seed (*see pp.328–329*) in a container in a cold frame as soon as it is ripe or divide clumps in summer (*see p.330*).

Hyacinthoides hispanica (Spanish bluebell)
‡40cm (16in) ↔10cm (4in)

Hyacinthus
Hyacinth

EARLY TO LATE SPRING

Possibly the most sweetly scented of all spring-flowering bulbs, hyacinths are grown for their densely packed flowerheads in white, pink, red, yellow, and shades of purple. Each sturdy flower stem rises up above the deep green, strappy leaves. All cultivated forms derive from *H. orientalis*, growing 20–30cm (8–12in) tall. Make a virtue of their slightly unnatural appearance by using them in formalized spring bedding displays, with polyanthus (*see Primula, pp.260–261*), winter-flowering pansies (*see Viola, p.282*) and tulips (*see pp.278–279*).

■ **HARDINESS** Fully hardy ✳✳✳ in the ground, but may be damaged by frost if grown in containers outdoors.
■ **CULTIVATION** ■ **Plant** bulbs 10cm (4in) deep and 8cm (3in) apart in autumn. Grow in well-drained, reasonably fertile soil in sun or partial shade. Protect container-grown bulbs from excessive winter wet. ■ **For forcing**, plant specially prepared bulbs in containers in autumn; use bulb fibre in bowls with no drainage holes. Keep in a cool, dark place for 6 weeks and bring into light and warmth when shoots are 2.5cm (1in) tall. After flowering, plant bulbs outside in a secluded spot to produce smaller flower clusters.

Hyacinthus orientalis 'City of Haarlem' ♀
‡20–30cm (8–12in) ↔ 8cm (3in), flowers in late spring

Iberis
Candytuft

LATE SPRING TO EARLY SUMMER

Clusters of small, often scented flowers almost conceal candytuft's low mounds of spoon-shaped, dark green leaves. This group of spreading perennials and bushy annuals flower in shades of white, purple, red, or pink from late spring until early summer. Evergreen *Iberis sempervirens*, 30cm (12in) tall, produces round heads of densely packed, white flowers, while compact *I. umbellata* has flowerheads in pinks and purples. Perennial forms of candytuft are good for rock gardens and walls. Grow annuals as bedding or in containers; good companions include other hardy annuals such as nigellas (*p.244*).

■ **HARDINESS** Fully hardy ✳✳✳ to frost-hardy ✳✳.
■ **CULTIVATION** ■ **Grow** in poor to reasonably fertile soil that is moist but well-drained, in sun. After flowering, trim perennials back to tidy. ■ **Sow** seed of annuals where they are to grow (*see p.329*), in spring or autumn. Sow seed of perennials in containers in a cold frame in autumn (*see pp.328–329*).
■ **Take** softwood cuttings in late spring, or semi-ripe cuttings in summer (*see pp.329–330*).

Iberis umbellata
‡15–30cm (6–12in) ↔ to 23cm (9in), annual, with a mixture of pink, lilac-purple, and white, scented flowers ✳✳✳

Impatiens
Busy Lizzie

Free-flowering even in shade, busy Lizzies are among the most useful plants for long-lived summer colour. They produce a profusion of flowers, in reds, purples, pinks, and white, and many bicolours, from early summer into autumn. Most are annuals, or tender perennials grown as annuals. All have brittle, almost succulent stems with fleshy leaves. The New Guinea hybrids (*Impatiens schlechteri*) and *I. walleriana* varieties are valuable in borders and containers in shady spots; try some unusual types in a windowbox or in pots to bring their flowers nearer the eye.

■ **HARDINESS** Fully hardy ✱✱✱ to frost-tender ✿.
■ **CULTIVATION** Grow in soil enriched with well-rotted organic matter in partial shade, with shelter from cold winds. In pots, use loam-based compost and keep well watered; feed with a balanced fertilizer every week. ■ **Sow** busy Lizzie seed (*see pp.328–329*) at 16–18°C (61–64°F) in early spring. ■ **Take** softwood cuttings (*see pp.329–330*) in spring and summer to overwinter. ■ **Moulds** (*see pp.332–333*) may affect flower buds in damp conditions; pick them off promptly and healthy ones should follow.

***Impatiens niamniamensis* 'Congo Cockatoo'**
↕90cm (36in) ↔35cm (14in), erect, short-lived perennial ✿

Inula

These robust, herbaceous perennials produce a mass of yellow daisies with prominent, yellow centres and narrow, dainty petals. The flowers are borne singly or in flat-topped clusters throughout summer. The leaves are large at the base, becoming progressively smaller up the stem. Heights vary tremendously, from *Inula ensifolia* 'Compacta', only 15cm (6in) tall and suitable for a rock garden, to towering species such as *I. magnifica*, growing to 2m (6ft) tall, which with their rather coarse foliage suits the back of a border or a wild garden. Grow medium height inulas in an informal border, with other summer-flowering perennials. Some species can be invasive, but can be controlled by digging out unwanted clumps.

■ **HARDINESS** Fully hardy ✱✱✱ to frost-hardy ✱✱.
■ **CULTIVATION** Grow all but rock-garden species in deep, fertile, well-drained soil, in full sun or partial shade. ■ **Divide** perennials in spring or autumn (*see p.330*). ■ **Sow** seed (*see pp.328–329*) in containers in a cold frame in spring or autumn. ■ **Powdery mildew** can be a problem in dry conditions.

Inula hookeri
↕60–75cm (24–30in) ↔ 60cm (24in), softly hairy stems and leaves, flowers from late summer to mid-autumn ✱✱✱

Ipheion

The starry flowers of these plants sit like jewels among their grassy leaves in spring. This is a small group of bulbous perennials whose blue, violet, or white flowers are often strongly honey-scented. Most other parts of the plant, especially the leaves, smell of onions when crushed. The most commonly grown species, *Ipheion uniflorum*, may be small, but is sturdy and quickly clump-forming. These are beautiful plants for a rock garden, or can be used in a border to underplant herbaceous perennials such as hostas (*see pp.218–219*) and peonies (*see p.248*). They need winter protection in colder areas; if grown in pots and bowls, they can be brought under cover in winter.

■ **HARDINESS** Frost-hardy ✱✱ to frost-tender ✿.
■ **CULTIVATION** Grow in reasonably fertile, well-drained soil enriched with well-rotted organic matter, or in loam-based compost, in full sun. Plant the bulbs 8cm (3in) deep, 5cm (2in) apart in autumn. ■ **Provide** a mulch (*see p.326*) where temperatures regularly fall below -10°C (14°F). ■ **Divide** (*see p.330*) in summer, when the plants are dormant. ■ **Sow** seed (*see pp.328–329*) in containers in a cold frame as soon as it is ripe, or in spring.

***Ipheion uniflorum* 'Wisley Blue'** ♀
↕15–20cm (6–8in), leaves produced in late autumn, scented solitary flowers in spring ✱✱

Iris

Irises produce their distinctive, handsome flowers mainly from midwinter to midsummer on plants that vary greatly in height. Diminutive types such as *Iris danfordiae* and *I. histrioides* unfold their petals when snow may be on the ground. These are bulbous irises, one of the many types included in this wide-ranging genus. Other irises grow from rhizomes, fleshy stems that creep on or below the soil surface. Those with this kind of rootstock include the widely-grown bearded irises, with stiff, sword-like leaves, at their peak in early summer. Beardless irises lack the decorative tuft on the lower petals, but their flowers are often beautifully marked. They include early summer-flowering Siberian irises and moisture-loving water, or flag, irises. Those classed as crested irises also spread by rhizomes and produce showy but flatter-shaped flowers. There are many more garden-worthy irises besides. All are perennial, and a few are evergreen. Taller irises often make typical cottage-garden plants and have a stately presence in mixed or herbaceous borders. Smaller varieties tend to be best suited to a rock garden, raised bed, or container.

■ **HARDINESS** Fully hardy ✳✳✳ to frost-tender ✿.
■ **CULTIVATION** Different types of iris require different growing conditions, so check the label when you buy. ■ **Plant** bearded irises in well-drained soil in sun (*see below*). Moisture-loving species need the soil to be damp at all times and suit bog gardens or pond margins. Most types grow well in slightly neutral to slightly acid soil, but a few have special requirements: *I. laevigata* and Pacific Coast irises, for instance, need acid soil, and winter-flowering *I. unguicularis* needs alkaline soil and a sheltered site. ■ **Remove** faded flowers and spent flower stems if unsightly, but leave if you want the seedheads, as with *I. foetidissima*.
■ **Divide** rhizomes from midsummer until early autumn (*see below*).
■ **Sow** seed in containers in spring or autumn (*see pp.328–329*). Bearded irises are susceptible to rot if the soil is not well-drained.

Dividing and planting iris rhizomes

To divide Lift the iris and wash the soil from the roots. Split the clump apart with your hands or an old knife. Make sure there is one good rhizome with roots and leaves for each new clump. Use a sharp knife to trim the rhizome carefully. Discard any pieces that do not have any new shoots. Trim the roots by up to one-third, then cut down the leaves to 15cm (6in) to prevent wind rock. The leaves can act like sails.

To plant Water irises should be replanted in a basket if destined for a pond, or in damp ground. In baskets, use aquatic compost and a top-dressing of gravel to prevent the compost from washing away. Bearded irises need to be planted with the roots in the soil but the rhizomes set on the surface, 13cm (5in) apart. Firm in and water to settle the soil around the roots. Water regularly until established.

I. **'Alcazar'** ‡60–90cm (24–36in), bearded

I. **'Annabel Jane'** ‡1.2m (4ft), bearded, late spring

I. **'Early Light'** ♀ ‡1m (3ft), bearded, mid-spring

I. **'Eyebright'** ♀ ‡30cm (12in), bearded, early spring

I. **'Joyce'** ‡13cm (5in), dwarf bulbous, early spring

I. **'Katherine Hodgkin'** ♀ ‡13cm (5in), dwarf bulbous, late winter

I. **'Sable'** ‡60–90cm (24–36in), bearded, early summer

I. setosa ♀ ‡15–90cm (6–36in), beardless, late spring

I. 'Blue Denim' ‡40–45cm (16–18in), bulbous, late winter or spring

I. confusa ♀ ‡1m (3ft)

I. danfordiae ‡8–15cm (3–6in), dwarf bulbous, late winter

I. delavayi ♀ ‡1.5m (5ft), Siberian, summer

I. foetidissima ♀ ‡30–90cm (12–36in), beardless, early summer

I. 'George' ♀ ‡13cm (5in), bulbous, early spring

I. histrioides 'Major' ‡10–15cm (4–6in), dwarf bulbous, early spring

I. 'Jane Phillips' ♀ ‡60–90cm (24–36in), bearded, early summer

I. laevigata ♀ ‡80cm (32in), beardless water iris, early summer

I. magnifica ♀ ‡30–60cm (12–24in), bulbous, mid-spring

I. 'Natascha' ‡13cm (5in), bulbous, early spring

I. 'Red Revival' ‡60–90cm (24–36in), bearded, scented, late spring

I. sibirica 'Butter and Sugar' ♀ ‡70cm (28in), Siberian, mid-spring

I. sibirica 'Shirley Pope' ♀ ‡85cm (34in), Siberian, early summer

I. sibirica 'Wisley White' ‡1m (3ft), Siberian, early summer

I. unguicularis 'Mary Barnard' ♀ ‡30cm (12in), beardless, midwinter

Knautia

SUMMER TO AUTUMN

These charming plants are particularly suited to growing in a cottage garden, or a wildflower area, where their exuberant habit lends an air of informality to the planting. Garden knautias are perennials, but there are annual species. They have basal rosettes of simple, broad leaves that last through the winter and tall, slender stems. From summer to autumn, these bear numerous, long-lasting, bluish-lilac to purple flowers, similar to those of scabious (*see p.268*), that wave gracefully in the breeze and attract bees. If the plants flower profusely for 2–3 years, they may become exhausted and have to be replaced.

■ **HARDINESS** Fully hardy ✳✳✳.
■ **CULTIVATION** Grow in any moderately fertile, well-drained soil, preferably alkaline (limy), and in full sun. Knautias can be prone to rot in wet soils during winter. ■ **Dig in** plenty of coarse grit to improve drainage permanently on heavy clay soils. Raising the level of the soil by 5–8cm (2–3in) can also help to improve drainage. ■ **Sow** seed (*see pp.328–329*) in containers or take cuttings (*see pp.329–330*) from the base of the plant in spring.

Knautia macedonica
↕60–80cm (24–32in) ↔45cm (18in), flowers 1.5–3cm (½–1¼in) across in mid- and late summer

Kniphofia
Red hot poker, Torch lily

SUMMER TO AUTUMN

The spiky flowerheads in brazen hues and erect habit of these striking perennials reveal how they became known as red hot pokers. Most form large clumps with arching, strappy, light green or blue-green leaves. During summer, strong stems soar up to 2m (6ft) and bear flower spikes composed of many small, tubular flowers. They may be in shades of scarlet, orange, gold, white, or greenish-white – some flower spikes are bicoloured. There are also dwarf kniphofias that are no more than 50cm (20in) tall. Use these plants in borders to provide a vertical contrast to plants with broad foliage such as hostas (*see pp.218–219*).

■ **HARDINESS** Fully hardy ✳✳✳ to frost-tender ❀.
■ **CULTIVATION** Grow in fertile, well-drained, preferably sandy soil with plenty of well-rotted organic matter added to it before planting. Kniphofias prefer a sandy soil in full sun or partial shade. ■ **Protect** the plants from severe frost in the first winter by putting a layer of straw or leaves over deciduous plants, or tying together the stems of evergreens. ■ **Sow** seed (*see pp.328–329*) in containers in a cold frame in spring. ■ **Divide** (*see p.330*) established clumps in late spring.

Kniphofia 'Green Jade'
↕to 1.5m (5ft) ↔60–75cm (24–30in), evergreen, flowers fade to cream and then white in late summer and early autumn ✳✳✳

Kniphofia 'Bees' Sunset' ♀
↕90m (3ft) ↔60m (2ft), deciduous, flowers early to late summer ✳✳✳

Kniphofia 'Royal Standard' ♀
‡90–100cm (36–39in) ↔ 60cm (2ft), deciduous,
scarlet buds, flowers in mid- and late summer
✳✳✳

Kniphofia 'Ice Queen'
‡to 1.5m (5ft) ↔ 75cm (30in), deciduous, green
buds open to pale primrose, then to ivory, in late
summer to early autumn ✳✳✳

Lamium
Dead nettle

This group of annuals and perennials
are grown mainly for their very
decorative foliage, and make good
ground-cover plants among shrubs
and larger, vigorous perennials. The
leaves are roughly textured and, in
some plants, are mottled or tinted.
Lamiums have the distinctive square
stems of plants belonging to the nettle
family, but fortunately no stings. From
late spring until summer, the two-
lipped flowers are borne either singly
or in tiers in dense clusters or spikes.

Easily grown, the larger species can
be invasive in very rich soils, but less
so in poorer soils. Lamiums look
particularly good at the front of a
border or in a woodland setting with
light, dappled shade.

■ **HARDINESS** Fully hardy ✳✳✳.
■ **CULTIVATION** Grow vigorous species
of dead nettle in moist but well-drained soil in
shade. Dig out the spreading underground stems
(rhizomes) if needed, to keep them away from
less robust plants. Less vigorous lamiums prefer
sharply drained soil in full sun or partial shade.
■ **Trim** plants with shears in early spring or
in summer after flowering. ■ **Sow** seed (see
pp.328–329) in autumn or spring in pots in a
cold frame; take stem-tip cuttings (see p.330)
in early summer.

Lamium galeobdolon 'Hermann's Pride'
‡60cm (2ft) ↔ indefinite

Lamium maculatum
‡20cm (8in) ↔ 1m (3ft)

Lamium maculatum 'Album'
‡15cm (6in) ↔ 60cm (2ft)

Lamium maculatum 'Beacon Silver'
‡15cm (6in) ↔ 60cm (2ft)

Lathyrus vernus
Spring vetchling

This dense, clump-forming herbaceous perennial is related to the climbing sweet pea (*Lathyrus odoratus*) (*see p.123*). However, despite the plant's pea-like appearance it does not climb. In spring, it bears one-sided clusters of 3–6 flowers, poised above dark to mid-green pointed leaflets. The plant dies back in summer after flowering. Since the spring vetchling grows only 20–45cm (8–18in) tall and spreads to only 45cm (18in), it is suitable for rock gardens and woodland settings. It can also be grown in herbaceous and mixed borders, but the plants should be placed near the back of the border so that they are hidden when their foliage dies back. There is also a fine pink- and white-flowered form, *Lathyrus vernus* 'Alboroseus'.

■ **HARDINESS** Fully hardy ✳✳✳.
■ **CULTIVATION** Spring vetchlings prefer well-drained soil in full sun or partial shade. They will tolerate poor soil, but resent being disturbed or transplanted. ■ **Sow** seed (*see pp.328–329*) in pots in spring or directly into the soil where they are to grow.

Lathyrus vernus ♀
↕↔ 45cm (18in), flowers are 2cm (³⁄₄in) across

Lavatera
Mallow

The annual mallows have very similar flowers to the shrubby types (*see p.72*), and like them grow vigorously and flower very profusely in a single season, but once seed is set, they die. They produce masses of showy, open, funnel-shaped flowers in shades from white to pale pink to reddish- or purple-pink. The leaves are mid- to dark green with heart-shaped bases. The flowers are also good for cutting. Mallows grow wild in dry, rocky places and in the garden they thrive in sunny herbaceous borders or summer bedding displays. For a traditional cottage-garden look, grow them with other annuals such as calendulas (*see p.171*) and nasturtiums (*see Tropaeolum, p.277*).

■ **HARDINESS** Fully hardy ✳✳✳ to frost-hardy ✳✳.
■ **CULTIVATION** Grow in light to moderately fertile soil, in full sun. They can grow quite tall, and so may need supporting with twiggy sticks in exposed gardens. ■ **Sow** seed in containers under glass in mid-spring, or slightly later outside where plants are to grow (*see pp.328–329*).

Lavatera cachemiriana
↕ 2.5m (8ft) ↔ 1.2m (4ft), short-lived, woody perennial grown as an annual, flowers in summer, good as temporary hedge ✳✳✳

Leucanthemum

Robust and clump-forming, these perennials and annuals bloom for long periods in summer through to early autumn and the dense flowerheads are carried singly at the ends of long stems. The flowers are excellent for cutting. The dark green leaves are long and toothed. *Leucanthemum vulgare* is the common marguerite or ox-eye daisy, a classic plant for meadows and wildlife gardens, while *L. x superbum* cultivars (shasta daisies) are what used to be called *Chrysanthemum maximum* – also white-flowered, but usually with fancy petal details. Grow them in a wild or informal area, or in borders to lighten planting schemes.

■ **HARDINESS** Fully hardy ✳✳✳ to frost-hardy ✳✳.
■ **CULTIVATION** Grow in reasonably fertile soil that is well-drained, in full sun or partial shade. Taller plants may need support with twiggy sticks. ■ **Divide** perennials in early spring or late summer (*see p.330*). ■ **Sow** seed of annuals where plants are to grow, in spring. Sow seed of perennials in containers in a cold frame in spring or autumn (*see pp.328–329*).

***Leucanthemum x superbum* 'Horace Read'**
↕↔ 60cm (24in), double white flowers from early summer to early autumn

Leucojum

Snowflake

SPRING AND AUTUMN

Similar to snowdrops, although some are larger, these bulbous perennials flower at various times of year, giving more scope for pairing them with other plants. The flowers have attractive greenish spots on the tips of the petals. The slender, strappy leaves grow direct from the bulbs. The larger species are good in a border or near water, whilst the smaller species are ideal for a rock garden or alpine trough. *Leucojum vernum* and *L. aestivum*, both spring-flowering, associate well with other bulbs, such as crocuses (*see p.184*) and narcissus (*see pp.240–241*).

■ **HARDINESS** Fully hardy ✽✽✽ to frost-hardy ✽✽.
■ **CULTIVATION** Plant bulbs 8–10cm (3–4in) deep in autumn, in moist but well-drained soil in full sun. Add plenty of organic matter for *L. aestivum* and *L. vernum*, which need soil that retains moisture reliably. ■ **Sow** seed in a container in a cold frame in autumn (*see pp.328–329*), or remove well-rooted offsets (*see p.330*) once the leaves have died down.

Leucanthemum vulgare
‡30–90cm (12–36in) ↔ 60cm (24in), solitary white flowers with yellow centres in late spring and early summer

Leucanthemum x superbum 'Phyllis Smith'
‡90cm (36in) ↔ 60cm (24in), sturdy perennial with single flowers 10–13cm (4–5in) across ✽✽✽

Leucanthemum x superbum 'Wirral Supreme' ♀
‡90cm (36in) ↔ 75cm (30in), perennial with glossy leaves and dense, double flowerheads ✽✽✽

Leucanthemum x superbum 'Cobham Gold'
‡60cm (24in) ↔ 75cm (30in), perennial, double flowerheads on short stems, dark green leaves ✽✽✽

Leucojum aestivum 'Gravetye Giant' ♀
‡90cm (36in) ↔ 8cm (3in), the largest of the snowflakes, spring flowers are faintly chocolate-scented, likes damp conditions

Lewisia

SPRING TO SUMMER

These popular, hardy alpines are grown for the pretty, often bright colours of their flowers. There are both deciduous and evergreen kinds, forming either rosettes or tufts of fleshy leaves. The deciduous species are more commonly native to high meadows or to grassland, and will die down after flowering; the evergreens are found in shady crevices among rocks. Lewisias have many-petalled flowers in shades of pink, peach, magenta, purple, yellow or white – they are often striped. They bloom for many weeks in spring and summer. Grow them in a rock garden or in crevices in a dry-stone wall, with other rock plants and perhaps aubrietas (see p.165).

■ **HARDINESS** Fully hardy ✽✽✽.
■ **CULTIVATION** Grow in reasonably fertile, sharply drained, neutral to acid (lime-free) soil, in full sun or partial shade. Protect all lewisias from winter wet. In containers, grow in equal parts loam, leafmould, and sharp sand. ■ **Sow** seed in containers in a cold frame in autumn (see pp.328–329). Seed of L. cotyledon hybrids produces plants that may look different to their parents. Evergreens may produce plantlets around the main rosette of leaves, which can be removed and potted up in early summer. ■ **Slugs** and snails (see p.332) are likely to attack lewisia.

Lewisia brachycalyx ♀
‡↔to 8cm (3in), deciduous perennial, flowers often tinged with pale pink on short leafless stems in late spring and early summer

***Lewisia cotyledon* hybrid**
‡15–30cm (6–12in) ↔20–40cm (8–16in), evergreen perennial, yellow, orange, magenta, or pink flowers in late spring to summer

Lewisia 'George Henley'
‡10cm (4in) ↔10cm (4in), evergreen perennial, small rosettes but tall flower stems with many flowers from late spring to summer

Liatris

Blazing star, Gayfeather

LATE SUMMER TO AUTUMN

The tall flower spikes of liatris are unusual in that they open from the top of the spike downwards, instead of from the bottom upwards, giving them a distinctive bottle-brush shape that is emphasized by the appearance of the tightly packed flowers. These are produced on stiff stems in shades of purple and white, and are highly attractive to bees. Liatris grow wild on prairies and in open woodland. In the garden, they provide late-summer colour and are good for cutting, too. Try growing with perennials with open-faced flowers, such as erigerons (see p.197), coreopsis (see p.183), and geums (see p.210), to accentuate their striking form.

■ **HARDINESS** Fully hardy ✽✽✽.
■ **CULTIVATION** Grow in light, fertile, moist but well-drained soil in full sun. L. spicata needs soil that is reliably moist. In heavy soils, plant on a layer of coarse gravel to improve drainage, or plants may rot in wet winters. ■ **Divide** in spring (see p.330). ■ **Sow** seed in a container in a cold frame in autumn (see pp.328–329). ■ **Slugs**, snails (see p.332) and mice are likely to attack.

***Liatris spicata* 'Kobold'**
‡to 1.5m (5ft) ↔45cm (18in), broad, long-lasting flower spikes in late summer and early autumn

Libertia

LATE SPRING TO SUMMER

Valued for their striking forms, libertias have stiff, narrow, evergreen leaves that are a feature all year round. At the base, the leaves are leathery and long; those on the stem are smaller and more sparse. In late spring and summer, libertias produce slender spires of saucer-shaped, white, yellow-white or blue flowers. These are followed by shiny, light brown seedheads. The leaves and seeds of *Libertia ixioides* are tinted orange in late autumn and winter. These clump-forming perennials should be grown towards the front of a mixed or herbaceous border; they make perfect partners for the garden tradescantias (*see p.275*), and also look good with bronze-tinted grasses.

■ **HARDINESS** Fully hardy ✳✳✳ (borderline) to frost-hardy ✳✳, but with protection, all can survive all but the coldest winters.
■ **CULTIVATION** Grow in reasonably fertile soil enriched with well-rotted organic matter, in full sun. In frost-prone areas, protect with a thick mulch in winter. ■ **Divide** in spring (*see p.330*). ■ **Sow** seed in containers outdoors as soon as it is ripe (*see pp.328–329*).

Libertia grandiflora ♀
‡to 90cm (36in) ↔60cm (24in), forms dense clumps, flowers early spring to early summer ✳✳✳ (borderline)

Ligularia

MIDSUMMER TO AUTUMN

These architectural plants are large, robust, clump-forming perennials grown for their pyramid-shaped spikes of flowers, produced in shades of yellow and orange from midsummer until early autumn. Each individual flower is daisy-like, often with a contrasting centre. The large, usually rounded or kidney-shaped, mid-green leaves are equally bold. Ligularias look imposing grown in a mixed or herbaceous border, with other moisture-loving perennials such as astilbes (*see p.164*), daylilies (*see Hemerocallis, p.216*), and border phloxes (*see p.254*). Tall species, such as *Ligularia przewalskii*, need to be at the back of planting schemes. They also look very striking growing by a stream or pond, where they will enjoy the damp conditions.

Ligularia **'Gregynog Gold'** ♀
‡to 2m (6ft) ↔1m (3ft), rounded to heart-shaped leaves, flowers with brown centres in late summer and early autumn

Ligularia **'The Rocket'** ♀
‡2m (6ft) ↔1m (3ft), sturdy black stems, large, boldly toothed leaves with purple veins, tall "candles" of flowers with orange-yellow centres, flowers in early and late summer

■ **HARDINESS** Fully hardy ✳✳✳.
■ **CULTIVATION** Grow in reasonably fertile, deep and reliably moist soil, in full sun or partial shade. Provide shelter from strong winds, otherwise taller plants may need staking with twiggy sticks. ■ **Divide** in spring or after flowering (*see p.330*). ■ **Sow** seed of species outdoors in autumn or spring (*see pp.328–329*).

Lilium
Lily

SUMMER TO AUTUMN

Lilies have long graced gardens, both in the West and in the East, where many originate. Their appeal lies in their extravagant, often fragrant, summer blooms, which can measure up to 8cm (3in) across and over 10cm (4in) long. There are about 100 species; all are perennial bulbs. Some of the earliest in cultivation are among the most demanding, for instance the Madonna lily, *Lilium candidum*, which can be disease-prone. Others have definite preferences for acid or alkaline soil. Modern hybrids, however, tend to be vigorous, disease-resistant, and less fussy about soil. Lilies are available in most colours except blue, and the flowers come in four distinct shapes: trumpet, funnel, bowl, and turkscap, with swept-back petals. One of the easiest ways to grow them is in a container, but most do well in sunny borders; some, such as *L. martagon*, prefer dappled shade.

■ **HARDINESS** Fully hardy ✳✳✳ to half-hardy ✳, but young shoots may be damaged by frost.
■ **CULTIVATION** Grow in any well-drained soil enriched with well-rotted organic matter or in containers in good potting compost. On heavy clay soils, improve drainage by digging in plenty of coarse grit in the area of the planting hole. Most lilies prefer full sun, but some tolerate partial shade. ■ **Plant** bulbs in autumn or spring at a depth of 2–3 times their height; the distance between should be three times the diameter of the bulb. ■ **Water** regularly during dry spells in summer and feed with a high-potash fertilizer in the growing season. ■ **Stake** tall varieties in exposed sites. ■ **Deadhead** fading flowers before seed sets to maintain the plant's vigour. ■ **Sow** seed (*see pp.328–329*) as soon as it is ripe in pots in a cold frame. ■ **Detach** stem bulbils and bulblets from those cultivars that produce them (*see below*). ■ **Slugs**, snails (*see p.332*) and lily beetles may eat the plants and flowers. Pick off and destroy the bright orange beetles, or spray the plant with a proprietary insecticide.

Propagating from bulblets
Lilies such as *L. auratum*, *L. longiflorum*, and *L. speciosum* naturally produce bulblets (small rooted bulbs that grow into flowering plants in 3–4 years). They form below ground at the base of the main stem. Lift the parent plant in autumn, remove the bulblets and replant the mature bulb. Prepare pots of moist, loam-based compost. Insert bulblets to twice their depth, and cover the compost with a layer of grit. Label and keep in a frost-free place to plant out the next autumn.

Propagating from bulbils
Bulbils are tiny bulbs that form where the leaf stalks join stems of lilies such as *L. bulbiferum* and *L. lancifolium*, as well as *L. x testaceum*, and their hybrids. They ripen in summer, and produce flowering plants in 3–4 years. Take them only from healthy plants as they can transfer disease. Fill a pot with moist, loam-based compost and press the bulbils into the surface. Cover with a 1cm (½in) layer of coarse sand and label. Grow on in a frost-free place to plant out the next autumn.

L. African Queen Group ♀ ‡1.5–2m (5–6ft), scented ✳✳

L. 'Ariadne' ‡80cm–1.4m (2½–4½f scented ✳✳✳

L. Citronella Group ‡1–1.5m (3–5ft) ✳✳✳

L. 'Connecticut King' ‡1m (3ft) ✳✳

L. henryi ♀ ‡1–3m (3–10ft), neutral to alkaline soil, partial shade, late summer ✳✳✳

L. 'Journey's End' ‡1–2m (3–6ft), late summer ✳✳✳

L. 'Rosemary North' ‡90–100cm (36–39in) ✳✳✳

L. rubellum ‡30–80cm (12–32in), acid soil, partial shade, early summer ✳✳✳

auratum var. *platyphyllum*
1.5m (5ft), scented ✳✳✳

L. 'Bright Star' ‡1–1.5m (3–5ft), scented, lime-tolerant ✳✳✳

L. candidum ⚥ ‡1–2m (3–6ft), scented, neutral to alkaline soil ✳✳✳

L. chalcedonicum ‡60cm–1.5m (2– 5ft), any soil, sun or shade ✳✳✳

'Enchantment' ‡60–100cm (24–39in), good for cutting ✳✳✳

L. 'Fire King' ‡1–1.2m (3–4ft), good in containers ✳✳✳

L. Golden Splendor Group ⚥ ‡1.2–2m (4–6ft), scented ✳✳✳

L. 'Gran Paradiso' ‡90cm (36in) ✳✳✳

lancifolium ‡60cm–1.5m (2–5ft), acid soil, late summer ✳✳✳

L. martagon ⚥ ‡90cm–2m (3–6ft), rank scent, well-drained soil, sun or partial shade ✳✳✳

L. Pink Perfection Group ⚥ ‡1.5–2m (5–6ft), scented ✳✳✳

L. regale ⚥ ‡60cm–2m (2– 6ft), scented, full sun, midsummer ✳✳✳

L. 'Star Gazer' ‡1–1.5m (3–5ft) ✳✳✳

L. 'Sterling Star' ‡1–1.2m (3–4ft) ✳✳✳

L. superbum ‡1.5–3m (5–10ft), acid soil, late summer and early autumn ✳✳✳

L. tsingtauense ‡70–100cm (28–39in), acid soil ✳✳✳

Limnanthes douglasii
Poached egg plant
SUMMER TO AUTUMN

This is a fast-growing annual with sweetly scented flowers similar to those of buttercups from summer to autumn. It has yellow, glossy flowers with white tips to the petals. Although annual, it does self-seed prolifically. The flowers are rich in nectar and so are attractive to bees and hoverflies. Hoverflies are good allies to have in the garden as they consume many aphids over the summer. The poached egg plant makes neat, bright splashes of colour at the front of a herbaceous or mixed border – perhaps with other vividly coloured annuals, such as calendulas (*see p.171*) and nasturtiums (*see Tropaeolum, p.277*) – at a path edge, or scattered among paving. It makes an attractive rockery plant, although you will almost certainly find yourself weeding out surplus self-set seedlings.

■ **HARDINESS** Fully hardy ✱✱✱.
■ **CULTIVATION** Grow in fertile, moist but well-drained soil, in full sun. ■ **Sow** seed (*see p.329*) where plants are to grow in spring or autumn. Protect autumn sowings with cloches in frost-prone areas.

Linaria
Toadflax
SPRING TO AUTUMN

This is a large group of annuals, biennials, and herbaceous perennials. Their stems, which can be erect, trailing, or branched, are clothed with clusters of flowers that look like tiny snapdragons. They bloom abundantly from spring to autumn, in hues of white, pink, red, purple, orange, and yellow. The smaller species suit a rock garden or wall crevice. Taller annuals and perennials, such as *Linaria vulgaris*, are a popular choice for the foreground of borders, forming soft masses of colour that act as foils to plants with bolder flowers; they also grow and look well in gravel beds.

■ **HARDINESS** Fully hardy ✱✱✱ to half-hardy ✱✱.
■ **CULTIVATION** Grow in reasonably fertile, well-drained soil, in full sun. Divide perennials in early spring (*see p.330*). ■ **Sow** seed of annuals where they are to flower in early spring (*see p.329*). Thin the seedlings to around 15cm (6in). Sow seed of perennials in containers in a cold frame in early spring (*see pp.328–329*). ■ **Take** softwood cuttings of perennials in spring (*see pp.329–330*).

Linum
Flax
EARLY TO LATE SUMMER

These annuals, biennials, and perennials produce clouds of brilliantly coloured flowers on graceful, wiry stems. They appear from early to late summer, and are mainly in pale primary colours – yellow, blue, or red – or white. The flowers of *Linum perenne* last for only one day, but are replaced by more the next day. The perennials tend to be short-lived, but are easy to raise from seed. The smaller flaxes are at home in a rock garden, while the larger ones make a stunning display *en masse* in borders; grow in drifts among other herbaceous plants with soft outlines, such as cranesbills (*see Geranium, pp.208–209*) and monardas (*see p.239*). (*See also p.73.*)

■ **HARDINESS** Fully hardy ✱✱✱ to frost-hardy ✱✱.
■ **CULTIVATION** Grow in light, reasonably fertile soil enriched with organic matter in full sun. Smaller alpine species need sharply drained soil and protect from winter wet. ■ **Sow** seed in spring or autumn. Annuals can be sown where they are to grow; sow perennials in containers in a cold frame (*see pp.328–329*). ■ **Take** stem-tip cuttings of perennials in early summer (*see p.330*).

Limnanthes douglasii ♥
↕↔15cm (6in) or more, sprawling habit, ferny, yellow-green leaves

Linaria vulgaris
↕to 90cm (36in) ↔30cm (12in) ✱✱✱

Linum flavum 'Compactum'
(Golden flax)
↕↔15cm (6in), upright perennial, dark green leaves, dense flowers that open in summer sun ✱✱✱

Lobelia

SUMMER

Annual bedding lobelia is hugely popular, producing masses of flowers in the familier blues, but also pink, purple, and white. Use it in summer beds, as edging, or trailing from hanging baskets and windowboxes. Planted around the edges of containers, they are perfect partners for fuchsias (*see pp.56–57*) and other summer bedding. There are also hardier, perennial lobelias, from such diverse habitats as the meadow, riverbank, and woodland. They usually bear their flowers in erect spikes, in jewel-like shades of azure, violet, carmine-red, and scarlet.

■ **HARDINESS** Fully hardy ❊❊❊ to frost-tender ❀.
■ **CULTIVATION** Grow in deep, fertile, reliably moist soil, in sun or partial shade. *L. cardinalis* can be grown in baskets (*see p.321*) in water 8–10cm (3–4in) deep. Bedding lobelia flowers for longer in shade. In containers, it needs weekly feeding. ■ **Protect** perennials in frost-prone areas with a thick winter mulch (*see p.326*). ■ **Divide** perennials in spring; aquatics in summer (*see p.330*). ■ **Sow** seed of perennials as soon as ripe; annuals in late winter, at 13–18°C (55–64°F) (*see pp.328–329*). ■ **Slugs** are likely to cause damage (*see p.332*).

Lobelia **'Bee's Flame'**
↕75cm (30in) ↔30cm (12in), clump-forming perennial, dark leaves, tall flower spikes in mid- and late summer ❊❊❊

Lunaria

Honesty, Satin flower

LATE SPRING TO SUMMER

Flowers, seed pods, and leaves are all decorative in this small group of plants. They bear purple or white flowers in late spring and early summer, followed by flat, silvery or beige seed capsules, the sides of which fall to reveal a satiny inner membrane. The capsules last quite well into autumn, although for use in dried flower arrangements they are usually cut in late summer and dried indoors to avoid any damage from autumn weather. The leaves vary in shape and have toothed edges. Annual, biennial, or perennial honesty self-seeds easily and naturalizes well in a wild garden. It can also be grown in a shrub border or with herbaceous perennials like aquilegias (*see p.156*), lupins (*see right*), and poppies (*see Papaver, p.249*). Research has shown that ligularias may have a use in the production of some pharmaceutical products in the future.

Lunaria annua **'Variegata'**
↕to 90cm (36in) ↔to 30cm (12in), as well as white-edged leaves, this has more deeply coloured flowers than *L. annua*

■ **HARDINESS** Fully hardy ❊❊❊.
■ **CULTIVATION** Grow in fertile, moist but well-drained soil, in full sun or partial shade.
■ **Divide** *L. rediviva* (*see p.330*) in spring.
■ **Sow** seed (*see pp.328–329*) in a seedbed: *L. rediviva* in spring, and *L. annua* in early summer. If plants are stunted, pull one up to see if the roots are knobbly and deformed; if so, burn all affected plants; they may have clubroot (*see Crambe, p.183*), a persistent soil-borne disease.

Lunaria annua **'Alba Variegata'**
↕to 90cm (36in) ↔to 30cm (12in), the white flowers will be followed by seed pods that are silvery outside and inside

Lunaria rediviva (Perennial honesty)
↕60–90cm (24–36in) ↔30cm (12in), the flowers are fragrant; the seed pods of this species are more fawn-coloured than silvery

Lupinus
Lupin

EARLY SUMMER

The enduringly popular flower spikes of lupins provide some of the brightest colours to be seen in the early-summer garden. There are plenty to choose from, in almost any colour and even bicolours; they last well when cut. The attractive foliage is mid-green with lance-shaped leaflets; a rain shower will leave it starred with small, silvery droplets. Most lupins grown in gardens are stately perennials, to be paired with other classic herbaceous plants such as delphiniums (*see p.188*) and Oriental poppies (*see Papaver orientale, p.249*). However, there are smaller-flowered, less formal low-growing annuals.

■ **HARDINESS** Fully hardy ✳✳✳ to half-hardy ✳.
■ **CULTIVATION** Grow in reasonably fertile, well-drained soil in full sun or partial shade.
■ **Deadhead** (*see p.327*) for a second flush of flowers. ■ **Sow** seed, after soaking for 24 hours, in spring or autumn, outside or in containers in a cold frame (*see pp.328–329*). ■ **Take** cuttings of new shoots of named varieties in mid-spring (*see pp.329–330*). ■ **Slugs** and snails are likely to attack lupins. It is worth taking precautions against these pests. (*see pp.332 and 218*)

Lupinus **'The Chatelaine'**
‡90cm (36in) ↔75cm (30in), this crisp combination is popular and among the brightest of the bicoloured forms

Lupinus **Russell hybrids**
‡90cm (36in) ↔75cm (30in), among the earliest and most reliable of lupin hybrids, these have a wide colour range

Lupinus **'Noble Maiden'**
‡90cm (36in) ↔75cm (30in), the densely packed flower spikes such as this make a strong impact in the border

Lychnis
Campion, Catchfly

EARLY TO LATE SUMMER

Campions have bright summer flowers in shades of vivid scarlet, purple, and pink as well as in white. The flowers are usually tubular or star-shaped and borne singly or in small clusters. The erect flower stems make them ideal for cutting. Butterflies find the flowers attractive. The leaves may be hairy. Campions are biennial or perennial. Smaller species are pretty in rock gardens, and the taller ones are best in informal borders with other perennials including aquilegias (*see p.156*), lupins (*see p.234*), and Oriental poppies (*see Papaver orientale, p.249*). Some campions, such as *Lychnis chalcedonica*, have brittle stems and need the support of twiggy pea sticks.

■ **HARDINESS** Fully hardy ✳✳✳.
■ **CULTIVATION** Thrive in reasonably fertile, well-drained soil, in full sun or partial shade. Grey-leaved species produce the best leaf colour in well-drained soil in full sun. ■ **Remove** fading flowers regularly. ■ **Sow** seed in containers (*see pp.328–329*) in a cold frame when it is ripe or in spring. ■ **Divide** (*see p.330*) or take cuttings (*see p.329*) from new shoots at the base in spring.

Lychnis coronaria ♀ (Dusty miller, Rose campion)
‡80cm (32in) ↔45cm (18in), biennial or short-lived perennial, flowers in late summer

Lysichiton
Skunk cabbage

These strikingly shaped, colourful perennials flower in early spring. Dense spikes of tiny, greenish flowers are surrounded by elegantly sculptural, hooded bracts (modified leaves). These are followed by clusters of large, glossy, mid- to dark green leaves. The yellow skunk cabbage, *Lysichiton americanus*, is larger than the white-flowered *L. camtschatcensis*, which has 40cm (16in) hoods and leaves up to 100cm (39in) long; it has a height and spread of 75cm (30in). Both plants have a musky, some would say unpleasant, smell. Their native habitat is beside water, so grow them by a pond or stream along with *Caltha palustris (see p.172)* and other moisture-loving marginal plants.

■ **HARDINESS** Fully hardy ✳✳✳.
■ **CULTIVATION** Plant in fertile soil enriched with plenty of well-rotted organic matter, at the edge of a stream or pond, in full sun or partial shade. Allow sufficient space for the leaves to develop without swamping other plants.
■ **Remove** offsets *(see p.330)* at the bases of the main stems in spring or summer.

Lysichiton americanus ♀ (Yellow skunk cabbage)
↕1m (3ft) ↔1.2m (4ft), the flowers are up to 40cm (16in) long, leaves up to 120cm (48in) long

Lysimachia
Loosestrife

Loosestrifes are a large and varied group that includes many herbaceous perennials, and some evergreens. Flowers appear from mid- to late summer, and may be star-, saucer-, or cup-shaped; and they are usually white or yellow, but sometimes pink or purple. Larger loosestrifes are suitable for planting in damp herbaceous and mixed borders along with other moisture-loving perennials such as astilbes *(see p.164)* and border phloxes *(see p.254)*. They are happy in a bog garden or by pool margins and also look at home when naturalized in a woodland garden. Creeping Jenny (*Lysmachia nummularia*) makes a good ground-cover plant. *L. punctata* can spread and become a problem.

■ **HARDINESS** Fully hardy ✳✳✳ to frost-tender ❀.
■ **CULTIVATION** Grow in well-drained soil enriched with organic matter, in full sun or partial shade, and in a site that does not dry out in summer. ■ **Sow** seed in containers outdoors *(see pp.328–329)* in spring or divide plants in spring or autumn *(see p.330)*.

Lysimachia clethroides ♀
↕90cm (36in) ↔60cm (24in), spreading, hairy leaves, flowerheads appear mid- to late summer becoming upright as they mature ✳✳✳

Lythrum
Loosestrife

Even longer-flowering than their namesakes (*see left*), these upright annuals and perennials are valued for their slender spikes of pretty flowers in shades of purplish-pink, or occasionally white. Individual flowers are up to 2cm (³/₄in) wide, with 4–8 petals, and are borne along the ends of tapering, square stems in summer to autumn. The leaves are up to 10cm (4in) long and sometimes add to autumnal displays by turning yellow. Some of these loosestrifes flourish at the margins of streams and ponds. For a colourful display, combine with other flowering plants such as astilbes (*see p.164*), montbretias (*see Crocosmia, p.184*), and phloxes (*see p.254*).

■ **HARDINESS** Fully hardy ✳✳✳.
■ **CULTIVATION** These loosestrifes thrive in any fertile, moist soil in full sun.
■ **Remove** fading flowers to prevent self-seeding. ■ **Sow** seed at 13–18°C (55–64°F) in spring *(see pp.328–329)* or divide plants in spring *(see p.330)*. Take cuttings from new shoots at the base of the plant *(see p.329)* in spring or early summer.

***Lythrum virgatum* 'The Rocket'**
↕80cm (32in) ↔45cm (18in), clump-forming perennial, leaves 10cm (4in) long, flowers from early to late summer

Macleaya
Plume poppy

`EARLY TO MIDSUMMER`

These majestic herbaceous perennials are grown for their handsome foliage and graceful plumes of tiny, petalless flowers. The feathery flower plumes, in buff-white, cream, or soft apricot to coral pink, are carried on erect blue- or grey-green stems from early to midsummer, and appear to almost float above the foliage. The fine leaves, in grey-green to olive-green, are deeply lobed and may be up to 25cm (10in) across. Plume poppies can grow quite tall, up to 2.5m (8ft), so are best planted at the back of a border, where they have great presence; they can be invasive, however. Grow them in a spacious border with other summer-flowering perennials; they can also be used to subtle effect with tall grasses.

■ **HARDINESS** Fully hardy ✳✳✳, but the new growth may be damaged by late frosts.
■ **CULTIVATION** Grow in any soil that is moist but well-drained, in full sun or partial shade. Provide shelter from cold, drying winds. ■ **Divide** plants in spring or autumn. ■ **Sow** seed (see pp.328–329) in containers in a cold frame in spring. ■ **Take** root cuttings in winter (see p.330) or separate the rhizomes (see p.330).

***Macleaya microcarpa* 'Kelway's Coral Plume'** ♀
‡2.5m (7ft) ↔1m (3ft), grey-green leaves with buff to coral-pink flowers in early and midsummer

Malva
Mallow

`SUMMER`

Mallows are easy and rewarding plants to grow and flourish on the poorest of soils. This colourful group of annuals, biennials, and woody-based perennials produce leafy spikes of pink, purple, blue, or white flowers throughout summer on upright plants. The flowers are bowl- or saucer-shaped and last for many weeks, making mallows useful plants for mixed, annual, and herbaceous borders alike. Use them as gap-fillers among other summer-flowering plants such as campanulas (see p.173), phloxes (see p.254), and lilies (see pp.230–231), or for a more informal look, with flowering grasses such as *Lagarus ovatus* (see p.293).

■ **HARDINESS** Fully hardy ✳✳✳.
■ **CULTIVATION** Grow in any moist but well-drained soil in full sun. Provide some support especially if growing in fertile soil. Perennial cultivars and species are often short-lived, but they self-seed. ■ **Sow** seed of annuals where the plants are to grow, or in containers, in spring or early summer (see pp.328–329). ■ **Take** cuttings of new young shoots from perennials in spring (see p.329).

***Malva sylvestris* 'Primley Blue'**
‡to 20cm (8in) ↔30–60cm (12–24in), prostrate perennial

Maianthemum
False Solomon's seal

`MID-SPRING TO MIDSUMMER`

The lush foliage of these vigorous perennials is much like that of Solomon's seal (see *Polygonatum*, p.258) – hence the common name. The resemblance ends when they burst into bloom from mid-spring to midsummer, producing dense clusters of tiny, starry flowers at the tips of arching stems. The flowers are creamy white and have a delicate scent that hangs in the still, damp air of a woodland garden. Green berries follow that ripen to red in autumn. In favourable conditions, these trouble-free plants can be invasive, but are easily dug up if they spread too far. Use maianthemum with other shade-loving plants, for example ferns (see pp.300–309).

■ **HARDINESS** Fully hardy ✳✳✳.
■ **CULTIVATION** Thrive in moderately fertile, preferably slightly acid (lime-free) soil that has been enriched with well-rotted organic matter. Choose a position in full or dappled shade that is sheltered from cold winds. ■ **Sow** seed (see pp.328–329) in containers in a cold frame in autumn. ■ **Divide** the rhizomes of established plants (see p.330) in spring.

***Maianthemum racemosum* (False spikenard)** ♀
‡90cm (36in) ↔60cm (24in), clump-forming, leaves downy beneath

Matthiola
Gillyflower, Stock

LATE SPRING TO SUMMER

For sweet fragrance, few plants can better stocks. They include the dainty, annual, night-scented stock (*Matthiola longipetala* subsp. *bicornis*) and the chunkier gillyflowers (*M. incana*), widely sold as cut flowers. Both are essentials for a cottage-style garden. Gillyflowers, which include the popular Brompton stocks, although perennial are grown as biennials or annuals. There are tall and dwarf forms with single or double flowers in bright or pastel shades of purple, violet, pink, and white. Dwarf verieties are good in containers. Night-scented stocks come in similar colours and can be grown in pots, but must be direct-sown.

■ **HARDINESS** Fully hardy ✷✷✷ to frost-hardy ✷✷.
■ **CULTIVATION** Grow gillyflowers in any moist but well-drained soil in full sun; incana types tolerate partial shade. Tall forms may need some support. ■ **Sow** seed (*see pp.328–329*) of incana types for summer flowering in early spring at 10–18°C (50–64°F) and for spring-flowering outdoors in summer; overwinter in a cold frame to plant out the following spring. Sow night-scented stocks in situ and thin to 10–15cm (4–6in) apart.

Matthiola incana ♀
‡20–25cm (8–10in) ↔ to 25cm (10in), double flowers held in dense spikes 15cm (6in) tall, in late spring to summer ✷✷

Meconopsis

EARLY TO MIDSUMMER

This cosmopolitan group of plants includes both the cheerful yellow Welsh poppy (*Meconopsis cambrica*) and the sapphire-blue Himalayan poppy (*M. betonicifolia*); despite the must-have appeal of the latter, it must be said that the former is much easier to grow. However, if you have the ideal site – a cool, moist woodland garden, or a sheltered border that mimics these conditions, with soil rich in humus or leafmould – you can grow any meconopsis. Their silky flowers appear from early to midsummer. The plants may be short-lived, but all are worth it; some self-seed.

■ **HARDINESS** Fully hardy ✷✷✷, but frost may damage young growth.
■ **CULTIVATION** Grow meconopsis in moist but well-drained, slightly acid (lime-free) soil, in partial shade, with shelter from cold winds. ■ **Divide** established plants after flowering (*see p.330*). ■ **Sow** seed (*see pp.328–329*) in containers in a cold frame as soon as ripe, overwintering seedlings in the frame, or in spring. Sow the seed thinly, on the surface of the compost.

Meconopsis cambrica
‡45cm (18in) ↔ to 1m (3ft), in all but very dry soils

Meconopsis napaulensis
‡2.5m (8ft) ↔ to 1m (3ft), evergreen

Melissa officinalis
Lemon balm, Bee balm

SPRING TO SUMMER

The leaves of this popular herb give off a clear, fresh lemon aroma when they are crushed or brushed in passing. Apart from their scent, these bushy, upright perennials are grown mainly for their attractive nettle-like foliage, which is hairy and light to bright green, or splashed with golden yellow in variegated forms. The young shoots are popular ingredients in pot-pourri and herb teas. In summer, the plants also produce spikes of small, tubular two-lipped, whitish flowers, which attract bees. Grow in a herbaceous or mixed border or with other herbs in a herb garden. While they enjoy full sun, these plants are also useful for dry shade.

■ **HARDINESS** Fully hardy ✷✷✷.
■ **CULTIVATION** Grow in any poor soil in full sun, but provide protection from heavy winter rain. ■ **Cut back** hard after flowering to encourage a fresh flush of foliage and to prevent self-seeding. Variegated forms are better trimmed back before flowering to encourage bright foliage. ■ **Divide** (*see p.330*) as growth starts in spring, or in autumn. ■ **Sow** seed in containers in a cold frame in the spring (*see pp.328–329*) or transplant self-sown seedlings.

***Melissa officinalis* 'Aurea'** (Golden lemon balm)
‡to 1.2m (4ft) ↔ to 45cm (18in), hairy stems, off-white flowers in summer

Melittis melissophyllum
Bastard balm

LATE SPRING TO EARLY SUMMER

This herbaceous perennial is grown for its tubular flowers produced in late spring and early summer. *Melittis melissophyllum* occur in shades of pink and purple, or white with creamy white, marked with pink or purple, and they stud the stems, appearing in the leaf joints. The oval leaves are hairy and wrinkled; they have an aromatic or honeyed scent. Grow bastard balm in a cool border with other plants that are happy in light shade, such as bergenias (*see p.167*) and aquilegias (*see p.156*), or in a woodland garden. Its flowers will attract bees and other pollinating insects into the garden.

■ **HARDINESS** Fully hardy ✷✷✷.
■ **CULTIVATION** Grow in reasonably fertile, moist but well-drained soil, in partial shade.
■ **Divide** plants (*see p.330*) in spring as new growth begins. ■ **Sow** seed in a container in a cold frame as soon as it is ripe, or in spring (*see pp.328–329*).

Melittis melissophyllum
↕20–70cm (8–28in) ↔50cm (20in), woodland plant that can be found growing wild throughout most of Europe

Mimulus
Monkey flower, Musk

EARLY SUMMER TO AUTUMN

The numerous hybrid mimulus are grown as annuals for their bright flowers that bring cheer to containers or borders from early summer through to autumn. These are trumpet-shaped or tubular, in a variety of colours, and usually heavily freckled with a contrasting hue. The pale- to dark-green leaves often have silvery hairs. Mimulus often have a creeping habit, but may be upright and bushy; some are perennial. Most prefer moist or even boggy soil.

■ **HARDINESS** Fully hardy ✷✷✷ to frost-tender ✸.
■ **CULTIVATION** These plants need very moist soil in sun or semi-shade, although *M. cardinalis* will tolerate drier soil; the bedding hybrids and *M. aurantiacus* require well-drained ground and sun. Mimulus is short-lived, so it is worth propagating regularly. ■ **Sow** seed (*see pp.328–329*) of hardy species in containers in a cold frame in autumn or spring; sow tender bedding at 6–12°C (43–54°F) in spring.
■ **Root** softwood cuttings in early summer (*see p.330*). ■ **Divide** perennials (*see p.330*) in spring. ■ **Slugs** (*see p.332*) can cause damage.

Mimulus aurantiacus ♀
↕↔1m (3ft) ✷✷

Mimulus cardinalis ♀
↕1m (3ft) ↔60cm (2ft) ✷✷✷

Moluccella laevis
Bells of Ireland, Shell flower

LATE SUMMER

The extraordinary, leafy flowers and pale-green foliage are the attractions of this commonly cultivated annual – a favourite with flower arrangers. In late summer, it produces spikes up to 30cm (12in) tall that, near the tips, bear tiny, white or pink flowers cupped in large, green collars (called calyces). The calyces become white-veined and papery as the seeds develop and can be used in dried flower arrangements. The flowers are also fragrant. Moluccellas can be used to provide an eye-catching architectural addition to a border of more common bedding plants such as French marigolds (*see Tagetes, p.274*) or heliotropes (*see p.62*).

■ **HARDINESS** Half-hardy ✸.
■ **CULTIVATION** Moluccellas will grow in any moist, but well-drained soil in full sun.
■ **Sow** seed (*see pp.328–329*) at 13–18°C (55–64°F) in early or mid-spring, or in situ in late spring.

Moluccella laevis
↕60–90cm (24–36in) ↔23cm (9in)

Monarda
Bergamot

MIDSUMMER TO AUTUMN

With spidery flowerheads and lush foliage, bergamots enhance any garden. Most widely grown are the clump-forming, herbaceous perennials, but there are a few annuals. From midsummer to early autumn, they produce clusters of tubular flowers, in shades of crimson, pink, white, or violet, at the tips of the stems. The leaves of these plants are mid- to dark green and are often flushed purple. Bergamots are highly aromatic; both the leaves and flowers are used in the fragrance industry. Use these splendid plants in any border where they will attract bees to the garden.

■ **HARDINESS** Fully hardy ❋❋❋.
■ **CULTIVATION** Any moist but well-drained soil, that does not dry out in summer, is suitable – in full sun or dappled shade. ■ **Sow** seed (*see pp.328–329*) in a container in a cold frame, in spring or autumn. ■ **Divide** plants (*see p.330*) in spring before new growth begins. ■ **Slugs** may attack in spring. Powdery mildew may become a problem in dry weather (*see p.332*); mildew-resistant cultivars are available.

Monarda 'Cambridge Scarlet' ♀
‡90cm (36in) ↔ 45cm (18in), clump-forming perennial

Muscari
Grape hyacinth

SPRING

These bulbous plants, although rarely more than 20cm (8in) in height, are very versatile. In spring, and occasionally in autumn, grape hyacinths bear clusters of tiny flowers that are usually blue, but sometimes yellow, white, purple, or even black. Some species are very fragrant. The flowerheads are held above clumps of fleshy, mid-, blue- or grey-green leaves. Plant in large groups in a border, or beneath deciduous shrubs and trees. They are often grown naturalized in grass with other spring-flowering bulbs such as daffodils (*Narcissus, see pp.240–241*) and tulips (*see pp.278–279*). Some species are invasive.

■ **HARDINESS** Fully hardy ❋❋❋ to frost-hardy ❋❋.
■ **CULTIVATION** Plant bulbs 10cm (4in) deep in autumn, in well-drained soil, in sun or dappled shade. ■ **Lift and divide** (*see p.330*) every five years, in summer, to maintain vigour. ■ **Sow** seed in containers in a cold frame in autumn (*see pp.328–329*). ■ **Viruses** can occur: destroy any that are distorted, or marked with patches.

Muscari armeniacum 'Blue Spike'
‡20cm (8in) ↔ 5cm (2in), may form large clumps and become invasive, mid-green leaves in autumn, flowers in spring ❋❋❋

Myosotis
Forget-me-not

MID-SPRING TO MIDSUMMER

A large group of annuals, biennials, and short-lived perennials grown for their delightful flowers and hairy leaves. Most forget-me-nots have blooms in shades of blue, with white or golden eyes, but pink, yellow, or white varieties are available. The biennial *Myosotis sylvatica* and its cultivars, widely used in bedding schemes and containers, are also easy to grow in borders. The water forget-me-not (*M. scorpioides*) is happiest in mud or shallow water, and some of the small, mat-forming perennials, like the alpine forget-me-not (*M. alpestris*), prefer very sharply drained conditions. Nearly all self-seed freely.

■ **HARDINESS** Fully hardy ❋❋❋.
■ **CULTIVATION** Thrive in any moist but well-drained, not too fertile, soil, in sun or semi-shade. ■ **Sow** seed (*see pp.328–329*) in situ in spring. Seed of *M. scorpioides* should be sown in pondside mud. ■ **Divide** plants (*see p.330*) when they are dormant. ■ **Mildew** can create white patches on the foliage (*see p.333*) in damp conditions.

Myosotis sylvatica
‡12–30cm (5–12in) ↔ 15cm (6in), blue, occasionally white flowers from spring to early summer

Narcissus
Daffodil

WINTER TO SPRING

Daffodils and narcissi are the harbingers of spring. The flowers, in cheerful yellows, creams, and white, are a welcome sight after a long winter. The range of species and cultivars runs into thousands, varying widely in both height and shape, with flowers that may be borne singly or several per stem. All are bulbous perennials. The tall, showy varieties look splendid among shrubs in borders or used as spring bedding with polyanthus primulas. The smaller types are often at their most effective in drifts in grass or in a woodland setting, where they will gradually spread if left undisturbed. Dwarf types are suitable for rock gardens. Some, including many of the jonquil, tazetta, and poeticus narcissi, are fragrant. Grow these where you can catch their delicious scent, such as in a trough by the door. Some may also be "forced" (*see below*), grown indoors and made to flower early, usually for Christmas. Most daffodils also make fine cut flowers.

■ **HARDINESS** Fully hardy ✳✳✳ to half-hardy ✳.
■ **CULTIVATION** Tolerate a wide range of soil types, but most grow best in fertile, well-drained soil that is moist during the growing season. Position in full sun or partial shade. ■ **Plant** the bulbs to twice their own depth in autumn, slightly deeper in sandy soils and when naturalizing them in grass. ■ **Water** late-flowering daffodils during dry spring weather to encourage good blooms. ■ **Deadhead** faded flowerheads before the seedheads form, but leave the foliage to die down naturally (delay mowing if in grass). This helps the bulb build up food reserves (and so flower buds) for the following year. ■ **Feed** foliage until it dies down with a high-potash fertilizer to encourage subsequent flowering. ■ **Lift and divide** bulbs (*see p.330*) if flowering deteriorates, usually where bulbs become congested after four or five years. The tiny young bulbs can be grown on into new plants, which need three to four years to begin flowering. Poor flowering, or "blindness", may also be due to bulbs not being planted deeply enough and replanting may be necessary. Stunted, mottled, or streaked foliage is a sign of virus attack. Dig up and destroy infected plants.

Forcing daffodil bulbs

Step 1 Mix washed gravel with a little charcoal. Fill the container to three-quarters full of gravel. Make a gentle dip in the surface with your finger and place a bulb in it, "nose" upwards. Plant the remaining bulbs, making sure they do not touch each other.

Step 2 When you have finished planting, add water until it is just below the bottom of the bulbs. Unless you have prepared bulbs, which can be left in the light, cover the container with a black plastic bag, secure it with string, and stand in a cool, dark place.

Step 3 Check after about four weeks to see if they need more water. After 8–10 weeks, they should have grown 1–2cm (½–¾in) and can be brought into the light. As they grow taller, support weak leaves or stems, securing them to split canes with plant ties.

N. **'Actaea'** ♀ ‡45cm (18in), late spring, scented

N. **'Baby Moon'** ‡25–30cm (10–12in), late spring

N. **'February Gold'** ♀ ‡30cm (12in), early spring, can be naturalized in grass

N. **'Fortune'** ‡45cm (18in), mid-spring

N. **'Jack Snipe'** ♀ ‡20cm (8in), early and mid-spring, increases rapidly

N. **'Jenny'** ♀ ‡30cm (12in), early and mid-spring, can be naturalized in grass

N. **pipit** ‡25cm (10in), mid- and late spring

N. **romieuxii** ♀ ‡8–10cm (3–4in), early spring ✳✳

N. bulbocodium ♀ ↕10–15cm (4–6in), mid-spring, can be naturalized in grass

N. 'Cassata' ↕40cm (16in), mid-spring

N. 'Cheerfulness' ♀ ↕40cm (16in), mid-spring, scented

N. 'Dove Wings' ♀ ↕30cm (12in), early spring

N. 'Golden Ducat' ↕35cm (14in), mid-spring

N. 'Grand Soleil d'Or' ↕45cm (18in), mid-spring, scented ✳✳

N. 'Hawera' ♀ ↕18cm (7in), late spring ✳✳

N. 'Ice Follies' ♀ ↕40cm (16in), mid-spring, prolific

N. jonquilla ♀ ↕30cm (12in), late spring

N. 'Liberty Bells' ↕30cm (12in), mid-spring

N. 'Little Beauty' ♀ ↕15cm (6in), dwarf, early spring

N. 'Pencrebar' ↕18cm (7in), mid-spring, scented

N. 'Salome' ♀ ↕45cm (18in), mid-spring

N. 'Sweetness' ♀ ↕40cm (16in), mid-spring, vigorous, scented, long-lasting as a cut flower

N. 'Thalia' ↕35cm (14in), mid-spring, scented

N. triandrus ♀ ↕10–25cm (4–10in), mid-spring

Nemesia

SUMMER

Annual nemesias are popularly used as riotous summer bedding or container plants. They are easy to grow and produce abundant, brightly coloured flowers in an assortment of blues, reds, pinks, yellows, oranges, and whites. Many are bicoloured, too. The perennials are taller and less brash in appearance, flowering mainly in mauve and white; they may not survive cold winters unless grown in pots and brought under cover. Some of the newer named perennials are more reliably hardy, and will withstand being left in a sheltered position outside over winter, especially if given a protective mulch.

■ **HARDINESS** Frost-hardy ✽✽ to half-hardy ✽.
■ **CULTIVATION** Grow in any moist but well-drained soil in full sun. Nemesias may suffer from root rot in wet soils. ■ **Pinch out** the growing tips of annuals to promote a bushy habit and plenty of flowers. Ensure plants in pots are waterd regularly. ■ **Sow** seed at 15°C (59°F) from early to late spring, or in autumn (*see pp.328–329*). ■ **Take** softwood cuttings from perennials in late summer (*see pp.329–330*) and overwinter young plants in frost-free conditions.

Nemesia denticulata ♀
‡25cm (10in), perennial, ✽✽✽ but may need winter protection

Nemophila

EARLY TO MIDSUMMER

The slender, fleshy stems of nemophilas carry large, open flowers with distinctively marked petals. The flowers are saucer-shaped and usually blue or white, with veins, tints, patches, or centres in contrasting shades of blue, purple, white, or yellow. The showy blooms are set off by feathery, mid- or grey-green leaves. Nemophilas are low-growing annuals that bloom for several weeks in early to midsummer, with more flowers being produced in cool, moist conditions. They are useful for edging a path or filling gaps in the front of a border. Neat and compact, they also suit any type of container, or a rock garden that has moisture-retentive soil.

■ **HARDINESS** Fully hardy ✽✽✽.
■ **CULTIVATION** Grow in any moist but well-drained soil, or in loam-based compost, in full sun or partial shade. ■ **Water** well during dry spells, or plants may stop flowering. ■ **Sow** seed where it is to grow outdoors in spring or autumn (*see p.329*), in shallow drills about 15cm (6in) apart. Thin the seedlings along the rows to about the same distance. Will also self-seed freely.

Nemophila maculata (Five spot)
‡↔15–30cm (6–12in), named for the markings at the tips of its five petals, sometimes veined in mauve also

Nepeta

Catmint

EARLY SUMMER TO AUTUMN

The catmint best known for its strongly aromatic leaves is catnip (*Nepeta cataria*) which cats find hypnotic, but there are other varieties widely grown in gardens that are less appealing to cats. They are perennials with soft, silvery grey foliage and small, erect flower spikes in white and shades of blue, purple, and sometimes yellow. Most have a loose, spreading habit and act as good ground-cover plants since the dense growth

Nepeta govaniana
‡90cm (36in) ↔60cm (24in) ✽✽✽

Nepeta sibirica
‡90cm (36in) ↔45cm (18in) ✽✽✽

suppresses weeds. They can be used to line a broad, sunny path where their scent can be enjoyed whilst walking; some tiny species also suit a rock garden. Taller catmints are best sited in a mixed or herbaceous border.

■ **HARDINESS** Fully hardy ✳✳✳ to half-hardy ✳.
■ **CULTIVATION** Grow in any well-drained soil in full sun or partial shade. The more loosely growing, taller nepetas may benefit from staking (*see p.327*). ■ **Trim** the plants after flowering to maintain a compact habit and encourage more flowers. ■ **Divide** plants in spring or autumn (*see p.330*). ■ **Sow** seed in a container in a cold frame in autumn (*see pp.328–329*).

Nepeta subsessilis
‡to 90cm (36in) ↔30cm (12in) ✳✳✳

Nepeta 'Six Hills Giant'
‡90cm (36in) ↔60cm (24in) ✳✳✳

Nerine

AUTUMN

These bulbous perennials have the most unlikely flowers for autumn – delicate, trumpet-shaped clusters in bright pink, or occasionally crimson or orange-red. They cannot help but lend an invigorating, airy feel to the garden at a time when most other plants are fading. Nerines enjoy well-drained, dry conditions, and usually flourish under a south- or west-facing wall or in a sheltered rock garden. In most, only once the flowers open or even die down do the strappy, mid-green leaves start to emerge, making the bare-stemmed flowers stand out even more dramatically; they are stunning seen in isolated groups against dark soil, or plant them with other late-flowering bulbs, such as schizostylis and *Scilla scilloides* (*see p.269*).

■ **HARDINESS** Fully hardy ✳✳✳ to half-hardy ✳.
■ **CULTIVATION** Plant in well-drained soil in full sun in early spring. Site them carefully as they are best left undisturbed to form a large clump. In cold areas, provide a deep, dry mulch (*see p.326*) for protection. May need protection against slugs (*see p.332*).

Nerine bowdenii ♀
‡45cm (18in) ↔8cm (3in), robust plant, broad leaves to 30cm (12in) long, faintly scented flowers ✳✳✳

Nicotiana
Tobacco plant

SUMMER TO AUTUMN

The perfumed, trumpet-shaped flowers are the main reason for growing this group of annuals, biennials, and perennials. The flowers, in shades of lime-green, red, pink, apple-green, and white, last for many weeks over summer and autumn. They usually open fully only in the evening, when they release their heady scent, but some newer cultivars will open during the day if sited in part-shade. Although some are herbaceous perennials, most are usually grown as annuals and are raised from seed every year. Plant in groups for the best effect and site them on a patio or near the house to enjoy their rich evening fragrance. Contact with the foliage can irritate the skin.

■ **HARDINESS** Frost-hardy ✳✳ to half-hardy ✳.
■ **CULTIVATION** Grow in any moist but well-drained soil in full sun or partial shade. ■ **Stake** tall tobacco plants in exposed positions. ■ **Sow** seed at 18°C (64°F) in spring on the surface of the compost (*see pp.328–329*); they need light to germinate.

Nicotiana 'Lime Green' ♀
‡60cm (24in) ↔25cm (10in), upright annual, flowers 13cm (5in) long ✳

Nigella
Love-in-a-mist, Devil-in-a-bush

SUMMER

Nigella is available in several colours – white, mauve, rose-pink, deep pink, and yellow – as well as the original blue. Some seed mixtures, such as the popular Persian Jewels, produce flowers in several harmonizing shades. These bushy annuals flourish on rocky slopes and wastelands, and will grow almost anywhere. Their dainty summer flowers sit within a hazy ruff of feathery foliage (the "mist" of the common name), and are followed by inflated seed pods, equally good for cutting. Sky-blue 'Miss Jekyll' with yellow and orange eschscholzias (*see p.200*) makes a fine summery contrast. Both of these easy plants fill your garden with colour at very little cost since they self-seed freely.

■ **HARDINESS** Fully hardy ✳✳✳.
■ **CULTIVATION** Grow in any well-drained soil in full sun. ■ **Sow** seed where it is to grow (*see p.329*) in shallow drills about 15cm (6in) apart and thin seedlings to about the same distance. Seed can be sown in spring or autumn, but autumn-sown seedlings benefit from protection, for example with a cloche, over winter.

***Nigella damascena* 'Miss Jekyll'** ♀
‡ to 50cm (20in) ↔ to 23cm (9in), self-seeded offspring may flower in different shades

Nymphaea
Water lily

SUMMER

These herbaceous, submerged, aquatic plants grow from tubers or rhizomes (underground stems). Hardy varieties have mostly white, yellow, or crimson flowers that float on the surface and open during the day (unless overcast). Non-hardy tropical water lilies bloom either in the day or at night and the flowers, which include shades of blue, are held above the water. Water lilies look stunning in large ponds, and there are dwarf varieties to suit small pools. The handsome leaves of mymphaea cover the water and provide shade for fish and also have the effect of reducing algal growth in the water by cutting out sunlight.

■ **HARDINESS** Fully hardy ✳✳✳ to frost-tender ✿.
■ **CULTIVATION** Grow in still water in full sun at the correct depth for the variety. Plant hardy types in early summer in aquatic compost in planting baskets lined in hessian. Insert the rhizomes just under the soil surface and top-dress with gravel to help keep soil in place. ■ **Submerge** the basket so it sits with 15–25cm (6–10in) of water above it, placing on a stack of bricks if necessary. Gradually lower the basket, letting the leaves grow to the surface between each move, until it sits at the right depth. ■ **Remove** fading flowers, if possible, to encourage flowering. ■ **Divide** established plants after three or four years.

***Nymphaea* 'Fire Crest'**
↔ 1.2m (4ft) ✳✳✳

***Nymphaea* 'Virginalis'**
↔ 90cm–1.2m (3–4ft) ✳✳✳

***Nymphaea* 'Marliacea Chromatella'** ♀
↔ 1.2–1.5m (4–5ft) ✳✳✳

***Nymphaea* 'Laydekeri Fulgens'**
↔ 1.2–1.5m (4–5ft) ✳✳✳

Oenothera
Evening primrose, Sundrops

The delicate, papery flowers of evening primrose grace the garden from late spring until summer's end. Although individually short-lived, they are borne in such profusion that new flowers constantly unfurl to replace their predecessors. This varied group includes annuals, biennials, and perennials that produce yellow, white, or pink flowers. Some have the additional attraction of decorative, red or coral flower buds. Heights range from low-growing species suitable for rock gardens or raised beds, such as *Oenothera macrocarpa*, to border plants such as the tall, graceful wands of *O. biennis*, which grows to 1–1.5m (3–5ft) and spreads to 60cm (24in).

■ **HARDINESS** Fully hardy ✳✳✳ to frost-hardy ✳✳.
■ **CULTIVATION** Grow in well-drained soil in full sun – rock plants in a site not prone to excessive winter wet. ■ **Divide** perennials (*see p.330*) in early spring, or take softwood cuttings (*see pp.329–330*) from late spring to midsummer. ■ **Sow** seed in pots in a cold frame (*see pp.328–329*), of perennials in early spring and of biennials in early summer.

Oenothera macrocarpa ♀
‡15cm (6in) ↔ 50cm (20in), vigorous perennial with hairy, branching, red-tinted stems, flowers in late spring ✳✳✳

Oenothera speciosa 'Rosea'
‡↔ 30cm (12in), spreading perennial, a long flowering season from early summer to autumn, can be invasive, dislikes winter wet ✳✳✳

Omphalodes
Navelwort

Sprays of blue or white flowers that are similar to those of forget-me-nots (*see Myosotis, p.287*) are produced in spring and summer. The flowers are held on long, wiry, upright stems. This small group of annuals, biennials, and perennials, some evergreen or semi-evergreen, have a spreading habit that makes good ground cover. Some are suitable for shady borders where the plant choice is limited; companions could include hostas (*see pp.218–219*), carexes (*p.289*), or *Arum italicum* 'Marmoratum' (*p.160*). *Omphalodes linifolia* and *O. luciliae* prefer sun: grow them in a raised gravel bed or rock garden to enjoy the dainty flowers close up.

■ **HARDINESS** Fully hardy ✳✳✳.
■ **CULTIVATION** Grow *O. cappadocica* and *O. verna* in moist, fertile soil in partial shade. *O. linifolia* and *O. luciliae* require sun and well-drained soil or gritty compost (alkaline for the latter). ■ **Sow** seed (*see pp.328–329*) in spring; annuals where they are to grow, and perennials in pots in a cold frame. ■ **Divide** perennials (*see p.330*) in early spring. ■ **Slugs** and snails (*see p.332*) are likely to cause damage.

Oenothera fruticosa 'Fyrverkeri' ♀
‡30–90cm (12–36in) ↔ 30cm (12in), perennial, purple-brown flushed leaves, flowers from late spring to late summer ✳✳✳

Omphalodes cappadocica 'Cherry Ingram' ♀
‡25cm (10in) ↔ 40cm (16in), evergreen perennial, flowers in early spring

Ophiopogon
Lilyturf

SUMMER

The grassy leaves of these plants range in colour from an unusual shade of near-black to light green with cream, yellow, or white margins. In summer, they produce small clusters of bell-shaped, lilac, pink, or white flowers, followed by glossy, round, blue or black seed pods. Their unusual hues associate well with many other plants, including small grasses (*see pp.284–299*) such as *Lagarus ovatus*, brizas and carexes. Blue fescue (*Festuca*) makes a striking contrast to the dark 'Nigrescens'. Alternatively, use as a ground-cover plant. Although all are evergreen perennials, they can be raised from seed as summer bedding each year – the dark-leaved forms, planted *en masse*, form a stark contrast to brighter bedding, such as flame-coloured begonias (*see p.166*).

■ **HARDINESS** Fully hardy ✳✳✳ to half-hardy ✳.
■ **CULTIVATION** Grow in moist, but well-drained soil that is slightly acid (lime-free), in full sun or partial shade. ■ **Divide** plants in spring (*see p.330*) as the new growth appears. ■ **Sow** seed in containers in a cold frame (*see pp.328–329*) as soon as it is ripe. ■ **Slugs** (*see p.332*) can damage young leaves.

Ophiopogon planiscapus 'Nigrescens' ♀
‡20cm (8in) ↔15cm (12in), purplish-white flowers borne in summer, followed by round, dark blue-black fruits ✳✳✳

Ophiopogon jaburan 'Vittatus'
‡60cm (24in) ↔30cm (12in), white, sometimes lilac-tinted flowers in late summer and oblong, violet-blue fruits ✳✳

Origanum
Marjoram, Oregano

SUMMER

These perennials have aromatic foliage and tiny flowers that are usually pink, surrounded by bracts (modified leaves), which determine the dominant colour, in shades of purple, pink, or green. *Origanum laevigatum* 'Herrenhausen' has branched stems to 45cm (18in) tall, clothed with leaves that are flushed purple when young. *O. majorana*, *O. onites*, and *O. vulgare* are the well-known culinary herbs. Grow in a border or herb garden, and smaller species in a rock garden or in paving crevices. (*See also p.80*.)

■ **HARDINESS** Fully hardy ✳✳✳ to frost-hardy ✳✳.
■ **CULTIVATION** Grow marjoram in full sun in well-drained and, preferably, alkaline soil. ■ **Cut back** flowered stems in spring. ■ **Divide** (*see p.330*) or take cuttings (*see pp.329–330*) in spring. ■ **Sow** seed (*see pp.328–329*) in pots in autumn or at 10–13°C (50–55°F) in spring.

Origanum laevigatum ♀
‡50–60cm (20–24in) ↔45cm (18in) woody-based perennial ✳✳✳

Origanum vulgare
‡↔30–90cm (12–36in), woody-based perennial ✳✳✳

Ornithogalum
Star-of-Bethlehem

The silvery white flowers of these bulbous perennials are cup-, star-, or funnel-shaped, and borne on stout stems in spring and summer. They are occasionally scented. Each thick, long leaf curls to a point and some have a silver stripe down the centre. Plants vary in height from *Ornithogalum lanceolatum*, which is only 5–10cm (2–4in) tall, to *O. pyramidale*, which can reach up to 120cm (48in). Smaller species are suitable for a rock garden. *O. nutans* and *O. umbellatum* can be invasive; they are best naturalized in short grass or at the base of shrubs. Grow tender species in containers and move under cover in winter.

■ **HARDINESS** Fully hardy ✳✳✳ to frost-tender ❀.
■ **CULTIVATION** Plant hardy and half-hardy bulbs in autumn, 10cm (4in) deep in reasonably fertile, well-drained soil in full sun; some tolerate partial shade. Tender bulbs are best planted in spring, for summer flowers, in cool climates. On heavy clay soils, plant on coarse grit to improve drainage. ■ **Lift** and separate offsets (*see p.330*) when the bulbs are dormant in summer.

Ornithogalum narbonense
↕30–90cm (12–36in) ↔5cm (2in), long grey-green leaves, late spring and early summer flowers ✳✳✳

Osteospermum

Beguiling daisies with a satin sheen and soft evergreen foliage make these plants worthy of any border. Several new cultivars are brought out each year in an ever-increasing range of colours. The petals are sometimes spoon-shaped and either white washed with a delicate shade of violet, pink, lilac, or blue, or saturated with a single hue, from cream or magenta to purple. The central boss of each bloom has a contrasting tint. Osteospermums can flower from late spring until autumn. They include annuals and subshrubs, but perennials are most commonly grown in borders; half-hardy perennials are grown as annual bedding in cooler areas. They can become a little straggly, but are easily increased from cuttings.

■ **HARDINESS** Fully hardy ✳✳✳ to half-hardy ✳.
■ **CULTIVATION** Grow these in light, fertile, well-drained soil, in a warm, sheltered site in sun.
■ **Remove** fading flowers. ■ **Take** softwood cuttings in late spring and semi-ripe cuttings in late summer (*see pp.329–330*). ■ **Sow** seed at 18°C (64°F) in spring (*see pp.328–329*).

Osteospermum 'Nairobi Purple'
↕15cm (6in) ↔90cm (36in), spreading subshrub, flowers flushed white beneath ✳

Osteospermum jucundum ♀
↕10–50cm (4–20in) ↔50–40cm (20–36in), clumping perennial, flowers have bronze undersides ✳✳✳ (borderline)

Osteospermum 'Buttermilk' ♀
↕↔60cm (24in), upright subshrub, toothed mid-green leaves have pale yellow edges, flowers are bronze-yellow beneath ✳✳

Osteospermum 'Whirlygig' ♀
↕↔60cm (24in), spreading subshrub, flowers have slate-blue central boss ✳

Oxalis
Shamrock, Sorrel

SPRING AND SUMMER

Low clumps of pretty, clover-like leaves provide a fine setting for these plants' small flowers. These appear in spring and summer, and may be funnel-, cup-, or bowl-shaped and tinted in shades of pink, yellow, and reddish-purple. In dull weather, the flowers close up. Some oxalis are spreading weeds, and some of the ornamental types can also be invasive, and are best planted in isolation. Bulbous perennials, these plants may spring from tubers, rhizomes, or true bulbs. Many oxalis thrive in the free-draining soil of a rock garden or in a container. Others, such as *Oxalis acetosella* and *O. oregana* are happy in woodland or shady sites.

■ **HARDINESS** Fully hardy ✱✱✱ to frost-tender ❀.
■ **CULTIVATION** Woodland species need moist, humus-rich, fertile soil in sun or partial shade; hardy species need moderately fertile, humus-rich, well-drained soils in full sun.
■ **Sow** seed at 13–18°C (55–64°F) in late winter or early spring (*see pp.328–329*).
■ **Divide** plants (*see p.330*) in spring.

Oxalis adenophylla ♥
↕10cm (4in) ↔ to 15cm (6in), true bulb, prefers sun and free-draining soil such as a raised bed or rock garden ✱✱✱

Pachysandra

SPRING TO EARLY SUMMER

Good ground-cover plants, these low, bushy perennials quickly spread to create an evergreen, or semi-evergreen, carpet of dark or grey-green foliage. These leaves are sometimes toothed and cluster at the tips of upright, fleshy stems. *Pachysandra terminalis* 'Variegata' has pleasing white leaf margins. In spring to early summer, pachysandras produce small spikes of greenish-white female, and white male, flowers. Pachysandras are easy plants to grow and they look very much at home in shady areas or at the feet of flowering shrubs, for example rhododendrons (*see pp.92–93*) and camellias (*see pp.28–29*). Pachysandras spread particularly freely where the soil is moist and the conditions are humid.

■ **HARDINESS** Fully hardy ✱✱✱.
■ **CULTIVATION** Any soil is suitable – except very dry soil – in full sun or partial shade. Soil enriched with plenty of organic matter is best.
■ **Divide** established plants (*see p.330*) in spring or take softwood cuttings (*see pp.329–330*) in early summer.

Pachysandra terminalis
↕20cm (8in) ↔ indefinite, evergreen, leaves to 10cm (4in) long, male flowers in early summer

Paeonia
Peony

LATE SPRING TO EARLY SUMMER

With their spectacular blooms and bold, lush foliage, the many herbaceous perennial peonies remain a classic choice for any border. The flowers open from large buds, usually in early summer, and vary from single cups, some with golden stamens, to blowsy doubles. They range in size from 5cm (2in) to an impressive 20cm (8in) or more. The large leaves of these clump-forming plants are usually blue-, grey-, or dark-green, and deeply divided. Think carefully before you

Paeonia cambessedesii ♥
(Majorcan peony)
↕↔ 45–55cm (18–22in), leaves are purple-red beneath with purple veins, flowers up to 10cm (4in) across in mid- and late spring ✱✱✱

***Paeonia lactiflora* 'Sarah Bernhardt'** ♥
↕↔ 90–100cm (36–39in), vigorous, with mid-green leaves and erect stems, fragrant flowers are over 20cm (8in) across ✱✱✱

grow peonies – they are long-lived plants, and suffer if moved once they are established. (*See also p.81.*)

■ **HARDINESS** Fully hardy ✳✳✳ to frost-hardy ✳✳, but early flowers and young foliage may be damaged in a late frost.
■ **CULTIVATION** Grow in fertile, moist but well-drained soil, and dig in well-rotted organic matter before you plant. Choose a position in full sun or partial shade. ■ **Support** stems of peonies with very large flowers. ■ **Take** root cuttings (*see p.330*) in winter or divide the tuberous roots in autumn or early spring (*see p.330*). ■ **Peony wilt** may cause stems to blacken and flop: if a brown patch or grey, fuzzy fungal growth develops round the bases, cut affected stems back to healthy growth, beneath the soil if necessary.

Papaver
Poppy

LATE SPRING TO SUMMER

These cottage-garden favourites are beloved for their bright, papery, summer blooms. As well as the classic blood-red, poppies come in glowing oranges, and more subtle pinks, yellows, and white; many are smudged black at the bases of their petals. Each flower is short-lived, but is followed by many more, and later by striking, pepper-pot seedheads. The light to mid-green, often hairy or bristly, ferny leaves are very distinctive, even as seedlings. The flowers of annuals and

biennials are generally more delicate than the bold, brash blooms of the perennial oriental poppies, but they all have a place. Large poppies look good in any border; annuals thrive in a rock or gravel garden and self-seed freely.

■ **HARDINESS** Fully hardy ✳✳✳ to frost-hardy ✳✳.
■ **CULTIVATION** Grow in fertile, well-drained soil in full sun. ■ **Sow** seed (*see pp.328–329*) in spring: annuals and biennials in situ; perennials in a cold frame. ■ **Avoid** high-nitrogen fertilizers; they may cause flowers to fall early. ■ **Cut back** oriental poppies after flowering for a second flush. ■ **Divide** perennials in spring, or raise from root cuttings in autumn and winter (*see p.330*). ■ **Mildew** (*see p.333*) may be troublesome in damp summers.

Paeonia mlokosewitschii ♀
(Caucasian peony)
↕↔65–90m (26–36in), erect stems, leaves hairy beneath, flowers up to 13cm (5in) across in late spring and early summer ✳✳✳

***Papaver orientale* 'Cedric Morris'** ♀
↕45–90cm (18–36in) ↔60–90cm (24–36in), clumping perennial, hairy, grey leaves, 16cm (6in) flowers late spring to midsummer ✳✳✳

***Papaver orientale* 'Beauty of Livermere'**
↕45–90cm (18–36in) ↔60–90cm (24–36in), clumping perennial, flowers to 20cm (8in) across in late spring to midsummer ✳✳✳

***Paeonia lactiflora* 'Festiva Maxima'** ♀
↕↔90–100cm (36–39in), abundant mid-green leaves, fragrant flowers on strong, erect stems are over 20cm (8in) across ✳✳✳

***Papaver rhoeas* Mother of Pearl Group**
↕90cm (36in) ↔30cm (12in), annual, downy leaves, summer flowers in soft shades such as dove-grey, pink, and lilac-blue ✳✳✳

***Papaver orientale* 'Black and White'** ♀
↕45–90cm (18–36in) ↔60–90cm (24–36in), clumping perennial, large bristly leaves, flowers in late spring to midsummer ✳✳✳

Pelargonium
Pelargonium, Bedding geranium

SPRING TO AUTUMN

These popular plants are widely, but incorrectly, called geraniums. They are related to the cranesbills (*see Geranium, pp.208–209*), but are quite different in many ways, not least in being almost universally frost-tender. There is a huge range of pelargoniums to choose from, with beautiful flowers and attractive and often fragrant leaves. They are generally used as bedding plants, or in hanging baskets and other containers, producing dense clusters of bright flowers from summer until autumn. Flower forms vary from the double, heavily frilled 'Apple Blossom Rosebud' to the delicate 'Bird Dancer', and colours range from orange to pink, red or purple, in soft and restrained or bold and vivid shades. Most form upright, bushy plant, but there are also trailing forms (details of main types are given below).

■ **HARDINESS** Almost all are frost-tender ❄.
■ **CULTIVATION** Grow in fertile, well-drained soil, or in a loam-based or soiless compost. Position in full sun; zonal pelargoniums will tolerate some shade. ■ **Deadhead** regularly. ■ **Feed** with a high-potash fertilizer through the summer to encourage plenty of flowers. ■ **Lift** in autumn, and keep almost dry in a frost-free place over winter. Cut back the top-growth by about one-third and repot in late winter as growth begins.
■ **Take cuttings** in spring, summer, and autumn (*see pp.329–330*), but these need to be kept in a frost-free place over winter; young plants and plug plants are widely available in garden centres in early summer (*see p.316*). ■ **Sow** seed (*see pp.328–329*) with bottom heat in spring.
■ **Vine weevils** (*see p.332*) can attack if in pots. If plants suffer from grey mould (botrytis), cut out affected parts and treat with a fungicide.

The main types of pelargonium

Ivy-leaved pelargoniums These trailing perennials have clusters of single or double flowers in shades of red, pink, mauve, and purple or white. They resemble ivy in both their habit and the shape of their stiff, fleshy, evergreen leaves, 2.5–13cm (1–5in) long.

Regal pelargoniums Bushy, evergreen, and usually grown under glass, these bear dense clusters of single or double flowers to 4cm (1½in) across, in red, pink, purple, orange, white, or reddish-black. The rounded leaves are up to 9cm (3½in) long.

Scented-leaved pelargoniums Plant these in containers where you can touch them easily so the leaves release their scent. Each cultivar has its own perfume, from sweet to spicy or citrus. The leaves are usually mid-green, occasionally variegated, 1.5–13cm (½–5in) long, and vary in shape. The flowers are usually not very large.

Zonal pelargoniums The most popular of all the types, these are bushy, evergreen perennials with short-jointed stems. The round leaves are marked with zones of dark bronze-green; the flowers are single to fully double, in white and shades of orange, purple, pink, and scarlet.

P. **'Alberta'** ‡50cm (20in) ↔25cm (10in), zonal

P. **'Ann Hoystead'** ♀ ‡45cm (18in) ↔25cm (10in), regal

P. **Fragrans Group** ‡25cm (10in) ↔20cm (8in), pine-scented leaves

P. **'Friesdorf'** ‡20cm (8in) ↔13cm (5in) zonal

P. **'Mrs Pollock'** ‡30cm (12in) ↔15cm (6in), zonal

P. **'Old Spice'** ‡30cm (12in) ↔15cm (6i) spicy-scented leaves

P. **'Royal Oak'** ♀ ‡40cm (16in) ↔30cm (12in), spicy-scented leaves

P. **'Sefton'** ♀ ‡40cm (16in) ↔20cm (8in), regal

P. 'Apple Blossom Rosebud' ♀
‡40cm (16in) ↔25cm (10in), zonal

P. 'Clorinda' ‡50cm (20in) ↔25cm (10in), cedar-scented leaves

P. crispum 'Variegatum' ♀ ‡35cm (18in) ↔15cm (6in), lemon-scented leaves

P. 'Dolly Varden' ♀ ‡30cm (12in) ↔15cm (6in), zonal

P. 'Golden Wedding' ‡↔60cm (24in), zonal

P. 'Graveolens' ‡60cm (24in) ↔40cm (16in), lemon-rose-scented leaves

P. 'Lavender Grand Slam' ♀ ‡40cm (16in) ↔20cm (8in), regal

P. 'Lesley Judd' ‡40cm (16in) ↔20cm (8in), regal

P. 'Orsett' ♀ ‡70cm (28in) ↔50cm (20in), spicy mint-scented leaves

P. 'Polka' ‡50cm (20in) ↔25cm (10in), unique

P. 'Robe' ‡45cm (18in) ↔20cm (8in), zonal

P. 'Rouletta' ‡60cm (24in) ↔20cm (8in), ivy-leaved

P. 'Strawberry Sundae' ‡60cm (24in) ↔30cm (12in), regal

P. 'The Boar' ♀ ‡60cm (24in) ↔25cm (10in), trailing

P. 'Tip Top Duet' ♀ ‡40cm (16in) ↔20cm (8in), angel

P. tomentosum ♀ ‡90cm (36in) ↔75cm (30in), mint-scented leaves

Penstemon

MIDSUMMER TO AUTUMN

These flamboyant plants bring colour to the garden from midsummer, often lasting until the first frosts. Upright spires produce a continuous succession of tubular flowers, similar to foxgloves, in rich hues of purple, scarlet, pink, yellow, and white; many are bicoloured. This is a large group of mostly evergreen, bushy but neat perennials. They range from dwarf kinds around 15cm (6in) tall, that are suitable for rock gardens, to taller border plants of 60cm (24in) or more; these may need staking (*see p.327*).

The leaves may be narrow and up to 8cm (3in) long or oval, from 13cm (5in) long.

■ **HARDINESS** Fully hardy ✳✳✳ to half-hardy ✳.
■ **CULTIVATION** Border penstemons like fertile, well-drained soil in full sun or partial shade; dwarf and shrubby species need gritty, sharply drained, poor to moderate soil.
■ **Protect** plants with a dry mulch in winter in frost-prone areas. ■ **Deadhead** unless seed is needed. ■ **Sow** seed (*see pp.328–329*) in late winter or spring at 31–18°C (55–64°F).
■ **Take** softwood cuttings in early summer or semi-ripe cuttings in midsummer (*see pp.329–330*). ■ **Divide** plants (*see p.330*) in spring. To support clumps, put cane and twine or metal supports in place before penstemons grow too tall so they can develop a natural habit.

Penstemon 'Apple Blossom' ♥
‡↔45–60cm (18–24in), narrow leaves, white-throated flowers from midsummer to early or mid-autumn ✳✳✳ (borderline)

Penstemon 'Evelyn' ♥
‡45–60cm (18–24in) ↔30cm (12in), bushy, narrow leaves, flowers 2.5–3cm (1–1¼in), paler inside, midsummer to mid-autumn ✳✳✳

Penstemon 'Stapleford Gem' ♥
‡to 60cm (24in) ↔45cm (18in), large leaves, flowers 5–8cm (2–3in) long from midsummer to early autumn ✳✳✳

Penstemon 'Chester Scarlet' ♥
‡60cm (24in) ↔45cm (18in), large leaves and flowers 5–8cm (2–3in) long from midsummer to mid-autumn ✳

Penstemon **'White Bedder'** ♀
‡60cm (24in) ↔ 45cm (18in), large leaves, flowers become tinged pink as they age, from midsummer to mid-autumn ❈❈

Penstemon **'Pennington Gem'** ♀
‡to 75cm (30in) ↔ 45cm (18in), narrow leaves, flowers 5–8cm (2–3in) long from midsummer to early or mid-autumn ❈❈

Persicaria

SUMMER TO AUTUMN

Short, bottlebrush blooms – made of tiny pink, white, or red, funnel- or bell-shaped flowers that cluster tightly on wiry stems appear from summer to autumn. Persicarias also have pleasing foliage: with broad, long-stalked leaves at the base and smaller leaves clothing the fleshy stems. Many of these clump-forming perennials and annuals spread by means of creeping stems and can become invasive, but are easily kept under control if necessary. Ranging in height from 5cm (2in) to 1.2m (4ft), most are medium-sized and make an undemanding, weed-suppressing ground cover. Grow with phygelius (*see p.84*), and perennials like cranesbills (*see Geranium, pp.208–209*) and monardas (*see p.239*).

■ **HARDINESS** Fully hardy ❈❈❈ to frost-hardy ❈.
■ **CULTIVATION** Any moist soil in full sun or partial shade suits this plant; the best flower colour is obtained in full sun. *Persicaria bistorta* tolerates dry soil. ■ **Sow** seed (*see pp.328–329*) in a container in a cold frame in spring. ■ **Divide** perennials in spring or autumn (*see p.330*).

Persicaria bistorta **'Superba'** ♀ (Bistort)
‡to 90cm (36in) ↔ 45cm (18in), semi-evergreen, mat-forming perennial, autumn leaves rich brown, flowers over long period ❈❈❈

Petrorhagia

SUMMER

Closely related to gypsophila (*see p.211*) and dianthus (*see p.190*), these perennials and annuals are grown for their clusters of white, or occasionally pink or yellow, flowers that are borne all through summer. The delicate flowers are held on the tips of wiry stems above grassy leaves. Petrorhagias are best grown in a sunny position at the front of a mixed or herbaceous border, on a sunny bank, or against a wall. You could also grow them in a rock garden with other low alpines, such as dianthus and saxifrages (*see p.267*). Try planting petrorhagias in an alpine trough where the stems and flowers can be allowed to spill out and soften the trough's hard edges.

■ **HARDINESS** Fully hardy ❈❈❈ if soil is well-drained.
■ **CULTIVATION** Petrorhagias thrive in any poor to reasonably fertile, well-drained soil in full sun. ■ **Sow** seed (*see pp.328–329*) in a container in a cold frame in autumn. ■ **Take** stem-tip cuttings (*see p.330*) in early summer. ■ **Slugs** and snails (*see p.332*) can be a problem.

Petrorhagia saxifraga ♀ (Tunic flower)
‡10cm (4in) ↔ 20cm (8in), mat-forming perennial, long-lasting white or pink flowers – 1cm (½in) across – in summer ❈❈❈

Petunia

LATE SPRING TO LATE AUTUMN

Staple bedding and container plants, petunias are prized for their showy, velvety flowers. They may be single or double, and also often brightly veined or striped with a contrasting colour. There are two groups: Grandiflora types have large flowers up to 10cm (4in) across and include the Surfinias and others that are less weather-resistant. The bushier, and often more resilient, Multifloras bear masses of smaller blooms, to 5cm (2in) across. Trailing petunias are perfect for hanging baskets. Use Multifloras to carpet large beds or borders. Petunia leaves and stems are sticky and hairy. Many petunias are perennial, but most are grown as annuals.

■ **HARDINESS** Half-hardy ✳.
■ **CULTIVATION** Petunias enjoy light, well-drained soil or compost in full sun. Feed plants in containers with a tomato fertilizer every 10–14 days. ■ **Deadhead** regularly (*see p.327*) to keep them in bloom. ■ **Sow** seed (*see pp.328–329*) at 13–18°C (55–64°F) in autumn or mid-spring, or root softwood cuttings (*see p.329*) in summer. Overwinter seedlings under cover; plant out when all danger of frost has passed.

***Petunia* SURFINIA PURPLE** ('Shihi Brilliant') ♀
↕23–40cm (9–16in) ↔30–90cm (12–36in)

Phlomis

SUMMER

The herbaceous perennial phlomis are good year-round plants. Although the silvery or grey-green leaves die down in winter, the attractive seedheads remain to provide interest through the barest months. In spring, white-woolly young shoots emerge, to form an erect or spreading clump of foliage. Clusters of hooded flowers, somewhat like the dead nettle (*see Lamium, p.225*), are borne on tall stems in summer, and are usually white, dusty pink, or soft yellow. Phlomis is a good choice for hot, dry areas – for example, beside a patio or in a gravel garden – because their hairy leaves help them to retain moisture. They are also lovely planted in groups to form softly-coloured mounds in a sunny border. There are also shrubby types (*see p.83*).

■ **HARDINESS** Fully hardy ✳✳✳ to frost-hardy ✳✳.
■ **CULTIVATION** Grow in any fertile, well-drained soil in full sun, although *Phlomis russeliana* and *P. samia* will tolerate some shade.
■ **Sow** seed (*see pp.328–329*) at 13–18°C (55–64°F) in spring. ■ **Divide** (*see p.330*) large clumps, ideally in spring, but also in autumn.

Phlomis russeliana ♀
↕90cm (36in) ↔75cm (30in), upright, hairy leaves up to 20cm (8in) long, flowers from late spring to early autumn ✳✳✳

Phlox

SPRING TO AUTUMN

Phloxes are treasured for their flat, blue, milky- to bright pink, or red flowers, which are borne in fat clusters at the tips of tall stems. They are a diverse group that include spreading to erect, evergreen and herbaceous perennials, and some annuals. Spring-flowering, dwarf varieties, such as *Phlox subulata*, are perfect in a rock garden; early summer-flowering plants, such as 'Chattahoochee', prefer a woodland area, where their pale flowers seem to glow in the shade. Tall, midsummer-flowering phloxes, such as perennial *P. maculata* or *P. paniculata*, make a colourful addition to a sunny border. Annual bedding phloxes (forms of *P. drummondii*) flower from late spring to autumn.

■ **HARDINESS** Fully hardy ✳✳✳ to half-hardy ✳.
■ **CULTIVATION** Perennial border phloxes prefer well-drained soil in sun or partial shade; annuals and rock garden types need well-drained soil in full sun. Woodland phloxes such as *P. divaricata* require moist soil and shade.
■ **Deadhead** (*see p.327*) *P. maculata* and *P. paniculata* regularly. ■ **Sow** seed (*see pp.328–329*) of annuals at 13–18°C (55–64°F) in spring; that of perennials in containers in a cold frame when ripe, or in spring. ■ **Divide** tall plants in spring or in autumn, or take root cuttings in autumn or winter (*see p.330*).

***Phlox paniculata* 'Windsor'** ♀
↕1.2m (4ft) ↔60–100cm (24–39in), herbaceous perennial, ideal for a border, flowers from summer to mid-autumn ✳✳✳

***Phlox subulata* 'Lilacina'**
‡5–15cm (2–6in) ↔50cm (20in), dense,
mat-forming, evergreen perennial, flowers
in late spring and early summer ✳✳✳

***Phlox paniculata* 'Graf Zeppelin'**
‡1.2m (4ft) ↔60–100cm (24–39in), herbaceous
perennial, ideal for a border, scented flowers from
summer to mid-autumn ✳✳✳

***Phlox maculata* 'Omega'** ♀
‡90cm (36in) ↔45cm (18in), herbaceous
perennial, fragrant flowers in early and
midsummer ✳✳✳

***Phlox* 'Kelly's Eye'** ♀
‡10cm (4in) ↔30cm (12in), evergreen, mounding
perennial, long narrow leaves, flowers in late
spring to early summer ✳✳✳

***Phlox divaricata* 'Chattahoochee'** ♀
‡15cm (6in) ↔30cm (12in), short-lived, semi-evergreen
perennial, prostrate, purplish leaves, flowers summer
and early autumn ✳✳✳

Phuopsis stylosa

SUMMER

This is a mat-forming perennial with slender, branching stems bearing clusters of up to eight narrow, pointed leaves that have a musky fragrance. Over many months in summer, it produces a profusion of round heads of tiny, tubular-funnel-shaped pink flowers at the tips of the stems. These are delicately scented. Phuopsis spreads by rooting stems and makes a good ground-cover plant at the front of a border or on a sunny bank. You could also try it in a rock garden with other alpines such as phloxes (*see p.254*) and saponarias (*see p.267*).

■ **HARDINESS** Fully hardy ✳✳✳.
■ **CULTIVATION** This plant needs reasonably fertile, moist but well-drained soil, in full sun or partial shade. ■ **Cut** back the top-growth after flowering to maintain a compact habit. ■ **Sow** seed (*see pp.328–329*) in a container in an open cold frame in autumn. ■ **Divide** plants (*see p.330*) once established or take stem-tip cuttings (*see pp.329–330*) of *P. stylosa* from spring until early summer.

Phuopsis stylosa
‡15cm (6in) ↔ 50cm (20in) or more, individual flowers are 1.5–2cm (½–¾in) long

Physalis

Ground cherry

AUTUMN

With their striking seedheads, this group of upright, bushy annuals and perennials bring welcome colour to the garden in autumn. Clusters of tiny, white or cream flowers appear in the summer, but it is the seedheads that give these plants their impact. Vivid orange or scarlet, papery lanterns, or calyces, enclose bright red, gold, or purple berries. These lanterns retain their colour well when dried for decorative use or they may be left on the plant through winter to decay into skeletons, revealing the berries inside. The leaves often have silvery hairs. Physalis can be invasive in rich soils.

■ **HARDINESS** Fully hardy ✳✳✳ to frost-hardy ✳✳.
■ **CULTIVATION** Any well-drained soil in full sun or partial shade. ■ **Cut** stems for drying as the calyces begin to colour. ■ **Sow** seed (*see pp.328–329*) of perennials in containers in a cold frame in spring; sow seed of annuals where they are to grow in mid-spring. ■ **Divide** perennials (*see p.330*) in spring.

Physalis alkekengi ♀ (Chinese lantern, Japanese lantern)
‡60–75cm (24–30in) ↔ 90cm (36in) or more, vigorous perennial, lanterns 5cm (2in) across ✳✳✳

Physostegia

Obedient plant

MID- TO LATE SUMMER

Valuable in the late-summer border, the upright, herbaceous perennials in this group form dense clumps. Their flower spikes rise up in midsummer, crowded with almost stalkless blooms in shades of pink, lilac-pink, magenta-pink, or white. The flowers usually face in one of two directions; if they are moved on the stalks, the flowers remain in their new position, earning them the name of obedient plant. Like dead nettles (*see Lamium, p.225*), to which they are related, physostegias have square stems. The variably shaped leaves often have toothed edges. Physostegias spread by underground stems (rhizomes) and can be invasive in rich soils. Combine them with perennials such as phlomis (*see p.254*) and persicarias (*see p.253*). They are also good for cutting.

■ **HARDINESS** Fully hardy ✳✳✳ to frost-hardy ✳✳.
■ **CULTIVATION** Moderately fertile soil that is reliably moist, in full sun or partial shade. ■ **Sow** seed (*see pp.328–329*) in a container in a cold frame in autumn. ■ **Divide** (*see p.330*) in winter or early spring before growth starts.

***Physostegia virginiana* 'Vivid'** ♀
‡30–60cm (12–24in) ↔ 30cm (12in), toothed leaves to 13cm (5in) long, flowers from midsummer to early autumn ✳✳✳

Platycodon grandiflorus
Balloon flower

Large buds like miniature balloons give this plant its common name. The several cultivated forms of this perennial are grown for the pretty flowers borne in late summer, in blue, lilac-purple, pale pink, or white. The balloon flower varies in habit, but most form neat, compact clumps with toothed, blue-green leaves. These are lovely plants for a large rock garden or a border, and are also good for cutting. Try them with other herbaceous perennials, such as achilleas (*see p.140*), physostegias (*see left*), and lythrums (*see p.253*). Once they are well-established, the plants should not be moved because they do not recover well if their roots are disturbed.

■ **HARDINESS** Fully hardy ✳✳✳.
■ **CULTIVATION** The balloon flower prefers deep, fertile, well-drained but reliably moist soil, in full sun or partial shade. ■ **Support** the stems if necessary (*see p.327*). ■ **Sow** seed (*see pp.328–329*) in pots in a cold frame in spring. ■ **Divide** (*see p.330*) in summer or remove shoots rooted at the base in early summer and use as cuttings (*see p.330*).

Platycodon grandiflorus ♀
‡to 60cm (24in) ↔30cm (12in), compact clump, flowers to 5cm (2in) across

Polemonium
Jacob's ladder

Named for their distinctive leaves, these mostly clump-forming annuals and perennials are favourites in cottage gardens. The leaves are composed of many paired leaflets that resemble the rungs of a ladder, and are produced in rosettes, from which spring erect stems. The cup-, bell-, or saucer-shaped flowers of Jacob's ladder are borne in spring and summer and are either solitary or held in small clusters at the stem tips. Usually blue or white, they can be purple, pink, or yellow. Taller species of polemonium look good in a mixed or herbaceous border, with other spring- or summer-flowering perennials such as aquilegias (*see p.156*) or tradescantias (*see p.275*), while small ones look best in a rock garden. *Polemonium caeruleum* can be naturalized in grass in a wildflower garden.

Polemonium 'Lambrook Mauve' ♀
‡↔45cm (18in), also called 'Lambrook Manor', rounded mounds of neat leaves, free-flowering in late spring and early summer

■ **HARDINESS** Fully hardy ✳✳✳.
■ **CULTIVATION** Taller species thrive in any well-drained but moist soil in full sun or partial shade. Small species prefer very gritty, sharply drained soil in full sun. ■ **Deadhead** to prolong flowering. ■ **Sow** seed (*see pp.328–329*) in a container in a cold frame in autumn or spring. ■ **Divide** plants (*see p.330*) in spring.

Polemonium caeruleum (Greek valerian, Jacob's ladder)
‡30–90cm (12–36in) ↔30cm (12in), leaves 40cm (16in) long, flowers, rarely white, on ends of branching stems in early summer

Polemonium pauciflorum
‡to 50cm (20in), short-lived, leaves to 15cm (6in) long, red-tinted flowers single or in sparse clusters from early to late summer

Polygala

By far the most widely grown in gardens are the tiny rock polygalas, with their rich flower colours. *Polygala calcarea* and its varieties flower in particularly distinctive marine blues; use them to create pools of colour over pale stone chippings or, for a more unusual effect, dark slate or coloured glass pebbles. Commonly known as milkwort, this species was once used in herbal tonics for nursing mothers. *P. chamaebuxus* flowers in a mix of yellows; it also has white and bicoloured forms. Both these polygalas are evergreen, with small, leathery leaves, and flower in late spring and early summer. They are best grown in a rock garden, or in an alpine trough or sink garden.

■ **HARDINESS** Fully hardy ✿✿✿ to frost-tender ✿.
■ **CULTIVATION** Grow in moist but well-drained soil in full sun or dappled shade. In containers, use a soilless multipurpose compost, and top-dress with a layer of grit.
■ **Sow** seed in containers in a cold frame in autumn (*see pp.328–329*). ■ **Take** softwood cuttings in early summer or semi-ripe cuttings in mid- to late summer (*see pp.329–330*).

Polygala chamaebuxus var. grandiflora ♀
‡5–15cm (2–6in) ↔30cm (12in), spreading evergreen ✿✿✿

Polygonatum
Solomon's seal

Arching, leafy stems dripping with pendent flowers are the defining characteristic of most Solomon's seal – vigorous, clump-forming perennials with creeping, fleshy roots that thrive in shade. With their drooping habit, even the tallest ones have a shy look that is perfect for a woodland garden. The bell-shaped, subtly fragrant flowers that hang from the stems in spring and early summer are creamy-white or sometimes pink, with green markings, and are followed by red or black berries. Plant Solomon's seal among shrubs or beneath trees, or use them in pots on a shady patio to create a lush, textural display together with hostas (*see pp.218–219*) and ferns (*see pp.300–309*).

■ **HARDINESS** Fully hardy ✿✿✿ to frost-hardy ✿✿.
■ **CULTIVATION** Grow in moist soil or soil-based compost enriched with well-rotted organic matter, in deep or partial shade.
■ **Divide** large species (*see p.330*) as growth begins in spring, but take care not to damage brittle young shoots. ■ **Sow** seed in containers in a cold frame in autumn (*see pp.328–329*).

Polygonatum hookeri
‡10cm (4in) ↔30cm (12in), small, creeping perennial, flowers in late spring and early summer, needs rich soil ✿✿✿

Polygonatum stewartianum
‡20–90cm (8–36in) ↔25cm (10in), flowers from late spring to midsummer, followed by red berries with white spots ✿✿✿

Polygonatum hirtum
‡1.2m (4ft) ↔60cm (24in), erect zigzag stems, flowers from late spring to midsummer, blue-black berries ✿✿✿

Polygonatum x hybridum 'Striatum'
‡90cm (36in) ↔25cm (10in), brightens dark areas, flowers in late spring, the berries that follow are black ✽✽✽

Potentilla
Cinquefoil

SUMMER TO AUTUMN

Cinquefoil is a reference to the five-petalled flowers. The heavily veined foliage of these herbaceous perennials is reminiscent of the foliage of strawberry plants. These plants are valued both for their brightly coloured flowers and mid- to dark green foliage. Their saucer-shaped, single or double blooms are borne throughout summer and into early autumn. The smaller types suit a rock garden, while the taller, clump-forming potentillas are popular choices for beds, borders, and cottage gardens, where together with other late-flowering favourites such as asters (*see pp.162–163*) and chrysanthemums (*see pp.178–179*), they continue to warm up the fading garden into autumn with fiery shades of blood-red, burnt orange, and golden-yellow. (*See also p.87.*)

■ **HARDINESS** Fully hardy ✽✽✽.
■ **CULTIVATION** Grow in full sun and well-drained soil; flowering is better on poorer soils. ■ **Divide** (*see p.330*) in autumn or spring. ■ **Sow** seed in containers in a cold frame in autumn or spring (*see pp.328–329*).

Potentilla 'Monsieur Rouillard'
‡45cm (18in) ↔60cm (24in), bears semi-double, satin-petalled flowers from early to late summer

Potentilla 'Gibson's Scarlet' ♀
‡45cm (18in) ↔60cm (24in), extremely popular, flowers to 3cm (1¼in) across from early to late summer

Potentilla megalantha ♀
‡15–30cm (6–12in) ↔15cm (6in), widely available, hairy leaves, flowers from mid- to late summer

Primula
Primrose

EARLY SPRING TO EARLY SUMMER

There is a primula for almost every situation in the garden, and the majority are long-flowering and easy to grow. This diverse group of herbaceous perennials grows naturally in a wide range of habitats from boggy marshes to woodland and alpine areas. Most bloom in early spring and early summer, although a few flower from winter onwards. Their delicate clusters of flowers come in an appealing range of colours from deep purple and maroon through to pink, scarlet, and several shades of yellow, cream, and white. Garden primulas are divided into three groups (see below), although they do not include all species. Polyanthus types are the easiest to grow. Compact varieties make a bright display in containers, while more robust ones are suitable for the herbaceous border or cottage garden, or can be naturalized in lawns. Many primulas enjoy the dappled shade of the woodland edge, and work well planted with other woodland plants, such as lilies (see pp.230–231) and trilliums (see p.276). Water-loving candelabras thrive in bog gardens or on the banks of streams and ponds.

■ **HARDINESS** Fully hardy ✳✳✳ to frost-tender ❁.
■ **CULTIVATION** Grow primulas in full sun or partial shade, for the most part in moisture-retentive soil. ■ **Dig in** plenty of well-rotted organic matter before planting. Mix coarse grit into the soil or compost before planting alpine species. ■ **Water** plants well in dry weather.
■ **Deadhead** the flowers as they fade to prevent unwanted self-seeding, or allow seedheads to develop to collect your own seed. ■ **Sow** seed as soon as it is ripe (see pp.328–329). Scatter those of hardy species on the compost's surface in pots or trays and place in a cold frame.
■ **Divide** hybrids and cultivars between autumn and spring (see p.330).
■ **Vine weevil grubs** (see p.332) may eat roots, especially in pots.

Primula groups

Candelabra primulas These grow best in moist soil in a shady glade or at the edge of a pond. Robust perennials, they produce their rings of flowers, in many different colours, all the way up their sturdy stems. Candelabra primulas are deciduous and die back in autumn. Once established, plants will freely scatter their seed.

Auricula primulas The beautiful markings and colourings of many auriculas are a result of several hundred years of selection by enthusiasts. Choose those classed as border auriculas for general garden cultivation. They particularly suit cottage-style plantings.

Polyanthus group This group includes many of the most familiar primulas, including our native primroses and cowslips and the bright- and bold-flowered polyanthus that are used as biennials in spring bedding. When grown together in the garden, the two types will freely hybridize and may produce unique seedlings.

P. **'Adrian Jones'** ‡30cm (1ft) ↔25cm (10in), alpine auricula

P. **allionii** ♀ ‡10cm (4in) ↔20cm (8in) evergreen, flowers late winter

P. **'Buckland Wine'** ‡10cm (4in) ↔25cm (10in), polyanthus

P. **bulleyana** ♀ ‡↔60cm (2ft), candelabra

P. **florindae** ♀ ‡1.2m (4ft) ↔90cm (3ft), fragrant cowslip, for bogs and streams

P. **frondosa** ♀ ‡15cm (6in) ↔25cm (10

P. **prolifera** ♀ ‡↔60cm (2ft), candelabra, moist shade

P. **rosea** ♀ ‡↔20cm (8in)

. auricula var. **albocincta**
20cm (8in) ↔25cm (10in), evergreen

P. auricula 'Blairside Yellow' ‡50cm (20in)
↔30cm (1ft), border auricula

P. auricula 'Orb' ‡15cm (6in) ↔25cm (10in),
show auricula

P. beesiana ‡↔60cm (2ft), candelabra

. Crescendo Series ‡↔15cm (6in),
olyanthus

P. denticulata var. **alba** ‡↔45cm (18in),
drumstick

P. elatior ♀ ‡30cm (1ft) ↔25cm (10in),
evergreen, suits woodland

P. flaccida ‡50cm (20in) ↔30cm (1ft)

. Gold-laced Group ‡25cm (10in)
↔30cm (1ft), polyanthus

P. 'Guinevere' ♀ ‡13cm (5in) ↔25cm (10in),
polyanthus

P. 'Inverewe' ♀ ‡↔60cm (2ft), semi-
evergreen, candelabra

P. marginata 'Linda Pope' ♀
‡15cm (6in) ↔30cm (1ft), evergreen

. veris ♀ ‡↔25cm (10in), evergreen,
ragrant cowslip

P. vialii ♀ ‡60cm (2ft) ↔30cm (1ft),
moist shade

P. vulgaris subsp. **sibthorpii** ♀ ‡20cm (8in)
↔35cm (14in), suits woodland

P. 'Wanda' ♀ ‡15cm (6in) ↔40cm
(16in), evergreen, likes sun or shade

Pulmonaria

Lungwort

LATE WINTER TO EARLY SUMMER

Often handsomely spotted in silver or white, the deciduous or evergreen leaves were said in medieval times to resemble lung tissue and were used in remedies for chest complaints. Today, they make pulmonarias invaluable as ground cover that spreads slowly by underground stems (rhizomes). Their flowers are a welcome sight in the winter garden, continuing until late spring or even early summer. The delicate blooms may be blue, pink, red, or white and are held above the foliage in small clusters; they attract bees into the garden. Show off the flowers beneath deciduous trees and shrubs or with bulbs for a jewelled carpet.

■ **HARDINESS** Fully hardy ✲✲✲.
■ **CULTIVATION** Grow in moist, but not wet, humus-rich soil in full or dappled shade; *P. officinalis* tolerates sun. ■ **Cut back** after flowering to promote new foliage. ■ **Divide** (*see p.330*) every three to five years to keep plants healthy. ■ **Sow** seed (*see pp.328–329*) when ripe; seedlings will vary. ■ **Powdery mildew** may spoil leaves in dry weather.

Pulmonaria **'Lewis Palmer'** ♀
↕↔40cm (16in), flowers early spring

Pulmonaria rubra **'Redstart'**
↕40cm (16in) ↔90cm (36in), flowers late winter

Pulsatilla

SPRING TO EARLY SUMMER

Among the most beautiful of perennial alpine plants, pulsatillas have fine, ferny foliage, large, silky flowers, and round, fluffy seedheads. The leaves, buds, and petals are often covered with soft, silvery down. In spring and early summer, blooms appear in white or shades of yellow, pink, and purple – usually with a large, central boss of golden stamens. The flowers are followed by spherical seedheads with silver-silky, plume-like styles. As the seedheads develop, the flower stems grow even taller. Pulsatillas form clumps in a rock garden or at the front of a border, if you have well-drained soil, with other spring-flowering plants such as aubrietas (*see p.165*) or scillas (*see p.269*). In areas with heavy soil, it is best to grow pulsatillas in containers so they can enjoy free-draining soil and be moved easily to a position sheltered from the worst of the winter rain. Can cause mild discomfort if eaten.

Pulsatilla vulgaris ♀ (Pasque flower)
↕10–20cm (4–8in) ↔20cm (8in), young leaves very hairy, pale to deep purple flowers 4–9cm (2½–4½in) across, rarely white, in spring

■ **HARDINESS** Fully hardy ✲✲✲.
■ **CULTIVATION** Pulsatillas prefer fertile, very well-drained, gritty soil in full sun. They resent being disturbed; plant them out while they are young and site them carefully so they do not have to be moved. ■ **Sow** seed (*see pp.328–329*) as soon as it is ripe in a cold frame. ■ **Take** root cuttings (*see p.330*) in winter.

Pulsatilla halleri ♀
↕20cm (8in) ↔15cm (6in), violet-purple to lavender-blue flowers that are 9cm (3½in) across in late spring

Pulsatilla vernalis ♀
↕↔10cm (4in), semi-evergreen, flowers to 6cm (2½in) across in spring, requires sharp drainage and protection from winter wet

Puschkinia scilloides

This little bulb has a snowdrop-like flower, with each delicate white, or very pale blue, petal marked with a thin, dark blue stripe. The blooms are borne in thick spikes on arching stems in spring. Each bulb has two leaves. *Puschkinia scilloides* var. *libanotica* has smaller, pure white flowers. Puschkinias spread freely in a rock garden, or can be used for a pretty display beneath deciduous trees and shrubs before the leaf cover becomes too dense. They naturalize in short grass with other bulbs for a colourful carpet in spring. In common with other rock-garden or alpine plants, puschkinias can be successfully grown in containers; they enjoy the well-drained conditions, especially while dormant.

■ **HARDINESS** Fully hardy ✽✽✽.
■ **CULTIVATION** This plant likes any well-drained soil in full sun or dappled shade.
■ **Sow** seed (*see pp.328–329*) in a container in a cold frame in spring or autumn; seedlings may take 2–3 years to reach flowering size.
■ **Divide** clumps of bulbs (*see p.330*) as leaves die down in summer.

Puschkinia scilloides
↕20cm (8in) ↔5cm (2in), although larger clumps will quickly form

Ranunculus

Buttercup, Crowfoot

There are hundreds of types of buttercup – some are annuals and biennials – but herbaceous perennials are by far the most common; some are evergreen. They are very variable in habit, with widely ranging needs, so there should be one suited to any spot in the garden. Buttercups all bear cupped flowers, with bold central stamens, in spring, summer, or occasionally in autumn. They are mainly golden yellow, but white, pink, orange, or scarlet varieties are available.

■ **HARDINESS** Fully hardy ✽✽✽; *Ranunculus asiaticus* is half-hardy ✽.
■ **CULTIVATION** Buttercups have a range of cultivation requirements. ■ **Most species** are fine in fertile, moist but well-drained soil, in sun or semi-shade. ■ **Woodland** buttercups, which often have bronze-tinted leaves, need rich, moist soil in shade. ■ **Alpine** plants are small, with relatively large flowers, and require full sun and gritty, sharply drained soil, as do many of the tuberous buttercups. ■ **Aquatic** or bog plants are often tall and have lots of lush, bright green leaves. They need wet soil at the edge of a stream or pond. ■ **Sow** seed (*see pp.328–329*) of most buttercups in a container in a cold frame as soon as it is ripe. Alpine seed is best sown while it is unripe and its germination can be erratic and may take several years.
■ **Divide** (*see p.330*) all plants, except for alpines, in spring or autumn.

Ranunculus aconitifolius 'Flore Pleno' ♀ (Fair maids of France, Fair maids of Kent, White bachelor's buttons)
↕60cm (24in) ↔45cm (18in), flowers late spring

Ranunculus ficaria 'Brazen Hussy' (Lesser celandine)
↕5cm (2in) ↔30cm (12in), woodland type, flowers are borne in early spring, may spread rapidly

Ranunculus ficaria var. **albus** (Lesser celandine)
↕5cm (2in) ↔20cm (8in), woodland type, flowers in early-spring, may spread rapidly

Rheum
Rhubarb
SPRING TO AUTUMN

These impressive, clump-forming perennials have bold, handsome foliage and feathery flower plumes. The huge, rounded leaves, up to 90cm (36in) across, often emerge crimson-purple from bright red buds in spring. They mature to a glossy, dark green, but often retain a scarlet flush. In summer, large plumes of tiny pink, pale green, or cream flowers are held above the foliage on thick, hollow stems. Rheums revel in moist conditions: use them to create a lush display by a stream or pond, in damp borders or in woodland gardens. Although this group includes edible rhubarb, the ornamental varieties can cause severe discomfort if eaten.

■ **HARDINESS** Fully hardy ✳✳✳.
■ **CULTIVATION** Need deep, damp soil that has been enriched with organic matter, in sun or shade. ■ **Mulch** (*see p.326*) in spring to retain moisture. ■ **Sow** seed (*see pp.328–329*) in pots in a cold frame in autumn. ■ **Divide** the large, woody rhizomes (*see p.330*) in early spring.

Rheum palmatum **'Atrosanguineum'** ♀
‡2.5m (8ft) ↔2m (6ft), plumes of flowers up to 2m (6ft) tall in early summer

Rhodiola
LATE SPRING TO SUMMER

As long as they are grown in full sun, these perennials will thrive, and are useful for bringing subtle colour and texture into a rock- or gravel garden, or to the front of a mixed or herbaceous border. They form clumps of straight stems clothed in fleshy, grey-green leaves that complement plants with white flowers or silver foliage, such as artemisias (*see p.21 and p.159*). Each rhodiola stem is topped by a fluffy flowerhead of many tiny, yellow, green, orange, or crimson star-shaped flowers, with 8–10 prominent stamens. As well as flowers in late spring or summer, both the buds and seedheads provide ornamental displays.

■ **HARDINESS** Fully hardy ✳✳✳.
■ **CULTIVATION** Grow rhodiolas in any reasonably fertile soil in full sun. ■ **Sow** seed (*see pp.328–329*) in containers in a cold frame in spring or autumn. ■ **Divide** the rhizomes (*see p.330*) in spring or early summer.

Rhodiola rosea (Roseroot)
‡5–30cm (1½–12in) ↔20cm (8in), variable habit, leaves to 4cm (1½in) long with reddish-green tips, flowers in summer

Rodgersia
SPRING TO AUTUMN

A superb choice for moist soil, these vigorous, clump-forming perennials are valued for their fabulous foliage and tall flower spikes. The giant leaves are up to 90cm (36in) across, and are dark green and glossy. They are often boldly veined or wrinkled, especially when young, and occasionally tinged purple or bronze. Some varieties also display rich, reddish-brown autumn tints. The flower stems are often dark purple, and bear fluffy clusters of tiny, sometimes scented, blooms in summer, in shades of pink or white. Grow rodgersias by the edge of a pond or stream, or in a damp border.

■ **HARDINESS** Fully hardy ✳✳✳, although late frosts may damage young leaves.
■ **CULTIVATION** Reliably moist soil, enriched with well-rotted organic matter, in full sun or partial shade, with shelter from cold, drying winds is required. Drier soil is tolerated in shadier areas. ■ **Mulch** (*see p.326*) with a thick layer of organic matter in spring to help retain soil moisture. ■ **Sow** seed (*see pp.328–329*) in containers in a cold frame in spring.
■ **Divide** plants in early spring (*see p.330*).

Rodgersia pinnata **'Superba'** ♀
‡1.2m (4ft) ↔75cm (30in), new purple foliage (as shown) matures to dark green, stalks reddish-green, flowers in mid- and late summer

Roscoea

SUMMER TO AUTUMN

These tuberous perennials thrive in cool climates. They are invaluable in damp, shady borders where they are used to add a long season of bright colour to areas that are usually the preserve of shade-loving foliage plants, such as ferns (see pp.300–309) and hostas (see pp.218–219). Most roscoeas bear flowers all summer and into autumn, in shades of white, gold, or purple. They often start to bloom before the arching leaves, which reach up to 40cm (16in) long, are fully grown.

■ **HARDINESS** Fully hardy ✳✳✳ to frost-hardy ✳✳.
■ **CULTIVATION** Prefer a cool, sheltered, shaded site, in moist but well-drained, fertile soil. Dig in plenty of organic matter. ■ **Plant** tubers 15cm (6in) deep in winter or early spring. In very cold areas, plant even deeper: the insulation of the soil helps them survive temperatures down to -20°C (-4°F). ■ **Mulch** thickly (see p.326) with organic matter in winter in frost-prone areas. ■ **Sow** seed as soon as it is ripe (see pp.328–329) in containers. ■ **Divide** established plants (see p.330) in spring.

Roscoea cautleyoides ♀
↕55cm (22in) ↔15cm (6in), leaves 15cm (6in) tall at flowering, midsummer flowers are yellow, white, or purple ✳✳✳ (borderline)

Rudbeckia

Coneflower

LATE SUMMER TO AUTUMN

This large group of annuals, biennials, and perennials are grown for their large, brightly coloured daisies in late summer and autumn. They bloom in many shades from burnt orange to vivid yellow and last for many weeks. The prominent, conical centres may be black, brown, or green and give the plant its common name. Rudbeckias form leafy clumps with the flowers at the tips of sturdy, upright stems. The perennial *Rudbeckia hirta* and its cultivars are often used as annual bedding. Very easy to grow, rudbeckias provide a wonderful late burst of colour, try them with sedums (see p.270) and Michaelmas daisies (see Aster, pp.162–163). They are also good for cutting.

■ **HARDINESS** Fully hardy ✳✳✳ to half-hardy ✳.
■ **CULTIVATION** Reliably moist, heavy but well-drained, moderately fertile soil, in full sun or partial shade, is needed. ■ **Sow** seed (see pp.328–329) of perennials in containers in a cold frame in early spring. Sow seed of annuals at 16–18°C (61–64°F) in spring and plant out young plants when all threat of frost has passed. ■ **Divide** established plants (p.330) in spring or autumn.

Rudbeckia laciniata
↕1.5m–3m (5–10ft) ↔1m (3ft), loosely clumping perennial, flowers 8–15cm (3–6in) across in midsummer to early autumn ✳✳✳

Rudbeckia maxima
↕1.5m (5ft) ↔45–60cm (18–24in), perennial, large, waxy, grey-green leaves, flowers from midsummer to autumn ✳✳✳

***Rudbeckia laciniata* 'Herbstsonne'** ♀
↕2m (6ft) ↔90cm (36in), rhizomatous perennial, flowers 10–13cm (4–5in) across in midsummer to early autumn ✳✳✳

Salvia
Sage

SUMMER TO AUTUMN

The hardy culinary sage (*Salvia officinalis*), grown for its pungent leaves, is attractive enough for borders. Few of the herbaceous perennials are hardy, but will grace a sheltered spot with elegant flower spires in clear blues and reds. Salvias grown as annuals and biennials fall into two broad groups: the half-hardy, brightly coloured bedding plants typified by scarlet salvias, and hardy, more bushy plants in subtler colours, such as the clary sages, that look good in an informal or a herb garden. Hairy, woolly, or even white-mealy leaved salvias are more demanding, best grown in rock gardens or raised beds.

■ **HARDINESS** Fully hardy ✳✳✳ to frost-tender ❄.
■ **CULTIVATION** Grow in reasonably fertile, well-drained soil, in sun or partial shade. Small species with hairy leaves need sharply drained soil in full sun and protection from winter wet.
■ **Divide** perennials (*see p.330*) in spring.
■ **Take** cuttings from new shoots in spring or early summer (*see pp.329–330*). ■ **Sow** seed (*see pp.328–329*) of half-hardy annuals at 16–18°C (61–64°F) in spring. Sow hardy annuals in situ in spring.

***Salvia coccinea* 'Lady in Red'** ♀
‡40cm (16in) ↔ to 30cm (12in), erect, bushy annual with flowers 2cm (³⁄₄in) long from summer to autumn ✳

***Salvia patens* 'Cambridge Blue'** ♀
‡45–60cm (18–24in) ↔ 45cm (18in), erect perennial with true blue flowers from midsummer to mid-autumn ✳✳

Salvia fulgens ♀
‡50–100cm (20–39in) ↔ 40–90cm (16–36in), woody-based perennial with downy leaves and flowers in summer ✳✳

Salvia discolor ♀
‡45cm (18in) ↔ 30cm (12in), erect perennial bearing spires of very dark indigo flowers in late summer and early autumn ✳

Sanguisorba
Burnet

MIDSUMMER TO AUTUMN

For an unusual summer highlight in a moist border or corner of a garden, this small group of tall, clump-forming perennials is ideal. The wiry stems clothed with attractive leaves produce bottlebrush-like spires of small, fluffy flowers in red, pink, white, or greenish-white, with prominent stamens. The leaves are composed of toothed leaflets that are heavily veined and sometimes greyish. Burnets are suitable for mixed and herbaceous borders or particularly for naturalizing in a damp meadow or wildflower garden as they form spreading clumps. The flowers and foliage are good for cutting. Grow them with other perennials and with tall ornamental grasses (*see pp.284–299*).

■ **HARDINESS** Fully hardy ✳✳✳.
■ **CULTIVATION** Grow in any reasonably fertile soil that is moist but well-drained, in sun or partial shade. Taller species may need some support. In ideal conditions, plants may become invasive, but can be controlled by regular division (*see p.330*) in spring or autumn. ■ **Sow** seed in a container in a cold frame in spring or autumn (*see pp.328–329*).

Sanguisorba canadensis
‡to 2m (6ft) ↔ 1m (3ft), hairy leaves, flower spikes, to 20cm (8in) long, from midsummer to mid-autumn

Saponaria
Soapwort
SUMMER TO AUTUMN

The sap of soapwort was once used for laundering clothes as well as medicinally, for skin complaints. This group of sprawling and upright perennials is now grown for its profusion of tiny, pink to deep pink flowers in summer and autumn, as well as its ground-covering ability and for keeping down weeds. The plants thrive in sunny, dry sites. The low-growing, mat-forming species are excellent for the front of a border, perhaps spilling over paving, or in a rock garden. Grow taller ones with old-fashioned, pastel perennials such as pinks (*see Dianthus, p.189*).

■ **HARDINESS** Fully hardy ✳✳✳.
■ **CULTIVATION** Grow border perennials in reasonably fertile soil that is well drained and neutral to alkaline (limy), in full sun. Compact species such as *S. caespitosa* require sharply drained soil in a rock garden or between paving. Cut *S. ocymoides* hard back after flowering to maintain a compact habit. ■ **Divide** border perennials (*see p.330*) in autumn or spring.
■ **Sow** seed in containers in a cold frame in spring or autumn (*see pp.328–329*). ■ **Take** softwood cuttings in summer (*see pp.329–330*).
■ **Slugs** and snails (*see p.332*) cause damage.

Saponaria ocymoides ♀ (Tumbling Ted)
‡8cm (3in) ↔45cm (18in), mat-forming perennial, flowers in summer, can swamp small plants

Saxifraga
Saxifrage
SPRING TO AUTUMN

A staple of the rock garden, saxifrages are mostly low-growing plants that make dense mounds or mats of foliage, carpeting the ground or cascading down walls. There are more than 400 species, including evergreen, semi-evergreen, or deciduous perennials, biennials, and a few annuals. Arising from the foliage are masses of delicate, star- or saucer-shaped flowers in shades from white to lemon, bright yellow to rose, and indigo. Apart from rock gardens, saxifrages are grown in raised beds and alpine troughs and in alpine houses (unheated, well ventilated greenhouses). They are also often used to soften walls and paving. A few larger and more vigorous types, such as London pride (*Saxifraga* x *urbium*) and *S. fortunei*, make good path edgings or ground cover in borders and woodland gardens.

■ **HARDINESS** Fully hardy ✳✳✳; *S. stolonifera* and its cultivars are frost-hardy ✳✳.
■ **CULTIVATION** Saxifrages fall into four broad groups for cultivation. ■ **Group 1** need moist, well-drained soil in deep or partial shade. ■ **Group 2** prefer humus-rich soil, but with sharp drainage. Neutral to alkaline soil in light shade is best. ■ **Group 3** like fertile, well-drained, neutral to alkaline soil, with their roots moist. They tolerate full sun in cool areas. ■ **Group 4** require fertile but sharply drained, alkaline soil in full sun. Some will not tolerate winter wet. ■ **Sow** seed (*see pp.328–329*) in autumn in containers and put in a cold frame. ■ **Divide** herbaceous types in spring (*see p.330*). Detach single rosettes and root as cuttings (*see pp.329–330*) in late spring.

***Saxifraga* 'Apple Blossom'**
‡15cm (6in) ↔indefinite, suitable for crevices and borders, group 4

***Saxifraga* 'Tumbling Waters'** ♀
‡10cm (4in) ↔30cm (12in), group 3, mat-forming evergreen perennial with silvery-green leaves

***Saxifraga* 'Gregor Mendel'** ♀
‡10cm (4in) ↔30cm (12in), group 3, can be grown in crevices

***Saxifraga* 'Aureopunctata'**
‡30cm (12in) ↔indefinite, good for hanging baskets, group 3 or 4

Scabiosa
Pincushion flower, Scabious

MIDSUMMER TO AUTUMN

As the common name suggests, the centres of these plants' flowers look like pincushions. Whether you choose to grow the annuals, biennials, or perennials, each bears masses of delicate, solitary, sometimes fragrant flowers in summer to autumn. Shades range from lilac, purple, or white to deep crimson. Most of the leaves cluster at the bases of the stems. All attract bees and other beneficial insects into the garden. The tall-stemmed species, such as *Scabiosa caucasica* which has a height and spread of 60cm (24in), are good for cutting. Scabious blend in well in informal or cottage-garden plantings, in mixed borders, or in containers.

■ **HARDINESS** Fully hardy ✱✱✱ to frost-hardy ✱✱.
■ **CULTIVATION** Scabious prefer well-drained, moderately fertile soil that is neutral to slightly alkaline (limy), in full sun and with protection from excessive winter wet.

■ **Sow** seed (*see pp.328–329*) of annuals at 6–12°C (43–54°F) in early spring or where they are to flower in mid-spring. Sow seed of perennials in containers in a cold frame as soon as it is ripe, or in spring. ■ **Deadhead** to encourage more flowers (*see p.327*). ■ **Divide** established plants (*see p.330*) or take stem-tip cuttings (*see p.330*) of perennials in spring.

***Scabiosa caucasica* 'Miss Willmott'** ♀
↕90cm (36in) ↔ 60cm (24in), clump-forming perennial, flowers from mid- to late summer ✱✱✱

***Scabiosa* 'Butterfly Blue'**
↕↔40cm (16in), hairy, herbaceous perennial with branched stems, flowers to 4cm (1½in) across in mid- and late summer ✱✱✱

Scaevola

SPRING TO AUTUMN

Unusual, fan-shaped flowers in shades of purple-blue, lilac, or blue are produced by scaevolas in large numbers between spring and autumn. The flowers are borne singly or in clusters on slender stems, above spoon-shaped, mid-green leaves. Most are short-lived, mainly evergreen perennials. The perennial *Scaevola aemula* and its cultivars are most commonly grown in gardens. It is the only species that can be grown in temperate parts outdoors in summer and is generally treated as an annual. Grow scaevolas in mixed borders, in hanging baskets, or in large containers, where they make attractive specimen plants that can be moved under cover for winter.

■ **HARDINESS** Frost-tender ❀, but survives to -3°C (27°F) on sharply drained soil.
■ **CULTIVATION** Scaevolas require a well-drained, reasonably fertile soil, in full sun or partial shade. Use a loam-based compost for plants grown in containers; water freely in summer; and feed with a balanced fertilizer at monthly intervals. ■ **Sow** scaevola seed (*see pp.328–329*) at 19–24°C (66–75°F) in spring, or take softwood cuttings (*see pp.329–330*) in late spring or summer.

Scaevola aemula (Fairy fan flower)
↕↔to 50cm (20in), erect or prostrate, hairy stems, purple-blue or blue flowers to 2.5cm (1in) across in summer

Schizostylis coccinea
Kaffir lily

LATE SUMMER TO AUTUMN

Tall spikes of delicate, shimmering flowers in hot shades of red, pink, or scarlet make the kaffir lily a welcome addition to any garden. They resemble the gladiolus and are borne on stems up to 60cm (24in) in height, in late summer, autumn, or early winter, when there is little else in flower. A native of southern Africa, this vigorous, clump-forming perennial and its cultivars spread by means of underground stems (rhizomes). Try placing it in mixed borders with other late-flowering plants – for example Michaelmas daisies (*see Aster, pp.162–163*) or coneflowers (*see Rudbeckia, p.265*) – in containers, in waterside plantings, or by a sunny wall.

■ **HARDINESS** Frost-hardy to -10°C (14°F); flower spikes can be damaged by frost ✳.
■ **CULTIVATION** Grow in moist but well-drained, fertile soil in full sun. Support the flower stems if necessary with twiggy sticks in exposed gardens. ■ **Protect** with a mulch of organic matter in winter when the flowers are finished. ■ **Divide** (*see p.330*) in spring to maintain vigour. ■ **Sow** seed (*see pp.328–329*) at 13–16°C (55– 61°F) in spring.

Scilla
Squill

SPRING, SUMMER, AND AUTUMN

The dainty, diminutive flowers of scillas are extremely eye-catching, often with attractive, contrasting markings to the petals. They may be star- or bell-shaped, mostly in shades of blue but sometimes in purple or white, and are borne in loose or tight clusters amid strappy leaves in spring, summer, and autumn. Scillas are bulbous plants that will grow in a wide range of conditions and if left to their own devices, will self-seed freely. Naturalize the bulbs in grass, in rock or gravel gardens, or grow them in mixed borders, beneath deciduous shrubs and trees where they will receive plenty of light before the woody plants put on leaves. Scillas are also suitable for coastal gardens.

■ **HARDINESS** Fully hardy ✳✳✳ to frost-hardy ✳✳.
■ **CULTIVATION** Plant bulbs 8–10cm (3–4in) deep in late summer or early autumn, in well-drained, humus-rich, fertile soil that is in full sun or partial shade. ■ **Sow** seed (*see pp.328–329*) in pots and place in a cold frame. ■ **Divide** and pot up offsets (*see p.330*) when the bulbs are dormant in summer.

Scilla scilloides
‡15–20cm (6–8in) ↔ 5–10cm (2–4in) ✳✳✳

Scilla siberica '**Spring Beauty**'
‡20cm (8in) ↔ 5–10cm (2–4in) ✳✳✳

Schizostylis coccinea '**Major**' ♀
‡60cm (24in) ↔ 30cm (12in), flowers 5–6cm (2–2½in) across are borne on stiff stems in late summer

Scilla bifolia ♀
‡8–15cm (3–6in) ↔ 5–10cm (2–4in) ✳✳✳

Scilla peruviana '**Alba**'
‡15–30cm (6–12in) ↔ 5–10cm (2–4in) ✳✳

Sedum
Stonecrop

Sedums bring a range of textures and shapes to a garden; there are hundreds of annuals and perennials, many of which are succulent. There are low, creeping plants with tiny flowers that hug the ground, such as the common stonecrop (*Sedum acre*). This thrives in a rock or gravel garden, or in the crevices of paving or stone walls. The tall herbaceous perennials usually form architectural clumps, with large, flat heads of pink or white flowers. These provide late-season colour in summer and autumn, attract butterflies, and their tawny seedheads persist through winter. Sedums are often vigorous and very easy to grow.

■ **HARDINESS** Fully hardy ✳✳✳ to frost-tender ❀.
■ **CULTIVATION** Sedums like moderately fertile, neutral to alkaline (limy), well-drained soil in full sun, although vigorous plants tolerate light shade. ■ **Trim** spreading species after flowering to keep them neat. Support sedums with heavy flowerheads early on to stop the stems collapsing outwards. ■ **Divide** (*see p.330*) large herbaceous plants every 3–4 years in spring.
■ **Sow** seed in containers in a cold frame in autumn (*see pp.328–329*). ■ **Take** softwood cuttings of perennials (*see pp.329–330*) in early summer. ■ **Rots** may occur in wet conditions.

Sedum spathulifolium 'Cape Blanco' ♀
‡10cm (4in) ↔ 60cm (24in),
evergreen perennial, powdery bloom on leaves,
summer flowers, stands light shade ✳✳✳

Sedum spathulifolium 'Purpureum' ♀
‡10cm (4in) ↔ 60cm (24in), vigorous, mat-forming,
evergreen perennial, golden flowers in summer,
tolerates light shade ✳✳✳

Sedum spectabile 'Brilliant' ♀ (Ice plant)
‡↔ 45cm (18in), clumping, deciduous perennial,
flowerheads 15cm (6in) across in late summer,
seedheads persist, needs support ✳✳✳

Sedum populifolium
‡20–30cm (8–12in) ↔ 45cm (18in), deciduous
perennial with lax stems, fragrant flowers in late
summer and early autumn ✳✳✳

Sempervivum
Houseleek

These evergreen succulents are grown for their fleshy rosettes of leaves, which are often flushed red or purple, and sometimes thickly covered in hairs. There are numerous varieties with leaves of differing colours, sizes, and shapes. Although each plant is small, they spread across the soil by rooting stems, or runners, that produce new plantlets to form large mats of densely packed rosettes. In summer, starry, white, yellow, red, or purple flowers cluster on sturdy, fleshy stems. After a rosette flowers, it dies, but the gap is quickly filled by a new offset. Houseleeks thrive in rock or gravel gardens or containers, with other alpines such as saxifrages (*see p.267*) or pinks (*see Dianthus, p.189*). They are even used to clothe tops of walls or roofs.

■ **HARDINESS** Fully hardy ✳✳✳.
■ **CULTIVATION** Houseleeks grow in full sun, in poor, sharply drained soil and add plenty of grit or gritty compost. Shield hairy houseleeks from winter rain to avoid rots. ■ **Sow** seed (*see pp.328–329*) in pots in a cold frame in spring.
■ **Detach** rooted offsets in spring or early summer; they establish more quickly if kept out of direct sun.

Sempervivum arachnoideum ♀
(Cobweb houseleek)
‡8cm (3in) ↔ 30cm (12in), pink flowers

Senecio

There are hundreds of senecios, including annuals and biennials, shrubs, trees, and climbers. The shrubs are often grown for their foliage (*see p.100*), but the clump-forming annuals and perennials are valued for their daisies. They bloom from early summer until late autumn in shades of white, yellow, blue, crimson, and purple; usually with a golden yellow centre. Since senecios are so varied, check the label or with the nursery about each plant's needs. Generally, annuals are used as summer bedding or in containers; small perennials in rock or gravel gardens, and larger varieties in borders. Some senecios are quite tender, but can be grown in containers and moved under cover in winter.

■ **HARDINESS** Fully hardy ✽✽✽ to frost-tender ✿.
■ **CULTIVATION** May need gritty or moist, poor or moderately fertile, well-drained soil, in full sun or partial shade. ■ **Sow** seed (*see pp.328–329*) in spring at 19–24°C (66–75°F); seed of bog plants and alpines can be sown in a cold frame. ■ **Take** softwood cuttings (*see pp.329–330*) of perennials in early summer.

Senecio pulcher
‡45–60cm (18–24in) ↔ 50cm (20in), perennial, flowers in mid- to late autumn, survives winters outside in mild areas ✽✽

Sidalcea

False mallow, Prairie mallow

From early to midsummer, these annuals and perennials produce tall spires of long-lasting flowers. The petals are thin and silky and in clear shades of pink, purple-pink, or white. They often produce a second flush of blooms in autumn if the fading flowers are cut back before seeds develop. Another bonus is that the dense clumps of attractive, lobed or serrated, round leaves cover the soil and suppress weeds. Use sidalceas to add some height to a bed or border; they also are excellent for cutting.

■ **HARDINESS** Fully hardy ✽✽✽.
■ **CULTIVATION** A site in full sun, with moderately fertile, neutral to acid, moist but well-drained soil, enriched with organic matter, is best. Sidalceas tolerate a range of soils, but do not like to be too wet, especially in winter. ■ **Mulch** (*see p.326*) with straw or bracken where winters are cold. ■ **Cut back** stems hard after the first flowering. ■ **Sow** seed (*see pp.328–329*) in a container in a cold frame in spring or autumn. ■ **Divide** (*see p.330*) in spring or autumn. ■ **Remove** leaves affected by rust (orange-brown pustules); thin foliage to improve air circulation and help prevent a recurrence.

Sidalcea 'Oberon'
‡1.2m (4ft) ↔ 45cm (18in), rounded or kidney-shaped leaves, flowers in early and midsummer

Silene

Campion, Catchfly

There are hundreds of these annuals, biennials, and deciduous and evergreen perennials. They are grown for their pretty flowers with delicately notched or split petals. In summer, erect stems bear blooms, singly or in clusters, in shades from dark pink to pure white. Most are easy to grow; many are self-seeders. Deadhead regularly and use smaller perennials in a rock or gravel garden; place taller varieties in beds and borders. Annuals are often used as summer bedding. Some have sticky hairs on their leaves that trap insects – hence the common name.

■ **HARDINESS** Fully hardy ✽✽✽ to half-hardy ✽.
■ **CULTIVATION** Grow in moderately fertile, neutral to alkaline (limy), well-drained soil, in full sun or dappled shade. Smaller alpine species need gritty, sharply drained soil. *S. hookeri* prefers acid (lime-free) soil. ■ **Sow** seed (*see pp.328–329*) of perennials in a cold frame in autumn. Sow hardy annuals in situ in autumn or spring; half-hardy varieties at 16–19°C (61–66°F) in spring. Harden and plant out when threat of frost has passed. ■ **Take** new shoots from the base in spring and treat as softwood cuttings (*see pp.329–330*).

Silene schafta
‡25cm (10in) ↔ 30cm (12in), clumping, semi-evergreen perennial, flowers in late summer and autumn, good for rock gardens ✽✽✽

Silybum marianum
Blessed Mary's thistle
SUMMER TO AUTUMN

This tall, prickly biennial forms an impressive rosette of glossy, dark green, spiny leaves up to 50cm (20in) long in its first year, that are spectacularly veined and marbled with white. In the second year, large, slightly scented flowerheads appear throughout the summer and autumn. If you wish to keep the leaf variegation at its best and prolong the life of the plant, pinch out the flowers as they form. Silybums are excellent in groups in borders, where their architectural foliage contrasts with softer, round-leaved plants. Plant Blessed Mary's thistle singly in a gravel garden, so its handsome form can be appreciated.

■ **HARDINESS** Fully hardy ✳✳✳.
■ **CULTIVATION** Silybums prefer well-drained, neutral or slightly alkaline (limy) soil, in full sun. They dislike wet winters, so provide shelter if possible to avoid rots. ■ **Sow** seed (*see pp.328–329*) in situ, in spring or early summer, then thin seedlings to 60cm (24in) apart. If grown for foliage, sow seed under cover in late winter or early spring; pot up into 9cm (3¹/₂in) pots; harden off and plant out in spring.

Silybum marianum
‡to 1.5m (5ft) ↔ 60–90cm (24–36in)

Sisyrinchium
SPRING TO SUMMER

Pretty, star- or cup-shaped flowers are produced by these annuals and perennials in profusion over many weeks in spring or summer. They bloom in rich blues and mauves, or subtle yellows and whites, singly at the tips of stems or in tall flower spikes. The long leaves, which are sometimes variegated, form grassy clumps or large, iris-like fans. The spiky foliage complements that of ornamental grasses (*see pp.284–299*) or provides a textural contrast to plants with feathery or broad leaves. Smaller varieties are best in a rock or gravel garden where they can be left to self-seed; the tall sisyrinchiums hold their own in a border.

■ **HARDINESS** Fully hardy ✳✳✳ to half-hardy ✳.
■ **CULTIVATION** Poor to moderately fertile, neutral to alkaline (limy), well-drained soil in full sun, is required, with protection from extreme winter wet which encourages root rot. Some small or half-hardy sisyrinchiums are best grown in pots and moved under cover in damp winters. ■ **Sow** seed (*see pp.328–329*) in a container in a cold frame in spring or autumn. ■ **Divide** clumps (*see p.330*) in spring.

Sisyrinchium striatum '**Aunt May**'
‡50cm (20in) ↔ 25cm (10in), clumping perennial, flowers 2.5cm (1in) across borne in early and midsummer ✳✳✳

Solidago
Golden rod, Aaron's rod
LATE SUMMER TO AUTUMN

The warm yellow flowers of these vigorous, woody-based perennials appear in late summer to autumn borne in spikes or clusters, densely packed with tiny blooms, on stiff, upright stems. The leaves are usually mid-green. Species golden rods can be invasive, and although they can be controlled by digging them out, they are best reserved for wildflower gardens. Happily, many less unruly hybrids, with larger flowerheads, are available. They add late colour to the garden and are excellent for cutting. Use them with other autumn flowers such as rudbeckias (*see p.265*) and asters (*see pp.162–163*) among earlier-flowering plants for a prolonged seasonal display.

■ **HARDINESS** Fully hardy ✳✳✳.
■ **CULTIVATION** Thrive in poor to moderately fertile, preferably sandy, well-drained soil, in full sun. ■ **Deadhead** regularly to prevent self-seeding. ■ **Divide** (*see p.330*) plants every three or four years in autumn or spring to keep them healthy: discard the old, woody centres. ■ **Powdery mildew** may be disfiguring in dry summers.

Solidago '**Goldenmosa**' ♥
‡75cm (30in) ↔ 45cm (18in), compact bush, wrinkled foliage, 30cm (12in) long flower spikes in late summer and early autumn

x Solidaster luteus

MIDSUMMER TO AUTUMN

This hybrid is a cross between a solidago and an aster: as you might expect, it combines elements of both plants. Much like golden rod (*see left*), *Solidaster luteus* bears a profusion of tiny blooms in dense clusters from midsummer through to autumn. The flowers themselves are daisy-like, and similar to those of an aster (*see pp.162–163*). They open a pale, creamy yellow with a darker centre, which then fades as they age. The plant forms a clump with erect stems. Like both its parents, this perennial is a splendid choice for adding late-summer colour to a border, and also makes an excellent cut flower.

■ **HARDINESS** Fully hardy ✳✳✳.
■ **CULTIVATION** Moderately fertile, well-drained soil, in full sun or dappled shade, suits this plant. Take care not to over-fertilize the soil, because this encourages foliage at the expense of flowers. ■ **Divide** clumps in autumn or spring (*see p.330*) every three or four years to maintain vigour and discard the congested, woody centres. Take new shoots from the base in spring and treat as softwood cuttings (*see pp.329–330*). ■ **Powdery mildew** may be disfiguring in dry summers.

***x Solidaster luteus* 'Lemore'** ♀
↕↔80cm (32in), more spreading habit and a paler yellow than the species

Stachys

Betony, Hedge nettle, Woundwort

EARLY SUMMER TO AUTUMN

The main attraction of these plants are the large, felted or velvety leaves, which are usually covered in fine hairs; in some species, they are aromatic. Stachys include many make excellent ground-cover perennials such as *Stachys byzantina* of which 'Silver Carpet' is a non-flowering form ideal for edging. Their silvery foliage will complement many border plants: try crocosmias (*see p.184*), penstemons (*see p.252*), and shrub roses (*see pp.96–97*). The flower spikes, in white or shades of pink, purple, or gold, appear in summer and attract bees, butterflies, and other beneficial insects into the garden. Low-growing species, like *Stachys candida*, are good for dry banks or gravel gardens.

■ **HARDINESS** Fully hardy ✳✳✳ to frost-hardy ✳✳.
■ **CULTIVATION** Grow in well-drained, reasonably fertile soil in full sun. Smaller rock garden species need very sharply drained soil. ■ **Sow** seed (*see pp.328–329*) in a container in a cold frame in autumn or spring. ■ **Divide** plants (*see p.330*) in spring, as growth starts, or replant rooted sections from the outside of large clumps.

Stachys byzantina (Lambs' ears, Lambs' tongues)
↕45cm (18in) ↔ 60cm (24in), woolly pink-purple flowers from early summer to early autumn ✳✳✳

Symphytum

Comfrey

LATE SPRING TO LATE SUMMER

Prized for their shade tolerance, these hairy, clump-forming perennials make useful ground cover in a shady border or woodland garden. Although essentially coarse plants, they have decorative, crinkly foliage and pretty, long-lasting flowers in shades of bright blue, pale blue, cream, pale yellow, purple-violet, or white, and are borne in clusters amid the foliage from late spring to late summer. The leaves may be plain green, cream- or gold-variegated. Pick a site carefully because all but the variegated species can be invasive. Comfrey thrives beneath trees or in borders, where little else will grow.

■ **HARDINESS** Fully hardy ✳✳✳.
■ **CULTIVATION** Grow in moist soil in sun or shade, or in dry shade. ■ **Remove** flowers from variegated species for the best foliage colour. ■ **Divide** plants (*see p.330*) in spring; comfrey spreads by underground stems (rhizomes) and will reshoot from a tiny bit of stem left in the soil. Comfrey leaves make a rich, if smelly, liquid feed: one-third fill a bucket with leaves and top up with water. Cover and leave for 2–3 weeks, then use diluted one part comfrey liquid with two parts water.

Symphytum caucasicum ♀
↕↔60cm (24in) then spreads, clump-forming hairy perennial, erect then lax stems, rosettes of leaves, flowers from early to late summer

Tagetes
Marigold

For length of flowering and show of colour, marigolds have few rivals, and make excellent subjects for a formal bedding display. The many annuals and perennials are usually treated as half-hardy annuals and sown in spring. Germination is swift and they start flowering just a few weeks after sowing. The flowers, in a range of shades from deep orange to bright yellow, are produced from early summer until the first frosts of autumn. In some forms, they are single; in others they are like carnations. The ferny foliage is usually strongly aromatic. Taller African marigolds, with pompon flowers, are best grown in a border, but others, including French marigolds, are equally at home in containers or borders.

■ **HARDINESS** Half-hardy ❋.
■ **CULTIVATION** Any reasonably well-drained soil in full sun. ■ **Deadhead** regularly to prolong the flowering period and water freely in dry weather. If growing marigolds in containers, water them well, and feed with a balanced fertilizer at weekly intervals. ■ **Sow** seed (*see pp.328–329*) at 21°C (70°F) in spring.

Tagetes 'Lemon Gem'
‡23cm (9in) ↔to 40cm (16in), Signet marigold, flowers to 2.5cm (1in) across from late spring to early autumn

Tanacetum
Pyrethrum

Most species in this large, diverse group of annuals and perennials have finely cut, pungently aromatic leaves and daisy flowers in early and midsummer. Some flowerheads have a prominent central disc and others have small, double pompons. The ferny leaves are very decorative. *Tanacetum balsamita* smells minty and is an ingredient of pot pourri. Some species, such as *T. haradjanii*, are suitable for a rock garden, while others, such as forms of *T. parthenium*, can be grown in a herb garden or as an edging to mixed or herbaceous borders.

■ **HARDINESS** Fully hardy ❋❋❋ to half-hardy ❋.
■ **CULTIVATION** Grow these plants in any well-drained soil in full sun. Dwarf and silver-leaved species prefer sharply drained soil.
■ **Cut back** flowers of *T. coccineum* after flowering for further blooms. Self-seeds prolifically. ■ **Sow** seed at 10–13°C (50–55°F) in early spring (*see pp.328–329*). ■ **Divide** perennials (*see p.330*) or take new shoots from the base and treat as cuttings (*see pp.329–330*) in spring. ■ **Chrysanthemum eelworm** in the roots may cause leaves to turn brown and die from the base; destroy affected plants.

Tanacetum parthenium (Feverfew)
‡45–60cm (18–24in) ↔30cm (12in), bushy perennial, flowers in summer ❋❋❋

Thalictrum
Meadow rue

Thalictrums are a large group of moisture-loving perennials with delicate, grey-green foliage and airy clouds of tiny flowers from early to late summer. The numerous flowers may be coloured white, pink, and purple to yellow, often with showy central stamens, which create a fluffy effect from a distance. The leaves are composed of many fine-textured leaflets. They are mostly upright plants, although some, such as *Thalictrum kiusianum*, are mat-forming. Taller species are excellent in borders with perennials like achilleas (*see p.140*), sidalceas (*see p.271*), and golden rod (*see Solidago, p.272*). Small ones add grace to a shady rock garden.

■ **HARDINESS** Fully hardy ❋❋❋ to frost–tender ❀.
■ **CULTIVATION** Grow in partial shade, in moist soil enriched with organic matter. Small species like well-drained soil in cool, partial shade. ■ **Stake** taller plants. ■ **Sow** seed (*see pp.328–329*) in a container when ripe or in early spring. ■ **Divide** plants (*see p.330*) as growth begins in spring. ■ **Powdery mildew** can be a problem in dry soil.

***Thalictrum delavayi* 'Hewitt's Double'** ♀
‡1.2m (4ft) or more ↔60cm (24in), leaves up to 35cm (14in) long, long-lasting flowers from midsummer to early summer ❋❋❋

Tiarella
Foam flower

Frothy spires of tiny flowers appear to float above the foliage of these herbaceous perennials. The white or pinkish-white flowers are borne from late spring to midsummer. The foliage is also a valuable feature of these plants, being oval to heart-shaped and pale to mid-green with bristly hairs. In autumn, the leaves turn reddish-copper. Since the foliage is so dense, and some species have a spreading habit, foam flowers make attractive and effective ground-cover plants, particularly in a shady border or a woodland garden. They combine very well with other shade- or moisture-loving perennials such as coral flowers (*see Heuchera, p.217*), hostas (*see pp.218–219*), and speedwells (*see Veronica, p.281*).

■ **HARDINESS** Fully hardy ✷✷✷.
■ **CULTIVATION** Foam flowers thrive in any moist soil that has been enriched with well-rotted organic matter, in deep or partial shade. ■ **Protect** the crowns from winter wet if necessary. ■ **Sow** seed in a container (*see pp.328–329*) in a cold frame as soon as they are ripe. ■ **Divide** plants (*see p.330*) in spring.

Tiarella cordifolia ♀ (Foam flower)
‡10–30cm (4–12in) ↔ to 30cm (12in), hairy leaves bronze-red in autumn, flower spikes 10–30cm (4–12in) long in summer

Tolmiea menziesii
Pick-a-back plant, Youth-on-age

The appeal of this fast-growing, clump-forming perennial lies in its foliage. Its softly hairy, usually light green, pretty leaves produce new plantlets at the points where the leaf stalks and leaf blades meet, hence the name of pick-a-back plant. From late spring to early summer, it bears long clusters of up to 50 slightly scented flowers with purple-brown petals. *Tolmiea menziesii* and its cultivars spread by means of creeping stems. Use it as ground cover in a woodland setting with perennials such as coral flowers (*see Heuchera, p.271*) and foam flowers (*see left*).

■ **HARDINESS** Fully hardy ✷✷✷.
■ **CULTIVATION** Plant this perennial in moist soil in partial or deep shade. Full sun can scorch the leaves. For a container-grown plant, use a loam-based compost; water freely during the growing season; and feed with a balanced fertilizer weekly. ■ **Sow** seed (*see pp.328–329*) of pick-a-back plant in a container in a cold frame in autumn, or divide (*see p.330*) in spring. You could also try cutting off plantlets below a leaf in mid- to late summer and rooting them in the same way as a cutting (*see pp.329–330*) with the bottom leaf just covered.

***Tolmiea menziesii* 'Taff's Gold'** ♀
‡30–60cm (12–24in) ↔ 1–2m (3–6ft), leaves up to 13cm (5in) long, particularly prone to sun scorch

Tradescantia

The hardy tradescantias are very useful, clump-forming perennials, and although each flower is short-lived, they are produced in profusion in summer and much of autumn. The blue, purple, rose-pink, rose-red, or white blooms stud the mounds of matt-green, or occasionally purple-tinged, grassy foliage. Grow these easy-going plants in a mixed border, perhaps married with ornamental grasses such as hakonechloas (*see p.292*), or with other herbaceous perennials. The tender tradescantias are familiar as house plants with trailing stems and evergreen, often stripy or purple leaves. These also have a place outside in summer schemes, for example with fuchsias or busy Lizzies, or tumbling over the edges of hanging baskets or pots.

■ **HARDINESS** Fully hardy ✷✷✷ to frost-tender ❀.
■ **CULTIVATION** Hardy species prefer moist, fertile soil, in full sun or partial shade. ■ **Cut back** hard after flowering to prevent seed setting and for a further flush of flower. ■ **Divide** hardy tradescantias in spring or autumn (*see p.330*).

***Tradescantia* 'Purewell Giant'**
‡↔ 45cm (18in), flowers from early summer to early autumn ✷✷✷

Tricyrtis
Toad lily

SUMMER AND AUTUMN

Toad lilies have spectacular flowers, produced in white, shades of pinkish-white, or green flushed white or yellow, and frequently spotted with contrasting markings in pink or purple. They are star- or funnel-shaped and borne singly or in small clusters during summer and autumn. The leaves are often glossy, dark green to pale green, and usually clasp erect or arching stems. Some foliage is spotted or has prominent veins. Toad lilies are herbaceous perennials and particularly suitable for woodland gardens and shady borders. Try combining them with other perennials that enjoy moist, shady situations such as Solomon's seal (see Polygonatum, p.258).

■ **HARDINESS** Fully hardy ✳✳✳.
■ **CULTIVATION** Prefer moist but well-drained soil, that is humus-rich, in partial shade. In colder areas, grow late-flowering species in a warm, sheltered shrub border, protected from wind and frost, which could damage late flowers.
■ **Mulch** thickly with organic matter over the growing area in winter to protect the plants from severe frosts. ■ **Sow** seed as soon as it is ripe in a cold frame and overwinter seedling plants in frost-free conditions (see pp.328–329).
■ **Divide** plants (see p.330) in early spring while they are still dormant.

Tricyrtis formosana ♀
‡to 80cm (32in) ↔45cm (18in)

Tricyrtis hirta 'Alba'
‡to 80cm (32in) ↔60cm (24in)

Tricyrtis ohsumiensis
‡to 50cm (20in) ↔23cm (9in)

Tricyrtis macrantha subsp.
macranthopsis ‡to 80cm (32in) ↔30cm (12in)

Trillium
Wood lily, Trinity flower, Wake robin

SPRING

These spring-flowering plants of the woodland floor are prized for their curious three-petalled flowers held above the foliage, also grouped in threes. A small group of deciduous perennials, they are clump-forming and vigorous once established. The flowers, in white and shades of pink, dark red, and yellow, are held at the tips of slender stems in spring and summer. The rich or dark green leaves are sometimes mottled or marbled with silver or purple. Trilliums can be slow to get going, but once they are established resent being disturbed, so site them carefully. They are suitable for moist, shady borders or woodland gardens, in the company of plants such as hostas (see pp.218–219).

Trillium luteum ♀
‡to 40cm (16in) ↔to 30cm (12in), leaves palely mottled, stalkless sweet-scented flowers in spring

■ **HARDINESS** Fully hardy ✱✱✱.
■ **CULTIVATION** Grow in moist soil, preferably slightly acid (lime-free), in deep or partial shade. ■ **Divide** plants *(see p.330)* after flowering, preferably by lifting small, rooted sections; try to keep the central clump undisturbed. ■ **Sow** seed as soon as it is ripe in containers in a cold frame *(see pp.328–329)*. Plants may take up to seven years to reach flowering size from seed. ■ **Slugs** and snails can damage young leaves *(see p.332)*.

Trillium grandiflorum ♀ (Wake robin)
‡to 40cm (16in) ↔ to 30cm (12in), vigorous, with the largest flowers to 8cm (3in) long, in spring and summer

Trillium chloropetalum
‡to 40cm (16in) ↔ to 20cm (8in), with thick red-green stems and fragrant flowers in spring

Trollius
Globeflower
LATE SPRING TO EARLY SUMMER

Related to buttercups, these moisture-loving perennials take their common name from their bowl-shaped flowers. Flower colour ranges from pale cream to deep orange, with all shades in-between. The flowers may be single, semi-double, or double, and appear from late spring to early summer, borne on tall stems; single flowers often have prominent central stamens. The rosettes of mid-green leaves are much divided and often deeply cut, and may be glossy. Grow globeflower in a moist border, bog garden, or beside a pond or stream, with plants that enjoy similar conditions, like *Caltha palustris (see p.172)* or lysichitons *(see p.235)*.

■ **HARDINESS** Fully hardy ✱✱✱.
■ **CULTIVATION** Grow globeflowers in very moist soil, in full sun or partial shade. Cut back stems after the first flush of flowers to encourage more later. ■ **Divide** plants *(see p.330)* as new growth begins or after flowering. ■ **Sow** seed *(see pp.328–329)* in a container in a cold frame as soon as it is ripe, or in spring; it can take two years to germinate.

***Trollius* x *cultorum* 'Orange Princess'** ♀
‡to 90cm (36in) ↔ 45cm (18in), with glossy leaves, large at the base of the plant, and flowers in late spring and early summer

Tropaeolum
SUMMER TO AUTUMN

Nasturtiums are the most familiar of these vigorous, scrambling annuals and half-hardy perennials, grown for their cheerful, spurred flowers from summer until the first frosts of autumn. The trumpet-shaped flowers are borne in a variety of warm colours from red to orange and yellow, many bicoloured or with contrasting markings. The round or lobed, light to mid-green leaves are held on long stalks. The bushy plants are best with other annuals or as border gap-fillers. Those with trailing stems scramble over the ground or climb *(see p.132)*. Semi-trailing types are ideal for hanging baskets. Tender perennials grown in pots may be overwintered under glass.

■ **HARDINESS** Frost-hardy ✱✱ to frost-tender ✿.
■ **CULTIVATION** Grow in moist but well-drained soil, in sun or partial shade. Water plants in pots freely in summer; feed weekly with a balanced fertilizer. ■ **Sow** seed *(see pp.328–329)* of annuals where they are to grow, in mid-spring; sow seed of perennials in a container in a cold frame as soon as ripe. ■ **Blackfly** can occur *(see Aphids, p.332)*.

***Tropaeolum majus* Alaska Series** ♀
(Nasturtium)
‡to 30cm (12in) ↔ 45cm (18in), annual, variegated leaves ✱

Tulipa
Tulip

LATE WINTER TO LATE SPRING

Tulips have been prized for centuries for their brilliantly coloured spring blooms. They were one of the first of the many bulbous perennials to be introduced into western gardens from the eastern Mediterranean. Here, in the parched summer earth of their native lands, the sun "ripens" the bulbs, helping the buds to form that produce the following season's flowers. Single or double, these come in a dazzling array of colours, often fascinatingly flushed or streaked with other shades. Petals may be frilled, fringed, pointed, waisted, or tinged with green, as in the viridiflora types such as 'Spring Green'. The species tulips, for instance *Tulipa sprengeri*, *T. tarda*, and the Greigii types, are often the smallest and among the easiest to grow. They suit borders, rock gardens, and areas of naturalistic planting. The taller, more highly bred hybrids put on an eye-catching display, but flowers can diminish over the years and are best lifted (*see below*) or treated as annuals. All are excellent in pots.

■ **HARDINESS** Fully hardy ✻✻✻.
■ **CULTIVATION** Grow in well-drained, fertile soil in full sun. All tulips dislike heavy damp soil. Plant at twice the bulb's own depth in late autumn. ■ **Deadhead** to prevent seedheads forming, so concentrating the plant's energy into developing the bulb and next year's flower bud.
■ **Apply** a balanced liquid fertilizer once a fortnight after flowering until the foliage withers, to build up the bulb. ■ **Lift** bulbs (except for small species tulips) once the foliage has died down (*see below*), and discard or separate small offsets. ■ **Plant** large bulbs in late autumn. Grow on offsets in a spare corner until they reach flowering size (up to 7 years).
■ **Aphids** may spread an untreatable virus that causes petal streaking, which, although sometimes attractive, usually triggers a plant's decline.

Planting tulip bulbs for easy lifting

Most tall, hybrid tulip bulbs are best lifted once the foliage withers, then dried and stored until autumn. This, to some extent, mimics their natural ripening process in the wild and helps bulbs perform well for years, especially on heavy soils.

Planting tulips in a basket means they can be easily lifted after flowering and stored when not in season. Use a container with drainage holes – a lattice basket for pond plants is ideal. Lift carefully, so as not to damage roots grown through the basket. Bury the basket in a resting place in the garden so the top is just below the soil surface. Label it and water in well.

Tulips planted directly in the soil can be lifted with a fork. Shake off any soil and leave in a dry place to dry off. Remove withered leaves and flaking skin and throw away any bulbs showing signs of disease with soft spots on them. Keep in a cool, dark and dry place. Check at intervals for disease and replant in autumn.

T. acuminata ‡50cm (20in), early and mid-spring

T. **'Ancilla'** ♀ ‡15cm (6in), mid-spring, good for rock gardens

T. **'China Pink'** ♀ ‡50cm (20in), late spring

T. clusiana var. *chrysantha* ♀ ‡30cm (12in), early and mid-spring

T. **'Mount Tacoma'** ‡40cm (16in), late spring

T. **'Oriental Splendour'** ♀ ‡30cm (12 early spring, leaves marked bluish-purpl

T. sprengeri ♀ ‡50cm (20in), early summer, will self-seed in sun or partial shade

T. **'Spring Green'** ♀ ‡40cm (16in), late spring

T. **'Angélique'** ♀ ‡30cm (12in), mid-spring

T. **'Apeldoorn'** ‡60cm (24in), mid-spring

T. biflora ‡10cm (4in), late winter to spring, fragrant

T. **'Carnaval de Nice'** ♀ ‡40cm (16in), late spring

T. **'Douglas Bader'** ‡45cm (18in), late spring

T. linifolia ♀ ‡20cm (8in), early and mid-spring

T. linifolia Batalinii Group ♀ ‡35cm (14in), late winter to late spring

T. **'Madame Lefeber'** ‡35cm (14in), early spring, may need staking

T. praestans **'Van Tubergen's Variety'** ‡50cm (20in), early spring

T. **'Prinses Irene'** ♀ ‡35cm (14in), mid-spring, good for cut flowers

T. **'Purissima'** ♀ ‡35cm (14in), mid-spring

T. **'Queen of Night'** ‡60cm (24in), late spring

T. tarda ♀ ‡15cm (6in), early and mid-spring

T. turkestanica ♀ ‡30cm (12in), early and mid-spring, unpleasant fragrance

T. **'West Point'** ♀ ‡50cm (20in), late spring

T. **'White Parrot'** ‡55cm (22in), late spring

Verbascum
Mullein

SUMMER TO AUTUMN

These stately plants are grown for their tall flower spikes, densely set with saucer-shaped blooms from summer to autumn. The short-stemmed flowers occur usually in shades of yellow, but are occasionally purple, scarlet, brownish-red, or white. While the individual flowers are short-lived, there are always more opening to sustain the display. Most garden mulleins are vigorous, rosette-forming plants that are useful in any border, particularly in gravel and cottage gardens. The often woolly, silvery rosettes of leaves remain attractive into winter. They generally are not long-lived, being biennials, short-lived perennials, and some annuals. Mulleins self-seed prolifically if allowed to do so, although the seedlings may not come true.

■ **HARDINESS** Fully hardy ✽✽✽ to frost-hardy ✽✽.
■ **CULTIVATION** Grow mullein in well-drained, alkaline (limy) soil in full sun. Tall plants may require support, especially in rich soil. ■ **Sow** seed (*see pp.328–329*) of perennials in containers in a cold frame in late spring or early summer. Sow seed of biennials in early summer to flower the following year. ■ **Divide** perennials (*see p.330*) in spring. ■ **Take** root cuttings (*see pp.329–330*) in winter.

***Verbascum* 'Letitia'** ♀
‡to 25cm (10in) ↔ to 30cm (12in), dense, bushy evergreen, flower spikes to 10cm (4in) long all summer, needs sharp drainage ✽✽✽

***Verbascum* 'Cotswold Queen'**
‡1.2m (4ft) ↔30cm (12in), semi-evergreen, upright perennial with grey-green leaves, flowers from early to late summer ✽✽✽

***Verbascum chaixii* 'Album'** ♀
‡90cm (36in) ↔ 45cm (18in), rosette-forming, semi-evergreen perennial, flower spikes to 40cm (16in) mid- to late summer ✽✽✽

Verbascum nigrum (Dark mullein)
‡90cm (36in) ↔60cm (24in), rosette-forming, semi-evergreen or evergreen perennial, flowers midsummer to early autumn ✽✽✽

Verbena

SUMMER TO AUTUMN

This large group of annuals and perennials are invaluable, with dense clusters of long-flowering small flowers in shades of red, blue, pink, lilac, and violet borne on stiff, square stems. Verbenas fall into two main groups: the hardy perennials, such as *Verbena bonariensis*, will grow quite tall and bring height and an airy feel to a border, while the many shorter-growing, half-hardy perennials tend to sprawl. Grown as annual bedding they will add colour to containers and hanging baskets as well as the edges of borders. Grow perennials with tall plants like *Cynara cardunculus* (*see p.185*) and annuals with bedding plants such as pelargoniums (*see pp.250–251*).

■ **HARDINESS** Fully hardy ✻✻✻ to frost-tender ✿.
■ **CULTIVATION** Moist but well-drained soil in full sun is best. In containers, use a loam-based or soilless compost – water well in summer, and feed with a balanced fertilizer weekly. ■ **Sow** seed (*see pp.328–329*) at 18–21°C (64–70°F) in early spring. ■ **Divide** perennials (*see p.330*) in spring and take stem-tip cuttings (*see pp.329–330*) in late summer. ■ **Powdery mildew** can be a problem.

Verbena 'Peaches 'n' Cream' ♀
↕to 45cm (18in) ↔30–50cm (12–20in), sprawling perennial grown as annual ✻

Veronica

Speedwell

SPRING TO AUTUMN

The slender, graceful spires of veronica carry small, outward-facing flowers in intense or pastel shades of blue, pink, purple, or white. The numerous annuals and perennials in this group are mostly mat- or cushion-forming, but sometimes upright and branching. Their long or rounded leaves have toothed edges and are mid- to dark green, sometimes felted. Speedwells flower over a long period and are excellent garden plants, especially for the front of a sunny border. They make good partners for shrubby or perennial plants such as lavenders (*see p.71*) and cranesbills (*see Geranium, pp.208–209*). The smaller types are best grown in a rock garden.

■ **HARDINESS** Fully hardy ✻✻✻ to frost-hardy ✻✻.
■ **CULTIVATION** Alpine speedwells require sharply drained, poor to moderate soil, in full sun and protection from winter wet for those with felted leaves. Others like any fertile soil in full sun or partial shade. ■ **Sow** seed (*see pp.328–329*) in a container in a cold frame in autumn. ■ **Divide** perennials (*see p.330*) in spring or autumn. ■ **Powdery mildew** can occur in dry weather; remove affected parts.

Veronica austriaca 'Kapitän'
↕to 30cm (12in) ↔to 40cm (16in), mat-forming perennial with flower spires 10–15cm (4–6in) long all summer ✻✻✻

Veronica gentianoides ♀
↕↔to 45cm (18in), mat-forming perennial, dark green leaves, pale blue or, more rarely, white flowers in early summer ✻✻✻

Veronica spicata 'Rotfuchs'
↕↔to 30cm (12in), mat-forming perennial, spreads by rooting stems, flowers from early to late summer ✻✻✻

Viola

Pansy, Violet

The richly-coloured and open "faces" of these well-loved flowers bring cheer to the garden all year around. Hundreds of forms are available, with flowers in hues of gold, orange, crimson, purple, black, blue, lilac, and white; many are bicoloured and or even tricoloured. Traditional violas are compact, tufted perennials, with dainty, often scented flowers, such as the classic English violet, *Viola odorata*. This is an evergreen perennial with a strong, sweet scent and is a good ground cover for a shady spot. Garden pansies include the brasher, large-flowered hybrids, mostly unscented; they are grown as bedding, and include winter-flowering forms. There are also annual violas. Violas look extremely pretty as border edging or in hanging baskets and other containers.

■ **HARDINESS** Fully hardy ✽✽✽ to half-hardy ✽.

■ **CULTIVATION** Violas like fertile, humus-rich, moist but well-drained soil, in full sun or partial shade. Violas can be short-lived, so it is best to raise new plants regularly. ■ **Sow** seed (*see pp.328–329*) in late winter for summer flowers, or in summer for winter or spring blooms. ■ **Take** softwood cuttings of perennials (*see pp.329–330*) in spring or late summer.

***Viola* 'Nellie Britton'** ♀
‡15cm (30cm) ↔30cm (12in), clump-forming, evergreen perennial, abundant flowers, 2.5cm (1in) across, all summer ✽✽✽

Viola tricolor (Heartsease, Love-in-idleness, Wild pansy)
‡8–13cm (3–5in) ↔10–15cm (4–6in), annual, biennial, or short-lived evergreen perennial, flowers from spring to autumn ✽✽✽

***Viola* 'Jeannie Bellew'**
‡20–23cm (8–9in) ↔25–30cm (10–12in), bushy, spreading perennial, flowers from mid-spring to mid-autumn ✽✽✽

***Viola* 'Rebecca'**
‡10cm (4in) ↔25cm (10in), spreading perennial, heavily scented flowers – tinged blue in cold conditions – borne in summer ✽✽✽

***Viola* 'Jackanapes'** ♀
‡13cm (5in) ↔30cm (12in), clump-forming, short-lived, evergreen perennial, 2cm (³⁄₄in) flowers in late spring and summer ✽✽✽

Waldsteinia
Barren strawberry

LATE SPRING TO EARLY SUMMER

Excellent as ground cover for a shady spot, waldsteinias quickly carpet the earth with small tufts of lush, green foliage, which resembles that of the strawberry plant (*see Frageria, p.203*). The foliage is in turn smothered in bright yellow flowers, either singly or in small, loose clusters, from late spring to early summer. These trouble-free, herbaceous or semi-evergreen perennials cover the ground by means of creeping stems (rhizomes) that spread underground and produce a weed-suppressing mat. They can be invasive in favourable conditions. Waldsteinias are happy in a woodland garden, at the front of shady mixed beds, borders, or banks, or in herbaceous borders.

■ **HARDINESS** Fully hardy ✳✳✳.
■ **CULTIVATION** Any moderately fertile soil in full or partial shade suits this undemanding plant. ■ **Divide** mature plants (*see p.330*) in early spring. ■ **Sow** seed (*see pp.328–329*) in containers in spring or autumn and place in a cold frame overwinter.

Waldsteinia ternata
‡10cm (4in) ↔ 60cm (24in), vigorous semi-evergreen, leaves to 6cm (2¹/₂in) long, flowers up to 1.5cm (¹/₂in) across

Zantedeschia
Arum lily

SPRING AND SUMMER

These imposing, architectural perennials have lush foliage and large and elegant, funnel-shaped blooms. The flowers are borne in spring and summer on stems up to 90cm (36in) tall and are usually clear yellow, although white, pink, lilac, or dark purple forms are available. The large leaves are arrow-shaped and sometimes spotted. *Zantesdeschia aethiopica* can be grown in moist borders, where it can form large clumps, or as a marginal aquatic plant in water up to 30cm (12in) deep, in an aquatic basket (*see p.321*).

■ **HARDINESS** Fully hardy ✳✳✳ to frost-tender ❀.
■ **CULTIVATION** *Z. aethiopica* needs moist soil, enriched with organic matter, in full sun. In frost-prone areas, protect the crowns with a deep winter mulch. *Z. elliottiana* is best raised in pots under frost-free glass and stood outside for summer display. Use a soil-based compost and feed weekly at flowering time. ■ **Divide** (*see p.330*) in spring. ■ **Sow** seed (*see pp.328–329*) at 21–27°C (70–81°F).

Zantedeschia elliottiana ♀ (Golden arum)
‡60–90cm (24–36in) ↔ 20cm (8in), erect habit, leaves to 45cm (8in) long, flowers 15cm (6in) long in summer ❀

Bamboos and Grasses

Grasses are an autumn blessing: silhouetted against clear skies, their long-lasting, fluffy or feathery flowerheads help extend the season of interest and look just as graceful when they go to seed. Some also have colour to contribute as their foliage turns brown or bronze – and they hold these tones through the winter, giving structure during the bleakest months of the year.

Top: *Carex pendula*
From left to right: *Briza maxima*; *Hordeum jubatum*;
Pleioblastus auricomus; *Stipa gigantea*; *Sasa veitchii*

Choosing grassy plants

Ornamental grasses include several groups of grass-like plants. True grasses include lawn grasses; they may be annual or perennial and most have flowerheads formed of many tiny flowers in clusters or spikes. Bamboos are very large, handsome, evergreen grasses with segmented woody stems, or canes, and delicate, divided leaves. Many are vigorous and, once established, can spread over a large area. Rushes have tightly packed, upright leaves arising straight out of the soil. They prefer moist or wet conditions, and thrive in pond margins. Sedges are low-growing, usually perennial and evergreen, and valued for their foliage. Their stems feel distinctly ridged.

Planting ideas

Many grassy plants thrive in most situations. True grasses may tolerate very dry conditions, but rushes and sedges prefer moister soils. Before planting, however, it is a good idea to incorporate plenty of well-rotted organic matter into dry soils to ensure moisture retention. Heavier clay soils need coarse grit dug in to improve drainage. Grasses require little further attention, apart from cutting down old foliage in spring.

There are plenty of ways to use ornamental grasses, bamboos, and sedges. For example, large grasses like pampas grass (*Cortaderia*) and *Stipa gigantea* make excellent specimens in sunny gravel gardens. Alternatively, take advantage of the wonderful contrasts of foliage colour, shape, and height by planting them in drifts, creating a dedicated border that shimmers and changes with every passing breeze. Vary the pace by placing tall, bold grasses next to fine-leaved ones.

Grasses and sedges are equally at home in mixed or herbaceous borders. They provide the perfect foil to broad-leaved hostas or bright flowering annuals and perennials. Their slender stems allow you to glimpse other flowering plants through them, giving a light, airy feel to the planting. Tall grasses can be planted in clumps at intervals to act as focal points, or grown as a screen – bamboos with coloured stems are a handsome choice.

Pampas grass (*Cortaderia*) is a dramatic plant; it adds height to a border and the plumes last throughout the winter.

Pennisetum villosum
p.295

Festuca glauca *p.291*

Milium effusum 'Aureum' *p.294*

Deschampsia cespitosa 'Goldtau' *p.291*

Sasa veitchii *p.297*

Briza maxima *p.288*

Pennisetum alopecuroides 'Hameln' *p.295*

Carex pendula *p.289*

Cortaderia selloana 'Pumila' *p.290*

Semiarundinaria fastuosa *p.298*

Helictotrichon sempervirens *p.292*

Cortaderia selloana *p.290*

Schoenoplectus lacustris 'Zebrinus' *p.298*

Pleioblastus variegatus *p.297*

Lagurus ovatus *p.293*

Phyllostachys nigra *p.296*

Alopecurus
Foxtail grass

MID-SPRING TO AUTUMN

Foxtail grasses make low, loose, spreading clumps of flat leaves, and in spring and summer bear dense, narrow, hairy spikes of flowers that resemble a fox's brush. Although spreading, they are not invasive, so are suitable for borders and rock gardens. The tall flowering stems make them interesting plants for growing in containers. The blue-green perennial *Alopecurus lanatus*, with its leaves covered in fine hairs, hates winter wet so use in alpine-style rock gardens. The fine, striped foliage of the perennial *A. pratensis* 'Aureovariegatus' acts as a perfect contrast to plants with large, flat leaves, such as hostas (*see pp.218–219*). There are also annual foxtail grasses.

■ **HARDINESS** Fully hardy ✹✹✹.
■ **CULTIVATION** Grow in gritty, well-drained soil in sun or partial shade. On heavier soils, dig in coarse grit to improve drainage. ■ **Cut back** old foliage in spring to get the best foliage effect from new growth. ■ **Sow** seed (*see pp.328–329*) in containers in a cold frame as soon as it is ripe, or in spring. ■ **Lift** and divide the plants (*see p.330*) carefully in spring or early summer.

Alopecurus pratensis **'Aureovariegatus'**
↕ to 1.2m (4ft) ↔ 40cm (16in), produces spikes of flowers from mid-spring to midsummer

Briza
Quaking grass

LATE SPRING TO AUTUMN

The delicate shimmering effect created by the drooping heads of these grasses in the smallest summer breeze adds movement and interest to any border or rock garden, and gives the plants their common name. The flowers, almost hop-like, are tinged red-brown or purple when young, and turn straw-coloured in autumn. They are popular for dried flower displays, either in their natural state or dyed. The loose tufts of narrow leaves vary in colour from light green to blue-green. There are three commonly grown quaking grasses: the largest, *Briza media*, at 60–90cm (2–3ft), is a perennial, while *B. maxima* (*see below*) and *B. minor*, the smallest at 45cm (18in), are annuals.

■ **HARDINESS** Fully hardy ✹✹✹.
■ **CULTIVATION** All types require a well-drained soil. Grow the annual species in any such soil with a site in full sun; perennial species will tolerate a range of soils and a position in sun or partial shade. ■ **Sow** seed of annuals where they are grown in spring (*see pp.328–329*).
■ **Divide** perennials (*see p.330*) from mid-spring to midsummer.

Briza maxima (Greater quaking grass)
↕ 45–60m (18–24in) ↔ 25cm (10in), flowerheads from late spring to late summer

Calamagrostis
Reed grass

SPRING TO AUTUMN

The most widely grown reed grasses are cultivars of *Calamagrostis* x *acutiflora*. These are perennial grasses, generally slow-spreading and clump-forming, with particularly soft and elegant plumes of flowers. Their architectural forms add height to borders, while their open habits allow you to see other plants growing behind them. They give excellent value through the year, coming into growth early and bearing open clusters of summer flowers that slowly compress to become narrow seedheads that are retained through the autumn. 'Karl Foerster' has pink-bronze flowers fading to buff; 'Stricta' has red-brown flowers; and 'Overdam' has purplish summer flowers that fade to pale pink.

■ **HARDINESS** Fully hardy ✹✹✹.
■ **CULTIVATION** Grow in moist soil, ideally enriched with plenty of well-rotted organic matter, but all but the poorest soils are tolerated. Position in sun or partial shade.
■ **Leave** the season's growth uncut for winter effect, then cut down in early spring, before new growth starts. ■ **Divide** overgrown clumps in spring (*see p.330*).

Calamagrostis x *acutiflora* **'Overdam'**
↕ to 1.2m (4ft) ↔ 60cm (24in), pale yellow edges and stripes on the leaves, which fade to pink-flushed white as they age

Carex
Sedge

These grassy, tufted perennials are grown mainly for their form, and the colours or markings on their long, narrow leaves. There are many sedges in shades of copper or russet, and others striped with gold or silvery white. Mixed groups – for example, rich yellow *Carex elata* 'Aurea' next to the red-brown *C. flagellifera* – create unusual colour contrasts. Some also have attractive clusters of flowers, drooping in *C. pendula*, or spiky seedheads, like *C. grayi*. Most are evergreen, some deciduous, and while some prefer a damp spot, others are very unfussy.

■ **HARDINESS** All sedges described here are fully hardy ✻✻✻. Others from New Zealand, such as *C. conica*, *C. morrowii*, and *C. comans* 'Frosted Curls' are frost-hardy ✻✻, and benefit from a winter mulch.
■ **CULTIVATION** Sedges can be grouped by their differing cultivation requirements.
■ **Group 1** will thrive in any soil in sun or partial shade. ■ **Group 2** needs a moist, fertile, but well-drained alkaline soil and a position in sun or partial shade. ■ **Group 3** includes *C. flagellifera* and *C. siderosticha* 'Variegata' and requires fertile, moist or wet soil in sun or partial shade.

■ **Cut back** deciduous species in spring. Trim out any dead leaves on evergreen species in summer. ■ **Divide** plants (*see p.330*) between mid-spring and early summer. Aphids (*see p.332*) occasionally attack the bases of the stems.

Carex testacea
‡to 1.5m (5ft) ↔ 60cm (24in), group 1, evergreen

Carex oshimensis 'Evergold' ♀
‡30cm (12in) ↔ 35cm (14in), group 2, evergreen

Carex elata 'Aurea' ♀ (Bowles' golden sedge)
‡to 70cm (28in) ↔ 45cm (18in), group 3, deciduous

Carex pendula (Weeping sedge)
‡to 1.4m (4½ft) ↔ to 1.5m (5ft), group 3, evergreen, self-seeds freely

Chusquea

SPRING TO AUTUMN

This large group of bamboos form dense clumps of glossy, solid canes. They make distinctive evergreen specimens in a lawn or in a woodland garden, or can be grown with large ferns, such as *Woodwardia radicans* (*see p.309*), for dramatic, contrasting foliage effects. They are a good choice for a coastal garden. The hardy types, the most popular being *Chusquea culeou*, reach 6m (20ft). The stems are yellowish, with tapering, papery white leaf sheaths. These stay on the plant for the first year, giving an attractive striped appearance. Clusters of sideshoots grow from the leaf joints, bearing many thin, mid-green leaves. When leaves fall from the lower part of older canes, the branching growth and leaf stalks remain at the tips, giving them a "whiskery" look.

■ **HARDINESS** Fully hardy ✳✳✳ to frost-tender ✿.
■ **CULTIVATION** Grow chusquea in well-drained soil, enriched with plenty of well-rotted organic matter. Position in sun or partial shade, with shelter from cold, drying winds. ■ **Divide** clumps (*see p.330*) in spring.

Chusquea culeou ♀
↕to 6m (20ft) ↔2.5m (8ft), canes become very chunky, up to 3cm (1¼in) across ✳✳✳

Cortaderia

Pampas grass, Tussock grass

LATE SUMMER

Large and stately evergreen grasses, these are grown for their arching, ornamental foliage and large, feathery plumes of flowers in shades of white and silver. They form dense clumps of stiff, narrow, leaves with sharp edges (take care when siting it in family gardens), with flowers held on strong, upright stems above the foliage. The plumes can be used fresh or dried in flower arrangements. Pampas grass has a "retro" image, and still looks rather kitsch in a lawn or front garden, but it makes a fine full stop to a border, perhaps in front of a dark green hedge that will highlight its silvery plumes, or can be used to add often needed height and drama to a modern planting scheme of perennials and grasses.

***Cortaderia selloana* 'Pumila'** ♀
↕to 1.5m (5ft) ↔to 1.2m (4ft), flowerheads open in late summer ✳✳✳

■ **HARDINESS** Fully hardy ✳✳✳ to frost-hardy ✳✳.
■ **CULTIVATION** Grow in fertile, well-drained soil in full sun with plenty of space to develop.
■ **Protect** the crowns of young plants in their first winter, and plants of all ages in cold areas, with a winter mulch. ■ **Cut back** the old and dead growth in late winter or early spring; but take care because the leaf edges are sharp.
■ **Sow** seed (*see pp.328–329*) with bottom heat in spring. ■ **Divide** (*see p.330*) in spring.

Cortaderia selloana
↕2.5–3m (8–10ft) ↔1.5m (5ft), flower spikes, often flushed pink or purple, appear from late summer ✳✳✳

***Cortaderia selloana* 'Sunningdale Silver'** ♀
↕3m (10ft) or more ↔to 2.5m (8ft) ✳✳✳

Deschampsia
Hair grass
SUMMER TO AUTUMN

Cloud-like, airy flowerheads and graceful habits make these perennial grasses worth including in any garden. The tussocks of thread-like leaves may be evergreen or deciduous. Many of the hair grasses are cultivars of *Deschampsia cespitosa*, with flowers from silvery reddish-brown to gold, changing colour in autumn. This species grows up to 2m (6ft) tall, although it has several more compact varieties; *D. flexuosa*, at 60cm (24in), suits smaller gardens. All are effective alongside plants with open clusters of flowers, such as *Campanula lactiflora* (*see p.173*); the soft lilac-pink flowers of *C. lactiflora* 'Loddon Anna', for example, contrast perfectly with the flowers of *D. cespitosa* 'Goldtau'.

■ **HARDINESS** Fully hardy ✳✳✳.
■ **CULTIVATION** Best in neutral to acid soil. Dig in organic matter if your soil is light and sandy, to help retain moisture. Position in sun or part shade. ■ **Prune** old flowerheads in spring before new growth begins. ■ **Sow** seed in autumn or spring where plants are to grow (*see pp.328–329*). ■ **Divide** (*see p.330*) in spring.

***Deschampsia cespitosa* 'Goldtau'**
↕↔to 75cm (30in), reddish-silver flowerheads mature from early to late summer to golden yellow

Fargesia
YEAR-ROUND

These clump-forming bamboos have slender, arching stems and lance-shaped leaves growing from purplish sheaths. The large, striking *Fargesia murielae* makes a fine focal point or a hardy hedging or screening plant. The stems are white-powdery when young, maturing to yellow-green and then yellow. They arch under the weight of the leaves, which are up to 15cm (6in) long, with drawn-out tips. The leaf sheaths age to pale brown. For wonderful foliage contrast, grow it next to the bold gunnera (*see p.211*), although you will need a fair amount of space. The similarly large *F. nitida* has very slender, purplish canes and long, narrow leaves, which give it a more airy, delicate appearance, despite its hardiness.

■ **HARDINESS** Fully hardy ✳✳✳ to half-hardy ✳.
■ **CULTIVATION** Grow in fertile, moisture-retentive soil. Position *F. nitida* in dappled shade with shelter; *F. murielae* will tolerate full sun and windy sites. ■ **Divide** established clumps (*see p.330*). Take root cuttings (*see p.330*) of lengths of underground stem (rhizomes) in spring.

***Fargesia murielae* ♀** (Umbrella bamboo)
↕to 4m (12ft) ↔to 1.5m (5ft) ✳✳✳

Festuca
Fescue
EARLY SUMMER TO AUTUMN

Fescues are a large, varied group, deciduous and evergreen, mostly suited to sunny positions. They are grown mainly for the narrow, arching, smooth leaves, but also bear flowerheads that fade to golden shades. The densely tufted evergreen perennial *Festuca glauca* and its many new cultivars are very popular; the larger *F. amethystina*, which turns purplish after flowering, is also attractive. Grow fescues as edging or to provide a contrast to other smallish plants with bolder leaves: most are too small to make specimen plants. Blue flowers, like those of felicias (*see p.202*), complement the steely blue of *F. glauca*, while silver foliage plants, such as *Stachys byzantina* (*see p.273*), make a wonderful contrast.

■ **HARDINESS** Fully hardy ✳✳✳.
■ **CULTIVATION** Grow in poor to moderately fertile, well-drained soil, in full sun. ■ **Sow** seed (*see pp.328–329*) from autumn until spring in containers in a cold frame. ■ **Divide** (*see p.330*) in spring every two to three years to maintain good foliage colour and keep plants vigorous.

***Festuca glauca* (Blue fescue)**
↕to 30cm (12in) ↔25cm (10in) evergreen, violet to blue-green flowerheads in early and midsummer

Glyceria maxima
Sweet grass, Manna grass
SPRING TO LATE SUMMER

This is a dense, vigorous, spreading perennial. Unusually for grasses, it grows naturally not just along the damp edges of ponds or streams, but also in shallow water, to a depth of 75cm (30in). There are many forms, but the only one widely grown is *Glyceria maxima* var. *variegata*. This has narrow, strappy leaves; tinged with pink when they emerge in spring, they later become deep green striped with white. Plume-like clusters of green to purplish-green flowers appear in mid- and late summer on reed-like stems. It is useful for shading and softening the edges of a large pool, or in problem sites with wet soil, but with its invasive, spreading habit it may best be grown in a container or planting basket if the conditions in your garden suit it too well.

■ **HARDINESS** Fully hardy ✷✷✷.
■ **CULTIVATION** Grow *G. maxima* var. *variegata* in any moisture-retentive soil, or in water to 15cm (6in) deep, planted in an aquatic basket to restrict the spread of the roots. It also needs full sun. ■ **Divide** in spring (*see p.330*).

Glyceria maxima* var. *variegata
‡80cm (32in) ↔ indefinite, can become invasive both in ponds and in damp soil

Hakonechloa macra
Hakone grass
SPRING TO AUTUMN

This brightly coloured grass brings warmth and light to low-level plantings or the front of a border, forming a dense mound of narrow, arching, pale green leaves and producing reddish-brown flower spikes in summer. It is a deciduous perennial, flushed with orange and rust in autumn and slowly spreading to form mats. The leaves of hakone grass remain on the plant well into winter and often keep their colour, forming a bright splash in winter. This is one of the most attractive ornamental grasses to grow in containers on a patio, forming a neat, bushy mop of gently arching foliage that will almost completely cover its pot. There are several cultivars with differing variegation.

■ **HARDINESS** Fully hardy ✷✷✷.
■ **CULTIVATION** Grow in fertile soil enriched with well-rotted organic matter, or loam-based potting compost, in full sun or partial shade. ■ **Cut off** the old foliage of hakone grass in autumn if its winter show is not wanted, or in spring. ■ **Divide** plants (*see p.330*) in spring.

***Hakonechloa macra* 'Aureola'** ♀
‡35cm (14in) ↔ 40cm (16in), leaves flushed red in autumn, is best grown in partial shade

Helictotrichon
EARLY SUMMER TO AUTUMN

Forming tussocks of leaves in shades of blue-grey or mid- to light green, these grasses come from open sites, often with poor soils. They are particularly suited to the conditions offered by rock gardens or gravel plantings, but are happy in borders with well-drained soil. There are many perennial deciduous and evergreen species. In summer, nodding clusters of flowers glisten in the light; these age to a straw colour. *Helictotrichon sempervirens*, is especially popular, forming a dense, fine clump of tightly rolled leaves. Its flattened spikes of flowers, tinged with purple, have a graceful habit. These grasses make good specimens and associate well with purple or silver foliage plants.

■ **HARDINESS** Fully hardy ✷✷✷.
■ **CULTIVATION** Grow in well-drained, poor to moderately fertile soil, preferably alkaline (limy), in full sun. ■ **Cut back** dead foliage and flowers in spring. ■ **Sow** seed (*see pp.328–329*) in spring in containers in a cold frame or on a windowsill. ■ **Divide** (*see p.330*) in spring. Rust (*see p.333*) can be a problem, particularly in damp summers, but can be treated with a suitable fungicide.

***Helictotrichon sempervirens* ♀ (Blue oat grass)**
‡to 1.4m (4ft) ↔ 60cm (24in), evergreen, flower spikes in early and midsummer

Hordeum
Barley

This group of ornamental grasses contains about 20 annual and perennial species and includes the cereal crop, barley. The narrow leaves may be flat or rolled, and range from light to mid-green or blue-green. Flowers are produced in dense, cylindrical, or flattened spikes with distinctive long bristles. The type most often grown in gardens is *Hordeum jubatum* (see below). Squirrel tail grass is often grown as an annual with hardy annual "wild flowers" such as cornflowers (*Centaurea, see p.176*); a pretty look for a garden bordering open countryside. Many species are especially good to use in dried flower arrangements. They also look good growing in a wild garden or meadow planting, or among blue campanulas (*see p.173*).

■ **HARDINESS** Fully hardy ✳✳✳.
■ **CULTIVATION** Grow barley in moderately fertile, well-drained soil, in full sun. ■ **Sow** seed where it is to grow (*see pp.328–329*) in spring or autumn. ■ **Cut** flowerheads for drying before they are fully mature.

Hordeum jubatum (Squirrel tail grass)
↕50cm (20in) ↔30cm (12in), annual or perennial, red- or purple-flushed flowers from early to midsummer that fade to beige

Lagurus ovatus
Hare's tail

This annual grass grows naturally in open spaces in the Mediterranean region. It is valued for the appealing, softly hairy flowerheads that give it its name. These are pale green, tinged with purple, and mature to a pale, creamy buff colour in late summer and autumn. The flat, narrow leaves are pale green. A small and unassuming plant, hare's tail has most impact when planted in groups. It is best grown in drifts or among other hardy annuals such as calendulas (*see p.171*), cosmos (*see p.182*), and annual chrysanthemums (*see pp.178–179*). It also makes a useful gap-filler in mixed and herbaceous borders. The flowerheads can be used in fresh or dried flower arrangements.

■ **HARDINESS** Fully hardy ✳✳✳.
■ **CULTIVATION** Hare's tail prefers light, sandy soil that is well-drained and moderately fertile. Position in full sun. ■ **Sow** seed (*see pp.328–329*) in spring where the plants are to grow, or in containers in a cold frame in autumn. ■ **Pick** flowerheads to be used for drying before they are fully mature.

Lagurus ovatus ♀
↕to 50cm (20in) ↔30cm (12in)

Luzula
Woodrush

Valued for their tolerance of shade, these rushes provide good ground cover in woodland or mixed borders. Woodrushes are mostly evergreen perennials from heaths, moors, and scrubby woodland, forming tussocks of grassy leaves with white hairs on them, particularly along the edges. Clusters of tiny flowers are produced in spring or summer. The greater woodrush, *Luzula sylvatica*, will grow in dry shade and makes an excellent, weed-suppressing ground cover. Its leaves are glossy, dark green, and in mid-spring and early summer it bears chestnut-brown flowers in open clusters. Snowy woodrush, *L. nivea*, has pure white flowers that appear in early and midsummer.

■ **HARDINESS** Fully hardy ✳✳✳.
■ **CULTIVATION** Grow in poor to reasonably fertile, well-drained soil. Position in partial or deep shade; woodrushes can be grown in full sun where the soil is always moist. ■ **Sow** seed (*see pp.328–329*) in containers in spring or autumn. ■ **Divide** plants (*see p.330*) between spring and early summer.

***Luzula sylvatica* 'Aurea'**
↕to 70–80cm (28–32in) ↔45cm (18in), yellow-green leaves become bright, shiny yellow in winter, needs light, dappled shade

Milium
Wood millet

Mainly woodland grasses, these are a small group of annuals and perennials. The leaves are sometimes quite broad, and yellow-green to light green. Open, delicate flower clusters appear from spring to midsummer. Milium adds a bright splash of colour to herbaceous borders or the dappled shade at the edge of a woodland. Plants with dark green leaves, such as astilbes (*see p.164*) or some hostas (*see pp.218–219*), will highlight the leaf colour. *Milium effusum* 'Aureum' has smooth, flat, arching, golden leaves, at their best in early spring, fading slightly as summer goes on. Miliums associate well with other grasses such as pennisetums (*see facing page*) or woodrushes (*Luzula, see p.293*).

■ **HARDINESS** Fully hardy ✳✳✳.
■ **CULTIVATION** Grow in fertile, moist but well-drained soil with plenty of organic matter. Position in partial shade; may be grown in sun if the soil remains moist at all times. ■ **Sow** wood millet seed (*see pp.328–329*) outdoors in spring. ■ **Divide** (*see p.330*) in spring.and early summer.

***Milium effusum* 'Aureum'** ♀
(Bowles' golden grass)
‡to 60cm (24in) ↔30cm (12in), perennial with gold flower spikes from late spring to midsummer

Miscanthus

Graceful specimen plants in a lawn or in borders, these wonderful grasses add height without over-powering other plants. They bring movement and a rustling sound in the lightest breeze, and although they look delicate, the flowering stems stand up well to wind; this and their often fine autumn colour gives them added value late in the season. Miscanthus form large clumps of arching, narrow, light green foliage. Many cultivars of eulalia grass (*Miscanthus sinensis*) are widely grown. During late summer and autumn, they produce large, distinctive tassels of silky, hairy flowers, some red-tinted, others silvery. These grasses are deciduous, but the dying foliage of many develops russet or golden tints in autumn.

■ **HARDINESS** Fully hardy ✳✳✳ to frost-hardy ✳✳.
■ **CULTIVATION** Grow best in fertile, moist but well-drained soil in full sun. May be slow to settle in. ■ **Protect** from excessive winter rains. ■ **Cut** old foliage to the ground in early spring. ■ **Sow** seed (*see pp.328–329*) in spring in a cold frame or on the windowsill. ■ **Divide** plants (*see p.330*) as new growth emerges in spring.

***Miscanthus sinensis* 'Silberfeder'** ♀
‡to 2.5m (8ft) ↔1.2m (4ft), abundant flowerheads that age to silver and are retained into winter, particularly dislikes wet soil ✳✳✳

***Miscanthus sinensis* 'Zebrinus'** ♀
(Zebra grass)
‡to 1.2m (4ft) ↔1.2m (4ft), the most spreading of several striped cultivars ✳✳✳

***Miscanthus sinensis* 'Gracillimus'**
(Maiden grass)
‡1.3m (4½ft) ↔1.2m (4ft), dense, fine leaves with good bronze tints in autumn, may not flower in cooler summers ✳✳✳

Molinia caerulea
Purple moor grass
SPRING TO AUTUMN

Only this species is grown in gardens, but there are a number of different varieties. These are tall and slender grasses, making excellent structural plants for borders, or for the far edges of informal ponds. They are grown for their attractive habits, forming clumps of narrow, dark green leaves, and for dense, purple flower spikes, which are held on graceful, arching, golden stems from spring to autumn. The flowerheads and leaves in some cultivars turn shades of golden yellow in autumn, but the flowering stems do not usually last into winter. A beautiful way to highlight the purple flowers is by growing tall, pale blue delphiniums (*see pp.118–119*) behind it.

■ **HARDINESS** Fully hardy ✻✻✻.
■ **CULTIVATION** Grow in any moist but well-drained soil, preferably acid to neutral (lime-free), in full sun or partial shade. ■ **Sow** seed (*see pp.328–329*) in spring in containers in a cold frame or on the windowsill. ■ **Divide** (*see p.330*) in spring and pot up until they become established and then replant in the garden.

Molinia caerulea subsp. *arundinacea*
↕ to 1.5m (5ft) ↔ 40cm (16in), this subspecies and its cultivars are particularly noted for their autumn colour

Pennisetum
SUMMER AND AUTUMN

These ornamental grasses are grown for their feathery flowers or over-arching stems, produced in summer and autumn, and are popular in fresh and dried flower arrangements. Several types of these clump-forming perennials and annuals are grown in gardens. The evergreen fountain grass, *Pennisetum alopecuroides* (*see right*), which groes up to 1.5m (5ft) tall, has flat, dark green leaves, with bottlebrush-shaped, bristly flowerheads in shades of yellowish-green to dark purple. The smaller, deciduous fountain grass, *P. orientale*, has distinctive, pink flowerheads and combines well with Mediterranean plants such as lavenders (*Lavandula, see p.71*). Feathertop, *P. villosum* (*see below*), although a deciduous perennial, is often grown as an annual in cool climates.

Pennisetum villosum ♀ (Feathertop)
↕ ↔ 60cm (24in), flat leaves, soft flowerheads in late summer and early autumn, maturing to purple ✻✻

■ **HARDINESS** Fully hardy ✻✻✻ to frost-tender ❀.
■ **CULTIVATION** Grow in light, reasonably fertile soil in full sun. ■ **Cut back** dead growth in spring. ■ **Sow** seed (*see p.328–329*) in heat in early spring. ■ **Divide** plants (*see p.330*) in late spring or early summer.

Pennisetum alopecuroides 'Hameln'
↕ ↔ 50cm (20in), compact and early flowering, dark-green leaves turn golden yellow in autumn, may not survive cold, wet winters ✻✻

Phalaris arundinacea
Reed canary grass, Ribbon grass
EARLY TO LATE SUMMER

This spreading perennial and its cultivars are widely grown. It is an erect, evergreen grass with flat leaves. From early to midsummer, it bears narrow clusters of silky, pale green flowers that age to buff. It makes highly effective ground cover, crowding out weeds, and looks at home by a pond or stream. This grass can be invasive, so needs plenty of space or firm control: lift and divide regularly when growing in small spaces. There are several variegated cultivars. *Platycodon grandiflorus* (*see p.257*) is a striking plant to grow alongside these grasses – its blue flowers will be highlighted by the bright white stripes on the foliage.

■ **HARDINESS** Fully hardy ✳✳✳.
■ **CULTIVATION** Tolerates any soil in full sun or partial shade. Contain its spread if necessary by planting it in a sunken, bottomless half-barrel. ■ **Cut back** the dead foliage in spring. Variegated types may revert to plain green foliage in midsummer; cut down all but young shoots in early summer to encourage new, variegated foliage. ■ **Divide** plants (*see p.330*) from mid-spring to midsummer.

Phalaris arundinacea* var. *picta (Gardener's garters)
↕to 1m (3ft) ↔indefinite, variable, white-striped leaves, classic pond- and stream-side plant

Phyllostachys
Black, Golden, or Zigzag bamboo
YEAR-ROUND

Valued for their graceful forms, fine stems, and rustling foliage, these medium to large, evergreen bamboos can be included in almost any garden. They spread by underground stems (rhizomes) to form slowly expanding clumps, but can become invasive in mild gardens. Phyllostachys can be grown in either shrub borders or in containers outdoors. They also thrive in woodland gardens and have become popular as an elegant alternative to traditional hedging plants. These bamboos are particularly noted for

Phyllostachys nigra ♀ (Black bamboo)
↕3–5m (10–15ft) ↔2–3m (6–10ft), arching, slender young canes are green, turning to shiny black over two years

their grooved, beautifully coloured stems: brilliant yellow in *Phyllostachys aureosulcata* f. *aureocaulis* or purple in *P. violascens*. They often grow in a zig-zag fashion – hence one of their common names – and have a branching habit, bearing fairly small leaves.

■ **HARDINESS** Fully hardy ✳✳✳.
■ **CULTIVATION** Grow in well-drained soil enriched with well-rotted organic matter. Position in full sun or dappled shade. In containers, use a soil-based compost such as John Innes No.3 and feed with a liquid fertilizer monthly. ■ **Shelter** from cold, drying winds that can scorch leaf edges. ■ **Cut out** some of the old canes each year. ■ **Divide** clumps (*see p.330*) in spring.

Phyllostachys aurea ♀ (Golden, or Fishpole bamboo)
↕2–10m (6–30ft) ↔indefinite, upright young canes are mid-green, maturing to brownish-yellow

Pleioblastus

YEAR-ROUND

Most pleioblastus are dwarf only in relation to other bamboos, most being 1–1.5m (3–5ft) in height, although the pygmy bamboo, *Pleioblastus pygmaeus*, grows to only 40cm (16in) tall. This generally reduced stature makes them ideal bamboos for containers, as they will not appear top-heavy. Growing them in large pots also has the advantage of restraining their vigorously spreading habit, the pygmy bamboo being a particular offender in this respect. *P. auricomus* (syn. *P. viridistriatus*; *see p.284*) and *P. variegatus* are naturally more restrained. They make dense thickets of erect, leafy canes, and while they will thrive in open woodland glades, enjoying the shelter, they should be used cautiously in borders.

■ **HARDINESS** Fully hardy ✿✿✿.
■ **CULTIVATION** Grow in moist, well-drained soil enriched with well-rotted organic matter. Position in full sun or partial shade, sheltered from cold, drying winds that may scorch leaf edges. ■ **Restrain** their spread by confining the roots if necessary. ■ **Take** root cuttings in spring and plant out widely spaced, keeping the soil reliably moist until plants are established.

Pleioblastus variegatus ♀
‡75cm (30in) ↔1.2m (4ft), leaves hairy, pale green canes

Pseudosasa

YEAR-ROUND

Grown for their erect, woody canes, this small group of robust, thicket-forming bamboos require quite a bit of space. They do have features that strongly recommend them in spite of this, making excellent screening plants to hide ugly structures, such as sheds or compost heaps. Cooler climates help to keep them clump-forming rather than invasive, but *Pseudosasa amabilis* may look ragged if not sheltered. The leaf sheaths tend to remain on the stems for some time, giving a striped appearance. The leaves are generally large, lance-shaped, and mid- or dark green. Rarely, small spike-like green flowers are produced. Unlike many bamboos, these often survive flowering, although they are weakened.

■ **HARDINESS** Fully hardy ✿✿✿.
■ **CULTIVATION** Grow in moist but well-drained, fertile soil; *P. japonica* tolerates poor, dry, or wet soils. Position in sun or partial shade. ■ **Divide** the clumps (*see p.330*) in spring and keep the divisions moist until they are well established. ■ **Cut back** plants if they flower, and apply fertilizer and a deep organic mulch.

Pseudosasa japonica ♀ (Arrow bamboo)
‡6m (20ft) ↔ indeterminate, canes are olive green when young and mature to pale beige, stands up well to winds

Sasa

YEAR-ROUND

These thicket-forming bamboos are small to medium in height, and grown as much for their handsome foliage as for their canes. The leaves are large and turn white and dry around the edges from autumn onwards, giving a variegated appearance. Sasas are useful for ground cover, or as a hedge if you have the space. The moderately spreading *Sasa veitchii* is invaluable under trees, tolerating deep shade: its natural habitat is in damp hollows in woodland. More rampant is the broad-leaved *S. palmata* and the purple-streaked canes of *S. palmata* f. *nebulosa* are attractive, but this is definitely a bamboo to plant only where there is plenty of space.

■ **HARDINESS** Fully hardy ✿✿✿.
■ **CULTIVATION** Tolerant of most sites and soils, except for dry soils in full sun. Dig in well-rotted organic matter before planting. Contain its spread by growing in a large tub that has been sunk in the soil. ■ **Divide** plants (*see p.330*) in spring, or cut off pieces of rhizomes (underground stems).

Sasa veitchii
‡1.2–2m (4–6ft) ↔ indefinite, slender, purple canes are smooth and round with a fine bloom, bristly sheaths protect new leaves

Schoenoplectus

Bullrush, Club-rush

EARLY TO LATE SUMMER

This group of sedges includes both annuals and evergreen perennials, suitable for a bog garden or as aquatic plants in still or gently moving water. They are valued mainly for their stems and for their grassy leaves. Growing in planting baskets around the edges of a pond, the narrow foliage makes an interesting textural contrast to the broader leaves of water irises (*see pp.222–223*). The brown flowers are borne from early to late summer, but are a fairly low-key display. Among the most widely grown is the variegated club-rush *Schoenoplectus lacustris* 'Zebrinus': striking stems are reminiscent of tiny tide-marker poles rising from the water.

■ **HARDINESS** Fully hardy ✳✳✳.
■ **CULTIVATION** Grow in fertile, wet soil or in water to a depth of up to 30cm (12in) and in a position in full sun. ■ **Restrict** growth in small ponds by cutting back the roots every year. ■ **Cut out** any plain green stems to the ground on variegated rushes. ■ **Propagate** by uprooting and planting out sections of underground stem (rhizome) from mid-spring to midsummer.

Schoenoplectus lacustris 'Zebrinus'
‡1m (3ft) ↔ 60cm (24in), perennial, almost leafless stems arise at intervals from rhizomes

Semiarundinaria

YEAR-ROUND

These are tall, upright bamboos, forming thickets in warmer climates, but clumps in cooler climates. These bamboos are at home in a woodland garden, making elegant companions to slender, small-leaved trees such as birches (*Betula, see p.24*). Their strongly vertical forms also make fine informal screens if you have the space. The leaf sheaths often hang onto the canes by the bases for some time before falling. *Semiarundinaria fastuosa* is widely grown. The lower levels of its canes are bare of leaves, making it ideal to position among lower plants in a shrub border. The glossy, mid-green canes have purple-brown stripes that are most prominent when the leaves are young.

■ **HARDINESS** Fully hardy ✳✳✳ to frost-hardy ✳✳.
■ **CULTIVATION** Grow in well-drained, reasonably fertile soil, adding plenty of well-rotted organic matter. Position in full sun or light shade. ■ **Divide** clumps (*see p.330*), or uproot and plant out sections of underground stem (rhizome) in spring. Young shoots may be damaged by slugs (*see p.332*).

Semiarundinaria fastuosa ♀
(Narihira bamboo)
‡to 7m (22ft) ↔ 2m (6ft) or more, glossy, mid-green leaves ✳✳✳

Spartina

Cord grass, Marsh grass

SUMMER TO AUTUMN

Adaptable and hardy, these herbaceous perennial grasses are found in swamps, marshes, and wet prairies. They are grown for their arching leaves and make excellent ground cover at the margins of ponds. In damp soil, they spread quickly by underground stems (rhizomes); they tolerate all but the driest soils, however, and the drier the soil, the easier they are to contain. Cord grasses tolerate salty conditions well, making them useful in coastal gardens. Grow prairie cord grass, *S. pectinata*, alongside late-flowering perennials that come from similar habitats, such as heleniums (*see p.212*) and rudbeckias (*see p.265*).

■ **HARDINESS** Fully hardy ✳✳✳.
■ **CULTIVATION** Grow in reasonably fertile, damp to well-drained soil with plenty of well-rotted organic matter added to it. They prefer full sun but tolerate light, dappled shade. ■ **Cut down** the old foliage in early spring. ■ **Divide** clumps (*see p.330*) in spring. Young shoots may be damaged by slugs (*see p.332*).

Spartina pectinata 'Aureomarginata'
‡to 2m (6ft) ↔ indefinite, retains its yellow autumn leaves and elegant silhouette during winter

Stipa

Feather grass, Needle grass,
Spear grass

SUMMER TO AUTUMN

This large group of perennial grasses
includes evergreen and deciduous
types that form lax tufts of narrow
foliage, above which tall flower stems
rustle and wave. The growth habit
alone is appealing; the flowering
display in summer and early autumn
is spectacular, ranging from the
ethereal, drooping flowers of *Stipa
arundinacea* (syn. *Anemanthele
lessoniana*) to the feathery, upright
S. tenuissima and the towering stems
of *S. gigantea*. Elegant in dried flower
arrangements, many feather grasses
age to rich golden yellow and russet,
keeping their colours into winter.
There is a range of shapes and sizes
suitable for use in most situations.
Plant *S. gigantea* in a border with the
tall, open *Verbena bonariensis* (*see
p.281*) to lend an airy feel to the
planting scheme.

■ **HARDINESS** Fully hardy ✲✲✲ to
frost-hardy ✲✲.
■ **CULTIVATION** Grow in any reasonably
fertile soil that is well-drained, in full sun. Dig
in some coarse grit on heavier soils to improve
drainage. ■ **Cut back** deciduous species in early
winter or spring. ■ **Sow** seed in containers in
spring (*see pp.328–329*). ■ **Divide** plants (*see
p.330*) from mid-spring to early summer.

Stipa gigantea ♀ (Giant feather grass,
Golden oats)
↕ to 2.5m (8ft) ↔ 1.2m (4ft), evergeen or
semi-evergreen, purple-green flowers are
gold when ripe in summer ✲✲✲

Stipa calamagrostis
↕ 1m (3ft) ↔ 1.2m (4ft), deciduous, blue-green
leaves, summer flowerheads are silvery and buff
to purplish-tinted ✲✲✲

Uncinia

Hook sedge

SUMMER TO AUTUMN

Generally grown for their shiny and
richly coloured, grassy leaves, these
evergreen sedges are small perennials
with a loosely tufted habit, at home in
damp places. Upright, triangular to
cylindrical stems bear flowers in
narrow spikes, with male flowers at
the top and female flowers beneath
them, followed by the hooked, nut-like
fruits that give the plants their
common name. The most widely
grown hook sedges are the russet-
leaved *Uncinia rubra* and the smaller
U. unciniata, both of which resemble
the New Zealand species of carex (*see
p.289*) in many ways. Uncinias look
very attractive surrounded by a gravel
mulch, although the soil below must
be moisture-retentive.

■ **HARDINESS** Frost-hardy ✲✲.
■ **CULTIVATION** Grow hook sedge in
reasonably fertile, but well-drained soil,
containing plenty of well-rotted organic
matter. Position in full sun or dappled shade.
■ **Sow** seed (*see pp.328–329*) in heat in spring.
■ **Divide** well-grown plants (*see p.330*)
between spring and midsummer.

Uncinia rubra
↕ 30cm (12in) ↔ 35cm (14in), greenish-red or
reddish brown foliage, russet, then dark brown
to black flowers in mid- to late summer

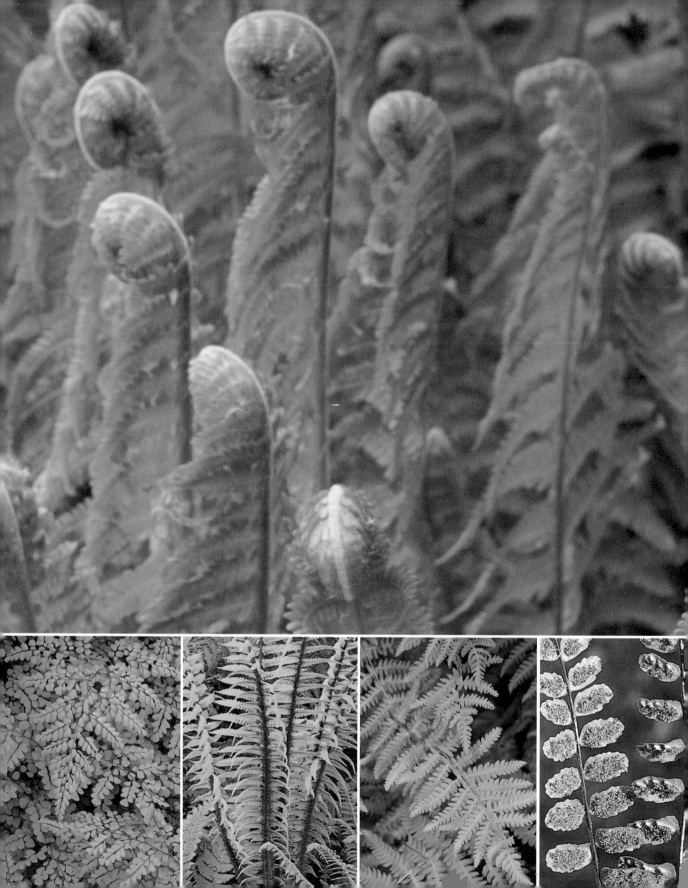

Ferns

With astonishingly varied shapes and habits, ferns often appear to defy attempts at generalization. They may be stiff and upright, or gracefully arching. Some ferns have tough, leathery, and glossy fronds; others are more dainty and fragile. And when it comes to colour, there's more choice than you might expect: ferns come in a vast range of different greens, often with subtle hues of silver and bronze.

Top: *Matteuccia struthiopteris*
From left to right: *Adiantum venustum*; *Dryopteris*; *Thelypteris palustris*;
Asplenium trichomanes; *Blechnum gibbum*

Choosing ferns

Ferns are perennial foliage plants: some are evergreen and others are deciduous. Unlike other plants, ferns reproduce by means of tiny spores that form on the undersides of the fronds; these fall from the plant when ripe, as part of the plant's reproductive process.

Many ferns are very attractive in spring as the new fronds unfurl; they often have a brown, furry coating that glows in the low spring sun, and makes them excellent companions for bulbs. The new fronds of the sensitive fern (*Onoclea sensibilis*) have a pinkish-bronze tint, and emerging foliage of Wallich's wood fern (*Dryopteris wallichiana*) is yellowish-green. Combine clumps of several types to create stunning textural contrasts.

Where to plant ferns

Hardy ferns are generally easy to grow in moist, shady areas. As they are quite tough, their needs are minimal and they need very little maintenance once they are established. Most ferns need a site in dappled, partial, or full shade – strong sunlight can scorch the thin fronds. The cold winds that blow over exposed sites can also cause scorching, so choose a sheltered spot. The few exceptions to this include lip ferns (*Cheilanthes*) and some polypodiums, which tolerate drier conditions and sun.

Good garden soil that is rich in organic matter is best for most ferns. Before planting, dig in as much well-rotted organic matter as you can to help the soil retain moisture. Humidity is important for ferns to thrive, so damp corners, bog gardens, and pond-side areas, with sheltered, still air, are ideal for lush foliage growth.

Making more ferns

The easiest way to propagate ferns is to lift and divide their clumps (*see p.330*). Some ferns, such as *Asplenium bulbiferum* and some polystichums, form bulbils on the fronds. Detach a frond of bulbils and peg it on to a tray of compost. Keep it watered, warm and well lit until plantlets form and root. Detach and pot up plantlets when they are big enough to handle.

The ferns' subtle shades of green and the contrasting colour and form of hostas gives this shady area plenty of interesting texture.

Athyrium filix-femina 'Frizelliae' *p.305*

Matteuccia struthiopteris *p.307*

Adiantum venustum *p.304*

Polypodium vulgare *p.308*

Onoclea sensibilis *p.307*

Asplenium ceterach *p.304*

Osmunda regalis *p.308*

Cryptogramma crispa *p.306*

Blechnum penna-marina *p.305*

Dryopteris wallichiana *p.307*

Asplenium scolopendrium *p.304*

Woodwardia radicans *p.309*

Blechnum gibbum *p.305*

Asplenium trichomanes *p.304*

Thelypteris palustris *p.309*

Polypodium glycyrrhiza *p.308*

Adiantum
Maidenhair fern
SPRING TO AUTUMN

Graceful, often finely divided foliage is the most desirable characteristic of this large group of evergreen, semi-evergreen, and deciduous ferns often grown as house plants. The fronds are usually mid-green, but may be paler green or even bronze-pink when young. They have black or brown-black stems which stand out well against the foliage. These ferns can spread widely by underground stems (rhizomes). They require shady areas, such as under trees or large shrubs, and also flourish beside water. Show off the delicate foliage by contrasting it with the bold foliage of plants such as hostas (*see pp.218–219*).

■ **HARDINESS** Fully hardy ✳✳✳ to frost-tender ❀.
■ **CULTIVATION** Grow hardy ferns in moist but well-drained, reasonably fertile soil in partial or deep shade. *A. capillus-veneris* likes moist, alkaline soil. ■ **Cut** old foliage from deciduous species in late winter or early spring. ■ **Divide** rhizomes in early spring every three or four years. Pull apart the rhizomes to obtain about three new ferns and replant, or grow them on in a pot of loam-based compost (*see also p.395*).

Adiantum venustum ♀ (Himalayan maidenhair fern)
↕15cm (6in) ↔indefinite, evergreen fronds 15–30cm (6–12in) long, bright bronze-pink in late winter and early spring ✳✳✳

Asplenium
Spleenwort
SPRING TO AUTUMN

This huge and varied group of ferns includes evergreens and semi-evergreens. The green fronds range in shape and texture from fine and feathery to long, pointed, and glossy. The hen-and-chicken fern (*Asplenium bulbiferum*) is one of many with fronds composed of tiny leaflets. Spleenworts grow from erect, sometimes creeping, rhizomes. Plant small species in wall crevices, or in a rock garden or alpine trough. Grow larger species in woodland or among shrubs in a shady border.

■ **HARDINESS** Fully hardy ✳✳✳ to frost-tender ❀.
■ **CULTIVATION** These ferns need partial shade and moist but well-drained soil, enriched with plenty of well-rotted organic matter. Most need an acid (lime-free) soil, but *A. ceterach*, *A. scolopendrium*, and *A. trichomanes* prefer alkaline (limy) soils. ■ **Divide** hardy species (*see p.395*) in spring every four or five years to obtain new plants with at least two leaves; replant them or pot up in loam-based compost.
■ **In wet winters**, *A. scolopendrium* is prone to rust disease; if you see orange or brown patches, remove the affected fronds.

Asplenium ceterach (Rusty-back fern)
↕15cm (6in) ↔20cm (8in), evergreen fronds up to 20cm (8in) long, rusty-brown scales on undersides ✳✳✳

Asplenium scolopendrium ♀ (Hart's tongue fern)
↕45–70cm (18–28in) ↔60cm (24in), evergreen, fronds 40cm (16in) or more long, prefers alkaline (limy) soils ✳✳✳

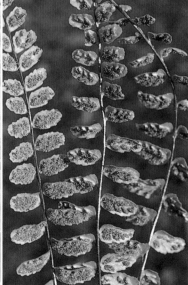

Asplenium trichomanes ♀ (Maidenhair spleenwort)
↕15cm (6in) ↔20cm (8in), evergreen or semi-evergreen, fronds 10–20cm (4–8in) long, rusty-red spores on undersides ✳✳✳

Athyrium
Lady fern

The lacy-leaved fronds of *Athyrium filix-femina* and its cultivars, and the silvery green, deeply divided fronds of *A. niponicum* mean that these deciduous lady ferns are decorative plants for shady areas. The midribs are reddish in colour, contrasting sharply with the foliage. The ferns are found growing wild in moist woodlands or forests, and they also look best grown in a woodland setting in the garden. You can create a natural-looking habitat for them by placing old logs in a shady border and planting the lady ferns among them as if they were growing among fallen trees.

■ **HARDINESS** Fully hardy ✳✳✳ to frost-tender ❋; *A. filix-femina* is hardy to -30°C (-22°F).
■ **CULTIVATION** Grow lady ferns in moist, fertile soil that is neutral to acid and enriched with plenty of well-rotted organic matter. Choose a site that is both shaded and sheltered. Lady ferns will tolerate all but the driest sites.
■ **Divide** hardy species in spring every four or five years. Use a spade to cut up larger clumps, obtaining several new plants with two or three leaves each. Replant in prepared ground.

***Athyrium filix-femina* 'Frizelliae'** ♀
(Mrs. Frizell's lady fern, Tatting fern)
↕20cm (8in) ↔30cm (12in), fronds 10–20cm (4–8in) long ✳✳✳

Blechnum
Hard fern

Some species of hard ferns have spectacular foliage, which bursts upwards and outwards in a fountain shape, sometimes from a small "trunk". This trunk is in fact an upright rhizome, up to 90cm (36in) tall, and covered in black scales; the fronds grow out from the top. Other species, such as *Blechnum penna-marina* have creeping rhizomes and are more suitable as ground-cover plants. Hard ferns are generally evergreen, with tough fronds standing through the winter. They flourish in moist soil under trees or in shady borders. The smaller species are also suitable for a shady corner in a rock garden.

■ **HARDINESS** Fully hardy ✳✳✳ to frost-tender ❋.
■ **CULTIVATION** Hard ferns like moist soil, preferably acid, enriched with well-rotted organic matter to retain moisture.

Blechnum penna-marina ♀
↕10–20cm (4–8in) ↔indefinite, creeping, fronds are 10–20cm (4–8in) long and glossy or matt, depending on the form ✳✳✳

■ **Grow** blechnum in pots of bark-based compost or ericaceous (lime-free) compost mixed with plenty of sharp sand or grit. Hard ferns need partial to deep shade. ■ **Grow** tender species in large pots and keep them in frost-free conditions over winter; in mild areas, they may survive winter outdoors if protected with straw held in place with netting. ■ **Divide** *B. penna-marina* and *B. spicant* in spring (*see p.395*); other species can be divided, but take longer to re-establish.

Blechnum chilense ♀
↕90cm–2m (3–6ft) ↔indefinite, trunk-like rhizomes, fronds up to 1m (3ft) long with scaly stalks ✳✳✳

Blechnum gibbum
↕↔to 90cm (36in), trunk-like rhizomes, fronds 90cm (36in) or more long, spectacular conservatory plant ❋ (minimum 18°C/64°F)

Cryptogramma crispa
Parsley fern
SUMMER TO AUTUMN

This delightful small fern is grown for its delicate foliage. The only cryptogramma commonly grown in gardens, it has deciduous fronds that turn an attractive, bright rust-brown during autumn. The old fronds usually persist all through winter. Since it is a fairly low-growing fern, the parsley fern is suitable for growing in a shaded crevice of a rock garden or at the front of a shady border. The lacy, pale green fronds make a good contrast to darker and bolder foliage on plants such as astilbes (*see p.164*) and rodgersias (*see p.264*).

■ **HARDINESS** Fully hardy ✳✳✳.
■ **CULTIVATION** This fern prefers partial or full shade in fertile soil that has been enriched with well-rotted organic matter to help retain moisture. The soil should be acid or neutral (lime-free), so if your soil is alkaline (limy) grow the fern in a container or a raised bed that contains ericaceous (lime-free) compost mixed with plenty of grit or sharp sand, or a bark-based compost. ■ **Remove** the faded fronds in spring before new ones grow. The parsley fern is deep-rooted and difficult to propagate by division.

Cryptogramma crispa
↕15–23cm (6–9in) ↔15–30cm (6–12in), fronds are up to 23cm (9in) long, grows well in poor soil such as in rocky outcrops and also fissures in rock

Cystopteris
Bladder fern
SPRING TO AUTUMN

The finely divided fronds of the bladder ferns make them a valuable asset in the garden. They are deciduous and their fronds grow in clumps or rosettes from fleshy stems (rhizomes), which may creep or grow upright above ground. The fronds tend to be pale or grey-green. These ferns will be happy in shady areas of a rock garden or under shrubs or trees. They also blend in well in a border or woodland area dedicated to ferns; such a planting will highlight their differing textures, forms, and shades of green, and make a restful feature.

■ **HARDINESS** Fully hardy ✳✳✳.
■ **CULTIVATION** Grow in fertile, moist soil, incorporating well-rotted organic matter to help retain moisture in partial or full shade. Provide shelter from cold, drying winds. ■ **Divide** rhizomes in spring (*see p.330*), planting them in the ground. ■ **Alternatively**, increase by using the bulbils that ripen on the undersides of the fronds from late summer. Peg each frond into a tray of compost. Once the bulbils have rooted, transfer the plants to 8cm (3in) pots of soil-less compost; keep them in frost-free conditions over the winter; and plant them out in spring.

Cystopteris fragilis (Brittle bladder fern)
↔20cm (8in), clump-forming with upright rhizomes, fronds are 15–45cm (6–18in) long

Dicksonia
YEAR-ROUND

Spectacular, tree-like forms and dramatic foliage distinguish these very large, semi-evergreen or evergreen ferns. They have thick, furry "trunks" formed from a mass of old stems and leaf bases. Each stem can be up to 60cm (24in) in diameter and has only a few roots – most of its nutrients are derived in the wild from decaying matter that collects in the fronds. The large, leathery fronds grow to 3m (10ft) and sprout from the top of the stem. The new fronds have a furry protective coating as they unfurl in spring. Dicksonias grow to their full height only in favourable conditions. Show it to its best advantage as a specimen or with other ferns in a shady border.

■ **HARDINESS** Frost-hardy ✳✳ to frost-tender ❄.
■ **CULTIVATION** Grow in fertile soil in partial or full shade. In spells of hot, dry weather, hose the trunk with water daily. ■ **Protect** the trunk and leaves in winter by attaching wire netting loosely around the trunk and over the crown and stuffing the gap with straw. ■ **Cut off** old fronds in early spring. They are difficult to propagate.

Dicksonia antarctica ♀ (Man fern, Soft tree fern)
↕to 6m (20ft) ↔4m (12ft), flourishes in a mild, damp climate sheltered from wind and sun ✳✳

Dryopteris
Buckler fern

This large group of ferns produces long, elegant fronds, often in a shuttlecock shape. Many retain their leaves over winter in mild, sheltered conditions, although they die down in less favourable climates. The evergreen fronds of the golden male fern (*Dryopteris affinis*) are pale green when young, contrasting with golden brown midribs. *D. erythrosora* has copper foliage in spring, turning dark green, with green midribs. The midribs of *D. wallichiana* are covered with brown or black scales, and are very striking in spring against the new yellow-green fronds; these age to dark green. With their distinctive shapes, they add height to a mixed fern border or in a shady border.

■ **HARDINESS** Most fully hardy ✳✳✳; a few are frost-hardy ✳✳ and frost-tender ✿.
■ **CULTIVATION** Grow these ferns in partial shade in soil with plenty of well-rotted organic matter to retain moisture. ■ **Shelter** from cold, drying winds. ■ **Divide** mature plants (*see p.330*) in spring or autumn every five or six years; use a spade for older clumps.

Matteuccia

Shuttlecock-shaped rosettes of upright, gently arching fronds are characteristic of the three or four species in this group of deciduous ferns. During mid- to late summer, smaller, dark brown fronds appear in the centre of each rosette; these are fertile fronds, while the green ones around the edge are sterile. The ferns spread by creeping stems (rhizomes) from which more fronds sprout. They are striking foliage plants for a damp, shady border in woodland or by water, and work well with other shade-loving plants such as rhododendrons (*see pp.92–93*).

■ **HARDINESS** Fully hardy ✳✳✳.
■ **CULTIVATION** Grow in moist but well-drained soil, incorporating well-rotted organic matter to help retain moisture. Matteuccias prefer neutral to acid soil in partial shade. If your soil is alkaline (limy), grow them in containers or raised beds containing ericaceous (lime-free) compost mixed with plenty of grit or sharp sand, or a bark-based compost. ■ **Divide** established clumps (*see p.330*) in early spring to obtain four or five new plants, each with at least two or three vigorous fronds.

Onoclea sensibilis
Sensitive fern

Upright and arching fronds up to 1m (3ft) long are produced by this single, deciduous fern. Its name derives from the fact that all its top-growth dies down at the first frost. In spring, its new, sterile fronds are sometimes pinkish-bronze; these turn pale green. They are very deeply divided, giving them a feathery appearance. In late summer, a number of fertile fronds with a contrasting, stiffly upright habit grow to 60cm (2ft). The sensitive fern thrives by the edge of water or in shady borders in damp soil. Try it with other shade- and damp-loving plants such as candelabra primulas (*see pp.260–261*).

■ **HARDINESS** Fully hardy ✳✳✳.
■ **CULTIVATION** Plant this fern in a sheltered site away from cold, drying winds. The sensitive fern prefers moist, fertile, acid (lime-free) soil in light, dappled shade; the fronds will be scorched if they are exposed to strong sun. ■ **Divide** established clumps (*see p.330*) in spring; ensure each new clump has at least two or three fronds.

Dryopteris wallichiana ♀ (Wallich's wood fern)
↕90cm (36in), sometimes to 2m (6ft) ↔75cm (30in), deciduous fronds 90cm (36in) long ✳✳✳

Matteuccia struthiopteris ♀
(Ostrich fern, Shuttlecock fern)
↕1.7m (5½ft) ↔to 1m (3ft), sterile green fronds 1.2m (4ft) long

Onoclea sensibilis ♀
↕60cm (24in) ↔indefinite, Sterile fronds grow from an underground, creeping rhizome; favours damp ground

Osmunda

SPRING TO AUTUMN

Osmundas are imposing, deciduous ferns, with upright, blue-green or bright green fronds, which fade to yellow or brown in autumn. In the centre of these sterile fronds are erect, fertile fronds that contrast pleasingly with the surrounding green foliage. In the royal fern (*Osmunda regalis*), they are brown or rust-coloured; the cinnamon fern (*O. cinnamomea*) is named after the rich colour of its fertile fronds. Use these large, architectural ferns as specimen plants in a mixed border or by a pond or stream. The royal fern also makes an excellent container plant provided that it is watered regularly, especially in warm weather. Its roots are fibrous, absorbing lots of water and, as osmunda fibre, they were used as orchid compost – although this practice is now banned.

■ **HARDINESS** Fully hardy ✳✳✳.
■ **CULTIVATION** Osmundas like moist, fertile, preferably acid (lime-free) soil in light, dappled shade. The royal fern does require a wet soil, but will do well in sun as long as the soil is moist.
■ **Divide** established clumps (*see p.330*) in autumn or early spring using a spade.

Osmunda regalis ♀ (Flowering fern, Royal fern)
‡2m (6ft) ↔ 4m (12ft), sterile fronds are 1m (3ft) or more long

Polypodium

YEAR-ROUND

These adaptable ferns make excellent ground cover with their spreading habit and beautiful, sculptural fronds. Many produce relatively long, arching fronds randomly from the creeping stems, or rhizomes. The fronds reach 60cm (24in) in the case of the southern polypody (*Polypodium cambricum*). Some have spores on the undersides of the fronds in contrasting colours. Unlike most ferns, polypodiums are also drought-tolerant and are happy in full sun. The mostly evergreen ferns in this group look particularly good growing in mixed borders or on a bank where ground cover is required. Their spreading habit helps to suppress weeds.

■ **HARDINESS** Fully hardy ✳✳✳ to frost-tender ❀.
■ **CULTIVATION** Grow polypodiums in well-drained, moderately fertile soil, with plenty of well-rotted organic matter added. On heavy clay soils, dig in coarse grit to improve drainage. *P. cambricum* prefers a neutral to alkaline soil.
■ **Site** in full sun or partial shade and provide shelter from cold, drying winds. ■ **Divide** in spring or early summer (*see p.330*) when the plants are four or five years old.

Polypodium vulgare (Common polypody)
‡30cm (12in) ↔ indefinite, thin to leathery fronds are 40cm (16in) long ✳✳✳

Polypodium glycyrrhiza (Licorice fern)
‡30cm (12in) ↔ indefinite, mid- to dark green fronds up to 35cm (14in) long, rhizomes have a sweet licorice taste ✳✳✳

Polystichum
Holly fern, Shield fern
YEAR-ROUND

The fine foliage of these ferns is usually arranged in shapely "shuttlecocks", forming exuberant bursts of often dark green fronds. The fronds tend to be highly intricate, especially in the soft shield fern (*Polystichum setiferum*) and its cultivars, and the leaflets may end in a sharp bristle, hence the common name of holly fern. This large group of mostly evergreen ferns includes plants that are 40cm–1.2m (16in–4ft) tall. These all combine well with other woodland plants such as hydrangeas (*see pp.64–65*) in a well-drained woodland planting.

■ **HARDINESS** Fully hardy ✳✳✳ to frost-tender ❀.
■ **CULTIVATION** Holly ferns prefer fertile soil enriched with well-rotted organic matter, in deep or partial shade. ■ **Protect** the crowns from excessive winter wet with a mulch of organic matter. In early spring, remove any dead fronds. ■ **Divide** the rhizomes in spring. In late summer or early autumn, detach fronds with bulbils and peg each frond into a tray of compost. Once they have rooted, transfer to 8cm (3in) pots of soilless compost with added grit; keep frost-free; and plant out in spring.

***Polystichum setiferum* 'Pulcherrimum Bevis'** ♀
‡↔ 60–80cm (24–32in), very rarely fertile ✳✳✳

Thelypteris palustris
Marsh fern
SPRING TO AUTUMN

This is a deciduous fern of swamps and bogs. In summer, if there is good light, fertile fronds, that are longer than the sterile ones, are produced. Spores are borne in abundance on the undersides of the leaflets, creating a brown haze over the ferns in late summer. Try growing this fern with other moisture-loving plants such as hostas (*see pp.218–219*), primulas (*see pp.260–261*), and marsh marigolds (*Caltha, see p.172*) at the edge of a pond. The marsh fern can be invasive, spreading by long, creeping underground stems (rhizomes), so allow it plenty of space, but it is also easy to keep under control by digging out unwanted pieces.

■ **HARDINESS** Fully hardy ✳✳✳.
■ **CULTIVATION** Grow the fern in any reliably moist, moderately fertile soil. ■ **Dig in** well-rotted organic matter to increase moisture retention, in sun or partial shade. ■ **Divide** in spring or summer (*see p.330*), replant and keep well watered, especially in summer.

Thelypteris palustris
‡60cm (24in) ↔to 1m (3ft), fronds up to 90cm (36in) long, a rare species that prefers marshy ground beside water

Woodwardia
Chain fern
SPRING TO SUMMER

Large, spreading, and arching plants, chain ferns are so-called because the spores are arranged on the undersides of the fronds in a chain-like formation. This small group of ferns includes evergreen and deciduous species. The intricate fronds are particularly attractive as they unfurl in spring. On their upper surfaces, small bulbils may be produced over the summer near the tips. The chain fern looks particularly natural near water, and it combines well with bold foliage plants, such as gunneras (*see p.211*), that also like moist soil.

■ **HARDINESS** Fully hardy ✳✳✳ to frost-hardy ✳✳.
■ **CULTIVATION** Chain ferns like neutral, reasonably fertile, damp soil in partial shade. In cold areas, shelter the ferns from cold, drying winds. ■ **Protect** over winter in frost-prone areas with a mulch of straw held in place with netting. ■ **Divide** in spring using a spade (*see p.330*) or sharp knife; replant in a similar site; or propagate from bulbils in late summer or early autumn. Detach fronds with bulbils and peg each frond into a tray of compost. Once rooted, pot into 8cm (3in) pots of soilless compost; keep frost-free over winter; and plant out in spring.

Woodwardia radicans ♀ (European chain fern)
‡2m (6ft) ↔3m (10ft), evergreen, each leaflet to 30cm (12in) long ✳✳

Caring for plants

Make sure the plants in your garden perform at their peak by giving them the attention they need, particularly in the growing season. In this chapter, you are guided through the basic principles of looking after plants, from what to look for when you buy them and assessing where to plant them, to all aspects of caring for them once they are in the ground.

Weeding, watering, composting, and raking up dead leaves are just a few of the tasks you need to perform regularly to help keep your plants healthy and your garden looking its best throughout the year.

Planning your garden

Whether adapting an existing garden or designing one from scratch, take time at the planning stage before rushing out and buying lots of plants. It will help you to avoid making costly mistakes and ensure you end up with your ideal garden.

First, make a rough sketch of your garden, preferably to scale on squared paper. Then list the things you want to include, how you want it to look, how you intend using it. With this information in mind, take another look at your sketch and see what changes need to be made.

Moving into a new house and then creating a garden from scratch can seem daunting. It does, however, have the great advantage of giving you complete freedom to develop your own design. Unlike an established garden that may be full of plants, a bare plot of freshly laid turf gives few clues as to what plants can be grown successfully. So it is essential to take into account the garden's location, effect of the local climate (see p.314), and soil type (see p.318) before buying any plants.

If you are redesigning an existing garden, don't be too hasty in your initial assessment of the site, as you may inadvertently remove some useful plants and features. Make changes gradually, over a full year if possible, adapting existing features to your plan.

Flowers and foliage come in an infinite palette of shades, providing the opportunity to experiment with colour schemes and moods in the borders. Do your homework before buying trees, shrubs, climbers, and perennials since these can be expensive and will form the permanent structure of the garden. By comparison, annuals and biennials – including bedding plants – last for one growing season and are much cheaper, so you can ring the changes from year to year.

The huge choice of herbaceous and bedding plants available makes planning a beautiful summer garden relatively easy. Colourful borders need not be a transient pleasure – there are many plants that provide interest over a longer period. As well as creating a permanent framework, trees and shrubs are often blessed with attractive spring blossom, followed in autumn by good leaf colour or berries and hips. There may also be attractive stems or bark to enjoy in winter. Keep the colour coming with spring bulbs.

When organizing the layout of your borders, try to show each plant to its best advantage. It is important not to place new plants too close together: allow room for them to reach their full size, even if it leaves a few gaps at first.

Choosing a style of planting

The plants are the most important element in a garden. There are many styles of planting to choose from and thousands of plants with which to plan a scheme. If you are looking for inspiration, one of the best ways to discover what style or theme would suit your plot is to visit gardens that

Assessing your priorities in the garden

▪ How will you use your garden?

▪ Do you enjoy gardening or just want a place in which to relax?

▪ Do you want to maximize your planting space or increase the amount of hard landscaping for a low-maintenance option?

▪ Is an outdoor entertaining or dining area required?

▪ Informal or formal? Which garden style do you prefer?

▪ What should the mood of the garden be – restful or vibrant?

▪ If children use the garden, do they need their own play area?

▪ Are new paths or steps needed?

▪ Are you happy to grow fruit and vegetables among other plants, or do you want a kitchen garden?

▪ Is there space for a utility area for a shed and compost bins? (Hide them behind hedges or trellis.)

▪ Do you want a pond or some sort of water feature?

▪ Do you want to position lights in strategic places to allow you to enjoy the garden during the evening?

In this formal garden, bricks are set into a sweep of stone slabs to warm up the colour and add texture, while plants lean out from their borders, disguising the hard edges.

are open to the public. Wandering around your neighbourhood and looking at other people's gardens will give you a good idea of different layouts and of which plants would be most happy growing in the local soil and climate.

Ideally, each plant you choose should remain attractive over many months, for example displaying spring blossom or autumn leaf colour as well as flowers.

Formality and order

Large areas of hard landscaping are often a feature of formal gardens, but although it allows for easy maintenance it can look clinical. A balance can be struck with planting. Bricks can be set into a sweep of stone slabs to warm up the colour and to add texture, while the hard edges of the paving may be softened by drifts of restrained planting spilling onto the stone.

Informal charm

In a cottage garden, on the other hand, the plants take centre stage and are allowed to self-seed where they will. Given a free rein, they will grow together to create borders with great appeal.

The free-flowing charms of the cottage garden call for an unforced naturalness and spontaneity, created by intermingling plants so that they appear to jostle for space.

Ponds and water features

A water feature always adds an extra dimension to a garden, whether it is a formal or natural pond, or a half-barrel of water. It is also a magnet for wildlife – birds will bathe in the shallows, while frogs and toads, which help to control slugs and snails, will become regular visitors.

Consider the style of pond you prefer and how it relates to the plan as they are not easy to move once installed. To help visualize it, mark the outline on the ground using a length of hose. Avoid siting it under a tree as falling leaves will foul the water.

Using containers

Bring colour right up to the windows of your house by planting containers with an ever-changing selection of plants, from spring bulbs and summer bedding, to shrubs and even small trees. Choose planters, pots, and windowboxes in materials that enhance, not compete with, the planting. Roots will quickly become restricted within the confines of a container, so replenish the nutrients in the compost and water regularly.

Using colour in the garden

Garden flowers come in an infinitely varied and dazzling array of colours and shades. However, foliage, bark, stems, berries, and seedheads can be colourful, too, and foliage and bark often have a longer season of interest than flowers. How you combine colour is a matter of personal preference, but there are a few ways to ensure successful planting schemes.

Many designers use a colour wheel for inspiration. This is simply a circle divided into six wedges, coloured in this order: yellow, green, blue, purple, red, and orange. Colours adjacent to each other create harmonious effects, while colours that oppose each other on the wheel make for lively contrasts. Yellows through to reds are warm and stimulating; while greens to purples are restful and cool.

The striking form of *Kniphofia caulescens* gives added impact to their fiery red colour, which is why they are so aptly named red hot pokers. Hot colours like this in a border always draw the eye.

Restricting the colour palette can produce a more pleasing effect than using very many colours, which often looks rather fussy. Strong colours attract the eye and so could be used especially successfully for specimen plants. Colour can be used to set a mood – reds, golds, and oranges, typical of a hot scheme, are exciting and dominant; while blues, soft pinks, and whites are soothing and subtle.

Foliage and form

Growing beautiful flowers is one of gardening's obvious pleasures, but you can have great fun designing with plants using their attractive growth habits and strikingly shaped or coloured foliage. Unlike a brief burst of flower colour, a foliage plant will offer a long season of interest. Plants with different types of foliage can be used to build up three-dimensional layers of texture, giving even a narrow border a more interesting feeling of depth and movement.

Create a collage of leaf shapes and sizes by planting spiky specimens, such as grasses (*see pp.284–299*) and yuccas, next to round-leaved cultivars, such as hostas (*see pp.218–219*) and bergenias (*see p.167*). Look, too, for subtle contrasts in leaf texture, such as glossy or hairy leaves, as well as striking variegation and complementary colours, ranging from silver and cream to purple and gold.

Climate and location

Not only does the weather dictate when certain jobs can be tackled in the garden, but the local climate will determine the types of plants that will thrive in your plot. Many plants are adaptable, but choosing ones most suited to your locality and garden aspect is fundamental to success. Providing suitable conditions for all the plants and matching as closely as possible their natural habitats, is challenging and satisfying.

The weather – temperature, frost, snow, rain, humidity, sun, and wind – affects how plants grow and dictates the length of the growing season. Only when the weather turns milder can we plant out tender bedding or start sowing seed outdoors. Colder areas tend to have later springs, sometimes weeks later than warmer areas farther south, as well as shorter growing seasons. Inland regions are often drier than areas by the coast. Although plants have to contend with salt spray and strong winds, coastal areas are also much milder.

You don't have to travel far, however, to discover significant variations in climate. There is a huge difference between the growing conditions on a sheltered valley floor compared to the exposed slopes of the surrounding hills. In the same way, while most of your garden may be warm and sunny, it may contain a range of microclimates, where the conditions are modified by factors such as the shelter of a warm wall or the heavy shade cast by an evergreen tree. Such areas need to be treated and planted differently.

Since the local climate will dictate which kinds of plants you can grow successfully, take time to find out what weather patterns you can expect over the course of the year. Consider joining a gardening club: gardeners are always willing to share their experiences and they will be a valuable source of information.

The dangers of frost

One of the greatest hazards that a gardener has to contend with is frost, especially in spring and autumn. An unexpected spring frost can destroy flower buds, ruining the display for the year.

Assessing your garden

Before making any changes to your garden it is worth assessing your surroundings to give yourself an idea of the plants you can grow.

■ How high above sea level are you? The higher you are, the colder it is because of exposure to strong winds.
■ Does the garden face north or south? In a north-facing garden, the shade cast by the house keeps the air cool and the soil moist. A south-facing garden is warm and sunny, but the soil may dry out in summer.
■ How shady is the garden? Is there heavy shade cast by established trees and shrubs or by the house?
■ Is the garden on a slope? Cold air will gather at the bottom of a slope to cause a frost pocket.
■ Does it get very cold in the winter or very hot in summer? Temperature extremes can stress plants and you may have to take extra care of them.

Tender, new shoots are also susceptible. Still, clear nights often signal that a frost is on the way, and quick action can protect vulnerable plants. If you cannot bring them under cover, loosely wrap them in some horticultural fleece, newspapers or a similar insulating material.

The incidence of late spring frosts in your area will determine the time at which it is safe to plant out tender plants, such as summer bedding. The onset of autumnal frosts will then determine the end of their growing season.

Where there are low points in the garden, frost pockets may form. Frost also collects at the bases of fences, walls, and closely planted, thick hedges, or even large objects such as a statue or solid seat. If there is a frosty hollow in the garden, avoid growing fruit there and choose plants that are fully hardy and will not suffer in low temperatures.

Hardiness of plants

The hardiness of a plant refers to its ability to withstand year-round climatic conditions, including frost, without any protection. Fully hardy plants withstand temperatures down to -15°C (5°F). Frost-hardy plants are happy in temperatures down to -5°C (23°F), whereas half-hardy ones prefer

Although it looks pretty, heavy snow can break branches. After a fall of snow, go out with a broom and knock it off the plant. If more snow is forecast, tie vulnerable branches into the main stem.

temperatures above 0°C (32°F) and are damaged by frost. Frost-tender plants need shelter in conditions that are cooler than 5°C (41°F).

Hardy plants need less nurturing because they survive without harm in the garden all winter. The more tender plants, on the other hand, have to be brought under cover before the first frost in autumn and can be planted out only when all danger of frost has passed, in spring. This obviously varies from one area to another, but is generally around late spring to early summer.

Helping plants to survive the winter

Young or slightly tender plants need protection to help them survive a severe winter. Protect top-growth by covering plants with horticultural fleece, hessian sacking, bubble plastic, or some layers of newspaper. Likewise, wrapping containers with hessian or bubble plastic protects the roots from freezing. This is a useful technique when the container is too large to take indoors. A double or triple layer of wrapping offers good protection.

Wrapping plants, such as tree ferns, in dry bracken or straw will trap any warm air escaping from the soil and provide valuable insulation on a cold night. When temperatures are above freezing, unwrap the plants to give them a chance to breathe and prevent the build-up of moulds and pests. A thick mulch of garden compost spread over the crowns of plants, such as herbaceous perennials that have died down over winter, will give protection from several degrees of frost. A mound of dried leaves, held in place over the plant with chicken wire, works well too.

Cloches, usually made of glass or rigid or film plastic, are excellent for keeping a few degrees of frost off plants. On exposed sites, protect the plants from cold winds with proprietary windbreaks or fine-mesh netting supported on stout stakes.

As well as making an attractive feature in a border, bell cloches offer effective winter protection for less hardy plants. Glass cloches are beautiful, but very expensive and vulnerable to breakage – plastic ones, like these, do the job just as well.

Over winter, frost-tender plants must be taken into a greenhouse or a conservatory where low-level heating will keep the temperature a few degrees above freezing.

The effect of wind on your garden

Strong winds can have positive benefits, helping to disperse pollen and seeds. However, they can be a destructive force causing damage to plants, especially young ones that have yet to become established. They can also discourage beneficial insects that help to control pests. Although they have a cooling effect on plants, strong winds also increase the rate at which water vapour is lost from plants' leaves (called desiccation), which causes browning and leaf drop.

When woody plants are exposed to strong winds, their top-growth becomes unbalanced, making the plants appear one-sided. The tips of shoots and leaves are also at risk of being damaged, or scorched. The higher the wind speed, the more damage is done, with stems being broken and, in severe cases, entire plants being uprooted.

Protect vulnerable plants with a windbreak. Choose a material that will allow about 50 per cent of the wind to pass through, because a solid structure will create problems of its own. Hedging plants are ideal, or choose open-weave fencing or special windbreak netting. For best protection, a windbreak should be 4m (12ft) tall, but a lower one would work well for smaller plants.

The effects of shade

Shady areas of the garden generally have dryish soil, and plants have to cope with very low light levels. The ground under trees poses a real challenge to gardeners because some types of tree and hedging plant, such as conifers and other evergreens, cast deep shadow and take lots of water and nutrients from the soil. The soil at the base of walls and fences can also be shady and dry. However, if the soil is enriched by digging in plenty of well-rotted manure or garden compost (*see p.319*), and any overhanging plants are judiciously pruned, a number of beautiful plants can be grown, for example *Cyclamen cilicium* (*see p.185*). You may also have areas of cool, moist, dappled shade – often under deciduous trees. In such conditions, there are plenty of woodland plants that will thrive.

Providing shelter

If you are planting on an exposed site, most young plants, especially evergreen shrubs and perennials, will require protection from strong winds and fierce sun until their root systems become established. If the garden does not enjoy the natural shelter of trees and hedging plants (*see above*), there are several temporary measures you can take.

Open-weave fencing or hurdles provide a suitable solution, as does planting fast-growing climbers to cover trellis panels. For an instant and economical fix, make a small windbreak using mesh and canes. For best results, erect the shelter on the windward side of the plant or, if fierce sun is the problem, on the sunny side.

Buying plants

The old saying, "You get what you pay for", is never truer than when buying plants. Buying quality plants from a reputable nursery is always money well spent as young plants must get a good start in life. You may be tempted by trays of bedding at knock-down prices, but they may have been on the shelf for ages, starved of food and water and so they will never grow as vigorously as good-quality stock.

When selecting a plant, look for one that is well-balanced, with plenty of healthy growth and, where appropriate, lots of flower buds. If the plant shows any symptoms of neglect – signs include algal growth on the compost, pests and disease, a stunted appearance, dry compost, and yellowing leaves – choose another one. Yellowing leaves may signify a lack of nutrients, a sign that the plant has not been looked after very well. Wilting leaves are caused by a lack of water; if the compost dries out too often the plant becomes stressed and vulnerable to pests and diseases.

Bare-root plants

Woody plants, including deciduous trees, shrubs, and roses, are often sold as bare-root plants. Grown in the ground rather than in pots, they are cheaper to produce in bulk and the nurseries can then pass on their savings to their customers. The plants also tend to be bigger and stronger than similarly priced container plants. Bare-root plants are available in nurseries (some of which are specialist), but they are generally sold by mail order (*see facing page*).

Bare-root plants are dug up in their dormant season, cleaned of soil, wrapped for posting, and dispatched in time for planting in early winter. Unwrap them as soon as they arrive and plant them immediately if conditions are favourable. If the soil is frozen, you can store them for a few days wrapped in damp newspaper in a cool shed.

A bare-root plant should have a good root system to support the plant. To encourage fibrous, feeding roots to form, trim the longest of the thick roots back hard. The branches will also have an evenly spaced framework. Plant without delay to prevent the roots drying out – they should then be well established before the spring.

Container-grown plants

Most plants are available in containers, from summer bedding in plastic strips to large shrubs and trees in pots. The big advantage to buying plants grown in this way is that the root system remains undisturbed during planting so that there is no check on growth. These advantages, however, may be outweighed by their premium price.

Most hardy container-grown plants can be planted out at any time of year. The exception is tender summer bedding, which often goes on sale in early spring. If you cannot resist buying early, grow the plants on under cover, and move them outdoors after the last frost, which is usually in late spring or early summer.

If you can, while at the nursery, gently knock the plant out of its container and inspect its root system. If lots of roots are growing through the drainage holes, or you find a solid mass of roots growing round the outside of the root ball, then the plant is pot-bound. Roots may also be visible on the surface of the compost. Severe

Nurseries sell bedding plants in polystyrene or plastic trays or strips. Push up gently through the holes in the base of the tray to free the plants without damaging their root systems.

constriction of roots may inhibit the plant's ability to take up water and nutrients. In this state, the plant's growth will have been severely stunted and it may never fully recover and thrive. In such an instance, don't buy it and look for a more cared-for specimen.

If, however, once you get home you find that you have to deal with a pot-bound plant, carefully tease out the roots and cut off some of the thicker sections. This will encourage new roots to venture out into the surrounding soil. Before planting it, soak the root ball in a bucket of water for a couple of hours and also water the planting hole thoroughly.

Plug plants

Pots of seedlings and plug plants are widely available, especially of bedding annuals and perennials. Plug plants can be bought from nurseries and garden centres and are also dispatched by mail-order companies from early spring (see below). Pot up or plant out plug plants as soon as possible (see p.320), and water them well.

Hippo plugs are more expensive than standard plugs; however, because they are larger plants, they should establish and flower more quickly.

Mail-order plants

If buying plants by mail order, always deal with a reputable supplier, placing your order early to get the ones you want. The plants will be dispatched in special packs, such as moulded containers or sealed plastic bags, designed to keep them moist. As soon as the plants arrive, open the package and check them, making sure that they are healthy with no signs of pests or diseases and, equally importantly, are the ones you ordered. Pot up the plants in potting compost and grow on for planting.

Plug plants have well-developed root systems, but the young stems and foliage are quite delicate. When potting on, it's best to handle them by the base to avoid damaging young growth.

Root-balled plants

Root-balled plants are grown in open ground rather than in pots. They are lifted with a ball of roots and soil, which is wrapped in net or hessian. Many shrubs and trees are sold in this way in spring and autumn by specialist nurseries, often by mail order. Check that the root ball feels firm and that the net is intact or the roots may dry out. Soak the netted root ball in water for a couple of hours, then unwrap and plant it immediately.

Bulbous plants

Spring-flowering bulbs, corms, and tubers are sold in autumn, whereas summer-flowering cultivars will be available in spring. Always buy bulbs as soon as they go on sale, when they will be in prime condition (firm, plump, and blemish- and rot-free with a clean, unbroken skin, or tunic) and plant them as soon as possible. The longer you delay, the more dried out they will become, and the plants will not perform as well. Inspect the bulbs and reject any that show signs of disease, such as soft or dark patches.

Water-garden plants

Always take care to introduce only healthy plants into a pond, otherwise the delicate ecosystem may be disturbed by pests or diseases carried in on the plants. Choose those with clean, green leaves and a good crown (the point where the leaves and roots meet) with several buds. If leaves are slimy or yellow, or if the water the plants are growing in is murky, then select another plant.

To fill a pond successfully choose a variety of aquatic types, such as marginal plants like irises (see pp.222–223) that need shallow water and deep-water aquatics like water lilies (see Nymphaea, p.244), that sit on the pond floor. Ensure that you plant them at the correct depth (see p.244).

The best time to buy aquatic plants is in late spring and early summer so they have a chance to become established before winter sets in. Most aquatic plants tolerate being out of the water for only a short time. Take them home in a plastic bag and put them into the pond as soon as possible.

Give hardy aquatic plants, such as this Nymphaea 'Laydekeri Fulgens', a good start by planting them in late spring or early summer. In this way, they will survive if the water freezes in winter.

Soils and compost

Soils are made from minute particles of rock and organic matter that has been broken down over time. Fertile soil is essential for healthy growth as it supplies plants with water, air, and nutrients. Not every type of soil is suitable for the widest range of plants, but almost any soil can be improved over time if garden compost is worked into it regularly.

It is important to know what type of soil you have in your garden so you can grow plants that thrive in it. The soil within the garden, however, can vary so you may have to choose different plants to suit each site.

What is soil pH?

It is relatively easy to determine your soil type and its pH. Before buying any plants, check the pH of your soil to ensure that they will thrive in it. The pH reflects the level of lime in the soil. Soils lying over limestone or chalk are rich in lime and known as alkaline, but soils over sand become acid. Soil pH is measured on a scale of 1–14. The optimum soil pH for plant growth is within pH5.5–7.5. Neutral soil, in which most plants thrive, has a pH of 7; soils of more than pH7 are alkaline (limy), while those of less than pH7 are acid (lime-free). Kits that indicate pH by reacting with soil and changing colour, are available from garden centres.

Soil pH affects the solubility of vital nutrients in the soil and their availability to plants. Acid and alkaline soils vary in the amounts of nutrients they contain. Plants like or tolerate different levels of lime; some, such as azaleas and many ericas, thrive only on acid (called lime-free) soils and others, such as clematis and pinks, are happy in limy soils.

Conditioning the soil

To ensure your plants get off to a good start, it is always worth conditioning the soil. There are many soil-conditioning materials available from garden centres. The best are bulky organic materials, like manures, composted bark, or garden compost, which improve the soil structure so that it drains freely but retains moisture in dry weather. Manures and compost also replace some of the nutrients taken up by plants or washed out of the soil. Organic matter must be well-rotted; if not, it will deplete the soil of nutrients as it rots.

Types of garden soil

The soil type you have largely dictates the plants you can grow. Soils in different sites, or even in different parts of a garden, vary in ease of cultivation, their fertility, and how easy it is for plant roots to penetrate. There are several basic kinds of garden soil.

■ Loam has an ideal balance of clay and sand particles. It is the perfect growing medium – rich in nutrients and with a friable, crumbly texture that allows good drainage and water-retention.
■ Chalk soil is free-draining and quick to lose moisture. It is reasonably fertile and contains lime so is very alkaline.
■ Clay soil is often very fertile, but slow-draining. Heavy clay soil can be difficult to work. If you open up its

structure by digging in grit and organic matter, plant growth will be vigorous.
■ Peat soil is acid and in winter can become waterlogged. It is high in organic matter and, if well-drained, provides good growing conditions. Add lime to grow more types of plants in it.
■ Sandy soil feels gritty and light, is easy to work, and warms up quickly in spring. Very free-draining, it dries out fast; nutrients can be washed out by rain and by watering, so it needs regular additions of organic matter and fertilizer.
■ Silty soil is silky to the touch. It can be badly drained, and when it is wet, packs down and becomes quite waterlogged. Improve it by adding plenty of well-rotted organic matter. Silty soil is also reasonably fertile.

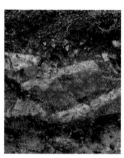

Chalk soil is pale, loose-textured, and full of chalk stones. The topsoil is usually shallow and has solid chalk rock beneath it.

Clay soil is heavy and cold. In dry conditions, it sets solid and cracks. Clay rolls into a soft ball that is shiny if smoothed.

Peat soil is spongy and holds a lot of water. Its dark colour is due to decomposed organic matter, which may still be visible.

The best time to incorporate well-rotted organic matter into the soil is during autumn. Scatter a thick layer all over the bed and fork it in. Alternatively, leave it as a surface mulch to protect the roots of vulnerable plants over winter.

You can greatly improve the drainage of heavy clay and silty soils by incorporating a 5–8cm (2–3in) layer of coarse grit or gravel. Digging in the gravel with a fork will open up the structure and facilitate the flow of water through the soil.

The more organic matter that you add to the soil, the more organisms such as bacteria and worms will populate the soil, help to work it, and improve its structure. Making garden compost is easy and costs nothing (*see right*).

Well-rotted horse manure is one of the best soil conditioners, but can be hard to obtain. Spent mushroom compost contains rotted manure and peat. It also has some lime, so do not use it where acid-loving plants are grown. Seaweed is an excellent conditioner because it makes the soil more friable and is rich in trace elements. Composted straw and leafmould use otherwise wasted resources, but they take two years to rot. Pelleted chicken manure adds vital nutrients, but has no conditioning value since the pellets have little bulk.

The importance of good soil drainage

The amount of water that is available to plants through their roots depends on the type of soil and how free-draining it is. In well-structured soils, like loam, sufficient water and air is held in the spaces, or pores, between the soil particles to supply most plants adequately.

A soil with poor structure may dry out very quickly or become waterlogged. For example, finely textured clay soils hold most moisture, but it is bound up in such

a way that it is unavailable to plants. The large pores of sandy soils make water easily available to plant roots, but it drains away quickly. Peat soils can become waterlogged, and compacted silt and clay soils are often poorly drained.

Digging in well-rotted organic matter will improve the structure of both clay and sandy soils. Drainage can also be improved by adding gravel.

Making garden compost

Even in the smallest garden, it is worth making your own compost – it enables you to recycle waste and return it to the garden in a form which is unsurpassed for improving soil structure and fertility. It also saves you the expense of buying proprietory soil conditioners.

To make good garden compost, you first need a suitable container. There are many compost bins on the market, but you can make one easily at home, for example from builders' pallets or old wood. The main thing to bear in mind is that the bin should be 1–1.5m (3–5ft) square, with fairly solid sides in order to retain heat and moisture. It should also have a cover; a piece of old carpet will do.

The best compost is made from mixing fast-rotting, succulent material, such as grass clippings and vegetable trimmings, with drier material, such as straw and

shredded newspaper, which is slower to decompose. Try to add materials in well-mixed layers.

Compost takes about a year to rot down, but the process can be speeded up if the heap is turned at least once to mix the contents thoroughly. The easiest way to do this, if space allows, is to have two bins, so you can turn the contents of one bin into the other. If the compost is slimy and smelly, mix in more "dry" material; if it is dry and not rotting, add sappy stuff.

Compost ingredients

Almost any material of organic origin can be recycled into compost. You can add any plant waste from the garden into the heap, except perennial weeds, seeds, and diseased material. Burn or bin these items; if they survive in the compost heap you may end up spreading weeds and diseases around the garden. Shred woody prunings, fibrous stems, cardboard, newspapers, and old clothing. Vegetable kitchen waste can also be used, but meat, fish, and cooked foods will attract vermin. Litter from small pets such as rabbits, guinea pigs, or birds is suitable, but not from cats and dogs. You can also add manure and autumn leaves.

After about a year, rotted compost is dark, friable, and odourless, and ready to use in the garden.

Planting basics

Give your plants a good start in life and there is every chance that they will grow strong and healthy. The first and most important step is to create a welcoming environment for their roots, encouraging them to spread out into the surrounding soil where they will take up water and nutrients.

All plants appreciate being planted in a suitable and well-prepared site. Generally, the better the soil, the quicker they will become established. Before starting to plant, clear the plot of any weeds that could compete with your plants for water and nutrients. Then take care to ensure that each plant has room to grow to its full size. Check the mature height and spread on the care label and mark it out around each planting hole. You can fill the gaps with bedding plants until they mature. If a plant outgrows its space, transplant it in autumn or spring: dig it up, saving as much of the root mass as possible, and replant it in a previously prepared site.

Plants always look more natural in a border when grouped in odd numbers because the brain automatically sorts even numbers into pairs.

Many trees and shrubs are planted in the same way as those grown in containers (*see right*), but bare-root and root-balled plants (*see pp.316–317*) require slightly different treatment. Plant bare-root plants in early winter so they can establish before summer. Even with careful handling, they may suffer some root damage. To encourage new growth, cut damaged or dry roots back hard; to compensate for the loss of roots, trim the top-growth back hard.

Root-balled plants are best planted in autumn or spring. After soaking the root ball, remove the netting and tease out the roots. Both root-balled and bare-root plants should be planted with the old soil mark level with the surface.

Planting container-grown trees and shrubs

Plant container-grown plants at any time, so long as the soil is not waterlogged or frozen, but the best results are from autumn or spring planting (*see below*). If you plant in summer you must keep the roots watered while the plant establishes itself. Before planting, prune out any dead or diseased growth and awkwardly placed shoots. Scrape away the top layer of compost from the pot to remove any weed seeds, then stand it in its pot in a bucket of water for two hours to soak the root ball.

Dig a good-sized planting hole. Fill the hole with water and allow it to seep away. Next, fork a thick layer of well-rotted farmyard manure or garden compost into the bottom of the hole to give the plant a good start. Shrubs also appreciate some slow-release fertilizer. If the soil gets very wet in winter, improve the drainage by forking in coarse grit. Gently knock off the pot and place the plant in the hole.

Planting at the correct depth is crucial to avoid a check in growth. With a few exceptions – such as some clematis (*see pp.118–119*), which like to be planted deep – you should keep the plant at the same depth as it was in its container.

It also helps to enrich the removed soil by mixing it with well-rotted organic matter. If the plant needs support, insert canes or stakes, taking care not to damage the root ball, and tie in the main stem.

Planting non-woody plants

The principles of planting are much the same for perennials, annuals, and other bedding plants as for shrubs (*see left*). However, these plants are more prone to drying out, so should be planted without delay. Some plants are sold in pots, but bedding plants are usually sold in modular trays, with one seedling per module to stop the roots being disturbed during planting. As soon as you buy bedding plants, give them a good soaking and plant them or, if there is still a risk of frost, pot them up separately to grow on under cover until it is safe to plant them out.

Planting climbers

The soil at the base of a wall or fence can be extremely dry because it is in a rain

---

How to plant a container-grown tree or shrub

1 Soak the plant's root ball in a bucket of water for a couple of hours before planting. Dig a hole that is at least twice as wide and one-and-a-half times deeper than the root ball. Fork in plenty of well-rotted organic matter and, if it is needed for improved drainage, some coarse grit.

2 Set the plant at the same depth as it was in its original pot. Use a cane to check that the root ball is level with the soil surface.

3 Fill in the hole with soil. Use your heel to firm the soil around the plant to remove air pockets.

4 Water the plant well to settle the soil, even if it is raining. Apply a 5cm (2in) layer of well-rotted compost or bark as a mulch over the root area to help retain moisture and suppress weeds.

To train newly-planted climbers, separate out the shoots and tie them into the supports, using garden twine. Canes angled towards the wall will encourage the shoots to grow towards it.

shadow, where rain rarely reaches the soil. When planting a climber, you should first improve the soil's moisture-retention by digging in plenty of well-rotted organic matter (such as garden compost). Follow the technique for planting a container-grown shrub (*see p.320*), but make sure that the planting hole is at least 30–45cm (12–18in) away from the wall. Also don't forget to angle the top of the root ball towards the wall, while keeping the crown of the plant level with the soil surface.

Before planting, fix up a support. The easiest system is horizontal wires through galvanized vine eyes in the wall, or trellis panels (*see p.327*) attached to battens.

Planting bulbs

There are a couple of important points to remember when planting bulbs. First, most should be planted at a depth equivalent to three times their size. For example, if a bulb stands 5cm (2in) tall, then there should be 10cm (4in) of soil on top of it, and the planting hole should therefore be 15cm (6in) deep. However, check the care label because some bulbs, such as nerines and some lilies, prefer to have their tops level with the soil surface. If bulbs are planted at the wrong depth, they may fail

to flower (a condition referred to as "blindness"). Blindness can also occur when the bulbs become crowded; lifting and replanting bulbs every three to four years should prevent this problem.

The second point to bear in mind is to check that the bulb is the right way up. This is easily done with true bulbs, like narcissi, but on corms and tubers the buds are not always very distinct.

The most natural way to grow bulbs is in large drifts in grass. There are two ways to do this – but first, cut the grass as short as possible. You will need to leave it uncut until the bulb foliage dies down in early summer.

With large bulbs, such as daffodils, informally scatter them over the chosen area. Check they are all at least 10cm (4in) apart and then plant each bulb where it fell. Use a bulb planter (*see below*) or trowel to dig a hole, insert the bulb, and replace the soil.

To plant a large number of small bulbs, such as crocuses, make an "H"-shaped cut in the lawn using a half-moon edger or spade. Turn back the turf flaps. Take out the soil to the correct depth if necessary; plant the bulbs about 2.5cm (1in) apart; then fold back and firm the turf.

A bulb planter takes out a neat plug of soil just big enough for one bulb. Push it vertically into the ground, giving it a firm twist before lifting out the plug of soil. If the planter doesn't have depth markings on its side, use a ruler to measure the hole. If it is too deep, top up with soil, compost or grit.

Preparing containers

Most plants grow happily in containers but they demand more attention than if they had been planted in the garden. Line the base with broken crocks to stop the drainage hole becoming blocked up with compost. Choose a loam-based compost as it holds nutrients and water longer than a soilless compost. Mix water-retaining granules and slow-release fertilizer into it to cut down on watering and feeding later.

Climbers need more attention to thrive. Choose the largest container you can handle: the more compost in the pot, the slower it will be to dry out. Insert the support system right at the start, so that plants can be trained to it. And keep the pots well watered, especially during dry spells; a decorative grit or pebble mulch may help conserve moisture.

Planting water-garden plants

The best planting times for aquatic plants are late spring or early summer. The majority of them benefit from being planted in a basket. There are many different planting baskets – the most common ones are made of plastic mesh and require lining with hessian to contain the soil. The mesh allows water to penetrate to the roots, while containing the growth of more rampant plants.

Partly fill the basket with soil and sit the plant so its crown is level with the top of the basket. Fill in soil around the roots and firm. Leaving the growing points exposed, top-dress with a thin layer of gravel to hold the soil in place. Soak the compost well before setting the basket in shallow water. Move into deeper water as the stems grow (*see p.244*).

Aquatic plants are generally easy to grow. You can use special low-nitrogen aquatic compost (too much nitrogen in water causes green algae to grow), but ordinary garden soil works just as well if no fertilizer has been added to it.

Pruning

If you grow woody plants, sooner or later you will have to prune them to keep them looking their best. Pruning is often regarded with dread by gardeners, but it really is just a matter of common sense and learning a few fundamental rules. Also, good-quality tools make the job easier.

Pruning encourages new, strong growth and increases the number of flowers, maintains a well-balanced shape, and keeps a plant to the desired size. The methods vary depending on the type of plant. It is most important in a plant's early years because it affects its future shape. By pruning out dead and diseased growth, you can also improve the health of an ailing plant.

It may seem contrary, but by cutting back a plant you encourage it to grow bigger and stronger, because it reacts by sending out new shoots from below the cuts. You can also persuade a plant to grow in a particular direction and regulate the quantity and vigour of that growth.

Before you start pruning, take a good look at the plant, giving some thought to the cuts you are about to make. If you rush in, you could end up with a badly shaped plant or lose a season of flowering because you have cut out the wrong stems.

Basic tools for pruning

If you invest in a few good-quality pruning tools, it will make your job much easier. Using good cutting tools will also ensure the pruning cuts are clean and heal quickly without becoming vulnerable to disease. For most pruning tasks, a pair of secateurs, a pruning saw, and perhaps some loppers are all you need. Use a tool suited to the stem size – if you try to cut a large stem with secateurs, you will damage it by making a blunt cut. Keep blades clean and sharp: blunt blades tear rather than cut, allowing disease to take hold.

Spring-flowering plants

It is best to prune spring- or early flowering plants after they flower and before they start to put on new growth. This is because their flowers develop from buds growing on the previous year's stems. If pruning is left too late in the season, you might remove next year's flowering shoots.

First thin out any old, damaged, and diseased wood. Then cut some older stems right back to the ground. Next, cut shoots with buds back to five or six buds, even if they have started to put on new growth at the tips. The following year's flowering shoots will develop from these buds.

Many spring-flowering shrubs can be trained flat against a wall. On planting, tie all the main stems and sideshoots into a support. Cut back any shoots that cannot be tied in to one or two buds and pinch out the tips of forward-facing shoots so that they branch sideways. Shorten the longest sideshoots, especially where growth is

---

Basic principles of pruning

No matter what type of plant you are pruning, certain basic principles apply. Fast-growing plants that put on more than 30cm (12in) growth in a year respond well to hard pruning. Slow-growing plants usually do not respond well to being pruned back hard, so avoid it unless absolutely necessary. When pruning to a single bud, make your cut at a 45° angle, 5mm (¼in) above the bud so any moisture runs off. For buds that are opposite each other, cut straight across the stem close to the bud tips.

■ When pruning dead or diseased wood, wipe the blades between cuts with a proprietary disinfectant in order to avoid spreading spores or infection to the next plant that you prune.

■ Crossing stems rub together causing chafing damage to bark, creating a wound where disease can enter.

■ Overcrowded stems are weak, block out light, and trap damp air which encourages disease. Thinning out such stems restores a plant's vigour.

■ After hard pruning, always give the plant a good feed and mulch, and water it if necessary. Inspect your plants regularly and take out any broken or damaged stems without delay to minimize the risk of disease (*see right*).

Remove dead wood to stop disease spreading, cutting back to a strong bud or the nearest healthy, new shoot.

sparse. In later years, after flowering, tie in new growth and cut back badly placed or overly long shoots. Take out any diseased or dead wood; checking ties are not too tight. Cut back the flowered shoots to 5–6 buds; some shrubs, such as flowering quinces (*Chaenomeles*) and pyracanthas, are pruned to 2–3 buds for prolific flowering.

Late-summer flowering plants

These plants produce flowers on growth made in the current growing season. Early spring is the best time to prune them, because it diverts each plant's energy to existing buds and gives it time to produce new flowering shoots from the buds.

Hard annual pruning suits many deciduous shrubs and climbers, such as caryopteris, ceanothus, *Hydrangea paniculata*, and phygelius – as well as many grey-leaved evergreens, for example lavenders. It produces the best-quality flowers and prevents the plant from becoming too big. Old or neglected late-summer flowering shrubs respond well to hard pruning.

In the first spring, aim to form a base of strong, woody stems from which spring-flowering shoots will grow each year. Cut out any weak or diseased stems and shorten the remainder to 15–45cm (6–18in), or if a large plant is required, to 1.2m (4ft). Prune in subsequent early springs before growth starts. Restore the original framework by pruning all the old flowering stems to leave two or three pairs of fat, healthy buds from the previous year's growth. At the same time, if it is necessary, thin out dense congested stems.

Early summer-flowering plants

Early summer-flowering shrubs, for example philadelphus and weigelas, and climbing plants are generally pruned in late summer, after flowering has finished. You

To encourage new growth on a mature shrub, after flowering cut out one in four of the old stems just above the base. Take care to leave a few strong buds on each. Shorten younger shoots by about a quarter.

should aim to open up the plant to allow in light and air and retain an uncluttered, balanced shape.

In the first year after planting, remove all weak and crossing shoots by cutting each out just above an outward-facing bud or at the base. Trim back any overlong shoots to within the overall outline, again cutting each to an outward-facing bud.

In subsequent years, thin out the plant by removing about one in four of the oldest stems, cutting them back to the ground. This makes room for new stems to grow from the base. Shorten younger stems to encourage flowering sideshoots. Wayward stems should be pruned back to maintain a good shape.

Hedges

Regular trimming not only keeps a hedge looking neat, it also promotes strong, dense growth and longevity. Use an electric trimmer and keep the blade parallel to the hedge for an even cut. Always wear eye and ear protectors and gloves, and sweep the blade away from your body and the cable. Aim to create a hedge that is wider at the base than at the top. It is less vulnerable to damage from snow and winds, and light can reach the lower branches.

Trim established evergreen hedges, for example privet and fast-growing conifers,

in late spring or early summer and again in late summer or in early autumn, while they are in growth. Deciduous hedges, such as beech and hawthorn, are best trimmed in summer with a second tidy up in autumn. Time pruning of flowering hedges to suit their flowering periods.

It is especially important to prune evergreen and coniferous hedges regularly, because very few will reshoot from old wood. When training an evergreen or conifer hedge, keep the sides trimmed, but allow the main stem to reach the desired height before pruning it.

Climbing plants

Many climbers, such as *Clematis montana* and rambling roses, make a lot of growth in one season. Prune spring-flowering climbers after flowering; summer-flowering plants in spring. Remove overlong shoots and unhealthy growth. However, do not over-prune summer-flowering plants because it will encourage leafy growth rather than flowering shoots. You can thin out congested climbers, but only once every three years or so.

Renovation pruning

Provided that plants are basically healthy, renovation pruning can spur strong growth and flower production. The most drastic pruning involves cutting all main stems to 30–60cm (12–24in) and is suitable for many deciduous plants like lilacs and buddlejas. For a staged renovation, each year prune half of remaining old stems, cutting them to ground level and thin out new growth arising from last year's cuts to two to three strong stems. This suits less vigorous woody plants, particularly evergreens such as rhododendrons, as it gives them a chance to recover.

The best time is in late winter or spring so the plants have a chance to put on new growth before the next winter. Not all old shrubs survive such drastic pruning, so be prepared for some losses.

Routine tasks

A little time spent regularly on maintenance, such as feeding, watering, weeding, mulching, and deadheading, will keep your plants in top condition so they perform at their best. Enjoy the chance these simple tasks give you to enjoy your garden.

Any job in the garden is easier if you use the correct tools. Essentials include a spade, a fork, a hand trowel and hand fork, and a hoe and short-tined rake for soil cultivation and weeding. Secateurs are needed to deadhead and prune plants and if you have trees, shrubs, or woody climbers, loppers and a pruning saw are useful. If you have a lawn, a good lawnmower and a long-tined lawn rake will help you to keep it looking good. Add to those a watering can and a wheelbarrow and you can undertake most routine tasks in the garden. Always buy the best-quality tools you can afford since cheap ones may last only one or two seasons.

Routine tasks can be minimized by making sure that plants are growing in a position with a soil and conditions that suit them (see Climate and location, pp.314–315, and Soils and compost, pp.318–319). If you grow a plant in an unsuitable site, it is unlikely to flourish and will need much more attention. It is also essential that plants have space to grow to maturity; you may be tempted to cram them in for immediate effect, but this will make them weak and more prone to attack from pests and diseases.

Above all, it is more effective and easier to care for your plants by doing a little quite often, rather than leaving tasks until the garden becomes neglected.

What to do when: a seasonal calendar

Spring
■ Cut back old growth left over the winter and clear away insulation put over and around plants.
■ As grass begins to grow, begin mowing lawns with the cutting blade set at maximum height; tidy up edges.
■ Feed and mulch all woody and herbaceous perennial plants as soon as soil starts to warm up.
■ Repot or top-dress plants that are grown in containers.
■ After they flower, prune spring-flowering deciduous shrubs and climbers (see pp.322–323); also prune late-flowering shrubs and climbers, all bush roses (see p.96), and groups 2 and 3 clematis (see p.118).
■ Prune or trim evergreens if necessary to keep their shape.
■ Divide clump-forming perennials, bamboos, and grasses.
■ Plant new plants and autumn-flowering bulbs, and seed.
■ Provide support now for perennials and biennials that will need it when they are fully grown.

■ In late spring, start to bring container-grown plants that have been overwintered under cover out into the garden.
■ Keep young and newly planted varieties watered regularly.
■ Keep on top of routine tasks such as deadheading and weeding; start to feed plants in containers.
■ Layer shrubs and climbers.
■ Plant, thin, and divide oxygenating plants in ponds.

Summer
■ Mow lawns regularly.
■ Clip hedges.
■ After they flower, finish pruning spring-flowering deciduous shrubs and climbers and group 1 clematis (see p.118).
■ Continue routine tasks such as feeding, deadheading, and weeding.
■ Prune Prunus trees and shrubs in midsummer to avoid infection by silver leaf and other diseases.
■ Take soft and semi-ripe cuttings.
■ In late summer, prune early summer-flowering deciduous shrubs and climbers (see pp.322–323).

Autumn
■ Keep up with routine tasks such as weeding and deadheading; but stop feeding plants.
■ Prune flowering hedges and rambling roses after flowering.
■ Clear dying growth of perennials and grasses, but leave it in cold regions to act as winter insulation.
■ Lift tender rootstocks, such as dahlias, and store over winter.
■ Mow lawns at maximum height.
■ Move tender plants under cover.
■ Plant hardy trees, shrubs, climbers, perennials, and spring-flowering bulbs; sow seed of hardy plants.
■ Take hardwood cuttings.
■ Clear out any leaves and dead material from ponds.

Winter
■ Plant hardy trees, shrubs, hedges, climbers, and perennials.
■ Brush snow from conifers.
■ Plan what seeds and plants you wish to order for next year.
■ Take root cuttings.

Using fertilizers

Plants need nutrients to encourage strong, healthy growth and plentiful flowers. Whether you use organic or non-organic fertilizers is down to personal choice. Organic feeds tend to release nutrients over a longer period; chemicals give a fast, but short-lived, boost to growth. Both are available as granules, powders, or liquids. Powdered or granular feeds, such as poultry pellets, can be scattered over the entire planting area or around individual plants as required.

Dry fertilizers, such as bonemeal, have to be watered into the soil, because plants can absorb nutrients only once they are dissolved in water. Liquid feeds are quick-acting and easy to apply, using a special hose-end applicator or watering can. Fertilizer pellets are useful for inserting into containers as they release their goodness slowly.

Apply fertilizers from mid-spring to midsummer, when the plants are growing rapidly and will benefit from extra nutrients. Take care when applying a concentrated fertilizer because it may scorch the stems and foliage of the plants. Always take heed of the manufacturer's instructions, and avoid the temptation to overfeed the plants; it is wasteful and only results in weak, sappy growth with fewer flowers.

Applying a top-dressing

Compost in containers becomes less fertile over time as its nutrients are taken up and used by the plant, and leached out by rain and watering. If the plant has not outgrown the pot and become root-bound, you can apply an annual top-dressing at the beginning of the growing season in order to replenish the nutrients. Remove the top layer of old soil, and replace it with fresh compost.

Alternatively, for shrubs and trees, you could use garden compost or composted bark. A mulch (*see p.326*) of bark chips or gravel will conserve moisture and give a decorative finish.

Rock-garden plants, especially alpine species, like well-drained soil; a top-dressing of gravel, pebbles, pea shingle, or even glass chips, avoids water puddling around the plants and causing rot.

Watering

How often you need to water will depend on the local conditions. Frequent rain should supply enough moisture, but in dry spells you may have to water beds, lawns, and containers daily. Some plants require moist soil and will quickly die if the ground starts to dry out, but others will be able to cope once they become established. New plantings are also at risk from drought until they form a strong root system.

Try basin watering (*see below centre*) to direct water to the roots. Another option is pot watering: sink a deep pot into the soil next to a plant; fill it with water and allow it to drain into the soil. Seedlings especially need constant attention – too much water and they will rot off, too little and they will quickly die. In summer, water in the evening or early morning. In the middle of the day, the heat increases evaporation so your efforts will be wasted, and water droplets act like lenses to scorch the foliage.

Hoses and sprinklers

Watering can be a time-consuming task, so consider investing in a hose that will carry water to where it is needed. Reinforced hoses are less likely to kink than the flat ones. Hoses that wind onto their own reels are easy to store. All should be fitted with a spray nozzle that can adjust the flow of water from a stream to a fine spray, so you can water appropriately (*see below*).

Some types of hose are laid around the garden as a permanent irrigation system controlled by a tap or a timer. Seep hoses let water ooze out along their entire length; drip hoses deliver water through holes to individual plants in beds or containers. Sprinklers can be used for large areas. Their fine sprays soak the soil evenly, but they are wasteful, and have to be moved often to stop puddles forming.

Liquid feed can be sprayed onto plants as a fast, effective pick-me-up if they are not doing well. Most is absorbed through the leaves, and any excess is taken up by the roots. To avoid scorch, apply in the evening or on dull days.

To create a water basin, plant slightly lower than the soil surface to create a hollow, or surround the plant with a raised dam of soil. Water into this basin so that all the water is directed straight to the roots, saving time and conserving water.

Take care when using a hose to water plants. A strong stream of water can erode soil from around the roots, leaving them prone to dry out. Alternatively, if the ground is hard, it may just run over the surface away from where it is needed.

Mulching

A mulch is a layer of material applied as a skin over the soil, and has many advantages over leaving the surface bare. Loose mulches maintain a more even soil temperature that is warmer in winter and cooler in summer than naked ground. The need for watering is reduced, because moisture cannot evaporate from the soil so readily. Mulches also help to suppress weeds, especially the sheet mulches such as landscape fabric and black plastic. The weeds are prevented from germinating by the lack of light, although some persistent perennial weeds such as dandelions may grow through a loose mulch unless the soil has been throughly weeded beforehand. Any weeds that appear after the mulch is laid will be easier to spot and remove. As well as being useful, mulches can also be very ornamental, especially if you use materials such as chipped bark, pebbles, or glass chips.

Types of mulch

There are many types of organic and synthetic mulch available, but to be effective it should be long-lasting and not easily dislodged by rain or blown away. Organic mulches such as compost will be

Spread organic mulch directly onto the soil to a depth of 5–8cm (2–3in) to control weeds or 10–15cm (4–6in) for winter insulation. Leave a 10cm (4in) gap around each plant to avoid rot setting in.

carried down into the soil by worms, improving the soil structure and replenishing nutrients – mulching and fertilizing in one. If using an organic material, make sure it has a loose texture that allows moisture to pass through easily.

Organic mulches, such as well-rotted manure, improve soil structure, but do not use mushroom compost for acid-loving plants. Grass cuttings are free, but may turn slimy or spread weed seeds. Bark chips look good and use an otherwise wasted resource, as do sweet-smelling cocoa shells. Sheet mulches are effective, but need disguising. Gravel is expensive, but makes a handsome mulch.

Applying and using mulches

A mulch stabilizes and maintains soil conditions, so the best time to apply one is in autumn or spring. At these times of year, the soil should be reasonably warm, not too wet or too dry, and free from weeds. A loose mulch, such as gravel, well-rotted manure, and chipped bark, can be applied by spreading it liberally around plants with a shovel and raking it level.

Sheet mulches of landscape fabric or plastic are easy to use if laid over a bed before planting. Cut the sheet so that it is at least 15cm (6in) larger on all sides than the area to be covered. Secure the sheet at the edges with pegs, or push the edges into the ground with the edge of a spade, making sure that it is taut. The plants can then be inserted through planting holes. If using black plastic, punch some holes in it so air and water can reach the soil.

Weeding

Any plant growing where it is not wanted can be called a weed, although they are often thought of as wild plants. In favourable conditions, some ornamentals such as *Alchemilla mollis* can be invasive. Weeds are a nuisance because they grow very fast, taking water, nutrients, and light from less vigorous, cultivated plants.

To use a hoe, walk backwards, pushing and pulling the blade along the surface, slicing off the tops of annual weeds. If it is hot, let the weeds wither, or if damp, remove them and add to the compost bin.

There are two types of weed: annual and perennial. Annual weeds, such as annual meadow grass, have thin, shallow roots and complete their life cycle within one year. Left to grow they will self-seed prolifically and grow rapidly, producing up to three generations in a season. If you don't allow them to seed, they are fairly easy to control.

Perennial weeds usually have deep, fleshy, or spreading roots, such as the common dandelion, or creeping underground stems, for example, ground elder. They are difficult to remove completely, and return year after year even if only a small piece of root is left in the soil after weeding.

Controlling weeds

The method of control you choose for your garden will depend on the types of weed, the scale of the invasion, and whether you are prepared to use chemicals.

If you want to avoid using weedkillers, then mulching (*see left*) as well as using ground-cover plants will prevent weeds taking hold. If a few annual weeds do appear, they are simple to deal with. Cut them down with a hoe, or pull them up by hand, before they set seed.

Small patches of perennial weeds can be dug out with a fork, but may reappear unless you remove every last bit of root. If there is a very bad infestation, then a drastic solution may be needed. A sheet mulch (*see facing page*), will kill most weeds if it is left in place over two seasons.

Inevitably, chemical weedkillers save a lot of time and effort. Many are effective only in early summer and should be used on a dull, dry day. Some weedkillers are selective and will kill only certain types of plants, so first identify the problem weed. Several applications may be necessary to clear persistent perennial weeds. Always follow carefully the manufacturer's instructions when using chemicals.

Individual weeds can be targeted, but if an area has more weeds than desirable plants, consider digging up the plants you wish to keep and treating the entire area. Before replanting the ornamentals, wash the soil off the root balls and check for and remove any perennial weed fragments.

Supporting plants

Many herbaceous plants need some support as they grow to prevent them from being snapped by wind or being flattened by heavy rain. Push supports

Link stakes come in varying heights and slot together easily to create a support. You can position them around any shape of clump. Insert to a depth of 10cm (4in) to keep them steady.

into the soil when the plant is no more than 30cm (12in) tall, so that it has time to grow through and disguise the support. If you delay staking the plant until it begins to flop, the supports will look obvious and unnatural.

Traditionally, bamboo canes are used – either singly for tall plants such as gladioli, or in a circle with twine for clumping plants. A more natural alternative is peasticks – twiggy branches usually discarded from coppiced shrubs. You could use large plastic or wire mesh stretched between canes; the plant stems grow through the mesh and obscure it. There are also many metal and plastic staking systems available that are re-usable and versatile. Small climbers, such as sweet peas, can be grown successfully over a wigwam of canes that are tied at the top with raffia, or over a wooden or metal obelisk.

Using trellis

Train climbers and wall shrubs on trellis used as a freestanding screen, fixed to battens on a wall, or to extend the height of a fence. Make sure the wood has been treated with preservative before it is covered by the plant. Most plants grown on trellis need to be tied regularly into the support; a loose figure-of-eight loop of twine will allow for stems to grow. Check the ties at least once a year and loosen any that are too tight.

Deadheading and pinch pruning

During the growing season, prolong each plant's flowering period by deadheading. This directs energy that would have gone into producing seed into forming more flowers. Try to get into the habit of deadheading whenever you go into the garden, and you will be rewarded with a constant and tidy display of flowers.

Removing the spent flowers of most herbaceous plants can be done by hand.

Some perennials, for example delphiniums, lupins, and oriental poppies, can be cut down to the base once the first flush of flower has ended to induce fresh foliage and a second display later in the season. Other plants, such as catmint, cranesbills, and pulmonarias can simply be sheared over once they have finished flowering.

To deadhead shrubs and woody climbers, use secateurs and cut back the flowered shoot to a healthy, outward-facing bud. The new shoot should grow in a direction that will enhance the shape of the plant. Remember that many plants, including some roses, achilleas, and grasses, should not be deadheaded if you wish to enjoy their decorative hips or seedheads in late autumn and winter.

You can also keep the foliage of plants, for example herbs, looking neat by pinch pruning. This is a similar process to deadheading, but involves removing the growing tips of shoots before flowering to encourage lots of new sideshoots and a dense, bushy habit. It is a technique often used with fuchsias and summer bedding plants early in the season; if you stop pinch pruning in midsummer, the plants will burst into bloom, producing a continuous mass of flowers.

Regularly remove withered flowers to prolong the display. On woody plants use secateurs, always cutting back to a strong, outward-facing bud as this will encourage open growth.

Raising your own

One of the great joys of gardening is propagating your own plants by taking cuttings, dividing, layering, and sowing seed. Not only are these techniques fun to learn, they will also save you a great deal of money – when compared with nursery plants, the price of a packet of seed is small.

You don't need to purchase much equipment to raise your own plants, nor do you need a great deal of space – a sunny windowsill will do – but you do need clean containers, good-quality, fresh compost (not salvaged from other pots) and, if taking cuttings, a clean, sharp knife. Poor hygiene is the prime enemy of young seedlings and cuttings, because it allows diseases such as rots to attack the vulnerable young plants.

New seedlings and cuttings need the correct balance of nutrients, a good supply of oxygen and moisture, and appropriate light and temperature levels. All you have to do is provide suitable growing conditions – nature will do the rest for you. Seed and all cuttings, except hardwood ones, succeed in the protected environment of a propagator. Create similar conditions by covering a pot with a clear plastic bag. Warming the compost gently will also help.

Division and layering (*see p.330*) are even easier ways of raising new plants, because they are undertaken outdoors, but these methods produce only one or a few new plants at a time.

Sowing seed in containers

Most plants are easy to raise from seed, including annuals, perennials, and even trees. If you have never sown seed before, it is best to buy packeted seed because it is quality controlled and comes with full instructions for each type.

The most natural way to grow seed is, of course, outdoors but by sowing indoors you have more control over the environment and each seed has a better chance of survival. Indoor sowings can also be made earlier than outdoor ones, getting the plants off to a good start.

Sow seed thinly to avoid problems with overcrowding. Fine seed will be easier to sow if mixed with sand. Whether you use a full- or half-sized seed tray will depend on the amount of seed that you are sowing. Many gardeners use modular trays or coir or peat seed blocks – if sown one per module, each seedling can grow to a good size before being disturbed. Biodegradable pots also avoid root disturbance because each seedling is planted out with its pot. Seedlings that develop long roots, such as sweet peas, are best grown in tall tube pots.

You can use recycled containers: yoghurt pots and foil trays work well (just make drainage holes), while cardboard egg boxes and toilet roll tubes make useful biodegradable modules.

Successful seed germination

A seed contains a plant in embryo and to kickstart it into life, it needs the correct balance of warmth, air, and moisture. You can usually achieve these conditions by placing pots or trays of seed in an electric propagator or heated tray, which provide "bottom heat", gently warming the soil to encourage germination. Alternatively, cover the container with kitchen film or a sheet of glass.

Some seed needs special treatment to trigger it into germination, for example, low light levels. A period of cold, to mimic winter, can be created by placing the seed container in the refrigerator or outdoors for a time. Some seeds with a thick coating need to be soaked before sowing. These details will be listed on the seed packet. As soon as the seedlings emerge, increase ventilation or remove any film, but keep out of the sun. If left covered, they may fall prey to damping off, a fungal disease that spreads fast in damp, still air.

Caring for seedlings

Seedlings should never be allowed to dry out, nor should they sit in wet compost, which is a breeding ground for diseases such as damping off. Watering from overhead can wash seedlings out of the

---

How to sow seed in a tray

1 Fill the tray with good-quality, fresh seed compost. Tap the tray firmly on the bench two or three times to settle the compost and scrape off the excess with a ruler. Press another tray on the surface to firm the compost to 1cm (½in) below the rim. Stand the tray in a reservoir of water until the surface is just moist.
2 Sprinkle seed thinly on the surface of the compost, then cover with a fine layer of sieved compost. Press large seeds into the compost, at a depth of twice their diameter; fill in the holes.
3 Water the surface of the seed compost with a fine spray. Cover the tray to prevent moisture loss and maintain an even temperature – use a sheet of glass, clear kitchen film, or a purpose-made plastic lid. If it is very sunny, shade the tray with paper to prevent it overheating.

When transplanting seedlings, gently hold them by their true leaves above the lower seed leaves, and carefully lever out with a dibber or pencil.

compost. Instead, stand pots and trays in clean tap water and lift out as soon as the surface of the compost starts to moisten. Allow any excess water to drain away.

Seedlings sown indoors tend to be taller and weaker than those sown outside. Gently stroking their tops 10–20 times a day with your fingers, or a piece of thin card, encourages shorter, sturdier growth.

Overcrowded seedlings compete for light, water, and space. They may grow leggy and more vulnerable to disease, so transplant or prick them out as soon as they have formed two true leaves above the first pair of seed leaves.

Select the healthiest, strongest seedlings to grow on and discard the rest. You can thin them out, by pulling out unwanted seedlings with tweezers, or transplant them into new containers of fresh compost. Insert them about 5cm (2in) apart with the seed leaves just above the compost. To prick out, use a dibber to ease the seedlings out of the old compost. Try not to damage any roots. Make a hole for each seedling, lower its roots into the hole, and firm gently by pushing in the compost from the sides. Pop them back in a ventilated propagator and shade from bright sun until they are established.

Hardening off

Young plants that have been indoors need to be acclimatized to the drier and cooler conditions of the garden. If this is not done, the young plants will be knocked back and suffer a check to their growth. It is best not to rush this final stage – known as "hardening off" – so allow a week or two for the process.

Wait until all danger of frost has passed before moving young plants outdoors. Choose a warm, dry, but dull day to commence hardening off. In the early stages, cover the plants with a layer of horticultural fleece to protect them from windchill, and keep them out of heavy rain or strong sun. Bring them back under cover at night for the first few days.

If the weather stays mild, leave them out overnight under a double, and then a single, layer of fleece. If the plants look healthy, finally remove it altogether. Your plants will be fully hardened off and ready for planting out.

Making use of plug plants

Raising plants from seed is very satisfying and it is still the only way you can obtain some of the more unusual plant cultivars. There is no denying, however, that it can be time- and space-consuming. Plug plants are a speedy alternative. These are young plants that have been grown in modules so they have a well-developed root system that forms an easy-to-handle plug. You can still enjoy potting up the plants and hardening them off. Pot up or plant out plug plants (*see p.317*) as soon as possible, and water them well.

Sowing seeds outdoors

You can create a colourful border full of hardy annuals by sowing seed directly outdoors. The sheer volume of seed sown (packets are still fairly cheap) will more than compensate for any seedlings you lose to pests and harsh conditions. Also, you do not have to worry about pricking out,

growing on, and hardening off the seedlings. Start sowing outdoors as soon as the soil has started to warm up in spring.

Give plants a good start in life by preparing the area thoroughly. Remove any weeds (which compete for water, light, and nutrients) and large stones, then roughly level the surface. Do this in autumn, or several weeks prior to sowing, so the soil has time to settle and any germinating weeds can be removed. Before sowing, rake the soil until it resembles fine breadcrumbs (known as a "fine tilth") and the surface is level. Water the plot well if it is dry, otherwise the freshly sown seed might dry out and die.

You can either sow seed in rows or broadcast sow. The latter is done simply by scattering seed as evenly as possible to fill each sowing area, then lightly raking over the plot to mix the seed into the soil. Rake the soil in two directions to ensure that the seed is evenly distributed. Broadcast sowing is quicker, but it is more difficult to spot weeds among the seedlings later.

Once the seedlings have appeared, thin them to leave the strongest ones at the correct spacings. Place your fingers around the base of each chosen seedling's stem to keep its roots firm as you pull out unwanted seedlings around it. Cover the seedlings with horticultural fleece to protect them from frost or heavy rain and from pests such as mice, birds, and cats.

Softwood, semi-ripe, and heel cuttings

A stem-tip cutting is the quickest and most successful way of propagating many perennials, shrubs, biennials, and alpines. It may be of soft or semi-ripe wood. A softwood, or slightly more mature greenwood, cutting is taken from the actively growing tip of a shoot in early summer. Look for strong, young growth, which will be a lighter green than older growth or wood. Later in the summer when the shoots begin to ripen or become woody and stiff, semi-ripe cuttings can be taken. Test stems by bending them – if they split, they are still soft, if they spring back they are semi-ripe.

When taking stem-tip cuttings, cut off shoots about 10cm (4in) long, just above a leaf joint and place in a bucket of water or plastic bag to stop them wilting. Trim all but the top 2–4 leaves and cut the end just below a leaf joint. Insert the cuttings in pots of moist, gritty cuttings compost, so that their leaves are not touching and are just above the surface.

You can dip the cuttings in fungicide to protect against rot and the ends in a hormone rooting compound to encourage rooting. You can also take cuttings of woody plants by making a heel cutting (*see below*). Cover a pot of cuttings with a clear bag to retain moisture, or put it in a propagator, in a warm, light place.

Hardwood cuttings

Hardwood cuttings are normally taken from the mature wood of deciduous and evergreen trees and shrubs from late autumn until winter. Hardwood in this context refers to shoots of the current season that have started to toughen up.

Look for stems that are the same thickness as a pencil. Cut them off just above a bud or leaf joint on the parent plant. Trim to 20–23cm (8–9in) and then cut off the bottom just below a leaf joint.

To make a heel cutting, select a new semi-ripe sideshoot about 10cm (4in) long. Gently pull it from the main stem with a small sliver of bark. Trim the bark with a sharp knife, to leave a small "heel".

Trim off any soft wood at the top to just above a leaf joint. Dip their bases in hormone-rooting compound and insert in a 15cm (6in) deep trench in a cool, sheltered spot. Keep them watered in dry spells. You could also root them in deep pots of cuttings compost in a cold frame.

Leave the cuttings undisturbed for a year, watering and weeding them. By the following autumn, they should have rooted and be ready to transplant.

Root cuttings

Grow fleshy-rooted perennials, such as eryngiums, from root cuttings. Dig round a plant in autumn to expose some roots. Cut off a few healthy, medium-thickness roots close to the crown. Wash off the soil and cut the roots in 5–10cm (2–4in) pieces. Dust with fungicide. Lay the pieces flat in a tray of cuttings compost and cover.

Dividing plants

This is the easiest way of propagating herbaceous perennials, grasses, ferns, and many alpine and aquatic plants. Most of them form mats or clumps, and as they grow the centre becomes congested and begins to die. Lifting and dividing a plant every three or four years, in autumn or early spring, restores its vigour and gives the plant a new lease of life. Plants that are borderline hardy or have large rhizomes are best divided in early spring.

When dividing a clump, always look for the natural divisions between the shoots. Replant only the young growth from the outside of a clump, or, for fleshy crowns, sections with healthy buds or roots.
Dividing by hand Pull apart small fibrous-rooted plants by hand; cut tough or tangled roots with a knife or secateurs.
Dividing rhizomes Use a clean, sharp knife to cut off young pieces with healthy buds, shoots, and roots from old, woody rhizomes. Replant the divided pieces on the surface so the sun can ripen them. To avoid wind rock, trim the leaves to 15cm (6in).

Large clumps are best divided with two forks. Push them back to back into the root mass and pull the handles apart to split the clump. Alternatively, cut the roots with a sharp knife or pruning saw.

Dividing bulbous plants

Many bulbs, corms, and tubers increase by producing offsets around the parent bulb or corm. These types of bulbous plant can quickly form congested clumps. Unless they are lifted every three or four years and divided, the plants will stop flowering.

After lifting, pull the offsets away from the parent bulb. Many will be small and may take three or four years to mature and reach flowering size. Grow them on in pots of gritty compost in a sheltered spot or cold frame. Replant large bulbs immediately, or if still in leaf, temporarily plant them in a corner of a border until they are needed. Insert a label so you don't forget where they are. Alternatively, clean off any soil and store the bulbs in a cool, dark place for replanting at the appropriate time.

Layering

Some climbers, such as ivies, and woody plants like heathers spread by rooting from their stems wherever they touch the soil. Layering takes advantage of this tendency. Select a low-growing stem, and wound it near a bud by scratching or twisting the stem. Bury the wounded part in soil mixed with grit and cuttings compost. Support the exposed shoot, which will receive nourishment from the parent plant while it develops roots. After 4–6 weeks, dig up the rooted shoot, cut off and plant out.

Avoiding problems

If plants are given the best possible growing conditions so that they are healthy and strong, they will be able to survive most pests and diseases. Some problems in the garden are almost inevitable, but the majority are easily kept under control, or cured and prevented from returning.

If your plants show signs of discoloured or distorted growth, or holes in leaves and flowers, they are usually caused by pests, diseases, or nutrient deficiencies. The best way to deal with these problems is to use an integrated approach, where cultural and organic methods are used to keep plants healthy, and chemicals are used only as a last line of defence.

Prevention is always better than cure; if given good growing conditions, plants will be strong enough to survive attacks without any lasting damage. Check plants thoroughly before you buy them for any sign of damage or disease, to avoid bringing problems into the garden.

Always keep cutting tools clean so they do not spread infection. Promptly remove yellowing leaves and faded flowers, and clear plant debris.

Be vigilant, squashing pests and cutting out diseased parts as soon as you notice them. Some pests and diseases are persistent on certain plants, such as blackspot on roses. If you find the same problem is returning year after year, it is worth obtaining a resistant cultivar. If you have to resort to chemicals, use a specific remedy if possible, and spray the entire plant thoroughly. If all else fails, you should remove the plant before the problem spreads.

Keeping a healthy garden

Thriving plants are better able to resist problems, so it is important to maintain a healthy garden. There are several important ways in which you can ensure that your plants continue to remain in top condition.

Plants that are growing in sites or conditions that do not meet their particular needs become stressed and more prone to problems. To avoid this situation arising, take care to choose plants that are suited to each aspect in your garden and to the local conditions (see Climate and location, pp.314–315). It is rare to find perfect soil; before planting, prepare it well (see Soils and compost, pp.318–319).

Pay attention also to watering and feeding your plants appropriately so that they do not suffer from insufficient or excessive water or nutrients (see p.325). It is essential, too, that you weed around your plants regularly so that they do not have to

Nutrient deficiency is usually first seen on leaves. Yellowing between the leaf veins, as shown here, indicates a lack of magnesium, which is used by the plant to make green chlorophyll.

compete with fast-growing invaders for vital light, water, and nutrients (see p.326–327).

Many pathogenic bacteria, fungi, and viruses are opportunists, and some infect a weak plant through an existing wound. Avoid giving them easy access by cutting cleanly when pruning (see p.322) and removing crossing branches that might chafe as they rub together.

Plants that are overgrown or are planted too closely often become weak and sickly, with elongated shoots as they fight for light. Fresh air cannot circulate freely around the stems and leaves, and the still, stagnant air encourages rots, moulds, and mildews. To avoid this, prune out congested growth (see p.322), divide herbaceous perennials (see facing page), and allow room for growth when planting any type of plant (see p.320).

Encouraging beneficial wildlife

The only good aspect of insect pests is that they attract lots of wildlife in search of a meal so do not be alarmed if you see a few pests about – allow their natural predators to take action before you think about resorting to chemical means. If you encourage a range of beneficial wildlife into the garden, the pests will be kept down to acceptable levels.

Water attracts lots of animals, including frogs and toads, which eat many pests that crawl on the ground. The hedgehog is also a valuable friend, and a pile of logs or leaves, or a thick hedge, can provide a home so it stays to eat your slugs. Ladybird larvae and adults feed eagerly on the scourge of almost every garden: aphids (see p.332).

Birds can damage some seedlings or edible crops, but this is more than made up for by the number of insect pests they eat. Attract birds by planting trees and shrubs that give cover or bear berries, for example rowans and cotoneasters.

How to control problems

By keeping a close watch on plants you can stop problems getting out of hand. If you see any pests, pick them off immediately. If you do spot symptoms of disease, remove the affected parts and burn or throw them in the rubbish bin.

Some plants are irrestistible to aphids: if you notice that a plant is particularly affected, consider planting French marigolds (*Tagetes, see p.274*) nearby; they will attract hoverflies, the larvae of which feed on aphids. Aromatic plants such as catmint (*Nepeta, see p.242*), and garlic may repel or confuse pests.

Predators or parasites of some pests can be introduced into the garden as a biological control. Nematodes (microscopic worms) can be watered onto the soil or compost to kill slugs or vine weevil larvae, but they often need high temperatures and consequently may be more effective in a greenhouse or conservatory than in the open garden.

If you do use chemicals, follow the manufacturer's instructions. Fertilizers cure deficiency diseases – if you can identify the missing nutrient, it is better to use a specific cure than an all-purpose feed. Organic pesticides, such as pyrethrum, made from plant extracts, and fatty acids, are available. Use them with the same care as any other chemical. A few inorganic pesticides are toxic to some ornamental plants. There is usually a list on the packaging; if in doubt, test the chemical on a plant before general use. Spray pesticides in the evening, when bees are not around, and in still weather so the wind does not carry spray where it is not wanted. Any old or unwanted chemicals should be disposed of safely; contact the local authority for advice.

Whole-plant problems

Occasionally you may notice that an entire plant is looking sick. The usual causes are incorrect watering, pests, disease, or nutrient deficiencies. Newly planted and container-grown plants often wilt because of drought or overwatering (*see p.325*). Check the soil or the compost and either give it a good soak or allow it to dry out, as appropriate.

Root diseases such as honey fungus and *Phytophthora* cause wilting, as do pests such as vine weevil (*see below left*). Lack of nutrients can make a plant sickly and yellow, but it should perk up after a liquid feed (*see p.325*). You will also find that clumping plants lose vigour unless they are divided regularly (*see also www.rhs.org.uk/advice/problems_tree.asp*).

Stem problems

The stems of a plant support the leaves and flowers and contain veins that transport water and food to and from the deepest roots and the tallest shoots. Because they are so important, damage to them may result in the loss of an affected plant. Pests that attack plant stems may eat the skin or bark, suck sap by piercing the veins, or in some cases tunnel right through, or live in, the stem. The wounds that they leave then provide doorways for diseases that can spread through the plant and quickly kill it.

Bad pruning and extremely cold, hot, or windy weather can also damage stems. Look out for dead, diseased, or damaged parts and cut out and dispose of them so problems cannot spread to other plants.

The following pests, disorders, and diseases are very common. Although they can be severe enough to kill, most will cause little long-term damage – especially if they are dealt with quickly – and some can be easily prevented.

■ Cuckoo spit is the foamy, protective coating made by froghoppers (small, jumping insects); it does little harm other than looking unsightly.
■ Frost damage can kill, but if only new shoots are affected they often grow back.

Number one pests

The most common garden pests crop up regularly from year to year. Slugs and snails attack a wide range of plants. They prefer seedlings and young or fleshy plants, and will eat large holes in leaves or stems or even the entire plant. You can hunt and destroy them under cover of darkness, make traps, or lay barriers (*see also p.218*). Vine weevil larvae (*see right*) cause considerable damage to container-grown plants by eating all the roots. The adults make notches in the leaf margins.

Aphids attack the soft shoots and buds of most plants, and spread virus diseases on their piercing mouthparts. Red lily beetles eat entire flowers and leaves. Deal with these pests by either picking them off or using a specific biological or chemical control.

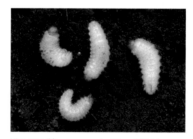

Vine weevil larvae are up to 10mm (½in) long, creamy white. The first symptom of these pests is sudden wilting. Biological control is available.

Aphids such as greenfly and blackfly suck sap from veins, leaving sticky honeydew behind on which sooty mould can develop.

If frost is forecast, move tender plants under cover and drape early blossom and new shoots of hardy plants with horticultural fleece.

■ Mildew is a white, powdery, fungal infection; it attacks plants that are already weak or congested so air cannot move around stems freely.

■ Dieback can occur if pruning cuts are made too far from buds.

■ Canker first appears as a zone of flattened, discoloured bark which later splits, forming a ring of flaky bark that kills the shoot. Canker affects many plants, especially apples and pears, and should be cut out.

Leaf problems

Foliage problems can take the form of discoloured, distorted, or damaged growth, or premature leaf fall. This not only spoils the plant's appearance, but also reduces its ability to thrive.

Fungi can cause moulds, mildews, rusts, or spots. They attack weak plants and are unsightly, but rarely deadly, although some, for example, silver leaf on plums and cherries, are fatal.

Bacteria can cause black spots on leaves; they are not raised or patchy like fungal spots, but appear more like dark shadows. Foliage with pale flecks, streaks, or mottling often has a viral infection.

Some pests, such as caterpillars, eat leaves and others, like leaf miners, burrow into them. Most plants can withstand an attack, but may become weak, which then turns them into an easy target for disease. Nutrient deficiencies – the usual cause of yellowing, or chlorosis – also compromise plant defences.

With all leaf problems, first try to identify the cause, and then take an appropriate course of action. Pest control or removal of affected foliage is often required. Never put diseased material on the compost heap because that will often spread infection (see p.319).

Lack of water, nutrients, light, and space all favour disease; and often pampering a plant by thinning stems, watering, and feeding, will make it strong enough to fight off infection.

If all else fails, chemical controls are often effective. Use one specific to the problem, following the manufacturer's instructions carefully.

Many disorders occur on the undersides of leaves, so be vigilant and occasionally check under leaves to make sure that there is no problem developing. If you use a contact fungicide or pesticide, spray the whole plant and make sure you include the undersides of the leaves as well. These are some of the most common problems.

■ Adult vine weevils are slow moving and eat irregular notches in leaf margins near ground; they should be destroyed before they lay eggs.

■ Fuchsia rust forms tiny, orange spots underneath leaves and is encouraged by damp air.

■ Rose blackspot causes dark blotches and early leaf fall.

■ Peach leaf curl results in distorted leaves, which may be flushed red.

■ Fungal leaf spot appears as rounded, brown or grey patches containing raised, dark spots.

■ Pelargonium rust develops as dark brown pustules, often arranged in rings, on lower leaf surfaces.

■ Geranium downy mildew shows as pale patches with white fungus on the undersides of leaves.

Flower problems

Most plants in the garden are grown for their flowers, and when problems such as pests, diseases, and the weather affect them, it spoils the show. If the first blooms are ruined, all is not lost; if you can cure the problem, you may find you can encourage another flush of healthy flowers by regular deadheading and feeding.

Discoloured flowerheads may be a sign of pests such as thrips – insects that suck sap from flower buds in hot, dry summers, causing white flecks on the petals.

Sap-sucking insects, such as aphids and thrips can distort or discolour blooms (see above); keep a watch for them and squash or spray them off. Other insects, such as earwigs, and also birds eat petals or buds before they open. Diseases can also be a problem, and those affecting flowers are particularly destructive if the weather is cool and damp. Symptoms to look out for include white spots, often edged with a darker ring, on the petals; these indicate the presence of grey mould (botrytis). Streaks or flecks, or deformed flowers, are usually caused by a viral infection.

Weather damage is a common problem for delicate blooms. The flowers of roses and other plants often fail to open if wet spells are followed by hot sun because of a condition known as balling. The damp bud is scorched by the sun and cannot open, causing the inner petals to rot. Flowers that open in early spring are often prone to frost damage, made worse by the morning sun. Cold, drying winds can scorch petals, turning them brown, so position early-flowering plants with care.

Remain observant so any problems can be overcome before they get a firm hold. If you fail to cure a disease, then it is best to admit defeat and throw away the affected plant before it contaminates others.

Plant selections

Every garden presents you with a different challenge. Some have heavy, seemingly unworkable soil; others excessive amounts of shade. The lists in this section are intended to help you identify plants for particular uses, such as herb and bog gardens, and for some of the most common problem areas, such as shaded and dry sites.

EXPOSED SITES

Gardens on hillsides or in flat, open areas regularly experience high winds. Create a shelterbelt using hedges and trees to filter the worst of the wind, and choose hardy plants that are able to withstand a battering.

Acer pseudoplatanus and cultivars
Achillea
Ajuga reptans and cultivars
Anchusa azurea 'Loddon Royalist' ♀
Anemone x *hybrida* and cultivars
Antirrhinum majus and cultivars
Arctostaphylos
Berberis
Bergenia
Bupleurum fruticosum
Calendula officinalis and cultivars
Calluna vulgaris and cultivars
Caragana arborescens
Carpinus betulus 'Fastigiata' ♀
Chaenomeles
Chamaecyparis obtusa 'Nana Aurea' ♀
Chamaecyparis pisifera 'Filifera Aurea' ♀
Clethra arborea
Colutea arborescens
Coreopsis 'Schnittgold'
Cornus
Corylus avellana 'Contorta'
Cotoneaster horizontalis ♀
Crataegus laevigata 'Paul's Scarlet' ♀
Cryptomeria japonica 'Elegans Compacta' ♀
x *Cupressocyparis leylandii* ♀
Cupressus macrocarpa 'Goldcrest' ♀
Deutzia
Echinops ritro 'Veitch's Blue'
Elaeagnus
Erica carnea and cultivars

Erigeron aureus 'Canary Bird' ♀
Erigeron 'Dunkelste Aller' ♀
Eryngium alpinum ♀
Eryngium x *oliverianum* ♀
Escallonia 'Apple Blossom' ♀
Eschscholzia californica ♀
Eucalyptus
Euonymus alatus ♀
Euonymus fortunei and cultivars
Euphorbia characias subsp. *wulfenii* 'John Tomlinson' ♀
Fagus sylvatica 'Dawyck Purple' ♀
Felicia amelloides 'Santa Anita' ♀
Ficus carica
Forsythia x *intermedia* and cultivars
Fraxinus excelsior
Fuchsia magellanica
Gaultheria
Ginkgo biloba ♀
Gleditsia triacanthos 'Sunburst' ♀
Griselinia littoralis ♀
Hamamelis
Helleborus niger ♀ and cultivars
Hippophae rhamnoides ♀
Hydrangea paniculata 'Grandiflora' ♀
Hypericum calycinum
Ilex aquifolium ♀
Iris sibirica ♀ and cultivars
Jasminum nudiflorum ♀
Juniperus
Kalmia angustifolia ♀
Kerria japonica and cultivars
Kerria japonica 'Picta'
Laburnum
Laurus nobilis ♀
Lavatera
Leucothoe fontanesiana 'Rainbow'
Limnanthes douglasii ♀
Miscanthus
Nepeta sintenisii
Nepeta 'Six Hills Giant'
Osmunda regalis ♀

Phalaris arundinacea var. *picta*
Phlox subulata 'Lilacina'
Picea abies
Pieris
Pinus nigra ♀
Populus x *canadensis* and cultivars
Potentilla
Primula
Prunus spinosa
Pyracantha
Quercus
Rubus cockburnianus
Salix alba
Sempervivum arachnoideum ♀
Senecio cineraria 'White Diamond'
Sorbus aria
Sorbus aucuparia and cultivars
Spiraea
Symphoricarpos x *doorenbosii* 'White Hedge'
Tamarix
Tanacetum parthenium and cultivars
Taxus
Tiarella cordifolia ♀
Tilia
Tsuga canadensis and cultivars
Ulex
Viburnum x *bodnantense* 'Dawn' ♀
Viburnum x *burkwoodii*
Viburnum opulus 'Compactum' ♀
Viburnum rhytidophyllum
Viburnum tinus 'Eve Price' ♀

SEASIDE GARDENS

Coastal areas suffer from winter gales and the scorching salt spray that they bring. Create shelterbelts by planting trees around the perimeter, and go for tough plants that conserve moisture.

Achillea
Allium
Alstroemeria

Anaphalis triplinervis ♀
Anchusa azurea 'Loddon Royalist' ♀
Anthemis
Anthericum liliago
Antirrhinum majus and cultivars
Arbutus unedo ♀
Armeria
Artemisia abrotanum ♀
Aster
Aucuba
Bergenia
Buddleja davidii and cultivars
Bupleurum fruticosum
Campanula
Centaurea 'John Coutts'
Choisya ternata SUNDANCE ♀ ('Lich)
Cistus
Cordyline australis 'Torbay Red' ♀
Cotoneaster
Crataegus
Crocosmia
Cupressus macrocarpa
Cytisus
Dahlia
Dianthus
Dierama pulcherrimum
Echinacea purpurea 'White Lustre'
Echinops ritro 'Veitch's Blue'
Elaeagnus x *ebbingei* 'Gilt Edge' ♀
Erica arborea var. *alpina* ♀
Erica carnea and cultivars
Erigeron 'Quakeress'
Erodium manescavii
Eryngium alpinum ♀
Escallonia 'Apple Blossom' ♀
Eucalyptus
Euonymus fortunei and cultivars
Euphorbia
Felicia amelloides 'Santa Anita' ♀
Ficus carica
Filipendula rubra 'Venusta' ♀
Forsythia x *intermedia* and cultivars

Fuchsia magellanica
Garrya elliptica
Gaultheria
Geranium
Gleditsia triacanthos
 'Sunburst' 🏆
Griselinia littoralis 🏆
Gypsophila 'Rosenschleier' 🏆
Halimium 'Susan' 🏆
Hebe
Hemerocallis
Heuchera
Hibiscus syriacus 'Oiseau
 Bleu' 🏆
Hippophae rhamnoides 🏆
Hydrangea macrophylla and
 cultivars
Impatiens
Iris
Juniperus
Laburnum
Laurus nobilis 🏆
Lavandula
Lavatera
Leycesteria formosa 🏆
Lonicera nitida
Lonicera x *purpusii* 'Winter
 Beauty' 🏆
Lychnis coronaria 🏆
Melissa officinalis 'Aurea'
Monarda
Oenothera
Olearia
Origanum
Pachysandra terminalis
Penstemon
Phormium tenax 🏆
Phygelius
Pinus nigra 🏆
Pittosporum
Populus tremula 🏆
Potentilla
Prunus spinosa
Pulsatilla
Pyracantha
Quercus ilex 🏆
Rosa (some)
Rosmarinus officinalis
Rubus cockburnianus
Salvia
Sambucus racemosa 'Plumosa
 Aurea'
Santolina
Sisyrinchium
Spartium junceum 🏆
Stachys
Tamarix
Ulex
Viburnum

DRY SUN
Situations prone to drought
include steeply sloping sunny
banks with rapid drainage; the
base of a warm south- or
west-facing wall; and shallow,
sandy, or stony soils in full sun.
Abelia
Acacia baileyana 🏆
Acaena saccaticupula 'Blue
 Haze'
Achillea
Agapanthus
Allium
Alstroemeria
Anchusa azurea 'Loddon
 Royalist' 🏆
Anthemis
Arabis
Arctotis
Armeria pseudarmeria
Artemisia
Asphodeline lutea
Brachyglottis 'Sunshine' 🏆
Buddleja
Bupleurum fruticosum
Buxus
Caryopteris x *clandonensis* 'Kew
 Blue'
Catananche caerulea 'Bicolor'
Ceanothus 'Blue Mound' 🏆
Centaurea
Cerastium tomentosum
Ceratostigma willmottianum 🏆
Chamaemelum nobile 'Flore
 Pleno'
Chrysanthemum segetum
Cirsium rivulare 'Atropurpureum'
Cistus
Clerodendrum trichotomum var.
 fargesii 🏆
Cotoneaster
Crambe cordifolia 🏆
Crocosmia
x *Cupressocyparis leylandii* 🏆
Cynara cardunculus 🏆
Cytisus
Dianthus
Diascia
Dictamnus albus
Draba mollissima
Echinops ritro 'Veitch's Blue'
Erica arborea var. *alpina* 🏆
Erica cinerea and cultivars
Erodium glandulosum 🏆
Erodium manescavii
Eryngium alpinum 🏆
Erysimum
Escallonia

Eucalyptus
Euphorbia
Foeniculum vulgare
 'Purpureum'
Fuchsia magellanica
Gaillardia grandiflora
 'Dazzler' 🏆
Gaultheria mucronata 'Mulberry
 Wine' 🏆
Gaura lindheimeri 🏆
Genista lydia 🏆
Geranium
Gleditsia triacanthos 🏆
Gypsophila 'Rosenschleier' 🏆
Hebe
Helianthemum
Hippophae rhamnoides 🏆
Hypericum
Impatiens
Ipheion uniflorum 'Wisley
 Blue' 🏆
Iris foetidissima 🏆
Juniperus
Kniphofia
Kolkwitzia amabilis 'Pink
 Cloud' 🏆
Lavandula
Liatris spicata 'Kobold'
Limnanthes douglasii 🏆
Linum flavum 'Compactum'
Lychnis coronaria 🏆
Melissa officinalis 'Aurea'
Nepeta
Nerine bowdenii 🏆
Oenothera
Olearia
Origanum laevigatum 🏆
Osteospermum
Papaver orientale and cultivars
Pelargonium
Penstemon
Perovskia 'Blue Spire' 🏆
Phlomis fruticosa 🏆
Phlox subulata 'Lilacina'
Phormium
Phygelius aequalis 'Yellow
 Trumpet' 🏆
Potentilla
Pulsatilla vulgaris 🏆
Quercus ilex 🏆
Ribes
Rosmarinus officinalis and
 cultivars
Salvia patens 'Cambridge
 Blue' 🏆
Sambucus racemosa 'Plumosa
 Aurea'
Santolina
Saponaria ocymoides 🏆

Sedum
Sempervivum arachnoideum 🏆
Spartium junceum 🏆
Spiraea
Stachys byzantina
Stipa
Symphoricarpos x *doorenbosii*
 'White Hedge'
Tagetes
Tamarix
Teucrium polium
Thymus
Tulipa
Ulex europaeus 'Flore Pleno' 🏆
Verbascum
Yucca gloriosa 🏆

DAMP SHADE
A cool, humid woodland
environment where the soil is
reliably moist all year.
Acer cappadocicum
Acer griseum 🏆
Acer negundo 'Variegatum'
Acer palmatum f. *atropurpureum*
Acer saccharinum
Alchemilla mollis 🏆
Alnus
Aruncus dioicus 🏆
Asplenium scolopendrium 🏆
Astilbe
Athyrium filix-femina
 'Frizelliae' 🏆
Aucuba japonica
Buxus sempervirens 🏆
Caltha palustris 🏆
Camellia japonica and cultivars
Cercidiphyllum japonicum 🏆
Clethra arborea
Convallaria majalis 🏆
Cornus canadensis 🏆
Crataegus
Daphne
Darmera peltata 🏆
Dicentra
Dryopteris wallichiana 🏆
Elaeagnus
Erythronium
Euonymus fortunei
Fatsia japonica 🏆
Fothergilla major 🏆
Gaultheria
Haberlea rhodopensis 'Virginalis'
Hamamelis
Helleborus
Hosta
Hydrangea
Hypericum calycinum
Ilex aquifolium 🏆

Iris sibirica ♀ and cultivars
Ligularia 'The Rocket' ♀
Lilium martagon ♀
Lythrum virgatum 'The Rocket'
Mahonia aquifolium
Matteuccia struthiopteris ♀
Metasequoia glyptostroboides ♀
Monarda
Osmanthus x burkwoodii ♀
Pachysandra terminalis
Picea
Pieris
Polystichum setiferum ♀
Populus
Primula (candelabra types)
Prunus laurocerasus ♀
Prunus padus 'Watereri' ♀
Quercus
Rhododendron
Rodgersia pinnata 'Superba' ♀
Rubus
Salix
Sambucus racemosa 'Plumosa
    Aurea'
Sarcococca
Sasa veitchii
Skimmia
Sorbus
Spiraea
Stachyurus praecox ♀
Symphoricarpos
Symphytum
Taxus baccata ♀ and cultivars
Viburnum davidii ♀
Viburnum opulus
Viburnum rhytidophyllum

DRY SHADE

The combined problems of shade and drought are often found by walls, and beneath thirsty, shallow-rooting trees.
Acanthus spinosus ♀
Ajuga reptans and cultivars
Alchemilla mollis ♀
Amelanchier lamarckii ♀
Aquilegia
Arum italicum 'Marmoratum' ♀
Astrantia
Aucuba
Berberis
Bergenia
Betula
Buxus sempervirens ♀
Cornus canadensis ♀
Cortaderia
Cotoneaster
Daphne
Dicentra formosa

Digitalis
Epimedium
Euonymus fortunei
Fatsia japonica ♀
Garrya elliptica
Geranium himalayense
Geranium macrorrhizum
Geranium nodosum
Hedera
Heuchera
Hippophae rhamnoides ♀
Ilex aquifolium ♀
Iris foetidissima ♀
Juniperus x pfitzeriana
Lamium
Lunaria annua and cultivars
Mahonia
Meconopsis cambrica
Melissa officinalis 'Aurea'
Milium effusum 'Aureum' ♀
Pachysandra terminalis
Pittosporum tenuifolium ♀
Polygonatum
Polypodium vulgare
Prunus laurocerasus ♀
Pulmonaria
Santolina
Skimmia
Symphoricarpos
Taxus baccata ♀ and cultivars
Teucrium polium
Thalictrum
Tiarella
Tolmiea menziesii 'Taff's Gold' ♀
Waldsteinia ternata

DEEP SHADE

Permanently shaded positions may be beneath evergreen trees, by high walls, and between tall buildings. Use plants and structures in light colours to help brighten up these areas.
Acer cappadocicum
Acer griseum ♀
Adiantum venustum ♀
Ajuga reptans and cultivars
Alchemilla mollis ♀
Aruncus dioicus ♀
Asplenium scolopendrium ♀
Astilbe
Athyrium filix-femina
    'Frizelliae' ♀
Aucuba japonica
Betula nigra
Blechnum
Camellia
Cercidiphyllum japonicum ♀

Cotoneaster
Cryptogramma crispa
Daphne
Dicentra
Dicksonia antarctica ♀
Digitalis
Dryopteris wallichiana ♀
Epimedium
Erythronium
Fatsia japonica ♀
Fothergilla major ♀
Gaultheria
Helleborus
Hosta
Hydrangea
Ilex
Iris foetidissima ♀
Iris sibirica ♀
Mahonia
Matteuccia struthiopteris ♀
Osmanthus x burkwoodii ♀
Pachysandra terminalis
Pieris
Polypodium vulgare
Polystichum setiferum ♀
Primula (candelabra types)
Prunus laurocerasus ♀
Prunus lusitanica subsp. azorica
Pulmonaria
Rhododendron
Rodgersia pinnata 'Superba' ♀
Rubus cockburnianus
Salix
Skimmia
Symphoricarpos
Symphytum
Taxus baccata ♀ and cultivars
Viburnum davidii ♀
Viburnum rhytidophyllum
Woodwardia radicans ♀

HEAVY SOILS

Heavy clay soils can be hard to work, but are often rich in nutrients. Select hardy plants, avoid alpines, and persist in digging in organic matter and grit in order to improve fertility and drainage.
Abelia
Acer
Aconitum
Aesculus
Ajuga reptans and cultivars
Alnus
Anemone x hybrida and
    cultivars
Aster
Aucuba japonica

Berberis
Betula
Campanula
Carpinus betulus 'Fastigiata' ♀
Chaenomeles
Choisya ternata SUNDANCE ♀
    ('Lich')
Colutea arborescens
Cornus
Corylus avellana 'Contorta'
Cotoneaster
Crataegus
Crocosmia
Cytisus
Darmera peltata ♀
Digitalis
Echinops
Eranthis hyemalis ♀
Erigeron
Escallonia
Eucalyptus
Forsythia x intermedia and
    cultivars
Fraxinus excelsior 'Jaspidea' ♀
Geranium
Hamamelis
Hedera helix and cultivars
Helenium
Helleborus
Hemerocallis
Hibiscus syriacus
Hosta
Hypericum
Ilex
Kerria japonica and cultivars
Laburnum x watereri
    'Vossii' ♀
Lysimachia clethroides ♀
Magnolia
Mahonia
Malus
Monarda
Osmanthus x burkwoodii ♀
Persicaria bistorta 'Superba' ♀
Physalis alkekengi ♀
Philadelphus
Populus
Potentilla
Prunus
Pyracantha
Pyrus salicifolia 'Pendula' ♀
Quercus
Ranunculus
Rheum palmatum
    'Atrosanguineum' ♀
Rhododendron
Rodgersia
Rosa
Rudbeckia

Salix
Sasa veitchii
Sidalcea 'Oberon'
Solidago 'Goldenmosa' 🏆
Sorbus
Symphoricarpos x *doorenbosii* 'White Hedge'
Symphytum caucasicum 🏆
Syringa
Tilia
Tradescantia
Waldsteinia ternata
Weigela florida

ACID (LIME-FREE) SOILS

Acid soils are typically very fertile, nutrient-rich, and moist with good drainage. You can create the right conditions for some acid-loving plants by planting them in containers of ericaceous compost.

Acer rubrum 'October Glory' 🏆
Betula
Calluna vulgaris
Camellia
Cassiope 'Edinburgh' 🏆
Cercidiphyllum japonicum 🏆
Corylopsis glabrescens
Cryptomeria japonica 'Elegans Compacta' 🏆
Daboecia cantabrica and cultivars
Erica
Gaultheria
Ilex aquifolium 🏆
Kalmia angustifolia 🏆
Leucothoe fontanesiana 'Rainbow'
Liquidambar styraciflua 'Golden Treasure'
Osmunda regalis 🏆
Pinus nigra 🏆
Populus tremula 🏆
Rhododendron
Skimmia
Trillium grandiflorum 🏆

CHALKY, ALKALINE SOILS

Soil over chalk and limestone is almost invariably alkaline (limy). It is usually fairly fertile, but can be shallow and consequently dries out quickly. In such cases, use drought-tolerant plants.

Acanthus spinosus 🏆
Acer cappadocicum
Acer griseum 🏆
Amelanchier lamarckii 🏆

Anthemis
Berberis
Buddleja davidii
Carpinus betulus 🏆
Catalpa bignonioides 🏆
Ceanothus 'Blue Mound' 🏆
Clematis
Corylus avellana 'Contorta' 🏆
Daphne mezereum
Dianthus
Eremurus robustus 🏆
Fagus sylvatica 'Dawyck Purple' 🏆
Fraxinus excelsior 'Jaspidea' 🏆
Gleditsia triacanthos 'Sunburst' 🏆
Hebe
Kolkwitzia amabilis 🏆
Laburnum x *watereri* 'Vossii' 🏆
Laurus nobilis 🏆
Liriodendron tulipifera 🏆
Malus
Paeonia
Papaver orientale and cultivars
Prunus (all Japanese cherries)
Pulsatilla vulgaris 🏆
Pyrus salicifolia 'Pendula' 🏆
Robinia pseudoacacia 'Frisia' 🏆
Saponaria ocymoides 🏆
Sedum spectabile 🏆 and cultivars
Spartium junceum 🏆
Syringa
Tradescantia
Verbascum

ROCK-GARDEN PLANTS

Rock gardens and raised beds provide good drainage and make an ideal showcase for small plants and alpines.

Ajuga reptans and cultivars
Arenaria montana 🏆
Armeria pseudarmeria
Aubrieta
Calluna
Cassiope 'Edinburgh' 🏆
Daboecia cantabrica and cultivars
Daphne cneorum
Dianthus
Erica
Erinus alpinus 🏆
Eryngium alpinum 🏆
Hebe pinguifolia 'Pagei' 🏆
Helianthemum
Juniperus communis 'Compressa' 🏆

Lamium maculatum
Lithodora diffusa 'Heavenly Blue' 🏆
Phlox subulata 'Lilacina'
Saponaria ocymoides 🏆
Saxifraga
Sedum spathulifolium 'Cape Blanco' 🏆
Thymus
Veronica spicata 'Rotfuchs'
Waldsteinia ternata

FRAGRANT PLANTS

To maximize your enjoyment of the wonderful aromas of scented plants, grow them near the house, or by paths.

Akebia quinata
Asphodeline lutea
Azara microphylla 'Variegata'
Buddleja
Chimonanthus praecox 'Grandiflorus' 🏆
Clematis armandii
Convallaria majalis 🏆
Corylopsis glabrescens
Cosmos atrosanguineus
Cytisus battandieri 🏆
Daphne
Dianthus
Hamamelis
Laburnum x *watereri* 'Vossii' 🏆
Lavandula
Lunaria rediviva
Malus floribunda 🏆
Monarda
Osmanthus x *burkwoodii* 🏆
Phlox paniculata and cultivars
Rosa
Sarcococca
Syringa
Wisteria floribunda

BOG-GARDEN PLANTS

All these plants like permanently moist soil. Some will even grow in very shallow water at the edge of a pond.

Aruncus dioicus 🏆
Astilbe
Caltha palustris 🏆
Cardamine pratensis 'Flore Pleno'
Cornus alba and cultivars
Darmera peltata 🏆
Eupatorium purpureum
Euphorbia palustris 🏆

Filipendula rubra 'Venusta' 🏆
Gunnera tinctoria
Hemerocallis
Iris ensata 🏆
Iris sibirica 🏆 and cultivars
Ligularia
Lobelia 'Bee's Flame'
Osmunda regalis 🏆
Primula bulleyana 🏆
Primula denticulata 🏆 and cultivars
Primula florindae 🏆
Primula rosea 🏆
Rheum palmatum 'Atrosanguineum' 🏆
Rodgersia pinnata 'Superba' 🏆
Salix alba and cultivars
Trollius x *cultorum* 'Orange Princess' 🏆

ORNAMENTAL HERBS

Good-looking culinary plants that are at home in the herb garden or the shrub border.

Anethum graveolens
Angelica archangelica
Borago officinalis
Calendula officinalis
Chamaemelum nobile 'Flore Pleno'
Foeniculum vulgare 'Purpureum'
Hesperis matronalis var. *albiflora*
Laurus nobilis 🏆
Lavandula angustifolia 'Hidcote' 🏆
Melissa officinalis and cultivars
Rosmarinus officinalis
Salvia officinalis
Thymus

SLOPING SITES

Ground-cover plants are ideal for slopes because they help to bind the soil, preventing erosion.

Ajuga reptans and cultivars
Bergenia
Cistus
Calluna
Clematis tubulosa 'Wyevale'
Epimedium
Gaultheria
Hedera
Hosta
Hypericum calycinum
Lamium
Potentilla
Tiarella
Thymus

Index

Acknowledgments

Picture credits

The publisher would like to thank the following for their kind permission to reproduce their photographs:

(Key: a-above; b-below/bottom; c-centre; f-far; l-left; r-right; t-top)

1 GAP Photos: Jerry Harpur. 2 DK Images: Photographer: Steven Wooster; Garden for Chelsea Flower Show 2002 by Tamsin Partridge. 4–5 Corbis: Mark Bolton. 6–7 GAP Photos: Elke Borkowski. 8 Jo Whitworth: (bl/Clerodendron). 8-9 Getty Images: Dave Zubraski (t). 12 Garden Picture Library: Jerry Pavia (bc). 22 Garden Picture Library: Neil Holmes (bc). 36 Jo Whitworth: (br). 39 Garden World Images: (fbr). 50 Garden Picture Library: Brian Carter (bl). 56 Garden Picture Library: Brian Carter (crb). 59 Garden World Images: (br). 67 Andrew Lawson: (bl). 70 Holt Studios International: Rosemary Mayer (br). 72 John Glover: (bl). 81 Annelise Evans: (br). 87 DK Images: Hopley's Plants, Much Hadham (bc). 88 Andrew Lawson: Bosvigo House, Cornwall (bl). 89 Andrew Lawson: (fclb). Photos Horticultural: (br/triloba). 94 Corbis: Frank Blackburn; Ecoscene (l). Garden World Images: (bc). 97 DK Images: R.N.R.S. St Albans (fbl). 102 Garden World Images: (br). 104 Garden World Images: (bc). 107 Garden World Images: (bc). 108 Photos Horticultural: (fbl). 111 DK Images: Cambridge Botanic Gardens (br). Eric Crichton Photos: (bc). 112 Suttons Seeds: (fbr). 112–113 GAP Photos: Neil Holmes (t). 118 Raymond Evison: (cra). 119 Raymond Evison: (bl/'Rouge Cardinal'). Roseland House Garden & Nursery, Truro, Cornwall: (clb/'Minuet'). 120 Suttons Seeds: (bl). 126 John Vanderplank, National Collection of Passiflora: (bc). 127 John Vanderplank, National Collection of Passiflora: (tl). 130 Garden World Images: (bc). 134–135 GAP Photos: Jerry Harpur (t). 140 Photos Horticultural: (bl). 142 Garden World Images: (bl). Photos Horticultural: (t). 144 Photos Horticultural: (t). 147 Garden World Images: (br). 150 Thompson & Morgan: (bc). 153 Photos Horticultural: (br). 154 Andrew Lawson: (t). 155 Thompson & Morgan: (cra). 156 Eric Crichton Photos: (br). 157 Photolibrary: David Dixon (br). 158 Garden World Images: (br). 159 Garden World Images: (br). Photos Horticultural: (bl). 169 Garden World Images: (bl). 171 Mr Fothergill's Seeds: (br). 174 Andrew Lawson: (bl). 175 Garden World Images: (br). 177 Andrew Lawson: (bl). 185 Photos Horticultural: (cla). 188 Garden World Images: (bc). 189 Garden World Images: (bl). Photos Horticultural: (tl). 193 Garden World Images: (br). 196 Photos Horticultural: (bl). 203 Wildlife Matters: (bl). 208 Eric Crichton Photos: (clb). Andrew Lawson: (bl). 209 DK Images: Hidcote Manor (cra/himalayense). Andrew Lawson: (crb/maderense). Photos Horticultural: (tl/'Biokovo'). 217 DK Images: Courtesy of Blooms of Bressingham (bc). 218 Andrew Lawson: (fbr). 222 DK Images: RHS Garden Wisley (crb/'Joyce'). 223 John Glover: (fclb/laevigata). Andrew Lawson: (cra/'Major'). Wildlife Matters: (fcla/foetidissima). 230 Clive Nichols: (cra/Citronella Group). 231 Garden World Images: (fbl). John Glover: (cla/'Fire King'). 244 Merebrook Online (www.pondplants.co.uk): Roger Kings (bc). 253 Garden World Images: (bl). 260 DK Images: Country Park Nurseries, Hornchurch (fcrb/frondosa). 261 DK Images: Barnsley House, Glos. (fclb/Gold-laced Group). 268 Garden World Images: (br). 269 Garden World Images: (tr). 274 Mr Fothergill's Seeds: (bl). 276 Photos Horticultural: (bc). 286 DK Images: Steven Wooster. 302 GAP Photos: Jerry Harpur. 310–311 Corbis: Mark Bolton (t)

All other images © Dorling Kindersley
For further information see:
www.dkimages.com

Author's acknowledgments

Although my name sits on the cover of this book, writing a book is very much a team effort, and I wish to express my heartfelt thanks to all of the people involved. Firstly, I must thank David Lamb, Annelise Evans, Anna Kruger, Lee Griffiths, Alison Donovan, Letitia Luff, Louise Abbott and Pamela Brown. I thank all of them for their professionalism and patience, and for keeping me on the right track.

I also wish to thank the editorial team of Joanna Chisholm, Helen Fewster, Candida Frith-Macdonald, Diana Galligan, Gail Griffiths, Jonathan Hilton, Andrea Loom, Carole McGlynn, Simon Maughan, Christine Morley, Jane Simmonds, and Victoria Willan. Also special thanks to the RHS editorial team.

May I also thank the botanists at the RHS Garden, Wisley, for their generous help in providing information on some plants. I am sure they got tired of my incessant phone calls. And my thanks also to all the nurseries which I contacted for information on plants.

Finally, to anyone not mentioned, my apologies and sincere thanks.

Publishers' acknowledgments

Dorling Kindersley would like to thank Susanne Mitchell, Barbara Haynes, and Simon Maughan at the Royal Horticultural Society, Vincent Square for their time and assistance.

Editorial assistance Joanna Chisholm, Helen Fewster, Diana Galligan, Gail Griffiths, Jonathan Hilton, Andrea Loom, Carole McGlynn, Simon Maughan, Christine Morley, Jane Simmonds, Victoria Willan
Additional picture research Neale Chamberlain, Archie Clapton, Romaine Werblow
Index Hilary Bird

Revised edition 2009

Dorling Kindersley would like to thank Andrew Halstead and Chris Prior of the Royal Horticultural Society for their help in updating pest and disease advice for this revised edition.

Proof-reader Fiona Wild
Media resources DK Image Library